Canadian Cultural Poesis

Essays on Canadian Culture

Garry Sherbert,
Annie Gérin, and
Sheila Petty, editors

Wilfrid Laurier University Press

WLU

We acknowledge the financial support of the Government of Canada through the Book Publishing Industry Development Program for our publishing activities.

Library and Archives Canada Cataloguing in Publication

Canadian cultural poesis : essays on Canadian culture / Garry Sherbert, Annie Gérin, and Sheila Petty, editors.

(Cultural studies series)

Includes bibliographical references and index.

ISBN–10: 0-88920-486-1
ISBN–13: 978-0-88920-486-7

1. Culture — Canada. 2. Mass media and culture — Canada. 3. Arts and society — Canada. 4. Minorities — Canada. I. Sherbert, Garry Herald, 1957– II. Gérin, Annie, 1969– III. Petty, Sheila IV. Series: Cultural studies series (Waterloo, Ont.)

FC95.5C35 2006   306'.0971   C2005-906167-7

Excerpt on page 62 taken from "The Only Tourist in Havana Turns His Thoughts Homeward" from *Flowers for Hitler* by Leonard Cohen. Used by permission of McClelland and Stewart.

Excerpt on page 106 taken from Mike Bocking, "Step by Gruesome Step, One Man's Killing Spree," *Vancouver Sun* 8 April 1996, B2. Courtesy *Vancouver Sun.*

Excerpt on pages 107 and 108 taken from Mike Crawley, "Shooting Victim 'Let Down' by Vernon RCMP: Shooting Victim Isn't Looking to Blame Police, but Wants Protection for Women," *Vancouver Sun* 15 April 1996, A1. Courtesy Mike Crawley / *Vancouver Sun.*

Dedicated to the memory of
Irene Elizabeth Sherbert

Table of Contents

III (Dis)Locating Language

IV Cultural Dissidence

List of Illustrations

Preface

Garry Sherbert

THE ORIGIN OF THIS BOOK SPRINGS largely from the recognition that
until now there has been no textbook by Canadians, for Canadians, on
Canadian culture. When the call for essays on Canadian culture went out,
there were no rigidly preconceived ideas about what kind of thing we
were looking for. The essays gathered here contain something of a surprise
because they reveal a startling amount of concern for the issue of Canadian
national identity, albeit with a far more positive view regarding its absence
than one might expect. The very idea of producing a book on Canadian culture at a time when most Canadians still discuss the impossibility of even
finding a national identity presents quite a paradox and a challenge to
anyone writing an introduction to the subject.

This paradoxical fascination with an indeterminate Canadian identity
raises another point that concerns the formation of cultural studies as a new
discipline. Cultural studies already vigorously debates the extent to which
it fuels the fires both of "identity politics" (in which a social movement
advances the interests of a particular social group as opposed to the society as a whole), and of what some have called "culture wars" (ideological
struggles over cultural issues like abortion, gun control, and homosexuality). But, as different societies take on the rhetoric of multiculturalism—a
term invented in Canada—such conflictual political language seems
inevitable. If, as Northrop Frye suggests, "a nation's identity is (not in) its
culture,"[1] it is hardly possible to permanently separate identity politics
from culture in Canada. The point of *Canadian Cultural Poesis* then seems
less to find Canadian identity than to try to understand the open-ended,
negotiated nature of the process of identification. Many of the essays
found in this collection negotiate between different cultures in a Canadian context and appear to keep the question of nationalism suspended
between its opposing tendencies toward unity and plurality. For instance,
there are not only writers who question the policy of multiculturalism but
also francophone writers who address Quebec nationalism, and writers
who address the First Nations' struggle for autonomy. Although directed
primarily at English-speaking Canadians, the text leaves an open space
for cultural plurality and provides an occasion for its writers and its readers to "translate" themselves by crossing linguistic, political, and cultural
boundaries.

In the interest of maintaining the interdisciplinary nature of the subject
of culture, the editors have divided the material into the areas of media,

identity, language, and dissidence. These areas are focused enough to gather the essays according to their content, but sufficiently generalized to avoid locating them according to specific academic disciplines. The book strives not for the unity of some idea of culture but for *union* wherein the idea of culture is not made whole, but the idea of the whole is made possible. Cultural studies does not swallow the other disciplines, but respects their specific differences while providing a space for the disciplines to communicate with each other in a sustained and productive way. One way *Canadian Cultural Poesis* exemplifies this respect for disciplinary differences while promoting their interaction is by means of the "public art" or the visual artwork that introduces the subsections in the text. The artwork also emphasizes the organizing theme of the book, which is that cultural poesis is the simultaneous experience of making and being made by culture. Through the essays and the artworks, the text participates in the "making of culture," making and being made. The book is designed to provoke students into doing their own version of a poetics of culture whereby they experience making and being made through a critical or creative act. The text's value is that it exemplifies, for students, the many ways that the discovery of cultural studies can be made personally relevant. In every essay they write, or artwork they make, students engage in some act of identification with something other than themselves, an act affecting their identity, however minimally. In the act of making their own identity, students experience making and being made by culture through the new arrangements and relationships they invent through their critical or creative acts.

Notes

1. Northrop Frye, *The Eternal Act of Creation, Essays 1979–1990*, ed. Robert Denham (Bloomington and Indianapolis: Indiana University Press, 1993), 168.

Acknowledgements

AS WITH ANY BOOK OF THIS MAGNITUDE, the editors have many people to thank. We are immensely grateful for the financial support of the Research and Publications Committee of the Faculty of Arts at the University of Ottawa; and for the financial support of the President's Publication Fund and the Humanities Research Institute at the University of Regina. Furthermore, Garry Sherbert acknowledges Chris Elson, now at Dalhousie University, with whom the project of this book was first conceived. Without his willingness and intellectual courage to take on such seemingly impossible tasks, the project would never have gone forward. When Chris could not continue with the project, by extraordinary good fortune, Annie Gérin agreed to launch the project with Garry, at their first meeting at the house of former University of Regina president, David Barnard. It was Annie who suggested using original artwork, the funding for which she would like to thank the Dean in the faculty of Arts (Dean's Special Project Fund) at the University of Regina. Sheila Petty's collaborative experience, combined with her film and media expertise, was essential in making the book a reality. Once the call for abstracts went out, the work of Garry's student research assistants, Chris Moore, André Gareau, and, most recently, Deborah Manstan, proved indispensable. These three students were exceptionally talented and hard-working, and we could not imagine having worked through all the demands of this book without them. We would also like to thank Wilfrid Laurier's acquisitions editor, Jacqueline Larson, for her patience in helping with the revision of the introduction. We also deeply appreciate the impressive copy-editing work of Lisa LaFramboise and managing editor Carroll Klein's wisdom and encouragement in the final stages of getting the book into print. Finally, Sheila would like to thank Vaughn Borden for always being there, and Garry would like to recognize the support of Troni Grande, whose contribution also kept the book moving forward at times when the labour seemed too great.

Garry Sherbert
Annie Gérin
Sheila Petty

Introduction

A Poetics of Canadian Culture

Garry Sherbert

IT IS A COMMONPLACE IN INTRODUCTIONS TO CULTURE to quote Raymond Williams's observation that "culture" is one of the most complex words in the English language. The word means different things to different people. To an anthropologist or ethnographer, it can mean describing a cockfight in Bali in so detailed a way that the reader is given a sense of the Balinese view of the world. To others, culture can mean engaging in the creative arts, a privilege too often reserved for the wealthy few, or it can mean participating in a popular culture made from the commercialized products of an industrialized society. The word can also refer to the activity of cultivating, or improving, our individual selves. In all of these meanings, culture is usually opposed to nature, but such oppositional thinking often gets in the way of understanding the full range of the ways in which the natural and the cultural interact. Nothing, for example, could be more natural than having the bodily experience of feelings, but while feelings shape our way of dealing with the world, they are also influenced or shaped by objects we encounter in the world, as well as by our memory and past associations. The idea that our most intimate feelings circulate in public and that we are all emotionally invested in relations of power even leads one critic to write about a "cultural politics of emotion."[1] That emotion is involved in cultural politics raises the important question of whether culture is just given, and therefore determines all of our emotions and behaviour, or whether it provides us with choices by offering alternative ways of looking at the world.

1

Obviously, the way we define culture will have an enormous influence on the way we view society and our place as individuals within it. Williams, one of the founders of the cultural studies movement in Britain, gives four distinct meanings to culture, summarized by Terry Eagleton: "as an individual habit of mind; as the state of intellectual development of a whole society; as the arts; and as the whole way of life of a group of people."[2] The last definition of culture "as the whole way of life of a group of people" focusses on culture as social identity, and this is the idea that you will find explored in our book. The essays collected here arise mainly from the claim that all identity is socially, or culturally, constructed. Rather than seeing it as something natural, or essentially unchanging regardless of time or place, all of the writers in this volume see identity as a cultural artifact, shaped by social processes.

To say that identity is socially or culturally constructed does not mean that identity can be whatever one wants to make it. If, as one philosopher puts it, "you are what you eat," then, even though eating seems to be an entirely natural activity, we also find that our food preferences and the way we eat are shaped by social practices and cultural expectations. Indeed, the original definition of "culture" in Latin is "husbandry," or the "tending of natural growth," which, according to the Marxist critic Terry Eagleton, "suggests a dialectic between the artificial and the natural, what we do to the world and what the world does to us."[3] For example, when we name a child, we make or create a new, unique identity for that child. The act of naming, however, follows certain rules and conventions that control the process of naming. That is, a name places the new, singular identity within a family system and gender category already in the world. So the name represents both our attempt to make a new identity in the world and the world's effort to make its influence felt on this new identity at the same time. For Eagleton, and for the contributors of this anthology, the word "'culture' contains a tension between making and being made."[4] Our title *Canadian Cultural Poesis* conveys that tension in the word "poesis," which means "making" in the original Greek and is the basis of the English words for "poesy" and "poetry" (*Oxford English Dictionary*). *Canadian Cultural Poesis* refers to the "making of culture," or to the tension between making and being made by culture at the same time. This collection does not try to resolve that state of tension, but maintains it as an experience that the readers must pass through if they want to engage in cultural criticism.

What marks cultural poesis as Canadian is the fact that a politics of identity has been familiar to Canadians at the national level since the Second World War because of the uncertainty about our national identity.[5] Since there has always been a plurality of cultures competing for national attention, Canada has been characterized by the lack of a single, national identity. Canada includes a number of social groups that claim the universal-izing language of nationalism, such as "Quebec Nationalists," "First Nations," and even, as one of our essayists states, "Queer Nation." This cultural plurality means that, instead of a universal Canadian identity, the universal is now seen as a contested site of power: the power to represent a whole society or national identity. Many of the writers in our text show that, like individual identity, national identity is constructed and contingent, or dependent upon circumstances.

One of the ways the writers here reveal the constructed nature of national identities is by exposing the antagonistic relationship that these nationalisms have with each other. Since there will always be competing nationalisms, no one national ideology can be taken as universally true for all cultural groups. Even though some thing or group may temporarily represent a universal or dominant Canadian identity, there is no particular thing or group that must necessarily, and permanently, be its true embodiment.[6] When one social group dominates the social and cultural landscape by winning the consent of other social groups, this political arrangement is called "hegemony."[7] Some aspects of the social and cultural experience will always necessarily escape the dominant group's version of reality, and it is this leftover that permits a critic of culture to question the legitimacy of that group's claim to power. The Canadian government, for instance, long defined the identity of Native groups in terms of "bands" and "tribes" through the Indian Act, until First Nations defined themselves in terms of "nationhood." Ironically, the First Nations continue to consent to the paternalistic hegemony of the Indian Act, because they believe that it protects them better during their struggle towards self-government than the new Canadian constitution. In other words, the hegemonic relationship between First Nations and the Federal government, like all hegemonic relationships, is temporary and contingent because it depends less upon coercion for maintaining the dominant group's power than upon winning consent. Rather than covering over the social divisions by declaring one group's account of reality as objectively true, cultural poesis challenges every group's version of reality as partial, a socially constructed fiction that never explains the social totality.

There are two basic consequences to saying that identity is socially constructed. First, national identity is no longer imagined as "fixed and historically given but as something in the process of becoming."[8] Second, a socially constructed identity is always a mixture of various cultural differences. For instance, in this collection, Zoë Druick and Patsy Kotsopoulos attest to the struggles of Canadians to maintain their cultural independence and define themselves against the overwhelming influence of American culture, especially in media such as cinema and television. Canada's ongoing struggle to define its uniqueness demonstrates that identity is relational, meaning that a group's identity is defined by its similarity to and difference from the identity of another group. Or, as writer and filmmaker Trinh T. Minh-ha puts it (quoting an African proverb), "'A thing is always itself and more than itself.'"[9] Minh-ha suggests that identity is a process of identification, always travelling elsewhere, always crossing boundaries. Identity, in other words, is always a mixture and an incomplete hybrid. As many of the essays in this collection show, hybrid identities are therefore not a marginal phenomenon. In fact, "hybridity" names the place where all individual, cultural, even political, identities are produced.

The question of identity and its relation to representation is central for cultural studies. In terms of the traditional disciplines, cultural studies has been described as a non-disciplinary discipline.[10] Whether we trace its roots back to anthropology, sociology, English literary studies, or, as Stuart Hall has done, to postwar Marxism in Britain, the study of culture comes from the realization that "questions of power and the political have to be and always are lodged within representations."[11] For Hall, one of the founders of this new non-disciplinary discipline, to do cultural studies is to raise questions about, or to "theorize power—politics, race, class and gender, subjugation, domination, exclusion, marginality, Otherness, etc."[12] If we define cultural studies, as Chris Barker has done in his fine introduction to the discipline, as centred on "questions of *representation*, that is on how the world is socially constructed and represented to us and by us,"[13] then we have returned to the question of our title, cultural poesis: how do we make culture and how does culture make us?

The phrase "cultural poesis" has been used in anthropology by James Clifford to indicate that the representation of another culture in ethnography is never a detached, scientifically objective act of observation, but an inventive art saturated with the cultural biases and personal perspective of the ethnographer.[14] As Clifford puts it, "'Cultures' do not hold still for their photographs."[15] Clifford adopts the idea of cultural poetics from the work of the new historicist Stephen Greenblatt, for whom the term refers, like Eagleton's definition, to the notion that we make and are made by culture.[16] But if we are made by our culture, then how do we as individuals or groups find a space within which to make our own identities? How do we even resist simply being assimilated into the dominant culture?

Consider the question of whether an individual is made by consumer culture, or can make his or her identity out of that consumer culture. A consumer culture is one where our values and social practices are mostly defined by our relation to consumption rather than by systems of meaning like citizenship or religion. As consumers, we are encouraged to express our uniqueness by identifying with and then buying certain brand names, or labels. In fact, as Naomi Klein has shown in her book *No Logo*, corporations like Disney, Nike, Starbucks, or Virgin no longer sell products but rather the brand itself.[17] By associating the brand with a lifestyle, corporations transform consumers into "walking billboards." Corporations search desperately for the "coolest" lifestyle trend, which turns out too often to be associated with the poorest African Americans, such as in the case of rap culture, and then that lifestyle is marketed to middle-class white America. Ironically, even gay identity is pirated by corporations to sell television programs and alcohol despite its controversial nature (given the recent negative reaction to gay marriage). Cultural identity itself becomes a commodity, merely providing the content for the culture industry.

We are largely made by consumer culture, and the "culture industry"— a popular culture that has been commodified and homogenized by capitalist corporations—presents a serious obstacle to individuals and social groups when they try to form their own independent identity.[18] On the one hand, it is clear that the culture industry exerts a tremendous influence on the shaping of our identity; but, on the other hand, surely individuals and social groups can and do still resist being completely assimilated by consumer culture. In fact, some cultural critics emphasize our ability to resist being entirely shaped by ideological forces. If we use what consumer culture gives us, and create something new out of it, we will not only be made by culture, but we will be contributing to making it ourselves. John Fiske, a well-known critic of popular culture, has outlined how consumers can exercise this form of resistance: "In industrialized society the people make their culture out of the resources that are not of their own making and are not under their control."[19] For example, he cites the way women use popular television programs like *The Newlywed Game* to question the dominance of masculine values. Popular culture is, for Fiske, "the art of making do with what is available."[20] But, as Fiske admits, making do is an "'art of being in between.'"[21] Fiske argues that we as consumers must work within and against the dominant capitalist ideology that saturates our society.

Understanding the interaction between ideology and the formation of identity helps to explain the problems faced by individuals who struggle to resist hegemonic cultural forces. An ideology may be defined broadly as any system of ideas we use to make sense of the world we live in. A more well-known definition by Louis Althusser describes ideology as the imaginary relationship individuals have to their real conditions of existence.[22] Althusser makes a strong case for our being made as individual subjects by ideology and its various institutional apparatuses, when he says that we are called into our social roles, or "interpellated."[23] Our earlier example of naming children at birth is an example of interpellation (being "called" or "summoned" in such a way that we must conform to prescribed social categories). Take the way we are made to conform to society's gender roles: whether someone declares, "It's a girl" or "It's a boy," interpellation, or conditioning the child to accept the heterosexual norm of gender, has already begun.[24] The same social conditioning can occur with regard to an individual's religious beliefs. A child cannot understand moral abstractions or the concept of a "God," and yet by attending church and performing repeated acts of prayer and worship, that child internalizes his or her family's religious convictions. Our identity is therefore determined by our repeated, ritualistic social behaviours before we are even aware enough of our identity to challenge it.

However, we can be made consciously aware that ideology is at work when we see a disconnection between what an ideology claims about reality and how we ourselves perceive reality. The essays here by Jayne Wark and Joanne Lalonde, for example, examine this disconnection when gender identities deviate from the ideology of patriarchy (that is, a society where a masculine point of view becomes the accepted norm). Wark and Lalonde write about the ways that art may challenge the compulsory norms of heterosexuality in a patriarchal system, through the performance, or playful reinvention, of gender roles and codes that fall outside traditional definitions of femininity or masculinity. The traditional notion that the most natural relationship is a heterosexual one with a member of the "opposite sex" proves to be just an imaginary relation that, through repeated enforcement of social norms, has been taken as "real."

If the ideological system, as Althusser suggests, is an imaginary relation, then it is not a true representation of reality, but a matter of interpretation or belief. Indeed, ideology comes about as the result of a claim made by a given social group to legitimize its social, political, or cultural supremacy. One critic argues that "any authority always claims more than what we can offer in terms of belief."[25] The hegemonic group introduces ideology to fill the gap in belief, to supplement belief, and meet the claim to legitimacy.[26] In this sense, they advocate their belief system as valid beyond doubt. Advertising is notorious for making exaggerated claims by which to promote a commodity and the values associated with it. Political parties also routinely make promises that are not fulfilled. Some of the authors in this book, such as Susan Lord, Jasmin Yiwani, and Cecil Foster, will show, similarly, that the Canadian government claims to provide equality for all ethnic or cultural groups through its policy of multiculturalism, but that reality does not always show the government living up to its claim. The failure of the government to fulfill its claim of equality among the different cultures may lead to a gap in its credibility, but this failure does not prevent it from continuing to use culture as a means to legitimate its power.

An ideology is fully realized when people identify with it and act on it, giving it material form through social practices. These social practices can range from an economic purchase to a political action. A gender ideology, for instance, may be materialized or embodied when a person acts on an ideal of a male or female gender with which he or she identifies. A "tomboy," for example, is a girl, but as a girl she crosses the lines of gender ideology by exhibiting, or identifying with, behaviours traditionally associated with boys. Other acts of identification may take a political form, like participating in a political protest. Similarly, as Fiske observes, a commodity is "ideology made material"[27] because it gives the capitalist ideology a material form. We can alter a commodity to adapt it to our particular needs and thereby resist capitalist ideology. Fiske uses the example of tearing or bleaching our jeans, or wasting time at the video arcade to resist the protestant work ethic. We may even celebrate, with Fiske, the ability of the consumer to take some creative mastery back from the culture industry. Others, however, question whether this celebration of what one critic calls "'consumer sovereignty'"[28] is not still complicit with the consumer culture it seeks to resist.

Indeed, as Cynthia Sugars reminds us in her analysis of the popular beer commercial, "The Molson Rant," we can experience simultaneously a loss and a gain from a single act of cultural identification. A commercial that has enjoyed wide, national success, "The Rant" depicts "Joe Canadian" mockingly defending Canadian cultural distinctiveness against the assimilation and misunderstanding of Americans. This commercial stands as a prominent example of the culture industry's effective intervention in the Canadian political discourse of identity. One could view the commercial in positive terms, because like any social authority it provides an ideological model that supplies a ready-made identity for a community at a time when it feels threatened by a lack of identity.[29] Alternatively, the identity claim presented in the Molson Rant can be seen as imposed, fixed, and rigid. The national symbols of Canadian identity exploited in the commercial, from the beaver to the maple leaf, can influence the audience beyond the ironic humour of the commercial's ostensible purpose to sell beer. Does this commercial signify a loss of identity because it exposes Canadian identity as a fiction constructed from worn stereotypes? Or does it provide us with the opportunity to construct a new identity because we identify with it? This remains an open question. The commercial does, nonetheless, illustrate that no single act of creative consumption completes our sense of identity because of the gap between the representative of identity and the people it is supposed to represent.[30]

Rather than swinging back and forth between making and being made by culture, and resolving nothing, cultural poesis allows both to happen at the same time by dwelling on the space in between the two processes.[31] How is it possible for us as cultural critics to be both inside and outside the culture we are criticizing? The critic must know something about the popular culture and yet maintain a certain critical distance in order to criticize it. The point of this anthology is not to choose between being immersed in the market forces of the culture industry or being completely outside them, but to occupy the split between the two. However impossible this place is to maintain, the paradoxical position of the cultural critic can be articulated, as Robert Young states, only through an "'ambivalent relation to an other that it can neither fully assimilate nor totally exclude.'"[32] It is precisely this ambivalence that so many of the authors in this book attempt to write about, whether their chosen field is media, language, identity, or politics. In fact, *Canadian Cultural Poesis* is a text replete with words that argue for and against something at the same time, words like *irony, fetish, paradox, ambivalence, parody, doubleness,* and *dialectics*.

Canadian Cultural Poesis has been organized as a text around four areas that affect social identity or culture: the media, identity (both individual and social), language, and the politics of cultural representation. Although the essays in this collection spring from traditional disciplines such as law, psychology, sociology, or the visual arts, they all move toward some kind of liminal space between academic disciplines and cultural fields. There is a mixture of established scholars who are known for being innovative in their respective academic areas, and newer scholars who bring fresh perspectives and renewed vigour to ideas already implicit in the culture. As a group, the new voices in this text intensify the overall focus on the political nature of the struggle to construct cultural identity. All the writers, however, are united in their movement beyond the horizon of their specific academic and cultural contexts toward unexpected, new objects of knowledge. The text as a whole is therefore interdisciplinary, not only because the essays come from a broad range of the traditional disciplines, but also because many of the essays are interdisciplinary in themselves. They combine literary and visual cultural elements, for example, or they make more generally available aspects of culture associated with a specific cultural sphere, such as commercials, gay identity, technology, or ethnic norms of humour. To borrow from one of our own authors, Jeanne Randolph, interdisciplinarity can be understood as the ability of the critic to transform a particular piece of culture into a "transitional object." Just as an infant uses a transitional object such as a blanket or teddy bear to cope with external social pressures, so artists and critics use their work as a transitional cultural object to adjust to changes in reality. Those working within a given discipline may find that interdisciplinary work functions as a transition between an inside—whether that inside is a person's subjective feelings, a specific field of knowledge, or a particular culture—and the acceptance of reality on the outside. This book should, then, have an appeal for anyone interested in cultural studies, Canadian studies, women's studies, communication studies, and the interdisciplinarity that necessarily comes with these areas of study. More traditional disciplines such as English and French literature, visual arts, film, sociology, and others may also find this text of value for contributing to an understanding of cultural difference and for exploring the ways in which their object of study fits within a broader concept of culture.

Our four sections serve to direct the inquiries found in each contribution beyond their own particular scope, but they also provide a centre of gravity to organize the diversity of the ideas and approaches. Each subsection will be introduced here through a description of each essay according to its grouping. These summaries will give the reader an idea of the variation within the essays assembled in each section, but the emphasis will fall on the surprising continuities and abiding themes (though many of the essays in one section could just as easily be placed in more than one section). All the essays, for instance, explicitly or implicitly, encounter at some point a conflict between the particular and the universal, whether it takes the form of an antagonism between the individual and the social, the regional and the national, or some other conflict between the local and the global. Since nothing makes the distinction between the particular and the universal, the local and the global, more difficult to maintain than the media, we will begin there.

Media and Its (Dis)Contents

The first section is entitled "Media and Its (Dis)Contents" because these essays examine the capacity of various media to be both a positive and negative influence on the content of the "imagined communities" in a Canadian context.[33] The title can also be read as an allusion to Sigmund Freud's classic text on culture and its repressive effects on the unconscious mind in *Civilization and Its Discontents*[34] because, despite acting as a kind of social control, the media cannot always control the effects of what it says on society. On the frontier between public and private space, a battle rages over surveillance technology. Gary Genosko outlines some of the strategies used by various activists to resist the disciplinary gaze—the fixed, controlling look of surveillance technology—by creating a distance, their own space between surveyor and surveyed. Against this one-way form of surveillance, Genosko proposes three different kinds of resistance: web activists, or "hacktivists" who use viruses to interrupt the surveillance system and free workers by creating downtime; neo-situationists who criticize the ideology of transparency that compels us to give up our privacy by putting on a theatre of the absurd before the camera; and finally, the work of Steve Mann, a performance artist-cum-activist, who assumes the role of a "video vigilante" by wearing his own miniaturized, wearable cameras to make various private businesses accountable for their surveillance practices. Genosko's essay most clearly illustrates "the art of being in between" mentioned above, by showing how popular culture might resist the culture industry. The art of counter-surveillance is, for Genosko, a "tactic of the weak"[35] because it does not produce the resources of popular culture, but it does make culture from those resources.

Other essays in the section can be read as protests against, or as simple acknowledgements of, the power of the media and technology to dislocate the uniqueness of individuals or local identities and make them more universally available. For example, the ironic discourse of cartooning in Canada has become very complex with the recognition that humour is culturally determined, and therefore Canadian humour often reflects a plurality of ethnic norms. Beverly Rasporich reveals that when the dominant discourses are challenged by the irony and satire of Quebec, First Nations, or Japanese-Canadian cartoonists, readers need to be aware of an incongruity between the ideal and the real. In other words, readers need to employ simultaneously their own cultural norms and other divergent Canadian cultural norms to understand the humour. Awareness of incongruity in humour exposes us to the contingency and multiplicity of the ideals and norms, or ideology, in our society and provides a much-needed critical distance from that ideology. Rasporich finds the acceptance of contingency and multiplicity that characterizes postmodern irony to be embodied in the Native figure of the trickster, who, to venture a little beyond her essay, says, "*Whatever* you do, I am going to do something else."[36] Like the other authors in this section, Rasporich searches for ways to articulate the contradictions that all media must face in the frontier between the individual and the social, between the public and the private, as well as between particular cultural identities and more universal national identities.

Collective memory projects produced for Canadian television, such as the *Heritage Minutes* and *Canada: A People's History*, demonstrate, according to Emily West, that the universal category of "the people" is a site of struggle for particular political interests. Both historical narratives attempt to rise above political and cultural differences by appealing to our common humanity or everyday heroes. West's essay tries to maintain a position that recognizes both the necessity and the danger of these memory projects as examples of popular culture and as contributions to Canadian identity. She acknowledges that such historical narratives are necessary imaginative constructs without which individuals might not believe in their nation and therefore make the kind of sacrifices that nations require of their citizens. At the same time, she reminds the reader that these histories reflect present political interests and are not to be viewed as free of ideological inflection.

Zoë Druick in her essay suggests that any place becomes a site of contestation and questions whether a particular, regional identity is destroyed by the abstractions of the media and its universalizing power, or enhanced by making us more aware of its uniqueness. She examines the central role that technology, particularly film and television, has played in the historical development of Canadian identity, and she concludes that the government has a long tradition of promoting Canada's local distinctiveness for national and international audiences. Contrary to its public declarations against the deleterious effects of American culture on national identity, the Canadian government's strategy has been deliberately to situate Canada within a global context by courting Hollywood and making it an integral part of Canadian culture. Canada's renowned policy of multiculturalism itself gets implicated in the government's willful participation in this process of "glocalization" by global corporations that treat national and local particularity as merely parts of a larger but more homogenized world picture.

Finally, Yasmin Jiwani reminds us of our duty as cultural critics to be vigilant regarding the ethnocentrism of a news media that generates a story when reporting events concerning particular ethnic groups outside the supposedly universal domain of the dominant culture. This essay gives three examples of "cultural racism" in the Canadian news media, a practice that hides racist explanations of non-white domestic violence against women behind cultural interpretations in order to avoid exposing the racist ideology of the dominant white culture. Focussing on events in British Columbia during the 1990s, including the Vernon Massacre, the shooting of Sharon Velisek, and the murder of Reena Virk, Jiwani argues that the massacre is represented as a result of the ethnic practices of arranged marriages in order to relocate the violence outside the dominant culture. The shooting of Velisek and murder of Virk, however, suppress the issue of the women's ethnicity to avoid the appearance of racism on behalf of the police in the first case, and the racially motivated violence of the white, teenage females who murdered Virk in the second case.

Performing and Disrupting Identities

The second section, entitled "Performing and Disrupting Identities," specifically investigates the ways in which individual and national identities are socially constructed. The essays in this section, following social constructionists like Judith Butler, Ernesto Laclau, and Chantal Mouffe, show that identity is performed and not an unchanging, naturally occurring essence. Cynthia Sugars, for example, proposes that the Molson's commercial called "The Rant" betrays a deep ambivalence about Canadian identity because it celebrates our identity while exposing it as a mere fiction. The Canadian in the commercial, who rants patriotically, paradoxically mocks Canadian identity; yet, judging by its popularity, the commercial also exhibits a furtive desire in Canadians to become more patriotic, more flag-waving, like, for example, the Americans. So the apparent self-deprecating irony of "Joe Canadian" declaring his national pride affirms the very identity it denies. This milestone in Canadian popular culture demonstrates the paradox that we can deceive ourselves by means of the truth because we become something by pretending we already are that. The contradiction in our "quiet pride" about being Canadian is played out in a fantasy that allows us to claim a unified national identity and simultaneously question its very existence.

Another kind of ambivalence in Canadian identity arises from the manner in which Canada treats its northern territories as both frontier and homeland. Alastair Campbell and Kirk Cameron record the history of a land exploited for its natural resources and yet promoted, in the case of Nunavut, as a model of Aboriginal self-government. In Campbell and Cameron's view, the North exemplifies the complex way that cultural identity is made and being made, for rather than allowing themselves to be colonized, the Yukon, Nunavut, and the Northwest Territories have found ways to get the federal government to accept negotiations based on Aboriginal title to the land and the inherent right to self-government. With modified structures of governance such as consensus government rather than the traditional party system, Aboriginal people have shifted the frontier-homeland relation from that of a centre dominating the margins, to that of a self respecting the cultural difference of the other. The northern political experience has changed the North from being an internal colony; the frontier is reversed by making the Canadian federal framework the place where a more radical democratic project of reconciling equality, collective rights, and cultural differences has found a home.

The next two essays examine the issue of gender identity as performance. Jayne Wark explores gender through the use of clothing and the body in performance art, while Joanne Lalonde explores transvestism through video confessions by contemporary artists. Both essays disclose the power of parody, paradoxically, to affirm the limits of gender identity produced by heterosexual social norms through the very act of transgressing them. Wark recounts a short history of performance art in Canada to prove how difficult it is for visual artists to intervene in a popular culture dominated by the mass media. The use of parody to resist the influence of sexual stereotypes or the male-female gender binary imposed upon us by the fashion industry sometimes backfires in performance art. For example, the use of leopard skin worn by female performance artist Kate Craig in the 1970s can be interpreted as being too invested in male sexual fantasy, rather than being an exaggeration of it designed to expose the objectification of women. A more effective parody of society's control of gender norms through clothing are the three popular figures in the 1980s performed by Tanya Mars. Mars chooses the clothing of females who refuse to submit to social conventions: the fairy-like dresses of the sixteenth-century's "Virgin Queen," Elizabeth I; the excessive and defiant sexual masquerades of Hollywood actor Mae West; and the unadorned Alice in Wonderland, who mocks Freud by searching for her lost male sexual organ.

The use of parody to question the supposed naturalness of the sexual categories in our gender ideology emerges again in Joanne Lalonde's anatomy of transvestism, particularly in the media of video confessions by artists. The medium of video enables a kind of self-representation that uncovers a split self, a self trying to integrate a figure of otherness that Lalonde refers to as a "video alter ego." In the quest for identity, a desire for the other gender turns into an identification with the other gender. This desire for the other can manifest itself in the form of transvestism, which Lalonde breaks down into three categories: drag queens, who are usually men dressed as women; female impersonators, who imitate conventional stereotypes of femininity; and she-males, who deliberately reveal attributes of both sexes to create the effect of ambiguity rather than deception. Although achieved in different ways, transvestism highlights the socially constructed nature of gender categories, such as in the case of the she-male, where the noticeable male attributes create a gap in the representation's plausibility. The fragmented style of the video and the fictionalized biographies in the confessions also combine to question the transparency of the televisual medium and its naturalizing, or realistic, effects.

In a daring comparison, Jason Morgan makes gay activism in the "Queer Nation" movement a model to show Canadians how to transform their lack of national identity and feeling of marginality into something productive. Offering a more inclusive model of nationalism that accepts difference and plurality, as opposed to the homogeneity of the "many as one" variety found in Canadian multiculturalism, Morgan argues that a lack of identity is not a failure but a productive rejection. Since the idea of a homogeneous nation contradicts the multiculturalism upon which it relies to define itself, Canadians are better off embracing difference and transgressing a normative basis for identity like the "perverse" gay and lesbian identities must do to survive. With filmmakers like Atom Egoyan,

Denys Arcand, and John Greyson to exemplify his argument, Morgan rejects the patriarchal anti-heroism in the "loser paradigm" of Canadian identity so that he can move from its futility and inferiority toward a more creative, performative Canadian national identity. This new "perverse" identity reinvents itself by means of a fantasized, consciously constructed historical past that disrupts and undermines the uniformity of our imagined national identity. As with the other writers in this section, the failure to embody an ideal (in this case, a national one) is taken as an opportunity for "culture jamming," or disrupting the homogeneity and heterosexuality of the public space in which the national imaginary is constructed.

(Dis)Locating Language

"(Dis)Locating Language," the third section, looks into the ways that we live, move, and have our being in language. As the primary medium through which meaning is produced and communicated within a group, language enjoys a privileged position in the study of culture; but, however much the identity of a particular individual or group depends upon a certain language to ground its identity, that linguistic identity is never permanent or pure. Monolingual anglophones who call themselves "Canadian," for instance, carry a trace of the First Nations in their identity because the name of our country derives from the Iroquoian word *kanata*, meaning "village." The essays in this section study the different effects that language can have on groups living within it and the various uses to which it is put in order to create unity or division within a community.

Jeanne Randolph's essay develops a mode of writing that she calls "ficto-criticism," which sees art as a transitional object between the subjective, inner world of our psyche and the objective, external world, an object that makes it possible for us to accept the demands and traumas imposed upon us by reality. Randolph takes object-relations theory, originating in the field of psychoanalysis from the work of D.W. Winnicott, and applies it to any creative act in the realm of culture, including her own essay, which combines the art of writing and art criticism. Anything invested with significance by our imagination can serve as a transitional object. The transitional object is an intermediate, and therefore paradoxical, area of experience between reality and fantasy. The therapeutic effect of the transitional object often depends upon the substance of illusion to help us adapt and adjust to reality. Since the task of accepting reality is never completed, we constantly resort to intermediate areas of experience like art and literature to work out the possibilities presented by a given reality through play, or "illusion," a word that derives from the Latin *ludere*, meaning "to play" (*Oxford English Dictionary*). The cultural significance of ficto-criticism becomes greatly extended when the capacity of art to embody, and thereby collectively share, our subjective experiences and creativity in some external object is generalized to technology.

In her essay on the way the print medium of the novel mediates the history of Quebec national identity, Ceri Morgan charts the changing cultural geography of Quebec, especially in relation to gender. Her historical narrative begins with the Quiet Revolution in the 1960s, during which Quebec witnessed the rise of the nationalist novel, or *le texte national*, in writers such as Jacques Renaud. The search for a nation in the 1960s is characterized by anti-urbanism, and a bi-ethnic model that splits francophones from anglophones, and from the more culturally heterogenous space of Montreal. Morgan argues that this bi-ethnic model leads only to fragmentation. The next phase marked by Morgan is the feminist fiction of women writers like Anne Hébert and Marie-Claire Blais, who attack not only the domestic violence of nationalist texts, but also their patriarchal structure and romanticizing of the rural. After the Quebec referendum over the issue of sovereignty association in 1980, and in spite of prior legislation designed to strengthen the French language, there emerges a much more radical challenge to nationalist discourse. Writers like Francine Noel, Hélène Monette, and Dany Laferrière introduce non-white, non-European characters with hybrid, fragmented identities that open up new cultural frontiers and spaces within the Quebec national imaginary.

Patsy Kotsopoulos investigates the political and economic issues surrounding the adaptation of Lucy Maud Montgomery's enormously popular literary classic *Anne of Green Gables* to the television screen. Caught between the cultural specificity of the Edwardian period on Prince Edward Island and the pressure to produce generic settings for global consumption, Montgomery's text exemplifies the risks involved in any Canadian art transformed by international success. Kotsopoulos outlines three styles of adaptation. In the first, the source novels are updated, resulting in a liberal feminist romance suitable for modern audiences. In the second, Montgomery's texts undergo a deregionalization, creating a regionless romance for a geographically and culturally diverse audience. Finally, a revisionist romance adapts the novels by rewriting the past to redress historical injustices, such as the exclusion of the Mi'kmaq culture in PEI, injustices either ignored or perpetuated by Montgomery's original text. Kostopoulos raises the serious question of whether it is better to see the costume drama construct a more politically correct, but indistinct, contextless past, or faithfully reproduce the specific past, in all its gender and racial exclusiveness.

Showing the way in which competing cultural discourses seek to persuade or compel popular consent, Carol Corbin's essay studies the struggle for hegemony between the traditional, patriarchal discourse and the newly emergent discourse influenced by feminism in a Nova Scotian fishing community. It is an open question as to whether the traditional word "fisherman," popular among the local community members, enjoys hegemony, or whether the degendered, government-sanctioned word "fisher" does. Corbin pays close regard to the local community's resistance to domination by the central government through its official language, even though it may not be in its long-term interest, especially for the local women, to do so. In fact, Corbin notes how she herself feels bound to use the word "fisherman" to gain acceptance in the local community, despite the compromise it represents to her academic training and feminist beliefs. Corbin's argument underscores the need to avoid simplistic models that see individuals as merely unwitting accomplices in their own domination. Instead, Corbin suggests that we need to understand the complexity of hegemonic relations in their specific social contexts within an open, democratic society.

Martin Arnold gives an account of an "aesthetics of the wonderful," translating *estetiku divnosti*, a theory of art formulated by Czechoslovakian experimental musician Rudolph Komorous, who now lives in Canada. Associated with the group of visual artists in Prague known as "Smidra," the aesthetics of the wonderful offers an experience of the strange or the unknown through art as distinguished from the transcendental or the miraculous associated with religion. As examples of art that produce the feeling of wonder, Arnold cites fireworks and unorthodox sound effects such as the musical language of jazz played with a bowed saw and synthetic sounds produced by holding a speaker inside the mouth cavity. The subjective effect of wonder is evoked by artistic events that defy comprehension and resist analysis. The unknowability of the wonderful is other to, or goes beyond, everyday reality. The wonderful arises not from belief in another world, but from the experience of other possibilities in this one. On the edge between the important and the trivial, the known and the unknown, the real and the imagined, the wonderful may be described as a paradigmatic cultural experience of the new and the singular, which allows us to invent ourselves as an other people.

Finally, Annie Gérin examines a fundamental paradox facing all public art, especially public memorials, which is that the art must somehow maintain or repeat its identity while remaining open to the changes in the cultural context surrounding it. Gérin illustrates her point by looking at politically motivated public art in Quebec, an art that assumes a coincidence of linguistic identity and territory only to find that the culture of Quebec is not always homogeneous over a given time and space. Because they are made from long-lasting materials, memorials can be used as a way of taking control of public space. The memorials in Gérin's examples impose the French language upon non-francophones and prevent them from participating in the artistic experience. Gérin makes her case with Roger Langevin's monument to the fervently nationalist poet Felix Leclerc and the Quiet Revolution slogan "Maîtres chez nous" or "Masters in our own house." A more inclusive example, Gilbert Boyer's "Comme un poisson dans la ville," or "Like a Fish in the City," is a series of plaques, each with an inscription in the French language (though Boyer has used English in other works) that invites the viewers to reimagine their cultural habitat. Boyer attempts to demonstrate how public art, despite the durability of its materials, can not only keep an open relation to language but also invite the viewer to participate in the production of the artistic event by remaining open to the changing context and chance encounters. However, because Boyer uses inscriptions in French, his work never fully achieves this goal of openness.

Cultural Dissidence

The final section, "Cultural Dissidence," covers a series of more explicitly political conflicts to show how challenging it is to hold the cultural imaginary of our Canadian communities open to cultural dissent and otherness, even though justice demands it. Ironically, recent developments in political theory seem to have caught up to the traditional Canadian debate over our lack of national identity by claiming that complete unity, or closure, of any society is impossible anyway.[37] No particular thing or group can ever stand permanently for a whole nation or for some universal national identity. Cecil Foster argues, for instance, that the celebration of Black history in Canada is a form of recognition that has only served to expose the hierarchy of race and the limits of multiculturalism. The idealistic goals of justice and equality for every individual regardless of their ethnic origin have not been realized because Blacks in Canada have not achieved their share of social justice, which includes the economic equality, and social mobility needed to fully actualize themselves. While Canada boasts of being the first multicultural state, Black History Month celebrates the historical achievements of Blacks such as Malcolm X, Nelson Mandela, or Martin Luther King, who are not even Canadian. The celebration of Black history, furthermore, homogenizes people of African ancestry into a single ethnicity despite the significant cultural differences between, say, Caribbean, American, and African cultures. Foster compares Black History Month to the medieval carnival that acknowledges the exclusion of marginalized groups by ironically reversing their socially marginal position for only a brief period of time. A genuine politics of recognition would not impose an identity on Black Canadians but would allow them to determine their own destiny and give them the equality of opportunity they need to feel a sense of belonging.

In her essay on the fortress at Louisbourg in Cape Breton, Nova Scotia, Erna Macleod demonstrates the difficulties of trying to decolonize representations of history within a colonial site that symbolizes the imperial ambitions of the "two founding nations," the French and the English. Given the demands of a nation that identifies itself with multiculturalism, historians at the reconstructed fortress must negotiate between a fair representation of cultural differences and the double danger of romanticizing a Eurocentric past while at the same time promoting a superficial fascination with exotic images of otherness. Romanticizing another culture or exploiting it merely for the exotic nature of its cultural difference objectifies non-dominant cultures and perpetuates their oppression. Macleod's interviews with the historians reveal an ongoing struggle to represent adequately the perspective of the Mi'kmaq Nation, the history of slavery, and women's history at the fort, without fueling twenty-first-century cultural conflicts. In fact, the very efforts to elide ideological conflicts between cultural groups show that, although the fortress has been transformed from a military installation to a museum, Canada's historical identity, like the fortress, remains a site of conflict.

Eric Sherbert's essay takes up the need for an Aboriginal charter of rights. Given the history of unjust exclusion of Aboriginal peoples from the Canadian system of justice, the protections provided by the Canadian constitution and its Charter of Rights and Freedoms are seen as inadequate. Rights are legal or moral claims to something that is due us, particularly the claim to justice, whether it be the state of being entitled to a privilege, immunity, or authority to perform some act, such as a woman's right to vote, or the Aboriginal right to hunt and fish. When certain social norms or rules are declared unjust, a person or group claiming a given right appeals to values to generate a new set of norms and rules, a situation that well describes the movement toward an Aboriginal charter. The values put forward by the First Nations for an Aboriginal charter would be based on their own cultural values, referred to as "inherent right," or those traditions or practices regarded as an integral part of their distinctive culture. Recounting the history of Canadian legal doctrine that attempted either to assimilate First Nations or exclude them by forcing them on to reserves, Sherbert proposes alternative human rights principles for a charter based on Aboriginal culture, such as the model of the circle, symbolizing equality.

In Susan Lord's analysis of the discourse on multicultural identity in Canadian cinema, the Gothic emerges, in the cultural encounter between the female, white prairie settler and the First Nations, as a means of opening our imagined national identity to its own otherness. Lord traces the history of the various government strategies for containing cultural difference. The "pass law" during Canada's colonial period, for instance, did not permit Aboriginal people to leave reserves without a pass, whereas the present-day policy of multiculturalism creates anonymous, generic citizens by treating everyone's cultural difference as something we all have in common. Treating the past as the unconscious part of our present identity, the Gothic challenges the governmentally managed version of Canadian historical identity that sees the past as a relatively peaceful, melodramatic, domestic scene in which the settler's labour wins over the vast spaces of empty land. Filmmakers like Anne Wheeler offer a Gothic account of a violent past that has been repressed and forgotten, but which returns by haunting the present in the form of terrifying encounters with a threatening and mysterious Native other. Canadian Gothic film often raises the spectre of a ghostly Native figure who, mourning a ruined civilization and conquered past, calls out for justice, troubling the conscience of the white settlers' descendants whose national myth of multiculturalism is disturbed by the nightmare of history.

Carol Payne looks into the government's use of still photography in the nineteenth century to construct Canadian nationhood under the guise of scientific discourse, photographs ostensibly used to map territory but ultimately designed to advance the cultural program of imperialism and subjugate Aboriginal peoples. Through the act of naming, mapping appropriates the land from the First Nations, and the supplementary photographic images taken by groups such as the Royal Corps of Engineers, the Canadian Pacific Railway, and the Geological Survey of Canada reinforce the claim of ownership over the land. Payne chooses one photograph depicting three unnamed "Chippewas" apparently mourning before a gravesite to illustrate the nineteenth-century anthropological attitude towards Natives as a vanishing race. She interprets the mechanically reproduced image further as an emblem of Aboriginal annihilation and colonial ascendancy, especially in the areas of science and technology. To expose the apparent neutrality of photography, contemporary Aboriginal artists like George Littlechild and curators like Jeff Thomas at the Canadian Museum of Civilization employ photography that reclaims agency for the Aboriginal subject and subverts colonial control over Aboriginal identity.

All of the essays in this anthology challenge the traditional notion of the universal as a norm that is imposed by some dominant group colonizing, or taking over, other cultures. Against the imperialism of any "particularism masquerading as the universal,"[38] the essays in this text propose a concept of universal identity that emerges out of a socially specific context of struggle. For instance, liberal individualism, defined as a system that places the rights of the individual over that of social groups, is charged with masquerading as a universal when it claims to remain neutral in the "private" matters of religion or culture. Liberal individualism reveals its bias by siding with the individual against the group claims. A truly democratic society must preserve the universal as an absence, or empty place, in order to protect and maintain the cultural plurality. The advantage of seeing the absence of a full identity as an empty place to be temporarily filled in by some group representing the universal is that it not only allows different cultural groups to struggle for democratic control, or dominance, but it also helps keep the national community open to cultural differences. Accepting the lack of a universal Canadian identity as an empty place therefore offers a more hospitable version of cultural identity because it compels all Canadian cultural groups to negotiate their identities on an ongoing basis. Negotiating a provisional identity demands that a cultural group perform an obligation or duty both to the universal and to the particular poles of national identity. More precisely, maintaining a provisional identity demands a "double duty"[39] from all social groups toward maintaining their own particular identity and that of others. Living on the borderline between the universal and the particular means welcoming different things or groups to represent Canadian cultural identity in order to adapt to changing social contexts. Canadian cultural poesis may then be described as an act of hospitality, the invention of new gestures, new ways of welcoming the marginalized other, the stranger, and the foreigner, in order to construct new cultural arrangements between the universal Canadian identity and their own particular identity. An act of hospitality defines a poetics of culture, for in the act of making an identity, that identity is also made by the other through the new relationship forged in the act.[40]

The contributors to this anthology are Canadian intellectuals and artists who were brought together not only to focus on cultural issues in a Canadian context, but also to stimulate further investigations into the complexities and contradictions of Canadian cultural pluralism. The contributors are aware that by analyzing Canadian culture they are also producing Canadian culture. To help remind the reader that *Canadian Cultural Poesis* as a text is also an artifact that participates in the making of culture, we have included four original projects, works of "public art" that take visual culture to task on its own terms. They explore how some contemporary visual artists re-present Canadian culture, influencing how Canadians *see* themselves. The art and the essays in this anthology show that Canadians see themselves as more than they are today, as something other than what they are. In the words of one Canadian cultural critic, "the real identity of all nations is the one we have failed to achieve."[41] To understand *Canadian Cultural Poesis* as it is used in this book means that we have to look at this failure to reach our ideal not as merely negative but as an opportunity to make and remake our identity in a more inclusive way.

Notes

1 Sarah Ahmed, *The Cultural Politics of Emotion* (New York: Routledge, 2004).

2 Terry Eagleton, *The Idea of Culture* (Oxford: Blackwell, 2000), 35.

3 Eagleton, 2.

4 Eagleton, 5. Eagleton defines the relationship that culture has with nature in the paradoxical terms of a "supplement," a term that he borrows from Jacques Derrida's book, *Of Grammatology*, trans. Gayatri Spivak (Baltimore: Johns Hopkins University Press, 1976). Derrida defines the supplement as a process that does not allow a thing, such as nature, to be self-sufficient, or maintain a clear-cut distinction with something outside it, for the "supplement adds itself, it is a surplus.... But the supplement supplements. It adds only to replace" (144–45). What appears to be a superfluous addition to something is also essential to define its identity.

5 Ian Angus, *A Border Within: National Identity, Cultural Plurality, and Wilderness* (Montreal and Kingston: McGill-Queen's University Press, 1997), 3.

6 I am following Ernesto Laclau's definition of the hegemony as one in which a particular thing or group performs the impossible role of representing a universal or national identity. There is no particular group that must necessarily be the embodiment of the true, universal, national identity even though some thing or group may temporarily function as a universal. In other words, no particular group necessarily embodies the universal, national identity because some other group could serve in its place. The universal is always an "incomplete horizon" or a "symbol of a missing fullness." See Ernesto Laclau, *Emancipation(s)* (London: Verso, 1996), 28.

7 Antonio Gramsci's definition of hegemony assumes the competition of social groups for dominance, which leads to one dominant group organizing and gaining the consent of other groups. *Selections from the Prison Notebooks of Antonio Gramsci*, ed. Quintin Hoare and Geoffrey Nowell Smith (New York: International Publishers, 1971), 80n49.

8 Jon Stratton and Ien Ang, "Multicultural Imagined Communities: Cultural Difference and National Identity in the USA and Australia," *Multicultural States: Rethinking Difference and Identity*, ed. David Bennett (London: Routledge, 1998), 157.

9 Trinh T. Minh-ha, "Other Than Myself/My Other Self," *Travellers' Tales: Narratives of Home and Displacement*, ed. George Robertson, et al. (London: Routledge, 1994), 11.

10 Chris Barker, *Cultural Studies: Theory and Practice* (London: Sage, 2000), 5.

11 Stuart Hall, *Stuart Hall: Critical Dialogues in Cultural Studies*, ed. David Morley and Kuan-Hsing Chen (London: Routledge, 1996), 274.

12 Hall, *Stuart Hall*, 274.

13 Barker, *Cultural Studies*, 8. Emphasis in original.

14 James Clifford and George E. Marcus, *Writing Culture: The Poetics and Politics of Ethnography* (Berkeley: University of California Press, 1986), 16.

15 Clifford and Marcus, 10.

16 Clifford, "Introduction: Partial Truths," 3, 24. For the phrase "poetics of culture," see Stephen Greenblatt, *Renaissance Self-Fashioning: From More to Shakespeare* (Chicago: University of Chicago, 1980), 5.

17 Naomi Klein, *No Logo* (New York: Picador, 1999).

18 Theodor W. Adorno and Max Horkheimer, *Dialectic of the Enlightenment*, trans. John Cumming (New York: Continuum, 1986), 120–67. Especially relevant to this introduction is Adorno and Horkheimer's claim that the culture industry's homogenizing effect of making particular things according to a model is the "false identity of the general and the particular" (121).

19 John Fiske, "Popular Culture," *Critical Terms for Literary Study: Second Edition*, ed. Frank Lentricchia and Thomas McLaughlin (Chicago: University of Chicago Press, 1990), 326.

20 Fiske, "Popular Culture," 326.

21 John Fiske, *Understanding Popular Culture* (Boston: Unwin Hyman, 1989), 36. Fiske is quoting Michel de Certeau, *The Practice of Everyday Life*, trans. Steven F. Rendell (Berkeley: University of California Press, 1984), 32.

22 Louis Althusser, *Lenin and Philosophy and Other Essays*, trans. Ben Brewster (London: New Left Books, 1971), 153.

23 Althusser, 162–63.

24 Sara Salik, "Introduction," *The Judith Butler Reader* (Oxford: Blackwell, 2004), 7.

25 Paul Ricoeur, "Ideology and Utopia as Cultural Imagination," *Being Human in a Technological Age*, ed. Donald M. Borchert and David Stewart (Athens, OH: Ohio University Press, 1979), 115.

26 Paul Ricoeur, *Lectures on Ideology and Utopia*, ed. George H. Taylor (New York: Columbia University Press, 1986). In his introduction to Ricoeur's lectures, Taylor describes ideology's role as a "needed supplement to belief that will fill this gap, [the gap between belief and an ideological claim]" (xvii).

27 Fiske, *Understanding Popular Culture*, 14.

28 Jim McGuigan, "Cultural Populism Revisited," *Cultural Studies in Question*, ed. Marjorie Ferguson and Peter Golding (London: Sage, 1997), 143.

29 Paul Ricoeur, *Lectures on Ideology and Utopia*, 261.

30 Laclau, 65. Laclau's discussion of identification as a process of supplementation is relevant here (98–99).

31 Herman Rapaport criticizes Stephen Greenblatt and others for their failure to resolve the dialectical swinging back and forth between making and being made in culture. See Herman Rapaport, *The Theory Mess: Deconstruction in Eclipse* (New York: Columbia University Press, 2001), 121.

32 Robert C. Young, *Torn Halves: Political Conflict in Literary and Cultural Theory* (Manchester: Manchester University Press, 1996), 98. Robert Young is quoting Samuel Weber, *The Legend of Freud* (Minneapolis: University of Minnesota Press, 1982), 33.

33 Benedict Anderson, *Imagined Communities: Reflections on the Origin and Spread of Nationalism,* Rev. ed. (London: Verso, 1991), 13.

34 Sigmund Freud, *Civilization and Its Discontents*, trans. James Strachey (New York: Norton, 1962), 59.

35 Michel de Certeau, 37.

36 Jimmie Durham, "Free Tickets," *Marginal Recession: An Installation by Edward Poitras* (Regina: Dunlop Art Gallery, 1991), n.p.

37 Ernesto Laclau and Chantal Mouffe, *Hegemony and Socialist Strategy: Towards a Radical Democratic Politics* (London: Verso, 1985), 114.

38 Charles Taylor, *Multiculturalism: Examining the Politics of Recognition*, ed. Amy Gutman (Princeton: Princeton University Press, 1994), 44. For another critique of liberal individualism's failure to remain neutral to group rights, the work of Will Kymlicka is indispensable. See especially his argument that liberal individualism, which regards the

protection of individual freedom as paramount, must change by also protecting group rights and transform itself into a "liberal culturalism": "The New Debate over Minority Rights," *Canadian Political Philosophy*, ed. Ronald Beiner and Wayne Norman (Oxford: Oxford University Press, 2001), 162.

39 Jacques Derrida, *The Other Heading: Reflections on Today's Europe*, trans. Pascale-Anne Brault and Michael B. Naas (Bloomington: Indiana University Press, 1992), 80.

40 Jacques Derrida says that "An act of hospitality can only be poetic": Jacques Derrida, *Of Hospitality: Anne Dufourmantelle Invites Jacques Derrida to Respond*, trans. Rachel Bowlby (Stanford: Stanford University Press, 2000), 2.

41 Northrop Frye, *The Modern Century: New Edition* (Toronto: Oxford University Press, 1991), 123.

1 Media and Its (Dis)Contents

My Grandmother's Violin
Frances Dorsey

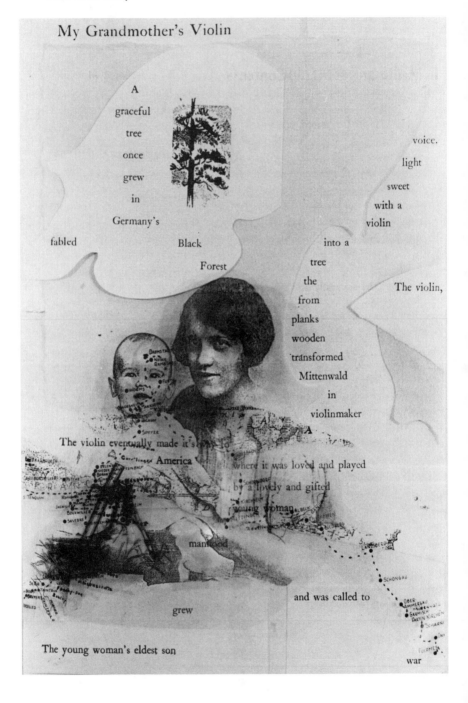

My Grandmother's Violin

A graceful tree once grew in Germany's fabled Black Forest

voice. light sweet with a violin

into a tree the from planks wooden transformed Mittenwald in violinmaker

The violin,

The violin eventually made it's way to America where it was loved and played by a lovely and gifted young woman

manhood

grew

and was called to

The young woman's eldest son

war

trees shot

shot trees

trees trees

trees trees

trees shot

shot shot

shot trees

trees trees

trees shot

shot shot

shot trees

trees

trees

The son fought his way across Europe,
shot apart the trees
of the Black Forest

and marched victoriously
into
Mittenwald

long silent, lay still and
slowly
dried
and
cracked.

Many years later the broken violin came
to the great grandaughter
of the gifted and lovely young woman

The violin was repaired but

The young woman, grown old and

care-worn,

the

music

had

gone

out

of

slipped

it

away

The violin set up a

     u   z   n

  b   z   i   g

in the chords of the the soldier's daughter,

The daughter of the soldier
held the violin
and s l o w l y drew the bow.

delicately,

haltingly,

the music

    drips

      drips

The
violin

the

places
in
the

of

the

soldier's

daughter

    the   back

    daughter

    of the

    soldier   into the violin.

    peeps

    into the

    silent

    heartstrings

    of the

    beautiful,

     gifted

       young

         woman.

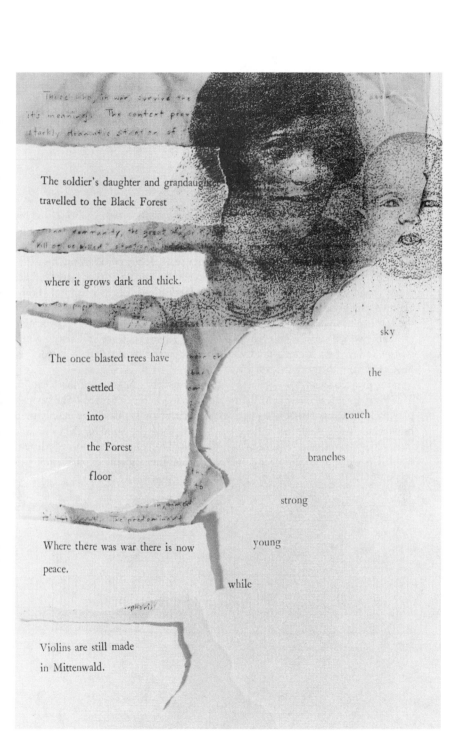

The soldier's daughter and grandaughter
travelled to the Black Forest

where it grows dark and thick.

The once blasted trees have

settled

into

the Forest

floor

Where there was war there is now

peace.

Violins are still made
in Mittenwald.

sky

the

touch

branches

strong

young

while

Frances Dorsey

In common with many of my generation, I grew up with a father who relived his World War II combat experience daily. He would never speak of the war. But he could not tolerate sudden loud noises, jingoistic political talk, or being woken up from deep sleep. Just before his death, he unexpectedly began to recount his experiences to his family and friends and work on essays addressed to a larger public. A few months later, I discovered quite a bit of writing, as well as a handful of tiny, yellowed snapshots of too-young soldiers. These were taken in Germany, after the war had ended. These fragments were poignant. They were silent yet evocative of a time which unleashed events and consequences that are still shaping our worlds today. As a second-hand witness I felt singed by the flames of war, yet protected from the burn marks.

This project tells the story (real and imagined) of my grandmother's violin. This instrument was made in Mittenwald, Germany, in the mid-1800s. She stopped playing it when my father went overseas as a rifleman. Ironically he mainly used his weapon to shoot up trees in the Black Forest, where the wood for the violin was most likely harvested a century before. The allied forces later conquered Mittenwald. The work is a composition of type, photographed Japanese paper, and violin contours. It tells a simple story about an instrument and a war.

1 (Im)Possible Exchanges

The Arts of Counter-Surveillance

Gary Genosko

It [a tactic] must vigilantly make use of the cracks that particular conjunctions open in the surveillance of the proprietary powers. It poaches in them. It creates surprises in them. It can be where it is least expected. It is a guileful ruse. In short, a tactic is an art of the weak.[1]

Introduction

SOCIAL THEORISTS CONSIDER SURVEILLANCE to be a key institutional dimension of many contemporary, technologically advanced, capitalist societies. Resistance to surveillance has not, however, taken the form of a mass oppositional social movement. The study of counter-surveillance has tended to focus on specific campaigns of resistance in urban centres against particular technologies, as well on disparate groups who perform their resistance as a kind of neo-Situationist protest before public video cameras. It is against this background that I want to critically analyze the activities and publications of University of Toronto engineer Steve Mann and his development of wearable personal technologies that permit him to "shoot back" at surveillance cameras.

Mann has an unfortunate tendency to blame front-line workers in the service sector for their own oppression, figuring them as agents of surveillance. His recent response to this charge was to caricature it as a reductionistic, left-wing defence of "workers" that failed to grasp his goal of psychically liberating individuals in the name of the protection of a "humanistic space" otherwise under constant pressure from intrusive surveillance technologies.[2] Mann's efforts lack a theoretical appreciation of a microphysics of power that cannot be frozen in such an opposition, and his tactics are overly symmetrical and beholden to an insufficiently analyzed image of "mirroring." Nevertheless, his efforts expose a fundamentally important point: the need for reciprocity in a distanciated form of observation (anonymous surveillors operating at a distance from those under surveillance) that does not permit reciprocal exchange (i.e., the exchange of visual information issuing from surveilled to surveillor).

Mann may not appreciate the thesis on power elaborated by Michel Foucault, who suggests that if power is a relational energetics, then it is everywhere and opposition to it is also everywhere; hence it does not pool in one place. Neither does Mann reflect on the discursive production of subjectivity and knowledge about it that invalidates his essentialistic conception of the subject. Those social theorists who ask why there is not a social movement against surveillance also fail to grasp this point in posing the question in the form of a sociological lament. By "shooting back" at unidirectional mechanisms of distanciated observation by means of his own innovative engineering designs, Mann attempts to steal away a surveillance system's monopoly over disciplinary gazes. He has understood this much: surveillance systems, no matter how much they allow for participation, attempt to make reciprocity impossible.

Counter-Surveillance in Social Theory

Social theories of surveillance and counter-surveillance have made productive use of Anthony Giddens' concept of time-space distanciation and the social relations resulting from this crucial feature of modernity. Giddens develops the concept of distanciation through an analysis of the *disembedding* of social activities from specific places or locales (their situatedness).[3] Disembedding is a phenomenon resulting from the emptying of time and space and the possibilities revealed in their separation (the separation of when from where), that is widely referred to either as space-time compression or implosion, and accomplished with technological advances in transportation and communication.[4] Hence, video surveillance is described in terms of an asymmetrical relation between surveillor and surveilled, a distanciated form of observation in which reciprocity (exchange of visual information issuing from the watched to the watcher) is thought to be difficult if not impossible.[5]

However, on the question of social movements, Giddens has proved less responsive since he mechanically maps types of social movements onto the institutional dimensions of modernity, aligning labour against capital, ecology against industry, peace against military power, and free speech and democratic rights movements against the constraints of surveillance.[6] For Giddens, surveillance is one of the key institutions of capitalist modernity, and free speech and democratic rights movements arise in direct response to an institution of modernity whose historical roots, while apparently deep, embrace an unwieldy range of phenomena. The idea of "answering back" to surveillance as an institution is a springboard to the debate around resistance arising from Giddens's work.[7] If certain technologies are defined along Giddens's lines through the concept of distanciated observation, response becomes extremely difficult and, perhaps most importantly, counter-surveillance is limited to a small group or individual affair rather than a widespread practice. Care must be taken not to accept this ontological positioning as definitive.

Still, social theorists have been struck by the absence of a broadly based, unified social movement specifically contesting the rise of societies of surveillance. Resistance to the diverse modes of surveillance, new social relations, and subordinations of the information economy by individuals, groups, and institutions have, however, certainly proliferated and become more and more commonplace, even if these lack a unique, unifying imaginary or shared organizational base. Attention has turned to specific, spontaneous mobilizations that pose a range of challenges from the non-serious to serious: from teenage pranksterism to workplace avoidance tactics.[8] Such theorists have not of course been blind to the burgeoning governmental privacy bureaucracies, not to mention non-governmental watchdogs, as a dominant form of resistance to surveillance. On a day-to-day basis, investigative journalism also plays an important role, as does web activism around privacy issues and cyber protest in all its diversity. Privacy legislation, initially figured as a form of resistance, tends to crowd out the social-movements approach. The legal remedies for individuals (dating from the American juridical perspective of the early 1970s) have included no end of legal speculations around torts such as dollar compensations for wrongdoings linked to intrusive surveillance, non-legislative solutions, contracts and warranties, and the fiduciary obligation of the data-holder or handler to use personal information only for the benefit of the subject. These legal remedies include legislative relief from data gathering, a relief that implies the implementation of a wide range of acts (freedom of information, freedom from commercial solicitation, fair credit reporting, and varieties of consent and refusal of consent mechanisms).[9]

In order to clarify my approach, I want to suggest that privacy legislation is not obviously a form of resistance; using Giddens's terms, I want to situate privacy legislation, especially its legal and policy dimensions, squarely in the institutional domain of surveillance and administrative power. The oft-noted enabling and constraining elements of surveillance—increasing involvement, but veering dangerously toward totalitarianism—place privacy legislation, the protection of personal information, and legal recourses to freedom of information in the domain of self-reproducing, yet enabling *institutional* aspects of surveillance. We are still faced with the problem of a sociological analysis of resistance to surveillance, and in this approach we may want to regain certain privacy discourses, especially those of the non-governmental organizations that more closely correspond, in their express aims, to the resistance model advocated by Giddens. But the characteristics of these forms of resistance involve oppositional identities that are not stable from the outset (contra classist apriorism). New context-dependent identities are only won through struggles of articulation in the "moving equilibria" of the field of antagonisms of hegemonic power (struggles articulating the range of differences, shifting boundaries, relative unities, and elastic hierarchies [subordination by consent] from which they derive their character, and importantly, create problems around identity formation).[10] The language of new alliances, rainbow coalitions, transversal connections, alternative flows, and remakings of territories and singularities in the processes of subject-formation[11] all speak of the fluidity and plurality of the ideological field in which resistances arise. The idea, then, that there is a one-to-one correspondence between institution and social movement is incoherent in these terms. Sensing this incoherence, social theorists like David Lyon have noted that many of the counter-surveillance activities performed by small groups and individuals have no formal connections with privacy bureaucracies or official lobbies but respond, instead, on the ground to the technologies of surveillance whose intrusion into the corners of everyday life seems to intensify and perfuse through new technologies with alarming regularity.[12]

In the British sociological literature of surveillance, highlights of specific campaigns of resistance in urban centres (London and Brighton) against particular technologies have been documented. For instance, actions include stickering, public performances, mischief created by false crime scenarios against Closed Circuit Television (CCTV) networks, anti-CCTV workshops at the big English summer youth festivals such as Glastonbury, and political support from the Green Party (UK).[13] Ecology is not a singular political value but reveals certain orientations that intersect with local anti-technological struggles and from which may emerge antagonistic actions resisting certain visible manifestations of surveillance (e.g., the stand-alone surveillance camera tower refigured as a May pole). Yet one of the features of these actions is that they are short-lived, tend to quickly disperse and go into hiding, and display a lively artistic, often playful, character. It is this temporal dimension that interests me here. I want to regain it through consideration of three diverse examples, but under the guidance of the theoretical considerations of ingenious retakings of time in a space that is not under one's control and weak, oppositional, tactical practices studied by Michel de Certeau and Jean-François Lyotard, among others.[14]

The first study is recommended by Gilles Deleuze—the creation of interruptive vacuoles of noncommunication in a society characterized by control and communication; the second is a neo-Situationist street performance by the Surveillance Camera Players; the third and main study concerns Mann's development of wearable personal technologies that permit one to "shoot back" at surveillance cameras.

Interrupting Control and Communication

Gilles Deleuze maintains that Michel Foucault had already left behind disciplinary society in his conception of panopticism for one of continuous control and instant communication—not an iron cage, but a wired cage—a control society based not on confinement but on the opening of hitherto closed sites (distance education, community care, decentralized labour in electronic cottages).[15] This announced the displacement of disciplinary societies based on confinement by control societies that capitalize on the breakdown of institutional sites with "free-floating," open systems. These are "just as rigorous as the harshest confinement," but are based on *modulations* (alterations according to circumstances) rather than *moulds* (firmly set and into which one must be made to fit). Modulations entail continuous assessment, postponement of every end, and passwords that allow coded "dividuals," as Deleuze calls them, to move from one complementary institution to another or, conversely, to fall between them. Deleuze emphasizes continuity and integrated circuitry within an intensified discipline adapted to institutions without walls. In an interview with Toni Negri, Deleuze addresses the issue of resistance to such ceaseless control, even though he is not especially hopeful: "Computer piracy and viruses, for example, will replace strikes and what the nineteenth century called 'sabotage' ('clogging' the machinery). You ask whether control or communication societies will lead to forms of resistance that might reopen the way for a communism understood as the 'transversal organization of free individuals.' Maybe, I don't know."[16] Later, against the hegemony of communication he raises this idea: "The key thing may be to create vacuoles of noncommunication, circuit breakers, so we can elude control."[17] This creativity breaks communication at some point by establishing *cavities* through which messages either fail to pass or pass all too well. An example of the latter is a kind of Deleuzean "hacking" (a curiosity about technology leading to experimental exploration and rule-breaking) that eludes control temporarily without destroying the network, in the case of computers; rather, the network's ability to identify a hacker is broken by the creation of a vacuole of the sort known as an "unauthorized access device…

which masks the user's true identity,"[18] but allows one to make use of the technology. The vacuole-barrier-mask (Steve Jobs and Stephen Wozniak's famous "blue boxes" for "phone phreaking," and all subsequent boxes—red, beige, brown, coffee) does not mask the hacker's actions, which may be monitored, but for a certain time at least, divorces such actions from the body of the actor-hacker performing them. An example of a vacuole as non-communication suggests more virulent forms of network attacks of the sort developed by "hacktivists" (those who use computer networks for political protest), such as the creation of disturbances through denial of service attacks (using FloodNet software that swarms sites and saturates lines), actions redirecting browsers to alternative sites, replacement of site contents ("spoofing," virtual graffiti), and worms and viruses (autonomously propagated or encouraged through user stupidity) whose eradication may require network shutdowns.[19] The result is "Freedom Downtime," as a recent issue of 2600: The Hacker Quarterly, stated on the cover (Summer 2000) in support of the documentary film of the same name.

My approach to the question of creating vacuoles is concerned not with the spatiality of a cavity but with temporality (e.g., "stealing time" from university mainframes and causing downtime). The temporality of small, weak, cunning instruments may be brought to bear upon magisterial discourses, not from some exterior position, but from within. These may operate for no more than "a fleeting instant... unsettling the magisterial position and the assumptions underlying it."[20] In short, a disturbance or interruption is created whose outcome is a temporally defined release within a surveilled space. A Deleuzean-inspired hacktivism is an art of time, a surreptitious incursion that retakes time against the process of production toward different ends. The vacuole is the gap between authentication and identification; the time-span of that gap is limited before the "bug" (computer virus) is linked to an offline body. Indeed, each time a major virus such as Melissa (1999), Iloveyou (2000), or Anna Kournikova (2001) circulates, the drama of detection is measured in days (Onel de Guzman was apprehended in seven days), and wild speculation of the number of computers infected and users affected, costs in dollars to remedy the situation, and the percentage of systems shut down (value judgements about a code's maliciousness) give the narrative structure. Short tactical incursions do not, in an absolute way, substitute non-communication for communication. Rather, the goal from the hacker's perspective is to maintain anonymity or defer the inevitable apprehension, and, as detection time diminishes, to write a program language that leaves less and less of a signature, an identification, a style of aberrant decoding, that is recognizable by investigators steeped in tracking bugs and analyzing strings (lines of code) of programming language.

Why time? As de Certeau clarified, it is the proper dimension of tactics: exercise minimum force, augmented by memory and knowledge, at an opportune moment, taking as little time as possible in order to maximize the effects of one's tactical incursion. And then disappear into the vacuole.[21]

Neo-Situationist Responses to Surveillance

At 1:00 p.m. (Eastern Standard Time) on Tuesday, 30 November 1999, the Surveillance Camera Players < http://www.panix.com/~notbored/the-scp .html> performed an anti-WTO (World Trade Organization) play in front of a surveillance camera overlooking Fifth Avenue in NYC that uploaded every thirty seconds to the following website: < http://www.irational.org/cgibin /cctv/cctv.cgi?action=console_frame&location=0 >. From this website a direct fax could be sent to the local precinct of the NYC Police Department reporting any suspicious behaviour.

When is a surveillance camera the occasion for a performance rather than the detection of suspicious behaviour and the protection of commodities and consumers? Scenes of detection from the classic Orwellian Telescreen to the security consoles of art galleries, to the cramped little dramas unfolding around Automated Teller Machines (ATMs)—and coming soon to biometric Rapid Pay Machines (RPMs)—have become topics for recent e-work; but using apparatuses of surveillance for performance pieces is still relatively rare. It is, however, an art that has been practised by the Surveillance Camera Players (SCP) of New York City since 1996.

Co-founders Bill Brown and Susan Hull combine community activism, Marxian-inspired sociological critiques of the diminishment of privacy and personal freedom in the information age, and avant-garde aesthetic practices. They are street performers and agitators who refuse to work in theatres or performance spaces proper. The work of the SCP constitutes an attempt to take back the right to assemble in a public place and sends a pointed message to those guards and police monitoring these places. The plays/performances are short and silent, using printed boards with bubbles and captions borrowed from comic books to convey dialogue, scene changes, and political messages, and the players are all amateur actors. This is not "content" for the amusement of the surveillors. It is what Brown calls "message" rather than method acting.

This kind of "programming" is a variation on "culture jamming" which envisages both the corruption or jamming of existing mainstream media content and the provision of new, critical content with its feet firmly placed in the radical and politically advanced aesthetic tradition of the Situationist International. The Situationist International was born in 1957 in Cosio d'Arroscia, Italy, and later became associated with avant-garde practices on the left bank in Paris during the 1960s. The language preferred by the SCP, who are definitely Not Ready for Prime Time, is that of rerouting and diverting means of social control by exploring their hitherto unappreciated opportunities for subversive activities. The emphasis is on the action—the performance as the creation of a situation that transforms everyday life—directed back at the surveillors by the surveilled. However, this return is theorized in terms of a critique of the ideology of transparency that valorizes clarity and visibility and problematizes opacity and obscurity: before the surveillance camera any act that does not conform in advance to the expectation of non-privacy is suspect and subject to discipline according to the operational codes of the surveillors.[22] To conform is to become transparent, to give up secrecy. Although the rhetoric of transparency is based in international economic relations, it is used to disguise the political dimension of accountability that is imposed as a condition of participation. Transparency also suggests promises and rewards: security, participation in decision-making, and sharing of resources.

Importantly, the SCP reject the tactic of inflicting "reciprocal transparency" on surveillants, which I will discuss in my third study, on the grounds that opacity can be revolutionary (figured in the masked faces of the Zapatistas[23]). Resistance to globalization that imposes transparency under the rules of uniformity and open accountability (rendering Chinese firms "transparent to the eyes of the World Trade Organization") is not to be reproduced in a "never-ending struggle for 'accountability.'" This position puts the SCP at odds with Steve Mann.

The performance pieces are produced as a critique of the social effects of a society of surveillance in which interpersonal interactions have been grossly distorted in many complex ways, from the flagrant abuse of such cameras under the pretext of security by unscrupulous employers for voyeuristic purposes in women's washrooms, to the production of potential criminals by police interpretations of groups of certain kinds of persons as deviant (the poor, Black, Aboriginal youth, or anyone for that matter who is not properly participating in consumer society or who already answers to the abstract profile of a likely suspect). Like the psychogeographers of the Situationist International floating around Paris, gathering the "ambiences" of urban locales for their signature driftworks—imaginary maps of the real world—the "stage" of the SCP is the surveilled space before the camera and their natural milieux are subway platforms, street corners, sidewalks, and, of course, the Internet.

The guerrilla programming of video surveillance equipment has included performances of such works as Alfred Jarry's important play from 1896

Ubu Roi, whose original excrementitious opening salvo of "Merdre!" caused a riot, and is here rendered as a delinquent "Fuk!" (Ubu's favourite exclamation); a version of Edgar Allan Poe's "The Raven" reduced to rotating posters in which an actor labelled "Poe," holding either the image of a fashion model or a woman's mask, also holds aloft a placard reading "O Lenore!" while a nameless actor brandishing either a death's head mask or a drawing of a raven holds up a poster with a speech bubble that reads "Nevermore"; a robust *Waiting for Godot* that features two actors wearing signs identifying them as Estragon and Vladimir, respectively, who chase one another or sit under a third person labelled "a tree." All these works were "adapted" for the little camera by Art Toad (Bill Brown's alias) and demonstrate the importance of short interventions of no more than 10 minutes, the "silent treatment" of modernist texts for the silent street stage and the significance of posters. Brown does not like the term "adaptation" and prefers to liken his work to "attacks" on existing works.

These works warrant the label "guerrilla" since they are performed by anonymous actors, using (let us say) weak tactics of popular resistance; but these tactics are weak in the sense that they are momentary, unfinished, and unpolished. The guerrilla programming of surveillance cameras is an art of time, of the timely manoeuvre, because it lacks a space of its own, a proper autonomous place, over which it has control. The scp does not take control of the camera—it is merely borrowed. Do they fill the frame? Yes, they occupy it with a new content, but only momentarily. Tactically, guerrilla programming retakes time from the surveillance mechanisms of an environment policed in the name of business interests, incorporated city services, and security operations. Indeed, this is a sophisticated, reflexive art of weakness: "The very inadequacy of the scp's theatre of cruelty—the fact that it seems powerless to actually stop generalized video surveillance—is actually its strength."[24] This is precisely what is meant by using the tactical strength of the weak and deploying timely maneuvers as opposed to occupying a strategic site and bringing it under one's control.

Personal Technologies

Toronto-based engineer Steve Mann (fig. 1) has developed a counter-surveillance tactic of "shooting back" at surveillance cameras with his Wearable Wireless Webcam, a personal technology[25] that he developed at MIT's Media Lab and the University of Toronto. Many of the documents on his sprawling website address his response to ubiquitous surveillance, primarily in commercial environments, with varying degrees of sociological naivete, homespun philosophy, borrowed aesthetics (photogrammetry in

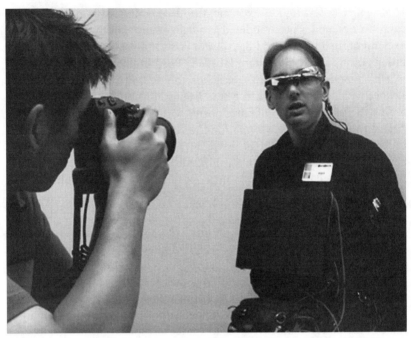

Figure 1   Steve Mann, *Privacy Issues of Wearable Cameras versus Surveillance Cameras*, 2001 (courtesy Gallery TPW, Toronto).

the manner of David Hockney's photography becomes pencigraphic image composition—the progressively seamless joining of many images into one image), and a rhetoric of contempt (for the establishment), but mostly with "techno-fixes" (technological solutions): "Miniaturization has turned the technology into an equalizer rather than an oppressor.... The problem of surveillance contains its own solution."[26]

Mann likes clichés such as "turning the tables" and the like to describe what he does. His sense of resistance is worked out far from the technological frame of reference. Symmetry of response is the central principle in his arsenal, buffeted by fairness, equality, independence (plurality of individual cameras providing evidence as opposed to a single source "Big Brother" system), and honesty (Mann is sensitive to editing as a form of falsification of evidence). Mann's counter-surveillance is a variation on a privacy solution, but his imaginary marks it off from legislative remedies. He has us wonder about fairness in the context of imagining that only wearable cameras were permitted in the society of surveillance. In this scenario, "privacy equals seclusion. Observation needs company." Observation implies a kind of group co-operation in the service of reducing crime, but without a theory of community or the social or indeed policing. A crime-fighting ethos certainly animates many of Mann's statements ("Who's Afraid of Wearable Wireless Webcam?"), and he creates a persona of a cyborg in a battle with the dark forces of corporate paranoia—the number of times he repeats the mantra-like phrase "ceiling domes of wine-dark opacity" is in itself a fairly conventional, yet poetic invocation of the enemy using typical light-and-dark metaphors.[27] As I suggested in my introductory remarks, the symmetry of response (Mann-the-cyborg-PhD and the apparatuses that have him under surveillance) is problematic. In a field of diffused power relations you cannot pin down the enemy. By the same token, you cannot line up a superhero cyborg and a master mechanism of surveillance.

Critics of Mann's brand of counter-surveillance have pointed out that his tactic of "looking back" is aimed only at front-line personnel (shop clerks),[28] whom he stigmatizes as collaborators with that vague bogey, the "Establishment": "one should not feel that it is a violation of an employee's privacy to Netcam an employee of a shop that uses video surveillance. That employee, by supporting an organization that uses video surveillance, has violated your privacy. Supporting an organization means cooperating with it (e.g., working for it, even though paid to do so)."[29]

In the tertiary sector (retail shops are Mann's great haunting grounds), insecure employment with minimal benefits is the norm, disaffection is high, and working conditions are often poor (see fig. 2); but devoid of sociological

"Shooting Back 1"

FIGURE 2 Steve Mann, *Privacy Issues of Wearable Cameras versus Surveillance Cameras*, 2001 (courtesy Gallery TPW, Toronto).

imagination, Mann's reactionary politics are given full vent. Elsewhere, he is content to catalogue abuses of video surveillance by "organizations" as he calls them (some private, some public) in employee locker rooms and quasi-public toilets, and fire exits illegally chained shut. This signals for him the existence of a problematic "centralized infrastructure" (an unanalyzed theory of power, in other words, inherited from George Orwell's critique of totalitarianism and applied to the contemporary social field). For Mann, the technological imagination, by contrast, knows no limits.

The most problematic element in Mann's work is clearly the figure of the clerk or floor manager and his inability to appreciate conditions of employment in the tertiary sector (not to mention that these front-line representatives of so-called totalitarian systems of surveillance—"attendants/maintainers/supporters of the video surveillance superhighway"[30]—are themselves subject to surveillance, a point especially important for all security personnel including police officers.[31] Mann may not understand the socioeconomic conditions of his favourite stomping grounds, and he may even believe they are non-reflective (he typically refers to them as "blind") about their situation and the implications of surveillance, but his laudable activist goals suggest that these problems are surmountable.

It is evident that Mann has learned something important from the retail environments he likes to haunt, for he understands one implication of the commercial discourse of personalization all too well. He maintains that the revolution in personal, portable computing, the advent of smart spaces, has not been personal enough: "neither laptop computers...nor ubiquitous multimedia computing/surveillance offer the kind of truly personal environment that would best suit our needs."[32] Multi-functional (integrated functions, unobtrusive design) clothing is Mann's response to smart surveillance environments; what Mann calls "personal imaging" enhances visual awareness of surroundings (and memory of them) rather than diminishing it, like personal sound systems such as Walkmans and arcade-style virtual reality technologies. Mann is specifically interested in the potential of "visual memory prosthetics" such as face recognition (in response to widespread use of face recognition systems and related smart CCTV systems around the world in airports and casinos, and by police organizations) but from a "first-person" rather than a "third-person" perspective: "if face recognition is used ubiquitously by ordinary individuals as part of their day-to-day living, it will give rise to a more democratic society in which policemen, as well as ordinary citizens (and shopkeepers as well as shoppers, bank tellers as well as bankers) will be recognizable and accountable for their actions." This technodemocratic argument is staged in response to Privacy International's call for public debate on burgeoning CCTV systems and their prohibition on privacy grounds. Becoming less intentionalist in inspiration, this argument suggests a concomitant shift away from the scapegoating of front-line personnel discussed above. Mann has derived several experiments such as the Maybe and Probably Cameras (Diffusionist actions in which security personnel are spotted by shoppers and wired cyborgs outfitted with Mann's gear remain uncertain if their personal gear is operative and actually transmitting images to a remote site), and *My Manager* (more expressly Reflectionist since it shoots back at "the Panopticon" with methods of its own). These experiments situate Mann as a recording probe, a mere servomechanism, whose wearable technologies may or may not be transmitting images to the web (this is what he means when he claims to be a robot, or a puppet controlled by a remote camera operator). Mann has devised these experiments in such a way that he must appeal, like so many of the clerks he confronts, to "his manager" to determine if his systems are operative. Still, even these tactics operate within the symbolic economy of the mirror. Mann videotapes front-line staff and transmits the images back to his "manager," who requires him to wear a special outfit and absolve himself of responsibility for this activity. Mann may offer to such staff if they object to Mann's presence and activities, a Request for Deletion form that they can submit to his "manager" since Mann himself cannot delete the images he merely records and transmits.

Mann's recent experiments such as "Can Humans Being Clerks Make Clerks Be Human? Exploring the Fundamental Difference between Ubi-Comp and WearComp"[33] have tested the results of this erasure of intentionality (what he calls "reduction of existentiality"). Mann still remains fixated on front-line staff in the figure of the clerk, but he attempts to formally account (a ranking scale from one extreme of physical violence to the other of funding Mann's research projects) for and register their reactions to his experiments in counter-surveillance. The overtness or obviousness of his activities is an independent variable, itself a function of other variables such as the *perceived validity* of the activity: for example, in videoconferencing with his partner about a purchase, acceptability increased the more that Mann appeared to be required to perform such an activity (existentiality), while singling out an individual was much less acceptable than recording a total field with a wearable cam (selectivity). The Maybe Cameras exploited the Existentiality Axis, while the Selectivity Axis was adjusted by various devices, some handheld, some with obvious blinking light-emitting diodes, various versions of Tilt-Pan-Zoom domes (as a pendant, on a backpack, etc.) (see fig. 3). Ultimately, Mann confirmed his hypothesis that the degree of overtness exists in inverse proportion to existentiality and selectivity (overtness achieving acceptability as existentiality and selectivity diminish). This attempt at quantifying the problematic of the clerk is a step forward from the scapegoating characteristic of Mann's

FIGURE 3   Steve Mann, *Smart Clothing*, 2001 (courtesy Gallery TPW, Toronto).

work in the mid-nineties. Mann still rehearses the notion of the difference between *being human* and *being a clerk* or *being an individual* and *being a clerk* but at least attempts a space for transformation: "the individual human becoming a clerk forces the clerk to become an individual human and make responsible decisions outside the scope of just being a clerk." I am working on the assumption, mentioned above, that the problematic of the clerk is surmountable and that Mann's work will tend more and more to loosen itself from the deleterious consequences of its lack of sociological imagination. A final note on the clerk is in order. It is a distraction of the first order that exemplifies the unfortunate effects of Mann's mirror metaphors. The mirror incorrectly gives the impression that the abstraction of data from persons as data shadows under the gaze of video cameras and face recognition technologies, not to mention "dataveillance" technologies, produces recognizable doubles. I cannot develop this point here, but suffice to say that the combinatorial codings, combinations, categorizations, and matchings of systems of abstraction produce non-iconic data shadows: even if you caught a glimpse of your double, there is no reason to assume that you would recognize yourself.

Let us go back, then, to the big picture. Mann wants to return the gaze of a largely invisible apparatus that renders surveilled subjects visible with an equivalent apparatus that renders visible its exposed technologies (the cameras themselves and front-line employees), by similar means but without the same invisible infrastructure, that is, by downloading and posting images of the shootback on a non-password protected website. This is a kind of counter-gift that is overly symmetrical and mimetic, what the SCP decry as meeting transparency with transparency and thereby multiplying surveillance. To employ Baudrillardian terms, it fails to escape the logic of the disciplinary gaze by merely repeating and extending it. Despite this,

Mann has grasped one essential point: the need for reciprocity when a distanciated form of observation does not permit it. By giving back distanciated observation of his own design, Mann attempts to steal away the non-reciprocity and unidirectionality of the disciplinary gazes. His response may be too strong, too closely linked to the model he is critiquing. For he seems to desire no more than a transfer, through decentering and multiplication, of power.

The question that fascinates Jean Baudrillard is whether a counter-gift can draw a system onto a different plane, making it strange to itself in as much as it is obliged to accept such a counter-gift in a circuit of exchange that it had hitherto controlled by prohibiting exchange or by blocking the possibility of a circuit. This is the problem of reciprocity.[34] The key point is the counter-gift's ability to make a system of disciplinary-distanciated observation acknowledge the obligation to receive (the counter-gift of "shooting back"). First, then, is the obligation to receive and, then, caught in the circuit of exchange, having been drawn into a different domain, the system experiences the obligation to repay, ultimately leading to the decentralization of surveillance networks, open access to security systems by those surveilled, and Mann's dream of reciprocal accountability, dignity, and so on, all of which is spelled out in Mann's plans for a mass counter-surveillance action, National Accountability Day (24 December) in which the prohibition of taking pictures of surveilled establishments and their apparatuses of surveillance will be broken: "Shoot Authority First, Question Authority Later."[35] At the very least, Mann hopes to provoke dialogue and discussion between the security establishments and civil liberties/activist organizations around the question of widespread urban video surveillance. Further, Mann effectively exploits a truism of surveillance—that "anyone who directly challenged, by gesture or deed, the right of the cameras to monitor them was especially subject to targeting."[36] Mann draws security personnel into the open, and thereby draws attention to himself, allowing him greater scrutiny in an exchange of sorts, even if this only means a close-up shot of a hand being placed over his camera lens. Mann's tactic of exposing video surveillance systems is more active and truly exchangist than civil liberties projects. For instance, the case of the NYC Surveillance Camera Project of the New York Civil Liberties Union raises awareness of video surveillance by mapping and categorizing by proprietorship in addition to calling for legislation to limit their use, all of the surveillance cameras in Manhattan, which number in the thousands and are undoubtedly increasing geometrically after the events of 9/11.[37]

Concluding Remarks

Does shooting back have a rhythm, an "accented beat" of social rearticulation, in Baudrillard's language?[38] Has Mann sensed the existence of a
"scansion" in which "something is given in the same movement and following the same rhythm. Otherwise there is no reciprocity and it is quite simply not given"?[39] The existence of such a rhythm does not guarantee that
exchange will be successful, and this lack of guarantee is both a weakness
and a strength. Shooting back, despite its many problems, awakens a possibility kept dormant by the disciplinary gazes of power. If we are to
believe Foucault, power is not uniform, Big-Brotherish, but is produced by
force relations immanent to a specific sphere.[40] Shooting back responds to
the irreversibility of the disciplinary gaze and its monopoly over the power
to render things visible, by responding to surveillance as if it were issuing
a challenge and by breaking through its tyrannous ubiquity with technical
creativity. The rhythms of surveillance-counter-surveillance are irregular
and ragged, but this is the temporal dimension that I regain from Mann's
counter-gift of his wearable webcams. Despite the differences between the
SCP and Mann, these forms of web-supported counter-surveillance actions
are fleeting but linger electronically away from the scenes of performances
that are not their own, and have a rhythmic irregularity (aside from a few
marked days of protest and announced events) that provide tentative models open to creative derivations, extensions, and reappropriations.

While reflecting on the relationship of his work to that of Jennifer Ringley of JenniCam fame,[41] Mann overcomes the limitations of the heroic
techno-individual and achieves a kind of symbolic pact with those who
interact via email with him as they watch the continuous feed from his
WearComp gear on the web. The "scansion" of this exchange is nothing
less than what Mann imagines as a "cyborg community" whose interactiv-
ity (immediate response and genuine *communication*) would be "real."[42]
Mann's recent work reflects on more than two decades of counter-surveillance experimentation with personal technologies and the factors shaping the kind of social interactions resulting from them. Within the terms of
exchange, counter-gifts of counter-surveillance actions have, like all practices, if we listen to Pierre Bourdieu for a moment, a timing—selecting an
occasion on which to retort, carefully calculating the effects of delaying,
waiting for an opportune moment, and seizing it. Time as rhythm has
"social efficacy"[43] and time-sensitive practice resists totalization, objectification, codification, and homogenization. A temporal dimension of
exchange introduces uncertainty (that is, Mann is chastised by those visiting his website for "ogling cleavage"). Counter-surveillance tactics must
remain weak and deploy time rather than attempt to mobilize space, which

FIGURE 4 Steve Mann, *Steve Mann's Prior Art Opening*, 2001 (courtesy Gallery TPW, Toronto).

they do not have at their disposal, perhaps except in the form of storage banks. In Mann's recent exhibition in Toronto, "Steve Mann: Prior Art: Arts of Record for Personal Safety" (see fig. 4), curator Kathleen Pirrie Adams commented on the question of surplus: where do all the images go that are collected by surveillance cameras around the world? Such excess raises questions of "saving and/or deleting and/or taping over."[44] Mann leaves a "public record" of his experiments in cyborgspace as an antidote to the "accumulation of secret dossiers."[45]

In the first hacktivist study undertaken here, control and communication are broken by cunning attacks that neutralize targeted networks for a time; in both the video surveillance examples, distanciated observation is decoded in terms of a weak content-based appearance and disappearance, and a challenge to formulate a response and initiate an exchange through the return of a counter-gifting action to a limited system of linked points of a relational power, whose rhythm constitute its temporality.[46] While the SCP exploited existing video surveillance with "revolutionary" content, Mann has issued experimental counter-gifts of his own engineering—a more formal response—that challenges factory-produced "smartness." Mann does not so much break communication as attempt to dupe networked surveillance systems in given environments into participating in the very thing they try to secure as non-participatory.

Notes

I would like to thank Bridget Indelicato at Gallery TPW, Toronto, for providing images from the exhibition "Steve Mann: Art of Record for Personal Safety." All images used courtesy of Gallery TPW.

1 Michel de Certeau, *The Practice of Everyday Life*, trans. Steven F. Rendall (Berkeley: University of California Press, 1984), 37.

2 Steve Mann with Hal Niedzviecki, *Cyborg: Digital Destiny and Human Possibility in the Age of the Wearable Computer* (Toronto: Doubleday, 2001), 117.

3 Anthony Giddens, *The Consequences of Modernity* (Stanford: Stanford University Press, 1990), 17–20.

4 Anthony Giddens, "Time and Space: Time-Space, Structure, System," *The Giddens Reader*, ed. Philip Cassell (Stanford: Stanford University Press, 1993), 178–79.

5 Clive Norris and Gary Armstrong, "Introduction: Power and Vision," *Surveillance, Closed Circuit Television and Social Control*, ed. Clive Norris, Jade Moran, and Gary Armstrong (Aldershot: Ashgate, 1998), 4–5.

6 Giddens, *Consequences*, 159.

7 David Lyon and Elia Zureik, "Surveillance, Privacy, and the New Technology," *Computers, Surveillance and Privacy* (Minneapolis: University of Minnesota Press, 1996), 12.

8 David Lyon, *The Electronic Eye: The Rise of Surveillance Society* (Cambridge: Polity, 1994), 175–76; David Lyon, *Surveillance Society: Monitoring Everyday Life*, (Buckingham: Open University Press, 2001), 35.

9 See Arthur R. Miller, "Computers, Data Banks and Individual Privacy: An Overview"and John P. Flannery, "Commercial Information Brokers," both published in *Surveillance, Dataveillance and Personal Freedoms: Use and Abuse of Information Technology*, ed. Staff of the Columbia Human Rights Law Review (Fair Lawn, NJ: R.E. Burdick, 1973), 11–22 and 215–47.

10 Ernesto Laclau and Chantal Mouffe, *Hegemony and Socialist Strategy: Towards a Radical Democratic Politics* (London: Verso, 1985), 168–71.

11 Félix Guattari and Antonio Negri, *Communists Like Us: New Spaces of Liberty, New Lines of Alliance*, trans. Michael Ryan (New York: Semiotext(e), 1990), 141.

12 Lyon, *Surveillance Society*, 133.

13 Simon G. Davies, "CCTV: A New Battleground for Privacy," *Surveillance, Closed Circuit Television and Social Control*, ed. Clive Norris, Jade Moran, and Gary Armstrong (Aldershot: Ashgate, 1998), 243–54.

14 Especially significant is the work of de Certeau, *The Practice of Everyday Life*; Jean-François Lyotard, "On the Strength of the Weak," trans. Roger McKeon, *Semiotext(e)* 3.2 (1978): 204–14; see also Gary Genosko, "The Struggle for an Affirmative Weakness," *Current Perspectives in Social Theory* 12 (1992): 179–94.

15 Gilles Deleuze, "Control and Becoming" [Interview with Antonio Negri] and "Postscript on Control Societies," *Negotiations 1972-1990*, trans. Martin Joughin (New York: Columbia University Press, 1995), 174–75.

16 Deleuze, 175.

17 Deleuze, 175.

18 Douglas Thomas, "Criminality on the Electronic Frontier: Corporeality and the Judicial Construction of the Hacker," *Information, Communication and Society* 1.4 (1998): 392.

19 See Dorothy Denning, "Hacktivism, and Cyberterrorism: The Internet as a Tool for Influencing Foreign Policy," 2000 <http://www.infowar.com/class_2/00/class2_020400b_j.shtml>.

20 Lyotard, "On the Strength of the Weak," 213.

21 de Certeau, *Practice of Everyday Life*, 82ff.

22 Surveillance Camera Players, "Time in the Shadows of Anonymity: Fighting against Surveillance Cameras, Transparency, and Global Capitalism." <http://www.panix.com/~notbored/transparent.html>. I have developed an analysis of "transparency" as a contemporary code that allows for the redefinition of all that is opaque (corruption, bribery, and even the secrecy of social relations themselves) as "terrorist" in an unpublished paper entitled "The Imposition of Transparency in Canada after 9/11," presented in the "Terror of Civilization" panel in the Canadian Political Science Association Congress Meetings 2002, Toronto.

23 The reference to the Zapatistas is again used in the SCP's explanation of its debts to Artaud's Theatre of Cruelty, especially the possibility of scripting and performing Artaud's *The Conquest of Mexico* and linking his sense of the necessity of indigenous forms of revolution with Zapatista tactics. Of equal significance is the SCP proposal to use Artaud's ideas of the priority of mise en scène over the script (already written), a theatre without texts, readers, interpreters, masterpieces, and even language: "Let the surveillance camera see all of it: the blank boards; the notepads full of sketches; the pencils, magic markers and spray-paint cans; and the hours of effort, discussion and deep concentration, as well as the show, 'the finished product,' itself " (Surveillance Camera Players, "Time in the Shadows").

24 Surveillance Camera Players, "The Surveillance Camera Players' Theatre of Cruelty" <http://www.panix.com/~notbored/artaud.html>.

25 In *The Consumer Society* (London: Sage, 1998), 88–90, Baudrillard addresses the paradox of personalization as a constraint internal to consumption understood as a form of social control. Based on the semiotic principle that no unit in a system has meaning in isolation because it is only defined negatively on the basis of what it is not, products (understood as signs) let you be yourself by constructing a synthetic personality, where one does not exist, by means of signs. This overly reflexive strategy involves the consumption of industrially manufactured differences, not genuine, metabolic, conflictual differences between persons, in conformity with an abstract model; both effectively require persons to relinquish any "real singularity" as they personalize themselves in greater and greater proximity to the abstract model in question. Mann's arguments in favor of the superiority of his WearComp system over HandyCams, for instance (*Cyborg*, p. 166ff), have an unintentional promotional tenor to them. WearCam as opposed to HandyCam merely places Mann and his creations in the production of differences that is the hallmark of consumer society. One might go further in this Baudrillardian critique and suggest that personalization by means of the WearComp system creates, as Mann suggests, "a new level of personal privacy," with the consequences that it erects signs of a privacy that it restores but only after the elimination of privacy in a surveillance society. Personal privacy thus becomes a prestige good.

26 Steve Mann, "Privacy Issues of Wearable Cameras Versus Surveillance Cameras," 1995 <http://www.wearcam.org.netcam privacy issues.html>.

27 Steve Mann, "Privacy Issues."

28 Heather Cameron, "Private Eyes, Public Eyes: Photography and the Surveillance Society," *Reflex Photo* 2 (2000): 13.

29 Steve Mann, "'Smart Clothing': Wearable Multimedia Computing and 'Personal Imaging' to Restore the Technological Balance Between People and Their Environments," 1996 <http://wearcam.org/acm-mm96/index.html>.

30 Steve Mann, "'Reflectionism' and 'Diffusionism': New Tactics for Deconstructing the Video Surveillance Superhighway," *Leonardo* 31.2 (1998): 93–102. <http://eyetap.org/wearcam/leonardo/my_hack_at_leonardo_html/index.htm>.

31 Richard V. Ericson, and Kevin D. Haggerty, *Policing the Risk Society* (Toronto: University of Toronto Press, 1997), 35.

32 Steve Mann, "Smart Clothing."

33 Steve Mann, "Can Humans Being Clerks Make Clerks Be Human? Exploring the Fundamental Difference between UbiComp and WearComp," *Informationstechnik und Technische Informatik* 43.2 (2001): 97–106. <http://wearcam.org/itti/itti.htm>.

34 Jean Baudrillard, *Symbolic Exchange and Death*, trans. Ian Hamilton Grant (London: Sage, 1993), 37. I explicate this theory in great detail in my essay "Undisciplined and Undisciplinable: Baudrillard's Radical Anthropology," *Undisciplined Theory* (London: Sage, 1998), 12–47. Baudrillard's most recent deployment of his theory of symbolic exchange appeared in his controversial response to the events of 9/11, "L'esprit du terrorisme," *Le Monde* (November 2, 2001). The counter-gift of death is the spirit of terrorism unleashed against a hegemonic world system that wants to expunge death, suicide and evil from its ranks. The terrorist attack on the twin towers of the World Trade Center—symbols of the operational involution of a system ruled by digital logic—was a symbolic counter-gift that shifted America onto a domain in which it became strange to itself. This challenge obliged a response superior in kind, in other words, the collapse of the towers.

35 Steve Mann, "Shootback Accountability Theatre, 1998 <http://www.wearcam.org/gat.htm>.

36 Clive Norris, "The Usual Suspects," 1997 <http://merlin.legend.org.uk/~brs/archive/stories97/Suspects.html>.

37 New York City Surveillance Camera Project, "Overview: New York City: A Surveillance Camera Town" <http://www.mediaeater.com/cameras/overview.html>.

38 Baudrillard, *Symbolic Exchange*, 131.

39 Baudrillard, *Symbolic Exchange*, 40.

40 Michel Foucault, *The History of Sexuality*, Vol. 1 (New York: Vintage, 1980), 92.

41 Jennifer Ringley, "JenniCam, life-online" <http://www.jennicam.com>.

42 Mann, *Cyborg*, 133–38.

43 Pierre Bourdieu, "The Work of Time," *The Gift: An Interdisciplinary Perspective*, ed. afke Komter (Amsterdam: Amsterdam University Press, 1996), 136.

44 Kathleen Pirrie Adams, "Prior Art: Art of Record for Personal Safety," 2001, Gallery TPW, <http://www.existech.com/tpw/essay.html>.

45 Mann, *Cyborg*, 139.

46 Mark Poster launched a critique of postmodernist naïveté, aimed specifically at Jean-François Lyotard, based on the utopian assumption of free access to databases "that does not take into account the performative effect of the discourse of databases, their ability to constitute subjects." Privacy legislation and freedom of information struggles misunderstand the character of databases and do not enable a critical understanding of the new subject formations of the information age, but rather rehearse the myth of the autonomous individual who gains power through manipulating the knowledge held in databases. This critique may be applied to Mann, especially his comments about the public nature of his web broadcasts and his storage of information. Databases, as a form of discourse, produce subjectivity and ways of knowing and experiencing. New knowledges about cyborg realities, for instance, produce new effects of power through new technologies. See Mark Poster, "Databases as Discourse; or, Electronic Interpellation," *Computers, Surveillance and Privacy*, ed. David Lyon and Elia Zureik (Minneapolis: University of Minnesota Press, 1996), 189–90.

2 Canadian Humour and National Culture
Move Over, Mr. Leacock

Beverly Rasporich

Canadians Discover Their Funny Bone

WHEN I WAS A GRADUATE STUDENT IN THE 1970s writing a dissertation on Stephen Leacock, an early-twentieth-century Canadian humorist, I was the butt of a repeated joke. When I told inquirers that my subject was Canadian humour, they inevitably burst into laughter, exclaiming that mine was going to be a short study, or that Canadian humour was surely an oxymoron, a contradiction in terms. At that time, the myth of the mirthless Canadian was widespread in the popular imagination. Since then, Canadians have discovered that they do indeed have a funny bone. In high culture, particularly literary studies, irony and its relationship to a collective Canadian imagination and the national identity have been the subject of ongoing sophisticated analyses. In mass culture, that is American popular culture, Canadian comedians have achieved unparalleled success and recognition. The continuous exodus of comics to Hollywood, such as John Candy, Martin Short, Dave Thomas, and Scott Thompson, who cut their comic teeth in Canada on such homegrown television programs as *SCTV* and *Kids in the Hall*, have led Canadians to believe that they may have a superior sense of humour, one that gives them a comic edge south of the forty-ninth parallel.

Comedians and cultural critics alike have suggested that this kind of success is based on the duality of our colonial experience and imagination in English Canada; ours is a broad, sophisticated perspective that internalizes the British tradition of absurdist humour, while at the same time absorbing American comic traditions from a thoughtful, often parodic, distance.[1] If Canadian comics abroad have an amazing double-sightedness, Canada at home also has an outstanding repertoire of humour, which currently functions in a multitude of communities and finds comic, ironic, satiric, and parodic expression in a variety of genres. Oral folk tales and jokes, stand-up comedy, musical performances, cartoons, paintings, contemporary art installations, folk-art works, radio, television, theatre, and a national literature with a remarkable, indisputably rich vein of irony are some of the venues by which Canadians demonstrate their love of laughter. The Internet, too, is creating new joke-sharing communities. I recently received a humorous email directed to all those who live, or have lived, in Thunder Bay. The humour here is informed by a widely held tenet of the national identity: that we are a northern frontier people living in a vast, inhospitable landscape. The message begins with "You know you are from Thunder Bay when ..." and lists such one-liners as

1. You measure distance in hours.
2. You know several people who have hit deer more that once.
3. Your grandparents drive at 100 kilometres per hour through 13 feet of snow and a raging blizzard—without flinching.
4. You know all four seasons: Almost Winter, Winter, Still Winter, and Construction.

This equation of Canada with northernness is very much bred in the cultural bone, beginning with the nationalist agenda of the "Canada First Movement" in the period after Confederation (1867). Historian Jack Bumsted points out that the pan-nationalist Canada Firsters were "convinced that Canada needed a distinctive culture, and it developed the concept that the nation's geography made it inevitable that it should be northern" and "it was not a far jump from northern geography to racialist ideas." One of the Firsters' members, Robert Grant Hamilton "insisted in a lecture eventually published as a pamphlet, that Canada 'must ever be a Northern country inhabited by the descendants of Northern races.'"[2]

For Arun P. Mukherjee, the mythology of the Great White North itself, a concept she describes as "an affectionate appellation used by Canadians to denote the long, wintry face of Canada," invites a discussion about racial valuing. She notes that, from a non-white point of view, there is potential irony in this colourless phrase. For her, it points to a marginalized discourse of irony directed by non-whites in a juxtapositional and parodic way towards the sacred national cows of dominant Canadians. She explains the ways in which this gets expressed: "For example, July 1, the erstwhile 'Dominion Day' and present 'Canada Day' has been called

'Humiliation Day' by Chinese Canadians—because to them the day is the anniversary of the infamous Chinese Immigration Act." First Nations people also parody Canadian patriotism: "Native Canadians create a similar parodic dissonance when they rewrite the national anthem by changing 'our home and native land' to 'our stolen native land.'"³ It is this evolving complexity of Canadian humour signified by the country's growing articulation of minority voices that I wish to address here, primarily in relation to national culture in English-speaking Canada.

National Culture and Political Cartooning

To begin with, the concept of national culture is an abstraction, a mythology—even an ideology—that consciously or unconsciously serves the needs of nation-makers. In the worst of times, it is used towards undemocratic purposes. One thinks automatically of Nazi Germany with its brutal hegemonic cultural imperatives. In my view, however, national culture is not simply determined and imposed on us by educators, policy-makers, and politicians; it is also an evolutionary, organic process, with a complex, transformational history in this country, a process that has startlingly different definitions in English and French Canada, and that shifts in part in relation to the will of the nation's peoples and their circumstances. Hockey, for example, has been a longstanding, regionally inclusive feature of Canada's national culture; but taken out of our arenas by being franchised as a North American sport, and no longer played as it once was as an all-consuming winter pastime on ponds, sloughs, and outdoor rinks, hockey has lost something of its national panache.

While sports have been important contributors to national culture and the national identity, there is no question that politicians set the national agendas—and in Canada, where there is a rich visual and cultural tradition of political cartooning, our cartoonists comment on them for us. Because humour is so deeply rooted in cultural values, attitudes, and realities, it can be a highly effective means of myth-making, of telling us who we are or ought to be, in a variety of forums, including the national arena. Depending on the genre and nature of the humour and the point of view of the humorist, of course, humour can invite a variety of audience responses, including affirmation, accommodation, protest, challenge, or even revolutionary change. Political cartooning is a genre that has periodically articulated radical, excoriating humour with serious consequences. Political cartooning, which began in the eighteenth century with the stinging political satires of James Gillray in England directed against Napoleon and the French, was, from this outset, a form of humour more hostile than genial.[4] It is a tradition that suits Sigmund Freud's theory that jokes can be the means for the release of aggression. In Canada, the cartoonist's pen has periodically had political impact. Jean-Baptiste Côté, one of the editors of *La Scie—The Saw*, the first bilingual comic journal in Quebec (1863), was arrested by the police for publishing a cartoon of a Quebec civil servant asleep at this desk.[5] The famous Quebec artist and cartoonist Robert LaPalme contributed to the beginning of the Quiet Revolution in Quebec through his incisive satirical interpretations of Quebec society, including a personal attack on a dominant political leader of the day, Quebec premier Maurice Duplessis.[6] There is a strong moral streak in political cartooning, and its mass media audience, largely informed through newspapers, expects it to point out injustices perpetrated on the average man by those who have power over them.

Political cartooning in major newspaper chains across the country has, at one level, been the spine of our political culture. Despite its more radical moments, it has always been the alter ego of the major political figures in the country, who have curiously tolerated and enjoyed the attention. These power brokers have been, and largely remain in 2002, white men. The history of this genre, particularly when it looks inward to the nation's business, is largely that of white male cartoonists taking as their subjects white male politicians who dominate the political arena in both English and French Canada. There have been some uncomfortable moments for racial minorities too, as when Henri Julien caricatured Wilfrid Laurier's cabinet in a series called the "Bytown Coons" in the *Star* from 1897–1900. This comic imaging and ridiculing of cabinet ministers through the presentation of them in black face, speaking in "niggah" dialect, was enormously popular with the Canadian public and speaks of the racial attitudes of the day.[7]

In *The Hecklers: A History of Canadian Political Cartooning over Two Centuries in Canada*, or to take a more recent illustration, *The Year 98 Portfolio in Canadian Caricature*, there are few examples of minority cultures or women's points of view. Of the approximately 167 cartoonists featured in *The Hecklers*, only the works of four women are included, and theirs are marginal citations. Of the forty-two cartoonists featured in the portfolio, only one is a woman.[8] In *The Hecklers*, the singular minority culture perspective presented consists of cartoons by Everett Soop, the Blood cartoonist from southern Alberta, who cartooned for a number of years for the Native newspaper the *Kainai News*. Soop's inclusion is significant because, unlike other minorities, Native peoples have always played a prominent role in Canadian literature and history. Still, the audience for Soop's cartoon, originally published in the *Kainai News*, was not meant to be the cultural majority, but a specific segment of the Native population.

The cartoon of the Alberta Heritage Fund as a piggy bank with an "Indian" receiving only what comes out of the pig's butt end is typical of Native irony directed at white political culture. It is also characteristic of the deeply embedded scatological humour of the Native peoples that was first censored by the Jesuit fathers, who simply left out the humour of bodily functions in their recordings of Native myths and legends. Even though Soop has a place in the national history of political cartooning for satirically "mooning" mainstream culture, as well as his own Native peoples, it is unlikely that the majority of Canadians today would respond to his cartoons as expressive of the national interest.

In order to derive genuine pleasure from humour—to get the joke— the audience needs to understand the cultural context and, most importantly, to identify with the community the humour addresses. As the French philosopher Henri Bergson explained in *Le Rire*, a person must first belong to the parish in order to appreciate parish laughter.[9] At the same time, the relationships between settler cultures and the Native peoples are changing as the First Nations achieve a newfound political and cultural authority. Perhaps it is possible that a more inclusive Canadian national parish may evolve to more fully accommodate and empathize with Native points of view and their expression in humour.

In fact, the question that arises from the lack of minority and women's perspectives in Canadian political cartooning is whether this particular comic form can survive today as an arm of national culture. Social psychologists argue that, pared to its essence, humour is a socio-cultural and group phenomenon that shares common language, experience, attitudes, and value systems. The successful joker is in complicity with his or her audience, reflecting the group back to itself, whether positively or negatively.[10] In a postmodern nation of fragmented ethnic, religious, and gender communities, the survival of political cartooning as a national force may depend on the genre's ability to embrace multiple perspectives—and for the Canadian public to sympathetically identify with them. Moreover, whatever the cartoonist's parish, she or he has to have a publishing venue to amuse us; with the increasing monopolization of newspapers in the hands of a few and Canadian publishing houses continually at risk, one wonders if the political cartoonist will have the opportunity to engage us at all. As the author of the introduction to *The Hecklers* explains, political cartooning came of age in the twentieth century and "presumably it will endure in its present form as long as newspapers remain important channels of political information and opinion."[11]

Laughing at the Americans

The national parish is the largest audience for humour in Canada that one can imagine. Thus its comic glue needs to be applied with broad strokes. Not surprisingly, in the history of Canadian humour in high and popular culture, beginning with Thomas Haliburton's satire of the archetypal American in *The Clockmaker*, with its narrator Sam Slick (1863), we have come to laughingly preserve and protect ourselves against the ever-present threat of domination by the United States by throwing comic darts at the Americans. In the past at least, by using humour to proclaim our difference, we have cemented our national identity. Again, this attitude is rooted in Canadian history, and humorists have not been alone in defining national culture through being "un-American." As a colony of Great Britain, Canada saw its early imperialist leaders decry the Americans and the threat of annexation to the United States. This is reflected in Canadian cartooning, where our relationship to the United States has been a dominant theme of the genre for over 150 years. The influential cartoons of J.W. Bengough, who strenuously opposed a popular plan to annex Canada to the United States in the mid-nineteenth century, exemplify early anti-American sentiment. In *A Pertinent Question*, from 1869, an early cartoonist articulated the feelings of the Canadian people on a possible union with Brother Jonathan, a comic archetype of the United States who later developed into the more familiar Uncle Sam (fig. 1).

From the 1950s on, historians, authors, and literary and cultural critics—and popular humorists—have been especially alive to Canadian-American relations. They have speculated on and championed our differences. In the 1980s, books of humour designed for the popular market in Canada and published by Mel Hurtig, a Canadian nationalist, entertained Canadians by asserting our differences and lampooning our relationship with the United States. In Eric Nicol and Dave More's *The US or Us, What's the Difference, Eh?* Canadians exhibit, among others, these national characteristics: we are better beer drinkers, less sexed, less patriotic, less brutal, and more law-abiding than our American neighbours.[12] Here, too, Canadians are as much the butt of the joke as the Americans, but to use a Canadianism, "it makes no never mind." The Canadian readership can revel in knowing who they are, that their national identity "has legs." Moreover, Canadian humour has often taken an ambivalent approach to its American subject. Haliburton's Sam Slick was admirable for his energy, know-how, and incredible money-making talents, even as he projected a moral laxity and threatening presence. Thus, in the chapter "Have Some American Media, M'dear" in *The US or Us*, Canada is typically represented as the poor cousin; given the availability of US television in Canada, "the

A PERTINENT QUESTION

MRS. BRITANNIA. — "IS IT POSSIBLE, MY DEAR, THAT YOU HAVE EVER GIVEN YOUR COUSIN JONATHAN ANY ENCOURAGEMENT?"

MISS CANADA. — "ENCOURAGEMENT! CERTAINLY NOT, MAMMA. I HAVE TOLD HIM WE CAN <u>NEVER</u> BE UNITED."

FIGURE 1 Unknown, *A Pertinent Question*, 1869.

amount of American TV programs sold to Canadian networks is a tribute to US technology in recycling garbage"; and given the low budgets of the CBC, "The American show features glamorous women wearing expensive furs. The Canadian: Just the fur. Usually with the fox still in it."[13] Still, even if we both admire and envy Americans for being richer, we resent their power. In *The Maple Laugh Forever*, poet Joe Wallace penned a version of the popular joke told by many Canadians: that when the United States sneezes, Canada catches a cold.

Ours is a sovereign nation
Bows to no foreign will
But whenever they cough in Washington
They spit on Parliament Hill.[14]

One of the most popular ways of tweaking the Americans is to expose their lack of understanding of Canada. The exposure of American ignorance about Canada allows Canadians a superior laugh—and national cohesion. This continued to be played out in Canadian culture in the Canadian television comedy show *This Hour Has 22 Minutes* where the segment "Talking to Americans" was extraordinarily popular and was initiated by viewer demand.[15] Rick Mercer, the comic, goes to the United States and interviews Americans about their knowledge of Canada, exposing their ignorance to laughing Canadians at home; Mercer also takes great delight in revealing American values as being different from those in Canada, at least as Canadians perceive and mythologize them. One of these differences is the view of ourselves as peacekeepers compared to the Americans, whom we see as militaristic. When Mercer asks, "Should America be bombing Bouchard?" and "Should America be bombing Saskatchewan?" the American answers, "Yes" and "Absolutely," underline this difference while addressing through humour the nation's early fear of American takeover.

An intriguing question for the student of the national parish and its humour is, who is the audience for American-focussed humour in Canada today? Specifically, given the tremendous influence of American popular culture, our increasing dependence on the American economy, a cultural policy towards immigrants that celebrates difference rather than assimilation to a national dream, and since September 11, the censorship of Canadian mockery of anything American, will there be a continuing audience for a humour that lampoons our American cousins? In other words, will the majority of Canadians continue to want a separate identity? Laughing at the Americans may be no laughing matter, for as John Morreall explains, "The person with a sense of humour can never be fully dominated, even by a government which imprisons him, for his ability to laugh at what is incongruous in the political situation will put him above it to some extent, and will preserve a measure of his freedom—if not of movement at least of thought."[16] Should Canadians come to the point where they laugh completely *with* the Americans and never *at* them, then the last laugh may be on us.

Irony—A Canadian Literary Tradition

The literary critic Bill New in *Borderlands*, examining the significance of the US border in Canadian cultural history, points to irony as a primary means by which "we walk the border." The point of our ironic view of the Americans, he suggests, is twofold: "(1) it confirms a sense of cultural separateness by implying a superiority of knowledge; and (2) it reconfirms what for Canadians has become a characteristic idiom—an oblique discourse, a communication by indirection, which of course only works if the power to interpret such obliqueness is culturally shared."[17]

Irony is not, of course, the exclusive idiom of Canadians. It has been a longstanding tool for withstanding domination and a method of signalling discontent. For example, Jonathan Swift's *A Modest Proposal* to have the English breed Irish babies as a solution to Ireland's economic woes in the eighteenth century is a classic example of taking an ironic stand against imperial authorities. In its simplest definition, irony as a situational and rhetorical device underlines the difference or the incongruity between expectation or appearance and reality, between the ideal and the real, between what is hoped for and what is possible. Wearing his cloak of irony, the ironist presents his audience with a double vision and doubled interpretation. Arguably, given our colonial status of being in the middle of things, first as a colony of Great Britain, and then as a satellite of the United States, irony came quite naturally to the Canadian psyche. Beginning with Stephen Leacock, a master ironist and cultural hero, irony has emerged as a strong feature of Canadian literature and what we call postmodern culture in North America and Europe.

While postmodernism is a debatable concept, it is generally accepted that in the literary and visual arts, irony, and her sister art of parody, are important defining features. Postmodernism in the arts is also said to reject the metanarratives of the past with their codes of universality and coherence, and to embrace fragmentation and multiple perspectives. In the literary and visual arts of high culture, irony can be a complex trope, and many theorists have speculated on its various uses. Linda Hutcheon, who has commented extensively on the nature and function of irony, has discussed, too, its changing nature and definitions. Of particular interest is her discussion of irony as it is expressed in premodernist, modernist, and postmodern art. Generalizing from Alan Wilde's study *Horizons of Assent: Modernism, Postmodernism and the Ironic Imagination*, she suggests that postmodern "irony is radical in its awareness of contingency and multiplicity, that it does not seek to recover ideals or norms, or transcend a fragmented world as do earlier forms of irony, but rather accepts doubleness and instability."[18] This is a useful general observation for a discussion of the development of the ironic tradition in Canada, particularly in relation to literary high culture and recent postmodern expressions. While Stephen Leacock's irony in the first half of the twentieth century is largely rooted in Christian idealism and an attempt to recover social control and order, later authors who write in a postmodern world in the late twentieth century, particularly as the "ethnic other," create ironies where doubleness and instability are accepted. Indeed, the minority writers' doubled cultural identity may be a root source of postmodern artistic expression. They are representatives of the postmodern reality of the ex-centrix, or the margins becoming the centre.

Stephen Leacock (1869–1944) is a national institution in Canada. In the first half of the twentieth century, he established himself as a genial humorist of international reputation through numerous volumes of humour and his bestselling work, a book on political economy. A university professor at McGill, Leacock was a member of Canada's cultural elite. He was a leading citizen of the majority Anglo-Canadian Christian culture of his time and a politically active and influential Conservative who also wrote, besides humour, serious books and articles that sought to define Canada and its nationhood, and shape political thought. While many of his volumes parodying and burlesquing popular fiction and literary classics are now outdated, a number of his works have remained humorously relevant and two, at least, are classic expressions of Canadian culture. In 1895, Leacock wrote the comic sketch "My Financial Career," which, in 1962, was made into an animated film by the National Film Board.[19] Leacock's creation of a man who goes into a bank and is overwhelmed by the institution and its authority was a major event in the development of North American humour. Leacock's "little man," whose mission is to deposit money but who is so shaken by the teller that he ends up ironically taking all of his money back out, heralded the birth of a comic archetype and the beginning of a parade of little men in Leacock's work and in American humour. The American public, confronted by new technologies and the complexities of modernity, responded with nervous laughter to these comic shadows of themselves, to Leacock's little men, to Charlie Chaplin's little tramp and to the American humorist Robert Benchley's oppressed and neurotic characters.[20]

Leacock's little man, however, was neither solely a continental phenomenon nor as anxiety-ridden as his later American counterparts. He had a stubborn Canadian dimension. As the critic R.E. Watters saw it, Leacock's little man archetype was rooted in the ironic posture that reflected the inner strength of a small nation that had survived the imperialism of larger powers. Watters also suggested that although Leacock's little men may appear powerless and subordinate, they, like the narrator of

"My Financial Career" who resolutely decides to bank no more, are in control themselves.[21] Watters's interpretation of Leacock's "national little man" is certainly in accordance with the humorist's serious views about Canada's place on the world stage. Although he was a firm believer in the British Empire, he rejected a subordinate position and foresaw Canada eventually evolving into an equal partner. Thus Leacock said, "I am an Imperialist because I will not be a Colonial."[22]

The internal confidence of Leacock's ironic narrators undoubtedly also rests on their creator's membership in the dominant Anglo-Canadian elite. This positioning is mirrored in his Canadian classic *Sunshine Sketches of a Little Town* (1912), an ironic reflection on life in small-town Canada, originally commissioned by the *Montreal Star* as "typically Canada" and adapted for both CBC radio and television in the 1950s.[23] Leacock's fictional small town of Mariposa (based on Orillia, Ontario, where he had a summer home) projects a Canada that is decidedly white, Anglo-Saxon, and Protestant. Here, there are no racial or ethnic minorities, no Native peoples, and the Church of England is an imposing structure on Mariposa's shady streets. Leacock's vision of Canada was based on the modernist's faith in universality. A singular, coherent society would be achieved by assimilation of all foreigners to the dominant culture. In his book *My Discovery of the West*, for example, he asserts, "The last thing these foreigners want to do is to go back home. They all want their children to learn English and to be English-Canadians.... As it is they all want to learn to play hockey.... In other words they want to be like us. Can you blame them? Leave them alone and pretty soon the Ukrainians will think they won the battle of Trafalgar: and if the President of the Rotary Club is a Bulgarian all he will ask is to forget it."[24] At the same time as Leacock was mythologizing Anglo-Canada in *Sunshine Sketches of a Little Town*, he was a critic of its turn-of-the-century, parochial small-town life; some of the leading citizens of Orillia were sorely offended by his interpretations of them, and understandably so. While for the most part the humorist treats his subjects affectionately, the central voice of the fiction is paternalistic, at a superior distance. As an ironist, Leacock had a moral imagination and a reformer's soul. Thus the incongruity between the ideal and the real is clearly presented, for example, in the political allegiances of his Mariposans in the chapter "The Great Election in Missinaba County." Here there is little ambiguity in the doubleness, the puncturing, and the ironic reversals that the reader is asked to make, and the underlying message for the Mariposans is that they could do better.

If Leacock made us chuckle at our own parochialism in *Sunshine Sketches,* he also initiated a tradition of irony for other authors to build upon. Although our literary tradition in English Canada has been dominated by an Anglo-Canadian sensibility until the mid-twentieth century, the literary scene broadened in the second half of the century to include other cultural heritages and points of view. Most notable have been writers of Jewish background. These include such famous literary figures as Irving Layton, Mordecai Richler, and Leonard Cohen, who have not been shy about using irony and outright satire to critique the historical and contemporary values of the founding French and Anglo-Canadian cultures.

Leonard Cohen, a novelist, poet, and internationally known songwriter and performer, has actually become, among the sixties generation, a symbol of the ironic Canadian and a national hero. Cohen, who is considered to have written the first postmodern novel in Canada in *Beautiful Losers*, is a remarkable ironist. His popular persona, that of the romantic ladies' man, is one that has a tongue-in-cheek quality and that offers paradoxically both a serious presentation and an ironic send-up of the romantic, brooding, melancholy lover. As well as appealing to middle-aged women across Canada with this somewhat humorous romantic fantasy, Cohen has penned ironic literary works that are broad in scope. Often serious in intent, they express his multiple identities and appeal to a number of parishes, including national, Quebec, and Jewish audiences. In this excerpt from the 1961 poem "The Only Tourist in Havana Turns His Thoughts Homeward," Cohen playfully and ironically undermines Canadian issues and prejudices with a series of injunctions to his fellow Canadians:

> let us sell snow
>   to under-developed nations,
> (Is it true one of our national leaders
>   was a Roman Catholic?)
> let us terrorize Alaska,
> let us unite
>   Church and State,
> let us not take it lying down,
> let us have two Governor Generals
>   at the same time,
> let us have another official language,
> let us determine what it will be,
> let us give a Canada Council Fellowship
>   to the most original suggestion,
> let us teach sex in the home
>   to parents,
> let us threaten to join the U.S.A.
>   and pull out at the last moment.[25]

In the poem "All There Is to Know about Adolph Eichmann" from his volume *Flowers for Hitler*, Jewish experience is the subject of the poem, which takes a darker ironic, postmodern turn. The irony here posits no ideals, no norms of character or behaviour. Rather, Cohen considers the Nazi Eichmann in his doubleness, as an average man and as a possible monster or madman. By questioning the latter, however, the poet overturns this possibility even as he affirms it. There are no sure answers here—only the acceptance of doubleness and ambiguity, and with it, the postmodern acceptance of the instability of human character and reality.

As one might expect, irony by minority culture writers in Canada is often directed inwards, towards issues and concerns of particular multicultural or religious groups and, very often, towards immigrant realities. Typically, writers from minority culture backgrounds walk in two cultural worlds. Like Hiromi Goto in *Chorus of Mushrooms*, they are inclined to consider the nature of Canada and what it means to be a Canadian with an ironic eye. Co-winner of the Canada-Japan Book Award and winner of the Commonwealth Writer Prize for Best First Book in the Caribbean and Canada Region, Goto writes fiction that explores poetically and with ambiguous irony the lives of three generations of Japanese-Canadian women in southern Alberta and their responses to an environment that demands their assimilation to the dominant Anglo-Canadian and Christian culture. For the youngest woman, the Canadian-born Murasaki, irony is a defence, and for her author, a means of underlining the racial and cultural barriers of Canadian society. In this fiction, the author-ironist presents no ideals of behaviour, no absolute standards. Her open-ended conclusion, two short pages of fragments of ironic conversation entitled "An Immigrant Story with a Happy Ending," is decidedly postmodern, her final few words metafictional and quintessentially those of the ironic Canadian: "An immigrant story with a happy ending. Nothing is impossible. Within reason, of course."[26]

The Trickster: A New Comic Hero for a Postmodern Age

Ironically enough for the national dream, postmodern ironic ambiguity in the Canadian arts is nowhere more dramatically expressed than in the new works of Native artists, and in the figure of the Trickster, an ancient Native concept known variously to Native tribes as Raven, Glooscap, Coyote, Nanabush, or Napi. The Trickster, a spiritual and shapeshifting presence of "serious fun," is central to Native mythologies; the Trickster has not only been revived by his own peoples but he is becoming increasingly well known to mainstream culture through the works of visual artists, writers, and dramatists of Native heritage, such as playwright Tomson Highway, who brought Nanabush to life for contemporary Canadian

FIGURE 2   Everett Soop, *Untitled*, 1972 (courtesy of the Glenbow Museum).

audiences in his award-winning play *The Rez Sisters*. At the very heart of Native cultures is the Trickster figure—and at the very heart of the Trickster is an ironic worldview. As Allan Ryan explains, quoting Lawrence Sullivan, the Trickster "is not only an ironic symbol but a symbol of irony."[27]

It is certainly not surprising then that the relationship of Native laughter to national culture, as with that of other minority groups, is fundamentally ironic and parodic, and that it is expressive of a Native way of being in contrast to national history, ideologies, and cultural practices accepted by the mainstream. Such is the case in a cartoon by Everett Soop (fig. 2).

Given their ironic puncturing of a Canadian metanarrative of national homogeneity, many Native artists today could be interpreted as being part of a contemporary postmodernism, while the Trickster itself allows for the multiple perspectives and ambiguous juxtapositions of the postmodern condition: "He [the Trickster] knows neither good nor evil yet he is responsible for both. He possesses no values, moral or social, is at the mercy of his passions and appetites, yet through his actions all values come into being."[28] While the Trickster is above all a spiritual Aboriginal concept capable of strengthening Aboriginal cultural identity, she or he can also provide cultural insights for what the First Nations see as the parallel nation of Canada. The Trickster is also an amazingly appropriate comic hero for the twenty-first century, particularly since the Trickster is without gender. Above all, the Trickster is one in a long line of celebrated cultural messengers, both in and out of mainstream culture in Canada, who, in a country that John Ralston Saul describes as "a permanently incomplete experiment,"[29] teaches us that the best way to deal with inconstancy and uncertainty is by doubling over with laughter.

Notes

1 Beverly Rasporich, "Canadian Humour in the Media: Exporting John Candy and Importing Homer Simpson," *Seeing Ourselves: Media Power and Policy in Canada*, 2nd ed., ed. Helen Holmes and David Taras (Toronto: Harcourt and Brace, 1996), 89–91.

2 Jack Bumsted, "Visions of Canada: A Brief History of Writing on the Canadian Character and the Canadian Identity," *A Passion for Identity*, 4th ed., ed. David Taras and Beverly Rasporich (Toronto: Nelson Thomson Learning, 2001), 19.

3 Arun P. Mukherjee, "Ironies of Colour in the Great White North: The Discursive Strategies of Some Hyphenated Canadians," *Double-Talking: Essays on Verbal and Visual Ironies in Contemporary Canadian Art and Literature*, ed. Linda Hutcheon (Toronto: ECW Press, 1992), 158–71.

4 Peter Desbarats and Terry Mosher, eds., *The Hecklers: A History of Canadian Political Cartooning over Two Centuries in Canada* (Toronto: McClelland and Stewart, 1979), 250.

5 Desbarats and Mosher, 63.

6 Desbarats and Mosher, 105.

7 Desbarats and Mosher, 68.

8 The cartoons here largely illustrate male roles and points of view. The prominently displayed cartoon on the back cover, for example, shows a "little" Joe Clark "wetting himself" in front of a United States/Canada free trade negotiating table while the American negotiator is a muscled Sylvester Stallone, sporting a machine gun, Rambo-style. While this is a traditional twentieth-century comic interpretation of Canada as a "little guy" (Canada was cartooned as a woman in the nineteenth century), it also portrays a confrontational male world.

9 Henri Bergson, "Laughter," *Comedy*, ed. W. Sypher (New York: Doubleday, 1956), 64.

10 C. Wilson, *Jokes: Forms, Content, Use and Function* (Toronto: Academic Press, 1979), 230.

11 Desbarats and Mosher, 11.

12 Eric Nicol and Dave More, eds., *The US or Us—What's the Difference, Eh?* (Edmonton: Hurtig, 1981), 15, 69, 87.

13 Nicol and More, 111.

14 Joe Wallace, "A Sovereign Nation," *The Maple Laugh Forever*, ed. Douglas Barbour and Stephen Scobie (Edmonton: Hurtig, 1981), 15.

15 Rick Mercer quoted in Derrick Toth, "Canada Baffles Americans," *Calgary Herald* 30 March 2001, E3.

16 Morreall quoted in Allan J. Ryan, *The Trickster Shift: Humour and Irony in Contemporary Canadian Art* (Vancouver: University of British Columbia Press, 1999), 229.

17 William H. New, *Borderlands: How We Talk about Canada* (Vancouver: University of British Columbia Press, 1998), 49.

18 Linda Hutcheon, ed., *Double-Talking: Verbal and Visual Ironies in Contemporary Canadian Art and Literature* (Toronto: ECW Press, 1992), 15.

19 David Legate, *Stephen Leacock* (Toronto: Doubleday, 1970), 32.

20 See Ralph Curry, "Robert Benchley and Stephen Leacock: An Acknowledged Literary Debt," *The American Book Collector* 7 (1957): 14. See also Norris Yates, *The American Humorist* (New York: Citadel Press, 1965).

21 R.E. Watters, "A Special Tang: Stephen Leacock's Canadian Humour," *Canadian Literature* 5 (1960): 21–32.

22 Leacock quoted in Bumsted, 21.

23 Legate, 256.

24 Stephen Leacock, *My Discovery of the West* (Toronto: Thomas Allan, 1937), 159.

25 Leonard Cohen, "The Only Tourist in Havana Turns His Thoughts Homeward," *A Passion for Identity: An Introduction to Canadian Studies*, 2nd ed., ed. David Taras, Beverly Rasporich, and Eli Mandel (Toronto: Nelson Canada, 1993), 149.

26 Hiromi Goto, *Chorus of Mushrooms* (Edmonton: NeWest Press, 1994), 212.

27 Lawrence Sullivan quoted in Ryan, 8.

28 Paul Radin quoted in Ryan, 7.

29 John Ralston Saul quoted in Adrienne Clarkson, "Installation Speech" in Taras and Rasporich, eds., *A Passion for Identity*, 4th ed., 11.

3 Collective Memory on the Airwaves
The Negotiation of Unity and Diversity in a Troubled Canadian Nationalism

Emily West

THIS ESSAY WILL LOOK AT TWO INSTANCES of national memory projects, or *lieux de mémoire*, taking place on television: the *Heritage Minutes* produced by the Historica Foundation, formerly known as the Charles R. Bronfman Foundation (CRB), and the Canadian Broadcasting Corporation's (CBC) documentary *Canada: A People's History*. The *Heritage Minutes* first aired in 1991 and since then have been a familiar feature on all the major Canadian television networks as well as in movie theatres.[1] To date the CRB has made sixty-five of these one-minute "commercials" for Canadian history, featuring an array of historical events and personalities. *Canada: A People's History* is a more recent and ambitious endeavour, setting out to dramatize Canada's entire history up until 1990 over seventeen episodes. Airing its first episode in October of 2000, and finishing in November of 2001, this $25 million project is a co-operative venture between English Canada's CBC and French Canada's network, Radio-Canada.

The *Heritage Minutes* and *Canada: A People's History* are both efforts to fill in the gaps of Canadian collective memory using the tools of popular culture. It is hardly news to many Canadians that national identity has long been an issue fraught with controversy and some angst, leading to a noticeable national conversation about Canadian history and heritage. Ideas about Canadian culture, who Canadians are, and what their relationship ought to be to the larger nation underlie not only media projects such as the ones discussed in this paper, but many government policies including trade and regulation of the airwaves and internet.

Cultural elites perceive a lack in Canadians' relationship to their past and have sought to address what they see as an insufficient shared collective memory. Some Canadians, including the producers of these programs, lament the failure in collective memory not just because of the intrinsic value of the nation's past, but because they see collective memory as instrumental in bolstering a sense of national identity, and ultimately as a functional component of national survival. In other words, as collective memory scholars have hypothesized, in collective memory projects such as these, the past gets enlisted to serve present interests, often of those in positions of power. As Barry Schwartz, a scholar of collective memory, explains, "Recollection of the past is an active, constructive process, not a simple matter of retrieving information. To remember is to place a part of the past in the service of conceptions and needs of the present."[2]

These memory projects are engaged in a balancing act between the very impulse for their creation—a desire for a shared memory and identity—and the need to recognize the importance of diversity within a unified conception of Canada. Because groups within Canada question the very desirability of national unity and the future security of the nation-state, these memory projects find themselves on somewhat shaky ground. In other words, the nationalist agenda of these memory projects presents a problem in Canada where the definitions of "Canada" and "Canadian," and the survival of the nation, are not necessarily consensual. However, these terms can be useful politically, and they convey a sense of feel-good national unity despite the almost infinite diversity of interpretations of how Canadians themselves understand their national identity. As a result, the *Minutes* and *A People's History* must walk a fine line between offering messages of diversity and unity, and therefore they seek to provide narrative accounts that make sense of both. This fundamental tension reveals itself not only in the content of these memory projects, but also in the discourse that surrounds them, from producers, audience members, and critics.

This essay will argue that these media memory projects demonstrate their awareness of the need to negotiate the balance between diversity and unity through their strategy of inclusion in the dramatic representations of Canada's past, and also by being careful to provide a mix of social history with the more traditional "national" history. These programs are structured in such a way as to self-consciously avoid the politically problematic appearance of offering a "grand narrative" of Canadian history, but as Jean-François Lyotard might predict, narrative is inherently both denotative and prescriptive.[3] In other words, narratives cannot represent "truth" or "facts" without some normative frame. In the case of the *Heritage Minutes* and *Canada: A People's History*, the unifying trope is framed in terms of our "common humanity," including universal topics of human interest such as courage, co-operation, sacrifice, and suffering. Gordon Henderson, senior producer of *Canada: A People's History*, explains the approach to making the various Canadian stories appeal to a wide and diverse audience: "We focus on what are the most important stories, the most interesting stories, human stories ... and then politics don't matter and agendas don't matter."[4] However, the seemingly "universal" aspects of the stories being told still exist within the larger framework and motivation for these projects—the continued success of Canada as a unified nation-state. To the producers' credit, there are many stories of dissent and injustice in these programs, such as the story of famed rebel Louis Riel, dealt with in both productions, or the internment of Japanese Canadians during the Second World War depicted in the documentary episode *The Crucible*.[5] However, these stories ultimately reside within a progressive narrative of the current state of the nation as the endpoint of the various dramas and sacrifices that went before it. Further, the way that these cultural productions, made in both English and French and broadcast nationally, symbolically unify the country through the simultaneous viewing from a "divided nation" cannot be ignored as a way that these memory projects meet their political aims.

Where is the proper location to observe something as immaterial and nebulous as the memory of a community? Indeed, a recurring question in collective memory studies is where to locate the transmission of memory. In *How Societies Remember*, Paul Connerton suggests that true memory is passed on through commemorative ceremonies and bodily practices.[6] Similarly, Pierre Nora theorizes that because modern societies privilege the new and innovative over the past, they have in effect "renounced memory."[7] He writes, "If we still dwelled among our memories, there would be no need to consecrate sites embodying them."[8] Now that the world changes too quickly for the past to be embodied in ritual practices and similar "organic" sources, Nora suggests that we locate it in *"lieux de mémoire,"* or self-consciously constructed repositories of memory, such as museums and monuments.[9] Work in collective memory is characterized by suspicion of the shift from the more "authentic" memory embodied in ceremonies and rituals to memory exteriorized in media, such as print and television. Lyotard suggests that the location of memory in narrative forms in general, as opposed to more "organic" sources, allows cultural forgetting and a problematic dependence not just on the legitimating structures of narrative, but also on the moment of reciting or receiving the narrative.[10] The *Heritage Minutes* and *Canada: A People's History* are examples of just such pieces of culture designed to promote Canadian collective memory and identity through the technique of dramatic narrative.

The Need for Canadian Lieux de Mémoire

The discourse of the producers of the *Heritage Minutes* and *Canada: A People's History* suggests that the impetus to create these memory projects lies in the belief that gaps exist in Canadians' knowledge of their history and, if only they could be filled, national identity (read "unity") could be fortified. The initiators of both of these projects cited their belief that Canadians found their history "boring" as a compelling reason to undertake the task of filling in the gaps of Canadian memory. Further, Charles R. Bronfman, initiator of the *Heritage Minutes*, points in particular to the education system which he argues has failed in teaching Canadians their history. To illustrate his point, Bronfman points to his own Heritage Quiz, which he funded to ask Canadians about their knowledge of the "basic facts" of the nation's history. He was dismayed to learn, for example, that 40 percent of the representative sample of Canadian adults and children did not know that John A. MacDonald was Canada's first prime minister.[11] Like Bronfman, Mark Starowicz, executive producer of *A People's History*, describes the documentary's aim "to show that Canadian history is not boring."[12]

Bronfman, Starowicz, and others believe that the normal mechanisms of collective memory, such as the education system, rituals, ceremonies, and everyday practices, have failed, leaving them to take it upon themselves to fill in the gaps. This view is also shared by historian Irving Abella, who writes, "For too long Canadians have dismissed their history as boring and lifeless, as if some potent industrial-strength cleanser had been poured on it and bleached out its colour and drama. *A People's History* has provided a powerful antidote. It has restored our history to us with all its vibrancy, surprises and humanity."[13] Like Starowicz and Bronfman, Abella argues that while Canada's *true* history is interesting, in the past Canadians have not been exposed to its full "colour and drama." Critics, observers, and some viewers hail the *Minutes* and the CBC documentary for the way they have re-injected interest and intrigue into Canadian history. For example, the *Ottawa Citizen* writes, "there is a void that must be filled, and *A People's History* may help do that."[14]

On the whole, the comments of viewers of *A People's History* on the CBC's message board also commend the program for the way it brings Canadian history to life. Contributors to the board often blame the education system for their own and others' lack of knowledge about the past, and congratulate the series for addressing this need. One posting reads, "To my mind, the series is a lot more fascinating than the history I learned during my school days. Thank you to the CBC for putting together this ambitious work for us, the viewing public."[15] Another posting says, "All I know is that this is the closest I have ever come to 'really' understanding what the history of this country is all about."[16] Yet another viewer writes, "The first part of this series has greatly expanded my knowledge and interest in our history. I have learned from the few short hours of the series many events and the people in those events, that the school system never once mentioned to me."[17] The numbers appear to back up the overall popularity of the series. The CBC/Radio-Canada report that "An astounding 15 million Canadians—one out of two—tuned into the series" over the first nine episodes.[18]

"Giving Our Past a Future"[19]

The question remains, why are these individuals and organizations so concerned about Canadians' ignorance of the country's past? Some of the figures involved in these projects seem to be suggesting that they see a strong collective memory and shared understanding of the past as crucial to the very survival of Canada. Of course, this sentiment is hardly unique to Canada. For instance, concern that people do not know enough about their history is also pervasive in the United States. Historian Michael Frisch describes the ideas underlying the movement to improve history education in the US: "The final proposition...is that unless there is a drastic change in the quantity and quality of the teaching of history, the only issue will be whether we collapse from internal disintegration before we are overwhelmed by economic and political threats from without."[20] Put this way, the idea that history education could be a sufficient, or effective, force against the very disintegration of the nation seems rather overstated.

However, the existence of this debate does suggest that people think collective memory can be a very powerful force. This idea is reflected in the work of memory scholars, who argue that in fact collective memory is functional in the maintenance and strengthening of the nation or the group. Barbie Zelizer summarizes this approach, saying, "Rather than be taken at face value as a simple act of recall, collective memory is evaluated for the ways in which it helps us to make connections—to each other over time and space, and to ourselves. At the heart of memory's study, then, is its usability, its invocation as a tool to defend different aims and agendas."[21] The suggestion of collective memory studies, then, is to resist seeing memory projects in a taken-for-granted fashion, as if their content and presentation were somehow inevitable, "natural," or free of ideological inflection. Rather, we are urged to notice what political agenda or goal motivates and frames the cultural production in question. In the case of memory work relating to the nation-state, the goal or purpose is generally directed towards the strength and survival of the group. Jacques LeGoff addresses the difficulty facing a group with a lack of collective memory, writing, "the *known* or *recognized* absence or brevity of the past can also create serious problems for the development of a collective mentality and identity—for instance in young nations."[22] If we agree with Benedict Anderson that nations are merely imaginative constructs, communities that we can never truly know or see, but that we agree to put our faith in, then the need for *lieux de mémoire*, or sites of collective memory, is even more apparent.[23] Collective memory can be understood as an important imaginative construct without which individuals might not "believe in" their nation and might therefore be less likely to make the kinds of sacrifices—of time and money, even bodily sacrifices—that nations periodically require of their citizens in order to survive.

Nora also casts *lieux de mémoire* as defenders of group identity when he writes that "These bastions buttress our identities, but if what they defended were not threatened, there would be no need for them."[24] The notion that the *Heritage Minutes* are responding to a threat is reflected in their slogan, "Giving our past a future."[25] This slogan makes an unequivocal statement about the agenda of the *Minutes*, implicitly suggesting that maybe, without these *Minutes* or similar efforts to revitalize collective memory, Canada's future as a nation would be in danger.

Thomas Axworthy, executive director of the CRB Foundation, articulated his understanding of memory to the importance of national survival in a speech to the Canadian Club of Toronto: "What we remember, what we stress as significant, what we omit from our past, and what we don't know or understand about the stories of our fellow inhabitants, is critical to our ability to endure as a collectivity."[26] One of Canada's leading historians, Desmond Morton, observed in the same issue of the *Toronto Star* featuring Axworthy's speech that, "As Canada once again threatens to disintegrate, a host of history and heritage organizations have emerged or revived with nation-saving concerns."[27] These collective memory projects, then, are framed not just as interesting but as important, even crucial, to the survival of the nation. Similarly, the *Toronto Star* review of *Proud and Free*, a production that introduced a new set of *Heritage Minutes* to the Canadian public in 1995 just a few months before the Referendum, expressed the following sentiment: "In form and content, *Proud and Free* is a reminder of how anxiously yet tenuously we hold on to our notions of cultural integrity, to our extraordinary and mostly unsung history, to our fragmented heritage, to our land. And in a TV universe about to be bombarded by foreign satellite channels, it raises the question of how important Canadian content is."[28] Here a number of sore points for Canadian national identity are touched on: the difficulty of hanging onto "cultural integrity" in the face of bombardment from American and foreign media, the fragmentation of our society, and our lack of connection with our history.

Of course, no one should be surprised that the CBC, whose mandate rests on its delivery of Canadian content, should be so invested in the idea that television documentaries have a role in the formation of national identity and strength. As long as the Canadian culture industries depend to some extent for legitimacy and financial support on their reputation as the carriers and protectors of Canadian heritage, they will presumably continue to have a vested interest in making connections like these between popular depictions of the past and the larger interests of the nation. Perhaps the CBC says it best when it states, in the 2000–2001 Annual Report, that "Only CBC/Radio-Canada could risk dedicating the resources to develop a bilingual epic history of Canada. It is a prime example of our contribution to national consciousness and identity."[29]

Balancing Acts

A fundamental difficulty facing these heritage projects then, and perhaps any heritage project, is a definitional one. The *Minutes* and *A People's History* undertake to show Canadians that their history can contribute to a unifying collective memory, when it is not completely clear what the boundaries of "Canada" are and whether there truly is a Canadian "collective" that can be understood to share a history, and therefore to share memories based on the past. Zelizer argues that the tension between the particular and the universal is ever-present in collective memory, because the cohesion of collectivities is usually more idealized than realized.[30] In the case of Canada, where the question of unity and the future shape of the country rarely leave the national agenda, the ability of collective memory projects to be "simultaneously particularistic and universal" is especially challenging.[31] Rex Murphy, journalist and CBC "talking head," encapsulates the political situation nicely when he says, "Canada is a country in which a simple word like 'we' has not yet achieved a fully satisfactory emotional—and, in some cases—political definition."[32]

At the risk of simplification, conventional knowledge suggests that Canadians pride themselves on being tolerant and welcoming of diversity, and congratulate themselves on their "multicultural mosaic" in comparison to what they perceive as America's "melting-pot" model of assimilation. However, if it is part of the so-called "Canadian character" to be so tolerant, even supportive of diversity, why the concern by organizations such as the Historica Foundation, the Dominion Institute,[33] and historians in general about the lack of knowledge of the "facts" of federal history such as the date of Confederation, and the further worry that historical knowledge varies greatly by region? Axworthy's 1997 speech about the *Minutes* seems to confirm that the implicit goal of the *Heritage Minutes* is to overcome the "fissures" compromising Canadian unity, and further, that the power of collective memory might be the answer to this dilemma: "If the foundation of our country is cracked—if our citizens cannot speak to each other, if there is no common point of reference, if there is no sharing of values, if there is no partnership of purpose, if we do not know or appreciate each other's stories—then no amount of constitutional jerryrigging can overcome the fissures of this San Andreas fault."[34]

LeGoff suggests that contemporary interest in the past is often associated with social conservatism and nostalgia, and with groups who are worried about their diminishing power and relevance.[35] Along the same lines, Frisch fears that the renewed interest in American history is a thinly veiled ethnocentric, even racist, response to the rise in social history which is more inclusive of different, often marginalized, groups, at the perceived expense of what would be the "genuine" or "really important" political and military history.[36] This debate about what history should look like has also been raging in Canada, most notably fuelled by historian Jack Granatstein, who in 1998 released a book titled *Who Killed Canadian History?* in which he responds to the proliferation of social history in Canada.[37] Granatstein accuses historians who concentrate on the experiences of different groups organized by class, ethnicity, and gender of neglecting the important questions of political and military history, and ultimately, of failing their responsibility to Canada as a nation.[38] He has famously lamented the lack of studies of the nation-building variety in light of a historical establishment that promotes work such as a history of "housemaid's knee in Belleville in the 1890s."[39]

The *Minutes* and *A People's History* fit in well with this larger trend of highlighting diversity and difference in historical work. However, the difficulty remains of whether it is really possible to promote pride and knowledge of the collectivity and simultaneously of diverse identities within the collectivity.

Inclusive Interpretation of Canada

By making as inclusive an interpretation of what "fits" into the story of Canada as possible, both these media initiatives strategically avoid making too narrow a definition of what "counts" as Canadian. For example, both programs take the current land borders of Canada, and map them backwards in time as a way to place boundaries on what people and events will be included in their productions. Hence, *Canada: A People's History* begins the story of Canada approximately 15,000 years ago, the time of the hypothesized immigration of people from Siberia across the Bering Strait. In this way, the political unity that the producers hope for, for the present and future, is projected back onto the past as a way to portray events as part of a coherent narrative.

This same principle seems to be in operation in the *Heritage Minutes*, as illustrated by the fact that inclusion in a minute seems to rest less on being a Canadian citizen or resident, or having relevance to Canadian issues per se, than on having taken place within the borders of what now defines Canada. Hence, the second earliest chronological *Heritage Minute* features the Vikings briefly settling in Newfoundland a thousand years ago.[40] Another *Heritage Minute* revisits Newfoundland in 1901, to dramatize Italian Guglielmo Marconi receiving the first radio message sent across the Atlantic Ocean.[41] Similarly, the Jackie Robinson *Minute*, described on the Historica website as when, "In 1946, Montréal Royals players and fans welcome the first African-American player, marking the beginning of the end of major-league baseball's colour barrier," was remarked on in the press as a strange choice for a Canadian historic moment.[42]

The effort of these productions to avoid seeming like they are offering a "grand narrative"[43] of Canadian memory or identity is highlighted by a slogan that appears towards the end of every *Heritage Minute*—"A *Part* of our Heritage" (italics mine).[44] While the official or privileged Canadian identity has historically been associated with white, Anglo-Canadian culture at the expense of other groups, notably French Canadians and First Nations peoples, the *Heritage Minutes* website draws attention to its inclusive approach to telling the story of Canada by organizing the various minutes by chronology, region, and theme.[45] The kinds of themes that the minutes are grouped into reflect the issues of diversity that the *Heritage Minutes* are invested in addressing, with unifying themes such as "Canadian Symbols" and "Building Democracy" listed side by side with themes highlighting difference and identity, such as "First Nations" and "Multiculturalism."[46]

Canada: A People's History also emphasizes its inclusion of different groups in the story of Canada, both in the content of the documentary and in the process of creating it. In particular, the promotional materials surrounding the production have drawn attention to the fact that this documentary was the first co-production between the CBC and its francophone counterpart, Radio-Canada.[47] From the program *The Making of Canada: A People's History* and the program's website, we learn that the producers consulted with historians and experts from many different groups in order to represent the past from multiple points of view.[48] We also learn that the French- and English-speaking producers sat down to come to consensus about what stories would play well to both audiences.[49] The *Heritage Minutes* have also been careful to consult with the relevant groups for their productions, even changing minutes based on their feedback, as they did for the "Nitro" minute which depicted the exploitation of Chinese-Canadian workers in building the Trans-Canada railroad.[50]

The historical figures who "speak to us" in the CBC documentary and through whose eyes we see the past include women, First Nations, and French-Canadian, as well as Anglo-Canadian people. Of course, despite the CBC's apparent efforts to be as inclusive and comprehensive as possible, viewers have expressed concern that certain groups or events have been given short shrift. For example, viewers from the Atlantic provinces complain on the documentary's electronic message board that the history of that region has received inadequate representation.[51] One viewer from New Brunswick writes on the CBC message board, "I have been sitting waiting for some reference to MY people's history...I realize that in such a broad treatment there will be some, even many, editing choices which will offend but these slights/oversights are absolutely unconscionable.... So far, I view this series as another example of Upper Canadian arrogance and willful neglect."[52] Similarly, some First Nations viewers have complained that there has not been enough coverage of their past, or have expressed concerns about the accuracy of the depictions. One viewer responds to the previous posting, writing "I too have been waiting for *my* family, the Mi'kmaq Nation, to be depicted in the series."[53]

The work of these media producers to incorporate and celebrate diversity has not prevented the *Minutes* from being read as anti-sovereigntist propaganda in Quebec. In 1999, the Quebec legislature proposed that they make their own *Heritage Minutes* "to counter the federal commercials."[54] Even though the Quebec legislature was not strictly correct in identifying the *Heritage Minutes* as "federal commercials" in that the project is not funded by the federal government, it does seem to be the case that a number of high-profile federalists are involved in the project. First of all, the movers and shakers at the CRB most certainly fall into the Canadian unity camp. Charles Bronfman, an anglophone Montrealer, has been quite clear about his hopes for Canadian unity,[55] as has Tom Axworthy, executive director of the CRB Foundation, former aide to federalist prime minister Trudeau and brother of former minister of Foreign Affairs Lloyd Axworthy. It is also not surprising to learn that Jack Granatstein, of *Who Killed Canadian History?* fame, is on the advisory council.[56]

Unsurprisingly, some members of the francophone community have also made complaints about the CBC documentary. The Carleton University History Collaborative reports that in the hour-long radio talk-show formats that Radio-Canada held after each episode, although generally the response was similar to that of English Canada, there was some discussion about "the whole enterprise being just another federalist plot to subvert a sovereigntist agenda."[57] On the other end of the political spectrum, some viewer commentary on the CBC message board bemoans the "political correctness" of the series, complaining that the attention to the suffering and "victimization" of different groups in Canada's past has resulted in too little time devoted to the military sacrifices and victories of the Second World War.[58]

As to whether these programs' representations of the "facts" of history are biased towards central Canada or are slanted towards a federalist stance in some "objective" sense, it is very difficult to conclude. Against whose standard of "reality" do we measure the events that have been included, and how many sympathetic depictions of anti-federalist personalities and movements balance out other narratives that are pro-Canada? Rather than pronounce definitively on this question, this author would redirect attention to the fact that representations of the past serve as a lightning rod around which grievances of both the past and present can be aired. Judgements of "fairness" are subjective, and consensus about them gets worked out through discourse that is inevitably mired in the politics of the present. However, we can observe how these programs seek to manage the kinds of critiques described here, ones that their producers have no doubt anticipated, through their content.

Balancing National and Social History

Another way that these media productions negotiate the tension between diversity and unity is to emphasize the stories of ordinary people, whom we might consider "everyday heroes," engaged in struggles that are universal to the "human condition" rather than particular to the history of Canada as a nation. While the programs seek to represent a variety of groups from Canada's past, they also invite audiences to identify with the stories of the individuals they portray, even if we do not share their gender, race, or class identity. Executive producer Mark Starowicz explains, "That, for me, is the dramatic centre, that if you're in Calgary, you will be moved by the story of the dispossessed and the wretched of Paris that came here with nothing but a wilderness. And that if you're in Quebec City and in St. Jerome, the story of the Selkirk settlers is just as moving and just as extraordinary as the story of the filles du roi, because it's human … just the drama of hope and love and war and loss."[59] As a result, while the *Heritage*

Minutes do feature some political figures and well-known "heroes" of Canadian history, such as Baldwin and LaFontaine, English- and French-Canadian politicians who co-operated in the nineteenth century to bring about democratic reforms, they also emphasize the "everyday" heroes.[60]

For example, one of the *Minutes* listed under the theme of "Heroes" "Recounts the tenacity of one family as they save themselves and their farm animals from the devastating fire of 1870," taking the bravery and will to survive of one family as a narrative of the "human spirit" that we can all relate to, standing in for the bravery and fortitude of all who came before us.[61] In another *Minute*, "Soddie," we watch the superhuman efforts of a family of European immigrants during their first year on the prairie, building their first home "out of the same sod they break to grow their crops."[62] The structure of the *Heritage Minutes*, where each story gets its own self-enclosed sixty seconds of narrative, implies that acts of everyday heroism such as these are equally deserving of their own *Minutes* as stories about great inventions or political agreements. While there are *Minutes* such as "Valour Road" that highlight the courage and sacrifice of three Winnipeg neighbours, all of whom were awarded the Victoria Cross for their part in the First World War, there are also many *Minutes* devoted to the somewhat more everyday brand of heroism and innovation of individuals and groups.[63] From the Canadian who invented the multiplex movie theatre to the First Nations peoples who taught early settlers how to make maple syrup, the *Heritage Minutes* emphasize social and cultural history as much if not more than the more traditional, political and military history.[64] From the Historica Foundation's website, we are asked, "What is a hero? *Heritage Minutes* present heroism in many forms, from comic book superheroes to courageous individuals who have risked their lives to save others. You might say that every *Heritage Minute* portrays Canadian heroes."[65] In fact, it is noteworthy that not one *Heritage Minute* features a Canadian prime minister as its main character, despite Charles Bronfman's concern that Canadians are innocent of the "basic facts" of Canadian history.

The makers of *A People's History* seem to use similar strategies of balancing the "national" with the "social" as the *Heritage Minutes*. The documentary, like the *Minutes*, seeks to fill in the gaps of history that the education system has left open, by filling in some of the human interest and creating a connection to our forebears that mere knowledge of the facts of history might not normally include. The episodes weave together the experiences and events featuring the kinds of people who already have their names in history books, along with the perspectives of the ordinary folk, whom we happen to know about because they have left us their stories in documents such as letters, diaries, and court transcripts. In fact, the mantra of the series is "Canadian history, through the eyes of the people who lived in."[66] Actors speak the actual words of the people they are playing, found in these various historical documents, or passed down through the oral tradition. Often these characters are not the famous protagonists that we have read about in history books, but the "regular" people who observed these events. Hence, we hear from John Cabot's first mate about the explorer's first encounter with Canada.[67] Similarly, we get a personal perspective on the Battle of Lundy's Lane because we see it through the eyes of a young woman picking her way through the field after the fighting, looking for her husband.[68]

In fact, the documentary's decision to feature ordinary folks so prominently has led to the notable absence of some well-known Canadian historical figures, such as Laura Secord. Credited with warning the British against a potentially devastating attack by the Americans during the War of 1812, Secord enjoys an unusual amount of fame for a Canadian hero, perhaps thanks in part to the fact that her name is now used by a popular confectionary company. However, she does not make it into the documentary's account of the War of 1812, losing out in the compromise between valorizing traditional "heroes" and creating new ones.

The visual iconography of the CBC documentary complements its overall approach. Opening credits, website graphics, and book designs use montage to juxtapose close and medium shots of the "people" of history, both famous and anonymous. Further, in the episodes themselves, especially before photographs and film are available, the characters of the past speak to the audience directly with a steady gaze, drawing us into their stories through dramatic portrayals. In this way, the documentary "re-peoples" Canada's past.

However, the *Minutes*' and the documentary's balancing act between political/military and social history, and their widest possible interpretation of what "counts" as Canadian, cannot fully resolve the tension between competing identities that often lead to competing interests. Any attempt to define what is "Canada" and who is "Canadian" can get them into trouble. Even while these memory projects try to avoid rigid definition, exclusivity, and grand narratives, they inevitably exhibit the present-mindedness and partiality that are an inescapable aspect of remembering and representing the past. As apolitical as claims to representing the universally interesting story of the human spirit appear to be, the motivation behind both these programs to bring Canadians together by getting them to share their past, and their decision to take "Canada" as the organizing unit of representation, gives even images of dissent and conflict a place in a progressive narrative of survival in nationhood. It appears that Starowicz, at least, is aware of this situation. Before the series began to air, he wrote in the

Globe and Mail, "*Canada: A People's History* is going to evoke and illustrate Canadian history by using the personal testimony of those who lived it. We will be informed by the present, but move into the frame of the past.... All documentary involves selection and exclusion, and thereby judgment and unconscious and cultural bias. That's why we call it *a* history, not *the* history."[69]

"Sharing our past" is a major trope of both the *Heritage Minutes* and *Canada: A People's History*. Especially for the documentary, there has been a good deal of commentary about how important it is for "all" Canadians to be able to view the same stories in their own languages. Of course, this formulation leaves out those Canadian citizens and residents who do not consider either official language to be their own. Claude Saint-Laurent, the general news director for Radio-Canada, explains on the CBC website, "For once ... let's put the same story on both networks at the same time and let both of our people see the same story."[70] Discourse such as this points to the ritual importance of all members of the group to be watching the same content at (about) the same time, "communing" through the same media channel, even if they do interpret what they see differently. Those involved with the CBC project have pointed out how rare it is for "all" Canadians to hear each other's stories through this most important of communication channels, television. This documentary seems to make reality the hopes of some cultural elites for television and the internet, that they can be a kind of "electronic agora." The co-production and co-viewing of the documentary makes an important symbolic statement about unity, fitting in with the motivation for producing it in the first place.

Conclusion

The terrorist attacks in the United States on 11 September 2001 and their aftermath make the questions of nationalism, patriotism, and collective memory, and the uses to which these things are put, even more salient. When looking at memory projects, we should ask who and what makes it into the collective memory of a nation, and how these shared scripts and frameworks for action play themselves out in the present. Why have other events and realities failed to stick so strongly in popular consciousness, and how can we understand collective forgetting? And finally, when national unity and consensus about who "we" are and where "we" come from seem so crucial to the survival of the group, what is lost in terms of recognizing difference and allowing dissent?

While on the surface, the *Heritage Minutes* and *Canada: A People's History* seem like quintessentially postmodern productions drawing on multiple perspectives and in many ways resisting a straightforward narrative of Canadian history, they are simultaneously born out of a prototypically modern impulse to restore the unity and strength of national identity and connection to the past. Even while we view past conflicts and injustices, such as the execution of Louis Riel or the Canadian government's repeatedly broken promises to First Nations peoples, the overall tone of these productions succeeds in remaining "feel good." By organizing these programs as stories of human sacrifice and achievement, these memory projects efface the way in which all this generically human suffering and sacrifice is located in a progressive narrative which has a specific endpoint—Canada as a nation-state. Further, both these media memory projects aim to literally unite Canadians in the act of viewing, such that independently of how citizens interpret the content they see, French- and English-speaking Canadians from right across the country have the potential to "share their past" in the viewing moment.

As self-conscious repositories of memory, and as potential shapers of identity and consciousness, the *Heritage Minutes* and *Canada: A People's History* have undertaken projects with potentially far-reaching ramifications. The Historica Foundation's description of the *Heritage Minutes* project hints at the role these kinds of media initiatives may have in affecting collective memory, that perhaps these programs "have themselves become part of Canadian heritage."[71]

Notes

1 Historica, "History of the Minutes," 14 February 2002 < http://www.histori.ca >.

2 Barry Schwartz, "The Social Context of Communication: A Study in Collective Memory," *Social Forces* 61 (1982): 374.

3 François Lyotard, *The Postmodern Condition: A Report on Knowledge*, trans. Geoff Bennington and Brian Massumi (Minneapolis: University of Minnesota Press, 1984), 31.

4 CBC, "Behind the Scenes—About the TV Series; Step by Step: One Story, Many Perspectives," 14 February 2002 < http://www.history.cbc.ca/history >.

5 *Canada: A People's History*, Episode 9, "From Sea to Sea," dir. Jim Williamson, CBC, 2001; and Episode 14, "The Crucible," dir. Susan Teskey, CBC, 2001.

6 Paul Connerton, *How Societies Remember* (New York: Cambridge University Press, 1989), 7.

7 Pierre Nora, *Realms of Memory: Rethinking the French Past*, vol. 1, trans. Arthur Goldhammer (New York: Columbia University Press, 1996), 6.

8 Nora, 2.

9 Nora, 6–7.

10 Lyotard, *Postmodern Condition*, 22–23.

11 Elspeth Cameron, "Heritage Minutes: Culture and Myth," *Canadian Issues* 17 (1995): 16.

12 Chris Cobb, "CBC's Greatest Story Ever Told," *Ottawa Citizen* 8 October 2000, A10.

13 Irving Abella, "The Greatest Show Unearthed," *Globe and Mail* 15 November 2000, A15.

14 *Ottawa Citizen*, "Better than a Heritage Minute," 24 October 2000, A16.

15 CBC, "CBC Message Board," 4 December 2000 <http://www.cbc.ca/mycbc/do/newslet ter.cgi>.

16 CBC, "CBC Message Board," 4 December 2000 <http://www.cbc.ca/mycbc/do/newslet ter.cgi>.

17 CBC, "CBC Message Board." 26 September 2001 <http://www.cbc.ca/mycbc/do/newslet ter.cgi>.

18 CBC, "A Great Success Story: *Canada: A People's History/Le Canada: Une Histoire Populaire*," CBC/Radio-Canada Annual Report 2000–2001, 14, 14 February 2002 <http://cbc.radio-canada.ca/htmen/6_2_00.htm>.

19 Historica, "Historica—A Web Site Dedicated to Canadian History and Heritage," 14 February 2002 <http://www.histori.ca>.

20 Michael Frisch, "American History and the Structures of Collective Memory: A Modest Exercise in Empirical Iconography," *Journal of American History* 75 (1989): 1131.

21 Barbie Zelizer, "Reading the Past Against the Grain: The Shape of Memory Studies," *Critical Studies in Mass Communication* 12 (1995): 226.

22 Jacques LeGoff, *History and Memory*, trans. Steven Rendall and Elizabeth Claman (New York: Columbia University Press, 1992), 2.

23 Benedict Anderson, *Imagined Communities: Reflections on the Origin and Spread of Nationalism* (New York: Verso, 1991), 6.

24 Nora, 7.

25 Historica, "Historica—A Web Site Dedicated to Canadian History and Heritage."

26 Tom Axworthy, "Memories Shape the Way We See Ourselves," *Toronto Star* 26 September 1997, A28.

27 Desmond Morton, "A Shared Past Is a Nation's Compass," *Toronto Star* 26 September 1997, A28.

28 Greg Quill, "Historical Vignettes Given a Dignified Debut," *Toronto Star* 3 May 1995, E1.

29 CBC, "A Great Success Story: *Canada: A People's History/Le Canada: Une Histoire Populaire*."

30 Zelizer, 230.

31 Zelizer, 230.

32 Quill, E1.

33 The Dominion Institute is another organization that has initiated projects to promote Canadian heritage and unity, such as a poll asking Canadians to nominate national heroes in 1999 <www.thememoryproject.com>.

34 Axworthy, A28.

35 LeGoff, *History and Memory*, 16.

36 Frisch, 1153.

37 Jack Granatstein, *Who Killed Canadian History?* (Toronto: HarperCollins, 1998).

38 A.B. McKillop, "CHR Forum: Who Killed Canadian History? A View from the Trenches," *Canadian Historical Review* 80 (1999): 270.

39 McKillop, 273.

40 Historica, "Search by Chronology," 14 February 2002 <http://www.histori.ca>.

41 Historica, "Search by Chronology," 14 February 2002 <http://www.histori.ca>.

42 "Robinson Slept Here," *Ottawa Citizen* 8 August 1997, A13.

43 Lyotard, *Postmodern Condition*, 15.

44 Historica, "Marconi," 18 February 2002 <http://www.histori.ca>.

45 Historica, "Heritage Minutes," 14 February 2002 <http://www.histori.ca>.

46 Historica, "Search by Theme," 14 February 2002 <http://www.histori.ca>.

47 Cobb, A10.

48 *The Making of Canada: A People's History*, dir. Mark Starowicz, CBC, 2001. CBC, "Behind the Scenes—About the TV Series," 14 February 2002 <http://history.cbc.ca /history>.

49 CBC, "Behind the Scenes—About the TV Series; One Story, Many Perspectives," 14 February 2002 <http://history.cbc.ca/history>.

50 Janice Dickin McGinnis, "Heritage Minutes: Myth and History," *Canadian Issues* 17 (1995): 30.

51 CBC, "A People's History of Central Canada ... Only" 14 February 2002 <http://www.cbc .ca/mycbc/do/newsletter.cgi>.

52 CBC, "Canada: A People's History: Discussion Forums: What Did You Think of Episode One?" 18 February 2002 <http://www.cbc.ca/mycbc/do/newsletter.cgi>.

53 CBC, "Canada: A People's History: Discussion Forums."

54 "PQ Debates Horses to Healthcare," *Montreal Gazette* 25 April 1999, A5.

55 Elspeth Cameron, 15–16.

56 Historica, "Governance," 14 February 2002 <http://www.histori.ca>.

57 Carleton University History Collaborative, "Press Reaction: The Reaction to Canada, A People's Reaction," 18 February 2002 <http://www.carleton.ca/historycollaborative>.

58 CBC, "Canada: A People's History: Discussion Forum: Episode 14: The Crucible," 18 February 2002 <http://www.cbc.ca/mycbc/do/newsletter.cgi>.

59 CBC, "Behind the Scenes—About the TV Series; Step by Step."

60 Historica, "Search by Theme," 14 February 2002 <http://www.histori.ca>.

61 Historica, "Search by Theme."

62 Historica, "Search by Theme."

63 Historica, "Search by Theme."

64 Historica, "Search by Theme."

65 Historica, "Search by Theme."

66 CBC, "Behind the Scenes—About the TV Series; Telling the Story."

67 *Canada: A People's History*, Episode 1: *When the World Began...15,000 B.C. to 1800 A.D.*, dir. Andrew Gregg, CBC, 2000.

68 *Canada: A People's History*, Episode 7: *Rebellion and Reform, 1815–1850*, dir. Peter Ingles, CBC, 2001.

69 Starowicz, D3.

70 CBC, "Behind the Scenes—About the TV Series; Step by Step: One Story, Many Perspectives," 14 February 2002 <http://history.cbc.ca/history>.

71 Historica, "History of the Minutes," 14 February 2002 <http://www.histori.ca>.

4 Framing the Local
Canadian Film Policy and the Problem of Place

Zoë Druick

CANADIAN FILMS ARE RARITIES IN CANADIAN THEATRES. In video stores across the land, Canadian films are categorized as "foreign." In contrast to the obscurity of domestically produced feature films, Canadian-made animation and documentary shorts, often produced by the National Film Board, are found in many Canadian classrooms, as well as other non-theatrical settings. Recognizable Canadian locations are often used in films made by Hollywood production companies, and even by the Indian equivalent, Bollywood. Recent Hollywood films that use Canadian locations include *3000 Miles to Graceland*, *Battlefield Earth*, *Exit Wounds*, *The Sixth Day*, *Finding Forrester*, *X-Men*, and *Saving Silverman*. Jackie Chan's *Rumble in the Bronx* may present the most outlandish example of the globalization of film production and film markets in the 1990s: the film features a star who began his career in Hong Kong action films making a Hollywood product set in New York but obviously filmed in Vancouver, with that city's distinctive mountain-ringed harbour unco-operatively requiring viewers to suspend their disbelief. The objective of this chapter is to think through these contradictions of visibility and invisibility, which are ultimately the contradictions of Canadian film culture. Beyond sketching the history of Canada's film policies and film industry, I aim to situate film studies and policy studies in relation to currents of thought in geography and anthropology, in order to explore the use of filmic signification in the production of local, national, and global identities.

Modernity is seen to have brought about fundamental technological and phenomenological displacements of time and space. In many ways, the fragmentary, displaced, technologized Canada is a perfect manifestation of the modern. Canada's largest immigration boom came during the years 1880–1918, the period in which historian Stephen Kern locates the perceptual shifts characteristic of modern life.[1] In the main, these shifts include some experience of space being diminished, conquerable by means of the technologies of train, telegraph, telephone, radio, and film, and later car and airplane, as well as the standardization of time. Modernity is thus equated with the introduction of certain new technologies that seem impervious to place and time and that connect people in globally unified time and across no-longer-insuperable distances. The problems of the Canadian nation are problems of modernity: the attempt to found an organic nation-state that is nonetheless reliant upon time and space-altering technologies to cohere.

How have the "problems" of the Canadian nation been expressed? From a centralizing, nationalist point of view, it is a problem that region, language, and American media may exert pulls upon Canadian identity: "In Canada, the attempt to address the question of national identity is complicated by the dualism of French and English Canada, by regionalism and multiculturalism, and by a ready acceptance of American popular culture on the part of most Canadians,"[2] notes one recent commentator. These conditions are only problems, I posit, in relation to an ideal notion of what a nation should be: monolingual, monocultural, bounded, and impervious to other nations' cultural products. The answer to these concerns in Canada has often been the assertion of national identity as a progressive, anti-American strategy. As Albert Moran observes, however, this involves implicit decisions about what authentic national culture is: "championing national cinemas in the face of the power of Hollywood may seem politically progressive ... [but] considered from a sub-national or multicultural perspective such a defense is more problematic."[3] Indeed, national identity is a provisional and often disputed category, whose inclusions and exclusions are always politically loaded decisions.

The Canadian nation is in many ways a study in the application of communication technologies to questions of difference that present a problem for governance. The challenges of an enormous land mass, an administrative state without a singular national sentiment, a legacy of colonial genocide, and masses of immigrants seem to call out for an administrative solution. The perceived lack of national identity presents a problem repeatedly addressed with technological solutions. Communication technologies seductively promise to expedite solutions to these complex problems in a way that can be budgeted for and expected to produce immediate effects. Yet, as Michael Dorland has noted, "For all its technical achieve-ments, Canada remains a fragile communicative entity, plagued by recur-ring problems of national identity, both internal and external."[4]

Despite all this thinking about communications technology as the solu-tion for problems of Canadian national identity—or, indeed, because of it—there is a well-established strand of thought in Canada about how this modern "technological nationalism"[5] effaces authentic experiences of place. Perhaps most famously, Northrop Frye wrote, "It seems to me that Canadian sensibility has been profoundly disturbed, not so much by our famous problem of identity, important as that is, as by a series of paradoxes in what confronts that identity. It is less perplexed by the question of 'Who am I?' than by some such riddle as 'Where is here?'"[6] Not long after-wards, Margaret Atwood agreed with Frye's focus on place in the fragmen-tary Canadian imaginary, characterizing Canadians as "lost." She went further to suggest that Canadian survival depended on cultural location: "What a lost person needs is a map of the territory, with his own position marked on it so he can see where he is in relation to everything else.... For the members of a country or a culture, shared knowledge of their place, their here, is not a luxury but a necessity. Without that knowledge we will not survive."[7] Both writers blamed the encroachment of American popu-lar media for the production of placelessness in Canadian lives.

These famous lines arose out of essays written during a resurgence of Canadian cultural nationalism on the left in Canada at around the time of the country's centenary. Admittedly, there is something compelling about their sentiments; yet they risk lapsing into an implied comparison to a stable, premodern, more authentic experience of place, where life was presumably lived with a map, to paraphrase Atwood. Their sentiments were very much of their time. Looking at the industrial, urban landscape of southern Ontario in the 1970s, geographer Edward Relph concluded that modern life was a "universal wasteland" in which contemporary peo-ple had an inauthentic sense of place.[8] Joshua Meyrowitz formulated one of the most extreme descriptions of this modern condition: "our world may suddenly seem senseless to many people because, for the first time in mod-ern history, it is relatively placeless."[9] These writers express the mournful critique of destructive modernization responsible in their view for the eradication of difference and uniqueness, seen to be the very stuff of iden-tity.

Out of these concerns came the Canadian truism that we are a nation of authentic regional differences and a state-enforced national unity. Frye asserts, "the question of Canadian identity...is not a 'Canadian' question at all, but a regional question."[10] Further, Frye polarizes culture and pol-itics: "identity is local and regional, rooted in the imagination and in works of culture; unity is national in reference, international in perspective, and rooted in political feeling."[11] Linda Hutcheon has recently reinscribed Frye's point: "Canada can in some ways be defined as a country whose articulation of its *national* identity has sprung from *regionalist* impulses: the ex-centric forces of Quebec, the Maritimes, the west. Its history is one of defining itself against centers."[12] In both of these assessments the local, or regional, is proposed as an authentic site of identity-formation and cultural creation in opposition to a national political agenda of false unity. This seems to be a compelling solution to the "problems" of the Canadian nation. Yet how authentic is the local? Indeed, how do we define the local?

In recent geographical and anthropological writing, there is a general dismissal of the concept of the local as independent from either the global or the nation-state that mediates between the two. Geographer Doreen Massey alerts us to the facile association of place with authentic community: "an (idealized) notion of an era when places were (supposedly) inhabited by coherent and homogeneous communities is set against the current fragmentation and disruption. The counterposition is anyway dubious, of course: 'place' and 'community' have only rarely been coterminous."[13] For his part, Roland Robertson proposes, "much of the talk about globalization has tended to assume that it is a process which overrides locality.... This interpretation neglects...the extent to which what is called local is in large degree constructed on a trans- or super-local basis."[14] According to Robertson, the local is best considered as an aspect of globalization,[15] rather than its antithesis. Far from being mutually exclusive, then, the terms actually infer one another.

It is important to separate the fact that modern landscapes are comprised of standardized multinational features, such as McDonald's and Wal-Mart, from the feeling of displacement that Relph and Meyrowitz express or the notion of authentic locality that we hear from Frye and others. Massey has suggested that when there is talk of dislocation we ought to ask *who* feels dislocated and invaded, and by what or whom?[16] Perhaps unsurprisingly, the root of Canadian placelessness is often attributed not only to American consumer culture, but also to the coeval disruptions of immigration, euphemistically known in recent years as multiculturalism. The response is often renewed attention to carefully selected heritage, or "tradition," combined with a "celebration of diversity." The ideology of "official" multiculturalism in Canada[17] is a discourse of tolerance for a folklorist other that attempts to fend off perceived threats of cultural difference.[18] Homi Bhabha notes that the liberal endorsement of "cultural diversity" is always accompanied by a corresponding containment.[19] Paying lip service to multiculturalism is a tactic that simultaneously reinscribes one ethnic norm as dominant. The common Canadian line that we are a nation of immigrants obscures the special status accorded to French and English in our linguistic, cultural, and political landscapes. Official multiculturalism attempts to contain ethnic disruptions to constructions of authentic experiences of Canadian regional heritage.

Nations are most often the rallying point for discussions of uniqueness and locality: "Modern nations have tended to promote discourses concerning their own unique difference, a practice much encouraged in and by the great globalizing thrusts of the late nineteenth and early twentieth centuries."[20] Paradoxically, then, far from destroying local difference, globalization has attempted to create a template in which national and local particularity can take shape as fragments of a larger picture. Even McDonald's follows the tactic of "glocalization,"[21] tailoring its offerings to particularities of local taste. For many contemporary anthropologists, traditional ideas about discrete peoples and unified cultures are no longer tenable.[22] Like "place" and "identity," "culture" is now seen as a site of difference and contestation, not just coherence and order.[23] This process-based notion of meaning and place implicates the media as a significant aspect of contemporary identity.

The field of communication studies began between the two world wars with a generally suspicious attitude toward the media. Not only had the mass media altered people's perceptions of space and time, but the media were also held responsible for destroying the premodern sense of place, with the resultant destruction of community and identity. In Canada, theorists often came to precisely these conclusions. Harold Innis made a "plea for time" in a world where empires are built on space-dominating technologies.[24] Marshall McLuhan was terrified of the "global village" and the post-literate electronic era he helped usher into popular consciousness.[25] In its 1951 *Report*, the Royal Commission on National Development in the Arts, Letters, and Sciences (known as the Massey-Lévesque Commission) gave the ominous warning, "Hollywood refashions us in its own image."[26] Canadian media commentators combined their sense of threat from the American media with support for indigenous control of the means of production. In the Canadian case, the media are presented alternately as saviours or eroders of national culture in a high-stakes game of identity.

The distinction between creator and destroyer of national culture, as well as between inside and outside of the national group, has to be challenged by more complicated notions of culture and identity, which take account of the productive and authentic place of the media in that process. Frederic Jameson gives this process the useful term "cognitive mapping." According to Jameson, "all forms of aesthetic production consist in one way or another in the struggle with and for representation."[27] Cognitively, we rely upon forms of signification for the production of meaning. Representational practices, such as the visual media, are thus constitutive aspects of our experience of self and place. As John Durham Peters has noted, we "see proximate fragments with [our] own eyes and global totalities through the diverse media of social description."[28] Yet one is not more authentic than the other. Local, national, and global combine in our formulations of "identity" and "place," in appropriately complex ways.

The importance of processes of signification, such as film, for the ongoing struggles over the production of cultural meaning is underscored by Raymond Williams, who insists that means of communication are *primary* forms of social production, not secondary derivatives: "Communication and its material means are intrinsic to all distinctively human forms of labour and social organization, thus constituting indispensable elements both of the productive forces and of the social relations of production."[29] Williams suggests that culture is not so much the reflection of the material world, as it is one of its constitutive parts. In terms of state interest in this field, Canada is not unique. Insofar as they regulate and organize cultural production, all nation-states attempt to intervene in the production of social being and consciousness; indeed, "If state-identifying peoples stopped the state-creating schools, newspapers, radio, television, films, sports, armies and police, most states would disappear within a short time."[30]

The Canadian government has intervened in the production of cultural identity through a variety of film policies with regional, national, and international implications. As argued above, the categories of local, national, and global cannot be clearly separated. The challenge of media representations to a nationally based policy is that the global has become a "graphic part of our local experience."[31] For example, recent postnationalist work has suggested that it is almost impossible for any country that boasts a film-consuming public to claim that Hollywood film is not somehow a part of its own national film culture. Albert Moran has declared, "Hollywood is no longer out there, beyond [our] borders, but is instead very much a component of [our] own national cinema."[32] This view holds significant implications for the analysis of Canadian film policy. The production of nationality in Canada has long been a strategy of "locality" in a global or international context. The international "promotion of locality"[33] has meant that local identity is formed into internationally expected configurations of uniqueness.

Early in the twentieth century, Canada was the first nation to take up film-production and distribution as a major government enterprise.[34] As early as 1901, the Canadian government had become involved with film as a promotional instrument to encourage immigration.[35] The Ministry of the Interior, concerned with settlement of the prairie provinces, collaborated with the Canadian Pacific Railway (CPR), whose film activities had begun three years earlier,[36] to promote frontier living. These efforts, directed particularly at England and France, continued sporadically through the first decade of the century:[37] "In this process of persuasion, the motion picture was to play a key role, being used first by the CPR and later by governments themselves and other railways. The effectiveness of these films was to be remembered later by officials of the federal government when they were considering the establishment of a permanent government film bureau in 1917."[38] In 1917, the Canadian Government Motion Picture Bureau (CGMPB) was formed under the auspices of the Department of Trade and Commerce. The first declared purpose of government film production was promotional, to publicize Canada and Canadian products abroad as part of exhibits at trade fairs. After the enhancement of trade, the bureau's next objective was the attraction of immigrants. Later, as the tourism industry grew, the bureau's films aimed to promote American sport and leisure in Canada. These objectives are reflected in films such as *Conquest of the Forest* (1928), *The Seasons of Canada* (1930), and a long-running series, *Seeing Canada* (1919–1939).

The CGMPB produced films about places in Canada that would be perceived by Americans as places to visit, by Europeans as places to settle, and by Canadians as part of a burgeoning sense of national identity. The government Film Acts of 1939 and 1950 are significant for the space they open up for the production of regionality in Canada. The 1939 Film Act, which founded the National Film Board (NFB), calls for a focus on regionality, so that Canadians "in all parts of Canada" can "understand the ways of living and the problems of Canadians in other parts."[39] Substitute "nation" for "parts of Canada" and it becomes clear that Canadian film policy presents a microcosm of international cosmopolitan discourses of consuming discrete national and regional cultural formations. Among the first NFB productions was a film called *Peoples of Canada* (1941). A synopsis published by the National Film Society in that year describes the film as a "documentary film show[ing] the different nationalities which make up the population of the Dominion of Canada." This effort was followed up by *Canadians All* (1943), a film promoting tolerance of cultural differences in Canada, especially for nationalities such as German and Italian, tarred by association with wartime enemy nations. This film was accompanied by a booklet published by the Nationalities Branch of the Department of War Services.[40] Both of these films use a nascent multiculturalist discourse to emphasize the need for tolerance towards internal others with bounded cultural and regional locations.

In 1950, after the onset of the Cold War, the Film Act was revamped to reflect the international circulation of images in the "national interest ...

designed to interpret Canada to Canadians and to other nations."[41] The revised act reflected the discourse of the United Nations that had taken hold in the postwar period, wherein local particularity was groomed according to narrative and symbolic conventions of international culture.[42] Throughout the late 1940s and 1950s, the NFB produced films that emphasized local differences as the basis for admittance into national and international communities.

Canadian cultural policy treated domestic multiculturalism as an internal United Nations. The 1940s saw a proliferation of NFB films about diverse forms of internal folk culture, such as *Iceland on the Prairies* (1941), *Gaspe Cod Fishermen* (1944), and *Eskimo Arts and Crafts* (1944). In the postwar period, there was a preponderance of trans-Canada films replaying the colonization of Canada, such as *Trans-Canada Express* (1944), *Passport to Canada* (1949), and *Trans-Canada Journey* (1962). (There were, in fact, so many of these films that Buster Keaton came to the NFB in the 1960s to make a trans-Canada spoof called *The Railrodder*.) Reflecting the social statistics and opinion polls that helped create their scripts, these documentaries choose a typical character or group to represent each region.[43] As these examples indicate, film policy in Canada actively used cognitive mapping to craft and promote the specificities and uniqueness of multicultural communities, and regionally specific places contextualized in an overarching narrative of nationhood.[44] The films thus seem to document previously existing regional identities that they are actually helping to produce through active representation.

What connects the film acts and the National Film Board films to Hollywood is their contrived complementarity.[45] Hollywood has long considered Canada to be part of its domestic market and, through unwillingness to regulate film production, distribution, or exhibition to any significant degree, the Canadian state has substantially concurred. By the late 1940s, Canada entered into a secretive "Co-operation Project" with Hollywood wherein Canada agreed not to put limits on profits earned by US films shown in Canada in exchange for Canadian references in American films.[46] At precisely this moment, the Massey-Lévesque Commission was decrying Hollywood's deleterious effects on Canada and a policy commitment to maintaining the National Film Board was being renewed. The unavoidable conclusion is that Hollywood is not an infringement into Canadian film culture so much as it is an integral part of that culture.

In 1956, the NFB headquarters were moved from Ottawa to Montreal. This move has alternately been perceived as centralizing and/or regionalizing the board: centralizing because it was a move that consolidated the NFB's operations in a single, dedicated facility; regionalizing because it meant the accelerated development of the French production side of the board, culminating in a series of the board's most celebrated films. Film-makers such as Gilles Groulx, Michel Brault, and Denys Arcand both experimented with documentary form and made films that served as weather vanes for the nascent Quiet Revolution. Ronald Dick character-izes these films as "regional": "They did not interpret Canada to Quebec, but Quebec to Quebecers, and to anyone else who cared to watch," he writes.[47] Despite Dick's assessment, such regionalism was in fact a clear ful-fillment of the NFB's mandate.

Over the course of the next decade, production and distribution offices opened in cities across the country. One of the most compelling examples of regionalization was the series of films produced during the 1960s by Colin Low under the rubric of Challenge for Change/Société Nouvelle. This project used newly accessible portable video equipment to create regional portraits in areas with social problems. Fogo Island, a remote fishing community in Newfoundland with severe work shortages and attendant social problems, served as the template for this approach. Dick describes this project as marking a new "tendency to see subjects in regional terms, addressing regional problems, and giving films a regional form. Sympathy with groups and individuals thinking 'regionally' was evident."[48] Colin Low would go on to be instrumental in making regionalization offi-cial policy at the NFB.[49]

In 1972, the Secretary of State, the department in charge of cultural agencies, reviewed film policy and published a report entitled "Global Film Policy" that indicated the government's support for the establish-ment of regional presence for the NFB.[50] The result was the creation of five regional offices: Atlantic, Quebec, Ontario, Prairie, and Western. Further, in 1976 the NFB adopted a five-year plan for regionalization:[51] "The objec-tive of this policy, in keeping with the role of the NFB, is to provide each region the opportunity to interpret a regional subject to a national audience or a national subject from a regional point of view."[52] The language of regionalization used by the head of production at NFB's Vancouver office is telling. Asked why there should be regional offices, he replied, "Because Canada is 3,827 miles wide. Because, for all the efforts of the CBC, the NFB, the CNR and Air Canada, for all the telephone and teletypes, newspapers, magazines and books—for all these methods of communication—there is still a huge gulf in realities and attitudes between Canadians in different regions."[53] Toward the end of this five-year period, Low remarked some-what defensively that the regional films that had resulted from the policy were not merely of regional interest, but had great potential to communi-cate at the national and international levels as well.[54] Yet he need not have been so defensive. Within the terms established here, this policy was the log-ical extension of the promotion of local distinctiveness for a national and international audience. The policy opens up the space in advance for appropriately distinct regionalism to come into existence.

Just as in the late 1940s there was a contradiction between government film policies for renewed support for the NFB and for the Co-operation Project with Hollywood, the late 1960s and 1970s saw an increasing rift between educational expectations for regional NFB productions and a new emphasis on domestic feature film production. In 1968, with the establishment of the Canadian Film Development Corporation (CFDC), the federal government began to make a concerted, if half-hearted, attempt to fund feature films.[55] Policy changes in the 1970s made film production a tax shelter and brought about the production of a raft of Hollywood-style films, the most infamous of which was the male adolescent fantasy *Porky's*.[56] This characterization does not necessarily lead to the most common assessments of these films as crass commercialism debasing an otherwise pure Canadian culture. Rather, the fact that Hollywood had long been a part of Canadian film taste became, if not more obvious, then certainly less obscured since, for the first time, Canadians became producers as well as consumers of mainstream, trashy commercial cinema.

With the transformation of CFDC into the more television-oriented Telefilm Canada in 1984 came a new period in Canadian film culture and yet another contradiction: the production of a plethora of American television knock-offs and the flourishing of indigenous art house auteurs, such as Patricia Rozema and Atom Egoyan, whose aesthetic sensibilities can be traced to international rather than specifically Canadian film culture. Indeed, although rooted in Toronto's art scene, their films proclaim their cosmopolitanism by obscuring their geopolitical location. Between 1967 and 1997, CFDC and Telefilm funded 1,600 television programs and series, and nearly seven hundred feature films,[57] many of which were co-productions with other countries. The state funding certainly affected production, but has had less impact on distribution and exhibition. The government commitment to put Canadian stories into an increasingly international media landscape was somewhat unconvincing. Indeed, with an explosion of Hollywood-style productions, as well as a multitude of co-productions with France and other countries, the conundrum of exactly what constituted a distinctive Canadian story was brought into sharp relief.

Where Canadian film policy has tried to redress questions of underproduction, the government has consistently backed away from interfering with American control over distribution and exhibition. In the late 1980s, as Hollywood companies, along with most multinational corporations, decentred their production in order to corner global markets, Canada became the site of a good deal of Hollywood production, acquiring the nickname Hollywood North.[58] This incursion of American production in

Canadian locations continues to be facilitated by government policies putatively designed to encourage an indigenous film industry by, in effect, forming a Canadian infrastructure funded by American companies. These economic incentives have translated into an influx of American production, currently constituting one third of Canada's $1.4 billion film and television industry,[59] which has been called a Canadian subsidy for Hollywood production.[60] The result has not been a collateral increase in domestic production, however, but rather a boom in foreign productions at the expense of domestic ones.[61] This confirms the traditional political economic view of Canadian film culture as little more than a "branch plant" of Hollywood.[62] However correct such thinking is from an economic standpoint, culturally it resorts to the presumption that there is a singular, authentic Canadian culture that is being suppressed or thwarted. A more productive way to think about the current situation might be to consider the politics of the spaces available for cultural production, many of which are provided, directly or indirectly, by government policy shaped by conflicting economic and cultural goals.

Knowingly or not, many, if not all, Canadians have had the uncanny experience of seeing Canadian places masquerading as American locations in American films and television shows. Presumably these locations have been used because of the assumption of placelessness discussed above. As cities around North America and the world acquire the same postindustrial sprawl, the same downtowns featuring the same international style architecture and the same suburban malls, they become interchangeable sets for interchangeable, mass-produced genre pictures. Indeed, the arrival of Indian, or Bollywood, film production in Canada[63] underscores the domination of global cinema by a few major world centres, including New York, Hong Kong, and Bombay as well as Hollywood.[64]

The plethora of Hollywood films shot in Canada is a graphic reminder of the illusion of an autonomous Canadian film industry that was not reliant upon the American one. Indeed, our notion of our own national distinctiveness, comprised of regional differences and placed in an international context, is a story, as well as a productive cognitive map, that has served us well in our attempts to apprehend both Canada and ourselves. Becoming aware of our reliance upon acts of signification for placemaking and processes of identification can make us more tuned in to the productive role cultural policy can play in temporarily reconciling contradictions and attempting to make spaces available for particular forms of cultural production.

Rather than suggest that contemporary Canadian audiovisual culture is inauthentic or masks a real understanding of Canadian homes, regions, or even the nation, it is more challenging to think about how a sense of identity, place, and culture is bound up in processes of technological modernity that are at once local, national, and international. These processes tie the Canadian state and economy into global contexts that ironically seem to demand authentic forms of locality even as they promote transnationality through flows of money, people, goods, and images.[65] Canadian film policy, like the discourse of Canadian nationalism, often seems saturated by contradictions between economy and culture, between narratives of the nation and the cultural differences that challenge neat boundaries between peoples, identities, cultures, and places. Recognizing the foundations of these contradictions in modern nation-building and its "strategy of culture"[66] gives us some perspective with which to "map" the multifaceted Canadian case.

Notes

1 Stephen Kern, *The Culture of Time and Space, 1880–1918* (Cambridge: Harvard University Press, 1983).

2 Ted Magder, *Canada's Hollywood: The Canadian State and Feature Films* (Toronto: University of Toronto Press, 1993), 11.

3 Albert Moran, "Terms for a Reader: Film, Hollywood, National Cinema, Cultural Identity, and Film Policy," *Film Policy: International, National, and Regional Perspectives*, ed. Albert Moran (London: Routledge, 1996), 10.

4 Michael Dorland, "Cultural Industries and the Canadian Experience," *Cultural Industries in Canada*, ed. Michael Dorland (Toronto: Lorimer, 1996), 348.

5 Maurice Charland, "Technological Nationalism," *Canadian Journal of Political and Social Theory* 10 (1986): 296–220.

6 Northrop Frye, *The Bush Garden: Essays on the Canadian Imagination* (Toronto: Anansi, 1971), 220.

7 Margaret Atwood, *Survival: A Thematic Guide to Canadian Literature* (Toronto: Anansi, 1972), 18–19.

8 Edward Relph, *Place and Placelessness* (London: Pion, 1976), 79.

9 Joshua Meyrowitz, *No Sense of Place: The Impact of Electronic Media on Social Behaviour* (New York: Oxford University Press, 1985), 308.

10 Frye, *Bush Garden*, i.

11 Frye, *Bush Garden*, ii.

12 Linda Hutcheon, *The Canadian Postmodern* (Toronto: Oxford University Press, 1988), 4; italics in original.

13 Doreen Massey, *Space, Place, and Gender* (Minneapolis: University of Minnesota Press, 1994), 146.

14 Roland Robertson, "Glocalization: Time-Space and Homogeneity–Heterogeneity," *Global Modernities*, ed. Mike Featherstone, Scott Lash, and Roland Robertson (London: Sage, 1995), 26.

15 Robertson, 30.

16 Massey, 212–48.

17 Himani Bannerji, *The Dark Side of the Nation: Essays on Multiculturalism, Nationalism and Gender* (Toronto: Canadian Scholars' Press, 2000).

18 Slavoj Žižek, "Multiculturalism, or, the Cultural Logic of Multinational Capitalism," *New Left Review* 225 (1997): 37.

19 Jonathan Rutherford, "The Third Space: Interview with Homi Bhabha," *Identity: Community, Culture, Difference* (London: Lawrence and Wishart, 1990), 208.

20 Robertson, 41.

21 Robertson.

22 Akhil Gupta and James Ferguson, "Culture, Power, Place: Ethnography at the End of an Era," *Culture, Power, Place: Explorations in Critical Anthropology*, ed. Akhil Gupta and James Ferguson (Durham: Duke University Press, 1997), 3.

23 Gupta and Ferguson, 5.

24 Harold Innis, *The Bias of Communication* (Toronto: University of Toronto Press, 1951).

25 Marshall McLuhan, *Understanding Media: The Extensions of Man* (Toronto: Signet, 1964).

26 Canada, Royal Commission on National Development in the Arts, Letters, and Sciences, Report (Ottawa, 1951), 50.

27 Frederic Jameson, "Cognitive Mapping," *Marxism and the Interpretation of Culture*, ed. Cary Nelson and Larry Grossberg (Urbana: University of Illinois Press, 1988), 348.

28 John Durham Peters, "Seeing Bifocally: Media, Place, Culture," *Culture, Power, Place: Explorations in Critical Anthropology*, ed. Akhil Gupta and James Ferguson (Durham: Duke University Press, 1997), 79.

29 Raymond Williams, "Means of Communication as Means of Production," *Problems of Materialism and Culture* (London: Verso, 1997), 50.

30 Bernard Nietschmann, "Authentic, State, and Virtual Geography in Film," *Wide Angle* 15.4 (1993): 12n2.

31 Peters, 82.

32 Moran, 7.

33 Robertson, 37.

34 Charles Backhouse, *Canadian Government Motion Picture Bureau, 1917–1941* (Ottawa: Canadian Film Institute, 1974), 5.

35 Peter Morris, *Embattled Shadows: A History of Canadian Cinema 1895–1939* (Montreal: McGill-Queen's University Press, 1978), 32.

36 Morris, *Embattled*, 30.

37 Morris, *Embattled*, 28.

38 Morris, *Embattled*, 33.

39 Canada, National Film Act, Statutes of Canada (Ottawa, 1939), 103.

40 N.F. Dreisiger, "The Rise of a Bureaucracy for Multiculturalism: The Origins of the Nationalities Branch, 1939–45," *On Guard for Thee: War, Ethnicity, and the Canadian State, 1939–45*, ed. Norman Hillmer, Bohdan Kordan, and Lubomyr Luciuk (Ottawa: Canadian Committee for the History of the Second World War, 1988), 6.

41 Canada, National Film Act, Statutes of Canada, Vol. 1 (Ottawa, 1950), 3.

42 Julian Huxley, *Unesco: Its Purpose and Its Philosophy* (Washington, DC: Public Affairs Press, 1948).

43 Zoë Druick, "'Ambiguous Identities' and the Representation of Everyday Life: Notes Toward a New History of Production Policies at the NFB of Canada," *Canadian Issues* 20 (1998): 125–37.

44 Homi Bhabha, *Nation and Narration* (London: Routledge, 1990).

45 Peter Morris, "Backwards to the Future: John Grierson's Film Policy for Canada," *People and Institutions in Canadian Film History*, ed. Gene Walz (Montreal: Mediatexte, 1986), 17–35.

46 Pierre Berton, *Hollywood's Canada: The Americanization of Our National Image* (Toronto: McClelland and Stewart, 1975).

47 Ronald Dick, "Regionalization of a Federal Cultural Institution: The Experience of the National Film Board of Canada, 1965–1979," *Flashback: People and Institutions in Canadian Film History*, ed. Gene Walz (Montreal: Mediatexte Publications, 1986), 109.

48 Dick, 112.

49 Dick, 113.

50 Dick, 121.

51 Dick, 121.

52 Dick, 122.

53 Dick, 120.

54 Dick, 127.

55 Magder, *Canada's Hollywood*; Michael Dorland, *So Close to the State/s: The Emergence of Canadian Feature Film Policy* (Toronto: University of Toronto Press, 1998).

56 Wyndham Wise, "Canadian Cinema from Boom to Bust: The Tax-Shelter Years," *Take One* 22 (1999): 17–24.

57 Tom McSorley, "Critical Mass: Thirty Years of Telefilm Canada," *Take One* 22 (1999): 30.

58 Mike Gasher, "The Audiovisual Locations Industry in Canada: Considering British Columbia as Hollywood North," *Canadian Journal of Communication* 20.2 (1995): 231–54.

59 Doug Saunders, "The Myth of Hollywood North," *Report on Business* 17.10 (2001): 97.

60 Saunders, 97.

61 Saunders, 100.

62 Harold Innis, *The Strategy of Culture* (Toronto: University of Toronto Press, 1952); Manjunath Pendakur, *Canadian Dreams and American Control* (Detroit: Wayne State University Press, 1990).

63 "Hollywood North Is Brimming to Become Bollywood West," *Canadian Press Newswire*, 4 June 2001. 4 October 2001 <http://www.lib.sfu.ca/cc4201a/conv95241.conv>.

64 Arjun Appadurai, "The Production of Locality," *Counterworks: Managing the Diversity of Knowledge*, ed. Richard Fardon (London: Routledge, 1995), 218.

65 Arjun Appadurai, "Disjuncture and Difference in the Global Cultural Economy," *Public Culture* 2.2 (Spring 1990): 1–23.

66 Innis, *Strategy of Culture*.

5 Framing Culture, Talking Race
Race, Gender, and Violence in the News Media

Yasmin Jiwani

Culture is one of the two or three most complicated words in the English language. —*Raymond Williams*[1]

Culture, this acted document, thus is public, like a burlesqued wink or a mock sheep raid. Though ideational, it does not exist in someone's head; though unphysical, it is not an occult entity.
                                                              —*Clifford Geertz*[2]

ALTHOUGH THE TERM "CULTURE" has a long and involved history shaped by material events as well as disciplinary perspectives,[3] it remains a highly fluid discursive category of common-sense thought containing within it a range of connotations that can be used strategically to define various groups and nations. Indeed, it is the very fluidity of "culture" that makes it so accessible and available to institutions such as the mass media to communicate notions of "us" and "them."

This chapter begins by interrogating dominant representations of "culture" in Canadian society. The latter provides a contextual background to understanding the various mediated representations of different groups that are prevalent within contemporary news media coverage. Thereafter, two different sets of news stories concerning systemic and intimate forms of violence involving women of colour are discussed. The chapter concludes with an analysis of the use of culture to dismiss and trivialize violence against women of colour and/or to erase the impact of racism.

Official Representations of Culture

At an official level of government discourse, Canada is characterized as a multicultural society. The different groups that inhabit the imagined space

The research for this paper was made possible by funding from the Social Sciences and Humanities Research Council of Canada, Strategic Theme Grant #829-1999-1002.

of Canadian national identity are given due recognition in terms of their multiplicity of origin and different social practices. Yet this multiplicity is also structured hierarchically, with the cultures of the two "founding" nations—the English and the French—being accorded greater dominance and legitimacy, albeit to varying degrees depending on one's geographical location. These dominant cultures provide the backdrop against which other cultures are assessed and ranked in terms of their legitimacy and the recognition given to their part in shaping the nation's identity. Hence, given their status as "founding" cultures, the dominance of the French and English serves to shape the context in which the rest of the "other" cultures are allowed to operate and their distinctiveness tolerated. This is most apparent in the structures and systems by which difference is defined and contained.

Existing critiques of multiculturalism have highlighted the various ways in which non-dominant cultural groups are subordinated and the manifestations of cultural identity are distorted in order to fit into the prevailing and tolerated notions of cultural difference. Thus, non-dominant cultural identities and expressions are confined to what has been described as "ethnic exotica"—the diet, dance, and dress signifying different and quaint cultural traditions.[4] Contained within this category, cultural differences are neutralized and converted into non-threatening displays of diversity, affirming the values of Canadian tolerance and benevolence. Cultural differences that cannot so easily be denied or erased are then used to symbolize those behaviours that are "unCanadian" or those that do not belong in the symbolic territory of the imagined Canadian identity.[5]

Problematizing "Culture" within "Multiculturalism"

While the official government discourse argues for a view of Canada as a multicultural nation, the definition of culture within that discourse is problematic on several grounds, some of which are alluded to above. For one, such a social construction relies on the notion of cultures as monolithic entities—as wholes that are uncomplicated by internal differences and bound by uniformly accepted conventions and rules that are ostensibly located in such markers as historically based cultural traditions, including diet, dance, and dress. This privileging of a primordial notion of culture as simple ethnicity fails to take into consideration a variety of factors that influence cultural interpretation and practice, such as class differences, generational differences, and political differences. As well, these dominant representations exclude recognition of the diasporic[6] nature of cultural groups, discounting how they change in different contexts and how they maintain ties with each other through transnational networks of communication. Further, the dominant discourse on culture negates any competing notion of cultures within dominant cultures, whether this is the corporate culture, youth culture, women's culture, and so on. Alternatively, the construction of a dominant culture also renders invisible the sub-cultural groups within it—groups that have been previously colonized and assimilated into a larger dominant group.

Clearly, "culture" is much more than ethnicity. Culture, according to Geertz, can be defined as constituting the "webs of meaning" by which we make sense of the world around us.[7] It is through the language of representations that we make culture and make cultural sense, but how are dominant representations conveyed to make certain definitions of culture more legitimate and credible than others? In our common-sense notions of world, why are some groups deemed cultural groups and others not? Why is it that the corporate culture is not recognized or treated in the same way as an ethnocultural group, given that both are "cultural?" These questions are all the more pertinent when we consider that groups create webs of meaning that on the one hand are specific to their particular location in the society, and on the other hand contribute to and draw from a shared framework of meaning or shared conceptual maps, as Hall refers to them, that constitutes society as a whole.[8]

Media Representations and Culture

In part, our familiarity with dominant notions of culture is derived from the messages that we receive through the mass media about "culture" and cultural groups. Stuart Hall argues that what the media "'produce' is, precisely, representations of the social world, images, descriptions, explanations and frames for understanding how the world is and why it works as it is said and shown to work."[9] Hence, the kinds of meanings of particular constructs that the media choose to privilege are those that acquire a certain taken-for-granted meaning and become part of our "common-sense" stock of knowledge over time. These are the categories that we tend not to interrogate but simply use as signs to understand the world. To some extent, these representations are not simply produced by the media in a vacuum but are grounded in the repository of our historically sedimented stock of knowledge. In other words, they refer to the ways in which these concepts were articulated at one time and the particular connotations they were imbued with. As they acquire legitimacy and currency, these representations tend to be reproduced over time and, in the process, reinforce our collective stock of knowledge.

Hall's definition is instructive as it sheds light on the historicity of common-sense knowledge as well as its continuous reproduction in society. He argues that

> contemporary forms of common sense are shot through with the debris and traces of previous, more developed ideological systems; and their reference point is what passes, without exception as the wisdom of our particular age and society, overcast with the glow of traditionalism. It is precisely its "spontaneous" quality, its transparency, its "naturalness," its refusal to be made to examine the premises on which it is founded, its resistance to change or to correction, its effect of instant recognition, and the closed circle in which it moves which makes common sense, at one and the same time, "spontaneous," ideological and unconscious. You cannot learn, through common sense, *how things are*: you can only discover where they fit into the existing scheme of things.[10]

The Mass Media as Public Texts

The mass media draw from and reinforce common-sense knowledge through the circulation of products that constitute "public texts."[11] These texts are public precisely because they are shared and draw from a shared conceptual map of meaning. Within the range of media programs and formats, news and current affairs programming provides "everyday accounts" of the world as framed by those who have symbolic power.[12]

As bits of common sense, representations, especially in the media, often function as shorthand devices, communicating in a condensed manner elements or figures that stand for a "general truth" and/or evoke a chain of associations embedded in our collective imagination.[13] In so doing, representations involve both connotative and denotative elements.[14] Signs that have acquired particular historical associations and that stand for a larger concept are selected and combined in ways that enable the representation to "make sense." Harve Bennett, the producer of the popular television series *The Six Million Dollar Man* and *The Bionic Woman*, describes this process in terms of communicating an Arab identity as follows: "Let me put it this way—do you know how to play charades? ... You don't go for the meat of the material. You do a pantomime of a guy in a burnoose [Arab or Moorish cloak]. But it's sign language and that's the trouble. That's the temptation. Put him in a burnoose and we'll all know who he is."[15] The visual character of media such as film and television makes the art of representations simple on the one hand and complex on the other as we, the audience, are required to make sense of the representation in relation to our particular semantic vocabulary of signs and the collective stock of knowledge that we inherit from society at large. Consequently, images that have acquired certain shared meanings are then read in both ways, depending on the location of the audience, and also read in ways that contribute to a shared understanding.[16]

Stuart Hall et al.[17] and Teun van Dijk[18] argue that the mass media work in concert with other dominant institutions, such as the government. In so doing, they amplify the dominant definitions and interpretations espoused by elite institutions.

"Race," Racism, and the Media

Over the last decade, there has been an increasing amount of attention devoted to the representation of visible minority groups in the Canadian mass media.[19] Many of these studies highlight the stereotypical representation of people of colour in a variety of different media. As well, studies concur that representations of minorities tend to cluster around the themes of crime and deviance, ethnic exotica, athletic prowess, and societal achievement, thereby constructing them as "other"—different from "us." Within this context, there has been a strong association between people of colour and immigration, evoking a host of negative associations cohering around fears of invasion, illegal entry, and opportunistic behaviour, all of which are seen as threatening Canadian identity and its imagined national traits. Indeed, the very term "immigrant" has come to connote people who are non-white.[20] What is critical to note is how these negatively inscribed representations have contributed to particular notions of racism, wherein racism is seen as a natural response to a perceived condition of cultural invasion and dilution, and/or an individualistic response based on ignorance or membership in an extremist organization such as the Ku Klux Klan. In this sense, the privileging of certain kinds of interpretations of racism has served to deflect attention from it as a systemic and institutionalized phenomenon involving collusion and complicity with the state and other elite institutions in society.[21]

For our purposes here, the issue is how the notion of "culture" enters into this description of racialized "others," and further, how it is used to underscore their "otherness." In other words, how do the media, through their circulation of public texts, produce and reproduce particular notions of "culture" and to what end?

Interestingly, while earlier dominant discourses referring to racialized groups relied on the notion that there were different "races" in the world,[22] more contemporary usages utilize other categories to signify "race." In part, the reluctance to use "race" as a descriptive label is based on the lack of its scientific validity. Instead, there is an increasing tendency within dominant institutions to signify "race" by using terms such as "immigrant" and to refer to those who are constructed as "others" in terms of their language, ethnic origin, and practices, as well as religion. British theorists such as Paul Gilroy[23] and Stuart Hall[24] have referred to this as "cultural racism." Gilroy states that the new racism "tends to deny that 'race' is a meaningful biological category. 'Race' is seen instead as a cultural issue."[25] The base co-ordinates of racism are still intact under the guise of culture as the aim of the discourse is to highlight the superiority of the dominant group and the inferiority of others.

Cultural Racism

If modern-day racism revolves around culture as the defining point to suggest the inferiority of some groups and the superiority of others, then what particular definitions of culture are being privileged here and under what circumstances? Sherene Razack notes that "Culture becomes the framework used by white society to pre-empt both racism and sexism in a process that I refer to as culturalization."[26] It is thus instructive to examine the different contexts in which the banner of "culture" is evoked to "explain" the behaviour of racialized "others."

In her analysis of cases involving refugee claimants who are victims of gender-based violence, Razack notes a strategic use of culture that not only fits within the western gaze but serves to reinforce it. As she describes it,

> Women's claims are most likely to succeed when they present themselves as victims of dysfunctional, exceptionally patriarchal cultures and states. The successful asylum seeker must cast herself as a cultural Other, that is, as someone fleeing from a more primitive culture. That is to say, it is through various orientalist and imperialist lenses that women's gender-based persecution becomes visible in the West. Without the imperial or colonial component, claims of gender persecution are less likely to succeed and asylum is denied.[27]

The focus on "primitive" and patriarchal cultures occurs against the backdrop of a dominant culture that positions itself, through contrast, as progressive and egalitarian. Hence, the West is seen as being devoid of patriarchal institutions and norms, and free of any form of gender-based violence. The "others" are then constructed as being "backward" and traditional, oppressing their women in ways that are stereotypically imagined by the West.

The following example illustrates the process of culturalization as it occurs in the media's rendering of an account concerning the murders of nine family members in Vernon, British Columbia. The news accounts analyzed are drawn from the *Vancouver Sun*, since it is the dominant paper in the province where the murders occurred. Further, being a part of the Southam newspaper chain at the time, the *Sun*'s coverage was reported in other papers throughout the country. While the analysis provided below is not intended as a claim towards generalizability, it nonetheless highlights the various ways in which this process of culturalization is rendered commonsensical in print media and further, makes salient the intersecting influences of racism and sexism in the portrayal of stories concerning racialized immigrant women and girls.

Cultural Racism in the Media: The "Vernon Massacre"[28]

On 5 April 1996, Mark Chahal drove to his estranged wife Rajwar Ghakhal's family home in Vernon, BC. On reaching the driveway, he shot her father and proceeded into the house to murder eight other family members, wounding two others in the process. The murders hit the headlines the next day. The *Vancouver Sun* headlines read: "Killer Had Threatened Family: Nine Die in Canada's Second-Largest Mass Murder on the Eve of a Vernon Wedding, and the Murderer Commits Suicide. Killer Apologizes in Suicide Note."[29] The front-page article went on to describe the murders in greater detail. Underscoring the description were persistent references to the family's ethnicity. For instance, the article mentions the presence of the Indo-Canadian community in the area where the murders took place, the anticipated wedding of one of the family members at the local temple on a religious holiday, and aspects of the Sikh religion as follows: "Vaisakhi marks the anniversary of the formation of the Khalsa, the five symbols of Sikhism, by Guru Gobind Singh, who was the 10th and final guru of Sikhism." In addition to the ethnic and religious background of the family, the article also references the immigrant origins of the estranged wife's father, stating that, "Harjinder Singh Brar headed to Karnail Gakhal's home seconds after he heard of the shooting. Brar and Gakhal had been friends for 20 years since they both immigrated from India's Punjab state to BC's Interior in search of a better life."

On the same day, another article began the story with the following description: "The blood on the aggregate concrete was that of Karnail Gakhal, the head of a quiet Sikh family who lived at the home."[30] Two days later, in another story, the victims are described as "all members of a prominent Indo-Canadian family."[31] In the same story, the reporters bring up the issue of arranged marriages as a possible reason for the tragedy, stating that, "According to people who know the family, Chahal was abusive to his arranged bride from the day they were married; on their wedding night he allegedly called her a 'slut' and beat her."

The theme of arranged marriages is reiterated in another story reported on the same day in the B section of the newspaper. Reporter Mike Bocking noted that

> Only two years ago Chahal married Rajwar in the Vernon Sikh temple. Now the entire Gakhal clan was gathering in Vernon to celebrate the marriage on Saturday of his ex-wife's younger sister, Balwinder. Rajwar's parents, Karnail and Darshan, are pillars of the Vernon Sikh community and Balwinder's marriage will be their community's social event of the season, with as many as 400 guests expected to attend.
>
> They are a traditional family and are founding members of the Vernon Sikh temple. The marriages of their three oldest daughters were arranged. Although Balwinder's wedding is an arranged marriage, the 24-year-old pharmacist is excited about her future, which includes moving to Toronto and starting a new life with her engineer husband.[32]

Within three days of the murders, the media had proffered explanations that cohered around a culturalized interpretation of the tragedy. References to the family's immigrant background, Sikh religious tradition, and the custom of arranged marriages served not only locate the murders on a cultural terrain, but also to suggest that the custom of arranged marriages, close-knit community life, and religious adherence were to some extent responsible for the ensuing violence.

The privileging of a cultural explanation subsequently became an issue of contestation. This can be seen in the media's attempt to present a balanced perspective by the inclusion of a more subjugated interpretation in the form of the oppositional voices of South Asian feminists and anti-violence workers. Thus, on the same day that Mike Bocking's article appeared, a smaller piece including an oppositional perspective was inserted on the same page. However, even in this story that focusses on the dangers of stereotyping, reporter Kevin Griffin states that "Indo-Canadian" counsellors "also say that particular cultural and family values can influence how some men carry out, and women react to, domestic violence." After interviewing Sashi Assanand and Mobina Jaffer, both well-known activists in the South Asian community, the reporter adds that "Ten bilingual and bicultural counsellors in Assanand's organization helped 1,180 women in 1994–95, in 18 languages ranging from Cantonese and Vietnamese to Spanish and Punjabi." Once again, the women are described in cultural terms and violence is safely relocated to the cultural terrain.[33]

In the stories that followed, the *Vancouver Sun*'s filter shifted to include a focus on the RCMP's role. In particular, the issue of gun control and the issuance of two gun permits to Mark Chahal became the topics of coverage. However, even within this framing, the cultural angle of the murders was retained by referring to Rajwar Ghakhal, the estranged wife, in terms of her reluctance to have the police initiate any action in response to her numerous complaints because of how it might affect her reputation in the Sikh community. By September 1996, the dominant frame of the story had shifted to the issue of gun control and to the findings of the inquest ordered by the government.

The Sharon Velisek Story

In light of Razack's observation regarding the use of cultural explanations to evacuate sexism and racism as possible explanations of gendered violence, it is worthwhile examining other stories concerning violence against women. Less than two weeks after the Vernon tragedy made headlines, Sharon Velisek, another victim of male violence, reported her story to the media. Velisek had been shot by her ex-boyfriend in November 1995; he had subsequently shot himself. Prior to that, she had complained to the RCMP detachment in Vernon on numerous occasions but had not received an adequate response. The media reports on the Velisek case do not mention her cultural background, her ethnic community, or her religious affiliation. Rather, the stories concentrate on the events leading up to her attempted murder and highlight the lack of police action. The following example typifies the kind of reporting that the *Vancouver Sun* undertook in its coverage of the Velisek case:

> VERNON—Vernon RCMP failed to act decisively on stalking complaints by a woman whose ex-boyfriend later shot and nearly killed her with a sawed-off shotgun, she has charged.
>
> Vernon resident Sharon Velisek complained seven times in a month-long period last fall that Larry Scott was following her, making nuisance phone calls and committing vandalism.
>
> Police did not arrest Scott and on November 22, he hid in the darkness behind Velisek's house and confronted her in her carport. The first blast from his sawed-off 12-gauge shotgun shattered her left arm and knocked her to the ground. He stood over her, held the shotgun to her right shoulder and shot again, blasting away four ribs and most of her right lung. Perhaps thinking he had already killed her, he turned the gun on himself and fell to the ground dead, his head slumped on Velisek's shoulder.
>
> That night, RCMP told reporters that Velisek had complained about Scott but did not want them to do anything. That's also what Vernon RCMP say

Rajwar Gakhal wanted. Her estranged husband, Mark Vijay Chahal, later obtained handgun permits from the police and killed Gakhal and eight members of her family here on Good Friday.

The police response to the Gakhal case is one of the reasons why Velisek decided to tell her story. Today she is sending a letter to Attorney-General Ujjal Dosanjh that asks for a "hard, honest look at the problems which exist in the RCMP detachment in Vernon when dealing with cases like mine."

"I don't want the action to be to figure out who's to blame here," she said in a weekend interview. "What I want is to show the real problem here is the system. It doesn't protect women."[34]

The story continues with Velisek as an active agent providing her own response to the situation. Although the reporter describes Velisek as a mother of four and provides some background to her relationship with Larry Scott, he also includes a synopsis of the escalating violence that characterized their relationship, highlighting the lack of police response.

The absence of a cultural explanation as a cause of violence in the Velisek case may have to do with her "unmarked" appearance—she is not a racial minority belonging to a community or religious tradition that constitutes the popular and common-sense notion of a cultural "other." Rather, she embodies the stereotype of the dominant culture that remains invisible to scrutiny. If we are to use a culturalized explanation, however, then Sharon Velisek's experiences of violence could be seen as emblematic of Canadian culture. Such a viewpoint was not advanced by the media on the probable grounds that it would reflect negatively on the dominant culture and also draw attention to the systemic barriers that underpin women's inequality and vulnerability to violence. However, the validity of a cultural explanation even in this context eschews the widespread and global nature of gender-based violence. It also negates the notion of the plurality of cultures that exist within the Canadian nation-state.

Erasing "Race" and Racism in the Murder of Reena Virk

On 14 November 1997, fourteen-year-old Reena Virk was brutally murdered in a suburb of Victoria, British Columbia. Reena was first beaten by a group of seven girls and one boy, all aged between fourteen and sixteen.[35] The media coverage of the murder was extensive and spanned the regional, national, and international press. The event incited a moral panic centring on the perceived increase in "girl-on-girl" violence despite evidence that clearly indicated that the murderers were of both genders.

From a cultural perspective, the interesting aspect of the Reena Virk case is that the media did not explicitly mention her cultural background or dwell on it. Instead, the consistent use of visual images of Reena accompanying the various stories provided the necessary "filler," highlighting her South Asian origins. Descriptions of Reena constantly focussed on her overweight appearance, emphasizing that she was five feet, two inches tall and weighed two hundred pounds. Further, the media constantly highlighted her lack of acceptance within her peer group, indicating that the latter was predicated on her appearance and size. The construction that emerged in these initial news accounts was that Reena "didn't fit." The media failed to interrogate at the outset the normative standards that precluded Reena from fitting in. This filter is apparent in the following headline of a story by reporter Marina Jimenez which appeared on the front page of the *Vancouver Sun* just days after the discovery of the murder: "Slain Teen Misfit Remembered."[36]

Interestingly, while Reena's ethnic background was not explicitly discussed, her family's religious affiliation was highlighted in a number of different articles. The news accounts suggested that Reena's inability to both fit into the dominant culture and to comply with her own family's rigid strictures may have been a result of their status as Jehovah's Witnesses. These stories nonetheless highlighted the family's immigrant status, drawing attention to the fact that the family had immigrated to Canada from India when Reena was a small child. The reference to cultural difference is implicit in this background.

The dominant filter used by the media in explaining the Virk murder was the notion of increasing girl violence, as is apparent in the following headlines from the *Vancouver Sun*: "Girls Killing Girls a Sign of Angry Empty Lives"[37]; "Teenage Girls and Violence: The BC Reality."[38] In part, this filter served to deflect attention away from male violence and from the normative standards in society that sanctions that violence. But why did the media shy away from forwarding a culturalized explanation of violence? The reluctance to use a cultural frame may have to do with Reena's status as a young woman of colour murdered by two white individuals. To have dealt with the issue of culture would have foregrounded the issue of racism and Reena's racialized difference as a contributing factor to her victimization.

The use of culture and cultural differences within this context would have resulted in a situation where the media would have had to confront the issue of racism. Given that both of Reena's murderers were not members of a defined hate group and both fitted in within the normative notions of youth, the only explanation that could be advanced was either "girl-on-girl" violence, or the catch-all category of "bullying." Indeed, subsequent coverage of the murder and the trials of both the accused (Kelly Ellard and Warren Glowatski) focussed on bullying and anti-bullying measures.[39] As van Dijk has pointed out, the denial of racism is a significant discursive move on the part of the media in order to legitimize the status quo and its world view.[40] In this instance, highlighting cultural differences would have meant that the non-acceptance of members of different cultural communities (as a function of racism) is a reality that shapes the lives of girls like Reena Virk and renders them vulnerable to violence.

Conclusion

The above examples illustrate the ways in which specific definitions of culture are used and, in some cases, evacuated from the kinds of explanatory frameworks offered by the media. As with the official government discourse on culture, the media tend to identify culture as that which is visible and different from the norm. The norm, in this case, remains invisible in the background but nevertheless serves as a benchmark by which to assess and evaluate the differences of those whose "cultures" are considered to be an "other." In the case of the Vernon tragedy, the cultural signifiers used throughout the reportage clearly position the murders as arising from a cultural practice of arranged marriages, which is then located as being a feature of the Sikh religious tradition. The Velisek incident serves as a stark contrast, demonstrating how the same issue has no cultural overtones when it concerns an individual who cannot be identified as being different or an "other." Finally, the analysis of the murder of Reena Virk points out how a cultural explanation is explicitly avoided in order to occlude issues of racism and racialized difference, and to privilege the dominant filter of girl violence or the filter of bullying. In the last instance, the emphasis on girl violence and bullying served to legitimize dominant definitions of youth violence as emerging from deviance and individual psychopathology rather than as symptoms of a social order that determines and contains youth in ways that are detrimental.[41]

The various ways that culture is used or rendered absent in these accounts also demonstrate how the dominant culture sees itself through the lens of the mass media. In the case of the Vernon tragedy, the media consistently emphasized the cultural background of the victims so as to highlight how the practice of arranged marriages is oppressive and different from the egalitarian and progressive ways in which the dominant society encourages heterosexual unions. Similarly, the constant emphasis on immigrant backgrounds of both the Ghakhal and Virk families serves to underscore their status as "others"—unlike Canadians who are not immigrants by virtue of being born in the country and who are, therefore, not problematic in the same way. Implicit in these stories is the notion that immigrants who are visibly and culturally different cannot "fit in" and, hence, their inability to fit in makes them a target of violence. The responsibility for perpetuating such violence is thus strategically avoided. It is not the responsibility of the state or of Canadians at large to prevent such violence. Rather, such responsibility remains an individual problem.

An ethnic interpretation of culture thus offers a way through which the dominant media can amplify differences to define "others" in society. It also becomes a way in which to neutralize the charge of racism. For simply by pointing out cultural differences, the media can refrain from using the explicit language of "race" and, at the same time, attribute to culture pejorative connotations that underscore the superiority of the dominant group. Culture thus becomes a way of talking "race," but at the same time, it dismisses and erases the notion of racism. This is particularly true in the context of modern-day racism, where groups are treated differently and denied access on the basis of their cultural differences. Nonetheless, the use of culture to signify ethnic differences is highly potent. If such a definition were to be diluted by including other forms of culture—i.e., sub-cultural groups, then ethnicity/culture would no longer have the charge that it does in the dominant public and official discourse.

Notes

1 Raymond Williams, *Keywords: A Vocabulary of Culture and Society* (New York: Oxford University Press, 1983), 87.

2 Clifford Geertz, *The Interpretation of Cultures* (New York: Basic, 1973), 10.

3 Susanne Schech and Jane Haggis, *Culture and Development: A Critical Introduction* (Oxford and Massachusetts: Blackwell, 2000).

4 Kogila Adam Moodley, "Canadian Multiculturalism as Ideology," *Ethnic and Racial Studies* 6.3 (1983); and Karl Peter, "The Myth of Multiculturalism and Other Political Fables," *Ethnicity, Power and Politics*, ed. Jorgen Dahlie and Tissa Fernando (Toronto: Methuen, 1981). For more recent critiques of multiculturalism, see Himani Bannerji, *The Dark Side of the Nation* (Toronto: Canadian Scholar's Press, 2000); Frances Henry, "Canada's Contribution to the 'Management' of Ethno-Cultural Diversity," *Canadian Journal of Communication* 27.2/3 (2002): 231–42; and M. Nourbese Philip, *Frontiers: Selected Essays and Writings on Racism and Culture, 1984–1992* (Stratford, ON: Mercury Press, 1992). For a more critical overview of studies pertaining to the representation of racial minorities in the Canadian media, see Minelle Mahtani, "Representing Minorities: Canadian Media and Minority Identities," *Canadian Ethnic Studies* 33.3 (2001): 99–133.

5 I use the term "imagined" in reference to Benedict Anderson's notion of the nation as being derived from a sense of an imagined community. As he states, "It is *imagined* because the members of even the smallest nation will never know most of their fellow members, meet them, or even hear of them, yet in the minds of each lives the image of their communion" (6). In Anderson's definition, the nation is "imagined" as being limited (by defined geographical boundaries), as sovereign and as constituting a community. Benedict Anderson, *Imagined Communities: Reflections on the Origin and Spread of Nationalism* (London: Verso, 1991).

6 The term "diasporic" is used here to refer to those groups sharing common cultural traditions that have migrated, either forcibly or voluntarily, in response to global and historical conditions such as slavery, war, and underdevelopment. The Black diaspora refers to the forcible relocation of Africans from Africa, through the institution of slavery, to different parts of the world. For more information on diasporic communities and transnational media, see Karim H. Karim, "From Ethnic Media to Global Media: Transnational Communication Networks among Diasporic Communities," *International Comparative Research Group, Strategic Research and Analysis, Canadian Heritage, Report No: WPTC-99-02*, June 1998, 10 December, 2001 <http://www.transcomm.ox .ac.uk/work ing%20papers/karim.pdf>.

7 Geertz, 5, 145.

8 Stuart Hall, "The Work of Representations," *Representation, Cultural Representation and Signifying Practices*, ed. Stuart Hall (London: Sage and The Open University, 1997), 15–74.

9 Stuart Hall, "The Whites of their Eyes: Racist Ideologies and the Media," *The Media Reader*, ed. Manuel Alvarado and John O. Thompson (London: British Film Institute, 1990), 11.

10 Stuart Hall, "Culture, the Media and the 'Ideological Effect,'" *Mass Communication and Society*, ed. James Curran, Michael Gurevitch, and Janet Woollacott (London: Sage, 1979), 325–26.

11 Simon Cottle, "'Race,' Racialization and the Media: A Review and Update of Research," *Sage Race Relations Abstracts* 17 (1992): 4.

12 Harvey Molotch and Marilyn Lester, "News as Purposive Behaviour: On the Strategic Uses of Routine Events, Accidents and Scandals," *American Sociological Review* 39 (1974): 101–12; Teun A. van Dijk, "Mediating Racism: The Role of the Media in the Reproduction of Racism," *Language, Power and Ideology*, ed. Ruth Wodak (Amsterdam and Philadelphia: J. Benjamin, 1989); and Teun A. van Dijk, *Elite Discourse and Racism*, Sage Series on Race and Ethnic Relations 6 (Thousand Oaks, CA: Sage, 1993).

13 Bill Nichols, "Embodied Knowledge and the Politics of Power," *CineAction* 23 (1990–91). 14–21.

14 Roland Barthes provides a succinct analysis of the constituent elements of signs in terms of their denotative and connotative elements. Roland Barthes, *Mythologies* (London: Paladin, 1973).

15 Jack Shaheen, *The TV Arab* (Ohio: Bowling Green State University Popular Press, 1984), 5.

16 In fact, the debate on the agency of the audience, that is, the power to exercise its own interpretations vis-à-vis interpretations or readings privileged by the media text, has been the focus of numerous studies. For more information, see David Morley, *The Nationwide Audience: Structure and Decoding* (London: British Film Institute, 1980), as well as the discussion on spectatorship by Ella Shohat and Robert Stam, *Unthinking Eurocentrism, Multiculturalism and the Media* (London and New York: Routledge, 1994).

17 Stuart Hall, Chas Critcher, Tony Jefferson, John Clark, and Brian Roberts, *Policing the Crisis* (London: MacMillan, 1978).

18 Van Dijk, *Elite Discourse and Racism*.

19 The following research studies document some of the recent developments and advances in this area: Mahtani, "Representing Minorities"; Augie Fleras, "Walking Away from the Camera," *Ethnicity and Culture in Canada: The Research Landscape,* ed. J.W. Berry and Jean Laponce (Toronto: University of Toronto Press, 1994), 340–84; Augie Fleras and Jean Leonard Elliot, *Unequal Relations: An Introduction to Race, Ethnic and Aborigi-*

nal Dynamics in Canada, 2nd ed. (Scarborough, ON: Prentice Hall, 1996); Frances Henry et al., *The Colour of Democracy: Racism in Canadian Society* (Toronto, ON: Harcourt Brace Canada, 1995), 231–56; and Frances Henry and Carol Tator, *Racist Discourse in Canada's English Print Media* (Toronto: Canadian Race Relations Foundation, 2000). <http://www.crr.ca/Load.do?section=26&subsection=38&id=322&type=2>.
    Yasmin Jiwani, "By Omission and Commission: 'Race' and Representation in Canadian Television News," (Dissertation, School of Communication Studies, Simon Fraser University, 1993); John Miller and Kimberly Prince, *The Imperfect Mirror: Analysis of Minority Picture and News in Six Canadian Newspapers* (Toronto: School of Journalism, Ryerson Polytechnic University, 1994) <http://www.cna-acj.ca/client/cna/cna.nsf/web/diversity andcdndaily>.

20 Yasmin Jiwani, "The Media, 'Race' and Multiculturalism," *Proceedings of the BC Advisory Council on Multiculturalism* (Vancouver, BC: Multiculturalism BC, 1995), 11–18 <http://www.harbour.sfu.ca/freda/articles/media.htm>.

21 van Dijk, *Elite Discourse and Racism*.

22 For a more extensive discussion on the historical evolution of the concept of "race," see David Theo Goldberg, *Racist Culture, Philosophy and the Politics of Meaning* (Massachusetts and Oxford: Blackwell, 1993); and Karim H. Karim, "Constructions, Deconstructions, and Reconstructions: Competing Canadian Discourses on Ethnocultural Terminology," *Canadian Journal of Communication* 18.2 (1993) <http://www.cjc-online.ca/>; Robert Miles, *Racism* (London and New York: Routledge, 1989).

23 Paul Gilroy, *"There Ain't No Black in the Union Jack": The Cultural Politics of Race and Nation* (Chicago: University of Chicago Press, 1987).

24 Stuart Hall, Convocation Address at the University of Massachusetts at Amherst, 1989.

25 Gilroy, 60.

26 Sherene Razack, *Looking White People in the Eye: Gender, Race, and Culture in Courtrooms and Classrooms* (Toronto: University of Toronto Press, 1998), 60.

27 Razack, 92–93.

28 This analysis is based on newspaper accounts from the *Vancouver Sun* printed in the immediate aftermath of the murders.

29 Mike Bocking and Kim Bolan, "Killer Had Threatened Family: Nine Die in Canada's Second-Largest Mass Murder on the Eve of a Vernon Wedding, and the Murderer Commits Suicide; Killer Apologizes in Suicide Note," *Vancouver Sun* 6 April 1996, A1.

30 Susan Balcom, "'Small-Town' Vernon in Shock over Massacre," *Vancouver Sun* 6 April 1996, A3.

31 Stewart Bell, Lindsay Kines, Mike Bocking and Petti Fong, "How Did Killer Get Gun Permit? Family and Friends Ask That Question, Saying Police Already Knew Mark Chahal Had Made Threats to His Estranged Wife; Wife 'Was Too Terrified' To Press Charges," *Vancouver Sun* 8 April 1996, A1.

32 Mike Bocking, "Step by Gruesome Step, One Man's Killing Spree," *Vancouver Sun* 8 April 1996, B2.

33 This culturalized explanation of the murders resulted in a submission to the *Vancouver Sun* that highlighted the pervasive and endemic nature of gender-based violence in Canadian society. See Yasmin Jiwani, "Violence against Women Is Bigger Than…Class, Racial or Religious Affiliation," *Vancouver Sun* 13 April 1996, A25. For more details on gender-based violence in Canadian society, see Yasmin Jiwani, "Mapping Violence: A Work in Progress," Report presented to the Federal Action on Family Violence Prevention in British Columbia, December 2000 <http://www.harbour.sfu.ca/freda/articles/fvpi.htm>.

34 Mike Crawley, "Shooting Victim 'Let Down' by Vernon RCMP: Shooting Victim Isn't Looking to Blame Police, but Wants Protection for Women," *Vancouver Sun* 15 April 1996, A1.

35 For a more extensive analysis of the media coverage of the murder of Reena Virk, see Yasmin Jiwani, "Erasing Race: The Story of Reena Virk," *Canadian Woman Studies* 19.3 (1999): 178–84. For a more detailed analysis of the court proceedings, see Brenna Bhandar, *A Guilty Verdict against the Odds: Privileging White Middle-Class Femininity in the Trial of Kelly Ellard for the Murder of Reena Virk* (Vancouver, BC: FREDA Centre, 2000) <http://www.harbour.sfu.ca/freda/articles/bhandar.htm>.

36 Marina Jimenez, "Slain Teen Misfit Remembered," *Vancouver Sun* 25 November 1997, A1.

37 Janet Steffenhagan, "Girls Killing Girls: A Sign of Angry Empty Lives," *Vancouver Sun* 25 November 1997, A1.

38 Marina Jimenez, "Teenage Girls and Violence: The BC Reality," *Vancouver Sun* 1 December 1997, A1.

39 The "bullying" filter continued to be a pervasive theme throughout the two years of coverage in the *Vancouver Sun* dealing with the Reena Virk murder.

40 van Dijk, *Elite Discourse and Racism.*

41 See Bernard Schissel, *Blaming Children: Youth Crime, Moral Panics and the Politics of Hate* (Halifax: Fernwood, 1997).

II Performing and Disrupting Identities

20-minute visualizaton: Sandee, Lee, Sandra, Seema
Joanne Bristol

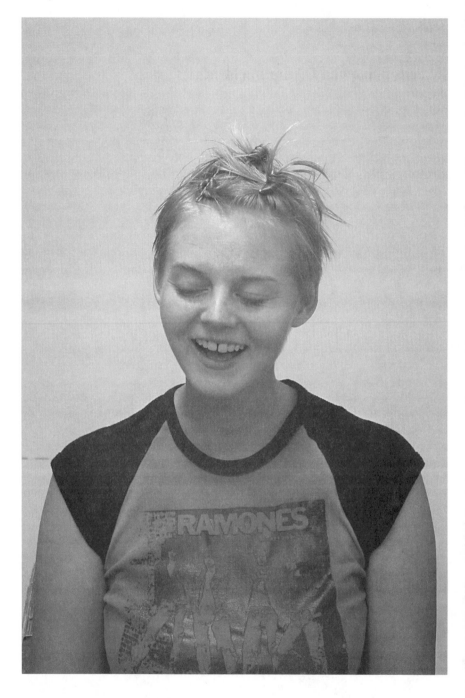

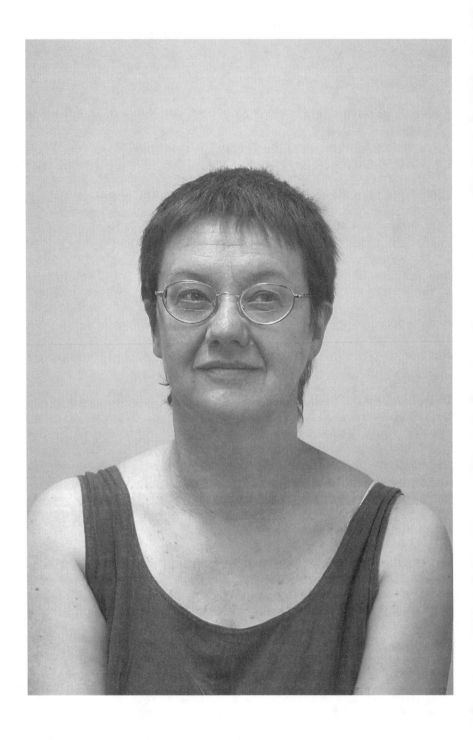

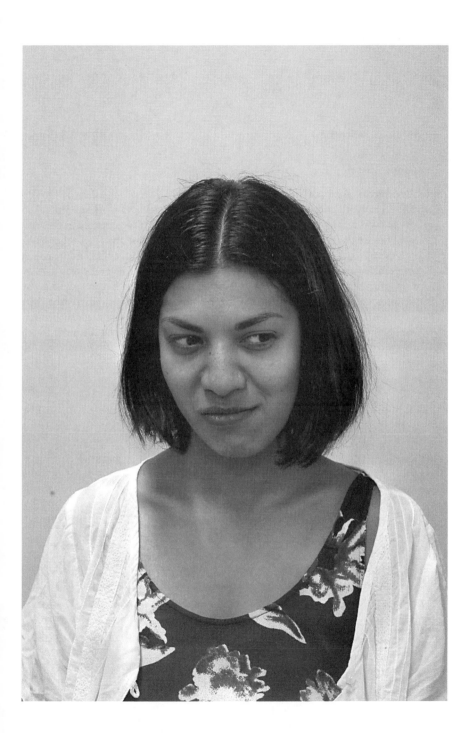

Joanne Bristol

The project presents an enactment of my relationship, as a visual art teacher, to students. The work consists of a series of portraits of students I worked with, taken just as I was leaving a teaching position in the Visual Art Department at the University of Regina. I asked each student to think of the most amazing, thoughtful, ambitious, moving artwork they could imagine making, if they had no financial, temporal, spatial, or other obstacles. I took their photos several times as they were going through the process of visualizing this artwork. We then looked at the photos together and I asked them to choose the one that best represented their process of imagining, or somehow captured the spirit of the imagined project. Though I was curious to know what they had imagined, I asked them not to tell me.

6 Marketing Ambivalence
Molson Breweries Go Postcolonial

Cynthia Sugars

A CENTRAL PARADOX OF CONTEMPORARY POSTCOLONIAL THEORY, in Canada and elsewhere, is that while its origins lie in the various nationalist decolonization movements of the period following the Second World War, its current incarnation is marked by a disenchantment with nationalism and its attendant colonizing effects. This has led to any number of disagreements about the role of the nation in postcolonial approaches to Canadian culture: from Enoch Padolsky's characterization of postcolonialism as not being sufficiently concerned with the "local" or the "national," to Larry McDonald's suggestion that postcolonialism in Canada has strayed from its true nationalist purpose, to Thomas King's (and others') accusation that Canadian postcolonialism is too national an approach.[1]

It is true that contemporary formulations of the postmodern or postcolonial character of Canadian culture have called for an interrogation of nationalist cultural discourse. This can be attributed in part to the influence of various poststructuralist attempts to deconstruct the admittedly restrictive and exclusionary metanarratives of national unity. The aspiration for the unifying potential of a shared national consciousness has been prohibited within recent postcolonial debates that are indebted to the extended critiques of twentieth-century nationalisms launched by such theorists as Frantz Fanon and Homi Bhabha. These debates are driven by an awareness of the ways that various asymmetries of power are perpetuated through narratives that attempt to enforce a group identity. If nationalism has become unacceptable in the wake of the resurgence of religious fundamentalism and ethnic nationalism around the globe, so has the academic community condemned emotional appeals to the homogenizing and necessarily exclusionary discourse of national identity. Wary of the perils of cultural-nationalist uniformity, various literary critics, such as Frank Davey—and Northrop Frye before him—have eagerly set out to define Canada in terms of its "post-national" character.[2]

However, contemporary theorizing about a postcolonial and/or postmodern Canada is nevertheless complicated by the continued appeal of popular representations of Canadian national and cultural identity, an appeal that one cannot dismiss out of hand by attributing it to a false consciousness on the part of certain unenlightened segments of the Canadian populace. The current demand, amongst the general public, for a reopening of discussions of Canadian identity and nationhood demonstrates that a commitment to the nation remains a compelling force for many Canadians. The proliferation of these cultural phenomena is evident not only in the spate of popular books on the subject (see, for example, Pierre Berton's *Why We Act Like Canadians*, Daniel Francis's *National Dreams*, Rudyard Griffiths's *Great Questions of Canada*, Geoff Pevere and Greig Dymond's *Mondo Canuck*, Patrick Watson's *The Canadians*, and Morton and Weinfeld's *Who Speaks for Canada?*), but also in the numerous satirical meditations, popular anthologies, national quizzes, documentaries for *The National*, CBC radio cross-country checkups, trivia games, television documentaries, comedy sketches, beer commercials, and innumerable discussions of Canadian literature that deal with the subject.

In taking a postcolonial approach to Canadian culture in this essay, I am implicitly invoking the ways both critical and celebratory approaches to the nation are central to the postcolonial enterprise.[3] To launch a critique of national constructs is not the same thing as rejecting them out of hand; likewise, to applaud certain instances of nationalist cultural expression is not to embrace them unquestioningly. By noting that Canadian cultural discourse has long been committed to promoting notions of national distinctiveness and national identity-making, I am not suggesting that it has consistently done so in a naively patriotic way, or that it has not often expressed skepticism about the very endeavour of national imagining. I state this at the outset because there is an assumption at large that one must either reject the appeals of national identity constructs out of hand, or risk becoming complicit with an outmoded, homogenizing system marked by intolerance and intellectual naïveté. This issue requires renewed attention today in what many identify as the contemporary postnational, yet nevertheless, inordinately national, global era.

My focus in this essay will be one specific example of nationalist imaging that highlights this incongruity at the core of Canadian nationalism, and, by extension, of postcolonial discourse more generally. Molson Canadian Breweries's now-infamous beer advertisement, "The Rant," exemplifies a central paradox of the Canadian postcolonial context. On the one hand, the ad is committed to a defence of a distinct Canadian national-cultural identity; on the other, it accomplishes this message through its evocation of an identity that may not exist. Because the ad dramatizes an integral ambivalence towards nationalism, it is interesting as a particular kind of postcolonial text: one that exhibits a yearning for a unifying national narrative alongside a problematization of such a quest. It is therefore an example of a compromised postcolonialism. This paradox highlights the lines where national identity and global capital meet. If it reveals the fact that both at home and abroad, nationalism sells, it may also be true that the international purview of the postnational and/or postcolonial is always contaminated by its nationalist foundations—which is also to recognize that even as the nation-state remains under interrogation, it still asserts itself in the dissemination of Canada as a global commodity.[4]

Some years ago, as a rookie teacher of an undergraduate literature class in British Columbia, I referred to Al Purdy as a Canadian nationalist. The phrase instantly provoked snorts of derision from one of my students. "What is so funny?" I asked, thinking that, yes, there was a case to be made for Purdy's sardonic undercutting of national symbols, and that perhaps I had been over-simplifying. "Isn't that an oxymoron?" the student asked. "What?" I responded, intrigued by the idea of Purdy as Canadian oxymoron. "Canadian nationalist."

Years later, I am still thinking about this question. There is some truth to the proposition, after all, despite the fever of nationalist sentiment that has dogged Canadian cultural expression from its beginnings. To a degree, Canadian culture has always been compromised by an epistemological scepticism, obsessed, one might say, by the possibility of its non-existence: why is there something rather than nothing? Yet what do we call it when one's national identity is defined by a negation of one's non-identity? In other words, the term "Canadian" might appear nonsensical if there is no clear national identity to which it refers. Does this double negative render "Canadian nationalist" redundant rather than oxymoronic? Can it be both? If Canadian nationalism, like all nationalism, represents an "imagined community" rather than an empirical reality, as Benedict Anderson argues, it might nevertheless have all the more force because it is virtual.

This epistemological scepticism is sometimes conjoined with a suspicion about the links between nation and culture more specifically. The interrogation of Canadian cultural nationalism found explicit expression in

A.J.M. Smith's division of Canadian poetry into "native" and "cosmopolitan" traditions in the 1940s.[5] More recently, one sees it in the frequent invocations of a paradoxical Canadian amorphousness: an invocation of the apparent absence of a definable Canadian culture/identity as evidence of a distinct Canadian expression and state of mind. Earle Birney's famous formulation of our being haunted by a "lack of ghosts" is one such example, as is Robert Kroetsch's account of Canada's definitive lack of a national metanarrative.[6] Dennis Lee's identification of Canadian "cadence," which in his account is characterized by the "silence" that marks Canadian colonial space, also celebrates the paradoxical character of Canadian national culture.[7] By a curious extrapolation, the Canadian nation has come to be characterized as a sort of disunified psychic space, subject to the "mental" ills of the classic fragmented subject. Thus, Margaret Atwood describes the "national mental illness" as "paranoid schizophrenia."[8] Postcolonial theorists of Canadian settler-invader ambivalence describe a similar phenomenon, whereby the poles of empire and indigene have been internalized to create the constitutive ambivalence and splitting of the Canadian psyche. Because the settler subject is at once both the colonizer and the colonized, the separation between the national Self and its extra-national Others becomes untenable.

If this represents a having-your-cake-and-eating-it-too approach to Canadian culture, it nevertheless has clear metaphorical appeal in that it describes the duplicity embedded within every national self-representation: the recognition that the nation, by definition, is not only exclusionary, but dependent on that exclusion for its actual and conceptual existence.[9] In a Canadian context, this uncertainty is compounded by yet another contradiction: the fear that the nation is not identifiably (and singularly) distinctive in any way, and the coinciding sense that there *is* something (however ineffable) distinctive about Canadian culture. The more that Canada is identified as lacking in culture, the more that absence is identified as characteristically Canadian; the more amorphous the culture, the more it must be fixed within national boundaries. This might also suggest that the more insecure or resistant one is about the notion of Canadian identity, the more identifiable, as Canadian, one becomes. One finds this sentiment expressed in Robert Kroetsch's assessment of Big Bear: "he became the archetypal Canadian by refusing to become a Canadian."[10] Thus might the national skeptic become the most "Canadian" figure of all: both embarrassingly colonial and astutely postcolonial in his/her recognition of the ambiguity of the spectre of Canadianness. Ultimately, the most Canadian thing of all may be to be as un-Canadian as possible.[11]

Stating the Canadian cultural-national problematic in these terms introduces a number of theoretical and pedagogical questions: what is it that we are doing when we set out to teach or interpret or disseminate a national culture? Are the ramifications of the linkage of culture and nation what we address when we investigate a cultural text from a postcolonial perspective? And how do we engage critically, perhaps even postcolonially, with instances of contemporary nationalist expression without discarding them altogether? I shall be touching on each of these problems in the course of analyzing Molson Breweries' particular brand of Canadian identity.

The paradox of a unifying Canadian ambivalence is central to Molson Breweries' "I am Canadian" ad campaign. Launched in 1994 and reaching its height in the famous "Rant" advertisement aired on national television (and in movie theatres) in March 2000, the campaign tapped into the subjugated nationalism lurking in the Canadian psyche at a period when nationalist sentiment was thought to be all but extinct. Of course, Molson's had been using a "'Canadian pride' platform" to sell their product well before this.[12] The company's prime product is called "Canadian"; it sponsors *Hockey Night in Canada* and the Molson Indy, not to mention the prestigious Molson Prize for contribution to the arts; and, in the 1980s, Molson's became a national-cultural symbol through its association with the beer-drinking Canadian archetypes Bob and Doug MacKenzie on SCTV. Molson's had all but cornered the market in Canadian patriotism: "The firm that brought you Canada's first beer (1786) and, for a time, its most glorious hockey dynasty (Les Canadiens) now brings you Canada's most in-your-face patriotism. Never mind beer, Molson has become the purveyor of the national dream," wrote one reviewer for the *Calgary Herald*.[13]

Publicity manager Michelle Robichaud stated that there was nothing subtle about the Molson "Rant,"[14] and indeed, on the surface, the "text" of the ad appears straightforward. The scene opens with a darkened stage, probably a movie theatre,[15] on which stands a solitary microphone. Enter average "Joe Canadian," dressed in jeans and lumberjack shirt, who shyly begins to address the various stereotypes of Canadian identity. His monologue builds to a crescendo, a "rant," as he enunciates the numerous ways Canadians are different from Americans. In the process, images of his text are flashed on an immense screen behind him. The "rant" culminates in Joe's final assertion—"I am Canadian!"—and concludes with him mumbling "thank you" and sheepishly walking off the stage.

My interest is not so much in the nationalist jingoism of the advertisement, but rather in its method—the way that the ad was able to (re)package Canadian nationalism to make it palatable to the seemingly "postnational" audience of the late twentieth century. In effect, by marketing a certain narrative of Canadian postcolonial identity and by dramatizing a central conflict within postcolonial expression more generally, Molson's was able to tap into the conflicted nationalist subtext that informs Canadian culture and identity. Through its self-referential stance, the ad performs a version of national skepticism, for even as it promotes Canadian nationalism, it dramatizes a debunking of national identity constructs. To adapt Homi Bhabha's phrasing, "The Rant" is a nationalist text that performs Canada as a nation "which is not one."

In a very obvious way, then, "The Rant" invites a postcolonial analysis. A postcolonial commendation of the text might celebrate it as an instance of Canadian expression in the face of American cultural imperialism. It might highlight the ways it pokes fun at national stereotypes and utilizes the celebrated mode of Canadian self-deprecating irony. The ad also attends to the important issue of language, and how a former British colony makes the English language its own. Thus, for instance, Joe rants about how we use the word "chesterfield" to mean "couch," and say "zed" instead of "zee."[16]

A postcolonial critique of the advertisement might comment on the ways it espouses conventional liberal values and does so from a young, white, middle-class, Anglo male perspective. The ad, then, speaks to only a select segment of the Canadian population. In one swoop, it excludes Canada's Inuit peoples by distancing "Joe Canadian" from those who eat whale blubber and live in igloos. It evokes a history of conquest and settlement in its allusion to fur traders and lumberjacks, and hence sets itself squarely within the context of European colonialism (Joe, you might say, is the prototype of the white, male settler subject). The speech, in fact, is set to the soundtrack of the stirring anthem of British imperialism, Sir Edward Elgar's pomp and circumstance march, "Land of Hope and Glory." It excludes many recent immigrant groups through Joe's claim to speak English and French as his native tongue, and in the clearly Anglo-Saxon names of other Canadians that he may or may not know personally: Jimmy, Sally, or Suzie, and so on. Finally, despite its nod to French Canada, the ad could not be marketed in Quebec, for obvious nationalist (perhaps even postcolonial) reasons.[17] All of this confirms what Himani Bannerji says about the selective nature of the national imaginary: "It is obviously a construction, a set of representations, embodying certain types of political and cultural communities and their operations."[18] Despite its apparent claims to an encompassing and inclusive Canadian identity, "The Rant" calls attention to the gaps within the national rhetoric, spotlighting the very people who are outside its marketing (and nation-making) radar. Some Canadians, the ad suggests, are more Canadian than others. If "The Rant" can be deemed postcolonial at all, it is surely as an instance of a compromised postcolonialism through its invocation of a nation that disavows its fraught origins. In this way, it dramatizes the dilemma at the core of postcolonial theory itself, what Alan Lawson identifies in terms of a "double

FIGURE 1   "Joe Canadian," 2001 (courtesy Rod MacIvor and the *Ottawa Citizen*).

move [that] might recognize the resistance in nationalisms while recognizing their concomitant containment."[19]

And yet, despite these omissions, the advertisement went on to become something of a national rallying cry, inspiring imitation and citation across the country. Even Canada's Heritage Minister, Sheila Copps, presented it at the Congress for the International Press Institute in Boston that year. Outside of Quebec, it quickly burgeoned into a national phenomenon—played or performed in hockey stadiums across the country where it received repeated standing ovations, performed in movie theatres, at one point garnering more applause than Julia Roberts.[20] Even more remarkable, Joe Canadian was transformed into a national icon. Soon after the ad was broadcast on national television, Jeff Douglas (the actor who performed "The Rant") was hired to perform the skit live, at hockey games, fundraising events, and finally at selected venues across the country on Canada Day that year. Love it or hate it, the ad has become a national pop-culture milestone: "We're hard-pressed to recall a commercial that's ever burrowed into the Canadian psyche so deeply," wrote Stan Sutter in *Marketing*.[21] Its text, its reception, its reification—all are object lessons in the making of a national metanarrative at an historical juncture when such an endeavour would have been thought impossible.

The genius of the Molson ad was its awareness of the paradox inherent in the enterprise of national image-making. But how was it able to communicate this message so effectively? Why, precisely, did Joe Canadian's rant provoke the unprecedented response that it did? Pam Blackstone, in the *Victoria Times Colonist*, puzzled over the phenomenon: "Why do we respond to this advertisement with such primal ferocity? Why does it speak to our Canadian souls so compellingly? I find myself cheering along with it, which—when you think about it—is pretty ridiculous. I'm cheering a beer ad, for Pete's sake."[22] In part, the ad accomplished its effect less through the character of Joe Canadian (despite his subsequent immortalization) than through its performance of specularity and projection. In the process, it provided Canadians with a glimpse of their own self-performances as reluctant postcolonials. Through its dramatization of ambivalence, the ad ensured one thing: to at least some degree, "we" were all Joe Canadian.

The effectiveness of the ad's theatricality is highlighted if one postulates alternative scenarios for the narrative. If the ad had simply been staged with a Canadian Joe speaking directly to the camera, would it have been as effective? This was the approach used in a subsequent Molson television commercial, "Here's to You, Canada," in which a Scottish man in a bar, speaking to the camera, toasts all of the things he loves about Canada. The result is saccharine at best. If, alternatively, "The Rant" had represented an American proclaiming his or her national identity, it might have elicited little more than a "so what" from its viewers. The success of the ad was related to two features: (1) the ad's conjuring, and coinciding denial, of a recognizable series of Canadian icons and fetish objects tied to a very specific conglomeration of assumptions and associations; and (2) its self-reflexive dramatization of the rant as a staged performance.

In many ways, "The Rant" worked because it expressed the unspeakable. At the outset, it invokes the celebrated insecurity that Canadians feel about their national identity. As he walks onto the stage, Joe is embarrassed by the promotional plug he is compelled to undertake; he is reluctant, modest. In attitude, he is very much an "average" Canadian, which also means that he represents the very stereotype that he is countering through his rant. Thus, Joe is claiming a clear Canadian identity, for he performs himself *as* colonial (both in dress and in demeanour). In part this may be the inevitability of colonial self-constitution, as Dennis Lee so clearly articulated it in the early 1970s. In Lee's account of the Canadian's difficult problem of speaking in "colonial space," he notes that all that is possible is a projection of voicelessness: "perhaps the colonial imagination is driven to recreate, again and again, the experience of writing in colonial space."[23] The image of Canadian non-existence may, in the end, be the only projection possible, since there is no essence that the image can invoke.

The same holds true for the stereotypes themselves. Joe rants about what he is not, while all along these images are flashed, larger than life, onto the screen behind him (images of lumberjacks, igloos, etc.), solidifying in the viewer's mind the very association of Canada with these images.[24] The filmic projection of these images behind the speaker duplicates the ad's performance of psychic projection—that is, a rejection (via denial) and coinciding affirmation of a series of unwelcome associations with Canadian national identity. By attributing these assumptions to a mythic American "Other," the ad was able to assist Canadians' rejection of their own complicity in these (often well-loved) stereotypes. Furthermore, the film's fetishization of these images *as* images highlighted their simulacral nature: the fact that they are artificial yet powerful reifications of nationalist desire. Much like Terry Goldie's account of the images of aboriginals in Western culture, these images lead back to an entire intertextual array of Canadiana iconography that exists as a self-generating body of textual signifiers. The images and stereotypes of Canadianness that Joe conjures for the audience, even as he rejects each in turn, may, paradoxically, be as close to the Canadian as you can get. The ad thus documents one of the central fears that lies at the heart of Canadian national culture: "Canadian" may in the end exist as image only. To use Slavoj Žižek's account of reflexive mimicry in *Looking Awry*: Canadian national identity may appear to be a fiction, but do not be fooled, it *is* a fiction. Canadian national culture may spotlight more starkly than others the contradiction at the core of national identity constructions: the desire for a nameable essence which can be approached but never secured. This is in part what Alan Lawson is referring to when he speaks of the settler locale as that place where the transactions of power between vying identities and interests are most visible.[25]

In the end, the concept "Canadian" in the ad is no more or less real than before Joe Canadian stood up to proclaim its existence. He has become just one more in a series of Canadian images, especially through his appeal to the time-worn tradition of defining Canada by what it is not. One can imagine what the next step in the process might be. The next time an average Canadian mounts a stage to proclaim the national narrative, he or she might include in the series of negations: "I am *not* Joe Canadian." Ultimately the ad reveals a basic tenet of subliminal (and not so subliminal) advertising: one can proclaim one's Canadian identity, and still be a colonial nonentity... one can have one's beer, and drink it.

The role of the series of invoked, and subsequently rejected, Canadian fetish objects is central to this process. On the one hand, these symbols and objects are conjured in an account that claims to de-fetishize Canadian identity. However, one cannot de-fetishize an object by marshalling it in its own dismantling. On the contrary, as a symbol that invokes two contradictory positions at once (an affirmation and a negation), the fetish is the ideal trope for invoking what one at once wants to claim (as Canadian) and reject (as colonial).[26] The national fetish symbol (beaver, lumberjack, etc.) enables a disavowal of the colonial moment (just as other imperial fetish objects—the map, the compass, and so on—did the same thing) in the same move that allows one to claim Big Bear as an "archetypal Canadian." This process facilitates "the slippage from invader to peaceful settler,"[27] which is then tidily contained under the label "Canada." An "amnesia of colonialism," to cite Linda Hutcheon, is thus performed in the very act of performing the Canadian as postcolonial.[28]

"The Rant," which swiftly became a fetishized text in its own right, thus enacts the function of the fetish object. By promoting what on the surface it purports to be contesting, it enables viewers to have it both ways: to trumpet their Canadian identity while rejecting such patriotic outbursts as suspect and mildly ridiculous. In the first instance, the very designation of the narrative as a "rant" renders the performance eminently un-Canadian. In order to assert his identity, Joe must wax patriotic and behave "like an American."[29] Steven Pearlstein noted how what was most remarkable about the *reaction* to the ad (and, we might say, about the ad itself) was that: "it is so un-Canadian. Ever since they fled the American colonies to support their king, English-speaking Canadians have shunned the kind of flag-waving, chest-thumping, We're-the-Best-at-Everything nationalism practised to the south. Along with gun control and national health care, a studied anti-jingoism has been a central feature of the moral superiority that Canadians feel toward the United States."[30] Paradoxically, the ad suggests that the more Canadian one proclaims oneself to be, the more one is not very Canadian at all. This was clear in Molson's hesitation to launch a nationalist campaign in the first place. While already marketing the slogan "I am Canadian," the company had decided to shelve the nationalist agenda because it was felt that it would not appeal to the apathetic mindset of Canadian youth. The impetus for the ardent nationalism of "The Rant" was sparked accidentally when young Canadians were spotted at the 1999 Woodstock festival with "I am Canadian" painted on their clothes and faces.[31] The fact that a nationalist agenda was initially deemed too "un-Canadian" an approach tells us something about the ad's widespread appeal: once again, it speaks the unspeakable. In this case, the unspeakable was not solely an outspoken patriotism, but also an underlying fear that ultimately, Canadians are not that much different from Americans after all. If the ad is set in the context of the oppositional nature of Canadian definitions of national identity—defining ourselves by what we are not—its repressed awareness that we are not substantively different from Americans underscores the need to be ranting about one's national identity in the first place. Michael Adams noted how "the ad reflects...the narcissism of small differences."[32] If one can only voice one's Canadianness by behaving as an American, this suggests that the Canadian is forever condemned to be "almost different but not quite."[33]

The effectiveness of the ad also lay in its staging, that is, in its dramatization of a performance. The context of the advertisement is not just that of a man proclaiming his Canadian identity; it is a dramatization of that proclamation—hence the stage, the microphone, and the cheers and applause that greet Joe's performance. In a sense, then, Joe's performance becomes a postcolonial rescripting of Homi Bhabha's notion of colonial mimicry, itself a performing of identity. While Bhabha analyzes the ways the colonized mimics an image of the colonizer, theorists of settler-invader postcolonialism, such as Stephen Slemon and Alan Lawson, have written about the ways the colonial subject is caught between the poles of the mimicking process itself. As these critics describe the dilemma, the settler subject is condemned to mimic both the imperial centre and the indigenous inhabitants of the settled landscape, neither one providing a secure sense of belonging or identity. Since mimicry always involves a performance, one might be tempted to say that in this case what Joe Canadian mimics is a stereotype of the Canadian as colonial, which is also to say that he is engaged in a performance of postcolonial ambivalence.

As in the process of mimicry more generally, the ad highlights the performed nature of all national narratives. Aimed at a Canadian market, "The Rant" is very simply an instance of Canadians performing themselves to themselves. However, it accomplishes this self-representation very specifically, for it represents Canadians representing themselves to the (American) other. If it thus reveals an awareness of the inherent discontinuity of (Canadian) identity—the fashioned and performed nature of identity—it also expresses a desire to incorporate this discrepancy into a national script; and it succeeds in this project as well as it does by dramatizing the unsettling yet tantalizing uncanniness of the Lacanian gaze (an awareness of the self viewing the self). The projection of this uncanny experience into a containing performance space elicits what Christopher Bollas identifies as the internalized sense we all have of ourselves as both subject-self and object to that self. One finds this relation expressed in dreams and various aesthetic narratives: "In the dream I am simultaneously an actor inside a drama and an offstage absence."[34] If Joe is meant to function as a projected or objectified representation of the average Canadian's inner self, the ad also enables the viewer to indulge in a voyeuristic process of what Bollas calls "self-experiencing."[35] In "The Rant," we (Canadian viewers) watch Joe Canadian being looked at, which also means that we are positioned as watching ourselves playing the colonial object.[36]

Another way of stating this is that the postcolonial self gazes upon its (repressed) colonial object-self. What we witness in "The Rant" is not our Canadian identity being projected back at us, but rather a split projection of ourselves responding to that identity (for one can only assume that the applauding audience within the film are a group of Canadians), which is what contributes to the advertisement's unsettling *frisson* effect. The uncanny awareness of the self viewing the self not only provides one with a glimpse of what Jacques Lacan describes in terms of the Real (or Derrida as the supplement; or Bollas as the "unthought known"), that excess which self-identity must discard in order to achieve a sense of coherence, but it also highlights the "contradictory articulations of reality and desire" in every assertion of national identity.[37]

Thus, where "The Rant" so splendidly succeeded was in its re-enactment of the precariousness of national and subjective identity: the recognition that all identity is a construction; that the national imaginary is just that— a process of national image-*making*; that Canadians are ambivalent about the role of nationalism. It is a testament to the ingenuity of the script writers and producers that they were able to create an advertisement that incorporated these agonistic perceptions within an amusing and seemingly simplistic narrative.

Nevertheless, a niggling question remains: if Canadians are so ambivalent about patriotic exhibition, why did the phenomenon take off to the degree that it did? At the height of the ad's popularity, Joe Canadian/Jeff Douglas could incite patriotic fervour in audiences across the country when he appeared spontaneously at hockey games and other national events. How could "The Rant" incite Canadians to be so unlike themselves?

The answer lies in the nature of irony itself. Undeniably, "The Rant" takes part in the venerable tradition of Canadian self-deprecating irony, making the clichés of nationhood "implode under their own accumulated cultural weight."[38] It accomplishes this even as it invokes these symbols for their iconographic potential. When I discussed the ad with my graduate class in Canadian Postcolonial Theory at the University of Ottawa, the students without exception called attention to the tongue-in-cheek nature of the piece. Behind Joe's earnestness, they felt, stood the ad creators as trickster. Hence, the reverential invocations of the "noble" beaver, or the emblematic toque, sparked snickers throughout the group. As Stan Sutter noted about the ad's "hoser pitch," "give this thing credit for being smarter than it lets on. 'Rant' displays a winking, kitschy nationalism that undercuts (almost) the flag-waving sentimentality that, on its surface, the commercial seems to espouse. It's a uniquely Canadian mix of earnestness and irony."[39]

However, the success of the ad as an ironic text ultimately lay in its dramatization of the ambivalent function of the Freudian fetish object. Indeed, central to the performance of an ironized object-self is the paradox of the ironizing speech act: saying one thing while meaning another. Thus, similar to the operation of the fetish, the performance of self-irony initiates a process of doubling and disavowal. In the case of the self-deprecating Canadian, the player hopes that the viewer will believe the reverse of that which is being performed. That is, the performer or mimic assumes that the viewer will realize that he or she is not what is being made fun of. Hence, if you perform yourself as insecure (and colonial), you in fact hope that people will believe you to be confident (and postcolonial). If you insist on playing the hick, as so many Canadian comedians do, you hope that in fact your viewer/listener will see you as incisive and astute.[40] In psychoanalytic terms, this may represent a roundabout attempt to control the process of transference—a sort of "nod" between insiders (I know that you know, etc.)—and it has obvious parallels with the Freudian process of negation, which Freud identifies as the mental process whereby a person takes cognizance of something that is repressed only when the thought is negated or denied, in some way, as being true. The performance of self-irony is therefore also a mode of deception—of oneself, and of others. If, in Freudian terms, "leave my mother out of this" really means "I want to talk about my mother (but I feel it is unacceptable)," the protestation that "Canadians are not ranting patriots" may be saying "I want to rant about my national identity (but I feel it is unacceptable)." The Molson advertisement stages this suppressed desire by projecting it onto a fantasy stage (with literal projections behind the speaker, as though his own mental contents have been projected outside himself). The ad thus achieves an ironic inversion of what Sherene Razack identifies in terms of the ways we "perform ourselves as dominant":[41] Joe Canadian performs himself as subordinate in order to assert his dominance, which in turn confirms his positioning, internationally, as subordinate.

Slavoj Žižek's explanation of the processes of ironic self-mimicry is relevant to this double-speak of performative deception. In effect, Žižek is interested in the process of *affirmation* as attempted deception: "Man alone," Žižek attests, "is capable of deceiving *by means of* truth itself."[42] In such cases, he argues, "we effectively *become* something by pretending that we *already are* that."[43] What Žižek realizes is that performance is never a mere mask, but that the mask, while posing as a mask, can sometimes represent the reality. Thus, "My name is Joe, and I am Canadian" may be deciphered as "do not be fooled, I *am* a Canadian." The Molson ad carries this process of deceiving by feigning deceit one step further. Joe Canadian performs the proud Canadian by playing the colonial hick. Yet if both are a performance, which is the real Joe? He begins as a meek Canadian, becomes a ranting nationalist, and concludes as a meek Canadian. So which is he?

The ad struck a chord with Canadians for this very ambiguity. It spoke to the nationalist ranter within every meek Canadian, and allowed Canadians to maintain their claim to modesty (and quiet patriotism) while indulging in a fantasy of belting it out in the spotlight. And vice versa: at hockey games, for example, Canadians were able to proclaim their identity while comforting themselves with the "truth" that they were in reality a modest people. Jeff Douglas hit the nail on the head in his comment on the ad: "'This country has a legacy of pride, and what I like about it is that it's quiet pride.... Sometimes you just have to jump up and yell about it.'"[44] By performing—and allowing Canadians to perform—this form of national karaoke, the ad enabled them to play out their nationalist (and definitively American) fantasies while sheltering behind the security of their Canadianness. Witness how many Canadians learned the words to "The Rant" by heart. As Douglas himself noted in an interview, "this kind of fervour is inside all of us, but we're quiet about it."[45] The patriotic fervour, then, becomes a kind of return of the (not very) repressed Canadian nationalist, representing an "almost repressed but not quite" version of Canadian identity.

Glen Hunt, the creator of the ad, tells how he began by interviewing people on the topic of Canada: "They'd start out very demure, *very Canadian*, and then they'd just erupt into Canadian patriotism and get quite psyched."[46] The *Toronto Star*'s Peter Goddard summed up Joe Canadian's appeal in this way: "This guy's in severe denial. He must be one of us."[47] Not only does this suggest that the height of Canadian patriotism is to be un-Canadian, but it also points to the ways that we identify with the colonial in our postcolonial icons. What we find here are several levels of negation taking place at once. If the ad is ironic about hokey Canadian iconography, it is also ironizing the very process of negation itself, making the urgency of Canadian nationalist expression its target as well as endorsing it.

Ultimately, then, the ad, like its viewers, is undecided whether it is in fact ironic. As Ed McHugh asserts in his assessment, "it hits on our tendency to make fun of ourselves…while at the same time, taps into something deeper. As in damn right!"[48] It thus homes in on the paradox that is central to popular conceptions of Canadian national identity: we are boastful about our modesty. One sees this in any number of performances of Canadian hickness, where the Canadian holds it over his or her interlocutor while presenting him or herself as flagrantly colonial. This is, after all, the essence of the joke in Rick Mercer's *This Hour Has 22 Minutes* sketch, "Talking to Americans." The ultimate irony may be that Canadian self-denigration covers over a sense of superiority that nevertheless conceals a core of insecurity at the base of its investment in a cohesive national identity. To be a proud nationalist, in Canada, is to be non-nationalist, a non-Canadian. The ad brilliantly plays it both ways; the very nature of a "rant" encompasses both: loud assertiveness and defensive insecurity.

That "The Rant" became a self-generating phenomenon is further evidence of performance becoming reality; it became a fetish object in its own right. Live performances of the ad were staged across the country, including an occasion at Toronto's Air Canada Centre where Jeff Douglas "[did] the skit from his seat in the crowd while the ad play[ed] on the giant score board."[49] In each instance, Joe Canadian/Jeff Douglas was greeted with a standing ovation: "In hockey cathedrals across the land, I Am Canadian has become the common creed."[50] A few months later, Douglas was performing the skit on a whirlwind cross-Canada tour on Canada Day, beginning on Parliament Hill in Ottawa (see figure 1). Across the nation, fans gathered for his autograph. Yet without the illusion of embarrassed spontaneity dramatized in the ad, and the apparent free-association that accompanies it, the significance of the speech as an impulsive rant becomes meaningless. The ad, in effect, became the reality, proving Žižek's claim that we can "effectively *become* something by pretending that we *already are* that."[51]

Joe Canadian and Jeff Douglas both became national celebrities—and ambassadors for Canadian national identity.[52] Not only did Sheila Copps use the video in a speech in the United States, but Jeff Douglas appeared on the *Today* show on 24 April, promoting his message of Canadian uniqueness:[53] "This thing has taken on a life of its own," Douglas told Josh Rubin of the *Toronto Star*.[54] At one point, the ad's creator, Glen Hunt, was rebuffed when he claimed credit for writing the piece: "'No you didn't, Joe did,'" he was told by a recent convert.[55] Soon the actor, Douglas, began to perform himself as Joe Canadian, engaging in numerous profiles and interviews in which he gushed national pride: "I was paid to say that stuff, but I believe it," Douglas assured Craig Offman in an interview for *Time International*.[56] In the same interview, he was anxiously questioned about the possibility that he might be leaving for the United States. Meanwhile, the *Toronto Star* noted how, on a recent trip overseas, Douglas (like Joe) "wore the Canadian flag on his back."[57] A chain email was distributed asking people to add their names to an "I am Canadian" list.[58] People were able to recite the lines from memory. The Molson *www.iam.ca* website became an interactive space for nationalist rantings, and had been deluged with over 30,000 rants by June 2000.[59]

The phenomenon had ramifications beyond the entertainment industry. When it was discovered by *Marketing* reporter Mark Etting that the voice answering message at Molson's corporate offices pronounced "zee" for the letter "zed," the company swiftly changed their voice-mail system, as did numerous other firms across the country. Nortel, "after receiving several complaints about the US usage," promptly agreed to manufacture a Canadian version of their voice-mail systems.[60] Charles Gordon, writing in *Maclean's*, took "solace" from the ad as proof of the existence, and integrity, of Canadian culture: "Comfort should also be taken—perhaps 'courage' would be a better word—by Canadian broadcasters, publishers, artistic directors and others who make the decisions that govern our culture.... The signs are all around. Take it from Joe."[61] Ironically, the Ontario Harris government's attempt to take advantage of the wave of patriotic euphoria that followed in the wake of "The Rant" by requiring grade-school students to recite a pledge of citizenship met with adamant resistance. Harris had missed the ad's central ironic lesson, namely the ambivalence that lies at the heart of nationalism itself: "Is the point of this pledge to encourage national pride in our students," a letter to the *Toronto Star* asked, "or is it to foster a resentment of... authority in general? If it is the former, would it not be more productive to require our students to recite The Rant heard in the new Molson Canadian ad?"[62]

"The Rant" thus highlights a blurring of the lines where national identity and cultural representation meet. As Anne Lavack of the University of Winnipeg inquired about the Molson ad: "Does advertising lead, or does it just reflect what is already going on?"[63] Instead of thinking of the ways cultural practices reflect national identity, it might be more productive to follow Stuart Hall's articulation of the ways identity is itself a production which is "always constituted within, not outside, representation."[64]

When "The Rant" was shortlisted at the June 2000 Cannes International Advertising Festival, Brett Marchand praised the piece on the basis that "national pride is a basic message that can speak to individuals on a world wide level."[65] Here again, the national readily slides into the postnational. However, in an age of increasingly globalized uniformity, the vector of the nation may have become more important than ever. James Deacon quotes Hunt as saying that "young adults who grew up with the Internet's one-world view still long for their own specific identity." "The Rant," he suggests, filled in for this absence.[66] The continual re-storying of the national self thus becomes its most compelling, if suppressed, feature.

Yet what happens when a form of strategic and parodic mimicry (mimicking oneself as other) is what is being exported internationally—that is, when provincialism becomes cosmopolitan? If Canadian nationalist expression takes the form of a skepticism about that expression, this might render the doubter both embarrassingly colonial and astutely postcolonial. To put it another way, the Canadian might become postcolonial the more colonial he or she appears to be. If the postcolonial is in fact the colonial, and the national is as international as you can get, where, finally, does this leave honest Joe Canadian? On a stage in the dark, trumpeting his identity while fumbling to get out of the limelight.

Notes

1 Enoch Padolsky, "'Olga in Wonderland': Canadian Ethnic Minority Writing and Post-Colonial Theory," *Canadian Ethnic Studies* 28.3 (1996): 16–28; Larry McDonald, "I Looked for It and There It Was—Gone: History in Postmodern Criticism," *Essays on Canadian Writing* 56 (1995): 37–50; and Thomas King, "Godzilla vs. Post-Colonial," *New Contexts of Canadian Criticism*, ed. Ajay Heble, Donna Palmateer Pennee, and J.R. (Tim) Struthers (Peterborough: Broadview, 1997), 241–48. For additional critics who take issue with the links between postcolonial theory and nationalism in a Canadian context, see those items in the bibliography listed under Boire, Chanady, Hutcheon, Maracle, Miki, and Mukherjee. See also Laura Moss, *Is Canada Postcolonial? Unsettling Canadian Literature* (Waterloo: Wilfrid Laurier University Press, 2003) for a collection of essays that undertakes an extended interrogation of postcolonial discourse in Canada. For attempts to historicize the nationalist foundations of postcolonial theory in Canada, see Diana Brydon, "Introduction: Reading Postcoloniality, Reading Canada," *Essays on Canadian Writing*, 56 (1995): 1–19; Donna Palmateer Pennee, "Literary Citizenship: Culture (Un)Bounded, Culture (Re)Distributed," *Home-Work: Postcolonialism, Pedagogy, and Canadian Literature*, ed. Cynthia Sugars (Ottawa: University of Ottawa Press, 2004); Cynthia Sugars, "National Posts: Theorizing Canadian Postcolonialism," *International Journal of Canadian Studies* 25 (2002): 41–67; and Sugars, "Can the Canadian Speak? Lost in Postcolonial Space," *ARIEL* 32.3 (2001): 115–52. For a selection of representative essays in the field of Canadian postcolonialism, see Sugars, *Unhomely States: Theorizing English-Canadian Postcolonialism* (Peterborough: Broadview, 2004).

2 In his conclusion to the *Literary History of Canada*, Frye affirms the contemporary era as "post-Canadian." Northrop Frye, "Conclusion to a *Literary History of Canada*," *The Bush Garden: Essays on the Canadian Imagination* (Toronto: Anansi, 1971), 249. A few years later, in *The Modern Century*, he used Canada's constitutive diversity to make a case for Canada being "post-national." Northrop Frye, *The Modern Century: Whidden Lectures 1967* (Toronto: Oxford University Press, 1967), 17.

3 There have been extended debates about the precise definition of the term *postcolonial*: is it a temporal marker, a geographical designation (and, if so, which geographical regions are legitimately postcolonial?), a matter of content or subject matter, or a critical orientation (in most cases pointing to an oppositional postcolonial "politics")? In many instances these categories overlap. I am using the term here to suggest a methodological approach that includes a concern with such interconnected issues as national expression and identity, culture and imperialism, hierarchies of power and processes of marginalization, colonial history and instances of resistance, Native-settler relations, appropriation of voice, and neo-colonialism and racism.

4 The incongruity I am highlighting here took on even further ironic proportions when Molson Breweries merged with the American company, Coors, in July 2004. The merger met with innumerable cries of protest and wounded outrage, from family historian Karen Molson's comment that "Molson's has turned its back on its distinguished heritage" and initiated "a fundamental...loss to Canada" to the "ViveleCanada" website's call for a boycott of Coors-Molson products because of Coors's "un-Canadian" legacy of racism and intolerance. Joanne Laucius's article in the 20 July 2004 *Ottawa Citizen*,

entitled "I Am Canadian...Well, I Was," opens with the tongue-in-cheek line: "I am multinational." She proceeds to lament the fact that, despite the success of "The Rant" as "a cultural touchstone," the Molson-Coors merger demonstrates that "Canada is just not big enough" in terms of the global market. Andrew Mayeda, "Brewing a Rich Heritage," *Ottawa Citizen* 23 July 2004, D3; Joanne Laucius, "I Am Canadian...Well, I Was," *Ottawa Citizen* 20 July 2004, A1–A2.

5 See A.J.M. Smith's introduction to *The Book of Canadian Poetry: A Critical and Historical Anthology* (Chicago: University of Chicago Press, 1943), 3–31.

6 Earle Birney, "Can. Lit.," *An Anthology of Canadian Literature in English*, ed. Russell Brown, Donna Bennett, and Natalie Cooke (Toronto: Oxford University Press, 1990), 296; Robert Kroetsch, "Disunity as Unity: A Canadian Strategy," *The Lovely Treachery of Words: Essays Selected and New* (Don Mills: Oxford University Press, 1989), 21–22.

7 Dennis Lee, "Cadence, Country, Silence: Writing in Colonial Space," *Open Letter* 2.6 (1973).

8 Margaret Atwood, *The Journals of Susanna Moodie* (Toronto: Oxford University Press, 1970), 62.

9 For extended treatments of the inner contradiction of national constructs, see Homi K. Bhabha, "DissemiNation: Time, Narrative, and the Margins of the Modern Nation," *The Location of Culture* (London: Routledge, 1994), 139–70; and Chris Prentice, "Some Problems of Response to Empire in Settler Post-Colonial Societies," *De-Scribing Empire: Post Colonialism and Textuality*, ed. Chris Tiffin and Alan Lawson (London: Routledge, 1994), 45–58.

10 Kroetsch, 29.

11 This is an oblique allusion to Linda Hutcheon, *As Canadian as Possible... Under the Circumstances!* (Toronto: ECW, 1990).

12 Lara Mills, "Bud Light, Canadian Get Big Ad Push," *Marketing* 27 March 2000, 2.

13 Janice Kennedy, "Only in the Rest of Canada? Pity," *Calgary Herald* 29 April 2000, O2.

14 Quoted in Kate Jaimet, "'I Am' ... Is Back: Molson Relaunches Ad," *Ottawa Citizen* 22 March 2000, D1.

15 The ad first aired in Cineplex-Odeon theatres across the country and was designed so that it could be "acted" live in Canadian cinemas, with the images projected on a screen behind the actor. Connected to this interlayering of cinematic performances, the television version of the ad aired for the first time during the 2000 Oscars and was strategically poised to follow the Oscar performance of the much-hated *South Park* song, "Let's Blame Canada."

16 The latter, of course, distinguishes Canadian English from American usage, not British.

17 A number of newspaper articles commented on the disingenuous nature of the ad's supposed claim to embrace Quebec when Molson's Canadian is not even marketed in that province. As Kate Jaimet noted, "The ad will show across Canada, except in Quebec, where apparently the 'Je suis Canadien' slogan wouldn't go down too smoothly with beer drinkers"; Jaimet, D1. See also Peter Diekmeyer, "Should Marketers Fly the Flag?" *Montreal Gazette* 25 April 2000, D2; and Janice Kennedy, "Only in the Rest of Canada? Pity," O2.

18 Himani Bannerji, "Geography Lessons: On Being an Insider/Outsider to the Canadian Nation," *Dangerous Territories: Struggles for Difference and Equality in Education*, ed. Leslie G. Roman and Linda Eyre (New York: Routledge, 1997), 24.

19 Alan Lawson, "Postcolonial Theory and the 'Settler' Subject," *Essays on Canadian Writing*, 56 (1995): 30.

20 Ellie Tesher, "Moviegoers Save Their Cheering for Canada," *Toronto Star* 23 March 2000, A27.

21 Stan Sutter, "Canadian Beauty, eh?" *Marketing* 8 May 2000, 42.

22 Pam Blackstone, "Canada Rules the Web," *Victoria Times Colonist* 1 May 2000, A9.

23 Lee, 46.

24 See Henry Wong's comment on the ad's images: "the screen images intrigued me so much, I played it on slo-mo looking for Satanic messages. Instead, I managed to see images that were very humorous, very hip and, more importantly, very Canadian. I AM proud." Henry Wong, "The Creative Eye: Molson Canadian," *Marketing* 8 May 2000, 32.

25 Lawson, 22.

26 See Freud's "Fetishism" for an extended account of the dual functioning of the fetish object. According to Freud, the fetish is a figure of radical ambivalence, enabling both a disavowal and affirmation of something (classically, the event of castration) at one and the same time. Sigmund Freud, "Fetishism," Vol. 7, trans. James Strachey, *On Sexuality*, ed. Angela Richards (Hammondsworth: Penguin, 1977), 351–57.

27 Lawson, 28.

28 Linda Hutcheon, "'Circling the Downspout of Empire': Post-Colonialism and Postmodernism,'" *ARIEL* 20.4 (1989): 170.

29 Interestingly, the staging of the ad bears a notable resemblance to the opening of the film *Patton*, where the general mounts a stage and, standing in front of an enormous American flag, rants about America's proud identity. I am grateful to Nathan Bootsma, one of the students in my University of Ottawa graduate seminar, for calling my attention to the parallel. An article in the 24 July 2000 *People's Weekly* also drew attention to the "Pattonesque fashion" of Joe Canadian's rant. See "North Star: A Proud Nation Embraces Jeff Douglas, Thanks to a Rousing Canadian Beer Ad," *People's Weekly* 24 July 2000, 126. The lurking presence of this key intertext adds a whole other level to the ad's ambivalent relation to American cultural imperialism. This is true, as well, of the setting of "The Rant" to the British anthem "The Land of Hope and Glory." While on the one hand it invokes Canada's British roots (and hence again excludes Québécois and First Nations Canadians), it forms part of the timeworn tradition of appealing to Canada's British North American character in order to distinguish Canada more clearly from the United States (see Francis's *National Dreams* for an account of this dynamic). However, historically, such appeals to the validating power of the mother country condemned Canadian culture to international ignominy, stigmatizing it with the label of colonialism. Once again, the ad sought to kill two birds at once: it conjured Canadian (postcolonial) distinctiveness while invoking Canada's compromised (colonial) identity.

30 Steven Pearlstein, "They.Are.Canadian: An American Newspaper Looks at the Peculiar Canadian Phenomenon Known as Joe's Rant," *Calgary Herald* 30 April 2000, A14.

31 Paul Bunner, "You've Seen The Rant, Now Read The Rave: My Name Is Paul (Bunner), and I Too Am a Canadian," *Report Newsmagazine* [Alberta] 27.1 (8 May 2000), 2.

32 Quoted in Pearlstein, A14.

33 See Homi Bhabha's use of the similar phrase, "almost the same but not quite" (and variations upon this). Homi K. Bhabha, "Of Mimicry and Man: The Ambivalence of Colonial Discourse," *The Location of Culture* (London: Routledge, 1994), 85–92.

34 Christopher Bollas, *Being a Character: Psychoanalysis and Self Experience* (New York: Hill and Wang, 1992), 13.

35 Bollas, 3.

36 Compare Mike Roberts's description of the effect of the ad: "Kind of like an eight-year-old who sees herself on TV." Mike Roberts, "I Rant, therefore I Am...," *Vancouver Province* 7 May 2000, B4.

37 Homi Bhabha, "Of Mimicry and Man," 91.

38 Linda Hutcheon, *166*.

39 Sutter, 42.

40 This is the essence of the humour of such Canadian comedy programs as *The Red Green Show* and *This Hour Has 22 Minutes,* especially Rick Mercer's "Talking to Americans" segment in the latter program. Posing as a journalist/opinion-poller in the United States, Mercer plays the Canadian hick while in the process maintaining a stance of superiority in response to the flagrant displays of American gullibility that his performance evokes (in a sense, he is playing on American willingness to view Canadians as hicks). Many of Margaret Atwood's "performances" of Canada in Britain make use of a similar ironic doubling: a performed self-deprecation or coloniality that emerges out of what one might term a kind of postcolonial condescension.

41 Sherene Razack, *Looking White People in the Eye: Gender, Race, and Culture in Courtrooms and Classrooms* (Toronto: University of Toronto Press, 1998), 159.

42 Slavoj Žižek, *Looking Awry: An Introduction to Jacques Lacan through Popular Culture* (Cambridge: MIT Press, 1991), 73.

43 Žižek, 73.

44 Quoted in Kerry Gillespie, "How That Molson Ad Hit Our Nationalist Nerve with the Rant That Rocks," *Toronto Star* 15 April 2000, A30.

45 Marilyn Smulders, "He Is…Truronian," *Halifax Daily News* 15 April 2000, 25.

46 Smulders, 25 [emphasis mine].

47 Peter Goddard, "Canadian, Eh? Then This Rant's for You, Bud," *Toronto Star* 1 April 2000, M4.

48 Quoted in Smulders, 25.

49 Don Brennan, "Life Imitates Advertising," *Toronto Sun* 15 April 2000, N7.

50 Kelly Egan, "Things He Always Wanted to Say: 'I Am Canadian' Author Just Let It All Pour Out," *Ottawa Citizen* 19 April 2000, A3.

51 Žižek, 73.

52 Douglas himself, stupefied by his overnight rise to fame, observed in disbelief: "'I didn't think people would be writing letters to the editor, saying I should be enlisted to help with the national-unity crisis'"; see Pearlstein, A14. Some editorials even suggested that Douglas run for prime minister; see Adam Bryant, "Message in a Beer Bottle," *Newsweek* 29 May 2000, 43. In effect, the ad does not aim to do what its script proclaims (that is, to correct American misconceptions about Canada); rather, its aim is to provide an illusion of national coherence. In this, it was astoundingly successful. One newspaper article notes how it "succeeded in connecting Canadians sea to sea"; see Andy Nulman, "Peqs Appeal," *Montreal Gazette* 30 April 2000, C5. Another heralded "The Rant" as "the unofficial anthem north of the border"; see Bryant, 43. "The Rant," James Macgowan claimed in the *Ottawa Citizen,* "is the most popular and nationalistic utterance this country has heard since *O Canada*"; see Macgowan, "My Name Is Glen and I Am an Ad Guy," *Ottawa Citizen* 19 August 2000, E2. Likewise, the numerous parodic versions of "The Rant" that erupted across the country—"I am Albertan," "I am Quebecois," "I am Torontonian"—even as they highlighted regional divisions within Canada, nevertheless testified to the *national* impact of its message. For the Albertan, see Don Martin, "For the Benefit of Easterners, This Is an Albertan…"; *Calgary Herald* 6 May 2000: A3; for the Quebecois, see Nulman, C5; for the Torontonian, see Goddard, M4. Mike Roberts lists a number of parodies of the ad in his article for the *Vancouver Province,* "I Rant, therefore I Am…."; see Roberts, B4.

53 Mark Etting, "Ambassador 'Joe,'" *Marketing* 1 May 2000: 39.

54 Josh Rubin, "Beer Pitcher Wows ACC: Live Performance of Canadian Rant Rocks Leaf Fans," *Toronto Star* 16 April 2000, C3.

55 Macgowan, E2–E3.

56 Craig Offman, interview with Jeff Douglas, *Time International* 3 July 2000, 44.

57 Brennan, N7.

58 I received one of these emails from my fifteen-year-old niece. Following the text of "The Rant," the instructions read: "If you truly are Canadian, read this out loud at the top of your lungs, add your name and then send it on its merry way to as many Canadians as possible."

59 Goddard, M4.

60 Mark Etting, "The Power of Joe," *Marketing* 29 May 2000, 35; Mark Etting, "Truth about Molson," *Marketing* 10 April 2000, 47.

61 Charles Gordon, "Let's Hear It for Canada!," *Maclean's* 1 May 2000, 62.

62 Trevor Amon, "Rant Would Make Much Better Pledge," *Toronto Star* 4 May 2000, A29.

63 Quoted in James Deacon, "The Patriot Game: I. Am. A Beer Marketer," *Maclean's* 18 June 2000, 30.

64 Stuart Hall, "Cultural Identity and Diaspora," *Colonial Discourse and Post-Colonial Theory: A Reader*, ed. Patrick Williams and Laura Chrisman (New York: Harvester-Wheatsheaf, 1994), 392.

65 Quoted in "'Canadian' Beer Ad up for Award," *St. John's Telegram* 24 June 2000, 25.

66 Deacon, 30.

7 "The North"

Intersecting Worlds and World Views

Alastair Campbell and *Kirk Cameron*

Introduction

WHAT DOES "THE NORTH" MEAN TO CANADIANS? Nunavut, Yukon, and the Northwest Territories make up more than one third of Canada's land-mass; if the northern areas of the provinces are added, most of Canada is northern.[1] How does this geographical fact affect the way Canada defines its identity? In the English version of its national anthem, the entire nation is celebrated as "the True North, strong and free!" What does this mean to the residents of Montreal, Toronto, or Vancouver? Is Canada's northern character mainly in contrast to the United States, or is there another North, external to the urban milieu yet still connected to it?

Canada's geographical centre lies near Baker Lake, a predominantly Inuit community of about 1,500 people, but, to the vast majority of Canadians, Baker Lake is more remote than a foreign country. Together the three territories represent only about 3 percent of Canada's total population. Most Canadians live within 350 kilometres of the American border; their outlook is formed within this "southern" geopolitical zone. As a

The authors wish to acknowledge the many Northerners and northern specialists who have helped inform their views through the years. They also thank those who commented on drafts of this chapter or who provided information on particular points. In addition to the editor, Garry Sherbert, they include Jim Almstrom, Sheila Bassi-Kellett, George Diveky, Steve Iveson, Doug Kane, John Merritt, Michael Posluns, and Graham White. The errors are our own.

143

result, "for most Canadians the North remains an unknown quantity."[2] Those few in the south who are knowledgeable of the North are usually concerned with government, the armed forces, mining, hydrocarbon development, Aboriginal affairs, or environmental matters. Their views typically reflect their sectoral interests. Northerners, Aboriginal and non-Aboriginal, have other views. These are far from uniform and often contentious within the North itself. Nonetheless, however divergent their outlooks may be on particular matters, Northerners share a common sentiment: that their interests are misunderstood, misrepresented, or simply disregarded by decision makers and interest groups in southern Canada.

This chapter examines how the North of today has developed since European contact was initiated four centuries ago. It reviews how economic and political change in the non-northern world has impinged upon the North, affecting the intimate details of Aboriginal cultures, even extending to the determination of Aboriginal identity. It argues that Northerners, and in particular Aboriginal Northerners, have not been simply the passive recipients of unwelcome changes. In the fur-trade period, Aboriginal peoples proved themselves capable bargainers and established relationships with the traders that extended beyond bartering transactions. Later, they negotiated treaties with the Crown, and subsequently insisted that discussions held in the negotiating process, not simply the legal text, represented the true agreement. With Aboriginal peoples in the provinces, they repudiated the Canadian government's assimilationist policies, challenged government decisions in the courts, and became a factor in the national political arena. They contested major resource developments, reversed the government's position on the legal existence of Aboriginal title, and ultimately secured recognition in the Constitution of Canada. Canada's political culture was transformed in this process.

Land-claim agreements (modern treaties) now cover most of the North, and the northern political system is being restructured. Territorial political systems have been democratized, and a new territorial government, Nunavut, has been created in the central and eastern Arctic. In Yukon and the Northwest Territories, Aboriginal self-government agreements have been negotiated or are under negotiation. A new North is being built through changing political and economic relationships and is evident in new cultural and artistic forms.

Metropolis and Hinterland: Frontier or Homeland?

In 1974, Justice Thomas Berger began a public inquiry into the social, economic, and environmental impacts of building a natural gas pipeline down the Mackenzie Valley in the Northwest Territories. In contrast to the usual decision-making pattern, Berger took the step of having both informal discussions and formal hearings in a total of thirty-five western Arctic communities. This allowed him to examine a potentially massive capital investment in the context of long-term northern interests, as seen by Northerners, and especially by Aboriginal Northerners. His report highlighted two strikingly divergent views, captured in the title *Northern Frontier: Northern Homeland*:

> We look upon the North as our last frontier. It is natural for us to think of developing it, of subduing the land and of extracting its resources to fuel Canada's industry and heat our homes. Our whole inclination is to think of expanding our industrial machine to the limit of our country's frontiers. In this view, the construction of a gas pipeline is seen as the next advance in a series of frontier advances that have been intimately bound up with Canadian history. But the native people say the North is their homeland. They have lived there for thousands of years. They claim it is their land and they believe they have a right to say what its future ought to be.[3]

"The frontier" is a place where two realities meet, such as two states or two contrasting societies. The American historian Frederick J. Turner describes it as "the hither edge of free land," and "the outer edge of the wave—the meeting point between savagery and civilization."[4] He emphasizes the frontier as the most formative influence in the shaping of American history and national character: "The true point of view in the history of this nation is not the Atlantic coast, it is the Great West."[5] The frontier symbolizes discovery, adventure, self-reliance, and destiny: "we are a frontier-bred people and will never be satisfied with mere comfort and security."[6] The frontier pervades North American popular culture. From *Star Trek* to journalistic reports, we constantly encounter references to "new" and "final" frontiers.[7]

Canadian historians, more restrained than Turner, and with more attention to the North than to the "Great West," likewise have emphasized the importance of the frontier to the development of this nation. Kenneth McNaught, in *The Pelican History of Canada*, observes, "from the time of the earliest records Canada has been part of a frontier, just as in her own growth she has fostered frontiers. The struggle of men, and of metropolitan centres to extend and control these frontiers, as well as to improve life behind them, lies at the heart of Canadian history."[8] The statement that the concern of the metropolitan centres has been not only to control the frontiers, but also to improve life "behind" them, although ambiguous, paints a benign picture. Others depict the metropolis-frontier relationship in far harsher terms:

Metropolis continually dominates and exploits hinterland whether in regional, national, class, or ethnic terms.... *Hinterland* means, in the first instance, relatively underdeveloped or colonial areas which export for the most part semi-processed extractive materials—including people who migrate from the country to the city for better educational and work opportunities. Hinterland may also ... denote urban under-classes as well as rural peasantries and rural proletariats. *Metropolis* signifies the centres of political and economic control located in the larger cities. Further, the term may denote urban upper-class elites, or regional and national power structures of one sort or another.[9]

The above formulation is by the sociologist Arthur K. Davis. Historians Kenneth S. Coates and William Morrison describe the northern regions of the provinces in substantially consistent terms: "What we are currently seeing in the Provincial North is ... a continuation of a well-established process of systematic underdevelopment. The northern regions of the provinces have been rendered into internal colonies, their resources deemed to be available primarily for the benefit of the non-Natives in the South."[10] This presumption leads to unequal power: "The control exerted by outsiders, the impoverishment of the indigenous population, the emphasis on rapid, profit-oriented development, and the inability of local residents to control their destiny are readily evident."[11]

McNaught regards the extension of the frontier as part of the panorama of Canadian history. Davis, by contrast, emphasizes underlying, exploitive, politico-economic relations associated with it. Berger's view is not antithetical to either of these, but focuses on the Aboriginal view of the North as a homeland, not another's frontier, and still less as representing a "line" behind which life should be improved. Berger thus illuminates the enormous divide between Aboriginal and metropolitan views. The periphery of the metropolis is the centre for the Aboriginal peoples.

The Aboriginal Peoples

There are currently about 48,000 Aboriginal people in the three territories. In Nunavut, Inuit constitute approximately 85 percent of a population of 27,000, while Aboriginal people (mostly members of First Nations) number about 23 percent of 29,000 Yukon residents. Around 50 percent of the 37,000 residents of the Northwest Territories are of Aboriginal descent, and of the latter about 10,600 are Dene, 3,900 are Inuit and 3,600 are Metis.[12]

The foregoing introduces terms like "Dene," "Inuit," "Metis," and "First Nations." Our linguistic habits lead us to suppose such terms to be simply labels applied to pre-existing classes, or sets of objects, as "zinc" is applied to the mineral Zn, or "weeping willow" to *salix babylonica*. In socio-cultural contexts, however, the names used to describe ethnicities, cultural groups, or peoples do not simply *name* a pre-existing social or cultural reality, but themselves *participate in creating* that reality. Consistent with this proposition, terms used to identify groups in cross-cultural contexts will be found to be not readily translatable from one language group and cultural context to another. Thus an examination of the various English terms applied to the Aboriginal peoples, and Aboriginal self-designations, shows them to be cultural artifacts, each with its own history and contexts, creating no less than describing entities. These terms both reflect and structure relations within and between Aboriginal and non-Aboriginal societies. The terms change with the relations.

In the Sámi (Lapp) context, the Finnish social scientist Marjut Aikio cautions that "we should not forget the dynamics of ethnicity and the perpetual differences in degrees of belonging to an ethnic group."[13] Aikio nevertheless contends that "[although] the boundaries between groups may be hazy and difficult to define ... the cores of ethnic groups are nevertheless clear."[14] On the basis of this conclusion, Aikio proposes that persons may be assigned to an ethnic minority on the basis of one of four criteria: (1) self-identification; (2) ancestry; (3) special cultural characteristics, such as command of a language; or (4) existing social organization for interaction among members.[15] Other criteria could be added, such as community acceptance and legal designation, but the objective, static appearance of this listing may obscure the dynamics of group affiliation in intercultural contexts. Ethnic identity is expressed through numerous terms in various contexts, for particular purposes, and sometimes in a contradictory manner. Thus self-identification and identification by others may not correspond, though both are important in the process of group formation; nor are the various criteria Aikio lists equivalent in all contexts.

Aboriginal peoples in the North, as elsewhere in Canada, have their identity defined, in part, by legal criteria. Canada's Constitution Act 1867 refers to only one Aboriginal people: it assigns responsibility for "Indians, and Lands reserved for the Indians" to the federal government.[16] By contrast, the Constitution Act 1982 speaks of three Aboriginal peoples: Indians, Inuit and Metis.[17] These are legal terms, each with its own history and meaning that has shifted through the years. These terms were included in the constitution as part of the national pact-making process. All may be confusing in other contexts.

Of the three constitutional terms, "Inuit" is perhaps the least problematic, since it refers to a culturally distinct Aboriginal people, formerly known as "Eskimos," and is a self-designation, at least in the Canadian eastern Arctic. "Inuit" is a plural form of "inuk" ("a person" or "human being") in the Inuit language.[18] The term was primarily incorporated into

Canadian English in the 1970s, in a restricted ethnic sense, as a result of use by Inuit political leaders and subsequent adoption by academics and journalists.[19] It thus entered the political lexicon and found its way into legislation, finally to become standard Canadian usage.[20]

The word "Indian," by contrast, is not an indigenous term. Columbus thought that the West Indies formed a part of Asia, and throughout North and South America the term "Indian," or its cognates, came into general use to describe any of the remarkably diverse indigenous peoples. These included Inuit, who were referred to as the "Esquimaux Indians" in various proclamations and other documents from the eighteenth century on.[21] Indeed, in the eighteenth century, Pacific Islanders and Australian Aboriginals also were called "Indians."[22]

Over time, mainstream Canadian society began to see Inuit as distinct from other Aboriginal peoples. This occurred for a number of reasons: Inuit geographic remoteness, occupancy of areas north of the treeline, and distinctive cultural traits like the kayak and igloo.[23] As well, the Indian Act was not applied to Inuit.[24] A proposed amendment in 1924, intended to make it so apply, was abandoned in the face of opposition from the Conservative Party, former prime minister Arthur Meighen contending that "the best policy we can adopt towards the Eskimos is to leave them alone."[25] Thus, section 4 (1) of the present Indian Act, in language befitting an earlier era, declares that "A reference in this Act to an Indian does not include any person of the race of aborigines commonly referred to as Inuit."[26] Closely connected is the fact that, before the 1975 James Bay and Northern Quebec Agreement, treaties were not signed with Inuit. Legal and administrative differences thus reinforced cultural and geographic distinctions.

In the early 1970s, when Inuit began to form representative associations, they did not see themselves as status or Treaty Indians, nor as non-status Indians or Metis. Their distinct identity and concerns led them to form their own national and regional associations, separate from those of Indians and Metis.[27] Thus Inuit acted independently in the tempestuous national process that resulted in the Constitution Act 1982 and came to be listed separately as an Aboriginal people in section 35, implicitly holding Aboriginal and treaty rights, but distinct from Indians and Metis.

At about the same time as the Inuit political leadership came to reject the term "Eskimo," the Aboriginal peoples of the Mackenzie Valley began to refer to themselves, in English, as "Dene."[28] This word, also meaning "people," is likewise taken from their own languages and has won acceptance in English in the Mackenzie Valley and among those familiar with the region. In constitutional language, however, Dene remain "Indians." In Yukon, the more general term "First Nation" has been adopted, though more recently.[29]

Like "Indian," "Metis" is a term whose meaning changes according to time and context; but, like "Inuit" and "Dene," it has the characteristics of self-designation. Metis originally were persons of French and Aboriginal origin who began to form as a distinct social group in the Red River area towards the close of the eighteenth century. Some entered the Northwest Territories through the fur trade or after the rebellions of 1870 and 1885, when they settled in the southern part of the territory and, in many cases, married Dene. Other Metis entered the territory throughout the twentieth century, sometimes following jobs in the mining industry. Somewhat distinct were the "halfbreed" children of those fur traders and others (often non-French and non-Catholic) who similarly married Dene women and settled in the Mackenzie Valley.[30]

When the Dene in the Northwest Territories and adjacent areas signed treaties 8 and 11 in 1899 and 1921, some of those partly of Dene ancestry chose to place themselves outside the treaties. Instead of adhering to treaty, they accepted "scrip" in settlement of their Aboriginal claims. Scrip was a certificate, awarded on the basis of family size, that could be exchanged for cash or individual title to land.[31] Generally, the treaty commissioners appear to have encouraged persons of mixed ancestry, who "lived as Indians," to adhere to treaty rather than take scrip. However, scrip was sometimes chosen for its immediate cash value, because some preferred the full legal rights of citizens to the "wardship" of status Indians, and because there was no third choice.[32]

The distinction introduced by the treaty-making process, between those who chose scrip and those who adhered to treaties, was reinforced by the Indian Act. The treaties themselves did not make reference to the Indian Act, but the Act was the government's legal instrument for administering reserves, determining Indian status, and generally for administering Indian affairs. The Act specifically excluded from registration any person who had received scrip, and any descendant of such persons, and thus established a distinct class of persons of Indian ancestry who would not be legally recognized as Indians.[33]

As well, the Act provided that any Indian woman who married a non-Indian was to be deprived of her registered status. The intent was to assimilate, and the effect was to ensure a constant flow of persons, called "non-status Indians," from Indian to non-Indian legal status.[34] Many such persons, or their children, joined Metis organizations.[35] In 1985, Bill C-31 amended the Indian Act. Indian status was restored to women who had married non-Indians, and to their children.[36] As might be expected, many so affected, although accepting registration under the Indian Act, have continued to identify themselves as Metis and continue today to belong to Metis organizations in the Northwest Territories.

In this convoluted fashion has the metropolis classified, shuffled, and reclassified the Aboriginal peoples of the North, recognizing some as parties who must be negotiated with, treating these as wards, seeking to assimilate others, ignoring ("leaving alone") others again. These are the people whom the non-Aboriginal population has seen as the occupants of the hinterland, perhaps as obstacles to the advance of the frontier, perhaps in need of protection, but in any case, in the modern era, as ultimately dependent and requiring the advancement of the metropolis to improve their lives.

Aboriginal Cultures

A switch from political, administrative, and legal categories of the metropolis to the Aboriginal peoples' own languages, cultures, and associations reveals a diversity that matches poorly the above, politico-administrative terms.

Considered culturally, the Inuit occupy a distinct area extending north of the treeline from Greenland and Labrador to northern Alaska. Within this area they speak various dialects of a single language, closely related to other languages spoken in southwestern Alaska, the Aleutian Islands, and Siberia.[37] Linguists call this broader group the "Eskimo-Aleut," "Eskaleut," or "Eskimoan" language family.[38]

The Dene or Athapaskan languages extend from the interior of Alaska across most of Yukon, down the Mackenzie Valley and through the northern areas of the four western provinces. Athapaskan groups in the territories include Chipewyan, Gwich'in (Kutchin), Kaska, North Slavey (Sahtudene), South Slavey, Tagish, Upper Tanana, Tåîchô (Dogrib), Tr'öndek Hwëch'in (Han), Northern Tutchone, and Southern Tutchone. However, as Kerry Abel cautions, "[even] these divisions can be problematic because they oversimplify a complex and historically fluid situation."[39]

For example, the Great Bear Lake area is today referred to as the Sahtu region and the Aboriginal communities within it—the Sahtudene—are all signatories to a single land-claim agreement and are represented by the Sahtu Tribal Council. The term "Sahtudene" is apparently a recent contraction from "Sahtúgot'ine" ("Great Bear Lake People"), which has been extended from the name of a local group to cover the people of the entire region. The Sahtu land-claim agreement itself refers to the "Slavey, Hare and Mountain Dene of the Sahtu region,"[40] while linguists Michael Krause and Victor Golla refer to four groups—Slavey, Mountain, Bearlake, and Hare—as all speaking "closely related dialects of a single language."[41] Father Morice, writing a century ago, adds further complexity, and this complexity is not unique to the Sahtu.[42] Indeed, local people sometimes have difficulty in defining their group affiliations, in English, in terms that correspond to those of linguists and cultural anthropologists. Thus linguistic and cultural maps and charts, with labels affixed, on close examination resolve into a series of hazy, multicoloured dots that form a pattern only when viewed from a convenient distance.

Non-Athapaskan languages in the North are represented by Cree and Tlingit. Cree-speaking groups are distributed from the southern Northwest Territories across the northern regions of the provinces, from British Columbia to Quebec. Tlingit is spoken in Yukon, British Columbia, and Alaska. Tlingit began to replace the Athapaskan Tagish language in Yukon before European settlement, and the few persons today who still have some knowledge of Tagish are all Tlingit speakers.

This description of Aboriginal groups places particular emphasis on language. At a basic level, languages mark group boundaries and are thus tied to group identity. At a deeper level, some linguists maintain that cultural traditions and world views are expressed though particular language structures: "[The Inuit language is] a reflection of the most basic elements of the Inuit culture and world view...[and] plays a prominent part in building the Inuit cultural identity at its deepest level.... [The language's] semantic and cognitive structure ... in its integrity, is necessary to the maintenance of the Arctic people's collective identity."[43] The twentieth century has, in fact, seen the erosion of the Aboriginal languages in the North. The cultural frontier has been marked by the dominance of the metropolitan languages, primarily English. An Aboriginal language is now the mother tongue of only about 12 percent of the Yukon's and 30 percent of the Northwest Territories' Aboriginal people.[44] Information on the strength of the Inuit language is subject to various interpretations. A national Inuit-language comprehension rate of 90 percent of all Inuit is suggested, but fluency in children may be only at a level of 70 percent. There are marked regional variations.[45] Yet linguistic erosion does not seem to correspond to the loss of identity as an ethnically distinct group. In such circumstances other ethnic indicators, like those listed by Aikio for the Sàmi, assume greater importance. These include ancestry, self-identification, and community acceptance.

Among the terms of land claims agreements are formal processes for determining Aboriginal group affiliation. This corresponds to Aikio's fourth criterion. For example, the Nunavut Land Claims Agreement lists Canadian citizenship, self-identification, determination as an Inuk in accordance with Inuit customs and usage, and association with a Nunavut community or the Nunavut Settlement Area as criteria creating an entitlement to registration under the agreement. The criteria in other claims agreements are not dissimilar. The creation of such formal lists is linked both to the exercise of rights and the enjoyment of benefits under the agreements, and to the establishment of Aboriginal claims organizations as regional centres of authority and political voice.

The Homeland: The Perspective of the Aboriginal Peoples

It is often difficult for non-Aboriginal people, now primarily urban and often without intergenerational attachment to particular localities, to understand the Aboriginal relation to the natural environment. For hunting societies, however, the natural environment provides the cultural matrix. Anthropologist Marshall Sahlins has challenged a common misconception of hunting societies—often imagined as beset by hardship and hunger—by describing them as "the original affluent society,"[46] but the Aboriginal peoples' attachment to their environment is not simply a matter of the effective utilization of certain resources and an emotional attachment to the familiar. It is embedded in a particular world view, which traditionally included aspects that Europeans might term "religious" but which was not articulated as a doctrine nor expressed in a particular institutional setting.

A glimpse of this distinctive world view is provided in the following short account from Brochet, in northern Manitoba, in 1939. It records the frustration of a Catholic priest who had tried to teach the catechism to a Chipewyan girl:

> She looked very bright. Every day I took special care of this little one. I went over the questions and answers with her alone. You know, there is a part of our catechism where the question is asked, "What is the most beautiful thing that God created?" The answer is: "Man and all the angels." But do you think that I could teach this simple thing? ... Every time I asked: "What is the most beautiful thing God created?" she would look up at me and say: "*Idthen!*" the caribou![47]

The Dene girl's conception of beauty was embedded in a distinct cultural and natural experience, which she did not transfer to the context of an unfamiliar, abstract doctrine. Animals like the caribou, moose, muskox, seal, bighorn sheep, walrus, bear, various species of whale, bison, mountain goat, rabbit, ptarmigan, many varieties of fish, and migratory birds sustain the Aboriginal peoples of the North. Hence they see these creatures not only as intrinsic to their own existence, but as embodying the beauty of creation and as participating in it in a spiritual sense. Today, many Aboriginal people hold Christian and more traditional spiritual beliefs simultaneously. There is no doubt that many continue to see "the land" as a place of intrinsic beauty and perfection. Their existence is rooted there, and it is often seen as free from the imperfections and turmoil of the urban centre.

Affluence or Hunger?

However, to follow Sahlins by describing hunting societies, such as those in the North, as "affluent" not only challenges metropolitan views of progress—the improvement of life behind the frontier—but seems to accord poorly with the images of hunger and privation that haunt the history of the North. For example, Hudson's Bay Company employees estimated that almost one hundred Inuit in the southern Kivalliq[48] died of starvation in the winter of 1919—perhaps a sixth of the region's population.[49] Richard Harrington and Farley Mowat documented and publicized other cases of starvation as late as the 1950s.[50] Without doubt, until the most recent decades, northern Aboriginal peoples lived tough and demanding lives when judged by contemporary urban standards. Hunting deaths, infanticide, and the death of the aged, when food was scarce, are all well known, yet the starvation that occurred in the Kivalliq was not typical of the North. The heavy dependence of the Kivalliq Inuit on caribou and the vulnerability resulting from changes in migration patterns and caribou population fluctuations was not characteristic elsewhere. Some researchers suggest that, in areas like southern Baffin Island and the central Arctic (Victoria Island and vicinity), death from starvation was relatively rare.[51]

European First Contact and the Fur Trade

Naturally, the explorers who led the expansion of Europe from the close of the fifteenth century encountered peoples and environments to which they were unaccustomed. For the European, the North was initially seen as a harsh, dangerous environment into which one ventured on a voyage of discovery linked to economic and strategic ends: this view continues today. Such difficult environments were a challenge to simple survival, but they also provided opportunities for exploration and trade, and even for enrichment or heroic attainment. As early as 1527, an English book boldly proclaimed: "There is no land uninhabitable nor sea unnavigable."[52]

The dangers of sea voyages in the early period of European exploration and the losses of Arctic explorers at much later dates show that trepidation, in a little-known environment, was well founded. Later stages reveal the gradual discovery of how to survive and travel in the Arctic environment—

essentials that the Aboriginal peoples had known for centuries. For the Aboriginal peoples this was (and remains) the natural environment, and to live in it was normal, not the stuff of heroic tales. It is not, as Ray Price names it in his popular historical account, *The Howling Arctic*; it is closer to what Vilhjalmur Stefansson calls *The Friendly Arctic*.[53] This goes beyond two contrasting images of the natural environment—those of the native and the stranger; closely linked are conflicting and shifting views of economic interest, public policy, and social identity.

In 1670, King Charles II granted a Royal Charter to Prince Rupert and seventeen other noblemen and gentlemen to incorporate the Hudson's Bay Company. Significantly, even at this early date, events in the hinterland reflected distant geopolitical considerations. The beaver trade through Hudson Bay was not simply a local commercial interest. It was motivated as well by the English desire to improve trade with the Russians and thus to diminish reliance on the Dutch for Baltic timber, required for naval purposes.[54]

The Royal Charter granted the company enormously broad powers: "sole trade and commerce," exclusive fishing rights, all minerals, and appointment as the "Absolute Lordes and Proprietors" of the territory. The company was "virtually a sovereign state subject only to the supreme authority of the Crown of England."[55] The charter was an obvious colonial act: the assertion of sovereignty by a nascent metropolis over barely known territories comprising the economic frontier. Various views have been taken of it. Three centuries later, in the James Bay context, journalist Boyce Richardson described the charter as "the deadly work of a king."[56] This was when Justice Turgeon of the Quebec Court of Appeal concluded that "All Aboriginal right in the territory, if it ever existed, was extinguished by the decision of the King."[57] Generally, however, the courts have been unwilling to share such a sweeping conclusion. Most notably, in *Hamlet of Baker Lake v. Minister of Indian Affairs*, Justice Mahoney found that the Royal Charter did not extinguish Aboriginal title in the territories to which it applied.[58]

Historically, the more immediately relevant point is that the pace of development in the North did not match the sweeping terms of the charter. By 1682, the company had only about thirty employees and officers scattered around Hudson Bay. By 1749, when an attempt was made in the British Parliament to deprive the company of its charter, as a "nonuser," there were still only four or five forts on the coast and about 120 regular employees.[59]

From the Aboriginal peoples, the company and other traders obtained furs, pelts, winter clothing, venison, fish, geese, snowshoes, wood supplies, and labour. In return, the Aboriginal peoples could (according to the period) obtain items like firearms, kettles, needles, knives, cloth, beads, oatmeal, flour, tea, tobacco, and (in some periods) liquor. In the twentieth century, the range of goods expanded to include steel traps, sewing machines, gramophones, fiddles, canned food, and other consumer goods.

The fur trade and the trading associated with whaling have often been portrayed as exploitative. The notion of exploitation requires a judgement as to the fairness of transactions in an intercultural situation. One important difference between the commercial and Aboriginal traders is that the trading companies accumulated capital through their transactions whereas the Aboriginal parties, operating in a non-monetary hunting economy, simply bartered produce for goods. Obviously, there was a profit to the party trading for that purpose, and over the centuries the Hudson's Bay Company accumulated substantial capital interests. However, much of the company's wealth resulted from later dealings not directly associated with the fur trade. Writing in the latter part of the eighteenth century, Adam Smith remarks that the Hudson's Bay Company had "a considerable degree of success," but he adds that, making proper allowance for extraordinary risk and expense, profits did not appear much, if at all, to exceed "the ordinary profits of trade."[60]

In actual on-site trading, the relation between the Aboriginal people and the commercial traders (the latter in relative isolation in the North), was often one of mutual dependency, and the Aboriginal people showed themselves capable negotiators. To give one example, the anthropologist John Matthiasson cites the difficulties of a whaling captain in negotiating fur prices with Inuit in North Baffin Island, and remarks, "if exploitation did occur, it did not happen to naïve aboriginal peoples who did not understand the nature of an economic transaction."[61] It is important to recognize, however, that there was a good deal of variation from one region and one period to another. From the western Arctic there are many examples of whalers and free traders bartering liquor for furs at exorbitant rates.[62]

Trading transactions must be viewed in their social context. In some areas, medical care was purchased by traders, often from Aboriginal women.[63] Conversely, physicians on whaling ships provided medical care to Aboriginal people, sometimes travelling long distances to do so.[64] Also important were the frequent liaisons, including marriage in accordance with local custom, between traders and Aboriginal women. It is an indication of the status accorded to Aboriginal peoples in the fur-trade period that, at an early date, the Canadian courts recognized the legal validity of such marriages.[65] Thus the relationship between Aboriginal people and traders was not strictly economic, but occurred in a broader social and institutional context.

From a long-term perspective, the fur trade and the Royal Charter might be seen as the beachhead for future metropolitan dominance of the Aboriginal homeland, as in southern Canada; but profound changes in the European-Aboriginal relationship resulted less from the fur trade itself than from the global evolution of Euro-American society outside the North, namely technological innovation, the accumulation of capital, and population transfers between continents. A series of waves was generated in the world's economic and political system and washed across the North. The fur trade was the first. It preceded, but did not directly cause, the others.

The Hudson's Bay Company's charter was terminated following an 1869 agreement with the Canadian government. The latter, with some reluctance, negotiated a purchase of the company's rights under the charter in order to bring Rupert's Land and the North-western Territory under Canadian jurisdiction. In essence, the company surrendered its charter in exchange for a cash payment of £300,000 and land provisions that caused it to benefit enormously from the agricultural settlement of the West. After 1912, the company developed the chain of retail outlets, for which it is mainly known today, and the fur trade became an ever-diminishing component of its business. The company sold its fur auction houses and northern stores in the 1980s; today it does not operate a single store in any of the three territories.

The Inclusion of the Territories within Canada

When Rupert's Land and the North-western Territory were transferred from Britain to Canada in 1870, Canada was mainly interested in the Prairies, which were part of the transferred region and which faced American settlement. The experience of the Columbia and the American southwest showed that American settlement would likely be followed by annexation, and the vision of a nation extending from the Atlantic to the Pacific Ocean would be endangered.[66] That this was foremost in the mind of Canada's first prime minister, Sir John A. MacDonald, is apparent from his comment, "If Canada is to remain a country separate from the United States, it is of great importance to her that they should not get behind us by right or by force, and intercept the route to the Pacific."[67]

The future existence of the nation was thus seen to depend on the speed with which British subjects could expand across the continent and occupy it, physically and institutionally. At stake was the question of which metropolis was to control the western Canadian hinterland. The North, for the time being, was incidental to this issue. It was not suitable for agricultural settlement and the fur trade required the continuation of the Aboriginal relation to the land simply to function. As Berger remarks, "the objectives of the fur trade were best met by keeping the Indians on their land."[68] Matthiason comments that, for Inuit, the transfer of Rupert's Land and the North-western Territory was "nothing more than a formality... and would remain such for the remainder of the nineteenth century."[69] Although specific to Inuit, this comment is generally true for all the northern Aboriginal peoples; the 1896 discovery of gold in Yukon marked the first major change.

Aboriginal Title, Treaties, and Land Claims

Canada was not equipped to undertake settlement of the West by force in face of the hostility of the Aboriginal peoples nor was this British policy. Along with the doctrines of European discovery and sovereignty, the procedure of recognizing Aboriginal land rights has deep roots in British and Canadian history.[70] It is evident in the 1867 *Address to Her Majesty from the Senate and House of Commons of the Dominion of Canada*, which sought the transfer of Rupert's Land and the North-western Territory to Canada: "Upon the transference of the territories in question to the Canadian Government, the claims of the Indian tribes to compensation for lands required for purposes of settlement will be considered and settled in conformity with the equitable principles which have uniformly governed the British Crown in its dealings with the aborigines."[71] Consistent with this, the Canadian government's 1869 agreement with the Hudson's Bay Company, as well as the Imperial Order effecting the transfer, included a stipulation that all Indian claims to compensation for lands for "settlement" were to be dealt with by the Canadian government "in communication with the Imperial Government."[72]

Treaties with the Aboriginal peoples in the prairies followed, and were extended northward as gold, oil, and other resources became known. These treaties were negotiated as the government judged necessary and were motivated by a desire to maintain peaceful relations and respond to Aboriginal demands. The latter were not a minor consideration. In 1898, a gathering of about five hundred Aboriginal people at Fort St. John, British Columbia, refused to allow miners and police to pass through their territory en route to the Yukon goldfields, until a treaty was signed.[73]

The texts of treaties 8 and 11 in the Northwest Territories and adjoining areas were similar to those negotiated throughout the Canadian West. They were inconsistent with the hunting and trapping lifestyle of the Dene. The consistency of their written terms with those for the greater populations and agricultural regions of the south indicates a lack of understanding of, if not indifference towards, the northern environment and the hunting economies of the Aboriginal peoples.

Written contracts and similar agreements were not a part of the northern Aboriginal culture, and it seems clear that the Crown and the Aboriginal signatories could *not* have had a common understanding of the document to which their signatures were attached. Father René Fumoleau remarks that the text of Treaty 11 was "completely unfamiliar" to the Dene and was seen by them for the first time on the day the treaty commissioner arrived. He adds (writing in 1973), "Very few could read it then; most have not read it yet."[74] Except for political leaders, negotiators, and lawyers, this statement could doubtless be repeated today. Dene continue to regard the treaties as important for recognizing their rights and establishing their relationship with the broader society, but they do *not* identify the treaties with the written texts.

In 1959 the federal Nelson Commission, appointed to deal with the reserves provided for in treaties 8 and 11, found that "some bands expressed the view that since they had the right to hunt, fish and trap over all of the land in the Northwest Territories, the land belonged to the Indians. The Commission found it impossible to make the Indians understand that it is possible to separate mineral rights or hunting rights from actual ownership of land."[75] If this were the case in 1959, it is even less likely that the Dene signatories of 1921 or 1899 would have drawn such distinctions, for they spring from English property law, not from the Dene view of their relationship to their homeland. The incomprehension was mutual. Lord Haldane had cautioned in 1921 that "in the various systems of native jurisprudence throughout the Empire there is no such full distinction between property and possession as English lawyers are familiar with."[76] Underlying the lack of "understanding" was doubtless something more basic: the Dene's refusal to *accept* that the land had been surrendered to the Crown.

As a result of the Dene view that the treaties did not change their ownership of the land, the unsuitability of small, localized reserves, and the relatively sparse non-Aboriginal settlement, the sections of the treaties providing for the setting up of reserves were never implemented. The Nelson Commission found no Dene interest in residing on reserves, and this ultimately led to the opening of land-claims negotiations throughout the territories on a "comprehensive" basis, in the 1970s.[77] This occurred not only in Yukon, the Inuvialuit area, and Nunavut, where Aboriginal title could be asserted according to principles of British and Canadian law, but also in the Mackenzie Valley, where (in the federal government's view) Aboriginal title had already been surrendered by treaties 8 and 11 and the issuance of Metis scrip.

Progress in dealing with land claims in Canada was erratic through the twentieth century. The nadir was marked by a 1927 amendment to the Indian Act—aimed particularly at Aboriginal people in British Columbia—making it illegal to raise money to pursue land claims.[78] Following the Second World War, however, important changes were to occur in relations between the Government of Canada and the Aboriginal peoples. Canada shed its blood in two horrendous world wars, the Second waged with a genocidal regime. In the postwar period, approaches towards the Aboriginal peoples began to reflect ideals that had grown in the course of the war, and that were shown in the formation of the United Nations, the Universal Declaration of Human Rights, and the postwar dismantling of the old colonial empires.

The Canadian Bill of Rights, enacted in 1960, was a landmark in this process. It recognized certain basic rights "without discrimination by reason of race, national origin, colour, religion or sex," including "the right of the individual to equality before the law and the protection of the law."[79]

In the context of this evolving framework of human rights and citizenship, it was increasingly unacceptable to keep the Aboriginal peoples in a segregated, subordinate position. In 1951, substantial revisions were made to the Indian Act. Although it remained a heavy-handed, paternalistic document, the prohibition on the raising of money to pursue land claims was repealed, as were prohibitions of dances and ceremonies. Voting rights in federal elections were extended to registered Indians in 1960, and in provincial elections from 1949 to 1969.[80] In 1970, in a criminal law context, the Supreme Court of Canada found certain continuing provisions of the Indian Act—in this case the offence of intoxication in an off-reserve situation—offended basic rights guaranteed by the Canadian Bill of Rights.[81]

Yet it was not clear how to marry the principle of legal equality for all individuals with the special status of the Aboriginal peoples under doctrines of Aboriginal rights, the treaties, the Indian Act, and the constitution. Harry Hawthorn, an anthropologist at the University of British Columbia, proposed the expression "citizens plus" to do so: "Indians should be regarded as 'citizens plus': in addition to their normal rights and duties of citizenship, Indians possess certain additional rights as charter members of the Canadian community."[82] This formulation, attractive in its simplicity, was adopted by the Indian Association of Alberta in opposition to the federal government's 1969 White Paper on Indian Policy. It barely deals, however, with the difficult issue of the relation of individual to collective rights.

Prime Minister Trudeau exemplifies the intellectual conflict. In many respects the architect of the Canadian Charter of Rights and Freedoms,[83] Trudeau's early comments on Indian policy, as prime minister, are couched in terms of justice "in our time," "full status as Canadians," and opposition to such notions as recompense for past wrongs or any kind of special status: "It's inconceivable, I think, that in a given society one section of the society have a treaty with the other section of the society. We must be all equal under the laws and we must not sign treaties amongst ourselves."[84] His government therefore advanced the idea that the Aboriginal peoples would be best served by incorporating them within the general framework of Canadian society, on the same basis as other citizens: "Aboriginal claims to land…are so general and undefined that it is not realistic to think of them as specific claims capable of remedy except through a policy and programme that will end injustice to Indians as members of the Canadian community."[85]

The goal of ending injustice was laudable, but Aboriginal people saw the promotion of an abstract equality, through the repudiation of Aboriginal and treaty rights, as tantamount to dispossession. The White Paper was therefore counterproductive to its own objectives, for it stimulated the development of Aboriginal political organizations in determined opposition to it. Connected to this, over the next few years a number of crucial land-rights cases began to proceed through the courts. The Nisga'a of British Columbia argued that their Aboriginal title to the Nass Valley had never been surrendered and still existed.[86] In northern Quebec, the James Bay Crees challenged a massive hydroelectric project on a similar basis.[87] In the Northwest Territories, the Dene attempted to file a "caution" with the Registrar of Land Titles on the basis that the written texts of treaties 8 and 11 did not correspond with the verbal explanations and assurances given by the treaty commissioners, and that the Dene therefore had not surrendered their Aboriginal title to the Mackenzie Valley by signing them.[88]

None of these cases provided clear victories for governments, developers, or Aboriginal peoples. Their cumulative impact, however, was to shock a complacent society. The 1973 injunction won by the James Bay Crees against the James Bay Development Corporation and Hydro-Québec, although quickly suspended, was especially remarkable. A few thousand hunters and trappers, in the remote hinterland, could potentially disrupt massive capital investments. It became apparent that Aboriginal title was not a nebulous concept but was grounded in British and Canadian law. Hence Prime Minister Trudeau's remark, following the split decision of the Supreme Court of Canada in the Nisga'a case: "You have more legal rights than I thought you had."[89] The Government of Canada subsequently adopted a comprehensive land-claims policy and the first modern Aboriginal treaty in Canada, the James Bay and Northern Quebec Agreement, was signed in 1975. Other actions followed. Dene and Inuvialuit used the Berger inquiry to defeat the Mackenzie Valley Pipeline proposal, Inuvialuit

forced Dome Petroleum to stop drilling in the Beaufort Sea, and Inuit prevented uranium mining near Baker Lake.

It is ironic that Prime Minister Trudeau was later to secure, as his
crowning political achievement, the enactment of a Canadian constitution in which Aboriginal and treaty rights were recognized and affirmed.
Further, in 1983, he personally convened the first of a number of national
constitutional conferences, to which the Aboriginal peoples and the territorial governments were invited, to discuss the further definition of Aboriginal rights in the constitution. The Aboriginal peoples and the territorial
governments had broken into the exclusive club of "executive federalism." The attempt to exclude both again, through the 1987 Meech Lake
Accord, was to lead to the defeat of that accord. The Yukon government
led the attack on the accord, while its death knell was sounded by an Aboriginal Member of the Legislative Assembly of Manitoba, Elijah Harper.

Aboriginal and Public Government

The metropolis/hinterland relationship is today complicated by the evolving nature of Aboriginal politics and its relation to the mainstream political economy. As the political and economic structures shift, the line
between what is metropolis and what is hinterland also shifts. There are
today important institutions connected with both the Aboriginal heritage
and the economic mainstream. Are these to be considered part of the frontier, an extension of today's metropolis, or a new relationship in formation?
The latter is nowhere more clearly shown than in the new relationships
emerging through land claims and self-government agreements in the
North. Despite some similarities, the maturing political institutional framework in the territories and the approach toward recognition of Aboriginal
rights and interests, both within those changing structures and in new
Aboriginal governance structures, are following different paths in each of
the three territories.

Yukon most clearly corresponds in its governmental framework to the
provincial norm in Canada with a Legislative Assembly, Cabinet, and
party politics. An attempt has been made to reach a modus vivendi with the
Aboriginal peoples through the negotiation of comprehensive land-claim
and self-government agreements, to which the Yukon government is a
party. Land-claim negotiations began in 1973 and resulted in a 1993 Umbrella Final Agreement, which provides the framework for the fourteen
individual Yukon First Nations to conclude regional land-claim agreements. At the time of writing, eleven First Nations have completed such
agreements. Self-government is dealt with in distinct but complementary
agreements.

Under self-government agreements, First Nations will exercise self-government at the community level, with the authority to pass some laws that can supersede some federal and territorial laws on lands owned by First Nations. In addition, First Nations may pass some laws that apply to their citizens no matter where they live in the territory. This may be called "parallel self-government," in that the territorial public government and Aboriginal governments may legislate in the same field, but for different population groups, and their legislation will work in parallel. At the administrative level, program and services transfer agreements are being negotiated, through which linkages or separations of administration between public and Aboriginal governments are accomplished.

Nunavut stands at the other end of the continuum. The territory is remarkable in that it was established as a separate jurisdiction in 1999, as part of the settlement of the Inuit land claim. Here Inuit land claim beneficiaries are represented by a non-profit corporation, Nunavut Tunngavik Inc., and self-government is expressed through municipal governments, the territorial Legislative Assembly, and appointments to management boards provided for in the land-claims agreement. There are no discrete institutions of Inuit self-government, which is exercised mainly by weight of numbers (the 85 percent Inuit population) and through the appointment processes and consultative requirements that arise from the land-claims agreement.

The Nunavut Legislative Assembly operates like other legislative assemblies in Canada, but on the basis of "consensus government," meaning that political parties do not operate within it. Votes are taken within the assembly, however, and Cabinet needs the support of a majority of members. In contrast to other Canadian jurisdictions, in 2005 the assembly made changes to the territorial budget proposed by government, without bringing about the resignation of Cabinet or provoking a new election. The Inuit language is commonly used in the assembly.

The Northwest Territories stands between these alternatives. With almost equal Aboriginal and non-Aboriginal populations, the Northwest Territories' diversity is reflected in the emergence of regional land claims and self-government negotiations. Faced with oil and gas development in the Mackenzie Delta and Beaufort Sea area, in 1977 the Inuvialuit decided to immediately pursue a land-claim agreement separate from the Inuit of the central and eastern Arctic. The Inuvialuit Final Agreement was completed in 1984. Dene-Metis claims to the remainder of the Mackenzie Valley have also proceeded on a regional basis. The Gwich'in (1992), Sahtu (1993), and Tåîchô (2005) have completed land-claims agreements specific to their regions. All provide for self-government through the agreement itself (Tåîchô), through negotiations that are provided for in the agreements (Gwich'in and Sahtu), or through general undertakings in the agreement

(Inuvialuit). A completely different approach has been followed in the region around Fort Smith, where the Salt River First Nation ratified an agreement based on treaty land entitlement in 2001.[90] Yet other approaches are being followed by the Akaitcho First Nations (Chipewyans, and Tâîchô communities adjacent to Yellowknife), the South Slave Metis Tribal Council, and the Slavey in the Deh Cho region.

The Legislative Assembly of the Northwest Territories is like that of Nunavut, in that it operates by "consensus," rather than on a party basis. The assembly has been fully elected since 1975, with responsible government (Cabinet accountability to the Legislative Assembly) since 1986. Since the separation of Nunavut, Aboriginal languages are not often spoken within the assembly, although they are officially recognized. Outside the assembly, self-government arrangements are being pursued at local and regional levels. Throughout the past three decades there has been intermittent tension between Aboriginal groups and the Government of the Northwest Territories. The former, especially the Dene, have held (to varying degrees) that the Government of the Northwest Territories is a "creature" of Ottawa with no standing in the homeland. Yet since 1975 a majority of MLAs have been Aboriginal persons, and while elections may result in uncontested acclamation in some electoral districts (even in communities like Yellowknife), territorial election turnouts are generally comparable to those in the provinces.

Attempts have been made over the years to resolve the conflicting views of the Government of the Northwest Territories. Possibilities like a bicameral legislature or guaranteed representation for the major Aboriginal groups in the Legislative Assembly have been discussed, but results have been inconclusive. Among other considerations, for cost reasons the Northwest Territories' small population is not conducive to complex constitutional arrangements. The present focus of interest seems to be on self-government arrangements at the regional or community level, rather than on territory-wide constitutional innovations.

Common to all three territories are resource management bodies, created or recognized through land-claims agreements, with members appointed by the federal and territorial governments and the Aboriginal organizations. These are constitutionally protected independent bodies, which carry out governmental functions such as issuing water permits, undertaking land-use planning, reviewing resource development impacts, and establishing wildlife harvesting levels. Examples include the Yukon Environmental and Socio-Economic Assessment Board, the Inuvialuit Environmental Impact Screening Committee and Environmental Impact Review Board, the Mackenzie Valley Environmental Impact Review Board, the Nunavut Impact Review Board, the Mackenzie Valley Resource Management Board, the Yukon and Nunavut water boards, the Inuvialuit Game Council and Fisheries Joint Management Committee, and the Nunavut Wildlife Management Board.

This very general description of the fit between Aboriginal and public governments in the three territories indicates the changing metropolis-frontier/homeland relationship. As political structures emerge that mesh Aboriginal interests and the parliamentary system, the intelligibility of the metropolis-hinterland model begins to come into question. It becomes increasingly difficult to regard the Aboriginal groups as the necessarily subordinate occupants of the hinterland when modified governance structures and resource management systems are emerging. These are not simply imposed systems. Three decades ago, it was the Aboriginal peoples who induced a reluctant federal government to accept negotiations based on Aboriginal title; a decade later, they secured the recognition of Aboriginal and treaty rights in the Constitution of Canada; in the third successive decade they obtained federal acknowledgement of an inherent right of self-government and legislation to create a new territorial government in Nunavut. It has not been an uneventful process. In 1984, an assembly of Yukon First Nations voted against a comprehensive land-claim agreement that had been under negotiation since 1973. In 1990, a joint Dene-Metis assembly rejected a land-claim agreement negotiated for the whole of the Mackenzie Valley. Opinions may vary as to whether or not these were, in the circumstances, strategically wise decisions. Yukon's 1993 Umbrella Final Agreement, provides for self-government and more land than the rejected 1984 agreement, but also provides for a significantly lower federal cash settlement. Moreover, regionalized claims negotiations in both Yukon and the Northwest Territories remain incomplete. The key point is that it was the Aboriginal peoples who took these decisions.

Conclusion

The North has enormous subsurface resources: oil, natural gas, gold, silver, lead, zinc, diamonds, tungsten, and other minerals. Today's strong interest in these is fuelled by metropolitan needs. Enormous capital investments in the territories are expected over the next decade. For the Aboriginal peoples, this holds out an opportunity to secure benefits and employment, and create a sufficient regional economic base to escape the poverty and social problems widespread in the North. The pattern of resource development today differs from that common in the past, when the developer extracted the resources and left others to cope with the damages and environmental contaminants. There are contaminated sites throughout the North, some posing immense cost and technical problems for cleanup. But land-claim agreements and other measures now establish the Aboriginal peoples as regulators of, and parties to, the development process. In this way, environmental impacts may be controlled and northern benefits (royalties, contracts, and employment) secured from development.

A more difficult and looming problem is the contamination of the North from other regions of the globe (airborne pollutants such as dioxins) and climate change. These problems pose a major threat to the future of the North. The Inuit Circumpolar Conference has been playing an important role at the international level in ensuring that scientific data is gathered and publicized. This issue ultimately can be dealt with only through international action.

The gradual acquisition of business experience, with the financial resources provided through land-claim agreements, has led to the formation of Aboriginal development corporations and businesses that are reshaping the territorial economy. As only one example, three of the North's largest airlines—Air North, First Air, and Canadian North—are wholly or partly owned by Aboriginal corporations. Aboriginal economic institutions and capital are key to the economic diversification of the North. Tourism, arts and crafts, the film industry, northern foods, and commercial fishing are all potential growth areas. Such diversification is essential as an alternative to the boom-and-bust cycle that has typified the mining and hydrocarbon sectors. The outcome is not so much a compromise between interests as a reordering of political and economic relationships in which Aboriginal organizations now play a central role.

The changing metropolis-homeland relation goes beyond land, economics, and politics, however. In 2000, Michele Genest and Dianne Homan put out a call to Yukon authors for short stories and poetry to capture the tensions and linkages between wilderness and the modern urban, developed world.[91] Interestingly, their efforts capture the intersection of metropolis and homeland. The preface to the resulting anthology, *Urban Coyote*, portrays much of what is intangible in the northern world; for it is no longer simply hinterland, nor is it urban or metropolitan, in the sense of Toronto or Vancouver. In between is a world that brings together different cultures, different peoples: a world characterized by a profound sense of attachment to the land, yet a strong interest in the modern: "Urban Coyote? It is a title that captures...the sense of worlds intersecting—of bush meeting asphalt, of trapline meeting supermarket."[92] This meeting place is not simply physical but aesthetic and philosophical.

Considering the small population, there are remarkably vibrant, highly diverse arts communities in all the territories. In 1999, 27 percent of those surveyed in Nunavut indicated that they were involved in the production of northern crafts.[93] Across the North activities range from crafts, visual arts, local theatre, musical productions, through children's books like those of Michael Kusugak, to internationally recognized novels like Richard Van Camp's *The Lesser Blessed* and award-winning films like *Atanarjuat* (dir. Zacharias Kunuk et al.). These express the intangibles of change in the North, an evolution of the aesthetic, which originates in the homeland but exemplifies modernity. It is this shift between the two that is distinctive of the North today. The frontier (intellectual and aesthetic challenge) and homeland (centre of being) fuse.

The conception of the North as a frontier was born in European and Euro-Canadian expansion. The homeland of the Aboriginal peoples became the frontier of the metropolis, and on the frontier, in the homeland, the interests of the metropolis prevailed. Yet the Aboriginal peoples, accepting aspects of their transactions with the metropolis, were not simply the passive recipients of external decisions. The metropolis has had to find ways to accommodate the Aboriginal peoples. This has included incorporating them within the politico-economic system while accepting their distinctiveness. Not only has the metropolis brought change to the homeland; the homeland has brought about changes in the metropolis: in its body of law, its political culture, and its symbols like Inuit art, which has become a marker of Canadian national identity in the international forum. In the twenty-first century, one may find not only Azerbaijanis and Somalis in Nunavut, but Inuit who have sailed in the South China Sea, who are homeowners in New Zealand or who have worked in Africa. In the global village we may find an internet cafe more easily in Whitehorse than in Boston.

There remain enormous economic, political, social, and environmental problems to overcome; but there are now too many anomalies for a simple model of metropolis-hinterland dominance to accommodate. A "paradigm shift" is needed. The North is no longer a frontier of exploitation, nor a homeland under siege. However, not only a paradigm shift is needed: a redefinition of Canada's identity is required.

Notes

1   The meaning of "the North," including its "boundaries, dimensions and variations," is discussed by geographer Louis-Edmond Hamelin. The present chapter primarily concerns Canada's three northern territories, which share a distinct constitutional status. However, the northern areas of the provinces share many characteristics with the territories. Strictly geographical criteria place Arctic Quebec in a more northerly zone than southern Yukon or the Mackenzie Valley. Louis-Edmond Hamelin, *Canadian Nordicity: It's Your North, Too* (Montreal: Harvest House, 1978), xiv.

2   Hamelin, 15.

3   Thomas R. Berger, *Northern Frontier, Northern Homeland: The Report of the Mackenzie Valley Pipeline Inquiry*, Vol. 1 (Ottawa: Minister of Supply and Services, 1977), 1.

4 Frederick J. Turner, *The Frontier in American History* (New York: Holt, Rinehart, and Winston, 1962), 3.

5 Turner, 3.

6 Will Ferguson, *Why I Hate Canadians* (Vancouver: Douglas and McIntyre, 1997), 107.

7 As one example, see Gary Lamphier, "Nunavut: Canada's Final Frontier," *Edmonton Journal* 30 October 2003, Section H.

8 Kenneth McNaught, *The Pelican History of Canada* (Harmondsworth: Penguin, 1976), 7.

9 Arthur K. Davis, "Canadian Society and History as Hinterland Versus Metropolis," *Canadian Society: Pluralism, Change and Conflict,* ed. Richard J. Ossenberg (Scarborough: Prentice-Hall, 1971), 12.

10 Kenneth S. Coates and William Morrison, *The Forgotten North: A History of Canada's Provincial Norths* (Toronto: James Lorimer, 1992), 6.

11 Coates and Morrison, 9.

12 Population figures (here rounded) are those reported by Statistics Canada from the 2001 census. <http://www12.statcan.ca/english/census01/products/standard/themes/data products.cfm?s=1&t=45&alevel=2&free=0>. See also "Population by Aboriginal Identity and Community, Northwest Territories, Census 2001," NWT Bureau of Statistics T-Stat (Territorial Statistics On-Line), Government of the Northwest Territories. <http://www.stats.gov.nt.ca/statinfo/census%2001/ethnicity.xls>. Aboriginal data, Yukon Bureau of Statistics, Government of Yukon <http://www.gov.yk.ca/depts/eco/stats/cen sus01/aboriginal/pdf>.

13 Marjut Aikio, "The Finnish Perspective: Language and Ethnicity," *Arctic Languages: An Awakening,* ed. Dirmid R.F. Collis (Paris: UNESCO, 1990), 368.

14 Aikio, 368.

15 Aikio, 368. The first three characteristics are described as individual, the fourth as a group quality.

16 Canada, Constitution Act 1867, S. 91 (24). *Revised Statutes of Canada, 1985* (Ottawa: Queen's Printer for Canada, 1985) *Appendices*, Appendix II, No. 5. In the 1864 constitutional resolution and in the official French version of the British North America Act this section was expressed in French as "Les Sauvages, et les terres réservées pour les Sauvages."

17 Canada, Constitution Act 1982, S. 35 (2). *Revised Statutes of Canada, 1985, Appendices*, Appendix II, No. 44, Schedule B. The term "Aboriginal" entered the Canadian political and journalistic vocabulary after its 1982 adoption in the Constitution Act. Before that time it was mainly restricted to specific contexts, as in legal terms like "Aboriginal rights." It has since largely replaced the earlier "Native." The latter term was rejected by most organizations in southern Canada, which based their membership on the Indian Act. They viewed the term "Native," especially in government usage, as blurring the distinction between Metis and status Indians, and as diminishing the importance of Aboriginal and treaty rights. At a popular level, and in the titles of some organizations that did not accept Indian Act criteria, such as the Native Women's Association of Canada, the term "Native" has continued in use.

18 The Inuit language is called "Inuktitut" in the Canadian eastern Arctic. In the central Arctic it is "Inuinnaqtun," and in the Beaufort Sea area and the Mackenzie Delta, "Inuvialuktun" or "Iñupiatun," the latter term also being used in northern Alaska. In Greenland, the Inuit language is called "Kalaallisut" ("Greenlandic").

19 The term "inuk" (plural, "inuit"), meaning "person" or "human being," is found from Greenland to northern Alaska ("iñuk" and "iñuit"). In the Canadian eastern Arctic, it is also used in an ethnic sense in place of "Eskimo" and has been adopted into English in this sense. In the central Arctic (Victoria Island and vicinity), the equivalent "ethnic"

term is "Inuinnait" and in the Canadian western Arctic (Beaufort Sea area and Macken-zie Delta) "Inuvialuit" or "Iñupiat," the latter term extending into northern Alaska. In Greenland, "Kalaallit" ("Greenlanders"), is the self-designation of Inuit Greenlanders. Despite local variation, the Inuit Circumpolar Conference, representing groups from Greenland to Siberia, has adopted "Inuit" for international purposes.

20 The older term, "Eskimo" generally is thought to derive from one of the Algonkian languages, and to mean "an eater of raw meat," although not all authorities are in agree-ment. Used in English as early as 1584, it became standard in English, French, and other European languages for four centuries, and is still widely used outside Canada.

21 In 1939, the Supreme Court of Canada found that the term "Indian," as used in the Constitution Act 1867, included Inuit, since Inuit were called Indians when the Act was passed. *Re Eskimos, Canadian Native Law Cases*, ed. Brian Slattery and Sheila E. Stelck (Saskatoon: University of Saskatchewan, Native Law Centre, 1980–1991), Vol. 5, 123–49.

22 Alan Moorehead, *The Fatal Impact: An Account of the Invasion of the South Pacific, 1760–1840* (Harmondsworth: Penguin, 1968), 41, 59–60n, 148.

23 Although they shared some culture traits with adjacent Aboriginal groups, Inuit (prior to European contact) have been assigned by anthropolgists to a single, distinct culture area: "Distributed thinly over a vast area … [Inuit] have developed a culture at once broadly uniform in all its subdivisions and distinct in large measure from every other cul-ture of the world." Edward Weyer, *The Eskimos: Their Environment and Folkways* (New Haven: Yale University Press, 1932), 4. However, Wendell H. Oswalt cautions against "stereotypic Eskimo cultural characteristics." He points out, as one example, that the igloo (snow house) was used primarily in Canada and Greenland. Wendell H. Oswalt, *Alaskan Eskimos* (Scranton, PA: Chandler, 1967), 2–3.

24 The Indian Act is the central piece of federal legislation governing those Aboriginal peoples considered "Indian." No comparable legislation was enacted for Inuit.

25 Frank Tester and Peter Kulchyski, *Tammarniit (Mistakes): Inuit Relocation in the East-ern Arctic, 1939–63* (Vancouver: University of British Columbia Press, 1994), 19. Tester and Kulchyski remark that "Meighen's attitude amounted to neglect" (20). Beyond neg-lect, Meighen strongly opposed a distinct legal status for any Aboriginal peoples.

26 Indian Act, Revised Statutes of Canada, 1985, Vol. 5, c. 1–5, s. 4 (1). This section was introduced into the Indian Act in 1951.

27 The Inuit Tapirisat of Canada (now Inuit Tapiriit Kanatami) was established in 1971 to represent Canadian Inuit at a national level, the National Indian Brotherhood (now the Assembly of First Nations) in 1968 for status and Treaty Indians, and the Native Coun-cil of Canada (now the Congress of Aboriginal Peoples) in 1971 for non-status Indians and Metis. The Metis National Council, a distinct organization, was established in 1983 to represent strictly Metis concerns. The Labrador Metis Nation, affiliated to the Con-gress of Aboriginal Peoples, is unique among Metis organizations in describing its con-stituency as "predominantly of Inuit descent." The term "Metis" began to be used for some Labrador Inuit descendants around 1975.

28 The Indian Brotherhood of the Northwest Territories, established in 1969, formally changed its name to the Dene Nation in 1978.

29 The term "First Nation" has become widely used in Yukon and the Northwest Territo-ries, though often in political and administrative contexts. Some Aboriginal peoples, notably Inuit and Metis, do not designate themselves as First Nations, although the expression "Metis Nation" is used.

30 Richard Slobodin records the expression "Halfbreed" in his 1966 study, *Metis of the Mackenzie District* (Ottawa: Canadian Research Centre for Anthropology, St. Paul Uni-

versity, 1966). In 1981 he remarks that the term is "now considered as pejorative." "Subarctic Metis," ed. June Helm, *Subarctic*, Vol. 6 of *Handbook of North American Indians*, ed. William C. Sturtevant (Washington: Smithsonian Institution, 1981), 371.

31　Metis heads of families and their children under eighteen years of age were entitled to money scrip of $240 per capita or land scrip of 240 acres per capita.

32　A "ward" is a person, such as a minor, under guardianship or protection. The term is found in descriptions of Indian status up to the 1970s.

33　This section of the Indian Act was repealed in 1985; by that time, it had already played its part in determining membership of the status Indian charter group.

34　Up to 1985, the Indian Act provided for the loss of Indian status by women who married non-Indians, and the acquisition of Indian status by non-Indian women who married an Indian man. Among the individual effects flowing from the loss of status was the loss of the right to reside on reserve. In the Northwest Territories and Yukon, the only inhabited reserve under the Indian Act was at Hay River and was not established until 1974. Distinctions between non-status and status Indians were thus not as marked in the North as in southern Canada. However, even in the North, status under the Act affected entitlement to health care, hunting rights, eligibility for housing, and the right to participate in band-related matters such as elections.

35　In contrast to most Aboriginal political associations in southern Canada, the Council for Yukon Indians (now the Council of Yukon First Nations) merged the Yukon Association of Non-Status Indians and the status-based Yukon Native Brotherhood in 1975. In the Northwest Territories, the Indian Brotherhood accepted non-status Indians as full members from the mid-1970s, and operated a secretariat for land claims negotiations jointly with the Metis Association. However, the two associations did not merge.

36　In an environment of changing rights expectations, it became increasingly unacceptable for the Government of Canada to discriminate against Indian women who married non-Indians. In *The Attorney-General of Canada v. Jeanette Lavalle*, the Supreme Court of Canada found that the membership provisions of the Indian Act, based on gender discrimination, were tied to the constitutional position of Indians and were not overridden by the Canadian Bill of Rights. Slattery and Stelck, Vol. 7, 238–68. Subsequent years saw the deepening of sentiment within Canada against gender discrimination in general, and international embarrassment with the membership provisions of the Indian Act. In particular, in 1981, in *Sandra Lovelace v. Canada*, the Human Rights Committee of the United Nations found Canada in breach of Article 27 of the International Covenant on Civil and Political Rights. There was also, after 1982, an expectation that the membership sections of the Indian Act would be eventually struck down because of their conflict with Section 15 of the Canadian Charter of Rights and Freedoms, which provides for "the equal protection and equal benefit of the law without discrimination," including discrimination based on sex. Section 15 of the Charter was due to come into effect in 1985. The minister of Indian Affairs and Northern Development, David Crombie, therefore undertook consultations with Aboriginal associations and, partly on the basis of these often heated discussions, amended the membership provisions of the Indian Act in 1985.

37　Jacques-Louis Dorais identifies fifteen dialects of the Inuit language. Jacques-Louis Dorais, *Inuit Uqausiqatigiit* (Iqaluit: Arctic College, Nunatta Campus, 1990), 17.

38　The term "language family" refers to a group of languages which are considered by linguists to have common roots.

39　Kerry Abel, *Drum Songs: Glimpses of Dene History* (Montreal and Kingston: McGill-Queen's University Press, 1993), xvi. Ties between groups are shown by intermarriage, adoption, and the capacity of many older people to speak more than one Aboriginal language.

40 Preamble, Comprehensive Land Claim Agreement Between Her Majesty in Right of Canada and the Dene…as represented by the Sahtu Tribal Council (Ottawa: Public Works and Government Services Canada, 1993).

41 Michael G. Krause and Victor Golla, "Northern Athapaskan Languages," *Subarctic*, ed. June Helm, *Handbook of North American Indians*, ed. William C. Sturtevant (Washington: Smithsonian Institution, 1981), 79.

42 A.G. Morice, "Hare Indians," *The Catholic Encyclopedia*, ed. C.G. Herbermann et al., Vol. 7 (New York: Robert Appleton, 1910). <http://www.newadvent.org/cathen/07136b.htm>

43 Louis-Jacques Dorais, "The Canadian Inuit and Their Language," *Arctic Languages: An Awakening*, ed. Dirmid R.F. Collis, (Paris: UNESCO, 1990), 185–289, 207. See also Dorais, *From Magic Words to Word Processing: A History of the Inuit Language* (Iqaluit: Arctic College, Nunatta Campus, 1993), 73–90.

44 In the Northwest Territories, the proportion of Aboriginal persons aged fifteen and older who are able to speak an Aboriginal language has fallen from about 59% (1984) to 44% (2004). Within this group there is a marked decline from those aged 65 and older (almost 90%) to those aged 15–24 (approximately 26%). Tlicho is the most widely spoken NWT Aboriginal language (94% of those aged 15 or older). In Yellowknife and in the Mackenzie Delta and Beaufort Sea region, about 25% of Aboriginal persons of the same age group speak an Aboriginal language. See Government of the Northwest Territories, *Annual Report on Official Languages 2003-4* (Yellowknife: Northwest Territories, Minister responsible for Official Languages, October 2004), 30–32. 10 October 2005 <http:// www.gov.nt.ca./research/publications/pdfs/03-04annualreportofficial languagesen.pdf>.

45 Statistics Canada, *Aboriginal Peoples Survey 2001—Initial Findings: Well-being of the non-reserve Aboriginal Population*, by Vivian O'Donnell and Heather Tait, Housing, Family and Social Statistics Division, Statistics Canada, Minister of Industry, Ottawa 2003, 30. <http://www.statcan.ca/cgi-bin/downpub/listpub.cgi?catno=89-589-XIE2003001>.

46 Marshall Sahlins, *Stone Age Economics* (New York: Aldine, 1972).

47 P.G. Downes, *Sleeping Island: The Story of One Man's Travels in the Great Barren Lands of the Canadian North* (Saskatoon: Western Producer Prairie Books, 1988), 86.

48 "Kivalliq" has been adopted, since the Nunavut Land Claims Agreement, as the name of the region formerly known as "Keewatin."

49 See Kaj Birket-Smith, "Descriptive Part," *The Caribou Eskimos: Material and Social Life and Their Cultural Position*, trans. W.E. Calvert, Vol. 5 of *The Report of the Fifth Thule Expedition, 1921-24* (Copenhagen: Glydenalske Boghandel, 1929), 68. About 10 percent of Inuit in the Kugaaruk (Pelly Bay) area died from starvation in 1919-20. Asen Balikci, *The Netsilik Eskimos* (Garden City, NY: Natural History Press, 1970), 244.

50 Richard Harrington, *The Face of the Arctic: A Cameraman's Story in Words and Pictures of Five Journeys into the Far North* (New York: Schuman, 1952), Farley Mowat, *The People of the Deer* (Boston: Little Brown, 1952) and *The Desperate People* (Boston: Little, Brown, 1959).

51 George Diveky: personal communication based on unpublished research. Conversely, there are records of deaths in other areas. For example, Hudson's Bay Company and other records show starvation in the vicinity of Fort Norman in 1831, 1836-37, 1842, 1851-52, and 1892. These include thirty-two "or more" deaths in 1836-37, "over fifty" at Fort Good Hope and twenty-five at Fort Norman in 1842, and "many" in 1851-52. Beryl C. Gillespie, "Bearlake Indians," *Subarctic*, ed. June Helm, *Handbook of North American Indians,* ed. William C. Sturtevant (Washington: Smithsonian Institution, 1981), 328.

52 Winston S. Churchill, *A History of the English-Speaking Peoples*, vol. 2, *The New World* (New York: Dodd, Mead, 1956), 93.

53 Ray Price, *The Howling Arctic: The Remarkable People Who Made Canada Sovereign in the Farthest North* (Toronto: Peter Martin, 1970); Vilhjalmur Stefansson, *The Friendly Arctic* (New York: Macmillan, 1921). Although Stefansson is closer to the Aboriginal reality, both titles play to the southern audience. In this respect they epitomize two conflicting views of the North: "an over-idealized vision and an excessively pessimistic vision," Hamelin, 4.

54 E.E. Rich, *Hudson's Bay Company, 1670–1870* (Toronto: McClelland and Stewart, 1960), Vol. 1, 51.

55 Arthur J. Ray and Donald B. Freeman, eds., *"Give Us Good Measure": An Economic Analysis of Relations between the Indians and the Hudson's Bay Company before 1763* (Toronto: University of Toronto Press, 1978), 13.

56 Boyce Richardson, *Strangers Devour the Land* (Vancouver: Douglas and McIntyre, 1991), 316.

57 *La Société de développment de la Baie James v. Kanatewat et al.*, Slattery and Stelck, Vol. 8, 386.

58 *Hamlet of Baker Lake et al. v. Minister of Indian Affairs and Northern Development et al.*, 107 Dominion Law Reports (3d) 513 (Fed. Ct. Trial Div.), 1980.

59 Adam Smith, *An Inquiry Into the Nature and Causes of the Wealth of Nations* (Toronto: Encyclopaedia Britannica, 1952), 324–25. It may be added that, despite its charter, the Hudson's Bay Company faced powerful Montreal-based rivals such as the North-West Company. While the Hudson's Bay Company commanded Hudson Bay, its rivals penetrated the interior, including the Mackenzie Valley. Aware of the competition, the Aboriginal peoples used it to their own advantage. It was not until 1821 that the Hudson's Bay Company was able to consolidate, south of the treeline, by absorbing the North-West Company. On the Arctic coast, north of the treeline, whalers dominated most of the trading with Inuit until the first quarter of the twentieth century. The Hudson's Bay Company had little reason to develop links with this area before white fox skins had become a valued commodity and the competing whaling industry had vanished.

60 Smith, 325.

61 John S. Matthiasson, *Living on the Land: Change among the Inuit of Baffin Island*, (Peterborough: Broadview Press, 1992), 32.

62 Norman A. Chance, *The Iñupiat and Arctic Alaska: An Ethnography of Development* (Fort Worth: Holt, Rinehart, and Winston, 1990), 35.

63 Sarah Carter, "First Nations Women of Prairie Canada in the Early Reserve Years, the 1870s to the 1920s: A Preliminary Inquiry," *Women of the First Nations: Power, Wisdom and Strength*, ed. Christine Miller and Patricia Chuchryk (Winnipeg: University of Manitoba Press, 1996), 64.

64 Matthiasson, 34.

65 See *Connolly v. Woolrich and Johnson et al.* and *Johnstone et al. v. Connolly*, Slattery and Stelck, Vol. 1, 70–243.

66 "The Columbia" was that part of the contemporary United States west of the Rocky Mountains and north of latitude 42° north.

67 Macdonald to Watkins, March 27, 1866. Quoted in Lewis H. Thomas, "The Constitutional Development of the North-West Territories, 1870–1888" (Saskatoon: University of Saskatchewan, Department of History, MA thesis, 1941), 12. Thomas adds that the Executive Council of the Province of Canada expressed the same opinion on June 22, 1866. 3n, 12.

68 Thomas R. Berger, *Village Journey: The Report of the Alaska Native Review Commission* (New York: Hill and Wang, 1985), 78.

69 Matthiasson, 27.

70 See The Royal Proclamation, 7 October 1763, in Canada, *Revised Statutes of Canada, 1985, Appendices,* Appendix 11, No. 1.

71 Canada, *Address to Her Majesty the Queen from the Senate and House of Commons of the Dominion of Canada,* 16–17 December 1867, Canada, *Revised Statutes of Canada, 1985, Appendices,* Appendix No. 9.

72 Canada, Revised Statutes of Canada 1985, *Appendices,* Appendix No. 9.

73 Richard Daniel, "The Spirit and Terms of Treaty Eight," *The Spirit of the Alberta Indian Treaties,* ed. Richard Price (Edmonton: Pica Pica Press, 1987), 64.

74 René Fumoleau, *As Long As This Land Shall Last: A History of Treaty 8 and Treaty 11, 1870–1939* (Toronto: McClelland and Stewart [1975?]), 163.

75 Quoted in Fumoleau, 214.

76 *Amodu Tijani c. Secretary Southern Nigeria.* Quoted in Slattery and Stelck, Vol. 8, 208.

77 The federal government's land-claims policy distinguishes claims based upon continuing Aboriginal title ("comprehensive") from those arising under the terms of a treaty or breach of statutory obligation ("specific").

78 Indian Act 1927, s. 141. *Indian Acts and Amendments, 1868–1975: An Indexed Collection,* ed. Sharon H. Venne (Saskatoon: University of Saskatchewan, Native Law Centre, 1981).

79 Canadian Bill of Rights 1960, s.1., Canada, *Revised Statutes of Canada, 1985,* Appendix 4.

80 The extension of federal voting rights to Canadian Aboriginal peoples in 1960 may be compared to the dates for New Zealand Maoris (1867), United States Indians (1924), Greenlanders (1953), and Australian Aboriginals (1962). In the Northwest Territories, the first territorial elections were held in the Mackenzie Valley in 1951 and included Aboriginal persons as eligible voters. Aboriginal people in Yukon first exercised the right to vote in the 1961 territorial election. Aboriginal people were never excluded from the right to vote in Nova Scotia or Newfoundland.

81 *R.v.Drybones,* Slattery and Stelck, Vol. 6, 255–92. This case originated in Yellowknife, Northwest Territories.

82 Harry B. Hawthorn, ed. *A Survey of the Contemporary Indians of Canada: Economic, Political, Educational Needs and Policies,* Vol. 1 (Ottawa: Indian Affairs Branch, 1966–67), 13.

83 See the 1967 address to the Canadian Bar Association, "A Constitutional Declaration of Rights," in which Trudeau describes a guarantee "against discrimination based on race, religion, sex, ethnic or national origin" as "basic for any society of free men." *Federalism and the French Canadians* (Toronto, Macmillan, 1968), 55.

84 Pierre Elliot Trudeau, "Remarks on Aboriginal and Treaty Rights." Excerpts from a speech given 8 August 1969 in Vancouver, British Columbia. *Native Rights in Canada,* ed. Peter A. Cumming and Neil H. Mickenberg (Toronto: Indian-Eskimo Association of Canada in association with General Publishing, 1972), Appendix 6, 331.

85 Canada. *Statement of the Government of Canada on Indian Policy* (Ottawa: Department of Indian Affairs and Northern Development, 1969), 11. In contrast to the Canadian government's view that Aboriginal land claims were so vague as to be incapable of remedy, the American government placed a freeze on all federal land transfers to the State of Alaska until Congress acted on Aboriginal land claims in the state. The Alaska Native Claims Settlement Act was signed into law in 1971. See Berger, *Village Journey,* 87–88; Chance, *The Iñupiat and Arctic Alaska,* 150–66.

86 On the Nisga'a (Nishga) claim see Thomas R. Berger, "The Nishga Indians and Aboriginal Rights," *Fragile Freedoms: Human Rights and Dissent in Canada* (Toronto and Vancouver: Clarke, Irwin, 1981), 219–54. See also *Calder v. Attorney-General of British Columbia*, Slattery and Stelck, Vol. 7, 91–173. The Nisga'a signed a land claims agreement with the governments of Canada and British Columbia in 1999.

87 On James Bay, see Richardson; also *Gros-Louis v. Société de Développement de la Baie James et al.* and appeals, Slattery and Stelck, Vol. 8, 188–415. The Grand Council of the Crees (of Quebec) and the Northern Quebec Inuit Association signed Canada's first modern land claims agreement with the governments of Canada and Quebec in 1975.

88 Fumoleau; *Re Paulette et al.* and *Registrar of Land Titles, Re Paulette et al.* and *Registrar of Land Titles (No. 2)*, and appeals, Slattery and Stelck, Vol. 9, 288–415.

89 George Manuel and Michael Posluns, *The Fourth World: An Indian Reality* (Don Mills: Collier Macmillan Canada, 1974), 225.

90 The agreement provides for twenty parcels of reserve land around Fort Smith and in Wood Buffalo National Park.

91 Michelle Genest and Dianne Homan, eds., *Urban Coyote: A Yukon Anthology* (Whitehorse: Lost Moose, 2001).

92 Genest and Homan. Preface, np.

93 Stephen Vail and Graeme Clinton, *May 2001 Nunavut Economic Outlook* (Ottawa: Conference Board of Canada, 2002), 40.

8 Dressed to Thrill

Costume, Body, and Dress in Canadian Performative Art

Jayne Wark

THE HISTORY OF PERFORMANCE ART has become the focus of a considerable number of recent studies, after a long period of time when this practice was relatively marginalized in the literature on twentieth-century art. While these studies have made important contributions to our understanding of the development and role of performance art within this period, there continue to be areas of neglect. Several of these studies have addressed how the body functions in performance as a form of artistic language that "speaks" about ideas or experiences, not by embodying them in objects, as art has traditionally done, but by communicating them to audiences directly or by means of documentation of the event or action.[1] Other studies have considered how performance can undermine or provide alternatives to art's traditional prioritizing of static forms like painting and sculpture by emphasizing "liveness" or by setting up relationships between a performance activity and the objects or quasi-objects it uses or produces as the residual trace of an ephemeral event.[2]

These broad areas of study do encompass the two major trajectories performance art has followed in the period since the Second World War, especially since the 1970s when it became recognized as an art form in its own right. Two areas that have not been adequately addressed, however, include the role of costume and dress in performance, either as adornment of the body or as performative prop, and the particular characteristics of performance art that have emerged within the practice of Canadian artists.[3] My objective here is to begin to fill in these gaps by considering how costume

175

and dress have been used by some recent Canadian performance artists to enhance the body and its social meanings in order to enact critical investigations into the relationship between identity formation and the dominant socio-cultural norms.

These kinds of investigation can be traced not only to the psychologically inflected and often sado-masochist work of 1970s performance artists like Vito Acconci and Chris Burden but even more to the embrace of performance by women artists as they became politicized by feminism during that decade. For these feminist artists, the possibility of placing their bodies at the centre of their work held enormous potential as a way of becoming agents of their own representations in a politically conscious way for the first time in history. In so doing, these women artists were able to explore the gendered problematics that feminists were then investigating by posing questions about identity and subjectivity, embodiment and representation, and role-playing and authorial agency. Consequently, the interrogation of subjectivities, particularized not only by gender, but also by race, class, and sexual orientation, became part of a broad phenomenon in performance art as it developed from the 1970s into the present.

This interrogation coincided with the articulation of poststructural theories, most notably those of Judith Butler, that have converged to place the notion of "performativity" literally at centre stage.[4] The key point of Butler's theory is that there is no essence to identity or subjectivity, nor is there any inherent or natural correlation between sex and gender. Rather, we "perform" our subjectivities by means of stylized and repeated acts of speech and gesture that create the illusion of an abiding (gendered) self, an illusion that she describes as a form of "regulatory fiction" or "essence fabrication."[5] The radical proposition of Butler's theory is that, if identity is thus created through a process of reiterated performative acts, then it is also possible for performativity to be enacted in a countervailing way as "the discursive basis for an opposition" to imposed cultural norms.[6]

Although Butler herself distinguishes performativity from performance as a cultural form (for example, in theatre or art), this theoretical discourse has provided an important critical basis for interpreting contemporary performance art. Butler's distinction is based on her premise that performance constitutes a "bounded act" predicated on the conscious application of the performer's "will" or "choice" as a humanist subject, while performativity "consists in a reiteration of norms which precede, constrain, and exceed the performer."[7] Other theorists argue, however, that Butler oversimplifies the complexity of performance. Geraldine Harris, for example, has proposed that the performer who activates such will or choice in the bounded act of performance can indeed establish a critical distance from performativity by making it evident how it relies upon the appearance and effect of being "real."[8] Elin Diamond has also questioned Butler's rejection of performance as cultural form from discussions of performativity by asking, "why should we restrict its iterative sites to theory and to the theorist's acts of seeing?" She goes on to argue that theatre (and performance art, we might add), is theory too and that performance is the site where the concealed or dissimulated conventions of performativity "might be investigated and reimagined."[9]

These arguments provide strong support for the relevancy of articulating critical readings of performance in relation to poststructural theories of performativity. Indeed, much of the current literature on performance art incorporates theories of performativity in a central way by addressing how the body in performance can instantiate an interrogation of normative identity formations. But if the body is indeed the site where the particularities of identity are visibly marked, and thus the site from which they can be investigated, it is also indisputable that the body in performance is rarely unadorned. More often than not, the body is accompanied by various cultural artifacts, from simple street clothes to theatrical costumes to elaborate constructions that function as hybrids between prop and art object. Even when the body is naked, the performance context establishes a public setting, and thus implies a flaunting of flesh that goes against the culture's social restrictions. As Joanne Entwistle has noted in her book, *The Fashioned Body*, all human cultures require the social body to be dressed in some way. Bodies that appear naked in public risk censure, scorn, or ridicule.[10] So when naked flesh is exposed in performance, we read this as a deliberately disturbing and potentially subversive disruption that is as heavily coded as are the strictures of social dress. In performance that uses costume or dress, these codes are conveyed through the sartorial adornment of the body by means of which identity is negotiated or "performed" in the social sphere. As Kaja Silverman writes, "The male subject, like the female subject, has no visual status apart from dress and/or adornment.... Clothing and other kinds of ornamentation make the human body culturally visible ... clothing draws the body so that it can be culturally seen, and articulates it as a meaningful form."[11]

Because the literature on performance art has largely ignored the role of costume and dress, or treated it at best as accessory, the implications of Silverman's observation as it might pertain to performance art remain unexplored. As Silverman notes, it is not the body alone but rather its articulation by way of clothing and dress that brings about the interaction between the individual and the social. For those artists who use performance as a strategy for exposing or resisting the operations of normative "performativity," in Butler's sense of the word, the artifacts of costume and dress can be seen to effect a clash of meanings that can reveal the naturalizing imperatives and ideological constructs of sexual and social hierarchy. This strategy can be compared to Bertolt Brecht's well-known theatre technique of *Verfremdung* (alienation or estrangement). This technique was based on the principle that, in order for audiences to become critically and politically aware, they had to have their familiar understandings and expectations overturned through a process of estrangement that would dialectically bring about a bewildered insight into their own state of social alienation.[12] Brecht's purpose was to subvert the realist or naturalist styles of bourgeois theatre, where ideology is kept hidden, so as to make ideology visible and thus engage audiences in an active and self-aware process of ideology critique. Although Brecht's theory of alienation was created for theatre in the 1920s and 1930s, it has been widely incorporated into feminist art, film, and theatre theory and practice since the 1970s as a strategy for disrupting and revealing the ideological operations at work with the normative codes of representation and spectatorship.[13]

This strategy of alienation, which aims to reveal the gap between what is presented as naturally given or "real" and the conventions that both produce and obscure it, is pervasively evident in the work of the Canadian performance artists under consideration here. While this strategy for making ideology visible is by no means unique to these artists, what I would argue is distinctive and characteristic about their work is its sustained engagement with popular culture, its use of camp and drag to assert the visibility of queer and marginalized identities, and its use of parody and other forms of humour both as a means of rebellious effrontery and as empowering transformation. As I will argue further, the impetus for the use of such strategies by Canadian artists largely came from their acute critical awareness, which resulted from the proximity of American popular culture as a powerfully coercive model of normative ideology.

Performance art flourished in Canada, as elsewhere, during the 1970s, a decade that marked a major turning point in history. The ideals of civil society seemed everywhere in jeopardy as terrorists inflicted violence from Ireland to Iran to Quebec, and the American president, Richard Nixon, was run out of office under a humiliating cloud of lies and deceit. As performance art historian Kristine Stiles has noted, it was a time of such trauma, bitterness, and anger that, by the end of the seventies, "its immaterial internal pain was perfectly and self-destructively embodied in the material external sign of safety pins stuck through the flesh of young punks."[14]

Yet, apart from the FLQ crisis in Quebec, which must not be minimized, Canada seemed insulated from these world disasters. Ebullient from its triumphant premier on the world stage at Expo 67, and able to lay claim both to Marshall McLuhan as an internationally recognized guru of the new media culture, and to Pierre Elliot Trudeau as the sexy, charismatic political leader who cranked open the faucet for arts funding, Canada seemed poised to make its mark. Canadian artists were ideally situated to take advantage of new international currents in the art world. They had no indigenous avant-garde, and they immediately grasped the possibility of transcending regional isolation by linking up to what Fluxus artist Robert Filliou called "the eternal network."[15] This, along with sudden access to government funding for equipment and space for artist-run centres, created an atmosphere that was nothing short of euphoric. Ground zero for this euphoria was the establishment of the Intermedia Society in Vancouver in 1967. Dedicated to the creative fusion of disciplines and to an openness towards popular culture, the Intermedia Society held annual multimedia extravaganzas at the Vancouver Art Gallery and sponsored workshops by American dancers Deborah Hay, Yvonne Rainer, and Steve Paxton in 1968 and 1969.

These workshops introduced Vancouver artists to the improvisational, task-oriented approach to dance then current in San Francisco and New York, which aimed to take dance down from its pedestal and merge it with the rhythm and flow of ordinary life. Gathie Falk, for example, who was inspired both by Hay's dance methods and Allan Kaprow's perform-ance mode known as "Happenings," began to incorporate unexpected combinations of props, costumes, and songs in performances such as *Red Angel* (1971).[16] Behind a tableau of five red turntables, each mounted with a red parrot and playing a round from the song "Row, Row, Row Your Boat," Falk posed in a white satin dress with feathered wings. During the performance, the dress was removed, revealing a grey satin dress under-neath, and then passed through a wringer washer by an assistant. The performance concluded with Falk singing the tune's final round, "Life is but a dream," a phrase that evokes the bizarre and Surrealist-like incongruity typical of her work.

The theatricality and allusions to popular culture in Falk's *Red Angel* ran somewhat against the grain of critical discourse around avant-garde per-formance at the time. Kaprow, for example, embraced the realm of "every-day life" in the Happenings, but largely excluded specific references to popular culture itself.[17] The reappearance of an interest in theatrically and/or popular culture in the activities of another group of young Vancou-ver artists at this time was indicative, however, of an emerging character-istic of Vancouver performance. These artists, who included Glenn Lewis, Robert Fones, Gary Lee-Nova, Michael Morris, Vincent Trasov, Eric Met-calfe, and Kate Craig, were interested in Dada absurdity, puns, and pranks, and had a Warholian fascination with mass-culture imagery, especially its fetish and ritual characteristics.[18] In emulation of Marcel Duchamp's alter-ego, Rrose Sélavy, each member of the group invented a persona and name that referred either to the art world or mass culture: Marcel Dot (Morris), Art Rat (Lee-Nova), Dr. and Lady Brute (Metcalfe and Craig), Candy Man (Fones), and Mr. Peanut (Trasov).

The group was strongly oriented to performative activities, and several of their fictive identities were outfitted with costumes and props. Dr. Brute, for instance, who was derived from the erotic and kitschy cartoons Metcalfe drew as a student, wore a tuxedo, and his symbol, the leopard spot, was applied to all his creations, including the kazoo-saxaphone he played during his accomplished jazz performances.[19] Dr. Brute and the aliases of other group members functioned as a blank slate for personal mythology and provided an armature allowing them to explore alternative lifestyles and art forms, especially by means of appropriating motifs from popular culture.

Lady Brute, who was invented by Metcalfe's partner at the time, Kate Craig, also took the leopard spot as her defining symbol. Craig collected a vast inventory of leopard paraphernalia, mainly articles of women's clothing that Lady Brute wore in her appearances around Vancouver. The Brutes' fascination with the leopard pattern lay in its associations with camouflage, sexuality, and kitsch, which converged with their interests in glamour, power, and the banality of mass culture.[20] Leopard skin, however, is particularly associated with female sexuality, suggesting wildness, exoticism, and feline sensuality. As such, it has acquired a favoured place in the repertoire of fetishism. Following upon Richard von Krafft-Ebing's first modern psychological identification of fetishism as an irrational sexual overvaluation, Freud later pathologized it as symptomatic of male castration anxiety, while Lacan added that, among women, it is found only in lesbians.[21] These views have been challenged in recent years by feminist and queer theory that aims to unsettle the strict sexual coding and ideological assumptions about subjectivity and gender identity, as well as by the fashion industry, which has increasingly exploited the wardrobe of the fetish subculture since the 1960s.[22]

Craig's own view of Lady Brute and her fetishistic trappings was ambivalent. Unlike Metcalfe's view of Dr. Brute, Craig saw Lady Brute as a mask to be put on at will rather than a personification of self: "I never felt I *was* Lady Brute. One of the wonderful things about Lady Brute was that there was a stand-in at every corner. If I wore the leopard skin, it was only to become a part of this incredible culture of women who adopted that costume.... It was a way of exaggerating something that already existed in the culture."[23] While the leopard gear thus served both Craig and Metcalfe as a device to publicly disrupt middle-class propriety and to problematize the relation between self and image, Grant Arnold has noted that it was particularly significant for Craig as a way "to identify with a specifically female culture for whom images of glamour operate simultaneously as a form of social bondage and a potential source of power."[24] However, Craig also became aware that Lady Brute had been too invested in the fantasies of her male peers, and accordingly, she retired Lady Brute in a 1975 videotaped performance at Western Front called *Skins: Lady Brute Presents Her Leopard Skin Wardrobe.*

To distance herself from Lady Brute, Craig then created *The Pink Poem*, consisting of a collection of pink garments in which she "performed" in the course of everyday life. Pink was definitely not a colour with feminist cachet in the late 1970s, but given that her male colleagues "found it abhorrent," it could also be strategically disarming.[25] Craig explained, "I read that psychiatric and penal institutions often painted their walls pink because it was believed this gentle colour calmed people. In those days we women were trying to achieve certain goals in institutions dominated by men. My strategy was to wear pink clothing in order to calm them while making demands that may have caused them anxiety."[26]

The Pink Poem culminated in Craig's 1980 video called *Straight Jacket*, which featured a close-up view of a writhing body trussed in a pink satin straightjacket while a female voice sings plaintively about torture and duress. *Straight Jacket* came at the end of a two-year period in which Craig had produced strongly feminist videos, including *Delicate Issue* (1979), which stands as one of the most powerful confrontations in the history of feminist art between the body and the technological, voyeuristic gaze of the camera.[27]

Elsewhere in Canada, performance was entering one of its most active periods. In Quebec, where the Quiet Revolution had coalesced into a vigorous nationalism in the 1970s, performance was dominated by three main trajectories: the highly verbal approach of people like Jean Tourangeau and Richard Martel; the body and/or spatial manipulations of Monty Cantsin or Alain-Martin Richard; and the innovations in dance that traced their lineage from Françoise Sullivan through Tangente Dance in Montreal to people like Marie Chouinard, who has used costume in dance to stunning effect.[28] Chouinard's ability to blur the distinctions between dance and performance art is unique in Canada. She achieved notoriety for her "haiku" solo in 1980 when she urinated in a pail at the Art Gallery of Ontario, but it is her combination of rigorous physical "architecture," disdain for gendered conventions of dance, and animated use of costume, props, and embodied sound (breathing, screaming, erotic moaning) that have resonated within the art community.[29] In her piece s.t.a.b. (*Space, Time and Beyond*), created in 1986, Chouinard slithers and stalks the stage like a futuristic, androgynous lizard brandishing a six-foot, whip-like proboscis from her helmeted head. In *L'Après-midi d'un faune* (1987), a paean to Vaslav Nijinsky's famous dance for the Ballets Russes, Chouinard wears a costume with cloven hoofs and massages a rigid phallus while generating the score by means of a synthesizer connected to controls on her body. Such works not only strip away the romanticism and sentimentalism that lingers in much contemporary dance, but also treat the body as an ambiguous, denaturalized entity capable of radical performative transformation.

In English Canada, a vibrant performance scene emerged in Toronto in the late 1970s. This coincided with the arrival of punk, whose aggressive subcultural stylizations and anarchistic politics merged seamlessly with the burgeoning art scene to create the kind of collaborative tribalism seen earlier in Vancouver. One of the main ingredients of this heady brew was the presence of General Idea, a group whose members were A.A. Bronson, Felix Partz, and Jorge Zontal. Since the early 1970s, General Idea had used performance, most famously in their *Miss General Idea Pageants*, to create an art dedicated, with tongue in cheek, to glamour and style and inflected by their self-consciously queer identities. In a 1975 issue of their magazine, *File*, they declared, "We wanted to be famous, glamorous and rich. That is to say we wanted to be artists and we knew that if we were famous and glamorous we could say we were artists and we would be."[30] General Idea's acute awareness of the need to intervene in a culture dominated by media and images helped create an ironic, stylized, and highly parodic milieu in which fashion, art, cabaret theatre, and music merged not only in performance per se but also in the performativity of lifestyles, enhanced in their case by a self-fashioning explicitly aimed at a critique of assumptions about both art and popular culture. One example of this parodic approach was David Buchan's invention of the sleazy lounge-lizard, Lamonte Del Monte, who performed at the 1978 Tele-Performance event in Toronto singing popular songs accompanied by a series of costume changes including gold lamé vest and boots, camouflage gear, and a straightjacket with black vinyl pants cinched with rope at the crotch and ankles.[31] Buchan's louche antics and eroticized costumes can clearly be read as an assertion of the explicitly queer associations of camp as it has been reclaimed as a politicized practice by theorists such as Moe Meyer and others.[32]

At the same event, the Clichettes, a lip-synch group formed by Johanna Householder, Janice Hladki, and Louise Garfield (with Elizabeth Chitty), wore kitsch-punk trappings as they belted out the lyrics of Leslie Gore's song "You Don't Own Me" in a full-frontal feminist assault. On one level, these performances were a send-up of the trashiest aspects of what General Idea's A.A. Bronson called the "aggressive foreplay" of American popular culture.[33] On another, they were an impertinent affront to the way cultural

FIGURE 1 Marie Chouinard, *S.T.A.B.* (*Space, Time and Beyond*), 1986. Photography by Louise Oligny (courtesy Compagnie Marie Chouinard).

forms continued to be managed primarily by men, as well as being a gambit in the censorship wars that had just landed Toronto's *Body Politic* magazine in a court battle fighting a charge of obscenity.[34]

At the time, however, there was a tendency on the part of art critics and writers to dismiss the entertainment-oriented approach of such Toronto performance art as frivolous, decadent, and pandering to a capitalist paradigm.[35] This view shared certain premises with a cultural critique articulated in the late 1970s by Americans such as James Hougan and Christopher Lasch, who diagnosed a degeneration of culture whereby social alienation had led to self-absorption and a posture of cynical detachment.[36] Lasch argued that the use of parody in popular culture was especially indicative of this cynicism: "Many forms of popular art appeal to this sense of knowingness and thereby reinforce it. They parody familiar roles and themes, inviting the audience to consider itself superior to its surroundings."[37] A year later, Lasch's condemnation of parody was extended by Bruce Barber to this whole genre of Canadian performance that drew upon forms of popular culture: "Aping the Hollywood star system or Las Vegas night club acts is simply that—aping. Stylish and sophisticated it may be but criticism it is not." Parody, he argued, is simply inadequate as a mode of critique, "especially if we ever find out what our post-modern priorities should be."[38]

Paradoxically, however, parody was soon redefined as a specifically postmodern mode of criticism in Linda Hutcheon's 1985 book, *A Theory of Parody*. Hutcheon notes that parody has traditionally been denigrated because it is derivative in nature and depends upon already existing forms to fulfill itself. By contrast, however, she argues that parody can indeed be critically effective because it undermines the Romantic fallacy of originality, thus forcing "a reassessment of the process of textual production." By inserting itself into existing cultural texts and forms, parody exposes the power relationships between those social agents who possess the "original" and the others who possesses the parodic alternative.[39] In retrospective light of these observations, we can see more clearly how Canadian performance around 1980 was engaging precisely those techniques of parody described by Hutcheon as a way to undermine gender binarisms and normative sexual categories. From this perspective, such work can clearly be aligned not only with feminist rereadings of Brechtian theory, but also with Butler's poststructural theory of performativity as a way to "make trouble" for such ideologies, especially the fallacy of gender as an abiding or ontological essence of one's sex.

If we consider the impact of such theories on cultural thinking over the past two decades, and recall the extent to which fashion during this same period has apparently abandoned strict sex/gender codes, we might suppose that the liberatory dismantling of male/female binaries is well underway. In fact, however, this seems not to be the case. The preoccupation with gender binaries in dress is considered by fashion historians to be a modern phenomenon in Western culture, dating roughly from between 1200 and 1400. Prior to that time, clothing divided people along lines of social rank rather than gender. Since then, clothing has increasingly served to express a relationship between the individualized—and thus sexualized—body and the conventions of the social body.[40] Indeed, the conventions of gender remain central to modern dress and to making sense of it. As Entwistle notes, in spite of certain freedoms, "contemporary society remains preoccupied with sexual difference ... and fashion continues to play on gender, even while it periodically deconstructs it." She even goes so far as to say, "one might argue that gender is more significant today than it used to be."[41]

This knot of contradictions has become a focus for a number of performance artists since 1980 who have used costume and dress to scrutinize the relationship between embodiment, sartorial style, and identity. Foremost in this genre is a trilogy of works by Tanya Mars that speculate on the relation between women and power: *Pure Virtue* (1984), *Pure Sin* (1986), and *Pure Nonsense* (1987).[42] In each, Mars plays a different archetype of female political, sexual, and creative power while performing in a burlesque style that veers from mock seriousness to ribald but cutting vulgarity. Costume is crucial in these performances. In *Pure Virtue*, Mars plays Elizabeth I, the Virgin Queen whose accession to the British throne in 1558 necessitated wearing her chastity like a badge to set her apart from other women. By her clothes, however, Elizabeth signalled her acquiescence to conventions of femininity at a time when differentiation of the sexes by dress had become well established.[43] Throughout Mars's exploration of the queen's relation to power, her sumptuous dress is the primary signifier. Its splendour confirms the power of wealth and rank, and sexual power too. The aging queen dispenses advice on the merits of chastity, but also lifts her voluminous skirt to demonstrate how its loss may be concealed, a messy operation involving leeches and a raw chicken. Such deceptions, we might conclude, are the price to be paid for power.

Costume is similarly central in *Pure Sin*, in which Mars takes on the role of Mae West, the mouthy Hollywood goddess whose bawdy sexual power and defiant refusal to submit to conventions of demure femininity were legendary. In flamboyant dress and blonde bouffant wig, Mars evokes West's excessive and artificial femininity, which not only epitomized female masquerade but also legitimized camp drag for the popular culture.[44] Mars as West is the bodacious sex queen, and, sheathed in a column of green satin and tulle, she is the ultimate phallic woman. In *Pure Nonsense*, the dress

FIGURE 2 Tanya Mars, *Pure Sin*, 1986. Photograph by David Hlynsky (courtesy of the artist).

perhaps does not matter so much as what is under it. Here Mars plays Alice in Wonderland, who awakens from a dreamy idyll to be abruptly informed by Freud that she has lost her penis. Aghast, Alice sets off to find it, querying the inhabitants of Wonderland, who vex her with absurd answers to the riddle, "Why does a Venus not have a penis?" Refusing to submit to their Oedipal fantasies of sexual difference, however, Alice is mightily relieved when in the end she lifts her crinolines to discover an impressive rubber penis, a comic gesture that literally deflates the whole apparatus of phallocratic mastery and subordination.

Tanya Mars's parodic mockery reminds us of Freud's observation that "humour is not resigned; it is rebellious." Moreover, he said, the ability to be the object of one's own humour is empowering because it is the sign of "the victorious assertion of the ego's invulnerability."[45] This rebelliousness is also evident in the work of Saskatoon artist Lori Blondeau, who uses parody strategically to define a positive identity in the midst of a hostile social environment.[46] Blondeau's work has centred on the clash between her identity as a Native woman and the ideals of white femininity that dominate our culture. She has made satirical self-portraits as the cover girl of a mock magazine called *Cosmosquaw* and has posed with a surfboard, like a displaced *Baywatch* babe, on the bank of a frozen Saskachewan river wearing nothing but a fur bikini and mukluks. Like Mars, Blondeau shows that humour can indeed repudiate reality and thus enable the humourist to resist her or his own subjection. It is, finally, a way to to "make trouble" for the status quo of hegemonic power structures.

Winnipeg-based performance artists Shawna Dempsey and Lorri Millan have been making similar trouble for over a decade now. As emphatically "out" lesbians, their work confronts sexism, homophobia, and the social negotiations of identity. They use costume and dress as metaphor, symbol, or dramatic prop for narrative skits and vaudevillian gags that are wickedly parodic inversions of what is "normal," legitimate, and officially sanctioned. Nothing is sacrosanct in their comedic repertoire, including feminism's own conflicted ideals. In *Mary Medusa* (1991–93), Dempsey appears on stage as a floating head with a halo of rainbow dreadlocks, demanding to know, "Is a woman without a body still a woman? Without a body, does a woman in fact exist?"[47] After dropping a black robe to reveal a business suit, she expounds ironically upon her achievements as a self-actualized, modern superwoman before stripping down to her control-top pantyhose and confessing, "A woman out of control is a frightening thing, lusting after sex once a week, food, and chocolate cake." "Lots of chocolate cake," she coos, dropping to the floor and squeezing one between her thighs, moaning audibly.[48]

As the *Arborite Housewife* (1994), Dempsey wears a pink dress made from one of the new "wonder" materials that furnished the postwar suburban boom.[49] Reciting a parable about marriage being like driving the family car, she warns of the dangers that ensue if family members deviate from their proscribed roles; yet there is little danger of us taking her morality tale seriously, for it is as rigid and artificial as her dress. In *Growing Up Suite 1* (1996), however, Dempsey confides that such rigid and artificial constructions could also be the object of queer desire. As an adolescent in the late sixties, she did not know what erotica or porn were, but she did know what turned her on: the ladies in the lingerie pages of Eaton's catalogue wearing "industrial-strength underwear concealing unimaginable body parts so powerful they needed architecture to keep them in place." As always for Dempsey and Millan, humour cuts like a knife, serving both as a means to expose the cultural contradictions and confinements that oppress them, and as a force for a liberatory reimagining of possibilities.

In this study, I have considered how costume and dress have been used to generate meanings within the specific historical context of Canadian performance. What emerges as distinctive here is the pervasive use of humour and references to popular culture. Canadian performance came of age at a time when the assumptions of power and privilege accorded to normative identities were everywhere being called into question. By calling their own identities into question by way of humourous interventions into popular culture, these artists flaunted themselves with subversive theatricality. Their colonization of popular culture enabled them to avail themselves of its pleasures and artifice, and to enact a critical mimesis of its entertainment strategies so as to expose and politicize those power relations that construct the body as the site where difference and deviance are inscribed. Yet, as I have argued, it is not just the body itself that is at issue here, but rather the fashioning of the body/self through manipulations of costume, dress, and sartorial style. These performative manifestations not only rely upon modes of popular entertainment, but also actively assault those modes by way of the excesses of queer camp, the intertextual meanings of parody, the exaggerations of satire, and the defiance of self-mocking humour.

It is important to note, however, that humour is not inherently oppositional any more than the relation between art and popular culture is unproblematic. It is a relationship that embraces the indeterminacy and flow between categories, but what is always at risk is the ability of art to retain its critical edge. In the era of advanced capitalism, popular culture is a euphemism for the culture industry, and that industry is in the service of a bourgeoisie, or middle class, whose genius for survival lies in detachment and the absorption of subversive elements within the culture. Defiant

FIGURE 3 Lorri Millan and Shawna Dempsey, *Growing Up Suite 1*, 1996. Photograph by Don Lee, The Banff Centre (courtesy of the artists).

practices like queer camp and gender parody can expose the ideology that the dominant and official culture would like to keep hidden, but they can just as easily be used for banal or exploitative ends. When humour is used merely to make political criticism more palatable, which involves emphasizing form over content, then it has moved into the realm of detached aestheticism, which is, says Chuck Kleinhans, "essentially a training program for alienation" rather than a strategic use of alienation to bring about critical awareness.[50] That defensive and ultimately cynical tactic is not, however, what is at work in the performances of the artists discussed in this essay. Instead, they use humour to lure audiences in, either to elicit identification with their socially marginalized subject positions or to disarm potentially hostile audiences in order to take them by surprise with unruly acts and defiant words. Using popular forms of humour and entertainment allows these artists to speak through the language of the common culture in order to gain critical purchase on that culture. But at the same time, in order for such art to maintain its criticality, it must be deftly poised on the razor's edge between the seductive appeal and subversive potential of popular culture. And it is in that subtle interstice where the artists considered here have enacted their critical forms of play through the mediating effects of costume and dress. By thus working from within the realm of popular culture and utilizing its modes with critical self-consciousness, they have been able to effect a performative revisioning of alternatives to the repressive, coercive ideologies that those modes seek to normalize and stabilize.

Notes

1 See Amelia Jones, *Body Art: Performing the Subject* (Minneapolis: University of Minnesota Press, 1998); Kathy O'Dell, *Contract with the Skin: Masochism, Performance Art and the 1970s* (Minneapolis: University of Minnesota Press, 1998); Rebecca Schneider, *The Explicit Body in Performance* (London and New York: Routledge, 1997); and Amelia Jones and Andrew Stephenson, *Performing the Body/Performing the Text* (New York: Routledge, 1999).

2 See Paul Schimmel, ed., *Out of Actions: Between Performance and the Object, 1949–1979* (Los Angeles: Museum of Contemporary Art, 1998); Philip Auslander, *Liveness: Performance in a Mediatized Culture* (New York: Routledge, 1999).

3 The role of clothing and dress in relation to art has been explored in Nina Felshin, *Empty Dress: Clothing as Surrogate in Recent Art* (New York: New York Independent Curators, 1993), but this did not entail a specific consideration of performance art. Ginger Gregg Duggan has edited *Fashion and Performance*, a special issue of *Fashion Theory* 5.3 (2001), but the focus was on how performance has influenced fashion rather than on the role of fashion or dress in performance art. The only study I have found to address this topic directly is the very brief essay by Moira Roth, "Character, Costume and Theater in Early California Performance," in *Living Art Vancouver*, ed. Alvin Balkind and R.A. Gledhill (Vancouver: Western Front, Pumps, Video Inn, 1979), 89–91. The key publications on Canadian performance include A.A. Bronson and Peggy Gale, *Perfor-*

mance by Artists (Toronto: Art Metropole, 1979); Alain-Martin Richard and Clive Robertson, ed., *Performance au/in Canada, 1970-1990* (Quebec: Éditions Intervention; Toronto: Coach House Press, 1991); Brice Canyon, ed., *Live at the End of the Century: Aspects of Performance Art in Vancouver* (Vancouver: Visible Art Society and Grunt Gallery, 2000); and Tanya Mars and Johanna Householder, ed., *Caught in the Act: Canadian Women in Performance* (Toronto: YYZ Books 2004). These are all anthologies of short essays; a book-length historical study of Canadian performance has yet to be written.

4 For the concept of performativity as the basis of identity formation, see especially Judith Butler, *Gender Trouble: Feminism and the Subversion of Identity* (New York: Routledge, 1990) and *Bodies that Matter: On the Discursive Limits of "Sex"* (New York: Routledge, 1993). For a discussion of how the linguistic theory of "performative" speech acts articulated by J.L. Austin in *How to Do Things with Words* (Cambridge, MA: Harvard University Press, 1962) can be understood analogously in performance acts that open up unstable readings and thus bring about the possibility of creating new meanings and realities, see Peggy Phelan, "Reciting the Citation of Others; or, A Second Introduction," *Acting Out: Feminist Performances*, ed. Lynda Hart and Peggy Phelan (Ann Arbor: University of Michigan Press, 1994), 13-31.

5 Judith Butler, "Performative Acts and Gender Constitution: An Essay in Phenomenology and Feminist Theory," *Writing on the Body: Female Embodiment and Feminist Theory*, ed. Katie Conboy, Nadia Medina, and Sarah Stanbury (New York: Columbia University Press, 1997), 412.

6 Butler, *Bodies That Matter*, 232.

7 Butler, *Gender Trouble*, 25.

8 Geraldine Harris, *Staging Femininities: Performance and Performativity* (Manchester: Manchester University Press, 1999), 174-75.

9 Elin Diamond, *Unmaking Mimesis: Essays on Feminism and Theatre* (New York: Routledge, 1997), 47.

10 Joanne Entwistle, *The Fashioned Body: Fashion, Dress and Modern Social Theory* (Cambridge: Polity, 2000), 6-7.

11 Kaja Silverman, "Fragments of a Fashionable Discourse," *Studies in Entertainment: Critical Approaches to Mass Culture*, ed. Tania Modelski (Bloomington: Indiana University Press, 1986), 145.

12 For a summary of this principle in Brechtian theatre theory, see Reinhold Grimm, "Alienation in Context: On the Theory and Practice of Brechtian Theatre," *A Bertolt Brecht Reference Companion*, ed. Siegfried Mews (Westport, CT: Greenwood, 1997), 35-46.

13 See, for example, Laura Mulvey, "Visual Pleasure and Narrative Cinema," *Visual and Other Pleasures* (Bloomington: Indiana University Press, 1989), 14-26; Griselda Pollock, "Screening the Seventies—A Brechtian Perspective," *Vision and Difference: Femininity, Feminism and the Histories of Art* (New York: Routledge, 1988), 155-99; and Elin Diamond, "Brechtian Theory/Feminist Theory: Toward a Gestic Feminist Criticism," *A Sourcebook of Feminist Theatre and Performance: On and Beyond the Stage*, ed. Carol Martin (New York: Routledge, 1996), 120-35.

14 Kristine Stiles, "Uncorrupted Joy: International Art Actions," Schimmel, 241.

15 In 1965, Robert Filliou, along with Fluxus artist George Brecht, formed the idea of an "eternal network" as a way of linking artists to one another and to other social and ecological networks. For the impact of Filliou's ideas on Vancouver artists, see Sharla Sava, "As If the Oceans Were Lemonade: The Performative Vision of Robert Filliou and the Western Front," (MA thesis, University of British Columbia, 1996).

16 The premise for Kaprow's Happenings was derived from his understanding of Jackson Pollock's drip paintings as having signalled the deathblow to painting and left artists at

the point where they had to become preoccupied by the spaces and objects of everyday life. In his article, "The Legacy of Jackson Pollock," Kaprow proposed that "Objects of every sort are materials for the new art: paint, chairs, food, electric and neon lights, smoke, water, old socks, a dog, movies, [and] a thousand other things." Allan Kaprow, "The Legacy of Jackson Pollock," *Art News* 57.6 (1958): 56–57. Significantly, in this first articulation of a theory of performance in the post-war period, no mention is made of costume since the emphasis was decidedly on the ordinariness of "everyday life."

17 The antinomy between the authenticity of art and the artificiality of mass culture was clearly set out in Clement Greenberg's influential essay, "Avant-Garde and Kitsch," *Partisan Review* 6.5 (Fall 1939): 34–49. The dichotomy between the criticality of art and the passivity of the entertainment spectacle was further developed in Guy Debord's *La Société du Spectacle* (Paris: Buchet/Chastel, 1967). This opposition continued to shape critical discourse well into the 1970s.

18 Scott Watson, "Hand of the Spirit," *Hand of the Spirit: Documents of the Seventies from the Morris/Trasov Archive* (Vancouver: University of British Columbia Fine Arts Gallery, 1992), 9.

19 Scott Watson, "Return to Brutopia," *Return to Brutopia: Eric Metcalfe Works and Collaborations* (Vancouver: University of British Columbia Fine Arts Gallery, 1992), 14.

20 Watson, "Return to Brutopia," 19–20, and Grant Arnold, "Kate Craig: Skin," *Kate Craig: Skin*, ed. Grant Arnold (Vancouver: Vancouver Art Gallery, 1998), 5–6.

21 See Richard von Krafft-Ebing, *Psychopathia Sexualis with Especial Reference to the Antipathic Sexual Instinct: A Medico-Forensic Study*, trans. F.J. Rebman (1886; New York: Physicians and Surgeons Book Company, 1934), 218; Sigmund Freud, "Fetishism," trans. James Strachey, *On Sexuality*, ed. Angela Richards (Harmondsworth: Penguin, 1977), 351–57; and Jacques Lacan, "Guiding Remarks for a Congress on Feminine Sexuality," *Feminine Sexuality: Jacques Lacan and the école freudienne*, ed. Juliet Mitchell and Jacqueline Rose, trans. Jacqueline Rose (New York: Norton, 1982), 96.

22 See Marjorie Garber, *Vested Interests: Cross-Dressing and Cultural Anxiety* (New York: Routledge, 1992), 118–27; Valerie Steele, *Fetish: Fashion, Sex and Power* (New York and Oxford: Oxford University, 1996), 11–31; and Entwistle, *The Fashioned Body*, 191-207.

23 Kate Craig, quoted in Luke Rombout et al., *Vancouver: Art and Artists 1931–1983* (Vancouver: Vancouver Art Gallery, 1993), 262.

24 Arnold, 5.

25 Kate Craig, quoted in Arnold, 8.

26 Kate Craig, letter to author, 9 February 2001.

27 See Nicole Gingras, "The Movement of Things," in Arnold, 17–29; and Jayne Wark, "Kate Craig at Vancouver Art Gallery," *n.paradoxa* 2 (1998): 38–39.

28 See Alain-Martin Richard, "Québec, Activism and Performance: From the Acted-Manifesto to the Manoeuvre," Richard and Robertson, 41–47.

29 In 1982, for example, Chouinard was invited to Western Front, where she produced the video *Marie Chien Noir*.

30 General Idea, "Glamour," *File Megazine* 3.1 (1975): 21–22.

31 See Colin Campbell, "David Buchan: Lamonte Del Monte and the Fruit Cocktails," *Centerfold* 3.1 (1978): 29–32.

32 See Moe Meyer, "Introduction: Reclaiming the Discourse of Camp," *The Politics and Poetics of Camp*, ed. Moe Meyer (New York: Routledge, 1994), 1–22.

33 A.A. Bronson, "The Humiliation of the Bureaucrat: Artist-run Spaces as Museums by Artists," *From Sea to Shining Sea*, ed. A.A. Bronson et al. (Toronto: Power Plant, 1987), 164.

34 See Clive Robertson, "The Complete Clichettes," *Fuse* 9.4 (1986): 9–15. An account of *The Body Politic*'s various legal conflicts has been published online by one of its members, Rick Bébout; see "On the Origins of *The Body Politic*" at <http://www.rbebout.com/oldbeep/beepint.htm>.

35 This negative appraisal of General Idea and the performance genre they were associated with has begun to be reassessed. See Philip Monk, "Picturing the Toronto Art Community: The Queen Street Years," *C Magazine* 59 (1998), unpaginated insert to accompany Monk's exhibition by the same name at the Power Plant, Toronto. Monk acknowledges that the exhibition served, in part, to revise earlier dismissals of General Idea's "image manipulation" by himself and others, as, for example, in Dot Tuer's "The CEAC Was Banned in Canada," *C Magazine* 11 (1986): 22–37.

36 James Hougan, *Decadence: Radical Nostalgia, Narcissism and Decline in the Seventies* (New York: William Morrow, 1975), and Christopher Lasch, *The Culture of Narcissism* (New York: W.W. Norton, 1978).

37 Lasch, 95.

38 Bruce Barber, "Performance for Pleasure and Performance for Instruction," Balkind and Gledhill, *Living Art Vancouver* (Vancouver: Pulp Press, 1979), 78–81.

39 Linda Hutcheon, *A Theory of Parody: The Teachings of Twentieth-Century Art Forms* (New York: Methuen, 1985), 5.

40 Anne Hollander, *Sex and Suits* (New York: Alfred A. Knopf, 1994), 30–33.

41 Entwistle, 180.

42 For Mars's 1990 amalgamated performance of this trilogy, see Barbara Fischer, *Pure Hell* (Toronto: Power Plant, 1990).

43 Hollander, 45–48.

44 For the theory of female masquerade, see Mary Ann Doane, "Film and the Masquerade: Theorising the Female Spectator," *Screen* 23.3–4 (1982): 74–87, and "Masquerade Reconsidered: Some Thoughts on the Female Spectator," *Femmes Fatales: Feminism, Film Theory, Psychoanalysis* (New York: Routledge, 1991), 33–43.

45 Sigmund Freud, "Humour," trans. James Strachey, *Art and Literature*, ed. Albert Dickson (Harmondsworth: Penguin, 1985), 428–29.

46 See Lynne Bell and Janice Williamson, "High Tech Storyteller: A Conversation with Performance Artist Lori Blondeau," *Fuse* 24.4 (2001): 27–34.

47 All references to the texts of the Dempsey/Millan performances, including *Mary Medusa* (1991–93), *Arborite Housewife* (1994), and *Growing Up Suite 1* (1996), are taken from their video compilation, *A Live Decade: 1989–1999*, available from Finger in the Dyke Productions, Winnipeg.

48 See Pauline Greenhill, "Lesbian Mess(ages): Decoding Shawna Dempsey's Cake Squish at the Festival du Voyeur," *Atlantis* 23.1 (1998): 91–99.

49 Renee Baert, "Three Dresses, Tailored to the Times," *Material Matters: The Art and Culture of Contemporary Textiles*, ed. Ingrid Bachmann and Ruth Scheuing (Toronto: YYZ Books, 1998), 81.

50 Chuck Kleinhans, "Taking Out the Trash: Camp and the Politics of Parody," in Meyer, 197.

9 Figures of Otherness in Canadian Video

Joanne Lalonde
Translated by Janet Logan

IN THE HISTORY OF VIDEO ART, there is great interest in body representation. New technology in art production has created conditions conducive to exploring the complex nature of subjectivity and identity, and their various possibilities within a varied framework.[1] Discovering the self and confronting the world through the camera has been and still is a concern of young videomakers. The aesthetic practice of reifying the human body in video has rapidly become fertile ground for questioning traditional ways of representing the body. The significance of this phenomenon is understood also as a way of confronting the videographic double and thus impeding the body image's fluidity. The videotext can be an indispensable tool for elaborating a subject's identity; video mediation enables the artist's psychic self to apprehend the corporal self.

In the early years of video production, many artists used their own image as their subject matter; and at that time, many of them were also involved with performance and body art. Various strategies of self-representation such as personal storytelling, confessional video, presentation of daily tasks, and other variations on one's private life were all flourishing. In this general context, numerous Canadian video artists have worked with the issue of self-representation in relation to various figures of cultural and sexual otherness.

This text analyzes various practices that integrate the figure of the other as counterpart while exploring the self. I call this figure the "video alter ego." Through the division or splitting of the self, the alter ego becomes the strange other to whom one is linked. The terminology of this phrase is evidence then of two poles united in the same figure: a dual and often transient figure in various areas of an identity being constructed. Continuing in the tradition of artists' self-representation, forms of self-portraiture, and otherness, the ego personifies the various characters that the artist takes on, showing a desire for the other through many versatile images.

I will begin by looking at the work of Toronto videomaker Colin Campbell, whose work has repeatedly dealt with the subject of identity, especially sexual identity. Campbell was a pioneer artist in narrative video in Canada. Along with Lisa Steele, he was one of the first to explore forms of confessional video. These are narrative instances in the first-person singular, fictional autobiographies with tight framing, and close-ups or head-and-shoulder shots of the artist addressing the camera. Neutrality is shown in the camera work and in the unity of time and setting.

In many of Campbell's videos, we find transvestite characters openly questioning issues of gender and sexual identity.[2] Campbell does not really try to become a woman or deceive the viewer; in fact, while playing the female roles in his videos he never hides his male identity. To the contrary, his characters waver between several identity factors such as biological sex and performed gender or sexual behaviour, proposing complex figures that deliberately blur boundaries in the area of sexuality. Because the videomaker emphasizes the disguise and the artificial nature of his change from a male artist to a female character, his work takes a political stance and proposes a reflection on the social construction of masculine/feminine categories. He carries out a veritable sexual transformation, creating a parody that criticizes the allocation of these phallocentric, or even heterocentric, powers. Figures of dual sexuality, Campbell's heroines are highly controversial: they question the exclusivity of the elements that classify gender.

The discussion of Campbell's work will be followed by that of a younger generation of videomakers exploring the figure of the alter ego. In the tradition of *video drag*, I will look at Stéphane St-Laurent/Minnie St-Laurent's *Stand by Your Man* (1998) and work complementary to *drag butch* such as Cathy Sisler's *Mr. B.* (1994). The transvestite figure will also be examined in the context of a hybrid cultural identity. Videomaker Jorge Lazano explores this issue in *Samuel and Samantha* (1993). Here the ambiguity of sexual identity intensifies the problem of combining Latin American and Canadian cultures. Finally, the binary oppositions of male/female and East/West are distinctly found in Karen Kew and Ed Sinclair's *Chasing the Dragon* (1993), Paul Wong's *Miss Chinatown* (1997), and Michael Chaowanasai's *The Adventures of Iron Pussy 3* (2000). These videomakers explore stereotypes and caricature as elements that make up identity.

The Dual Figure or the Video Alter Ego

The origin of this figure in Canadian video is probably Colin Campbell's *Janus* (1973). Here the artist presents a sensual/sexual encounter between himself and his photographic double, stressing the narcissistic dimension of self-representation in video. *Janus* exploits the divided self and the confrontation with the other that is found later on in all the female characters the artist personifies, in his videos *The Woman from Malibu* (1976–77), *Modern Love* (1978–80), and *Rendez-Vous* (1997–2000), in particular, and in his concerns about transvestism generally. The divided self in *Janus* prefigures the female character's otherness as a way for the artist to show his differing views of the world.

Dot Tuer has already suggested that practices of transvestism in video, such as in Campbell's work, are evidence of a desire to be female that is similar to a desire for otherness.[3] The representation of a transvestite figure presents an internalized view of the other sex through the partial appropriation of traits. The impersonation transforms the sexual being, making the biological sex coexist with cultural conventions recognized as belonging to the opposite sex, thus constructing a two-sided figure. This transformation reveals the social construction of the gender categories it questions through a new rendering of sex, sexuality, and desire.

The notion of the alter ego in video implies the ever-changing nature of identity constructed from sexual characteristics, as in the example given or from other cultural elements. The two-sided figure combines subjectivity and otherness to explore the fluctuations of a constantly evolving identity. Strongly iconoclast, the video tradition often shows subversive intentions both in the types of figures represented and in the narrative structure used. This is true of the various performing bodies in the productions examined here. Far from being naive, this inquiry about the self-image openly questions the increasingly uncertain foundations of our mutating identities.

The Tradition of Heroines in Colin Campbell's Videos

Since *The Woman from Malibu*, Campbell has produced several models around the paradigm of the female alter ego.[4] This includes his most recent character, Colleena, in *Rendez-Vous*, who is a synthesis of the various figures the artist has personified. Campbell's interest in issues of sexual identity originated early on as he reflected on the identity of the subject in his work. Self-representation and the use of biographical material were significant leitmotifs right from the start in works such as *True/False* (1972), *Janus*, and *This Is an Edit—This Is Real* (1974). *True/False* is Campbell's first confessional video. Here he makes a number of autobiographical statements and then either confirms or denies them. The artist plays ironically on the ambiguity between reality and fiction, and he also exploits the medium's potential intimacy. The framing is a close-up, full face or in profile, which increases contact with the viewer. Campbell confesses to the camera, and by extension to the viewer, a type of confessional that is reinforced by the mug-shot format of the portrait. This shows that Campbell's notion of identity at this period already implied an artificial construction. Viewers find themselves in front of a fragmented self-portrait where they must reconstruct the elements of a split personality whose foundations are continually questioned. This confessional mode is used for many of his heroine portraits: his Woman-from-Malibu character, Mildred, is presented this way most of the time. Elements that determine the female personalities are also revealed in small snatches, a phenomenon emphasised by the video's episodic nature.

In *This Is an Edit—This Is Real*, Campbell comments on notions of truth and representation, an antinomy already pronounced in *True/False*. The video uses biographical material, mainly photographs inscribed with "This is an edit" or "This is real." At first, the character is represented with archival photographs, creating an endless process of reifying the character through video. The artist then places himself in front of the camera and presents different part of his anatomy in close-up while commenting intimately. These comments are always accompanied by the duality of "This is an edit" or "This is real," creating a state of suspension. The artist draws fictional material from his wealth of experience, but the biography implies a necessarily false dimension, so that the representation cannot be true. The doubly mediatized, photographic, and video portrait that Campbell gives of himself is fictitious. The Colin in the video is an artificial character, a video double that will be widely used in the future.

The notion of the video alter ego should be understood in this way because I believe it perfectly defines the tradition of heroines in Campbell's work. His exploration of the female figure goes beyond the radical exclusivity of sexual categories. The alter ego that Campbell constructs is an enigmatic figure, wavering between male and female poles. Campbell passes in transit between identities to become multiple, without fixing completely on one or the other sex, playing at being himself and another self. The notion of the video alter ego implies this movement at the centre of identity. In Campbell's work, this phenomenon is reflected in his representation of gender as well as in his intention, which is to present both his own character and his progressive transformation into a female persona. As I mentioned earlier, interest in self-representation in the history of video

FIGURE 1 *The Woman from Malibu*, Colin Campbell, 1976–77 (courtesy V-Tape)

art is very pronounced. The term "self-representation" here implies biographical work as well as the various fictions in which artists play the roles themselves. The image of the producing subject here becomes the work's support. Twenty-five years after Rosalind Krauss' seminal essay "Video: The Aesthetics of Narcissism,"[5] the issue of video narcissism is as pertinent as ever and should be considered in a broader perspective. This would be an overall investigation into the self through the fascination the self-image exerts, rather than the single classical viewpoint of love for the self and a libidinal investment in one's own image.

One of the most interesting hypotheses in the revision of psychoanalysis is that of according the "narcissistic conflict" (tensions and rivalry between the ego and the representation that the ego fabricates of itself) a dimension just as significant as what Freud recognized as the "Oedipus complex."[6] In a society controlled by a strict moral code, it is consistent to think of psychic conflicts as the repression of desire. During the last century, great changes have occurred in our identification markers: "until then [they] had maintained control of ideals and had influenced the role these ideals played in shaping character and upholding self esteem."[7] Because the self-image develops in a social context that imparts models and conventional types, this self-image inevitably evolves in this context. Is it not plausible then to think of the loss of numerous identification markers as central to a new restlessness, which the practice of video could show?

Mildred, the Woman from Malibu, is the first female alter ego model that Campbell used to experiment with in video self-portraiture. At first glance, this woman Mildred is very different from the videomaker, sociologically at least. The artist even denied any biographical intention at first, insisting on the accidental circumstances of his performance;[8] however, the Woman from Malibu physically resembles Campbell and my intention here is to draw attention to this self-representational dimension that precisely reflects the convention of transvestism.

Generally, transvestites construct a gender image and behaviour in opposition to their biological sexual identity. A performer establishes his or her prestige through the chosen image's stature and by his or her success in impersonating this figure. This is why transvestites often choose gorgeous models from the past or present. However, various attributes can be used in different ways to represent a female figure either partially or completely. Campbell, for example, chose to impersonate an ordinary American woman whom he created by the means of contradictory facts and hearsay in which gender categories are constantly changing.[9]

From among the main transvestite categories that Richard Docter[10] has determined and in which the ultimate objective is not transsexualism, I am retaining the following three generic types:

DRAG QUEENS: a slang term referring to transvestite prostitutes that have been broadened to include transvestites generally as well as those working in the entertainment world, in a *drag show*, for example. Some of these transvestites have had hormone therapy and are now called *hormone queens*. The term "drag" is not necessarily linked to a specific gender, even if it was used traditionally for male to female transvestism. The word "drag" effectively connotes homosexuality and at times the expression is even considered a synonym for female impersonators. Despite the homosexual connotation, many homosexuals are anxious to distinguish themselves from drag queens because they prefer men displaying their virility, according to Esther Newton:[11] "Being gay and doing drag are not the same. The relationship between homosexuality and sex-role identification is complicated."[12] Newton adds that, in homosexual terms, a drag queen is a male homosexual dressed as a woman, while a *drag butch* is a lesbian dressed as a man.

FEMALE IMPERSONATORS: often but not exclusively homosexuals. Transvestism is considered a way of life. These people are generally more comfortable in their female role, but they are not interested in a sex change. Often their sexual situation is linked to the entertainment world, but their lifestyle can persist outside their work. More precisely, the female roles adopted by impersonators are often parodies, representing conventional stereotypes of femininity. It is not a matter of reproducing the behaviour of a particular woman but rather of imitating an artificial category—the feminine—as if this could be presented a homogeneous manner: "Femininity can only be acted by a man."[13] This category is culturally produced and reflects its production context; therefore, North American female impersonators turn to symbols specific to our culture.

SHE-MALES: transvestites who openly present the attributes of both sexes as the name indicates. This type of overtly ambiguous transvestism stresses the uncertainty of sexual categories by making conventional types normally thought of as exclusive coexist.

Throughout his performances, Campbell keeps his pronounced male anatomical characteristics such as his voice, apparent hairiness, and absence of breasts, thus presenting himself as a she-male: the transvestite figure most openly exploiting the subversive representation of gender identity because it combines both the male and female nature. Campbell's image remains an outstanding vocal image throughout Mildred's actual performance: her main action being to recount her life. This Mildred character contains all the alter-ego forms that will recur in his work: a she-male retaining elements common to Campbell the subject;[14] female appropriations of cultural markers; confessional style video; splitting the displayed self by the means of transvestism.[15] This last element is important because it magnifies the apparent splitting in two of the video alter ego. Campbell is not content just to explore another feminized aspect of his personality; he also comments on the actual process of transvestism. This he carries out by creating distance and reflectivity through the specular effect of verbal language. This process intensifies the first splitting of the self already present in the alter ego.

With the reduplication of the double, viewers find themselves in front of two complementary but antinomic worlds where the artist wavers between two positions. Sometimes he is Mildred, and other times he is Colin becoming Mildred. The issue here is again a transitory structure: the representational scenes waver between the artist's two images, sometimes favouring the character and other times the figure of the actor, disrupting the coherence of the diegetic fiction.

When we consider the male/female duality in the power relations of these various practices, the male is usually presented as the controlling entity, occupying a superior hierarchical position. Newton points out that this hierarchical privilege is in fact relatively delicate regarding the given image of masculinity, in which a single female element succeeds in unbalancing the character's male identity. In the case of Robin, the second heroine Campbell impersonated, the fact of wearing male clothing does not in the least challenge the character's female identity because it is well established by the hair, body movements, and accessories.[16]

From the general categories of female impersonators, subcategories appear such as *street, stage,*[17] *drag,* and even *camp.* The *drag impersonator* indicates the general change from one sex to the other, usually from male to female. The *camp impersonator* works in the same way but more strongly exploits the incongruities in the character's presentation, having an affected or show-off nature for example. Drag and camp impersonators play on the theatricality of their roles, emphasizing the artificiality of their characters, and in this way they create distance.[18] The impersonation or definition of a character is made by constructing an appearance contrary to the basic biological facts. The nature of gender is cultural.

Female impersonators use parody in their practice of transvestism; they exploit the boundaries between the male and female poles and at the same time draw attention to the artificial dimension created by gender categories that appear free of sexual determinism. In this sense, these propositions are meant to oppose legitimate sexual codes. This is even more flagrant in the "she-male," who presents very pronounced gender markers of both sexes. The she-male does not attempt to conceal his biological male attributes such a beard, chest hair, and of course a penis. In addition to this, he usually wears flamboyant embellishments that are conventionally female such as makeup, accessories, and clothes. The she-male openly manipulates sexual codes and presents himself as a subversive figure.

Unlike female impersonators, the she-male does not conceal the masculine nature of his biological sex in order to reveal it in a shocking manner at the end of his performance. The male sex is displayed right from the start. The she-male exploits the incongruity between cultural gender markers and anatomical sex. He plays with his dual identity. The figure of the she-male typifies the phenomenon of wavering between genders very well. This process can be extended beyond appearances and also be used in the sphere of identity generally. Referring to the tradition of transvestism in video, Chris Straayer refined the category of she-male and proposed the notion of the *she-man,* reinforcing the power dimension given to the combined figure when male anatomy is presented as sexual authority.[19] The she-man has completely subordinated his female elements to his male power. This is in contrast to an emasculated dimension that could remain in the she-male figure.

In broader popular culture, the she-man is a new figure, markedly bisexual rather than androgynous, in which the performer completely integrates the attributes of the female sex and sexuality.[20] The she-man is not effeminate; both heterosexual and homosexual artists can impersonate him. The she-man's specificity is the great sexual potential and strength attached to his image. These powerful new subversive figures have appeared

FIGURE 2 "Hands"
from *The Woman
from Malibu,* Colin
Campbell, 1976–77
(courtesy V-Tape)

mainly in experimental film and video art productions. Straayer refers to the aesthetics of narcissism and video's tradition of intimacy to explain this phenomenon. Since its beginning, the video medium has been a favoured means for exploring identity while proposing a discourse counter to leading media tendencies, thus exploiting the medium's subversive potential. Many themes show concern for indefinable, indistinct boundaries and paradoxical representations. The figure of the she-man can be understood then as a symbol of this iconoclast tradition in video.

In Campbell's work, transvestism is always evident. The Woman from Malibu is never presented as a drag queen. He does not play with deception, and at times has characteristics belonging to both sexes: female accessories and posture, male hairiness and voice timbre. In this sense, the character is much closer to the she-male type because the sexual power and potential attributed to the she-man is lacking. Actually, the Woman from Malibu's sexual dimension is diminished through the ambiguity of gender identity. I mentioned above that Mildred's physical appearance is similar to Colin's, and as if through gender interference, the artist's male nature persists through his voice and body. Similar to the she-male and even to the she-man who precisely exploits the male body's erotic potential, the body's maleness is not denied. The male body remains present and is not made dependent on a gender's cultural features. Campbell exists as himself, actively experiencing life and, by extension, gender. This is where the richness of his representation is found. The male body is neither a passive tool nor easily malleable material. Its uncontrollable presence creates a gap in the representation's plausibility.

Campbell has impersonated three other female characters: Robin, Anna, and Colleena are all based on the same kind of travesty as the Woman from

Figure 3 "Hairbrush" from *The Woman from Malibu*, Colin Campbell, 1976–77 (courtesy V-Tape)

Malibu.[21] He has never impersonated a true drag queen character. His various representations are never plausible. The artist always stresses his anatomical male traits such as his male voice, hairiness, and his lack of breasts, which are present to distance the cultural conventions he resorts to such as clothing and accessories.

A retrospective look enables us to observe a development in Campbell's female images. His first heroine, Mildred, the Woman from Malibu, is a middle-class American woman with an unstable psychological nature: she is a character that is culturally very different from the artist. Robin and Anna represent transitional models, female figures gradually developing and becoming freer, opening up through their professional activities and breaking new ground with their amorous experiences. The last character, Colleena, is overtly a female alter ego; she is widely biographical and directly inspired by Campbell's lifestyle.

This leads to Campbell's work on identity and the effect of reality in his work. Since the first video art productions, artists have questioned the supposed transparency of television. Many of these artists have openly criticized television's ideologies, from its editorial objectivity to its dependency on commercials and viewer ratings. Campbell's work lies within this logic. He plays with irony, setting up a distance to verisimilitude and engaging firmly in the constructed dimension of video discourse. He puts forward the following paradox: the camera does not lie in that what the viewers see is false. One of Campbell's intentions is precisely to question the video medium's capacity to transmit an objective reality. At least, he seems to constantly create a gap in the representational illusion or the effect of reality, particularly through the representation and subversion of gender categories.

Displaying the Process of Transvestism

Following this logic, videomaker Jorge Lazano in *Samuel and Samantha* (1993) applies the process of transvestism in the same manner as Campbell. This video relies on the performance of a character with a split personality: Samuel Lopez is a student and Salvadorian political refugee and Lazano's alter ego, while Samantha Trensch is a transvestite and stage performer. The first sequences show Samuel telling his story about his problems, which result from his homosexual condition, his difficulties in reconciling his Canadian and Latin-American identities, and his break with his father. This is presented in the confessional mode developed by Campbell and Steele. Throughout his account, Samuel applies makeup and progressively becomes Samantha, all the while keeping the masculine tone of his voice. His performance seems very natural, and yet the female is constructed in contradictory factual and verbal ways: the story remains Samuel's with Samuel's voice interrupting images of Samantha at shows and parties.

One of the video medium's strengths is its denotative power. The images and the voice, worked here in the confessional tradition, amplify the representation's narrative impact. Again due to the confessional mode, the artist's narrative, both as Samuel and as Samantha, has the effect of being very sincere. What the camera records seems true because video, like film, has a naturalizing effect. In fact, what the camera records is more a fashionable naturalization of the dominant ideology.[22]

As is the case for *The Woman from Malibu*, viewers are confronted by the character's paradoxical dual nature, which wavers between these two identities without ever completely settling on a specific sex or identity. The play of irony regarding the image's plausibility remains striking, and the classic documentary strategy is increased twofold by this constructed character's artificiality. This is a reduplication of the splitting and a strategy of caesura. Samuel/Samantha is presented as a transitory being with several sexual and cultural identities. The split in the character's life is backed up by a semiotic break; a gap in the representational illusion or effect of reality is created by strong distancing elements such as the very process of transvestism.

Like the transvestite body, the enunciative stance is bipolar, wavering between male and female without completely abandoning traces of otherness, again taking the place of the video alter ego. In this context the transvestite figure is polemic. The transvestite refuses to obey conventional sexual norms. The transgression enables us to reconsider these norms and as Judith Butler has stated about the film *Paris Is Burning*, "a distance will be opened up *between* that hegemonic call to normativizing gender and its critical appropriation."[23]

In his videos, Campbell focusses on critically appropriating gender norms through the free circulation of artifice. As for Lazano, the voice is the representation's main dissonant factor. Mildred's voice is the narrator Campbell's voice, the only one not disguised. Mildred's voice is already an interpretation that deconstructs the camera's representation and in a sense contradicts the denotation. The voice emphasizes that it is not a woman speaking. There cannot be a straight denotation because immediate identification poses a problem. Because this is puzzling, viewers must go beyond the medium's reality effect and recognize what is wrong. Through dissonance, the voice becomes a crucial interpretative factor.

The Strange Other to Whom I Am Linked

Another confessional video with a dual figure is Stefan St-Laurent/Minnie St-Laurent's *Stand by Your Man*. All the characteristics of the confessional video are respected here using minimal staging. In his apartment, a male transvestite street impersonator, Stefan/Minnie, is lip-synching a song by Tammy Wynette, the singer he is trying to be. It is mainly the singer's voice that is heard, although the actor's voice gives a couple of short commentaries on his performance, which acts as a distancing element.

The performer repeats his performance several times in a temporal loop that becomes disturbing. As well as the very unkempt-looking female image that he displays along with significant male anatomical traits such as a penis and a flat chest, the character wears a denture that hampers his speech. Stefan/Minnie's scrawniness, neglected look, and denture all eliminate any eroticism or desirability the transvestite figure might have. The compulsive repetition of the sequences accentuates the parody and even the pathetic aspect of transvestism.

Cathy Sisler presented the rarer female drag butch character in *Mr B.* Mr B does not speak, and he wanders anonymously around the city. The relatively normal male types that Sisler resorts to are concerned as much with accessories—a hat and a large overcoat to disguise her body—as with behaviour—spitting and smoking. Few anatomical traits are exploited; the character simply has her hair cut very short and scratches her cheek as if her beard is itching. It is evident that when we try to distinguish what belongs to the male universe and what is part of the female world, using stereotypes becomes inevitable; and stereotypes are much more pronounced when they concern the conventional cultural markers of a gender, as we have seen in the chosen examples. However, this is a sensitive issue and can be tricky because some elements typically belonging to one gender category can slip into the universe of the other through fashion: earrings and ties, for example. The use of these types is nevertheless inevitable when defining characters, and I consider them here as a gender's social conventions and not as essential characteristics.

To make her character more convincingly male, Sisler constructs an identity by exploiting several cultural stereotypes: she creates a male gender fiction, mixing together pornography, Humphrey Bogart, *GQ*, and *Modern Bride*. Category takes precedence over the individual and type dominates the personality. Mr B is one *man* among many in the urban mass. Here, the ego is diluted through an increased number of alter egos. These men merge into a prototype that is homogenous at first glance: they wear similar clothes and adopt the same posture. Only the few surprised looks that Mr B receives remind us of the character's ontologically female nature, which is difficult for the audience to identify with, not so much because of her masculine look but because of her lack of individuality.

Parody of the Sexes

I will end on the aspects of parody and caricature used often in many of these performance videos. As I have already mentioned, Karen Kew and Ed Sinclair's *Chasing the Dragon*, Paul Wong's *Miss Chinatown*, and even Michael Chaowanasai's *The Adventures of Iron Pussy 3* employ stereotypes and caricature to shape the identities of their represented characters.

Chasing the Dragon openly questions notions of exoticism. On the one hand there is Cherry, a female impersonation of the typical Asian sexual stereotype, a gentle and submissive curvaceous beauty, and on the other, the representation of a fantasy, the stereotype of an Asian woman created through erotic conversations at 1-900-NUMBER. The videomakers are following along the lines of *This Is an Edit—This Is Real*, and are indicating the video image's artificial dimension, which is just as artificial as their image of the Asian woman—like all media representations, they are ultimately constructed. They present a fantasy rather than a character, because in the end Cherry is only an empty form of female otherness, a form that the user reconstructs through projections: a twofold category that is both cultural and sexual. Kew and Sinclair stress that an Asian woman in pornography represents exoticism for a Western man.

Similar intentions are found in *Miss Chinatown*. The work's title stresses the artificiality of racial identity and the sham of beauty contests and transvestite galas, which are criticized, deconstructed, and re-evaluated from several testimonies superimposed as cacophonic interview accounts. Cultural, racial, and sexual identities are placed on the same level, each as fabricated as the others. Composite identities are transformed through their borrowings, contrasting in this way with the ideal of a standardized, stable identity.

A genuine cartoon video, *The Adventures of Iron Pussy 3* uses carica-ture to represent characters, to recount the story, and to construct the video.[24] The action takes place in Bangkok[25] with Iron Pussy wearing all the conventional flamboyant paraphernalia of a transvestite, such as a wig, pink stockings, and red, high-heeled shoes. Here, homosexuals are rep-resented as shaved and muscular with tattoos, and go-go boys are young nymphets. The acting is exaggerated and nothing escapes the biting humour of this Kung-Fu melodrama that borders on the burlesque. It is through the characters' sexual masquerades, the use of irony, and commentary on the medium's reality that we can understand the intended parody in the pro-ductions analyzed. In most cases, the artists have set up an important sys-tem of distancing through varying voices: the representations stress the arti-ficiality of the gender identities, the presentations, and the characters' performances. In this sense, parody is a typical element in video represen-tations of the alter ego.

As Linda Hutcheon says, parody is a form of imitation involving a cru-cial ironic distance.[26] It is a "transcontextualization," a repetition with differences, and does not necessarily entail a dimension that ridicules the referent parody; this is what distinguishes it from burlesque. Parody does not destroy its subject: it reinterprets it in a way that is sometimes critical and subversive and at other times more conservative. Parody implies the transgression of an organized and acknowledged structure, a legitimate ref-erent, which through this process becomes denaturalized and transcontex-tualized. By highlighting and transgressing this legitimized form, parody creates a critical distance. This aspect is particularly significant when one thinks about the subversive impact that parodying gender has for the transvestite exploiting the figure of the alter ego.

In the case of transvestism, the referent here is not necessarily another undertaking but more a series of legitimate types that serve to define gen-ders. For the transvestite, the parodied referent is a naturalized common code, that is, the artifice or acquired behaviour presented as conditioned by sex and, by extension, nature. The transvestite's parody questions the sup-posed naturalness of sexual categories, indicating both the constructed dimensions of these categories and the naturalizing context in which they are often presented. The parody in transvestism is directed at the proposi-tion's content—the category—but it also criticizes the propositional form—

the naturalizing context. This is its great subversive power. Understood in this way, the video alter ego's dual figures thwart our basic cognitive schema of exclusive classifications, proposing an aesthetic blending of the sexes that is still difficult to define. In this way, instead of creating of a coherent and unified image, the various strategies of self-representation analyzed in this essay use enigma and doubt to make a subject's dissociate and split nature more contemporary, while revealing the artificial dimension of video realism.

Notes

1 The themes of intimacy, introspection, and subjectivity have been abundantly treated most notably in the seventies and eighties. An outstanding example of this is Kate Craig's *Delicate Issue* (1979, 12 min.). This is a video portrait of the artist in which the camera takes a voyeuristic point of view.

2 Campbell impersonated female characters mainly in the series of five videos about *The Woman from Malibu* (1976–77), in the two tapes *Modern Love* (1979), and *Bad Girls* (1980), in *Dangling by Their Mouths* (1981), and most recently in *Rendez-vous* (1997), *Deja Vu* (1998), and *Dishevelled Destiny* (2000).

3 Dot Tuer, "Video in Drag: Trans-sexing the Feminine," *Parallelogramme* 12.3, (February–March 1987): 24–29.

4 These are *The Woman from Malibu, The Temperature in Lima, Culver City Limits, Last Seen Wearing,* and *Hollywood and Vine.*

5 Rosalind Krauss, "Video: The Aesthetics of Narcissism," *October* 1 (Spring 1976): 50–64.

6 Jean-Claude Stoloff, *Interpréter le narcissisme* (Paris: Dunod, 2000). The author examines the pertinence of this slippage in the context of current psychoanalysis, which is no longer exclusively preoccupied with Freud's guilty subject, a prisoner of conflicts between drives and taboos. Psychoanalysis today is also interested in the tragic subject engrossed in an existential malaise and problems of fulfillment and self-image.

7 Stoloff, xii.

8 When I interviewed Campbell, he said he impersonated the heroine by chance because he did not have enough money to engage an actress.

9 Resorting to a gender's cultural markers, such as makeup, clothing, and accessories recognized as female.

10 Richard F. Docter, *Transvestites and Transsexuals: Towards a Theory of Cross-Gender Behavior* (New York and London: Plenum Press, 1988).

11 Esther Newton, *Mother Camp: Female Impersonators in America* (Chicago and London: University of Chicago Press, 1972), 3.

12 Newton, 34.

13 Jan Kott, *The Theater of Essence* (Evanston: Northwestern University Press, 1984), 124. Quoted by Alisa Solomon, "It's Never Too Late to Switch: Crossing toward Power," Ferris, 145. Solomon also notes that caricatured behaviour is seldom found in women personifying men: they attempt to imitate male gender rather than parody it.

14 These elements can range from anatomical markers to homonyms.

15 *The Temperature in Lima* and *Hollywood and Vine* present explicit sequences of transvestism. The viewer is confronted by the paradoxical dual nature of the character Campbell impersonates, both Campbell himself and Campbell progressively becoming the Woman from Malibu.

16 Robin is the heroine in *Modern Love* and *Bad Girls*.

17 Contrary to street impersonators, stage impersonators really perform their numbers in a show.

18 Newton, 104–107. She adds that the category *camp* first designates the incongruous relationship between the elements; it can be applied to the duality of gender's out-of-context elements but still imply a high level of artificiality. A link can be made with the more current term "queer": "Queer... means to fuck with gender.... It concerns 'gender fuck,' which is a full-frontal theoretical and practical attack on the dimorphism of gender- and sex-roles." Stephen Whittle "Gender Fucking or Fucking Gender?" *Blending Genders: Social Aspects of Cross-Dressing and Sex-Changing* Richard Ekins and David King, eds. (New York and London: Routledge, 1996), 202.

19 Chris Straayer, *Deviant Eyes, Deviant Bodies: Sexual Re-Orientations in Film and Video* (New York: Columbia University Press, 1996).

20 The term "androgyny" involves a connotation of sexual absence and is rarely used for a highly sexed individual. The term "bisexual," which overtly implies sexual activity, seems to me more appropriate. Marjorie Garber adds to this subject: "androgyny as a metaphor. A metaphor... consists of two parts: the work being used figuratively (the vehicle) and the idea that it is meant to convey (the tenor). Androgyny is sexy when it is the vehicle (the physical form of performance we see) and not sexy when it is the tenor (the idea or the idealization). When the performance is androgynous, it is frequently erotic; and its eroticism is often bisexual, appealing both to men and to women.... When 'androgyny' was not the vehicle of a metaphor but its tenor, however—when it denoted something like 'wholeness' or 'integration' of personality—it was determinedly unsexy. It meant, or is said to mean, or was said *only* to mean, stasis, not movement, and union, not desire. In other words, not lack but fullness." Marjorie Garber, *Vice Versa: Bisexuality and the Eroticism of Everyday Life* (New York: Touchstone, 1996), 233–34.

21 Anna is the character in *Dangling by Their Mouths*, and Colleena is the heroine in *Rendez-Vous*.

22 Concerning this, see Teresa de Lauretis, *Alice Doesn't: Feminism, Semiotics, Cinema* (Bloomington: Indiana University Press, 1984).

23 Judith Butler, *Bodies That Matter: On the Discursive Limits of "Sex"* (New York: Routledge, 1993), 137.

24 A series of three videos.

25 A reconstruction of Bangkok, showing a Western vision of the East.

26 Linda Hutcheon, *A Theory of Parody: The Teachings of Twentieth-Century Art Forms* (New York and London: Methuen, 1985), 6–7.

10 Queerly Canadian

"Perversion Chic" Cinema and (Queer)
Nationalism in English Canada

Jason Morgan

FOR THE LAST TWENTY-FIVE YEARS OR SO, mainstream English-Canadian films (those that have enjoyed a degree of financial and critical success) have demonstrated a preference for narratives originating at the margins of society. Necrophiliacs, pedophiles, and homosexuals populate these films, their images being used to tell stories that are strikingly different from most of those told by Hollywood. An example of this is David Cronenberg's film *Crash* that, in 1996, won a special jury prize at the Cannes Film Festival for "originality, daring, and audacity" while simultaneously being characterized by some critics as disgusting, subversive, and pornographic. Termed "perversion chic" by the media, this emergent sub-genre encompasses the works of such diverse directors as Atom Egoyan, John Greyson, and Lynne Stopkewich.[1]

Lee Parpart suggests that perversion chic cinema incorporates a concern with marginality, manifest in narratives of deviant sex and bodily transformation, with a distinctly Canadian sense of the realities of contemporary life. Taking part in "an inflationary trend that seems to be constantly upping the ante of allowable (perhaps even mandatory) eroticism in English-Canadian cinema,"[2] these films indicate that perverse desire seems to have some deep resonance with the creative minds in this country. Robert Lantos, CEO of Alliance Atlantis, has argued that this is a reaction to the dominance of American cinema within our national borders. Rather than compete with Hollywood, "there's only one direction we can go in, and that is with filmmakers who have powerful visions. There's a handful of

211

them in Canada. They tend to make dark movies, movies that are counter-Hollywood and anti-television."[3] Such a perspective, however, betrays a limited sense of Canadian artistic endeavours, suggesting that we are only capable of producing cultural texts that reflect our political and economic subservience to the United States. Perversion chic is much more daring than that.

The purpose of this chapter is to sketch out the framework for a new understanding of English Canadian "national" cinema.[4] If ours is a cinema of marginality—in terms of the stories it tells and its relation to Canadian audiences—then how might Canadians use these films, alongside other cultural texts and mythologies, in order to imagine the nation? Perversion chic films do not mirror a nation that is unable to define itself, but rather emerge from a national imaginary that is struggling to expand and disrupt the boundaries of nationalism. Instead of rejecting "nation" as an important category of analysis in an increasingly globalized cultural marketplace, I will argue that these films, as they consider novel approaches to the question of Canadian cultural identity, invoke a *queer nationalism* that emphasizes the subversion of dominant models of belonging by positioning intersection and difference as the foundations of community. By examining some of the representational strategies deployed by these films, I will demonstrate that Canada is a queer nation, one that defines itself not through homogeneity but through plurality and the very impossibility of the nation.

The "Absent Audience" and the "Loser Paradigm"

Benedict Anderson explains that nations must be understood as *imagined* political communities.[5] In this respect, the power of cinema derives from its role as the purveyor of public fantasies, representations that are rooted in a group mythology, and are hence consumed and emulated by the masses. Consequently, it can be argued that audiences watch "national" cinemas in order to recognize themselves and to imagine the nation and their place within it. Canadian film, unfortunately, suffers from a lack of recognition by national audiences; English-Canadian films occupy a marginal position in national movie-going practices. If Canadians spend more time watching American films than they do watching their own, then "a seat in a Canadian movie theatre is essentially a seat on international territory,"[6] offering the experience of being "anywhere" but here. Without Canadian films being viewed on Canadian screens, whose community do we imagine we belong to? While it is true that "Canada" exists as a discursive category despite its lack of representation in popular culture—

audiences are quite capable of reading "Canadianness" into and through texts produced outside the country—this still leaves us with a need to account for the place of films that are made by Canadians, about Canadians.

In order to get at this issue, I want to suggest that we can speak of national cinemas on a purely representational level. Chris Berry suggests that by limiting the definition of national cinema to the realms of consumption, we downplay "consideration of the ways in which these texts usually attempt to solicit recognition of membership in a collectivity and to signify that this collectivity extends to include both the audience and the film-makers.... *For whether or not such cinematic efforts to participate in the construction of collective agency are effective, this is their aim.*"[7] English-Canadian films are produced in the context of the Canadian symbolic: they reference the cultural narratives, mythologies, and world views of Canadians, and that necessarily distinguishes them from their Hollywood competitors. The "absent audience" cannot, then, be employed as a factor in the dismissal of a national cinema in English Canada.

What, then, is an English-Canadian image? If "national" cinema is supposed to present us with stories and characters in which we recognize ourselves, how do you accomplish this in Canada, a nation with an apparently chronic inability to define itself?

Attempts to define English-Canadian nationalism inevitably reference an apparent *lack* that undermines such efforts. Ian Angus explains this as a lack of temporal resources: "We can indulge neither in the myth of an ancient nation from time out of mind (as in Europe) nor in a revolutionary founding that might forge a new nation in an act of radical institution of a new order (as in post-revolutionary New World nations). The two main temporal rhetorics of nationhood are denied to us."[8] As a result, "geography becomes important for identity where history has failed to provide it."[9] In other words, unable to embody the homogeneity that supposedly comes with a unified national history, Canadian texts are prone to ponder the question "Where is here?" rather than "Who am I?"[10]

This line of reasoning has had two significant impacts on theorizing about English-Canadian identity. The primary effect is to produce the idea that Canada can only ever define itself oppositionally, by pointing out that which it is not. Our apparent lack of (temporal) culture and history forces us to rely upon (spatial) geography in order to delimit the "borders" of English Canada. This, however, positions us as symbolically inferior to those who possess both spatial *and* temporal referents (a sign of adherence to a "true" nationalism), countries such as the United States. Canada thus works as the secondary term within an international binary, producing the nation as a category of identification that is always already marginal.

The reliance on space also has specific effects on the character of English-Canadian representation. According to Janice Kaye, the Canadian hero (who, like the nation, is assumed to be male) "is allied with the female space and thereby feminized."[11] This "female space" is that of landscape or nature, which are often dominant, if not all-encompassing, metaphors in Canadian representation. Contrasted with the "masculine space" of culture (which, of course, Canada supposedly lacks), this results in national narratives of isolation, powerlessness, and difference: "This Canadian emotional paradigm is one of solitude and isolation; of an ever-present looming sense of the immense surrounding wilderness which can never be physically or even mentally encompassed; of a Nature which is treacherous, violent and unknowable; of self-repressive passivity and caution; of feelings of impotence and hopelessness and marginalization."[12] This "loser paradigm" positions Canada suggestively as a site of anti-heroism, arguing "Canadian art reflects a fixation on defeat and failure."[13] Because the heroic ideal, as a manifestation of patriarchal ideology, necessarily excludes the "feminine," Canadian "heroes" tend to be weak, plagued with self-doubt and crippled by their own excesses and, consequently, are prone to reckless self-destruction and sexual deviance. Canadian heroes embody an exclusion from the national ideal; they can only be, as Robert Fothergill has famously argued, "cowards, bullies, or clowns."[14]

If the "loser paradigm" demonstrates the uniqueness of English-Canadian cinematic images, Peter Morris contends that it is also restrictive. He explains: "insisting on that uniqueness meant occasionally ignoring films that did not fit the model, or discussing some films in terms of an inappropriate model. And, at the same time, it tended to limit debate on other possible thematic models."[15] Indeed, many of the films released in the last decade do seem to resist the "loser paradigm" in their dealings with the psychological issues surrounding the feminization of the protagonist and his/her association with landscape, in particular when dealing with various alternative or "deviant" manifestations of sexuality and gender. Moreover, it is important to remember that the attachment to landscape is mobilized as a strategy *against* the perceived lack of national culture in Canada. In order to understand the way in which the nation is imagined in Canadian cinema, and particularly in perversion chic films, we have to question whether failure to adhere to dominant models of the nation necessarily signifies a lack.

The "loser paradigm" suggests that it is precisely Canada's inability to define itself that structures our representations. Our failure to embody the ideals of the nation—the appeal to historical homogeneity to which the United States adheres with apparent ease—culminates in representative strategies that reflect a sense of futility and inferiority. In short, if Canada is a nation that is somehow lacking, and if this has become our defining characteristic, then the cinematic figures with whom we are supposed to identify cannot help but mirror this. In describing the representation of Canada in such terms, however, we are assuming that any deviation from the dominant understanding of nationalism signals a failure, an exclusion from the very category of the nation. Perhaps what is needed is not an explanatory model along the lines of the "loser paradigm," but an alternative view of the nation, one that can account for anti-heroic imagery without recourse to a narrative of marginality.

Queer/Nation

In order to talk about the perversion chic films as a national cinema we need to recast the terms by which we understand nationalism. The idea that nations are made up of homogenous populations, that national (historical) identification can override all other identity categories or histories with which an individual might associate him or herself (such as gender, ethnicity, and sexuality), is an outmoded idea, one that the everyday realities of Canadian politics proves. Multicultural policies that attempt to acknowledge the diasporic origins of most Canadians and the efforts to maintain linguistic and cultural unity in the face of divergent and increasingly regionalist visions of the country demonstrate the mythological nature of the "many as one" archetype of nationalism. If Canada is a country that, to some degree, revels in the heterogeneity of the Canadian national body, then new structures are required if we are to look at our indigenous films as representing not the failure to embody the national ideal, but the richness that comes in its rejection. To this end, I suggest that we turn to the insights of queer theory and recast the nation as a queer nation.

The idea of a "queer nation" materialized, in the late eighties, out of the practices of Queer Nation (QN), a group who attempted to integrate a postmodern awareness of the constructed nature of identity with the "street theatre" tactics made popular by AIDS activism. They were committed to disrupting the public spaces in which the naturalness of heterosexuality is assumed through various culture-jamming strategies. Rosemary Hennessy argues that the use of the term "nation" for QN "signals a commitment to disrupting the often invisible links between nationhood and public sexual discourse as well as transforming the public spaces in which a (hetero)-sexualized national imaginary is constructed in people's everyday lives—in shopping malls, bars, advertising, and the media."[16] As strategies that maximize visibility, the actions of QN sought to emphasize "the ambiguities of this sexual geography [as] fundamental to producing the new referent, a gay community whose erotics and politics are transubstantial,"[17] while bringing the invisible inconsistencies of identity construction into plain view for their (primarily) heterosexual audiences.

Although this organization eventually fell out of favour with the larger gay and lesbian community, disappearing from the political stage during the mid-nineties, the idea behind the movement has continued to spark the imagination of cultural theorists. David Savran claims that QN failed as a political movement not because its conception of the nation was faulty but because it was unable to fully realize it. He notes that what is most interesting about QN is "its expropriation of the discourse of nationalism in an era when, at least for most self-identified leftists, nationalism was (and remains) deeply suspect."[18]

Taking at face value Anderson's claim that "since World War II every successful revolution has defined itself in national terms,"[19] QN was an "attempt to queer America, to produce a counter-hegemonic patriotism that militates for a redefinition of the nation"[20] through the exploitation of the basis of nationalism. For Savran, "the name Queer Nation is oxymoronic, asserting both difference and sameness. Insofar as 'queer' designates a perverse or marginal positionality and 'nation' an affirmation of commonality and centrality, Queer Nation necessarily combined 'contradictory impulses.'"[21] In other words, nationalism is queer inasmuch as it works to reconcile that which can never be reconciled: the heterogeneous national body. The mobilization of a queer theory in a new understanding of the Canadian nation finds obvious parallels here. In essence, the project of rearticulating the nation within the Canadian context refers to the necessity of queering Canadian nationalism.

The term "queer" denotes both inclusiveness and transgression. Initially coined as an alternative to the repressive heterosexual/homosexual binary, it has been defined by Eve Kosofsky Sedgwick as "the open mesh of possibilities, gaps, overlaps, dissonances and resonances, lapses and excesses of meaning, when the constituent elements of anyone's gender, of anyone's sexuality aren't made (or *can't* be made) to signify monolithically."[22] This new grouping, which denies the need for binary thinking, allows queer theorists and activists to escape a system of cultural logic that secures the dominance of one group (men, heterosexuals) over another (women, homosexuals) by regulating the categories into which one is able to place oneself.

Sexuality is not, however, the only identity marker that defines individuals: identity spins off in a plurality of directions. "For people with multiple 'marked' identities," Lisa Duggan argues, "the [queer] political project begins at the level of the very problematic construction of identities and their relation to different communities and different political projects."[23] "Queer" is not limited to the realm of sexual representation; it is an *inclusive* category that can be applied to phenomena that "spins the term outward along dimensions that can't be subsumed under gender and sexuality at all: the ways that race, ethnicity, postcolonial nationality criss-cross with these and other identity-constituting, identity-fracturing discourses."[24] By acknowledging this, queer theorizing speaks to the fundamental contradictions (the innate "queerness") in the formation of any community, including the nation.

A queer form of inclusive identification, such as queer nationalism, is *transgressive* (rather than oppositional) because it does not merely absorb heterogeneous differences under a new homogenous banner, but instead foregrounds its internal contradictions. In this way, the nation can be imagined as inherently queer because, as Homi Bhabha argues, its existence fundamentally contradicts that upon which it relies to define itself.[25] While the hegemonic system of understanding dictates that the nation embody homogeneity ("e pluribus unum," or "the many as one"), this is always already distanced from the heterogeneous reality of the "many" that it seeks to constrain as "one." The nation is constantly pushed beyond its own "borders"; it simultaneously demands homogeneity and denies its possibility. In short, the nation is an impossible existence, yet one that continues to reproduce itself.

Insofar as it is a nation that is struggling to contain its own internal differences under the monolithic banner of the "nation," Canada already embodies queer nationalism. It is a model which accommodates the inconsistencies of this nation and facilitates the project of rearticulating the national symbolic in order to construct a nationalism in which the numerous constructions of difference that make up the Canadian national body are encompassed without being erased. Queer nationalism centres on a "war of representation," one in which the dominant discourses of the nation must be re-signified in order to become more inclusive of their disavowed queer content. In connection with a broader understanding of the term "queer," however, the very structures that are made to accommodate excessive difference are ruptured under the strain of this task, facilitating a new, queer model of community membership. In English Canada, then, the search for inclusive identity fields must also be articulated in this fashion: opening up the national narrative so that it might more effectively account for its own excess, its own queer existence. This is accomplished, to some degree, by the perversion chic films.

Camping the Nation

Perversion chic cinema is not a product of the "loser paradigm" but of a new, queer awareness of the nation that embraces contradiction and paradox at the expense of an imagined homogeneity. Useful here is Cynthia Fuchs's suggestion that, "reframed as resistance to cultural interpellations, an 'identity in the lack of identity' becomes an effective position from which to speak, destabilizing preconceived binary categories of self-representation."[26] The supposedly inherent English-Canadian lack of identity may be seen as productive; the representative use of the feminized hero subverts the normative system by which the nation is called into being. In what follows, I will examine two films from the perversion chic cycle (*Lilies* and *Love and Human Remains*) and highlight some strategies they use in order to represent English Canada as a queer nation, as both inclusive and transgressive.

My selection of *Love and Human Remains* (1993) and *Lilies* (1996) as exemplary of perversion chic cinema and its implicit project of critique is, in itself, rather queer. Neither achieved the international attention that prompted the creation of the term "perversion chic" (I am thinking here of the films of Cronenberg and Egoyan, in particular). Further, both films signal a cultural cross-pollination between the purportedly rigidly segregated spheres of English and French cultural production in Canada: *Lilies* was directed by Toronto-based John Greyson, but was translated from a French screenplay by Québécois writer Michel-Marc Bouchard, adapted from his play *Les Feluettes ou la répétition d'un drame romantique*. Similarly, *Love and Human Remains* was directed by Denys Arcand, a Québécois filmmaker best known for his French language films (*The Decline of the American Empire, Jesus of Montreal*), and was written by Alberta-based playwright Brad Fraser, based on his play *Unidentified Human Remains and the True Nature of Love*. While, consequently, neither is able to claim the (ultimately dubious) status of a "pure" English-Canadian text, these films do share several significant characteristics, given my wish to discuss these films as manifesting within the English-Canadian imaginary, that place them unmistakably within this "canon." Both, for example, are explicitly concerned with economies of desire in the formation of community. Both turn their attention to the darker sides of sexuality (resisting, at the same time, the urge to focus unproblematically on those common "perversions" most often selected by Hollywood). And, finally, both deploy these representations as strategies for an overtly queer political critique of the state of Canadian nationalism. It is this last point that forms the strongest basis for linking all the perversion chic films together, and that will thus be the focus of my analysis.

Greyson's *Lilies* problematizes conventional notions of national identity by physically mapping out temporal relations onto space. *Lilies* plays with conventions of gender, ethnicity, and sexuality through the performance of performance: the narrative centres around the production of a play, which is in turn the re-enactment of the events that have led up to the present of the film. The bodies of the actors (both literally and in the context of the narrative) come to signify the heterogeneous national body; throughout the narrative, certain meanings are inscribed upon these bodies, only to be struggled against and ultimately rejected by the characters. In short, *Lilies* demonstrates the impossibility of homogeneity when applied to the nation. The national body becomes a vessel that seeks to contain the excessive meaning released by the impossibility of the nation, one that always fails. The story hinges on Bishop Bilodeau's (Marcel Sabourin) presence at a prison in Quebec, 1952, to hear the confession of a past schoolmate, Simon Doucette (Aubert Pallascio). A reversal takes place during the confession in which the bishop finds himself trapped, watching a stage play performed by the inmates that recreates his culpability in the events that led to the death of Vallier (Danny Gilmore), Simon's lover and Bilodeau's rival for his affections, and the wrongful imprisonment of Simon for this crime in 1912.

Rather than simply use flashbacks to shift the action from present to past, Greyson opts to play both time periods in the same space, and on the same bodies. The film never lets us forget that we are watching a *performance*. The cast is composed entirely of men (as would be expected in a prison) who portray all the roles, including those of women. Even in the sequences filmed as former presents, men continue to play the roles of women (albeit in better costumes and makeup), a cinematic strategy that constantly and reflexively references the present as it explores the temporal and spatial elements that exceed it. This performative and historical overdetermination is a deliberate, and queer, reference to the narratives that English-Canadian nationalism cannot lay claim. Past and present cannot be clearly distinguished in *Lilies*, both in terms of the staging of the narrative, and quite concretely in the competing versions of the past that we encounter in the divergent interpretations of Simon and Bilodeau. The film goes so far as to reference this ambiguity directly, even as it continues to play out its teleology.

For example, Bilodeau, who strives to remain firmly rooted in the present, interrupts the play. At this moment, we see the performance delayed, characterizations dropped, illusions and technical errors are unveiled, and thus we are reminded that what we are watching is not in fact the cinematic representation of a past present, but a present performance of a fantasized past. During this particular disruption, Bilodeau scoffs at the romantic undertones attributed to the relationship between young Simon and Vallier. The actor playing the Comptesse de Tilly (Brent Carver) retorts by stating, "Simon may have stretched the truth a bit about his love story, but, it's so beautiful." The audience is reminded that memory and the apparent truth of history are two separate notions, and that what we are watching is the former, not the latter. History becomes a masquerade of the past in the present, of memory acting out the illusionary stability attributed to historical narratives. In short, *Lilies* critiques the truism that we are a nation that lacks temporal resources. Instead, it argues, we merely exist ambiguously in relation to *teleological* narratives of national history. This endows Canada with the ability to highlight the gaps in the logic of the nation by upsetting the linearity of history and by incorporating the spatial into the temporal. The use of such tactics in *Lilies* works to queer history, revealing it as being simply memory in drag.

Critical to a reading of *Lilies* is an understanding of its use of masquerade and drag. Marginal difference and the feminized masculinity of the "loser paradigm" are present in *Lilies*, but this excess does not signal lack. Instead, it speaks to the possibility of transgression through performance. Judith Butler has argued that gender is not ontological, but is instead performative: individuals signal their belonging to either masculinity or femininity through a repetitive process of imitating an idealized and ideological model of gender. Drag—because it approximates the same gendered ideal but does so as campy parody or, at the very least, as a performance that works against socially instituted gender norms—highlights the ultimately "wishful" and impossible nature of gender imitation. She explains:

> drag characterizes the wishful performative of gender as such, the production of "identity" through an imitation that seeks to approximate an ideal that is always already expropriated and elsewhere…. In this sense, drag is not a representation that falsifies or distorts an original but rather the enactment of a constitutive falsification or failure that undermines gender's claim to identity.[27]

In *Lilies*, with its rampant use of drag performance, it is not just gender that is subverted in this fashion, but also sexuality, ethnicity, and class. Such performative play is most evident in the character of Lydie-Anne (Alexander Chapman). She is English Canada personified: an embodied paradox who is radically heterogeneous while subverting the structures that would contain such unruliness. Lydie-Anne's body betrays her, exposing the same inherent contradictions that plague national identity. In this way, her presence in *Lilies* serves to undermine the assumptions of sameness, stability, and naturalness upon which national membership is founded.

Lydie-Anne's body cites marginality on three levels. First, as with all the actors, she is an inmate, a condition that implies not only a peripheral existence, but also a lack of control over her own body. Second, she is played by a male actor, hence servicing the subversive gender imperative fundamental to Butler's conception of drag. Third, she is Black, a fact that functions to erase any chance that we might forget her innate marginality, considering the care taken to elaborate her character's background within the Parisian aristocracy and the fact that the events in which she is implicated occur in 1912. Despite standing antithetically to dominant conceptions of the national subject (most often characterized by the triad of masculinity, heterosexuality, and whiteness), Lydie-Anne nonetheless masquerades as the centre. As the representative of upper-class Parisian society (signalled through her dress, her condescending mannerisms, and the fact that she arrived in a hot-air balloon), and contrasted to the provinciality of the denizens of Roberval, she clearly stands as difference, but one that works to alienate the multiple representatives of a common and thus minor existence. As a Black, gay, male prison inmate, however, Lydie-Anne cannot in fact lay claim to the dominant themes of national belonging. In the end, then, she is shown to embody the contradiction of a queer national subjectivity in English Canada: she is both colonizer and colonized, centre and periphery.

In short, the corporeal landscape of Lydie-Anne's conflicted physicality expresses the language of a queer nationalism. She is the nation in drag, embodying simultaneously the ideal and the innate contradictions that make it an impossibility. In English Canada, as in Lydie-Anne, the many are not one, but rather exist as many *within* one. The challenge taken up by *Lilies* is that of a relocation of difference within the hegemony of state-sanctioned national belonging. Difference is organized not in a manner that signals the familiar "difference as sameness" trope of policies such as multiculturalism, but rather starts at the significantly divergent point of "difference as difference," period. If the body of Lydie-Anne serves as a nexus at which contradictory singularities are sustained within a single subjectivity, it is not a condition that proves to be fundamentally debilitating. Instead, difference is reconfigured as that which stands as the essential foundation of (an always already queer) nationalism.

The strategies of masquerade and parody, and the revelation of the queerness of English Canada through the deliberately exaggerated performance of its contradictions are a common practice in the perversion chic cycle of films. In Arcand's *Love and Human Remains*, for instance, the exclusionary model of English Canada is also played out on the bodies of the actors. Although arguably this theme is carried throughout the narrative—the story follows the intersecting lives of a series of young Canadians as they grapple with their inability to form relationships and define themselves due to fear and insecurity—it is most tellingly evident in scene where the queerness of English-Canadian nationalism is referenced directly. Benita (Mia Kirshner), a prostitute who specializes in the enactment of her clients' sado-masochistic fantasies, recruits David (Thomas Gibson), a gay actor, to help her stage a scenario for one of her customers. We enter on a scene (within a scene) of her tied to a post in her ultra-modern living room, made up with exaggerated red lips and clownish pigtails as a stylized "saloon girl" from the Old West. Her client enters, dressed in a black leather cowboy costume. He slaps her, telling her that he is about to teach her how to behave "like a real woman." At this moment, David steps out of the hall closet (another queer twist on Canadian nationalism), the archetypal cowboy hero in white. "Just what the hell is going on here," he growls. David slams the other man to the floor, at which point the latter begins to grovel, pleading for his life before becoming obviously aroused and performing a kind of fellatio on David's white boot.

Although this scene plays for laughs in an otherwise darkly inflected film, its implications are significant. If in *Lilies* performance and parody are used to question the normative basis of the nation, and thus Canada's supposed inability to access it, in *Love and Human Remains* this is amplified to the point of camping the very question of what an English-Canadian image might look like. The recreation, a stylized Western scenario, complete with references not only to the "official" historical past but also to a cinematic genre past, clearly positions this scene as self-consciously reperforming a previous performance on multiple levels (the clichéd scene, the repetition of this client's fantasy, and David performing as an actor for the only time during the film). The history that binds these three characters together proves to be simply an imitation of the past. The overwrought inauthenticity of the scenario clearly references, like *Lilies*, the supposed Canadian lack of historical consciousness.

More importantly, all three actors embody elements of the Canadian imaginary à la "loser paradigm": the helpless (and ultimately unimportant) woman, the weak (and perverse) villain, and the symbol of law and order paradoxically housed in a "deviant" body. The fact that these, too, are parodied suggests the arbitrary nature of these images and their necessary contradiction to the complexities of the lives of those who mobilize them in order to imagine themselves into the nation. Sue-Ellen Case has argued that in camp, deployed as a political tactic, "a strategy of appearances replaces a claim to truth."[28] In other words, camp exploits the wishful nature of identity, revealing reality to be fragmentary and contingent rather than homogenous, unified, and subsumable under an ordered metanarrative. It is little wonder then that camp has been employed by queer activists (including QN) in order to draw attention to the inconsistencies that underlie the institutions and spaces of our culture. In much the same way, this scene questions the iconography that is said to make up the English-Canadian symbolic and highlights its role in the imagining and representation of the nation. The exaggeration of the performances, along with the decidedly subversive turn that the narrative takes, suggests that the nation might be imagined differently, calling into question the very idea of authenticity when applied to nationalism.

This becomes evident when we consider that this scenario aims at reducing Benita's client to a position of impotence and submission, a metaphor very much in line with the "loser paradigm" and its perspective on Canadian heroes. In the following scene, however, Benita points out that "at least he paid for it," instead of forcing it on someone "who wasn't into it." The act of acquiescence is suddenly imbued with empowerment, suggesting its always already queer nature. Weakness is made strength: the contradictions of the entire situation are made evident and a new reading is required. In short, with the intertextual references to elements of the national imaginary (and the positioning of the "loser paradigm" as part of that lexicon), the parodic play on them, and the revelation of the underlying structures of the scene, Arcand re-presents the nation along decidedly queer lines. The feminized hero is here revealed to be nothing other than a convention to be played with, a performance that fails to reflect the nation in any concrete way because it is stripped of any power to restrict meaning. In this way, *Love and Human Remains*, like all perversion chic films, transgresses English-Canadian mythology. It camps the nation and thus opens a space for a new conceptualization of nationhood based in contradiction and paradox rather than homogeneity.

In the perversion chic films, Canadian nationalism is demonstrated to be queer because it transgresses the normative basis of the nation. Belonging need not signal the repression of difference—instead, it is a shifting plane on which multiple differences can coexist simultaneously, articulating into a "whole" that carries with it none of the "permanence" of hegemonic constructs. Such a view of the nation, one that embodies the heterogeneity that denies the very possibility of the nation as it has been previously understood, subverts conventional nationalism and forces its rearticulation as a fundamentally queer construct. In this way, I contend that English Canada has managed to produce a truly national cinema, one that dwells not on our inability to adhere to dominant models of nationhood, nor one that rejects the concept in its entirety, but one that reflects our quest to redefine what it means to be a national citizen in the context of postmodernity and the rise of media and cultural globalization.

Notes

1 Brian D. Johnson, "The Canadian Patient," *Maclean's* 24 March 1997, 44.

2 Lee Parpart, "Cowards, Bullies, and Cadavers: Feminist Re-Mappings of the Passive Male Body in English-Canadian and Quebecois Cinema," *Gendering the Nation: Canadian Women's Cinema* (Toronto: University of Toronto Press, 1999), 59.

3 Johnson, 45.

4 The invocation of an "English"-Canadian cinema does, in some ways, maintain a problematic binary conceptualization of Canadian film production, one that sees all domestic cinema as falling into one of two categories, anglophone or francophone (this is explored in some depth later in the chapter). That this dualism ignores the ways in which language, history, and culture are intertwined, and effectively silences recent Canadian film narratives that operate within an allophonic cultural code—films such as Zacharias Kunuk's *Atanarjuat* (2001)—is not lost on me here. However, because the French/English split figures so prominently in the mainstream Canadian imaginary, and the group of films I am discussing in this chapter draw so explicitly upon it, I have reluctantly chosen to utilize this limited terminology for the sake of simplicity.

5 Benedict Anderson, *Imagined Communities: Reflections on the Origin and Spread of Nationalism* (London: Verso, 1991).

6 Charles R. Acland, "Popular Film in Canada: Revisiting the Absent Audience," *A Passion for Identity: An Introduction to Canadian Studies*, ed. David Taras and Beverly Rasporich (Toronto: ITP Nelson, 1997), 283.

7 Chris Berry, "If China Can Say No, Can China Make Movies? Or, Do Movies Make China? Rethinking National Cinema and National Agency," *Boundary 2* 25.3 (1998): 142; emphasis added.

8 Ian Angus, *A Border Within: National Identity, Cultural Plurality, and Wilderness* (Montreal: McGill-Queen's University Press, 1997), 142–43.

9 Angus, 114.

10 Peter Harcourt, "Imaginary Images: An Examination of Atom Egoyan's Films," *Film Quarterly* 48 (1993): 2–14. Northrop Frye is the first to put the question of Canadian identity as a matter of situating oneself within a certain context, or location: "[Canadian sensibility] is less perplexed by the question 'Who am I' than by some such riddle as 'Where is here?'" *The Bush Garden: Essays on the Canadian Imagination* (Toronto: Anansi, 1971), 220.

11 Janice Kaye, "Perfectly Normal, Eh? Gender Transformation and National Identity in Canada," *Canadian Journal of Film Studies* 3.2 (1994): 66.

12 William Beard, "The Canadianess of David Cronenberg," *Mosaic* 27 (1994): 118–19.

13 Beard, 118.

14 Robert Fothergill, "Coward, Bully, or Clown: The Dream-Life of a Younger Brother," *Canadian Film Reader*, ed. Seth Feldman and Joyce Nelson (Toronto: Peter Martin, 1977), 234–50.

15 Peter Morris, "In Our Own Eyes: The Canonizing of Canadian Film," *Canadian Journal of Film Studies* 3.1 (1994): 38–39.

16 Rosemary Hennessy, "Queer Visibility and Commodity Culture," *Cultural Critique* 29 (1995): 51.

17 Lauren Berlant and Elizabeth Freeman, "Queer Nationality," *Boundary 2* 9.1 (1992): 159.

18 David Savran, *Taking It Like a Man: White Masculinity, Masochism, and Contemporary American Culture* (Princeton: Princeton University Press, 1998), 281.

19 Anderson, 2.

20 Savran, 281.

21 Savran, 282.

22 Eve Kosofsky Sedgwick, *Tendencies* (Durham: Duke University Press, 1993), 8.

23 Lisa Duggan, "Making It Perfectly Queer," *Socialist Review* 22 (1992): 18.

24 Sedgwick, 9.

25 Homi K. Bhabha, "DissemiNation: Time, Narrative and the Margins of the Modern Nation," *Nation and Narration* (New York: Routledge, 1990), 291–322.

26 Cynthia Fuchs, "'Beat me outta me': Alternative Masculinities," *Boys: Masculinities in Contemporary Culture* (Boulder: Westview, 1996), 176.

27 Judith Butler, "Lana's 'Imitation': Melodramatic Repetition and the Gender Performative," *Genders* 9 (1990): 2.

28 Sue-Ellen Case, "Toward a Butch-Femme Aesthetic," *The Gay and Lesbian Studies Reader*, ed. Henry Abelove, Michèle Aina Barale, and David M. Halperin (New York: Routledge, 1993), 304.

III (Dis)Locating Language

Pull / Apart
Rachelle Vaider Knowles

o

l q

m

t a s

y u

u l

e

p r

Rachelle Viader Knowles

Pull: damage by abnormal strain
Apart: into pieces

11 Out of Psychoanalysis
A Ficto-Criticism Monologue

Jeanne Randolph

I HAVE HEARD IT SAID that there are three kinds of baseball umpires:

"Whatever they are I'll call 'em."

"I call 'em like I see 'em."

"They ain't nuthin' till I calls 'em."

The art writing I casually referred to in 1983 as "ficto-criticism" was meant to swoop like an unsynchronized pair of pigeons, up, down, and sideways between each of these positions, the boundaries between which make no difference to beasts with poor eyesight, pea brains, and the power of flight.

Forget the pea brain. The pea brain dimension of the simile is inaccurate. The notion of ficto-criticism I imagined at that time was the deliberate play of a psychoanalytic bricoleur with the structure of formal art criticism. And my playing was borne upon intellection, research, and contemplation. The research, I confess, was not academic, and was not in any sense directed by literary theory. This research was just a searching, a longing to engage object relations psychoanalytic theory with the downtown versions of art criticism that were published and discussed in the bars, kitchens, and occasionally small formal conferences along Queen Street West in Toronto from the 1970s through the 1990s.

If there was one thing I knew, it was a thing or two about object relations psychoanalytic theory. I paid attention to the writings of Melanie Klein and D.W. Winnicott. In *Playing and Reality*, which was a short collection of some of Winnicott's thinking, there were clinical metaphors and inventive ideas that I purloined because they seemed specially sensitive to artistic practice.[1] For example, I treated Winnicott's idea of "transitional object"[2] like Play-Doh™ and renamed it "an amenable object." In my essay with the title "The Amenable Object,"[3] I figured I was counterbalancing the effects of systematic Freudianism—and a few other "isms"—prevalent at the time. Driving the idea of a transitional object home to his readers, Winnicott was under the influence of Existentialist philosophy. For instance, Jean-Paul Sartre, in *The Psychology of Imagination*, had described phenomena that are "syntheses of external and psychical elements."[4] This description was just right for what Winnicott observed clinically as "transitional objects," by which he meant those cuddly things babies love, like plush toy bunnies or monkeys or lambs. These "stuffies" have sensory allure, softness, pliability, and vague faces, and they are also imbued with sentience and an array of moods and roles, as well as an identity. Winnicott described these pieces of cloth, tiny pillows or dolls, as protocultural productions. In my essay "The Amenable Object," I suggested that this was a good enough model for artworks, especially as experienced by audiences. Ficto-criticism was writing that was ambiguous, pliable, and yet pertinent enough that it also was amenable to an artwork's effects, to an artist's concerns, and to the reader's experience, education, and imagination. Basically, I had been astounded that art criticism in the late 1970s was naive about the relationship between subjectivity and objectivity. Ficto-criticism dramatized the spectrum that "lies" (in both senses of the word) between the two.

To me, at that time and to this time, ficto-criticism was not some kind of genre; it was a method, a method meant to raise critical consciousness. It was based on the hypothesis that *all* art critical texts inherently act out a subjectivized rhetorical form, whatever else they accomplish. Writing this monologue reminiscence now, I wish Ludwig Wittgenstein were around. Had he not wondered whether "Nothing is more important for teaching us to understand the concepts we have than constructing new ones."[5] Not that Wittgenstein wanted someone to believe him without thinking, and yet....

In spite of my claim that I was intent upon raising critical consciousness, and that I had a hypothesis—if not a conclusion—to proffer, if Wittgenstein were still alive and I could get hold of him, I would tell him about my psychoanalytic research and living among artists and living with their works. Maybe he would keep this promise he made: "Tell me *how* you are searching and I will tell you *what* you are searching for."[6] Here and now, since Wittgenstein is not available to make his judgement, readers of this reminiscence can.

In 1979, when I began writing about art, all the smart critics had taken a vow to uphold the honour of objectivity and go forth to struggle with the image. The formalists, the Marxists, the semiologists, and the Freudians formed a local and specific contingent along Queen Street West and marshalled serious arguments about the works of artists such as Jan Poldaas, Ric Evans, Robin Collyer, Ian Carr-Harris, and General Idea. The times were heterogeneous, but intellectuals, always numbered by the fingers of one hand, whether left or right, brought theory to art, and theory got out unscathed. Or so it seemed to me.

The first ficto-criticism I ever wrote, and I told artist Andy Fabo beside the refrigerator at a party with lots of people, I distinctly remember telling him that is what it was—ficto-criticism. Richard Rhodes, the critic who later became editor of *Canadian Art* magazine, had hosted this party at his apartment on Gore Vale across from Trinity-Bellwoods Park in Toronto. Stan Denniston had brought my first ficto-criticism as a stack of *Reminders*, just published (1983) for Stan's solo show at the Art Gallery of Greater Victoria. The exhibition curator, Greg Bellerby, had told me, "If I didn't like this thing you wrote for Stan's show, I wouldn't have published it." *Reminders* was written as somebody's little first-person-singular travelogue during her visit to New Orleans. As the somebody strolled around responding to the sights, she reflected about the images and method in the *Reminders* exhibition. Entry number six, "Wednesday, April 18th, 10:00 PM, Room 631," implied equality between criticism and visual art:

> The sales clerk in the money and weapons shop hadn't hurried me a bit today. Of course he had understood how important it is to choose just the right souvenir to take home when you say goodbye to the Vieux Carré. And then after I had purchased my souvenir, I had realized that it was to become my unexhibited addition of a third image to REMINDER #5, in which a view from the slope of Parc Mont Royal in Montreal has as its counterpart an overlook from the edge of Beacon Hill Park in Victoria. My little souvenir, a label from an old rye whiskey bottle, offered a scene from the top of Walnut Hill in Boston.[7]

Stan had begun a friendship at the Ontario College of Art (now the Ontario College of Art and Design) in 1973 with Bernie Miller, to whom I am mated for life. Stan was our thinking and drinking buddy, founding member of the Parkdale Photo League (1980–1982) at Stan's apartment on Cowan Avenue, where I and Bern, Elizabeth MacKenzie and David Clarkson, and sometimes Martha Flemming met to debate art and society. Stan and Bernie were on the board of YYZ Artist's Outlet for ages. Just to attend an opening and get a really good cappuccino (in the earliest eighties), we three would drive to Montreal and back in a day. We drove to Kent State and back in a day. Stan and Bern drove to the grassy knoll in Dallas, and to New Orleans for god knows what. We would do what loyal friends do as days and years go by.

This ficto-criticism I was concocting was meant to raise critical consciousness. It meant exploring the conditions that brought it into being, and the conditions in which this particular ficto-criticism sprouted included at the time a modernist premise: while criticism brings artworks into serious discussion, the hanky-panky between the critics and artists, which supposedly does not, is properly hush-hush. It was almost as if the critic should appear most interested in writing about a stranger's art for an audience of strangers (yet these strangers were somehow in the know). According to principles that I deliberately made up to accommodate horsing around with critical writing, this modernist assumption discredits the influences between artist lovers, artist drinking buddies, artist fellow workers, artist curators, artist ex's, artist writers, and an artist audience.

In my imagination, I began a list of so-called tenets of ficto-criticism, the first of which is that long-term loyalties and tenderness are what preserve an art scene from functioning like a corporation. One of the conditions for my writing ficto-criticism would be that loyalty and tenderness be shamelessly acknowledged. This self-imposed tenet was exaggerated for the *Joanne Tod* "diary" publication at the Southern Alberta Art Gallery in 1986. Bruce Grenville, another culture comrade who is totally valuable to the visual arts in Canada, later gave consideration to this aspect of ficto-criticism:

> *Joanne Tod* raises fundamental questions concerning the position of the writer in relation to the art and the artist. Here, Randolph introduces herself as the writer of the text, but her position is so overdetermined that she begins to subvert her own credibility. Among other things, she plays on the importance of her personal relationship to the artist, a knowledge that the traditional critic would not have divulged:
>
>> It would be only natural to assume that I am the subject of the painting "Miss Lily Jeanne Randolph," as my family nick-named me "Lily Jeanne," and only my closest friends know that. Ms Tod is, of course, one of my closest friends. Ms Tod needs me as a friend, but as an art critic, she does not really need me. I am only one art critic among many who might be similarly paid to write about her art. But wouldn't you suppose that if I am involved in her life and portrayed in her painting, I could write something about her work that is deeper than what others who are paid might write? I might know something unique, something personal, even something secret.[8]

I did presume ficto-criticism to be my own brain-child. Maybe it was not for all I know, but whether it was or was not in point of law my original

FIGURE 1 Joanne Tod, *Miss Lily Jeanne Randolph*, 1984. Photograph by Peter MacCallum (courtesy Joanne Tod).

proprietary invention, my own idiosyncrasies of composing it meant holding myself to another condition—my own subjectivity: eccentric, really smart, cajun-cowgirl, totally friendly, exhibitionistic at times, highly educated, landed immigrant. In my convoluted mind, passion for theory, being a passion, is a dimension of subjectivity. I know I am not at all a person who, according to object-relations psychoanalytic theory, is "so firmly anchored in objectively perceived reality that I may be ill in the opposite direction of being out of touch with the subjective world and with the creative approach to fact."[9] There! Through object relations, psychoanalytic theory trumpets the subjectivity of the cultural worker as a *contribution*. The phrase I must have repeated hundreds of times between 1982 and, say, 1992, was "what is objectively perceived is by definition to some extent subjectively conceived of."[10] How, I would ask again and again, could this not apply to contemplation of the visual arts? Winnicott managed to wriggle free of strict binary thinking and of categorical precision, and wrote that "maximally intense experiences [take place] *in the potential space between the subjective object and the object objectively perceived*, between me-extensions and the not-me. This potential space is at the interplay between there being nothing but me and there being objects and phenomena outside omnipotent control."[11] Why not try for this effect on the reader?

For ten years after *Reminders*, I constantly had to convince people that my method of ficto-criticism was not, no way, not simply, self-expressionism. I kept repeating this to audiences, and reciting over and over again about the object objectively perceived, nevertheless, being in some sense an object subjectively conceived of.

I suppose there will always be press releases and publicity, but reliable understanding of cultural work flourishes in discussion. And in those times, discussion would be conjured by organized meetings either unique or regular, formal or informal, in spontaneous conversation, and sometimes as a response to articles in *Vanguard* magazine or in *Parachute*. Tom Folland had taken the time and effort to write an essay for "Débats/Issues" in *Parachute* (Winter 1989) in which he developed the hypothesis that ficto-criticism was probably amoral. Tom was not persuaded by W.J.T. Mitchell, who in 1987 had written:

> We live in a golden age of criticism. The dominant mode of literary expression in the late 20th century is not poetry, fiction, drama, film, but criticism and theory. By "dominant" I do not mean "most popular" or "widely respected" or "authoritative," but "advanced," "emergent."…"Feminism"/ "Marxism"/"Post-structuralism"…all three transform the traditional role of critical exile into a professional, collaborative, encyclopedic project.[12]

This means that criticism is not simply an objective body of techniques but includes an autobiographical moment of self-criticism, an examination and acknowledgment of one's origins, position, commitments, and antipathies. Mitchell continues, saying "an ambition is most scandalous when it claims to free criticism from its traditional subordination."[13] At the time this was something! The question of ethics evoked by an *art critical methodology.* Six months later I sidled up to Tom at an opening at YYZ and said something like, "Hey, guy, you and me gotta talk," but it never happened.

I was getting invited to lecture about ficto-criticism more frequently after 1989, and at the University of British Columbia in the early 1990s, Serge Guibault, upon hearing me tell an audience my method, said what I was searching for was to legitimate myself as "a narcissistic Reaganite." This was something! The question of ethics evoked by an *art critical methodology.* Ficto-criticism had, however, ambled onto the Queen Street scene about the time of Reaganomics, real-estate agents, and upscale shopkeepers. Compared to the early days, to which Philip Monk's "The Queen Street Years" exhibition at the Power Plant paid tribute, ficto-criticism was—like postcolonial, feminist, queer, and Lacanian theory, and even identity politics—a mid-age spread, less sexy and too responsive to postmodernist provocations. Soon enough, by the mid-nineties—Hannah Arendt had cautioned about this (Maynard Krebs had parroted it)—the thirty-something artist-run population was losing *propinquity.* To earn a predictable income, to afford your rent, to raise your children, to hear some silence longer than the interval between the Queen West Streetcars, artists had to change their addresses. Ficto-criticism had been most organic when we had propinquity, but in the nineties ficto-criticism had to get amoeboid, and reach beyond.

In 1993, when Cyril Reade was artist-in-residence at La Chambre Blanche in Quebec City, he could choose whomever he wanted to stay as resident art writer for the eleven days preceding his installation there. Cyril and I had been acquainted since 1989 when he, with Alice and Mickey Mansell, had orchestrated "Dynamics of Criticism," a three-day residential workshop at some kind of 1940s-style Rotary Club boy's camp or something at Owen Sound, Ontario. Bruce Barber and I had convened the various sunny talks and discussions each day. As with Nicole Jolicoeur and our beautiful *Vérité Folle* publication (1989), the idea was that Cyril's and my "catalogue" would be autonomous, designed for visual and intellectual pleasure, not a literal record of how his exhibition was set up in the gallery. At La Chambre Blanche, Cyril and I designed our own publication, which we distributed ourselves. Thanks to the nearby stationer with colour photocopier, cool papers, and spiral bindings, we produced a limited edition of *Table Talk. Table Talk* was placed on a table in Cyril's exhibition, *Talking Tables*, at La Chambre Blanche. His exhibition was a meditation upon stories, planning, and arguments at the family dinner table night after night. Our publication, including two truly lovely photos of his exhibition tables, comprised seven vignettes that were meant to appear as excerpts from a potentially endless series. This ficto-criticism was searching out in the far hinterlands. Although there were leitmotifs, the reader or visitor to the gallery could imagine to have recurred around the family dinner table, *Table Talk*, once it left La Chambre Blanche, was an odd, oddly bound, autonomous group of unlikely tales. A career-mongering artist would never have stood for it. The conversations, the fussing with details, the celebration of the installation at La Chambre Blanche, remain among my unique memories of *la vie bohème*, but if a historian ever wanted to confirm facts about the *Talking Tables* exhibition by referring to the alleged "catalogue," well, they would get an eyeful of "the creative approach to fact," as Winnicott had phrased it.

The twenty-fifth anniversary of my immigration to Canada was approaching, and in a preconscious acknowledgment of the changing circumstances in my adopted Canadian neighborhood, I accepted an invitation to write ficto-criticism for Vera Frenkel, after Vera's astonishing *Transit Bar* had garnered much admiration at Documenta. *The Transit Bar* was an installation about emigration, flight from war, expatriate travels and life in the aftermath. In 1994, the Power Plant Gallery at Harbourfront and the National Gallery in Ottawa would each install a version of ... *from the Transit Bar*. I know perfectly well that Vera comprehends friendship and ethos as an admixture with histories. As a generous artist person, Vera understands how the visual arts and art criticism can be in a sisterly, not a boss-employee, relation. I wrote *Truth Disguised as Lie* as an homage to the ethical power of visual culture invoked by Vera's work. *Truth Disguised as Lie* is what a myth might be like if it were secular, idealizing one's own locale, and sharing illusions with old comrades.

As always, I had turned to object relations psychoanalytic theory to interpret the relationship between friendship and ethos, or the characteristic spirit or disposition of a community. What I will do to object-relations psychoanalytic theory is, sometimes where there is a general term, like "reality-acceptance," I'll imagine it as transformed, like from "reality-acceptance" to "adopted country acceptance," which is what I did for Vera. This rubberizing of theory in relation to artwork does not leave theory unscathed. Theory can be reconfigured by the ideas, images, and memories important to the artwork. *Playing and Reality*, Winnicott's psychoanalytic theory text (from which my method of ficto-criticism usually ventures forth) presented a relevant, amenable hypothesis:

> It is assumed here that the task of reality-acceptance [adopted-country acceptance] is never completed, that no human being is free from the strain of relating inner and outer reality [homeland and adopted land difference], and that relief from this strain is provided by an intermediate area of experience...which is not challenged (arts, religion, etc.) [in regard to whether it has validity for those immersed in it].[14]

Winnicott adds,

> I am here staking a claim for an intermediate state between a baby's inability and growing ability to recognize and accept reality [homeland and adopted land difference]. I am therefore studying the substance of *illusion*... which in adult life is inherent in art and religion....We can share a respect for *illusory experience*, and if we wish we may collect together and form a group on the basis of the similarity of our illusory experiences.[15]

Truth Disguised as Lie was written to proclaim the illusions that Vera and I are capable of propagating through cultural husbandry. *Truth Disguised as Lie* chronicled events—it elaborated illusions of events—in the decade-long development of a revolutionary movement supposedly initiated by Vera and me. Each supposed event had become the scene for a different precept of our cultural change project. For instance, "Precept #3":

A Fierce Miscreed (Precept #3: Art Is Not the Opposite of Technology)
What will be the medium of our revolution? The choosing of medium is an ethical judgement. Belief must find its embodiment. Communication is required. What communicative technology will be invested with the power to represent our beliefs? The technology will offer a position, a role, perhaps, an identity, to those who operate it, as well as to its audience. The communicative device positions and limits, as well as serves, its operators.

No technology is without a history. Newly invented technologies are born into the waiting arms of the ideology that conceived them. Whoever has in their era invested a particular communicative vehicle with the privilege to convey their values has left their history upon that medium. Tickertape. Radio. The megaphone. Bongo drums.

What medium embodies collegiality, sensuality, responsibility, curiosity, the accidental, compassion, hope, vulnerability? What medium prizes these? And what will happen to the medium in the future?[16]

What would happen if Vera and I decided upon conversation as our preferred medium? According to the *Truth Disguised as Lie* myth, the Canadian cultural revolution was getting so widespread that General Norman Schwartzkopf himself, Commander-in-Chief of Operation Desert Storm, was brought to Ottawa to turn the citizens against Vera and me. If you read our other precepts, see whether you embrace them yourself, and so, quietly in your own mind, you decide whether or not the revolutionary movement has propagated after all.

In 1998, the next time an offer was made to me to write with a ficto-criticism method, I wandered right back into "the hinterlands." To my everlasting chagrin, I caused surprise and disappointment, forcing Cheryl Sourkes into what I can only speculate was a pressurized, sleepless night. Sharon Kivland, with whom I had enjoyed a cup of tea at Bernie's and my old place on Sterling Road in 1996, had been introduced to me by Nicole Joliecoeur. Nicole and Sylvie Belanger brought Sharon over for tea in advance of a lecture Sharon was to give at the Ontario College of Art. Two years later Cheryl Sourkes telephoned me saying that the Toronto Photographers' Workshop was mounting an exhibition of Sharon's latest work but it could not be confirmed what pieces were in the show until two days before the opening. "This calls for ficto-criticism!" Cheryl had joked, and I agreed to write the text for the exhibition. Unfortunately, even though I knew that Sharon knew that I write ficto-criticism, maybe neither Sharon nor Cheryl really believed I would go ahead with it this time.

The essay "Something for All Ages" was about desire, the symbol for which was the history of the desire of many Western poets to make their own versions of love poem #51 by Catullus, itself a Latin version of a Greek poem by Sappho. I had estimated that in the past five hundred years, five hundred poets, including Shelley and Keats, had composed their own version of this poem.

Winnicott, who read the poetry of John Donne with unique appreciation, had, according to me, recognized (centuries later) the psychoanalytic implications of how the Metaphysical Poets (someone of whom no doubt also wrote a version of #51) worked with symbolism. Winnicott had realized that, like the Metaphysical Poets, it is possible for any citizen, and especially artists, to "develop a use of symbols that stand at one and the same time for external world phenomena and for phenomena of the individual person."[17]

Marius Bewley, the editor of the book *Selected Poetry* of John Donne, describes Donne as "a leader of the *avant garde* in late Elizabethan and Jacobean London. His audience was deliberately restricted to the happy few whose education, background, and position equipped them to appreciate and esteem the most difficult poet of his day."[18] What a dream it would be to earn such a depiction! Bewley clarifies Donne's metaphysical method:

> In scholasticism man is a composite creature made up of body and psyche between which an intrinsic union exists, and man has his complete identity only in terms of this union. Psyche and body together form one nature, and essentially human activity, including the emotions, proceeds from body and psyche in conjunction.
>
> [In "The Ecstasy" Donne] presents his lovers to us in a spring landscape, implied rather than described in the opening stanza…. Contemplating each other, the lovers fall into a trance, or more properly an ecstasy, for Donne is thinking of that term in mystical philosophy which describes the intimate union of the [psyche] with God—a state in which a knowledge or sense of God, short-circuiting the senses, is intuited directly. In the poem, however, not God, but each to the other, becomes the object of this exalted

way of knowing.... In their ecstatic state it is revealed to the lovers that their love ... is ultimately an activity of the [psyche].... Although the lovers have discovered their love to be [intrapsychic] in essence, it can be consummated and fulfilled only if they resort to their bodies, for it is man's [*sic*] unique distinction that in the duality of his composition heaven and earth meet. This duality is explicitly introduced in the lines referring to the spirits of the blood that knit the subtle knot which makes us man [*sic*]:

> "The Ecstasy doth unperplex"
>   (We said) "and tell us what we love;
> We see by this, it was not sex;
>   We see, we saw not what did move;

> "But as all several souls contain
> Mixture of things, they know not what,
> Love, these mix'd souls doth mix again,
>   And makes both one, each this and that.

> "A single violet transplant,
>   The strength, the color, and the size,
> (All which before was poor, and scant,)
>   Redoubles still, and multiplies.

> "When love, with one another so
> Interinanimates two souls,
> That abler soul, which thence doth flow,
>   Defects of loneliness controls.

>   . . .

> "But oh alas, so long, so far
> Our bodies why do we forbear?
> They are ours, though they are not we; we are
>   The intelligences, they the sphere.

>   . . .

> "As our blood labors to beget
>   Spirits, as like souls as it can,
>   Because such fingers need to knit
>   That subtle knot, which makes us man."

This [continues Bewley,] is not philosophical poetry in any real sense, although it uses the concepts and vocabulary of philosophy. Its use of them is invariably accompanied by a complex infusion of irony.[19]

In the above citation, I have altered Bewley's commentary in just the way I imagine Winnicott would have. Everywhere Bewley used the word "soul," I substitute the word "psyche." Anyway, the resultant "Something for All Ages" implicated, but did not describe, Sharon Kivland's work, and, frankly, avoided Lacanian theory like the plague.

"Something for All Ages" was a flop. Sharon was considerate and gracious, of course, about its exemplifying literally what I had termed since 1985 as "a parallel text." The text was based on the centrality of the concept of desire and its representation, not on the specificity of Sharon's art practice. It was generous of Toronto Photographers' Workshop actually to print the thing. At literally the eleventh hour, meanwhile, Cheryl herself had composed a second essay, "What Pictures Want," that covered the actual works in the exhibition and their theoretical context. I was saddened to have caused disappointment to Sharon and Cheryl.

Undeterred, however, even by guilt, I wrote a "parallel" text again in 1999. It was gorgeously designed into an artist's book by Joey Morgan. Joey had been commissioned to produce a new installation, *The Man Who Waits and Sleeps While I Dream*, at the MacKenzie Art Gallery in Regina. It coalesced out of Joey's research into dreaming. Joey had visited sleep laboratories too, and had gathered hypnogogic images and ideas, which culminated in an elaborate multimedia installation. Joey worked devotedly to transform the imagery, her audio soliloquy, and the ficto-criticism essay into, again, an autonomous publication that would be a visual and intellectual pleasure for readers.

Winnicott had said something about "dreaming and living," that they were "two phenomena that are in many respects the same,"[20] typical inside-out thinking, and I just knew this concept was relevant to Joey's exhibition. I never figured out how, and that is because it was all so … so … well, metaphysical, in a way, and I decided such was not the point.

The circumstances in which I composed the essay "Elizabethan Post-Modern" for Joey revealed the irony of my own life as a psychoanalytic thinker. On a mischievous impulse, I had applied for promotion from assistant to associate professor in the Department of Psychiatry at the University of Toronto. I was proposing a change in academic designation based upon my research on culture, not on the basis of teaching or clinical work. The department even had a category for me—creative professional development. Inwardly giggling, I would imagine the Department of Psychiatry committee members trying to scan the horizon of "the hinterlands" of psychoanalysis. "Psychoanalytic theory is part of psychiatry isn't it?" I would say to myself to rationalize what I was doing, and said soon after to a special colleague, Professor Dr. Gary Rodin, when he delivered the bad news. Whatever the pastureland is that stretches between the farm and the hinterlands, modern-day psychiatry won't step in cultural theory to get there. So my day-to-day intellectual exile was confirmed, and yet, paradoxically, I felt intellectually located, unnerving as it was. At first I believed that sometimes the strain of reconciling inner to outer reality is not worth it. Cogitating honestly, however, about the relations

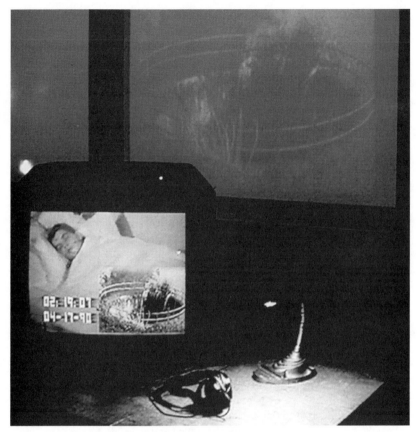

FIGURE 2 Joey Morgan, "The Man Who Waits and Sleeps While I Dream." Detail from *An Analysis for the Romantic Condition,* 2003. Photograph by Joey Morgan (courtesy of Joey Morgan and Centre D'Art Passerelle, Best, France).

between hard-core scientific ideology and the contradictions of making culture in a technological society, I finally accepted the wisdom of Winnicott: "Environmental influence, bad or even good, comes into our [lives] as a traumatic idea, intolerable because not operating within the area of [our] omnipotence."[21] Many a metaphysical trauma—just kidding! Many an environmental influence, bad or even good, comes into our lives as a traumatic idea—and if ideas were muscles, a whole passel of Canadian artists could train for Olympic weightlifting. Maybe there are ideas that the Department of Psychiatry committee deemed irrelevant, but with Joey Morgan the ideas would visually redouble still and multiply.

"Elizabeth Post-Modern" ends with Joey's prose, after my own paragraphs set it up:

Many of us today are impressed by technical apparatuses, yearning for mastery in physiological or chemical terms, and wishing to forget, as Freud himself most certainly did not, that "these terms too are only part of a figurative language."

For the scientist, [the patient in the sleep lab] who sleeps is performing and producing uniquely, all night, unabated. The scientist is expecting the man's immaterial plenitude to flood the chamber, the cot, the sheets, the white knit blankets, the electroencephalogram, the electrodes and wires, the sphygmomanometer, flood to the wall, through the glass, flood the data sheets, reading material, sandwiches, a clock. Five or six hundred minutes will accumulate.

Attending to this profusion is a woman who is paid to note and notice certain things. That woman, the monitor who is hired (free-lance, part-time) to collect the information for the research—depicted in this lab in these conditions, that woman's role reminds me of an artist's life, if not always, now:

> It's just that this is a lovely sort
> of peculiar circumstance.
> Maybe he doesn't ever think about me.
> Maybe once we've greeted each other,
> and I slip into the other room—
> maybe he forgets
> that I'm watching through the glass.
> I watch his body for signs
> of what his sleeping world is like.
> I used to think I could write my own novel
> or maybe some poetry
> in between your dreams.
> I guess I didn't count on being distracted.
> Maybe my own writing will come later
> when I'm more able to be alone.[22]

Then, as now, Winnicott's worry, about the empty patches in the psyche's garden that await new seedlings, seemed urgent: "In using the word culture I am thinking of the inherited tradition. I am thinking of something that is in the common pool of humanity, into which individuals and groups of people may contribute, and from which we may all draw *if we have somewhere to put what we find*."[23] Where, in the Canadian psyches, is there a place to put all the creations that Joey makes, every artist I know and do not know, all the imagery, all the ideas, mine included? We are the intelligences, and the Canadian pool of humanity is the sphere, and yet...???

Logicians, but not all philosophers, and certainly not Winnicott, hold to the *tertium non datur*, "the law of the excluded middle." It was generally thought to be a necessary truth, an indisputable law of logical thought: any proposition or statement whatever is either true, or, if not true, then false. The law of the excluded middle "seems," according to Richard Taylor, the first William H.P. Faunce Professor of Philosophy at Brown University, "in any case, quite unexceptionable."[24]

Meanwhile, wasn't it Wittgenstein who demonstrated that there is something in between logic and nonsense? Whoever demonstrated it, a ficto-criticism can be concatenated anywhere along that spectrum, from logically convincing to unciggerab ub ibbie defube. Nonsense is the true "hinterland strong and free" of language, yet the ficto-critical methodology I have perpetrated never treated the relationship between art writing and visual culture as nonsensical. The conditions to which ficto-criticism are held in my particular psyche are difficult, and do not adhere too well to the Reality Principle of time and money. For me, ficto-criticism is suffused with theory; theory is the ocean in which ficto-criticism paddles. I cannot imagine ficto-criticism without a corresponding theoretical system. And should not ficto-criticism require a patient commitment to the evolution of each artist's praxis? It surely requires a kindly relationship between the ficto-critical writer and the artist. Any ficto-criticism I had written in the twentieth century would materialize from an invitation by the artist, not a gallery, museum, or publisher. I composed ficto-criticism in an ambience of absolute trust between writer and artist. Such ficto-criticism does demand readers who can read between the lines. Ficto-criticism is not favoured by the humourless. And, its poison picked, ficto-criticism courts what Bewley said of John Donne's writing, "some snobbishness seems to have attached itself to the ability to do it."[25]

There is one last ficto-critical text to mention. According to Winnicott,

> It is creative apperception more than anything else that makes the individual feel that life is worth living. Contrasted with this is a relationship to external reality which is one of compliance, the world and its details being recognized, but only as something to be fitted in with or demanding adaptation. Compliance carries with it a sense of futility and is associated with the idea that nothing matters ... the link can be made, and usefully made, between creative living and living itself, and the reasons can be studied why it is that creative living can be lost and why the individual's feeling that life is real or meaningful can disappear.[26]

Late summer 2001 brought an invitation that required non-compliance with five-to-six-eighths of my own tenets of ficto-criticism. Somewhere, where I do not know, Winnicott had spoken of creativity as having an element of "ruthlessness," but Winnicott's inside-out thinking makes this kind of ruthlessness a socially desirable virtue. Winnicott implied that somewhere between good-enough compliance and good-enough ruthlessness, artists produce admirable work. Already reflecting upon this, I accepted an invitation to write for a group exhibition of artists whom I had never met and whose work I did not care all that much about. The artists obviously had no acquaintance with, let alone trust in, ficto-criticism (two of them were dead); it was the curator who had extended the invitation. Lisa Melandri, the curator at the Santa Monica Museum of Art, knew neither me nor my work, but she was gutsy. The exhibition was scheduled for the Moore College of Art in Philadelphia early in 2002, featuring the paintings of three women alumnae, Mary Cassatt (1844–1926), Alice Neel (1900–1984) and Karen Kilimnik (contemporary, age undisclosed). There had been nothing either Lisa or I could do but trust each other.

While staying in Vancouver at the brilliant Lorna Brown's house during the week before bounding onto a stage for "Acting Out, Playdoh™ and Doubt: a personal history of performative lecturing," there was time to switch from research to writing for Lisa. On a certain day in Lorna's study, I positioned myself such that a rare avalanche of sunlight thundered onto my retinas for five hours while I sat on a futon scribbling. The only thing I could think of was Mother Theresa. The title of the ficto-criticism composition for Lisa is "An Audience with Mother Theresa." This was based on the Saint of the Gutter's transient participation in each of the three artist's lives, unbeknownst to them. Supposedly, I knew about these transient incidents because I had interviewed Mother Theresa at Nirmal Hriday in Calcutta in August 1997. Why am I writing about this? I do not know, except historically speaking, this Mother Theresa thing was as true as ever to Winnicott's idea that to make culture we "develop a use of symbols that stand at one and the same time for the external world phenomena and for phenomena of the individual person."[27]

I remember back in 1982, written in "The Amenable Object" there was this idea: "It would be gripping indeed to read a critical review in which the writer is able to reveal in what way certain of his or her very own most hidden libidinal longings are linked to the quality of a particular artwork."[28] This here that you are reading now does not come close.

Notes

1 D.W. Winnicott, *Playing and Reality* (Markham, ON: Penguin, 1980).
2 Winnicott, 4.
3 Jeanne Randolph, *Psychoanalysis and Synchronized Swimming and Other Writings on Art*, ed. Bruce Grenville (Toronto: YYZ Books, 1991), 18.
4 Jean-Paul Sartre, *The Psychology of Imagination*, trans. Bernard Frechtman (New York: Washington Square Press, 1966), 25.
5 Ludwig Wittgenstein, *Culture and Value*, trans. Peter Winch, ed. G.H. von Wright (Chicago: University of Chicago Press, 1984), 74e.

6 Ludwig Wittgenstein, *Philosophical Remarks*, trans. R. Hargreaves and Roger White, ed. Rush Rees (Oxford: Blackwell 1975), 67.

7 Randolph, *Psychoanalysis and Synchronized Swimming*, 97.

8 Grenville, introduction, Randolph, *Psychoanalysis and Synchronized Swimming*, 13.

9 Winnicott, 78.

10 Winnicott, 77.

11 Winnicott, 118; emphasis in original.

12 W.J.T. Mitchell, "The Golden Age of Criticism: Seven Theses and Commentary," *London Review of Books* 25 June 1987: 16–17.

13 Mitchell, 16.

14 Winnicott, 15.

15 Winnicott, 3.

16 Randolph, *Symbolism and Its Discontents*, ed. Steve Reinke (Toronto: YYZ Books, 1991), 116–17.

17 Winnicott, 128.

18 Marius Bewley, introduction, *Selected Poetry*, by John Donne, ed. Marius Bewley (New York: New American Library, 1979), x.

19 Bewley, xvi-xviii.

20 Winnicott, 37.

21 Winnicott, 91.

22 Joey Morgan, "The Man Who Waits and Sleeps While I Dream," MacKenzie Art Gallery 1998, 16–17.

23 Winnicott, 116; emphasis in original.

24 Richard Taylor, *Metaphysics* (Englewood Cliffs, NJ: Prentice-Hall, 1963), 57.

25 Bewley, x.

26 Winnicott, 76–81.

27 Winnicott, 128.

28 Randolph, *Psychoanalysis and Synchronized Swimming*, 3–24.

12 Some Imaginary Geographies in Quebec Fiction

Ceri Morgan

SINCE THE QUIET REVOLUTION, the francophone nationalist assertion of the 1960s, questions around space, place, and identity have assumed a particular importance in Quebec politics and culture. The shift, at this time, away from a cultural nationalism that sought to protect the language, religion, and way of life of French Canadians throughout Canada, and towards a territorial nationalism that identified a francophone identity with the delimited space of the province of Quebec, is reflected in the epithetic slide from "Canadiens français" to "Québécois." Forty years on, efforts to promote a Québécois nationalism that is not bound up in an implicit assumption that the national subject will be of white, European descent point as much to the successes of the Quiet Revolution as to its failure to produce an independent Quebec. For at the same time as the attempts to make the term "Québécois" refer to all those living in the province of Quebec highlight the tensions inherent in what many regard as an ethnic nationalism, these debates also chart the shift in Quebec's political understanding of itself.[1] Whereas the nationalists of the Quiet Revolution were engaged in a search for the nation, there is a now an implicit assumption that this nation exists, if not in legal terms, then as a conceptual entity. This is the imagined nation theorized by Benedict Anderson, who argues that the rise of print capitalism, as represented by media like the newspaper, contributed to individuals thinking of themselves as being in a relationship of simultaneity with others within their community.[2] This horizontal temporal relationship is, simultaneously, a vertical one, since the nation is also imagined as "a solid community moving steadily down (or up) history."[3]

In this essay, I am going to look at some of the ways in which a particular kind of print medium, namely the novel, has mediated and contributed to Quebec's national imagining of itself since the Quiet Revolution. This piece is part of a growing interest in the spatial amongst critics of Quebec literature.[4] It is also part of a wider trend that seeks to address questions around the spatial by looking to cultural geography.[5] Within this wide-ranging discipline, a number of critics have been concerned with examining what Jack Warwick, in his analysis of representations of the North in French-Canadian and Québécois literature, terms "the geography of the imagination."[6] In her work on British and French travel writing between 1600 and 1830, Chloe Chard draws on Christian Jacob to describe what she refers to as imaginative geographies: "an imaginative geography marks out both a 'space of privileged projection for desires, aspirations, affective memory, the cultural memory of the subject' and, at the same time, a space governed by the demands of a field of knowledge."[7] Here, then, I am concerned with looking at the ways in which certain spaces or places within contemporary Quebec fiction become, at particular moments in time, privileged sites over which to map desires not only around the national but also around other positionings of identity.

Mapping Montreal during the Quiet Revolution

Montreal is the primary spatial referent to emerge in Quebec's francophone fiction of the last forty years. This is due to a number of factors, such as the city's being the cultural centre of Quebec, and the fact that, consequently, many writers and publishers are located there. However, it is the particular significance that is attached to Montreal that explains why it features so greatly in francophone Québécois literature. The city has tended to be seen as an obstacle to national independence, due in part to the historic presence of a significant anglophone community. Prior to the Quiet Revolution, it was this relatively small anglophone population that enjoyed most of the socio-economic power in the province. Many of this managerial and business-owning class lived on the west side of boulevard Saint-Laurent, otherwise known as the, or la, Main. The majority of the white francophones who made up the biggest percentage of the labour class lived to the east of this street. Montreal has historically been, and continues to be, an ethnically diverse city, and this is figured in its topography: in addition to the primarily white anglophone and francophone communities described above, there is, for example, a long-established Chinese community near the old port, a Jamaican community around NDG (Notre-Dame-de-Grâce), and an Italian community near Jean Talon metro station. The question of which majority language—French or English—is adopted by immigrants to Quebec with no prior knowledge of either has been a contentious issue. Indeed, Bill 101, the Charter of the French Language (1977), passed by the nationalist Parti québécois shortly after winning the provincial elections for the first time in 1976, sought partly to address the preference for English amongst many immigrants, who viewed the language as being ultimately more marketable than French.[8]

Nevertheless, discourses that pit a model of a multiethnic Montreal against the social homogeneity of the rest of francophone Quebec, which, for the most part, is situated along the Saint Lawrence River, are misleading. In addition to the anglophone communities in the Eastern townships along the US border, there are some anglophone villages on the Gaspé peninsula, as well as on the lower Saint-Lawrence. There are also a number of First Nations reserves, such as the Mohawk reserve in Kahnawake, near Montreal, and the Innu reserve at Sept-Îles, on the north shore. This social diversity is usually suppressed in the nationalist literature of the Quiet Revolution, which mobilizes the tensions between anglophones and francophones in Montreal as a metaphor for the wider national struggle between a francophone Quebec and an English Canada.

The literary genre that has since come to be known as *le texte national* adopts a bi-ethnic model of the city, with Montreal figured as being divided between a poor francophone east and a wealthy anglophone west.[9] This binary model functions as the framework for Jacques Renaud's *Broke City*.[10] Although Renaud described his novella as a purely personal piece of writing, it has been received as a nationalist text, due partly to the fact that it was published by Parti Pris. This publishing house was established around the same time as the cultural and political journal of the same name, which was founded in 1963. Theoretically informed by Marxism, psychoanalysis, Jean-Paul Sartre, and anti-colonial writers like Franz Fanon, Alberto Memmi, and Jacques Berque, those writing for the journal promoted secularization, socialism, and independence for Quebec.

In the course of *Broke City*, Johnny, Renaud's unemployed, anti-social, and extremely violent anti-hero, murders a drug dealer named "Bubbles" whom Johnny suspects of having an affair with his girlfriend, Philomena. Philomena, who supplements the income she earns at a cigar factory by turning tricks for drivers who offer her a ride, is actually having a relationship with Berthe, a middle-class student who has coerced the working-class woman into having sex with her in exchange for money. The two women are discovered by Johnny at the end of the novella, and he responds by assaulting Philomena before continuing his meanderings around Montreal.

Renaud's novella is typical of the nationalist, anti-urban writing of the 1960s, in that it mobilizes a mapping metaphor so as to carry out a symbolic reappropriation of Montreal—and therefore of Quebec as a whole—away from its anglophone ruling class.[11] Time and again, *Broke City* names particular streets and landmarks that would be very familiar to the domestic audiences at whom the novella was aimed. There are references to rue Saint-Denis, where Johnny lives, rue Duluth, where Philomena is staying with a friend, rue Clark, parc Lafontaine, and boulevard Saint-Laurent, or "the Main."[12] The majority of these are situated on Montreal's East Side in what were, during this period, francophone working-class neighbourhoods.

The effects of this quasi-obsessive naming of particular places in Montreal seem somewhat contradictory. On the one hand, at a time when Montreal looked like an English-speaking city, *Broke City* carries out a francophone recovery of the urban. In this respect, the novella can be compared with Hubert Aquin's *Blackout*, in which the francophone male protagonist asserts his national pride by having sex with and then killing his girlfriend in McGill University, the bastion of the middle-class anglophone society to which she belonged.[13] On the other hand, however, the francophone recovery of Montreal in *Broke City* is emphatically partial. This is suggested the morning after the murder. Sitting in parc Lafontaine, which borders the formerly working-class district of the Plateau, Johnny comments on the disparities between east and west Montreal: "The only difference between the orgies on the Plateau Mont-Royal and in Westmount is that on the Plateau you knock yourself out and in Westmount you tipple. On the Plateau you get plastered, in Westmount you get a little tipsy, and to do that you gotta hide yourself behind a ten-foot fence."[14] Although the English translation refers the reader to specific districts in Montreal, the French version alludes only to the more general categories of "east" and "west."[15] The absence of any direct references to anglophone neighbourhoods in Renaud's novella highlights Johnny's inability to roam the city in its entirety. This inability is suggested in the English translation by the allusion to the security measures adopted by the wealthy inhabitants of Westmount.

There is, then, a tension within *Broke City*, which is a common feature of *le texte national*. This genre often exaggerates its protagonists' sense of exile in order to emphasize more fully the oppression of Quebec's francophones. As Pierre Nepveu points out, a number of nationalist writers of the 1960s figured exile as a constitutive element of the colonized Québécois subject.[16] In so doing, they were informed by anti-colonial theories elsewhere in the French-speaking world, as well as by icons within Quebec's literary history, such as Émile Nelligan, who spent most of his life in a psychiatric institution. During the Quiet Revolution, these nationalist writers theorized colonization as having ensured that Quebec was cut off from history, caught in a temporal interruption that manifested itself in compulsive forms of behaviour such as the obsession with hate that comes to Johnny in the course of *Broke City*. Writing in 1976, Gilles Marcotte argues that this separation from history accounts for the focus on the spatial in this writing: "today's novelist, despite his desire for history, is closer to the cartographer, in that he wishes primarily to define a place, to 'construct the nation.'"[17] However, given that the search for the nation that we get in the anti-urban writing of the 1960s is characterized by a recognition of the impossibility of ever realizing this goal, the francophone recuperation of Quebec that is effected in this literature is extremely unstable.

The Anti-Domestic Novel, or Feminine Nationalist Writing

Le texte national is associated with the anti-urban writing of a number of male authors of the 1960s. This gendering of Quebec's nationalist literature has been critiqued by feminist scholars, as has the violence against women that typically informs it. In *le texte national*, the national struggle is frequently displaced onto the domain of sexual relations, with the male anti-hero only achieving a degree of self-assertion after he has raped or killed his female partner. The writing of the male nationalist authors and critics of the 1960s then mobilizes a misogyny that is at odds with the radical sexual politics that they otherwise espoused. Patricia Smart interprets this as an attempt to reject the castrating mother who was the flip side of the idealized maternal that informed French-Canadian nationalism.[18] This nationalism was based on Catholicism, an attachment to the land, and "the revenge of the cradle"—the maintaining of a high birth rate. Smart argues that, in making female characters the victims of a violence, which is figured as necessary for the self-assertion of the masculine protagonist, male writers of the Quiet Revolution effectively excluded women from the nationalist project. At the same time, she suggests that women writers within Quebec might have rejected the divisiveness that is inherent within nationalism: "Gabrielle Roy's *The Tin Flute*, Marie-Claire Blais's *Visions d'Anna*, and even "Speak White," Michèle Lalonde's famous nationalist poem, are examples of the profound malaise and even repugnance women seem to feel in relation to the borders that divide human beings and the wars and violence produced by national struggles."[19]

Smart is right to argue that Quebec women's writing is positioned differently than that by men with respect to the nationalist project of the 1960s. It is possible, nonetheless, to regard this difference as being as much a part of Quebec's nationalist literary canon as the anti-urban writing of authors like Jacques Renaud. The rejection of oppressive models of femininity bound up in French-Canadian nationalism that we get in women's writing of this period also represents an engagement with the modernizing impulses that informed the Quiet Revolution, since this was theorized by those writing for *Parti pris* in terms of a fundamental rejection of the past. Women's writing of the same period frequently subverts the formal conventions of Quebec's novel of the land, so as to critique the French-Canadian nationalist ideology that informed this genre. Writers such as Marie-Claire Blais and Anne Hébert set their novels within the rural, domestic space, which then becomes the locus for a critique of the figure of the happy, asexual mother that informed "the revenge of the cradle." Blais's *A Season in the Life of Emmanuel*, which charts a period in the life of a family in rural Quebec in the 1940s, is a playful, yet highly satirical reworking of the novel of the land.[20] Here, the domestic space is figured not as a source of comfort but as a place of overcrowding, poverty, and violence. This is underlined in the opening pages of the novel, when Grandmother Antoinette remarks to the newborn baby, Emmanuel, "you've picked a bad time to be born, we've never been so poor, it's a hard winter for everyone, the war, the food shortage, and you the sixteenth too."[21]

In contrast with the romanticized mother of "the revenge of the cradle," the mother in Blais's novel who, significantly, remains unnamed, is reduced to a shadowy presence, oppressed by years of multiple childbirth and sexual abuse. She is figured as being raped every night by her oafish husband, whilst her children listen at the door:

> At night [Emmanuel] slept in the same bedroom as his parents, cut off from his mother by his father's shadow, which filled all his dreams...with sacred terror. Several times, as he grew older, he was to see that brutal silhouette moving to and fro in the room. (Was he not the intruder, the giant enemy who raped his mother every night, as she lay moaning in a gentle whisper, "Please, the children are listening).[22]

The children, too, are subjected to the violence of their father and suffer regular beatings. The sense of claustrophobia within the domestic space is heightened by the representation of the land, which is figured as a desolate, snowy backdrop to the action, most of which takes place indoors: "the dark spread little by little over the hill, veiling the white forest and the silent fields."[23]

Despite the themes that Blais treats in her novel, the tone of *A Season in the Life of Emmanuel* remains ironic and humorous rather than desperate, since Blais uses a number of stylistic devices so as to subvert the realism of the novel of the land. As Mary Jean Green points out, Blais's novel inverts the traditional values of French-Canadian society.[24] Consequently, when the daughter, Héloïse, leaves to go to work in a brothel in town, this is figured as a preferable alternative to remaining in the domestic space and repeating the fate of her mother. At the same time, *A Season in the Life of Emmanuel* makes a parallel between the brothel and the convent, which Héloïse attended for a short time before being expelled for her erotic mysticism: "Before long, though never ceasing to compare life in the Tavern with her happy days spent in the convent, slipping from one form of contentedness into another ... Héloïse came at last to know the disturbing harmony of a satisfied desire."[25] Héloïse's move to the town represents an embracing of the urban by the end of Blais's novel, and is connected thematically with the optimism that comes with the beginning of spring and the beginning of Emmanuel's receiving some affection from his mother. In working in town, Héloïse, along with her brothers, Number Seven and Pomme, who have gone to work in the shoe factory there, are able to send money back home, thereby lessening the poverty of the family.

All the same, the embracing of the urban that we get in Blais's novel is a qualified one, since Pomme loses a number of his fingers in an industrial accident and Number Seven falls victim to the corrupt priest who previously helped to accelerate the death of his brother, Jean-le-Maigre. The children are represented as not being able fully to escape the fate expected of their social milieu: this is an ironic reprise of the novel of the land's emphasis on the continuity of an agricultural way of life; and yet it also has similarities with the claustrophobia that informed the anti-urban novels of the period, in which the anti-hero is caught up in a temporal circularity at the same time as he can only have limited access to Montreal. In this instance, however, it is woman who has no place to go since, as Green points out, Blais's novel does not propose that working in a brothel is a serious solution to women's oppression.[26]

Anne Hébert's *Kamouraska* also reworks the novel of the land from a feminine perspective.[27] Hébert's historical novel, which is based on a real-life event, is made up of a number of extended flashbacks. During these, the protagonist, Élisabeth, recalls her affair with a young anglophone doctor, George Nelson. Élisabeth first meets Nelson at Sorel, where she is staying at the home of her aunts, so as to avoid her violent and manic-depressive husband, Antoine Tassy. When she becomes pregnant with Nelson's child, Élisabeth and Nelson decide that they must kill Tassy. Nelson travels alone to Tassy's ancestral home in Kamouraska, a village on the lower Saint Lawrence, in a journey that Élisabeth imaginatively reconstructs. Although Nelson is successful in killing Tassy, the murder leads to the breakdown of the relationship between the two lovers. The doctor escapes to the United States to avoid arrest, but when Élisabeth tries to follow him, she is caught, and later put in prison. Due to her impeccable class background, Élisabeth is released after two months, and shortly afterwards marries Jérôme Rolland, so as to maintain her social standing. It is at a point eighteen years later, when Rolland is seriously ill, that the novel begins.

Like *A Season in the Life of Emmanuel*, *Kamouraska* highlights the oppressive nature of the domestic space. Tassy is described as subjecting Élisabeth to domestic violence, forcing her to have sex whilst holding a razor blade to her throat: "one night he knocks down the servant guarding the door. Tries to come over to my bed. I scream and scream.... The flash of a razor blade, just for an instant, right at my throat."[28] Élisabeth's marriage to Rolland is figured as an extension of her prison sentence: she responds to her dying husband's remark that she was fortunate in marrying him by claiming, "if not for you, Jérôme, I would have been free."[29] The repeated image of Élisabeth looking through the window at the world outside also contributes to the representation of the domestic space as one in which woman is confined.

At the same time as the domestic space is figured as one which imprisons women, the world beyond the home is represented as a place in which woman can only be a "stranger," or outsider.[30] This world is coded masculine, as is underlined in the description of Tassy's murder as "something that has to be settled man to man."[31] Hébert's novel, which has been compared with Emily Brontë's *Wuthering Heights* (1847), mobilizes the sense of threat that typically informs the gothic novel, locating this threat somewhere within the rural landscape. This is demonstrated in Élisabeth's recollections of her honeymoon trip to Kamouraska:

> Sainte-Anne, Rivière-Ouelle, Kamouraska!
> The hills loom up, rise out of the underbrush. Sudden whiteness, speckled with black. Layers of marbled rock, larded here and there with stunted trees. And close by, the forest.... The flat banks, stretching along the river. Reeds and rushes. And sea grasses, long-stemmed eelgrass, swaying in the wind. Like ripples along the water's edge.[32]

The lyrical description of the lower Saint Lawrence contains a sense of anxiety provoked by the unfamiliar landscape. This is the sensation of the uncanny, described by Freud as a recurring return of the repressed, which is linked to the castration complex.[33] By representing both the domestic and the rural spaces as unhomely (*unheimlich*), *Kamouraska* underlines the patriarchal nature of nineteenth-century bourgeois Quebec society. However, another, more shameful history haunts Hébert's novel. Arnold E. Davidson suggests that in both anglophone and francophone Canadian gothic literature, the wilderness is invoked as the underside of European settler discourses around civilization.[34] In this context, the uncanny gestures towards the anterior presence of indigenous peoples, which the dominant society seeks to suppress. Élisabeth's recollections then point to a murderous national past, which is signalled in the image of Tassy's bleeding body in the snow: "there, in the snow, I see a man all covered with blood. I see him there, stretched out forever."[35]

If *Kamouraska* criticizes the patriarchal nature of settler discourses, it also effects a degree of colonizing of its own. For at the same time as woman is figured as being out of place within the Quebec of the novel, the lower Saint Lawrence is represented as a space in which to inscribe white, bourgeois, feminine desire. In keeping with the conventions of the gothic novel, which both invokes fixed notions of place and identity and undercuts them, *Kamouraska* undermines the boundaries between the domestic space and the external world.[36] This is achieved through Élisabeth's imaginary reconstructions of her honeymoon trip to Kamouraska, and of Nelson's journey to and from this village: "names of villages clash in my head. Sainte-Anne-de Laval, Bécancour, Gentilly, Saint-Pierre-les Becquets…My love is on his way. Farther and farther."[37] By repeatedly inscribing Nelson's journey to and from Kamouraska, Hébert's novel makes use of a mapping metaphor similar to that used by the male anti-urban writers of the 1960s. In so doing, it continues to position Élisabeth ambiguously with respect to the class and community of which she is a part at the same time as it calls for the need for a feminine space within the Quebec nation.[38]

Badlands and Heartlands

Although there is an association between the farmed rural land and the feminine in Quebec's literary history, other places within the non-urban landscape are identified with a particularly virile tradition. The North, especially, tends to be linked with the coureurs des bois. These were the early francophone trappers, explorers, traders, interpreters, and guides who had regular social contact with indigenous peoples, and who operated outside of the strict religious and economic codes of the French colonial authorities. The macho space of the north is invoked in Claude Jasmin's *Don't Cry, Germaine*.[39] In Jasmin's novel, Gilles Bédard, the working-class protagonist, drives his wife—the Germaine of the title—and their children from Montreal to Percé, on the Gaspé peninsula. Ostensibly, this is in response to Germaine's wish that the family move to the area in which she grew up, and thereby leave behind the poverty that they suffer in the city. However, Gilles's real reason for making the journey, which he conceals from Germaine, is so that he can find the man whom he believes raped and murdered his eldest daughter, Rolande.

The revenge plot positions Jasmin's anti-hero within a cowboy tradition that is underlined by the character's comparing himself with the title character of the dubbed version of the US television series *Gunsmoke*: "I feel like Gunsmoke on the television, the one who stands up for himself, who settles his affairs like a man."[40] This western narrative is reworked from a Québécois perspective by casting Gilles as a modern-day coureur des bois, and by having Jasmin's protagonist look not to the west but to the North. In the US genre of the western, the so-called conquering of the west is nostalgically evoked. In the Canadian genre of the northern adventure narrative, the North is evoked in anglophone writing as the basis for a pan-Canadian identity, and in francophone writing as a means of differentiating Quebec from the rest of Canada. Both of these representations are problematic since they constitute the co-option by those living in the South of areas that are largely inhabited by Cree and Inuit populations through the kinds of imaginary projections described by Edward Said in *Orientalism*.[41]

Although Gaspésie does not correspond to the Great North in any real geographical sense, the area performs a similar imaginary function in Jasmin's novel, since it is invoked as a heartland that functions both as a refuge from the corrupting presence of Montreal and as a source of spiritual and cultural renewal. The term "heartland" is generally used to refer to areas where there is a particular strength of feeling, such as nationalist sentiment, as can be found in the region around Lac Saint Jean. However, I also use the term to suggest a particular attachment to place. Both of these senses are to be found in Jasmin's novel, which invokes the importance of Gaspésie within the Québécois imaginary as the birthplace of the nation, since it was at Gaspé, at the tip of the peninsula, that Jacques Cartier officially claimed the region for the King of France in 1534. At the same time, *Don't Cry, Germaine* stresses the natural beauty of the region and the leisure pursuits that it offers, contrasting it with the degrading urban environment of Montreal. In this way, on the family's arrival at Ste-Luce-sur-mer, Gilles comments on the disparity between the coastal village and the city street in which the Bédards had formerly lived: "the water is an amazing colour blue!... The swimmers are playing around—it's a wonderful image. A wonderful image of life. Nothing like Drolet Street."[42]

Ultimately, however, Jasmin's novel deploys the irony inherent in the road genre so as to undercut the romanticism of the rural that runs throughout much of the narrative.[43] Consequently, as the Bédards near their destination, Gilles finds that despite Gaspésie's natural abundance, unemployment is as much of a problem here as it is in Montreal. This is highlighted in the response that a man working in the garage at Ste-Luce-sur-mer makes to Gilles's remark that he is thinking of settling in the area: "Matane, Gaspé, Mont-Joli, Ste-Anne-des-Monts, everywhere's the same. Everywhere's finished."[44] In this way, *Don't Cry, Germaine* demonstrates that, in economic terms at least, the countryside has become an extension of the city.

The end of Jasmin's novel sees Gilles prepare to continue his travels, having discovered that he was mistaken in believing that his daughter was murdered. On the one hand, this highlights what was theorized as the exile suffered by Quebec's francophones under colonialism. This reading is strengthened by the novel's intertextual reference to Jack Kerouac and his seminal road novel, *On the Road* (1957). Both of Kerouac's parents were originally from Quebec, although they emigrated separately to the United States. *Don't Cry, Germaine* is then implicitly framed by the rural exodus of the late nineteenth century, when a number of francophones left Quebec to work in the industrialised towns along the US border. On the other hand, however, the ending of Jasmin's novel points to a tacit acknowledgement of the impossibility of Gilles's living up to his macho role model of the cowboy in the context of an economic climate in which Gaspésie is becoming more dependent on mass tourism for survival than on any other industry. The undermining of the romanticized heartland that we get in *Don't Cry, Germaine* then gives us an unstable reappropriation of the nation-space similar to that in Renaud's *Broke City* and, albeit from a rather different perspective, in Hébert's *Kamouraska*.

It is this instability that, in recent years, has been theorized as prefiguring the more self-conscious deconstruction of the national that we find in a number of examples of Quebec literature produced after 1980. These texts frequently seek to move away from the Quiet Revolution's implicit identification of the national subject with the white francophone of European descent. Writing for the now defunct trilingual journal *Vice Versa* in 1986, the Italo-Québécois writer Fulvio Caccia argued that the incompletion of the attempt to reappropriate Quebec on the part of the established francophone community was precisely what enabled this community to embrace other cultures.[45] In a similar argument, Nepveu suggests that literature of the Quiet Revolution "was already, in a way, *post*-Québécois."[46] By this, he does not mean the literature of this period represents a refusal of national concerns, but that it is characterized by a degree of fragmentation, irony, and self-reflexivity, whereby Quebec's so-called inability to enter into history is figured as both a catastrophe and as a springboard for the future. Although much of Quebec's nationalist writing of the Quiet Revolution has been seen as being engaged in a modernist play around identity, it does not fit neatly into this literary category. As Janet M. Paterson points out, it is difficult to think about postmodernism in the context of Québec, where there is no real tradition of modernist writing: "in Quebec, 'modern' and 'modernity' do not denote a well-defined literary period, as they do in the Anglo-American context. On the contrary, these versatile words usually designate part of the twentieth century or practices of the avant-garde."[47] Although only some of the work of the nationalist writers of the Quiet Revolution contains the stylistic devices which Paterson identifies as postmodern, such as intertextuality and a multi-voiced narrative, much of it appears to combine modernist and postmodern elements, so that the search for a unified national identity is also accompanied by an ironic recognition that a unified identity is not possible. In this sense, it anticipates the more properly deconstructive work of later writers, who engage in an opening of up the national so as to include all of those who live in the territory of Québec.

Post-1980: Feminist, Postfeminist, and Postcolonial Mappings of Montreal

In Quebec's recent history, 1980 was a defining year. The first referendum on sovereignty association, whereby Quebec would gain independence from Canada whilst retaining political and economic links with it, was rejected by 59.6 percent of the electorate.[48] This, in turn, contributed to a series of debates on what constitutes Québécois identity, and movement away from its association with the white francophone of European descent. Other factors that have contributed to the problematization of national identity include responses to Bill 101, a declining birth rate amongst white francophones, and increasing multiculturalism, particularly in the Montreal region.

A number of novels published since 1980 engage with the question of Québécois identity by calling into question the nationalist discourses of the Quiet Revolution, which, as a number of critics have pointed out, have come to represent the foundation narratives of contemporary Quebec. Many of these seem to rework the anti-urban novels of the 1960s, challenging the particular bi-ethnic model of Montreal, as well as the implicit identification of the national subject with the white, working-class male that typically inform these. One such example is Francine Noël's *Babel, Take Two, or We All Discovered America*.[49] Written in response to debates around Bill 101, Noël's novel gives us the diaries of Fatima Gagné, a speech therapist who works with aphasics in Montreal, and Louis Langevin, an architect, although Fatima is the main protagonist. Set between February 1988 and February 1989, the novel describes Fatima's relationships with her best friend Amélia, who is an immigrant of French and Spanish descent, with Linda, an aphasic, and with a number of men, including Louis Langevin. Fatima lives on the eastern outskirts of Outremont, somewhere near avenue du Parc. The area is inhabited by, amongst others, a post-Quiet Revolution francophone middle class; Black, Asian, and Greek communities who have adopted French as their second language; a Greek community whose second language is English; and a Hassidic community. These populations both complicate and contribute to older mappings of the city, which are represented by the working-class districts of Mile End and Côte-des-Neiges on one side of avenue du Parc, and by the bourgeois neighbourhood of Outremont on the other. For Fatima, the area functions as a kind of interface between cultures in a way that is representative of Montreal as a whole: "this neighbourhood has always been multi-ethnic, but over the last few years, it is Montreal as a whole which has become multicoloured."[50]

In contrast with Jacques Renaud's *Broke City*, in which boulevard Saint Laurent is figured as a barrier that separates francophones and anglophones, in Noël's novel, both the street on which Fatima lives and Montreal as a whole seem at first to function in terms of James Clifford's understanding of the "contact zone."[51] Clifford is informed by Mary Louise Pratt's definition of the contact zone as "the space of colonial encounters, the space in which peoples geographically separated come into contact with each other and establish ongoing relations, usually involving conditions of coercion, radical inequality, and intractable conflict."[52] Clifford extends Pratt's analysis to "include cultural relations within the same state, region, or city—in the centers rather than the frontiers of nations and empires."[53] The contact zone is a potentially radical space, since it enables cultural exchange within a context that takes account of the power differentials between the various groups engaging in this exchange. Noël's novel makes a parallel here between the staircases, balconies, and hotel rooms on and in which Fatima and Louis meet, and the border between the different social communities of Montreal represented by the area around avenue du Parc. The former constitute a series of "neutral zones" in which the young woman who rejects heterosexual monogamy and the wealthier, older, married man are able to carry out their relationship.[54] Implicitly, the area in which Fatima lives is figured as similarly neutral territory in which certain prejudices can temporarily be put aside.

Ultimately, however, *Babel, Take Two* returns us to a bi-ethnic model of the city. Fatima's understanding of the Babel myth is represented as a dream of perfect communication: "the founding people are at the same time different and similar, and their coming together is possible because, literally, they can speak to one another."[55] Nevertheless, French is invoked as the language of choice for communication amongst Quebec's various communities, thereby rendering any attempt at a two-way translation as tokenist as the greetings that Fatima makes to her Portuguese neighbours. Although there is an understandable anxiety around the future of the French language in Quebec and elsewhere in the French-speaking world, the solution that is proposed in Noël's novel serves, ultimately, to divide the Québécois between francophones of European descent on the one hand, and everyone else on the other.

It is precisely this dynamic that informs Dany Laferrière's *How to Make Love to a Negro*.[56] The narrator, a young, Black male immigrant to Montreal, is engaged in writing an autobiographical novel. In so doing, he hopes to achieve the financial success and social recognition that will enable him to escape the ethnic and economic prejudices that he is forced to suffer in his host country. *How to Make Love to a Negro* takes up the bi-ethnic mapping of Montreal that is found in the work of the anti-urban writers of the 1960s, replacing the dichotomy between white francophones and anglophones with a similar opposition between blacks and whites. The rundown apartment on rue Saint Denis in which the narrator lives is then contrasted with the middle-class homes in the west of Montreal that belong to the white anglophone women with whom he comes into contact: "Miz Snob has an MG. She lives next to the Outremont Cinema. Tree-lined streets. Near St-Viateur. French butcher shop. Greek pastry shop. Bookstore close by."[57]

In this novel, Laferrière, a writer of Haitian origin, ironically mobilizes a number of stereotypes. These include those that inform racist discourses by whites, such as the stereotype of the sexually insatiable Black male. At the same time, he mediates a number of discourses about whites on the part of people of colour. Finally, Laferrière also mobilizes a number of stereotypes around anglophones living in Montreal. This can be seen in the description of the narrator's visit to Miz Literature's family home:

> The luxury of soft Anglo-Saxon intimacy. Big red-brick house with walls scaled by ivy. English lawn. Victorian calm. Deep armchairs. Old daguerreo-types.... Portraits of young girls with long, fine, sickly features. Diplomat in pith helmet posted to New Delhi. Odour of Calcutta. This house breathes calm, tranquillity, order. The order of the pillagers of Africa. Britannia rules the waves. Everything here has its place—except me. I'm here for the sole purpose of fucking the daughter. Therefore, I too have my place.[58]

Here, Laferrière, who has described his novel as engaging with the contemporary realities of America rather than with Quebec in particular, combines a reflection on the operations of racism in Montreal society with a wider meditation on the Black condition. In this context, the sexually explicit nature of *How to Make Love to a Negro* reads as an ironic appropriation of the role attributed to the male of colour, both within Québécois culture and within white, racist culture more generally: "[Miz Sophisticated Lady] got right down on all fours and I took her then and there. To my own sweet rhythm…I carry her to the bed with no let-up in the rhythm, holding her at the end of my cock."[59]

As Anthony Purdy points out, the narrator's parodic adoption of the role of the hypersexual black male is accompanied by an undercutting of his authenticity as a black speaking subject.[60] For example, in response to being asked where he comes from, the narrator replies "on Thursday evenings I come from Madagascar."[61] In this way, Laferrière carries out a refusal of origin, thereby undermining any assumption that national identity is necessarily defined by the place in which you were born. However, the radical potentials of *How to Make Love to a Negro* as regards national belonging are mitigated by the fact that, its irony notwithstanding, the novel makes very difficult reading for a woman. Whilst the mobilization of a phallic subjectivity in Laferrière's novel highlights the racist workings of dominant discourses both within Québécois culture and within white, western culture more generally, *How to Make Love to a Negro* continues implicitly to position Quebec identity with respect to the heterosexual male.

A more radical problematization of the binary model of Montreal that informed the anti-urban novels of the 1960s occurs in Hélène Monette's *Unless*.[62] *Unless* is a multi-voiced novel narrated by three sisters, although it is the narration of the title character that predominates. Unless is a young francophone woman who works as a bicycle courier and lives on the east side of Montreal. She is represented as struggling to maintain her optimism in the face of the city's harsh economic climate and of her family's history of mental illness. *Unless* is a postfeminist reworking of *le texte national*. Here, I use the term to mean not "after feminism" but in the context of the deconstruction of the unified white, Western subject.[63] This is signalled in the opening sentences of Monette's novel, which read as an ironically simplified summary of the theoretical position of those who wrote for *Parti pris*: "to begin with, you have to feel ashamed. Then live in this neighbourhood and hit rock bottom. Then be proud of this neighbourhood and get back on your feet."[64] As a bicycle courier, Unless carries out a traversing of the city-space that was previously the prerogative of the male anti-hero of the national text. This is underlined when Galipar, a man whom Unless meets in a café, mistakes the courier's name for Ulyssette.[65] The allusion to James Joyce's *Ulysses* (1922), in which a male protagonist maps out Dublin by describing his meanderings around the city, works to challenge the authoritative male gaze, which also informed the writing of the *partipristes*.

The representations of place and identity that we get in Monette's novel are inscribed within a series of discourses around madness, and in particular, schizophrenia. Framed by this particular illness, the narrators symbolize the different personae belonging to someone with a multiple personality disorder, and it is not entirely clear that they do not have this function within the text. There is, then, little sense of a unified identity in *Unless*. The representation of Montreal is similarly fragmented. Drawing on feminist analyses of madness as "a female malady"—an ultimately self-defeating rebellion against patriarchal society—*Unless* mobilizes the danger inherent within the household so as to put into question any notion of the home as a bounded haven.[66] This is suggested through references to the mother's repeated psychiatric illnesses and absences when the children were growing up, and is underlined by the brother's committing suicide during a visit to his father. In this way, Monette effects a deconstruction of the subject of second-wave feminism, which tended to insist on the oppressive nature of the domestic space for women in a way that did not take account of the fact that this was largely a white, middle-class position.[67] For example, some feminists of colour have rejected this denigration of the domestic space, arguing that for many women, this is the only space in which they can feel some measure of safety and self-worth in a racist society.[68]

The opening up of the domestic space in *Unless* is accompanied by an opening up of the urban and national spaces. This is effected partly through an articulation of the interrelations between the local and the global, as in Unless's discussion with a psychiatrist, in which she talks about her first days in a baby unit and her separation from her mother: "it's insurmountable. It's forever. The glass. The distance. Chernobyl and Bhopal in my insurance plan."[69] The ironic critique of neo-colonialism that we get here and elsewhere in Monette's novel serves to figure madness partly as a symptom of the diseased world order that is late industrial capitalism. Finally, the description of both the family home and the city of Montreal as "nowhere" mobilize paranoia, which also serves to blur the boundaries between the inside and outside.[70]

This description is perhaps an allusion to Hubert Aquin's description of Quebec as a "non-country," as well as to the nationalist writer's representation, in *Blackout*, of madness as a congenital condition that entered the collective Québécois bloodstream following the defeat of the Patriot rebellion of 1837–38.[71] However, in making a number of references to "*risks within (the) blood*," Monette, like her predecessor, unwittingly mobilizes an implicitly homophobic discourse.[72] In recent times, parts of East

Montreal have become Montreal's gay village. This demographic is rather uncomfortably taken up in *Unless*, which, in representing madness partly as a condition of late industrial capitalism, seems to figure the AIDS pandemic as a metaphor for the collapse of the humanist subject. This is highly problematic, and is at odds with the radical sexual politics that the novel otherwise advocates.[73] Despite this tension, *Unless* affirms the need for some kind of politics of sex, class, and ethnicity at the same time as it puts the unified subject into question.

The Postnational Novel?

At the same time as a number of novels written in the 1980s and afterwards attempt to problematize notions around Quebec identity, there has also been a moving away from such concerns. This can be attributed to a waning of interest in the national question amongst Québécois.[74] However, the shift away from an engagement with the national question is also evidence of a self-assurance that was desperately sought in the affirmationist writing of the 1960s. The work of Quebec writers from outside the mainstream francophone community gives rise to a postnational literature whereby "post" does not signal "after," but rather a radical renegotiation of the national. Writing in 1993, Régine Robin concluded her study of recent trends in francophone Quebec literature, such as the deconstruction of the foundation myths of the Quiet Revolution on the part of the white, francophone community, and the notions of hybridity and transience that inform immigrant writing, with the question: "there would no longer be any 'pure' Québécois literature, nor neo-Québécois literature, no ethnicisation nor categorisation of writers and writings, simply writers from here?"[75] This is how we should approach Québécois literature: not as a body of writing associated with a particular ethnic group but as a literature of a particular moment in time: a literature of place.

Notes

1 For the debate around civic nationalism, see, for example, Michel Seymour, *Une identité civique commune* (Sherbrooke, QC: Sherbrooke GGC Éditions, 2001).

2 Benedict Anderson, *Imagined Communities: Reflections on the Origin and Spread of Nationalism*, rev. ed. (London: Verso, 1991).

3 Anderson, 26.

4 Recent examples include Jaap Lintvelt and François Paré, eds., *Frontières flottantes: Lieu et espace dans les cultures francophones du Canada/Shifting Boundaries: Place and Space in the Francophone Cultures of Canada* (New York: Rodopi, 2001); Rosemary Chapman, *Siting the Quebec Novel: The Representation of Space in Francophone Writing in Quebec* (Oxford: Peter Lang, 2000), and my doctoral thesis, Ceri Morgan,

"There's No Place Like Home: Space, Place, and Identity in the Contemporary Francophone Novel in Quebec," diss., University of Southampton, 1999.

5 "Cultural geography ... becomes the field of study which concentrates upon the ways in which space, place and the environment participate in an unfolding dialogue of meaning. This includes thinking about how geographical phenomena are shaped, worked and apportioned according to ideology; how they are used when people form and express their relationships and ideas, including their sense of who they are. It also includes the ways in which place, space and environment are perceived and represented, how they are depicted in the arts, folklore and media and how these artistic uses feed back into the practical." Pamela Shurmer-Smith, introduction, *Doing Cultural Geography*, ed. Pamela Shurmer-Smith (London: Sage, 2002), 3.

6 Jack Warwick, *The Long Journey: Literary Themes of French Canada*, 2nd ed. (Toronto: University of Toronto Press, 1973), 34.

7 Chloe Chard, *Pleasure and Guilt on the Grand Tour: Travel Writing and Imaginative Geography 1600–1830* (Manchester: Manchester University Press, 1999), 10. The citation is from Christian Jacob, *L'Empire des cartes: approche théorique de la cartographie à travers l'histoire* (Paris: Albin Michel, 1992), 16, Chard's translation.

8 Bill 101 made French the sole official language of Quebec, encouraged businesses to adopt a policy of *francisation*, ruled that public signs should be in French, and restricted the entry of immigrant children to English schools to those who had a parent who had attended an English-language school, and those who had begun their education in an English-language school outside of Quebec. The bill provoked an outcry amongst certain members of the anglophone and immigrant communities, and was revised after elements of it were declared unconstitutional by Canada's Supreme Court.

9 Jacques Godbout coined the term "le texte national" in reference to his novel *Salut Galarneau!* (Paris: Seuil, 1967). Ben-Zion Shek defines this genre as "describ[ing] novels that were mainly concerned with Quebec's place in Canada and the world—but in a more complex, contradictory, and tragic way." Ben-Zion Shek, *French-Canadian and Québécois Novels* (Toronto: University of Toronto Press, 1991), 53.

10 Jacques Renaud, *Broke City*, trans. David Homel (Montreal: Guernica, 1984); originally published as *Le Cassé* (Montreal: Parti pris, 1964).

11 I should point out that the anti-urban writing of the 1960s has a number of literary antecedents in the social realist literature of the 1940s, such as Gabrielle Roy's *Tin Flute*, trans. Alan Brown (Toronto: McClelland and Stewart, 1955); originally published as *Bonheur d'occasion* (Montreal: Beauchemin, 1945).

12 Renaud, 59.

13 Hubert Aquin, *Blackout*, trans. Alan Brown (Toronto: Anansi, 1974); originally published as *Trou de mémoire* (Montreal: Le Cercle du Livre de France, 1968).

14 Renaud, 87.

15 "La seule différence dans les orgies entre l'Est et l'Ouest c'est que dans l'Est on s'assomme et que dans l'Ouest on s'amuse." Renaud, *"Le Cassé" et autres nouvelles suivi de "Le journal du 'Cassé,"* Collection "projection libérantes" (Montreal: Parti pris, 1981), 77.

16 Pierre Nepveu, *L'Écologie du réel: Mort et naissance de la littérature québécoise contemporaine*, 2nd ed. (Montreal: Boréal, 1999).

17 "Le romancier d'aujourd'hui, malgré son désir de l'histoire, se rapproche du cartographe, en ce qu'il s'attache primordialement à définir un lieu, à 'bâtir le pays'," Gilles Marcotte, "Le Romancier comme cartographe," *Le roman à l'imparfait: La "Révolution tranquille" du roman québécois*, 2nd ed. (Montreal: Éditions de l'Hexagone, 1989); originally published as *Le roman à l'imparfait: Essais sur le roman québécois d'aujourd'hui* (Mon-

treal: Éditions la Presse, 1976), 244. Page citations are to the second edition. My translation, as are all other translations in this essay except where stated otherwise.

18 Patricia Smart, *Writing in the Father's House: The Emergence of the Feminine in the Quebec Literary Tradition* (Toronto: University of Toronto Press, 1991); originally published as *Écrire dans la maison du père: L'émergence du féminin dans la tradition littéraire du Québec* (Montreal: Éditions Québec/Amérique, 1988).

19 Smart, 92.

20 Marie-Claire Blais, *A Season in the Life of Emmanuel*, trans. Derek Coltman, 2nd ed. (Toronto: McClelland and Stewart, 1992); originally published as *Une saison dans la vie d'Emmanuel* (Paris: Éditions du Jour, 1965).

21 Blais, 7–8.

22 Blais, 101–102.

23 Blais, 14.

24 Mary Jean Green, "Redefining the Maternal: Women's Relationships in the Fiction of Marie-Claire Blais," *Traditionalism, Nationalism, and Feminism: Women Writers of Quebec*, ed. Paula Gilbert Lewis (Westport, CT: Greenwood, 1985), 125–40.

25 Blais, 116.

26 I am grateful to Katy Owen for this insight in relation to Green's essay.

27 Anne Hébert, *Kamouraska*, trans. Norman Shapiro (Toronto: Stoddart, 1994); originally published as *Kamouraska* (Paris: Seuil, 1970).

28 Hébert, 115.

29 Hébert, 31.

30 Hébert, 247.

31 Hébert, 188.

32 Hébert, 70.

33 Sigmund Freud, "The 'Uncanny,'" *Art and Literature*, trans. James Strachey, ed. Albert Dickson (Harmondsworth: Penguin, 1985), 426–33.

34 Arnold E. Davidson, "Canadian Gothic and Anne Hébert's *Kamouraska*," *MFS: Modern Fiction Studies* 27 (1981): 243–54.

35 Hébert, 25.

36 Cannon Schmitt, *Alien Nation: Nineteenth-Century Gothic Fictions and English Nationality* (Philadelphia: University of Pennsylvania Press, 1997).

37 Hébert, 190.

38 The novel makes a play around the question of Élisabeth's guilt, since she is figured as betraying her ethnic and linguistic community by having an affair with an anglophone. At the same time, the socialization that she receives as a bourgeois girl and young woman is represented as having done nothing but prepare Élisabeth for the behaviour that she displays as an adult.

39 Claude Jasmin, *Pleure pas, Germaine* (Don't Cry, Germaine) (Montreal: Parti pris, 1965). All references are to *Pleure pas, Germaine* (Montreal: Centre Éducatif et Culturel, 1974).

40 "Je me sens comme le Justicier, celui de la télévision, celui qui se défend, celui qui règle ses comptes comme un homme." Jasmin, 13.

41 Edward Said, *Orientalism* (London: Routledge, 1978).

42 "L'eau est d'un beau bleu d'empois chinois!... Les nageurs s'ébattent, c'est une belle image. Une belle image de la vie. Rien qui ressemble à la rue Drolet." Jasmin, 61.

43 The road genre evokes elements of the western at the same time that it demonstrates that, in the postmodern age, narratives around the establishment of a new social order in a natural paradise are no longer tenable. This is because the frontier has been paved over. Shari

Roberts, "Western Meets Eastwood: Genre and Gender on the Road," *The Road Movie Book*, ed. Steven Cohan and Ina Rae Hark (London: Routledge, 1997), 45–69.

44 "Matane, Gaspé, Mont-Joli, Ste-Anne-des-Monts, c'est toute la même affaire. On crève partout." Jasmin, 68.

45 Fulvio Caccia, "L'altra riva," *Vice Versa* 16 (1986): 44–45.

46 "Était déjà en quelque sorte *post*-québécoise." Nepveu, 16; Nepveu's emphasis.

47 Janet M. Paterson, *Postmodernism and the Quebec Novel*, trans. David Homel and Charles Phillips (Toronto: University of Toronto Press, 1994); originally published as *Moments postmodernes dans le roman québécois* (Ottawa: Les Presses de l'Université d'Ottawa, 1990), 5. Page citations are to the translated edition.

48 Colin H. Williams, "Quebec: Language and Nationhood," *Called unto Liberty! On Language and Nationalism* (Clevedon: Multilingual Matters, 1994). A second referendum in 1995 was won by a tiny majority of "no" votes, with 49.4 percent voting in favour of sovereignty association, and 50.58 percent voting against. Kenneth McRoberts, *Misconceiving Canada: The Struggle for National Unity* (Toronto: Oxford University Press, 1997), 187–231.

49 Francine Noël, *Babel, prise deux, ou Nous avons tous découvert l'Amérique* (Babel, Take Two, or We All Discovered America), (Montreal: VLB, 1990).

50 "Ce quartier a toujours été multi-ethnique, mais depuis quelques années, c'est Montréal tout entière qui devient bigarrée." Noël, 37. In this novel, Noël sometimes uses the feminine forms of the adjective to describe Montreal, in order to effect a playful, feminist reappropriation of the city.

51 James Clifford, "Museums as Contact Zones," *Routes: Travel and Translation in the Late Twentieth Century*, ed. James Clifford (Cambridge, MA: Harvard University Press, 1997), 188–219.

52 Mary Louis Pratt, *Imperial Eyes: Travel Writing and Transculturation* (London: Routledge, 1992), 6–7, cited in Clifford, 192.

53 Clifford, 204.

54 "Des 'zones neutres.'" Noel, 229.

55 "Les peuples constructeurs sont à la fois différents et semblables, et leur rassemblement est possible car, littéralement, ils sont *parlables*." Noël, 196; Noël's emphasis.

56 Dany Laferrière, *How to Make Love to a Negro*, trans. David Homel (Toronto: Coach House Press, 1987); originally published as *Comment faire l'amour avec un nègre sans se fatiguer* (Montreal: VLB, 1985).

57 Laferrière, 83.

58 Laferrière, 76.

59 Laferrière, 60.

60 Anthony Purdy, "Altérité, authenticité, universalité: Dany Laferrière et Régine Robin," *Dalhousie French Studies* 23 (1992): 51–59.

61 Laferrière, 82.

62 Hélène Monette, *Unless* (Montreal: Boréal, 1995).

63 In so doing, I am informed by Homi K. Bhabha: "If the jargon of our times—postmodernity, postcoloniality, postfeminism—has any meaning at all, it does not lie in the popular use of the "post" to indicate sequentiality—*after*-feminism; or polarity—*anti*-modernism. These terms that insistently gesture to the beyond, only embody its restless and revisionary energy if they transform the present into an expanded and ex-centric site of experience and empowerment." Homi K. Bhabha, "Introduction: Locations of Culture," *The Location of Culture* (New York and London: Routledge, 1994), 4.

64 "Pour commencer, il faut avoir honte de soi. Puis habiter ce quartier et débouler. Puis être fier de ce quartier et remonter la pente en soi-même." Monette, 9.

65 Monette, 11.

66 Elaine Showalter, *The Female Malady: Women, Madness, and English Culture 1830–1980*, 3rd ed. (London: Virago, 1988), 7.

67 See, for example, Dana Heller, "Housebreaking History: Feminism's Troubled Romance with the Domestic Sphere," *Feminism Beside Itself*, ed. Diane Elam and Robyn Wiegman (London: Routledge, 1995), 217–33.

68 See, for example, bell hooks, "Homeplace: A Site of Resistance," *Yearning: Race, Gender, and Cultural Politics* (London: Turnaround, 1991).

69 "C'est insurmontable. C'est toujours. La glace. La distance. Tchernobyl et Bhopâl dans mon plan d'assurance." Monette, 71.

70 "Nulle part." Monette, 60.

71 Hubert Aquin, "Profession: écrivain," *Parti pris* 1.4 (1964) 28, cited in Patricia Smart, *Hubert Aquin, agent double: la dialectique de l'art et du pays dans* Prochain épisode *et* Trou de mémoire (Montreal: Les Presses de l'Université de Montréal, 1973), 11. Monette's novel also makes an extra-textual reference to Aquin's suicide in 1977.

72 "*Les risques du sang.*" Monette, 62; Monette's emphasis. On the suppressed homophobia that informed the writing of the *partipristes*, see Robert Schwartzwald, "Fear of Federasty: Québec's Inverted Fictions," *Comparative American Identities: Race, Sex, and Nationality in the Modern Text*, ed. Hortense J. Spillers (London: Routledge, 1991), 175–95.

73 See Lee Edelman, "The Mirror and the Tank: 'AIDS,' Subjectivity, and the Rhetoric of Activism," *Writing AIDS: Gay Literature, Language, and Analysis*, ed. Timothy F. Murphy and Suzanne Poirier (New York: Columbia University Press, 1993).

74 The defeat of the Parti québecois in the provincial elections of April 2003 can be seen as pointing to a dissaffection with national independence. However, there has been renewed interest in this issue more recently, in response to the sponsorship scandal involving the allocation of public funds in a campaign designed to promote national unity following the 1995 referendum. Auditor General Sheila Fraser's report, published in February 2004, indicated that funds had apparently been given to supporters of the federal Liberal Party, sometimes for work that was not carried out.

75 "Il n'y aurait plus de littérature québécoise 'pure laine' ni d'écriture néo-québécoise, pas d'ethnicisation ni de catégorisation des écrivains et des écritures, simplement des écrivains d'ici?" Régine Robin, "Introduction: Un Québec pluriel," *La Recherche littéraire: Objets et méthodes*, ed. Claude Duchet and Stéphane Vachon (Montreal: XYZ, 1993), 309.

13 L.M. Montgomery on Television
The Romance and Industry of the Adaptation Process

Patsy Aspasia Kotsopoulos

LUCY MAUD MONTGOMERY'S BOOKS have always enjoyed consistent popularity, never going out of print. Yet the latter part of the twentieth century saw an upsurge of interest in Montgomery's stories. Beginning in 1985, interest from academics and fans alike was rekindled following the publication of the first four volumes of *The Selected Journals of L.M. Montgomery*. In popular culture, Sullivan Entertainment's wildly successful television adaptations of the *Anne* novels further fanned Montgomery's popularity in the late twentieth century and helped introduce the fictional Avonlea to a new generation. The Toronto-based production company created the critically acclaimed ratings hit *Anne of Green Gables* in 1985,[1] and followed it two years later with an equally successful sequel, *Anne of Avonlea*. Without these precedents, the television series *Road to Avonlea* (1990–1996) and *Emily of New Moon* (1998–2001) undoubtedly would not have been made.[2] Montgomery is big business not only in her birthplace of Prince Edward Island (whose tourism industry counts on her enduring popularity) but on the television screen as well.[3]

Several works of scholarly criticism bring to light issues regarding the effects of adaptation on the meaning of Montgomery's romances for con-

The author wishes to express her gratitude to those *Road to Avonlea* writers and executive producers who shared their insights on the making of the series. She also thanks the Social Sciences and Humanities Research Council of Canada for a doctoral fellowship that made this research possible.

271

temporary audiences. The academic literature on the Montgomery screen adaptations, to some degree, adopts literary formalism as its critical approach, focussing on point of view and narrative events, with an attempt to situate perceived differences in execution and meaning historically, mostly with respect to the (potentially) feminist portrayal of gender. The scholarly focus on gender is not surprising given the feminist interest in the works and life of Montgomery,[4] yet it does create some omissions. The main omission, save for Christopher Gittings's analysis of *Emily of New Moon*,[5] is the political-economic context in which these Canadian television productions occur. Consequently, we miss out on learning something about the conditions for Canadian television drama and their possible impact on meaning and content. Overlooked is the understanding that screenwriters are adapting for a television audience and not for an audience of readers—they are adapting for people who have not necessarily read Montgomery. Although Montgomery's name carries cachet because of her writings, it does so in Canada whether or not one has read her books. As Ann F. Howey states, "Sullivan's films depend less on faithfulness to source texts and more on the sheer recognition of name."[6] Moreover, writers and producers are additionally adapting for investors such as the Canadian Broadcasting Corporation, with its policy mandates, and for an anticipated export market, with its particular set of industrial demands.

In the scholarly literature on the Montgomery adaptations, what I call three styles of adaptation emerge. First, in the process of adaptation, Montgomery's source novels are contemporized, resulting in a liberal feminist romance suitable for a modern audience, as illustrated by the film versions of *Anne of Green Gables* and *Anne of Avonlea*. Second, Montgomery's texts undergo a deregionalization, creating a regionless romance appropriate for a geographically dispersed viewership—the audience for *Road to Avonlea*. And finally, adaptation rewrites the past in the effort to redress historical injustices either ignored or even perpetrated by Montgomery's original text. The result is a revisionist romance like the *Emily of New Moon* series. While my initial observations are more concerned with the meaning of romance than with the effects of the industry on the adaptation process, some conclusions can be drawn and elaborated in terms of the context for television production in Canada. Additionally, discussions of costume drama and the heritage industry help situate the Montgomery adaptations within wider trends in popular culture. They give a sense of the variety of meanings circulating around Montgomery's romances in contemporary Canadian culture and suggest points of address for the viewer.

A Liberal Feminist Romance

Susan Drain, Trinna Frever, and Ann F. Howey offer analyses of Sullivan's first two *Anne* films.[7] Their main contention is that, in the process of adaptation, the film versions effect two overarching changes to Montgomery's original texts. First, the films contemporize the novels' themes, making them relevant for a 1980s audience; and second, the adaptations squeeze the novels into a recognizable film genre, often drawing deliberately on cinematic predecessors for narrative conventions, thereby capitalizing on audience expectations. Their readings of the *Anne* films are consonant with the feminist literature on costume drama. This literature indicates that the Montgomery boom is not an isolated event must be situated within a broader cultural phenomenon of the 1980s and 1990s: the resurgence of the period piece in both film and television. The Montgomery adaptations participate in popular culture's renewed fascination with the past, or rather, the past as imagined from the point of view of the present. The costume drama gains special currency at this time with television hits like *Pride and Prejudice* (1995) and *Middlemarch* (1994), and screen successes from *A Room with a View* (1986) to *Howard's End* (1992).

The Montgomery adaptations belong to this cultural phenomenon, to the resurgent popularity of the costume drama, a genre with its own set of conventions including, most significantly, the use of a period setting to explore themes of contemporary relevance. Characters and situations are purely imaginary in costume drama, with the historical setting functioning as a dramatic, and even exotic, backdrop for romance, and sometimes adventure and intrigue. This loose treatment of history allows viewers to appropriate issues explored in the costume drama as contemporary to their own. As Marcia Landy explains, "The specific time of the events recedes, and they become ... transhistorical and timeless and, therefore, as relevant for the present as for the past."[8] In this way, the costume drama creates a sense of continuity between past and present through the portrayal of concerns having contemporary resonance—for instance, concerns about women's roles or the place of the family in society.[9] Such discussions of the costume drama demand a recognition of this genre as a particular kind of fantasy—one in which contemporary desires, anxieties, and fears find safe expression through displacement into a period setting.

Costume drama bears a special relationship not only to fantasy but also to adaptation. The period-piece revival owes a debt to second-wave feminism, which has brought attention to texts written by women in an attempt to reclaim women's past. As with the Montgomery adaptations, period pieces are often adapted from women's literature written in the 1800s and early 1900s, a literature that addresses questions of female

identity and female desire.[10] In costume dramas adapted from this literature, a double displacement is at work: not only the displacement of present-day concerns into a period setting, but the displacement of the original
text into a contemporary context. Films like *Sense and Sensibility* (1995)
and *Little Women* (1994), as well as television versions of *Jane Eyre* (1997)
and *Pride and Prejudice* (1995), tap into this phenomenon and create an
affinity between women's past and present struggles. To be sure, these
struggles are those of white, middle-class women seeking expression outside the traditional confines of domesticity and, therefore, they firmly situate these representations within a liberal feminist framework. The choice
of literature to adapt speaks to its white, middle-class concerns. Along
these lines, Stella Bruzzi discusses what she terms the "liberal method" of
costume drama, which "concentrates on finding a political and ideological affinity between the struggles of women in the present and figures from
the past." The liberal film, explains Bruzzi, "discerns patterns or draws out
meanings which at the time [in which the story takes place] may have
been obscured." The heroine of such a film is "both historical and contemporary, her struggle (with herself, her family and men) both parochial and
perennial."[11] For this reason, Andrew Higson calls the settings of these films
a "modern past" in which olden-day artifacts merge with contemporary
concerns, producing a pastiche of yesterday and today.[12]

In Frever's and Howey's analyses, Sullivan's *Anne* adaptations deploy
just such a "modern past." Frever and Howey argue that the *Anne* films
incorporate 1980s notions of womanhood in their construction of the
protagonist as "writer-heroine."[13] One of the ways Sullivan achieves this
is by changing the Alfred Lord Tennyson poem Anne enacts in *Anne of
Green Gables* from "Lancelot and Elaine," about a doomed romance, to
"The Lady of Shalott," about a creative woman struggling with the
demands of her artistic vocation. The choice of a different intertextual
heroine prepares the audience to accept Anne as artist-writer, explains
Howey, and marks an ideological shift from novel to screen further supported through additional changes. For instance, it is easier for Anne to get
published in the film than in the novel, and her literary accomplishments
are grander than in Montgomery's books.[14]

Frever argues that *Anne of Avonlea* cues us as to how to read the film
"through its emotional familiarity and through its establishment of a genre
context."[15] She shows how the film draws on cinematic predecessors as
intertexts, each showing "the complexities and the possible difficulties
faced by women who pursue their artistic ambitions while also seeking a
marriage accepting of those ambitions."[16] Following filmic precedents such
as *Little Women* (1933) and *My Brilliant Career* (1979), Anne's attempts
to publish her writing are a major plot thread in the second Sullivan film,

receiving greater attention than they do in Montgomery's original. These films want us to identify Anne as a writer, as a young woman with career ambitions, and as a female role model for contemporary viewers. To achieve this reorientation of identification, the adaptation makes changes to the source material resulting from the interaction of audience expectation, social history, and popular genre. Howey explains:

> Montgomery's *Anne* novels have influenced generations of girls but the social conditions of women's lives and changing ideas about women's roles influence the way Anne is interpreted and re-presented to the world. In adapting Montgomery's stories for a different medium and in targeting those adaptations for a broad popular audience, Sullivan effectively updates Montgomery's Anne to make her more consistent with contemporary, western ideas about women's roles after several waves of feminism.[17]

The screen Anne performs a balancing act different from her novelistic predecessor. In the books, Anne's literary ambitions fade as the duties of adopted daughter and schoolteacher, and later wife and mother, take over. Conversely, in the films, argue Frever and Howey, Anne's career ambitions are in the forefront. In fact, one of the ways Gilbert proves his worth as a mate is by appreciating Anne's artistic side and by encouraging her to pursue her writing. In the film, Gilbert encourages Anne to write about Avonlea, whereas in the novel a supportive teacher makes the suggestion.[18] For the cinematic Anne, career and marriage are simultaneously possible; not so for the novelistic Anne, and only with great emotional cost for the real-life Montgomery. Yet in her television incarnation, Anne can have it all; she is a modern woman as easily at home in 1905 as in 1985. The novels are thus adapted for an audience who wants Anne to have both career and marriage. As Frever puts it, "the creation of a heroine who pursues both marriage and career simultaneously speaks to contemporary visions of womanhood."[19] While the films address the same issues around career and marriage found in the Montgomery novels, these issues are given a different emphasis, creating new meanings more accessible to a late-twentieth-century audience.

Frever and Drain maintain that, in the effort to appeal to contemporary tastes, the Sullivan version reinforces Anne's relationship with Gilbert more than the novels do, but they disagree as to the ideological implications of this increased emphasis. Frever says that the television version opens up "the possibility of a marriage and a career which are not mutually exclusive, a possibility which was closed to the Anne of Montgomery's written text."[20] For this reason, Frever concludes that the televised Montgomery is a feminist text, more progressive than its original source. Conversely, Drain sees the adaptation as more regressive, "in some ways more old-fashioned, or even narrower, than the book,"[21] because Anne's character development, career interests, and involvement in a female community are sacrificed to the conventional love story in which "Gilbert is omnipresent." As Drain puts it, "the love story is the new heart of the television Anne."[22] In the process of adapting the original to the screen, Anne's story is squeezed into a familiar narrative trajectory, easily recognizable to a television audience. The result, states Drain, is "an exquisite romance, but the novel is a *Bildungsroman*. That reduction is, finally, a loss." For Drain, this message is a considerable departure from the novel, which suggests Anne's fulfillment is multifaceted, and that Gilbert is only a part of it rather than the key.[23]

Though Drain's account is more pessimistic than those of Frever and Howey, all three readings are nevertheless consonant with liberal feminist romance, or with the liberal method of costume drama. Significantly, none of these authors identifies the feminism at work in the adaptations as liberal. This method offers a safe version of feminism, one that is commonsensical by contemporary western standards, and one that, predictably, does not advocate a radical departure from how society is currently organized, arguing instead that women's enfranchisement is possible within existing social structures. According to Dinitia Smith, costume dramas fill the void in adult entertainment for predominantly white, middle-class women.[24] Given the presumed audience, not surprisingly, what is on offer is the liberal feminist concept that woman's fulfillment can no longer be confined to the home and must extend to both career (usually something appropriately middle class and "feminine" like writing) and romance (always of the heterosexual, matrimonial variety). Drain's reading of the screen version as more conservative than the original fits with this understanding of costume drama. Still, taken within the context of popular culture as a whole, costume drama is the only genre that guarantees women and their concerns are front and centre. Costume drama promises complex, intelligent, central female characters and an examination of gender and sexual politics not often found in films or series with a contemporary setting.

A Regionless Romance

Adaptation as liberal feminist romance is one way to interpret literary classics for the contemporary screen. The period setting provides both an exquisite backdrop for the exploration of contemporary gender and sexual politics and a lush escape from reality, making costume drama relevant and escapist at the same time. However, for some cultural critics, costume drama's use of a non-specific and spectacular past carries problematic implications. According to Higson, costume drama fetishizes the past as an object disconnected from history.[25] Martin A. Hipsky makes the same point that the setting is superfluous to plot; the setting becomes excessive spectacle, providing the audience with sensuous pleasure and with an escapist fantasy existing outside history.[26] These representations are often marked by a retreat to a pastoral condition, away from the taint of urbanization and industrialization, and the social ills associated with them.

This invocation of the past must be understood as part of a wider pop-cultural phenomenon, the heritage industry, which provides an intertext for the production of the Montgomery adaptations and contributes to the reading formation available to viewers. John Corner and Sylvia Harvey demonstrate that commercial activity around the past increased to an "unprecedented degree of activity" in the 1980s, particularly in the deindustrialized West.[27] This activity informs various cultural and economic practices, from the restoration of buildings both public and private, to the reconstruction of historical scenes on television and at the living history museum. Kevin Walsh discusses a related phenomenon within urban regeneration that he terms "heritagization," defined as "the ahistorical aestheticization of space, through the exploitation of historical images."[28] Heritagization wallpapers over urban decay and deindustrialization, while it simultaneously destroys regional identities in the production of a sanitized, standardized past.

Moreover, unprecedented technological changes in the mechanical reproduction of images means the past emerges as a part of media culture in ways not seen before, circulating through films, television shows, magazines, and fashions, which transform history into consumable images. Heritage critics such as Walsh argue that when historical images become commodified as mechanically reproducible consumer goods, the past is aestheticized, made non-specific and contextless.[29] Only certain images of the past come to have an exchange value on the market. Commodification results in the perpetuation of safe, pleasing images standardized through an aesthetic and ideological filter that removes the taint of history. What consumer culture offers is the look of the past.[30] The reproduction of such images makes us indifferent to the significance of the past since we are dealing with free-floating images of the past rather than the past to which they refer. In other words, commodification produces the past as an autonomous, decontextualized object severed from time and place.[31] The result is a regionless romance.

Heritagization plays a role in the creation and popularization of the regionless romance. Adaptation has a role to play here, too, in creating a non-specific past. Frever discusses this process in relation to *The Story Girl* (1911), the Montgomery novel from which early episodes of *Road to*

Avonlea are adapted.[32] She compares an early episode of *Road to Avonlea* called "The Story Girl Earns Her Name" to the original chapter of the same name. Frever argues, quite rightly, that the series abandons local lore and family legend, and the result is a loss of Island specificity. According to Frever, "several plot/production choices were made in the creation of this series that sadly betray the oral dimension of Montgomery's novel.... One of the most obvious and grievous changes was the decision to make Sara Stanley 'from away.' This decision completely berefts Sara of all the rich association with the Island, its language and its oral process, that is such an integral part of the novel."[33] In the television series, Sara comes from Montreal and is the daughter of a wealthy entrepreneur. Her Island cousins, whom she meets for the first time, acquaint her with the maternal side of her family and its rural way of life. In the novel, Sara is from Prince Edward Island and it is she who acquaints her two visiting mainland cousins, Bev and Felix, with the family and its Island history. Sara does this by telling stories: she is a consummate storyteller and orator, and her repertoire is drawn from family history and local lore. Sara's knowledge of the Island's past depends on these stories. Yet Sara's role as "storytelling ambassador" is "stolen" from her screen incarnation, says Frever, "by her removal from Island culture and placement as a visiting relative from Montreal."[34]

For Frever, the change from source to adaptation marks a rejection of the oral tradition and a loss of the Island's cultural and regional specificity: "The Sullivan adaptation, in its haste to embrace the mainland camera, misses the boat to the Island."[35] To be sure, Frever makes some important observations regarding the differences between the television episode and the Montgomery chapter, and their implications for meaning. However, Frever makes no attempt to understand the conditions in which the Montgomery adaptation takes place. Though she does not situate adaptation within a political-economic framework, we can still extrapolate some points from her work to shed light on the complexities of adapting regionally and historically rooted literature for a geographically dispersed, contemporary television audience.

Transforming Sara Stanley into a city girl from Montreal contemporizes the series' point of address. In effect, Sara is "us," the contemporary urban viewer with little or no experience of rural agricultural life. Her voyage of discovery, both personal and familial, becomes our voyage. Through Sara, a city dweller, we become acquainted with the small farming community of Avonlea. Moreover, while the novel is constructed from Bev's point of view, the series (at least the first four years of it) centres on the character of Sara, the lead in a coming-of-age drama. This departure from the novel is significant, as Bev the narrator is a boy. Constructing the series as a girl's rite of passage effectively secures the presumed female viewership of *Road to Avonlea* and capitalizes on the female audience for period pieces and costume dramas popular in the 1980s and 1990s, including the first two Sullivan *Anne* films.[36] CBC saw the *Anne* films and, likely by extension, *Road to Avonlea* as a part of the corporation's goal of increasing women's visibility on the network.[37] Heather Conkie, who wrote twenty-two out of ninety-one episodes, also points out that in adapting the stories to television, Sara was the obvious choice for main character as she is a typical Montgomery heroine—"incredibly active" in the book—whereas Bev "was a very passive kid."[38]

Gender is a factor in adaptation, perhaps not a deliberate one here, but present nonetheless. Yet other factors influence the adaptation process. The political-economic context of television production in Canada creates conditions that pressure a series such as *Road to Avonlea* to adapt source material for both domestic and export audiences. Export and co-production arrangements are meant to offset some of the exorbitant costs of producing indigenous television drama for a domestic audience as small as Canada's. *Road to Avonlea* is a CBC program, as well as a co-production with the Disney Channel. Throughout its seven-season run, Disney provided roughly 50 percent of the budget for *Road to Avonlea*.[39] Disney's deep pockets contributed to the series' high production values, unprecedented at the time in Canadian television drama. However, this co-production arrangement, while making the series possible, brought with it certain realities. The one I want to introduce is "cultural discount," as it has a significant bearing on the adaptation process and on the creation of the regionless romance. Colin Hoskins, Stuart McFadyen, and Adam Finn explain "cultural discount" as follows: "A particular television programme, film or video rooted in one culture, and thus attractive in the home market where viewers share a common knowledge and way of life, will have diminished appeal elsewhere, as viewers find it difficult to identify with the style, values, beliefs, history, myths, institutions, physical environment, and behavioural patterns."[40] Cultural discount can also apply to the diminished appeal of historically specific texts, regardless of the fact that book and reader may share national or regional origins.

In adapting Montgomery's characters and stories for television, a watering down of historical and regional specificity occurred, partly in response to requests from the co-producers—this according to Deborah Bernstein and Cathy Johnson, executives in charge of production for CBC and Disney, respectively, and present during the all-important development phase.[41] According to Bernstein, the corporation was concerned that the series retain "the flavour of Lucy Maud Montgomery," while also having "a contemporary flair." At Disney, Johnson says the desire was similar:

"regarding Montgomery material...it was understood that the entire thrust
of the series would transcend the era differences and be relevant today." In
the process, *Road to Avonlea* downplays aspects of Montgomery's writing.
For Bernstein, making Montgomery accessible included pruning anachro-
nistic features such as superstitious beliefs and negative attitudes towards
spinsters, and taking a more contemporary approach to gender relations.
According to Lucie Hall, story editor for the first two seasons, CBC specifically did not want *Road to Avonlea* to refer to prayer or superstition,
which formed a part of Montgomery's Scots-Presbyterian heritage and
the Island's culture. Hall says the request "imposed a revisionist view on
the written material" and "had everything to do with being in a modern
secular society, no matter what your religion."[42] The result is an Avonlea
that is more secular than the one found in Montgomery's books. Indeed,
Raymond Storey, a writer for the last four seasons, observes that prior to
Happy Christmas, Miss King, the Avonlea reunion movie he scripted,
"Christmas had never crossed the consciousness of these characters" and
the church was treated as the modern-day equivalent of a "community centre."[43] With this treatment, *Road to Avonlea* emphasizes the church's social
function over Presbyterianism's specifically religious aspects. Storey spec-
ulates that the point of treating the church in this way was to not have CBC
seen as "ramming Christianity down the throats of the general public" and
to avoid alienating members of the Canadian audience. The downside is
that differences within Canada's population and history are never considered, and instead are covered over through a bland homogenizing effect
that strips regions and communities of their specificity, both cultural and
historical. Such a public broadcasting philosophy, though having socially
progressive concerns around inclusivity, corresponds to the market's notion
of appealing to the lowest common denominator to maximize profits.
This activity is something of which Disney has been accused, particularly
with respect to its flattening of histories and cultures in its period animation.[44]

   As well, if Hall is correct, CBC may have been over-sensitive in that
Montgomery satirizes as much as she celebrates the church's role in the life
of PE Islanders. However, even such satire could be viewed as irrelevant to
the lives of most contemporary viewers not accustomed to the niceties of
rural Edwardian Canada and more interested in the homespun interactions
of family and friends within a community. Ultimately, what we see at play
in *Road to Avonlea* is a generic Montgomery rather than the Island Montgomery, which would help to explain Disney's support for the series. In fact,
Deborah Nathan, who worked on the series for four years in various
capacities as senior story editor, writer, and associate producer, suggests that
Disney executives "bought the series because it was quaint and colonial,

and the fact that it never really mentioned anywhere that it was Canada."[45] Storey concurs, and explains that details regarding Canadian history or the Canadian political scene of the early 1900s—the setting for *Road to Avonlea*—were to be avoided. However, he maintains, Disney welcomed examples of "Canadiana" such as showing the characters boiling maple syrup, waving the Union Jack, or making references to the British monarchy. Empire emerges as a pastoral utopia in *Road to Avonlea*: disconnected from history, protected from the taint of politics, and decorated with the emblems of a fetishized Canada.[46] *Road to Avonlea* corresponds with the characteristics critiqued by cultural critics who document Disney's stereotyping of national identities, its sanitization of histories, and its concomitant production of an innocent past rife with clichés.[47]

If deregionalization emerges as a style of adaptation, one that speaks to the political-economic context of television production in Canada, then what happens to our stories—the stories that reflect Canada, its regions and its history? What are the gains and the sacrifices in our cultural production when we create points of address for an export market? Questions of cultural specificity are complicated, and are not limited to Canada but have international significance, addressed in the literature on culture and globalization.[48] What is the effect of regionless "global" programming on local or national identities? Can we measure the effects only in terms of losses, or are there possible gains, not just economically but socially, in the apprehension of transcultural values? *Road to Avonlea* is a significant case study for exploring these questions because, paradoxically, Canadian viewers recognized the series as distinctly Canadian,[49] Americans made it the top-rated program on the Disney Channel, and over 150 countries purchased it for foreign distribution. In its transmission from novel to screen, Montgomery's story is indeed deregionalized as Frever argues, but *Road to Avonlea* appears to maintain some specificity for its Canadian viewers at the same time that it crosses the boundaries of nation and culture, defying the logic of cultural discount.

A Revisionist Romance

Liberal feminism and deregionalization are not the only ways in which adaptation responds to context. An interesting contrast is *Emily of New Moon*, adapted from the Montgomery novel of the same name. This series gives us a different picture of adaptation, that of a revisionist romance, much like the American television series *Dr. Quinn, Medicine Woman* (1993–1998), which revises American history with the creation of a multicultural frontier community where the racially intolerant are not welcome.[50] Similar to *Dr. Quinn* in this respect, *Emily* incorporates minority characters in the adaptation process in recognition of Canada's multicultural composition and fractious history. Gittings argues that the series thus revisions Montgomery for the nation, making her romance compatible with Canadian beliefs and attitudes in the late twentieth century.[51] According to Marlene Matthews, the series's producer, creator, and head writer (whom Gittings interviewed), adaptation had less to do with textual fidelity and more to do with historical fidelity.

For this reason, the series incorporates a Mi'kmaq boy, Little Fox, a character absent from Montgomery's novel, to recognize the significance of the Mi'kmaq on Prince Edward Island and to address past injustices in Canadian society, as symbolized by Emily's racist schoolteacher. Gittings sees the television invention of Little Fox as an acknowledgement of difference, of non-European identity as integral to the Canadian national narrative. The series also effects another change to the original: the Irish-Catholic priest of the novel, Father Cassidy, a minor character, is transformed into the French-Canadian Father Ducharme, a friendly, sympathetic confidante for Emily, whose family is resolutely Presbyterian. Emily goes against convention and often her family's wishes to include Little Fox and Father Ducharme in her imagined community—Emily's family is the Canadian family, as imagined in the late twentieth century. Gittings argues that Matthews reworks Montgomery to construct a romance that is self-consciously national with *two* founding nations and a *First* Nation. As Gittings states, "With the insertion of Little Fox, the rehabilitation of Montgomery as consumable national icon embracing French Canadian and First Nations' difference is complete."[52] This postcolonial Montgomery, a revisionist invention, is a far cry from the ethnophobic, even racist, Montgomery found in some of her writing.

Gittings makes the point that the series' inventions reference contemporary debates on native land claims, French-Canadian sovereignty, official multiculturalism, and the role of public broadcasting, which form "the dominant codes" of Canadian national identity. He situates the adaptation within the policy context of Canadian cultural production and within the mandate of the CBC, the broadcaster that originally aired *Emily of New Moon*. The "dominant codes" he identifies form intertexts that permeate *Emily of New Moon* with "the ideological content of federal policy" on national identity, multiculturalism, and public broadcasting, opening the series to other narratives of the nation, specifically the non-Anglo-Celtic elements of Canadian cultural identity and history.[53] Gittings surmises the effect:

> Like all historical novels or films, the CBC series reformulates the past, specifically Montgomery's representation of a Canadian past, based on pres-

ent concerns about the injustices suffered by groups read by the dominant as other to the nation. The television adaptation constitutes a melodramatic narrative of nation as a family, an ideological allegory that would sew into the cultural fabric of the nation those who have been excluded from an historically white Protestant fictive ethnicity that came to signify Canada in the nineteenth and twentieth centuries.[54]

In *Emily of New Moon*, adaptation revises the source text into a romance for the nation, one that is inclusive and open to diversity, and hence participates in contemporary cultural imaginings of Canada as a multicultural postcolonial nation—though not without problems. As Gittings mentions, Little Fox and Father Ducharme remain outsiders, on the margins of what is still the story of a white girl and her Anglo-Celtic protestant family. Nevertheless, Gittings argues that the changes to the original romance perform "the political work of making Montgomery more consumable as a national icon compatible with the nation's late twentieth-century diversity and official policy of multiculturalism."[55] Regardless of these aims, Gittings reports that the series' textual infidelities outraged some Montgomery scholars.

The revisionist romance illustrates the problems with the fidelity approach to adaptation and its criticism. Does textual fidelity justify the perpetuation of racist and exclusionary cultural practices and cultural canons, particularly on the part of the nation's public broadcaster? What justifies fidelity to Montgomery's vision of Canada now? While *Emily of New Moon* shows discomfort in perpetuating a white Anglo-Celtic protestant hegemony, neither Sullivan's *Road to Avonlea* nor its *Anne* films display such discomfort.[56] Although some Montgomery scholars express anger at textual infidelity, cultural critics representing the Centre for Resource-Action on Race Relations (CRARR) raise questions about the CBC's continued investment in the Montgomery adaptations and the vision of Canada's past they construct. At a 1998 CRTC hearing on television policy, Fo Niemi, CRARR executive director, presented the following statement:

> The best example of under-representation of diversity in English programming can be provided by the CBC: while substantial resources are devoted to the series *Anne of Green Gables* and the *Road to Avonlea*, there is, to this day, no national production of comparable value and budget on more important aspects of Canadian heritage and culture such as those stories dealing with the Chinese who built the national railway system in the West, Black loyalists who left the U.S. to settle in Ontario, Quebec and Nova Scotia, Jewish activists who fought for labour rights…or aboriginal soldiers who had to fight both Nazism in Europe and racism inside their Canadian armed forces during the Second World War.[57]

CRARR voices concern over the Montgomery adaptations for their perpetuation of a white past for Canada, one that excludes the nation-building contributions of non-white, non-Anglo Canadians. Where some cultural critics see the costume drama as constructing an indistinct, contextless past, others describe the production of a specific, racially exclusive past. Rather than imagining ourselves into Montgomery's words and her world, the screen versions provide us with a community already imagined for us, one which implicitly requires particular traits for belonging—whiteness being the most obvious and the most exclusive. Such imaginings of a national past have immense power, promoting feelings of community and belonging, or conversely, fragmentation and exclusion. The stories we tell ourselves about our past have implications for Canada today and tomorrow, and must be squared with the civic democratic goals of our public broadcaster. With the screen Montgomery, we are contending with not only an adaptation of a novel, but perhaps more pressingly, with an adaptation of Canada's past, making for a troubling public policy situation. For to whom does the nation's past, and by implication, its present and its future, belong?

Notes

1 In English-Canadian television history, Sullivan's two-part *Anne of Green Gables* holds the record for the most-watched Canadian miniseries, drawing 5.6 million viewers. Sid Adilman, "Ratings King," *Toronto Star* 16 January 1995: E7.

2 Additional Avonlea-related films include *Happy Christmas, Miss King* (1998) and *Anne of Green Gables: The Continuing Story* (2000). Of these Montgomery adaptations, Cinar and Salter Street produced *Emily of New Moon*. The others all belong to Sullivan Entertainment. Because my paper concerns criticism as much as adaptation, I do not discuss *Happy Christmas, Miss King*. Moreover, at the time of writing, Eleanor Hersey's observant analysis of the third Anne film did not exist. See Hersey, "'It's all mine': The Modern Woman as Writer in Sullivan's *Anne of Green Gables* Films" in *Making Avonlea: L.M. Montgomery and Popular Culture*, ed. Irene Gammel (Toronto: University Toronto Press 2002), 131–44.

3 The now-settled litigation between the PEI government and the Montgomery heirs over trademark rights, and the ongoing litigation between Sullivan Entertainment and Montgomery's descendants over profits from the adaptations, attest loudly to this phenomenon. See Doug Saunders and Gayle Macdonald, "Anne's Scary Stepparents," *Globe and Mail* 16 October 1999: C1; and Tracey Tyler, "Custody Battle over *Anne of Green Gables*: Trademark Tussle Worth Big Money," *Toronto Star* 6 March 1994: A1.

4 For examples, see Gabriella Ahmansson, *A Life and Its Mirrors: A Feminist Reading of L.M. Montgomery's Fiction*, vol. 1 (Stockholm: Uppsala, 1991); Mavis Reimer, ed., *Such a Simple Little Tale: Critical Responses to L.M. Montgomery's Anne of Green Gables* (Metuchen, NJ, and London: Children's Literature Association and Scarecrow Press, 1992); and Mary Rubio, ed., *Harvesting Thistles: The Textual Garden of L.M. Montgomery* (Guelph, ON: Canadian Children's Press, 1994).

5 Christopher Gittings, "Re-Visioning *Emily of New Moon*: Family Melodrama for the Nation," *Canadian Children's Literature* 91/92 (1998): 22–35. The article has been reprinted in *Making Avonlea*, 180–200.

6 Ann F. Howey, "'She look'd down to Camelot': Anne and the Lady of Shalott," paper presented at the L.M. Montgomery and Popular Culture Conference, University of Prince Edward Island, 2000. A version of this paper has since been published in *Making Avonlea*, 160–73.

7 Susan Drain, "'Too Much Love-Making': *Anne of Green Gables* on Television," *The Lion and the Unicorn* 11.2 (1987): 63–72; Trinna Frever, "Vaguely Familiar: Cinematic Intertextuality in Kevin Sullivan's *Anne of Avonlea*," *Canadian Children's Literature* 91/92 (1998): 36–52.

8 Marcia Landy, *Film, Politics and Gramsci* (Minneapolis: University of Minnesota Press, 1994), 135.

9 Stella Bruzzi, "Jane Campion: Costume Drama and Reclaiming Women's Past," *Women and Film: A Sight and Sound Reader*, ed. Pam Cook and Philip Dodd (Philadelphia: Temple University Press, 1993), 233–35; Landy, 126.

10 Along these lines, see Barbara Tepa Lupack, ed., *Nineteenth-Century Women at the Movies: Adapting Classic Women's Fiction to Film* (Bowling Green, OH: Bowling Green State University Popular Press, 1999).

11 Bruzzi, 233–34.

12 Andrew Higson, "Re-Presenting the National Past: Nostalgia and Pastiche in the Heritage Film," *Fires Were Started: British Genres and Thatcherism*, ed. Lester Friedman (Minneapolis: University of Minnesota Press, 1993), 109–29.

13 Frever, "Vaguely Familiar," 50.

14 Howey, 14–15.

15 Frever, "Vaguely Familiar," 42.

16 Frever, "Vaguely Familiar," 48.

17 Howey additionally conjectures that the emphasis on Anne's literary career may have as much to do with changing ideas of women's role in society as with recent interest in Montgomery as a woman writer, since the publication of her journals. To add to this observation, Sullivan's third *Anne* film seems to draw deliberately on Montgomery's real-life struggles as a writer, as documented in her private journals. Hersey maintains that the publication of Montgomery's selected journals was a direct influence on Sullivan's television adaptations; knowledge about Montgomery's career and personal struggles as a woman and a writer acted as deliberate intertexts through which the Anne character was re-envisioned.

18 Howey, 15–16.

19 Frever, "Vaguely Familiar," 47.

20 Frever, "Vaguely Familiar," 49.

21 Drain, 72.

22 Drain 67, 70.

23 Drain, 71–72.

24 Dinitia Smith, "Isn't It Romantic? Hollywood Adopts the Canon," *New York Times* 10 November 1996, sec. 4: 4.

25 Higson, 113.

26 Martin A. Hipsky, "Anglophil(m)ia: Why Does America Watch Merchant-Ivory Movies?" *Journal of Popular Film and Television* 22.3 (1994): 98–107.

27 John Corner and Sylvia Harvey, ed., *Enterprise and Heritage: Crosscurrents of National Culture* (London: Routledge, 1991), 49.

28 Kevin Walsh, *The Representation of the Past: Museums and Heritage in the Post-Modern World* (London: Routledge, 1992), 149.

29 Many of my observations here are indebted to the literatures on nostalgia, the historical film, and the heritage industry. See Malcolm Chase and Christopher Shaw, ed., *The Imagined Past: History and Nostalgia* (New York: Manchester University Press, 1989);

Robert A. Rosenstone, *Visions of the Past: The Challenge of Film to Our Idea of History* (Cambridge, MA: Harvard University Press, 1995); and Robert Hewison, "Commerce and Culture," Corner and Harvey, 162–77.

30 Along these lines, Canadian television critic Tony Atherton reports that one of the reasons producer Kevin Sullivan decided to stop making episodes of *Road to Avonlea* "was because he thought the show was getting more recognition for its costumes than its performances." Tony Atherton, "It's All in the Details, Avonlea Exec Says," *Montreal Gazette* 5 April 1999: B6.

31 Cavendish, Prince Edward Island, the home Montgomery immortalized as the fictional Avonlea, is a good example of this phenomenon. Within the shops, especially the Anne of Green Gables Store, the tourist can purchase an assortment of Avonlea merchandise from dolls to teapots. Jeanette Lynes coins the term "consumable Avonlea" to describe the commodification of the Green Gables mythology via this merchandise. For Lynes, merchandizing has resulted in the production of a mythology that is "at once regional—grounded in a specific locale—yet highly mobile or portable" (Lynes, 9–10). She refers to "dilution"—a marketing tool by which the more regionally grounded aspects of *Anne of Green Gables* are watered down—as a deliberate strategy whose purpose is to expand "the thematic range," and therefore the profit range, of products. Marketing deregionalizes Anne, makes PEI of minimal importance, and transforms Avonlea into a "floating signifier." Janice Fiamengo concurs, stating that tourists are just as happy to purchase Anne memorabilia from shops in Banff and Niagara Falls, as Cavendish or Charlottetown. This memorabilia, says Fiamengo, features the Green Gables house "disconnected from its particular environment and signifying an intense love of home not dependent on region or nation." Jeanette Lynes, "Consumable Avonlea: The Commodification of the Green Gables Mythology," *Canadian Children's Literature* 91/92 (1998): 7–21; Janice Fiamengo, "Belonging to the Land: Towards a Theory of the Popular Landscape in Green Gables," *Making Avonlea: L.M. Montgomery and Popular Culture*, ed. Irene Gammel (Toronto: University of Toronto Press, 2002), 7–21. Reprinted in *Making Avonlea*, 268–79.

32 Trinna Frever, "How the Story Girl Lost Her Stories," paper presented at the L.M. Montgomery and Popular Culture Conference, University of Prince Edward Island, 2000. Other Montgomery novels credited as sources include *The Golden Road, Chronicles of Avonlea*, and *Further Chronicles of Avonlea*. After the first two seasons, the series no longer relied upon the original texts, but used invented material that maintained continuity and invoked Montgomery's fictional world.

33 Frever, "How the Story Girl Lost Her Stories," 3.

34 Frever, "How the Story Girl Lost Her Stories," 4.

35 Frever, "How the Story Girl Lost Her Stories," 10.

36 Season summaries for the series obtained from CBC Research indicate that the largest segment of the viewing audience for *Road to Avonlea* is women over eighteen. They comprised 40 percent of the viewership consistently for the series' seven-season run.

37 Canadian Broadcasting Corporation, *Let's Do It: A Vision of Canadian Broadcasting Proposed by the CBC to the Federal Task Force on Broadcasting Policy* (Ottawa: CBC, 1985), 67–70.

38 Heather Conkie, personal interview, 9 October 2001. Conkie scripted the most episodes of any writer on the series.

39 Sid Adilman, "Road Getting Smoother for Avonlea Producer," *Toronto Star* 3 January 1995. In this *Toronto Star* interview, Kevin Sullivan discloses that each season of thirteen episodes cost roughly $15.6 million. Disney put up $8 million, nearly 50 percent of the

season's budget, while Telefilm Canada provided $2.5 million, and CBC covered the balance at around $5.1 million.

40 Colin Hoskins, Stuart McFadyen, and Adam Finn, *Global Television and Film: An Introduction to the Economics of the Business* (Oxford: Clarendon Press, 1995), 32–33.

41 Deborah Bernstein, personal interview, 4 October 2001; Cathy Johnson, email correspondence, 16 December 2001.

42 Lucie Hall, personal interview, 20 August 2001.

43 Raymond Storey, personal interview, 30 August 2001.

44 For a discussion of *Road to Avonlea*'s relationship to Disney, see Benjamin Lefebvre, "*Road to Avonlea*: A Co-production of the Disney Corporation," 1974–84; and my article, "Avonlea as Main Street, USA? Genre, Adaptation, and the Making of a Borderless Romance," in *Essays on Canadian Writing* 76 (Spring 2002): 170–94.

45 Deborah Nathan, personal interview, 10 September 2001.

46 Storey adds, "We soft-pedalled some of the Canadiana. Lucy Maud Montgomery's characters are rabidly anti-American. Rachel Lynde hates Yankees."

47 See Henry A. Giroux, *The Mouse That Roared: Disney and the End of Innocence* (Lanham, MD: Bowman and Littlefield, 1999); and Mike Wallace, *Mickey-Mouse History and Other Essays on American Memory* (Philadelphia: Temple University Press, 1996).

48 See Fredric Jameson and Masao Miyoshi, eds., *The Cultures of Globalization* (Durham, NC: Duke University Press, 1998); and John Tomlinson, *Cultural Imperialism: A Critical Introduction* (London: Pinter, 1991).

49 *TV Times* named *Road to Avonlea* the top Canadian television show of the twentieth century, the *Winnipeg Free Press* declared it "perhaps the most celebrated of all Canadian TV series," and *TV Guide* called it "probably Canada's greatest TV success." It is the winner of sixteen Geminis, awards that recognize excellence in Canadian television, and holds the record for the highest-rated Canadian drama series ever with 2.5 million viewers soon after its premiere.

50 See Bonnie J. Dow, chapter 5, "The Other Side of Postfeminism: Maternal Feminism in *Dr. Quinn, Medicine Woman*," *Prime-Time Feminism: Television, Media Culture, and the Woman's Movement Since 1970* (Philadelphia: University of Pennsylvania Press, 1996), 164–202.

51 Christopher Gittings, "Re-Visioning *Emily of New Moon*, 23.

52 Gittings, "Re-Visioning *Emily of New Moon*," 32–33.

53 Gittings, "Re-Visioning *Emily of New Moon*," 52.

54 Gittings, "Re-Visioning *Emily of New Moon*," 53.

55 Gittings, "Re-Visioning *Emily of New Moon*," 54.

56 There was some discomfort within the writing team regarding Avonlea's homogeneity. Over the years, story ideas were put forward to incorporate minority characters. According to Nathan and Storey, either Disney rejected these ideas as "not Avonlea," or they were disregarded in general as "token" and "contrived."

57 CRTC Public Notice 1998-44, Canadian Television Policy Review, CRARR Intervention, no. 13, 1998.

14 The Use of "Fisher" in a Nova Scotian Fishing Community
A Theory of Hegemony for a Complex Canadian Culture

Carol Corbin

Power Relations

THE CONCEPT OF HEGEMONY is about power in relationships. Relationships can be as large as relations between nations, such as the United States and Canada, or as small as an interpersonal relationship between two people. Power is exercised when people or groups of people interact—one usually has greater power than the other, although power can be shared equitably, too. Power can be acquired, exercised, and given in a number of ways,[1] and the contexts and identities within any relationship are constantly changing, thereby affecting the shape or appearance of hegemony. The word "hegemony" also has many definitions, as we shall see, but generally it means "leadership or predominant influence."[2] Through symbol systems we represent and enact both leadership and influence, and these qualities shape our relationships and our identities. Part of who we are is based on our taking power from and giving power to those with whom we interact.

This essay looks at the concept of hegemony in a Nova Scotia fishing community through the use of the word "fisher." Because of the complex nature of our society and our relationships today, with every person existing in multiple power relationships at the same time, we need to consider the various subject positions created in these relationships. Consider a small fishing community, located thirty-five kilometres from the main population centre on the Island of Cape Breton. The residents in this rural community live in networks of power relations with other rural communities, distant cities, and markets, and even, as a Canadian town, in relation to the power of other countries. As background to the daily interactions of everyone in Canada, diverse and vast networks of power shape and construct identities, create centres and margins, and establish the powerful that exercise influence or hegemony over the less powerful.

By taking a cultural approach to hegemony using Norbert Elias's "figurational sociology"—sociology based on networks of power[3]—we can construct a complex theory of hegemony that speaks to every person's individual subject position and the dynamics of power in relation to others. Elias's work helps explain how our choices can sometimes reinforce power relations that are not to our advantage—which means we are agents in our own domination. The people living in this fishing town are situated in a range of marginalized and empowered positions as they negotiate the messages and life choices they are faced with every day. For example, many offshore fishers were expected by their employers—the fish plants—to catch fish that were on the brink of extinction. These fishers knew that the long-term stability of their industry was jeopardized, but they had little power to alter the quotas and catch rates. They caught the fish in order to keep their jobs and feed their families, although most of them knew it was against their own greater interests.

Hegemony

The concept of hegemony has been useful to analyze how some people, discourses, and representations become more powerful than others. Concepts of hegemony change with the social, political, and economic context in which they are used, and, as recent discussions of the term suggest,[4] contemporary rhetoricians have not and probably will not come to agreement on one single form that it takes in today's conditions.

The term "hegemony," from the Greek word *egemon*, originally meant leader or ruler, usually ruling over a state other than one's own.[5] Isocrates uses the term in *Panegyricus* to refer to the influence or leadership that Athens had over the Aegean Islands. The various islands situated near Athens were convinced that they were better off joining Greece than remaining independent. They relinquished some of their autonomy in exchange for the protection that Athenian armies could provide. In some cases, hegemony meant simply "power over"—the original meaning of the word. An Aegean Island might be invaded by an Athenian army and then invited to join the Greek nation-state. The invitation was not without a certain amount of coercion or the exercise of power.

In the nineteenth century, the term still meant "political predominance,"[6] but by the twentieth and twenty-first centuries, as social and political worlds became more complex, the definition began to change. It came to mean "relations between social classes, as in *bourgeois hegemony*,"[7] and this expands the term from power relations between civic bodies like rulers and nation-states to relations between classes of people.

Antonio Gramsci's approach to hegemony in particular is a popular tool for cultural critics. Gramsci states, "the supremacy of a social group manifests itself in two ways, as 'domination' and as 'intellectual and moral leadership.' A social group dominates antagonistic groups, which it tends to 'liquidate,' or to subjugate perhaps even by armed force; it leads kindred and allied groups."[8] Thus Gramsci gives us two routes to hegemonic supremacy—domination and leadership.

Cultural critics have further broadened the Gramscian use of the word hegemony to mean the predominance of "a particular way of seeing the world and human nature and relationships" that depends "for its hold not only on its expression of the interests of the ruling class but also on its acceptance as 'normal reality' or 'commonsense' by those in practice subordinated to it."[9] Gramsci calls this "spontaneous consent."[10] That is, those who are out of power tend to go along with those who are in power often enough that it becomes common sense to do so. It becomes "naturalized."

However, when used in this broad cultural sense, hegemony is problematic on three levels.[11] The first problem is the elimination or reduction of subject agency in what is often referred to as *false consciousness*. The notion of false consciousness comes from the ideas of Karl Marx and Friedrich Engels and is the way they defined ideology. According to Marx and Engels, those with greater power have greater ability to construct the "truth" about a situation or knowledge, and therefore those with less power can never be sure of the "truth," since those with greater power will construct it to their benefit. This leads to a kind of false consciousness that is shaped by others rather than by oneself. Yet cultural critics often are admonished for suggesting that individuals make choices against their own best interests—that they are duped. Jackson Lears states that this aspect of Gramscian hegemony creates hostility among critics who are offended by the suggestions "that less powerful folk may be unwitting accomplices in the maintenance of existing inequalities."[12]

The second problem, as Gramsci, Lears, and Raymond Williams suggest, is that hegemony is not a "closed system of ruling class domination;"[13] it is a dynamic, endlessly changing system in which "new forms of cultural hegemony can bubble up from below."[14] Counter-hegemonic discourses can emerge that resist the sovereignty of the status quo. But when does one hegemonic discourse replace another, and which should be the target of today's criticism? The most common use of the term "hegemony" is in reference to the "hegemonic discourse" of capitalist ideology—the "political economy model." Capitalist ideology is the economic world view that allows the accumulation of capital (or money, stock, industries) by a few (capitalists) while others act in the role of labour for wages in capitalist-owned industry. It is based on market economics of supply and demand. Therefore, in theory, capitalism creates two basic classes: bourgeois (industry owners) and labour (industry workers). However, we know that the economy is more complex than that. The fishing industry, for example, exhibits a range of ownerships: from small family-run businesses to large multinational corporations. Labour, as well, is extremely diverse. Many fish plants are unionized, providing a powerful collective voice for workers; but deckhands on fishing boats are rarely unionized, and their employment security is often at the whim of the captain.

In order for hegemony to mean more than a simple dichotomy of oppressor (capitalist) and oppressed (labour), haves and have-nots, we need to unpack the complex relationships among people at various levels of power. Lears places hegemonic cultures on a continuum that runs from "closed" to "open." Closed cultures are tyrannical situations in which the oppressed have little vocabulary of resistance. A slave would live in a closed system, yet we know that even slave cultures resisted their oppression.[15] Open cultures are democratic situations where free choice is possible and "the capability for resistance flourishes."[16] Of course, the degree of openness or ability to resist authority will vary with each group to which an individual belongs. Aboard ship, deckhands could only complain so much about overfishing the depleted cod stocks before they were punished by the ship's captain or fired by the company. Yet in the pubs and around kitchen tables, many felt free to criticize the Department of Fisheries and Oceans (DFO) and industry policies.

The third problem with a theory of hegemony is that in non-coercive situations, persuasion is enacted in exactly the same way whether it is hegemonic discourse or counter-hegemonic discourse. Thus it becomes difficult to distinguish between types of persuasion that run the gamut from coercion, dominance, and influence to leadership and self-constraint. Consider for example that a sixteen-year-old Canadian girl's greatest desire is to be thin and to be popular among her friends. Most of her friends smoke cigarettes; her parents do not smoke cigarettes, so it seems to her that it is "cool" to smoke cigarettes because it is "bad." She is a consumer of both tobacco and anti-smoking advertisements. She wants to be "in" with her friends, take some chances, and maybe lose some weight, so she buys her first pack and lights up.

A cultural critic might want to analyze the advertising messages of the Canadian tobacco industry directed at young people, and in particular at young women in their quest for thinness, to uncover how they attain their hegemonic power. Clearly the tobacco industries operate in a capitalist society and hope to make money from their messages. They use persuasive images that they hope will naturalize smoking among young Canadians and generate a new pool of addicted smokers. We know that succumbing to these images could lead to a harmful or fatal addiction, and therefore it is not in one's best interest to acquire an addictive habit. Therefore, we can say that the young woman is in an oppressive situation even though she freely chooses to smoke.

Alternatively, a cultural critic could also analyze the messages that the Canadian government publishes to discourage young people from smoking. They too operate in a capitalist society, and they hope that by curtailing new smokers they can save taxes (not the young woman's taxes, because she does not pay any, but the taxes of those who do). The government, like the tobacco industry, attempts to naturalize its messages, and these messages are backed by an organization as powerful as the tobacco industry—the Canadian government. The government's primary reason for discouraging smoking is not because politicians or civil servants care personally about the nasty habits of young Canadians. They care about the high cost of health care that the Canadian government provides for smokers. Their motives may be just as pecuniary as the tobacco industry's. Although clearly these messages are competing with each other, are they not both hegemonic? Do they not both support a capitalist system? If so, which is the hegemonic message if two dominant powers are encouraging polarized courses of action? Which messages, from the perspective of the young Canadian woman, are expressions of the dominant ideology and which are not? In this case, she chose to smoke as a counter-hegemonic move against the "squareness" of anti-smoking propaganda. Smoking becomes an act of resistance.

As cultural critics, we are awash in competing discourses from different powerful interests seeking and compelling popular consent. Even in an "open" society where resistance is possible, there are coercive discourses that are backed up with violence. These messages intend to dominate and are designed for social control. Primarily they are the laws that the police enforce. For example, individual fishers are not allowed to take regulated fish species without a license, but corporations, that also must have licenses to fish, routinely and legally discard vast amounts of fish that an individual would be punished for taking home and eating. Fishery officers carry guns with which to back up their enforcement of Canada's regulations; but, these fishery laws, like other taken-for-granted regulations, tend to legitimate and further strengthen the dominant groups. In this case, the powerful fish-processing industry has greater say in the enactment and enforcement of legislation than do individual fishers. Yet we rarely question these sorts of coercive discourses, even though they act to restrict our freedom and support the status quo of those in power and those out of power.

On the other end of the continuum are the persuasive messages from people or institutions that we admire. We believe that we freely choose to follow them, and they seem to provide us with the best option for the moment. Gramsci calls this type of discourse *direzione* or "leadership" as opposed to domination.[17] It is in this realm of discourse that hegemony is most appropriately identified. The cultural critic attempts to identify what compels people to follow this leader or that message, because individuals adhere to a course of thought and action with the belief that for this moment, in this place, these discourses resonate with us and this course of action is our best choice.

By taking a complex approach to hegemony, we have a responsibility as cultural critics to fulfill the following tasks: first, to untangle the webs of competing discourses and consider their influence in a particular context; second, to expose the oppressive qualities of these discourses by tracing their ideologies and political roots; and third, to understand subject positions within the discursive constructs.

Norbert Elias and Figurational Sociology

In his two-volume work *The Civilizing Process* (1939), Norbert Elias explains how societies change and develop and how individuals relate to each other through and within figurations, networks, and social structures.[18] Every person, he believes, lives in networks of power that define or constrain the range of their possible actions. These patterns or "infrastructures of social relations"[19] are produced and reproduced through grammars of behaviour, which are learned and then internalized and naturalized. To understand how these grammars of behaviour work, Elias compares the cultural changes in manners between various European countries and over successive time periods within the countries. His theories of social relations based on medieval manners can help us understand the way fishers in Nova Scotia today relate to one another.

Elias is careful to point out that there is no clear beginning or starting point for human culture. To be human is to have culture, and concomitant with culture is language.[20] In addition, he states that we can never begin with a clean slate when we investigate a culture. We come to each investigation with our own ideologies, cultural concepts, and misconceptions; we cannot step completely outside of our cultural constraints to examine our own culture or other cultures. He also emphasizes that every different situation or context produces slightly different cultural properties and that no two contexts will ever produce identical behavioural results. Even in his studies of the middle ages, Elias recognizes that there were vast and unaccountable influences on every individual that were extraordinarily complex and constantly changing. No simple formula will depict the webs of individual and group associations.

Elias analyzes medieval treatises and books of manners, and traces the changes produced in court society and among the bourgeois as they aspired to participate in court life. Refined manners (courtesy) and polished speech were the keys to navigation among the nobility, yet, in order for members of the court to remain distinguished from those beneath them, they continuously assimilated or colonized habits and affectations from other courts and other classes. Thus, middle-class Europeans needed to believe in a permeable ceiling above them, a porous division between them and the court through which they could rise, while at the same time, they needed to distance themselves from the classes beneath them. When members of the court acquired slight variations in manners, nearly unnoticeable refinements or subtle shifts in gesture or speech, those outsiders aspiring to court circles were readily identifiable by their apparent crudeness of manner or speech, however nuanced. Elias traces this process through codes of behaviour: usages of silverware, manners at table, and affect display. In these medieval works, there is indication that the courtly class felt they were expressing their self-image in their artful and delicate mannerisms even as they used those affectations as class markers.[21]

During the economic and political changes of the Renaissance that shifted power from the court to the bourgeoisie, status in society became determined more by occupation and wealth than royal bloodline. Manners changed during this historic shift, but the same process occurred.[22] Those aspiring to moneyed circles needed to adopt the manners, habits, and behaviours of the moneyed circles. Their adoption of bourgeois style was a recognition of social power and an aspiration to claim part of it or to blend in with it. In his examples, Elias illustrates how an individual's behaviour often is controlled not by compulsion from without, but by self-restraint from within. Over and over again, what began as affectations of style and personal distinction became the social patterns that were internalized by those who wished not to resist dominance but to gain access to it. These codes of manners that Elias discusses so thoroughly can be seen in social relations today. Minor variations in one's speech, dress, or table manners reveal one's class, and they position one socially in relation to others. Even in fishing communities in Cape Breton, where, from a distance, there are more similarities than differences, slight differences in speech patterns or behaviours will reveal one's background and social status within the community.

These same patterns occur with variations between countries, cultures, time periods, and technical interventions. Elias calls this "social hegemony" and discusses it in terms of "group oppression" (or domination) and "group rise."[23] His description of "group rise" shows how those who have less power usually must find their vocabulary, their behaviours, and their manners from within the dominant group's realm in order to have a voice within the ruling discourses. Fishers in Cape Breton must continuously adapt their language to that of representatives of DFO, the powerful regulatory government agency, particularly when scientific information is introduced. As fishers aspire to gain influence with DFO representatives, they begin to incorporate DFO language into their own speech acts, rather than insisting on their own local vernacular. Internalization of one's inferior status and capitulation to dominant discourses do not bring about major social change, but they do allow members of oppressed or less powerful groups to ascend within the society that they had little part in creating.

Cultural patterns are not unidirectional; they are transmitted in various directions. The ruling class adopts working-class dress, the working class adopts ruling-class speech, and so forth, until it is sometimes difficult to attribute influence. This is as true in a fishing community today as it was in medieval and Renaissance Europe. Even though DFO enforcement officers have more power than fishers, they sometimes acquire wharf-side vernacular to be seen as "in the know" locally, just as fishers in the same way assimilate scientific terms. Both groups attempt to identify with the other if it is even temporarily to their advantage.

Elias's model of hegemony explains how individuals make choices that sometimes seem to work against their long-term interests, and how freedom even in a democracy is always constrained and negotiated. For example, most Cape Breton fishing families agree that the best way for their children to succeed in life is to get good educations. Nevertheless, the young, particularly young men, often leave school to take up fishing, because the force of tradition and peer pressure make it seem a reasonable choice, even though that choice usually means a fisher has few other career options in his or her life.

In a postmodern democracy such as Canada with proliferation of media and endless streams of messages, the sources of persuasion are too numerous to easily or clearly demarcate them as singularly dominant and hegemonic. Both industry and government sponsor messages to encourage Canadians to gamble their money in lotteries, purchase tobacco products, and give to charities—all with varying effects. Elias's contextualized, choice-based theory of hegemony allows for an examination of agency on the part of the individual while constructing a framework within which to judge harm and benefits of discourses and practices. It is the cultural critic's role to unravel the webs of persuasive discourses and identify and explicate the hidden oppression or potential benefits within these messages.

Mixed Subjectivities in Cape Breton

To illustrate how social hegemony can help explain individual behaviours in various power relations, I analyze the use of the word "fisher" and the terms used to describe and define the fishing occupation as they interact among people in a rural Cape Breton fishing community. The actors have multiple and mixed subjectivities, and they define themselves differently in relation to the category of "fisher." Within the relationships created by these discourses, hegemony is being acted out. At various levels of consciousness, actors make choices that sometimes capitulate to unspoken ideologies and at other times overtly resist those same ideologies. The acting out of power occurs through codes of behaviour, speech, gestures, and manners, and creates the fabric and character of society in every community.

Use of the term "fisher" represents the intersection of two primary subjectivities—class and gender—and the dynamics at work in this term illustrate the range of forces, including domination and empowerment, that affect those within the community. Use of the term occurs in social relationships through linguistic codes that structure each relationship. I explore some of the ways people are situated within the discursive subjectivities of the term "fisher" and the ways they select language based on Elias's notion of hegemony.

As I report local usages of terms related to fishing, I am surmising to a certain degree how people are selecting their vocabulary based on their mixed subjectivities. In addition, the hidden and subconscious nature of hegemony makes it a difficult concept to measure, and therefore I use anecdotal information based on my experiences and on participant observation as my data. The individuals I have observed and listened to work directly or indirectly in the fishery. My own subject position is that of a white, middle-class, feminist college professor living in this fishing community. Before moving to Nova Scotia, I used the term "fisher" instead of "fisherman" as an act of degendering my terminology, even though "fisherman" seemed easier and more natural because of its traditional usage. Like the word "farmer," "fisher" is genderless. We do not say "farmerman," even if the farmer is a man. I believe that to change society and create more equality for women, we should use degendered language whenever possible. I always use "fisher" in scholarly papers and in conversations with academic colleagues for my own feminist political reasons and in support of the dominant forms within the academic world.

However, when I am in conversation with local, non-academic people, I often use "fisherman" instead of "fisher." I do this because I come from elsewhere, and I want to gain acceptance in the local culture of my conversants. To many of my neighbours, the term "fisher" is an imposed and unnatural one with no connection to the "real" way people speak. Using "fisher" instead of "fisherman" is a mark of elitism or status that distinguishes those who use it from the ordinary people—in particular what I call the "fishers." Therefore, I often use the word "fisherman" in conversation because my conversants hold the power to accept me as one of them or to reject me as an elitist. In using "fisherman" instead of "fisher," I compromise my feminist political beliefs, and I do that for what may temporarily be a goal of greater personal importance: acceptance in the community where I live. Thus, I use both terms depending on the social group with whom I wish to belong and how I wish to position myself and construct my identity in the dialogue.

One of my male neighbours fishes crab and lobster, and I have had several conversations with him about the fishery. He is in his late thirties, well educated, and active in fishery politics. I use "fisher" with him, and he often uses "fisher" in conversation with me, although he occasionally uses "fisherman" as well. I attribute three reasons to his use of the term "fisher." First, he has upwardly mobile aspirations; he has a young family and hopes to make a good living. Therefore, he uses elite terms in hopes of social ascendancy. Second, as a spokesperson for local fishers, he deals with officials and scientists from DFO, which has degendered its language, and he adapts to their use of "fisher" to have greater affiliation with them. Third, he adapts to my usage because he sees me as linguistically correct. Although I may have little influence over his welfare or social status, I represent the university, and I sense that he wishes to be viewed as open-minded and progressive about gender relations. In some respects I am the coercive side of hegemony, since as a feminist I represent the social movement that has pressured DFO and the media to change their language use.

My other neighbour has never used the term "fisher." He is over seventy years old and has fished most of his life in Nova Scotia and Newfoundland. He feels no compunction to create stronger intellectual affiliation with me, nor does he become involved in many political or government issues. He has made a good living, is considered one of the town's "millionaires" and has little reason to aspire to a higher status position. When I interact with him, I usually convert to "fisherman" in order to establish reciprocity of usage and to diminish our differences. He is, after all, my next-door neighbour, and he has attempted to bridge our cultural differences in other ways. Even though my gendered usage of "fisherman" may be an act of submission to a male-dominated society, it is a choice I have made based on my particular relationship with this neighbour. I wish to build mutuality as a neighbour and not impose my way of speaking and my political affiliation on him. If I use "fisher," my neighbour might view me as an elite intellectual; but by not using it, I do a disservice to the politics of feminism.

Women who fish, for the most part, call themselves "fishermen," and I think there are several reasons for this. There are so few inshore women fishers that those who do this work prefer not to call attention to their gender by degendering their vocabulary. Identifying oneself as a feminist in this culture usually leads to jokes, derisive comments (labels like "feminazi"), and other forms of exclusion from predominantly male groups. A fisher must rely upon other fishers whether they are on the same boat or not, and to many it may be more important to maintain harmony and camaraderie than to make what seems to these women to be minor vocabulary changes, even though they may be in the best interests of women as a whole. Like many Canadians, these women dismiss language as insignificant in the "real" world. However, if language use were truly insignificant then degendering their language would not cause problems. But it does, and most women fishers opt to self-identify with the gendered "fisherman" especially when a word is threatening to co-workers.

I have never heard a fisher's wife use the term "fisher," and I suspect that is for a similar reason: to introduce gender politics into a patriarchal home would upset the delicate peace. Most women in this community assume "we know what is meant" by "fisherman"—that it includes women who fish as well as men. Many local women believe that feminist discourse has had little impact at the community level; they believe it has not helped women gain or keep jobs, nor has it liberated them from traditional work in the home. In fact, most of these rural women disavow any interest in or knowledge of feminism. It is a word akin to male castration, and in most of these women's eyes, their own best interests are served by not aligning themselves with any radical political movements. There is a certain security, although unfairness, in their subjugation. The men who gather in the pubs and on the wharves still constitute a powerful proscription of feminist ideology. These women know that they risk community cavilling if they more than joke about the liberation of women. They live in more traditional subordinate positions that fit neatly into the Gramscian hegemonic formula and for which academic language of oppression is most applicable. Yet, when a nineteen-year-old female fisher applied for a position with a local women's group, she referred to herself as a "fisherperson" in her application. She did this knowing that an all-female group would read her application and that this group could have feminist leanings. In her own best interests, in this particular context she degendered her language.

Fish-plant workers are primarily female, and, as with most factories, the women receive the lowest wages while the higher-paid management is primarily male.[24] These women too have complex subjectivities. Some have begun to identify themselves as "fishery workers." They find "fisher" awkward, and as one woman says, "fisher sounds like something that festers on my back." Many use the degendered "fishery worker" and apply it to all workers in the fishery. One feminist fish-plant worker and union representative corrects people who use "fisherman" and suggests "fishery worker" as a substitute. She has found it possible to make feminist word choices in part because she works in a female-dominated culture. Her use of "fishery worker" instead of "fisherman" has begun to spread among her female colleagues, especially, I believe, because she is seen as an influential voice within the fish plant.

The editor of the community newspaper intersperses both terms, "fisherman" and "fisher," in her columns. She believes that if she uses "fisher" exclusively, she will hear complaints from her male friends and family members. Yet she wishes to be fair about it; she states, "Not everyone who fishes is a man." Her mother, in fact, fishes with her father, and her mother has struggled to gain the respect she feels she deserves as an equal member of a male-dominated profession. She continues to argue to be granted a fishing license, but has met opposition she believes is based on gender. Her role as a fisher's wife is used by others to define her as "not-a-fisherman." She states that she does not mind being called either "fisherman" or "fisher."

Women fishers in another Nova Scotia community unanimously prefer to be called "fishermen." They state that "fisherperson" and "fisherwoman" "offend both the eye and the ear" and that a "fisher" is "a type of weasel"; but their presence on the water in a male-dominated industry is in itself an act of feminism, and from time to time they receive some unpleasant responses from their male counterparts. One woman said, "Sure, I got a few comments I'd just as soon forget ... but nothing serious, really." Another said, "When I worked in an office and [my husband] fished his licence, it was fine, but when I got my own licence, there were people who said there was no need for two licences in one household, that it was a no-no."[25] Social pressure constrains the lives of women in rural fishing communities in more traditional ways than in places where feminism has taken stronger hold, but social change may be pushing up from the grassroots, even as language change works its way into rural fishing towns from elite, academic, and government sources.[26]

These brief examples illustrate the way language establishes hegemonic relationships between people in interpersonal conversations, and how each choice of terminology is an act of power negotiation. Each linguistic choice reinforces or changes one's social status and identity within that context. People select their terminology based on their own personal aspirations, politics, and momentary needs, even if it sometimes means biting their tongues in order not to be accused of "stirring up trouble. " Additionally, fishers are influenced by media messages around them. Use of the degendered "fisher" reflects a class position superior to the traditional use of "fisherman," which one columnist calls a "fine, honourable, centuries-old, honest, descriptive and universally understood term."[27] Deakin feels that DFO's and the media's use of "fisher" is being imposed by a book-educated elite, who are willing to wipe out centuries of cultural usage and self-identification by individual subjects. DFO and the media, Deakin suggests, have capitulated to feminists and with them all sorts of other effete intellectuals whom Deakin describes as "Canada's English language revisionists," "that mysterious band of persons seemingly bent on eradicating the contiguous letters M-A-N from as many long-used, well-beloved words as they can find"—the "ardent proponents of gender-neutral language."[28]

It is possible that fishers associate the same "intellectuals" who are degendering the language with those who learned about fish only in books and then (mis)managed the cod stocks from Ottawa.[29] Through their lack of responsiveness to local cultural knowledge, this same book-educated group may be perceived to be destroying the very culture that uses "fisherman" instead of "fisher." Nevertheless, "fisher" has entered the linguistic realm of many fishing communities, and it has complicated the subjectivities of those who fish. Their self-identification and their relationships with others in the community and beyond are represented in these terms. Male resistance to linguistic change may reflect an inability or unwillingness to recognize gender injustices in the society that is couched in notions of a venerable "tradition."

Analysis

The words we choose are markers of our positions in relation to others. Words are not neutral; they are the very core of ideology. As the words we use change, society changes with them. We individually and collectively decide our visions of society—what parts we want to change and what parts we want to retain—and we base our linguistic choices on those visions. However, the language we use is always shaped by and within various relationships with others. We are born into a culture and a language that are not of our making, but as active agents we create and shape our identities, our relationships, and our futures through the words we choose.

Because the practices of the dominant culture and the dominant linguistic forms act to empower some people more than others, cultural critics must examine both the oppressive qualities of the dominant ideology and the way even minor linguistic changes can shift the balance of power ever so slightly. Hanging on to old, gendered forms of language continues to constrain women as they do work that is equal to men's. The Cape Breton fishery is a good example of a complex culture that clearly exhibits both gendered division of labour and gendered language; but it also incorporates "emergent" discourses as women make inroads into male-dominated jobs and as subtle changes in language take hold. This tiny power shift in this fishing community to the benefit of women may, however, be a result of the greater linguistic control exercised by the power of class. The hegemony of articulate, well-educated feminists will offer a path to liberation for women fishers while it renders obsolete the gendered, class-based, linguistic traditions.

As we attempt to understand how hegemony works, we must examine what Raymond Williams calls "something which is truly total ... which saturates the society to such an extent" that it is not enough for cultural critics to accept the world as it is, as a completed work. Rather our responsibility is always to question the assumptions and the "commonsense" of the discourses and symbolic practices that surround us, and recognize our individual power to affect the work in progress that is our culture.

Notes

1 J.R.P. French and B.H. Raven suggest these five sources of power: legitimate (based on an appointed, elected or designated position); referent (based on interpersonal attraction); expert (based on knowledge and experience); reward (based on ability to control resources); and coercive (based on the use of sanctions and punishments). J.R.P. French and B.H. Raven, "The Bases of Social Power," *Group Dynamics*, ed. J.D. Cartwright and A. Zander (Evanston, IL: Row, Peterson, 1962), 607–22. Michael Mann lists ideological, economic, military, and political as the sources of power. Michael Mann, *The Sources of Social Power* (Cambridge: Cambridge University Press, 1986), 518.

2 Jess Stein, *The Random House Dictionary of the English Language* (New York: Random House, 1973), 657.

3 Norbert Elias, *Power and Civility* (New York: Pantheon, 1982), 166.

4 Charles Lewis, "Making Sense of Common Sense: A Framework for Tracking Hegemony," *Critical Studies in Mass Communication* 9 (1992): 277–92; C.W. Condit, "Hegemony in a Mass-Mediated Society: Concordance about Reproductive Technologies," *Critical Studies in Mass Communication* 11 (1994): 205–30; and D. Cloud, "Hegemony of Concordance? The Rhetoric of Tokenism in 'Oprah' Winfrey's Rags-to-Riches Biography," *Critical Studies in Mass Communications* 13 (1996): 115–37.

5 Raymond Williams, *Key Words: A Vocabulary of Culture and Society*, rev. ed. (New York: Oxford University Press, 1983), 144–46.

6 Williams, 144.

7 Williams, 145, emphasis in original.

8 Antonio Gramsci, *Selection from the Prison Notebooks* (London: Lawrence and Wishart, 1971): 57–58.

9 Williams, 145.

10 Gramsci, 12.

11 There is a fourth problem with the term hegemony in that it is not falsifiable. That is, in scientific terms, you cannot prove its existence or non-existence because the results, conclusions, and circumstances would be the same in either condition.

12 T.J. Jackson Lears, "The Concept of Cultural Hegemony: Problems and Possibilities," *American Historical Review* 90.3 (1985): 573.

13 Lears, 571.

14 Lears, 587.

15 Robert Scott, *Dominance and the Arts of Resistance: Hidden Transcripts* (New Haven, CT: Yale University Press, 1990).

16 Lears, 574.

17 Gramsci, 104–106.

18 Norbert Elias, *The History of Manners* (New York: Pantheon, 1978), 224, 234.

19 Jorge Arditi, *A Genealogy of Manners* (Chicago: University of Chicago Press, 1998), 8.

20 Elias, *History of Manners*, 215.

21 Elias, *History of Manners*, 62.

22 Elias, *Power and Civility*, 307.

23 Elias, *Power and Civility*, 314–15. Elias's descriptions of "social hegemony" resemble Lewis's description of hegemony in a "culturalist" sense. Lewis states, "In culturalism, the key to analysis is everyday experience. The everyday practices people engage in and larger cultural patterns constantly intersect one another; determination is mutual and uneven." Lewis, 279.

24 R. Apostle et al., *Land and Sea: The Structure of Fish Processing in Nova Scotia: A Preliminary Report* (Halifax, NS: Gorsebrook Research Institute, 1985), 31.

25 "We All Leave the Wharf at the Same Time," *Coastal Community News* [Halifax, NS], November/December 2000: 5.

26 "Female Lobster Fishers in Maine," *Cape Breton Post* 10 June 2001, 17.

27 B. Deakin, "Politically Correct Should Let 'Fishers' off the Hook," *The Chronicle Herald* [Halifax, NS], 12 August 1997: B2.

28 Deakin, B2.

29 A.C. Finlayson, *Fishing for Truth: A Sociological Analysis of Northern Cod Stock Assessments from 1977 to 1990* (St John's, NL: Institute of Social and Economic Research, 1994).

15 Thinking the Wonderful
After Rudolf Komorous, beside the Reveries

Martin Arnold

I STUDIED MUSIC COMPOSITION with Rudolf Komorous in Victoria, British Columbia, between 1983 and 1988.[1] Komorous is a composer of experimental music who engendered in me an experimental sensibility. This essay, however, is not an appreciation of his singular accomplishments as a composer or as a teacher. It is also not about music composition, or even about music per se. Rather, what follows takes as its impetus ideas that Komorous took part in generating as a young man in the late 1950s. Living in Prague, he was a member of a group of artists who met regularly in the cellar of the Moravian Winery near Wenceslas Square and called themselves "Smidra." He was the only musician in the group, which was largely made up of visual artists. Together they developed an *estetiku divnosti*, a term that has come to be translated as "aesthetic of the wonderful." This essay wonders about the wonderful—its cultural politics and potentials.

Smidra's formulation of the *estetiku divnosti* is rife with theoretical valencies. This essay will follow some of these combinations, proposing connections between a variety of (perhaps incongruous) critical thoughts. Its purpose is not to explicate or contextually encompass the wonderful, but rather to problematize and enrich its conceptual possibilities. I think it is worth acknowledging explicitly from the onset that this essay operates as an example of critical work that finds its insight in exploiting connections between disparate theoretical disciplines and projects. This venture encourages hijacking salient observations made by gifted thinkers and putting

305

them to work, with other like materials, in ways that diverge from their generative intentions and may even be at odds with those intentions. These connections are not at all systematic. Throughout the writing of this consideration of the *estetiku divnosti*, many different possible combinations presented themselves. Some of these would have substantially altered the eventual focus of the study, others could still be fruitfully inserted were there no limit on the length of this essay.[2] None of the connections are necessary. That is, one connection does not lead consequently to the next to form a closed, complete argument. Opening up useable potentials is the goal of this work.

Divnosti—from *divny*—is most commonly translated as "strange," but it also appears as "bizarre" or "peculiar." A recent Czech recording of Komorous' early work translates *estetiku divnosti* as "aesthetics of curious things."[3] The shades of meaning implied by the complexity of translation fit well the kind of artistic engagement Smidra aspired to. The group's intention was "to drive every situation to its end-point, so that the serious and the trivial cannot be distinguished" as well as "to bring into play paradox and the mystifying, in the joy of experiencing the wonderful."[4] Komorous further explained in an interview that "the group's main philosophy was that things should somehow be driven on the edge—on that edge when you cannot really recognise what's serious, what's not serious; you know, what's true, what's not true; what's sort of from life and what is a sheer imagination. Simply that edge—because we thought that on that edge real things happen."[5]

Komorous brought the concept of the aesthetic of the wonderful to Canada. It continues to inform every piece he writes, and it informed his teaching methods. However, the aesthetic of the wonderful was not taught as a methodology or a compositional technique. It is not one. Moreover, while the music of many of Komorous's students evinces a skewed critical sensibility that could be viewed as stemming from this aesthetic, Komorous's teaching did not engender a style.[6] As the above suggests (and as this essay will explore), Komorous's wonderful destabilizes value judgements, fractures hierarchies, and breaks down dualities. Komorous was a highly trained European classical musician who had been formed in one of the major capitals of European classical music history, Prague. He taught from this classical background, yet constantly unsettled otherwise unscrutinized hierarchies—preferring Corelli or Zelenka to J.S. Bach, C.P.E. Bach or Haydn to Mozart, Schubert to Beethoven, Janacek to Bartok, or J.M. Hauer to Schoenberg. However, Komorous's thought is in no way intrinsically confined to the very limited realm of European aristocratic/ bourgeois music.

An aesthetic of the wonderful does not prescribe the kind of art it finds wonder in. Komorous could therefore fruitfully interact with students from a culture in which European classical music is essentially foreign, where it functions more like a rarefied commodity—ensconced in academies and elite institutions (largely defined by wealth)—rather than as a seminal part of a vital, local cultural history. He offered the possibility for his students to engage a radical, productive sensibility that could embrace any musical background or predilection, insisting only "that things should somehow be driven on the edge" of those predilections.

One of the most crucial aspects of the wonderful is that it renders irrelevant the cultural construct of high versus low art, or elite versus popular art. That is the kind of duality that cannot be established when the "serious and the trivial cannot be distinguished." As a performer and composer, I am currently working in Toronto with musicians who are radically experimental (in a sense that will be suggested below) and who come from various post-rock, post-punk, pre-jazz backgrounds. Most are active in the free-improvisation scene. A trio of these musicians, the Reveries, will serve as an example of how the "aesthetic of the wonderful" can manifest itself.

I think it is particularly significant to consider the aesthetic of the wonderful within the context of Canadian culture. It strikes me that much of the ongoing difficulty with trying to define a Canadian identity is due to what I perceive as a lack of a generalized narrative in this country that asserts the importance of being Canadian; there is nothing like an American Dream—which asserts itself relentlessly given its multifarious relationship to every imaginable kind of sales-cycle—or various historical/nationalist/racial European models. When such narratives are put forward in Canada, they are received as the opinion of an individual or community and scrutinized as such. This essay will consider what is at stake in whether one has a narrative or not, when I examine Norman Bryson's ideas below. These observations speak to my belief that there is a greater intrinsic, unselfconscious allowance in Canada to make work that is not exemplary, more than in any other nation in the world I can think of. A work here does not have to serve as an example of being Canadian or as an example of production that in some way resists or opposes that identity—no such identity exists. I am not suggesting that this is somehow more "wonderful" per se—and any Canadian can *choose* to make exemplary work of any sort. However, wonder, as we are considering here, can only arise when generative motivations and creative intents are not apparent. And so, as an example of all this, I would say that, while in no way do the Reveries sound "Canadian," I cannot think of another culture that their sound could have come out of.

In some sense then, "wonderful" is an extremely apt word to embrace the *estetiku divnosti*, even if its current usage has become largely banal, a limp superlative or an expression of delight. This is a far cry from its historically complex application as denoting "the wonderful," the passion of wonder in the presence of wonders, and whole orders of marvels—preternatural objects and occurrences. Indeed a *div*—the root of *divnosti*—is just that, a marvel/miracle/wonder. "Wonderful" is therefore a word that can be read as suggestive of that "edge" that Komorous referred to. It embraces the innocuous, a hackneyed term of appreciation, and a category that has historically been concerned with that crucial area between the known and the unknown.[7]

What is meant by wonders, the marvellous, *mirabilia,* has had a multifaceted history embracing radically different world views. In their exhaustive study *Wonders and the Order of Nature, 1150–1750,* Lorraine Daston and Katherine Park carefully and thoroughly emphasize these shifts and (often antagonistic) differences. At the same time, they make a general distinction between the nature of wonders as they were viewed during the Middle Ages and their status within the current order of nature: "Wonders tended to cluster at the margins rather than at the center of the known world, and they constituted a distinct ontological category, the preternatural, suspended between the mundane and the miraculous. In contrast, the natural order moderns inherited from the late seventeenth and eighteenth centuries is one of uniform, inviolable laws."[8] Wonders and marvels were not really supernatural, above (*super*) nature. Rather, they were preternatural, beyond (*preter*) nature, often just beyond, on the edge of the mundane. Miracles were understood as supernatural. They were direct acts of God. They were transcendent, flowing from a spiritual realm. Wonders were in the world, a part of the world, but somehow remarkably other to its regularly experienced operations. This otherness could include everything from "accidental" aberrations of nature like a six-fingered child or magnificently astonishing and wildly rare and exotic phenomena such as manticores and dragons.

One crucial aspect of Daston and Park's historical formulation is that a wonder, regardless of the form it took, was not impossibly breaking a law of nature, on the one hand, or within the laws of nature, on the other. These laws, as such, did not yet exist. Rather, in the Middle Ages there was a familiar world that existed and operated in a recognizable way. Wonders flickered or burst around the edges of this regular movement, defying familiarity and recognition (without being *super*-natural). This suggests a very different kind of human imagination than any modern formulation that Western culture might posit. It is an imagination that allows things to stay unexplained (even be essentially, ontologically unexplainable) yet cohabitate with us as part of a hypothetically perceivable reality. Wonders, and the wonder they elicited, existed as a true margin: "Wonders as objects marked the outermost limits of the natural. Wonder as a passion registered the line between the known and the unknown."[9]

Daston and Park point out that, in a number of medieval European languages, the same or very similar words were used for both objects (wonders) and the passionate reactions they gave rise to (the feeling of wonder), "signaling the tight links between subjective experience and objective referents."[10] A manifestation of these tight links can be observed in their presentation of a thirteenth-century catalogue of wonders compiled by an English nobleman, Gervase of Tilbury. It is a wildly varied collection of 129 "marvels of every province—not all of them, but something from each one:"[11]

> At first glance, this list appears incoherent. It included plants, animals, and minerals; specific events and exotic places; minerals and natural phenomena; the distant and the local; the threatening and the benign. Furthermore, Gervase had compiled his wonders from a wide range of sources. Many (dolphins, the phoenix, the portents) came from classical texts, while others were obviously biblical or belonged to the capacious Christian corpus of wonder-working sites, images, and relics. Still others, like the werewolves and *dracs*, had their roots in Germanic, Celtic, or other local oral traditions. Yet for all their diversity, Gervase stressed the coherence of this catalogue of wonders, locating it in the emotion evoked by all of them.[12]

It is significant that the criteria for being a wonder was, fundamentally, that it made one feel wonder. Indeed, other quasi-objective, analytical/hierarchical taxonomies (as in asking "how is it marvellous?" and "how marvellous is it?") were not really applied when it came to organizing an appreciation of the marvellous. Beyond the basic coherence of the passion of wonder, modes of grasping marvels were essentially local (that is, focussed on the marvel's peculiar locale) and particular. This is consistent with the medieval imagination. If one could more thoroughly, and in a generalizable way, grasp the essential nature of a wonder, then it would cease to be one; it would cease to inhabit that inscrutable margin between the mundane and the (theologically explicable) miraculous. That wonders are intrinsically ungraspable, that they resist analysis and classification, that they are defined through their subjective affects, and that they are radically specific and idiosyncratically local, are all crucial attributes in connecting this history of the marvellous to certain more recent aesthetic theories—in particular, to an *estetiku divnosti*.

With this connection, I do not propose any kind of direct link between the medieval wonderful and Smidra's wonderful. There was certainly no knowing appropriation of some idea of the medieval in Smidra's maxims and practices. However, as a theoretical tool, as a point of view from which to speculate and conjecture (that is, theorize), the history of marvels is highly useful. It allows us a glimpse of a profoundly different kind of sensibility, a different kind of human mind interacting with phenomena, imbedded within earlier moments of European cultural development. Moreover, I do not suggest that the aesthetic plays the same role or serves the same functions in the modern imagination as the preternatural did within the medieval world view. However, the accounts of the medieval mind moving into the experiential flux, found in the margin between the known and the spiritually transcendent and supernatural miraculous, provide a productive vantage point from which to consider phenomena that escape traditional aesthetic hierarchies and boundaries. These accounts of an imagination experiencing the passion of wonder in contact with the unknown give rise to an array of possibilities in thinking the unknowable in art.

To link unknowability to art brings to mind many disparate aesthetic theories. For example, in his book *The Sovereignty of Art: Aesthetic Negativity in Adorno and Derrida*, Christoph Menke presents two contrasting, pervasive models (ascribed to Arthur Schopenhauer and Friedrich Nietzche respectively) that stress the incomprehensibility of the aesthetic object. Menke points out that both models "initially share a premise: the location of the aesthetic object outside the realm of customary understanding."[13] The particular unknowability I am concerned with here, however, is the one imagined by Smidra. It is that mystifying location where the nature of an artistic phenomenon cannot be distinguished, where one cannot really recognize its values and purposes. I think of that edge on which Komorous has located his music as being related to that margin in which we have located the wonderful. His music is driven onto the edge just beyond where its workings can be comfortably intellectualized and just before it takes on the quasi-miraculous aura of some form of spiritual/transcendent/numinous unsayable meaningfulness.

As was stated above, one of the conceptual preconditions that allowed the medieval wonderful to exist in a somewhat amorphous margin was the lack of scientific laws (laws that the human mind can be certain are governing the order of nature whether a particular phenomenon is currently explainable or not). To further extend the metaphor of the medieval wonderful to art, it is relevant to conjecture what it is to experiment without the substrate of rational laws. Art theorist John Rajchman has recently published a book considering the thought of the late French philosopher, Gilles Deleuze: *The Deleuze Connections*. Throughout Deleuze's work, Rajchman finds a call for radical experimentation. Deleuze viewed experimentation as a continuous source of encounters with unprescribed possibilities that unravel the fabric of the known, the conceivable, and the projectable. This concept of experimentation is opposed to any kind of analysis that supplies data in the testing of pre-existing hypotheses, hypotheses that are based on laws.

Rajchman further states that Deleuze's "aesthetic takes the form not of a judgement, but rather of an experimentation and creation that defies judgement."[14] It is important to register that the aesthetic (from the Greek *aisthetikos,* to perceive) fundamentally refers to the act of apprehending art in general. Thus it is not the making of art that is being considered an experimentation and creation, but the experience of it. This notion already defies one pervasive formulation of art that views it as a medium that carries and communicates some kind of significant emanation from the artist that the viewer/listener/reader grasps and evaluates in order to ascertain its degree of beauty or sublimity. For Rajchman's Deleuze, "art (and thought) is never a matter of 'communication'.... For what [art] supposes is a condition of another kind, not transcendental, but experimental [or, perhaps, not 'miraculous,' but 'marvellous'].... In Deleuze's aesthetic, a 'will to art' is always concerned with the emergence of something new and singular, and requires us to 'invent ourselves' as another people."[15] For Rajchman, art is not *about* life. It does not somehow symbolize the artist's world view. Nor is art a rarefied object. It cannot be reduced to an epiphanal manifestation of artistic vision, held aloft for a consumer to admire. For Rajchman, art is preternatural, not supernatural. It is a psychic location that occupies the attention of someone who possesses the "will to art," and there are as many locations as there are people with the will to explore them. These are states of mind as "real" as any other, but which lie beyond the conventions and praxis of the field of daily experience that is often circumscribed by terms like "real life:"

> The aim of art is, through expressive materials, to extract sensations from habitual sensibilia—from habits of perception, memory, recognition, agreement—and cause us to see and feel in new or unforeseen ways.... Thus art is less the incarnation of a life-world [a kind of illuminating, if numinously poetic, representation of human experience, of humans' interaction with their world] than a strange [maybe as in *divnosti*] construct we inhabit only through transmutation or self-experimentation, or from which we emerge refreshed as with a new optic or nervous system.[16]

In relation to the conception of the miraculous presented above, Rajchman refers to some other pervasive philosophies of art as "aesthetic pieties." He states that "we must push sensation beyond transcendence where it becomes a matter of belief not in another world, but in 'other possibilities' in this one."[17] Obviously, these quotations suggest philosophical issues that reach far beyond the scope of this essay. They also certainly do not encompass the subtlety of investigative thought that surrounds them in Rajchman's text—these statements are not so stridently aphoristic in their original context. However, they serve to suggest that Rajchman locates

Deleuze's aesthetic in a place that is in many ways analogous to the medieval wonderful. It is a place of discovery without judgement, a margin outside of the mundane, away from habits of perception, memory, recognition, agreement. It is a place that exists outside of the miraculous, the transcendent, as "a matter of belief not in another world, but in 'other possibilities' in this one." This place is a "strange construct" set apart from laws of judgement, that stands away from pre-existing, a priori statutes of evaluation (whether considered transcendentally subjective or inescapably dictated by culture), which tend to envelope and synthesize any specific aesthetic experience within their precepts. Through Deleuze's writing, Rajchman sees art as a location where another imagination, another mind can be continually invented and reinvented. I think of it as a call to wonder, in every sense of the word.

The above concepts of art and of the wonderful begin to give an indication of what is at stake with my initial assertion that Rudolf Komorous is an experimental composer. Komorous creates sounding situations in which a listener can experiment and create. These situations encourage the listener to break through codes and representations, through pre-existing conditions of judgement. They require the listener to find new ways of experiencing what she or he is hearing. The goal of the musical experience is not to "make sense" of the composition and evaluate its success or failure. Experimenting within the music goes far beyond the synthesis of the unknown into the familiar. And I think this is what Komorous meant when he said "that things should somehow be driven on the edge—on that edge when you cannot really recognise what's serious, what's not serious; you know, what's true, what's not true; what's sort of from life and what is a sheer imagination. Simply that edge—because we thought that on that edge real things happen." The "things" that happen when one interacts with, and not merely reacts to, music moving on this edge are "real" in the sense that they embrace new becomings, generative experiences that push beyond interpretations and symbolically mediated representations. They are transmutations rather than translations. The music—that edge— is a location where a real, immanent experience takes place rather than a representation, however numinous and poetic, of someone else's life-world experience.

Deleuze's aesthetics embrace possibilities and potentials that are available through interaction with art in general, whatever the medium or the period of its creation. Yet this is a historically marginal point of view; artists and art lovers have rarely described their practices and aesthetic experiences in Deleuze's terms. Thus, Rudolf Komorous's music is generally considered to be distinctly idiosyncratic and, to some, perplexingly eccentric. Likewise, the *estetiku divnosti*, with its subtle but radical undermining and unravelling of traditional aesthetic codes of evaluation, is a marginal perspective, distinct from most other aesthetic theories.

How Komorous's wonderful distinguishes itself from other art-conceptions can be fruitfully considered in terms of what German philosopher and cultural critic Theodor W. Adorno referred to as reification. His use of the word in the context of observations about fireworks is particularly useful to further investigate the wonderful: "Ernst Schoen once praised the unsurpassable noblesse of fireworks as the only art that aspires not to duration but only to glow for an instant and fade away. It is ultimately in terms of this idea that the temporal arts of drama and music are to be interpreted, the counterpoint of a reification without which they would not exist and yet that degrades them."[18] When Adorno refers to duration he does not principally mean it in a statistical sense, as in the number of seconds the light of a pyrotechnic burst is visible for, or the number of minutes a given performance of a Beethoven piano sonata takes. Rather he thinks about duration in the sense of enduring, the way in which a work of art continues to be present in a way that can be possessed.[19] On this topic, I wrote in a different context that "Adorno is concerned throughout his writings with the ways that art is commodified and acquired, but here he is also talking about possession in terms of grasping/apprehending/comprehending the work of art. This is the "reification" mentioned—the considering or making of something abstract, concrete; taking an immaterial phenomenon to be an empirically graspable object."[20]

This reification is the process by which, for example, we are able to talk about a piece of music and refer to it as a unified object: a "work," a "piece," a "composition." For, like fireworks, a piece of music can never be apprehended as a complete work until it ceases to be empirically present. It cannot be fully grasped until it is finished, no longer sounding, done, complete. It only exists as a whole in a listener's memory. How this whole is formed in the memory, how it is stabilized to become an object one can discuss or, more pertinently, judge, is the "reification without which [the piece] would not exist." Returning to fireworks, Adorno writes, "The phenomenon of fireworks is prototypical for artworks.... Fireworks are apparitions par excellence: they appear empirically yet are liberated from the burden of the empirical, which is the obligation of duration; they are a sign from heaven yet artifactual [human-made], an ominous warning, a script that flashes up, vanishes, and indeed cannot be read for its meaning."[21]

A true post-Enlightenment thinker, Adorno breaks immediately into the realm of the miraculous—"a sign from heaven"—to find metaphors for an experience that bursts the membrane of the rationally containable mundane. His project cannot embrace the befuddling, incoherent margin of the wonderful. Nonetheless, the apparition Adorno writes about would be better considered as belonging to the marvellous. Indeed, his description of the aesthetic appreciation of fireworks essentially describes a wonder; "they appear empirically,"[22] they thoroughly belong to this world, and they are available for immediate contact. Yet, they defy the need to be explained and be possessed by the mind ("duration"). They fade away from the judgemental grasp of the laws of God/nature/culture. If Adorno gives a semantic nod to aesthetics that understand art as a kind of communication, ascribing to fireworks the aspect of "a sign," "a warning," "a script," he immediately modifies his insight by asserting that the explosion "cannot be read for its meaning." Another translation is even more explicit on this point: "[Fireworks] are both a writing on the wall, rising and fading away in short order, and yet not a writing that has any meaning we can make sense of."[23] While it might seem obvious that fireworks are not carriers of a meaning that lies outside of the empirical facts of their existence, it is significant that Adorno finds them prototypical for artworks in general. For Adorno, all art as it appears, as we perceive it as art,[24] is like fireworks. It constitutes an apparition, distinct and singular, rife with transient potentials and possibilities, but only those immanent to it. In other words, "It is not that something appears to us in the work of art, but rather it is the art work that appears (to us)."[25] But the mind tries to take hold of the experience and the apparition is reified. The glimmer gives way to a form and substance, a history and a cultural context. The experiment is over. Wonder gives way to intellectualization.

Rudolf Komorous's work sets in motion the continuation of this sense of apparition suggested by Adorno. Even if the musical apparition is imagined as continuously fading, the reverberations of its attacks (be they no more aggressive than whistles in the dark) continue to resonate, transmutating with the listener's transmutations.

One more theoretical shift will enable us to further think around (rather than think through) the *estetiku divnosti*. It takes us to an unlikely location: the study of a traditional art historical subject that might seem very far from the passion of wonder. It is an essay on still-life painting by Norman Bryson, "Rhopography," that takes its title from *rhopos*, meaning trivial objects, small wares, trifles. One of the main focal points of the essay is a very particular idea about narrative. Bryson suggests that to narrate is to assert importance ("and narrative works hard to explain why any particular story is worth narrating").[26] Stories are extracted from the infinite, chaotic jumble of experience, real and imaginary: "The concept of importance can arise only by separating itself from what it declares to be trivial and insignificant; 'importance' generates 'waste'.... Still life takes on the exploration of what 'importance' tramples underfoot. It attends to the world ignored by the human impulse to create greatness."[27] Bryson observes that still life defines itself not only through leaving out human subjects, but through representing objects adjunct to feeding and cleaning, two of the most general, basic, and obligatory areas of human activity. He follows his propositions with thorough interrogations of many celebrated still-life paintings, including works by Michelangelo Merisi da Caravaggio, Paul Cézanne, Juan Sanchez Cotán, and Francisco de Zubarán. In each of the paintings discussed, Bryson finds dominating, even heroic narratives embedded within the works. These are located not in the subject matter, but in the artistic strategies evinced by the paintings themselves. For example, in the work of Caravaggio and Cézanne, Bryson locates narratives about "the power of art to ennoble and elevate even a humble basket of fruit, or the capacity of art to embody and dramatise the detailed workings of the aesthetic consciousness."[28] The paintings assert the importance of the artists' visionary interaction with their life-worlds. With Cotán and Zubarán, the narratives, fuelled by religious zeal, are not so heroically individualistic but dominating nonetheless: "Defamiliarisation confers on these things [the objects depicted] a dramatic objecthood, but the intensity of the perception at work makes for such an excess of brilliance and focus that the image and its objects seem not quite of this world."[29]

It is only with the work of Jean-Baptiste Siméon Chardin that Bryson finds any breakdown of this pattern of evinced narrative:

> The central issue is … how to defamiliarise the look of the everyday without precisely losing its qualities of the unexceptional and unassuming … Chardin's solution to the problem of defamiliarisation is to cultivate a studied informality of attention, which looks at nothing in particular…. For this reason his canvases tend to avoid priorities. Even blank background— which, for example, in Caravaggio is left uniform and eventless—is filled with incident, with mysterious flickers and sparks of colour that can be as engaging to the eye as any of the presented objects. No single square inch of the painting has been declared unimportant, and the objects are not intrinsically more significant than the areas between them…. Chardin undoes the hierarchy between zones of the canvas which the whole idea of composition traditionally aims for—the regulating and directing of the gaze from what in a painting is of primary to what is of secondary or tertiary importance. He gives everything the same degree of attention—or inattention; so that the details, as they merge, are striking only because of the gentle pressures bearing down on them from the rest of the painting.[30]

Bryson is interested in work that slips away from narrative, a construct that establishes importance, extracted from the mess of experience. This "importance" is analogous to Adorno's "reification" or "judgement," which Deleuze's art-as-experiment defies. Bryson still seeks defamiliarisation, a break in the dull habits of engaging the world, but without "a reassertion of painting's own powers and ambitions, or [moving] into an overfocused and obsessional vision that ends by making everyday life seem unreal and hyper-real at the same time."[31] I am reminded here of Jacques LeGoff's observation that "the marvel barely ripples the tranquil surface of daily life. What is perhaps most troubling about medieval marvels is precisely the fact that they merge so easily with everyday life that no one bothers to question their reality."[32] In a sense, Bryson is looking for marvels not miracles. He is not looking for transcendence; he is looking for "other possibilities" in this world.

Bryson's rhopographical aesthetic and Komorous's *estetiku divnosti* are not synonymous. On the contrary, they are fascinatingly and instructively different. The insights that emerge from this difference must be left for another time. What rhopography and the *estetiku divnosti* have in common, however, is that they are both radically non-hierarchical and radically non-narrative (in Bryson's understanding of the word). Moreover, Bryson's discussion of narrative brings to light specific considerations that are crucial for thinking about my proposition that the apparitional quality of Komorous's music never subsides.

Most crucial is Bryson's formulation of the idea of narratives embedded in a work that have no direct semiotic relationship to the material subject matter (for example, Caravaggio's painting of a fruitbowl is not *about* a fruitbowl, it is about *his* painting of a fruitbowl). These are stories about the creative motivations and processes being enacted. Indeed, this idea of narrative would be a fruitful starting point for any discussion of meaning in music. There is a lot of theory written about how music might be considered meaningful. As Georgina Born puts it, "Throughout history there have been two recurring kinds of universalising theory of musical meaning: that music represents the emotions, and that music is... 'sounding mathematics.'"[33] Explaining how the first of these theories might actually function in any sensible way, or how the second is at all congruous with intuited musical experience, has never been satisfactorily explicated. Indeed there is a lot of theory, most often written by philosophers or literary critics, that celebrates the intrinsic meaninglessness (in a semiotic sense) of music. However, what Bryson illuminates is the degree to which such concerns are beside the point. Regardless of how difficult it is to assert how music is meaningful, as a practice, music is most often firmly locked in the embrace of narratives located in formal elements and procedures, and appurtenance to an aesthetic tradition. In other words, as with still life, it does not matter what the content of a piece of music might be said to be; its production is infused with codes and conventions that authorize its importance. These codes are recognizable and supply the criteria by which to judge the success or failure of a piece. Tastes differ and so too will a given listener's judgement, but regardless, most music will evince the narratives by which it will be reified. Komorous is right: wonder occurs when judgement is rendered irrelevant, when "the serious and the trivial cannot be distinguished."

There is therefore a crucial link between the *estetiku divnosti* and rhopography: "The concept of importance can arise only by separating itself from what it declares to be trivial and insignificant." The concept of triviality can therefore only arise as a waste by-product of importance. When the serious and the trivial cannot be distinguished, both can disappear and any elements/events/becomings can intermingle with "the same degree of attention—or inattention." This fundamental inability to judge is absolutely critical to the *estetiku divnosti*.

Komorous's music has evolved through a number of phases, and many different stylistic strategies have been deployed throughout this history: true minimalism (spare sounds utterly exposed, as opposed to its current usage as denoting extreme repetition); poised, elegant textures worthy of Franz Joseph Haydn or Franz Schubert yet insidiously skewed; evocative melodies, redolent with Czechness, which inscrutably dissolve into prosaic, generic ascending scale passages and then suddenly evaporate; deliriously dreamlike waltzes and boogie-woogies; nightingale bird calls and grinding ratchets effortlessly intermingling with virtuoso lyricism or lush, hanging harmonies rolled on a vibrato-drenched electric piano. This list never needs to end, for Komorous's music is a gloriously bottomless pit of details. Like Gervase's list of wonders, these details embrace evenly the grand and the demure (and everything in between and scattered all around). Moreover, this list is not simply applicable to charting Komorous's historical development. Any of these attributes can be observed uncontentiously coexisting within a given work taken from any stage of his career. Komorous's compositions are radically local. Each piece defines its own distinct parameters. There is no single strategy that can be generalized for the way he brings elements together. Yet, as with medieval catalogues of wonders, Komorous's body of work displays a psychedelic coherence of character engendered by the wonder each piece elicits. Profoundly different textures and gestures can be starkly abutted without ever authoring a sense of dramatically pregnant contrasts. In this context, the experimental listener can engage with loud and soft, stasis and movement, major and minor for their specific properties rather than for their culturally conditioned narrative manipulations. Komorous somehow presents the most basic harmonies in such a way that I feel I have never heard them before. It is striking, for example, that the usually easily graspable difference between harmony and orchestration is often utterly confounded in his work. To say that music is "about" anything is to introduce a narrative.

Komorous's music leaves his motivations profoundly unknowable. Komorous's music is not about wonder; it allows wonder.

At this point it would make sense to explore in more detail how this wonder manifests itself in specific compositions by Rudolf Komorous. However, such an exploration would open itself to specialized technical considerations that require a certain kind of musical training, for Komorous's "wonderful" inhabits a margin at the edge of European aristocratic/bourgeois composition. However, there are edges to every recognizable musical practice. For example, the Reveries are a group of Toronto-based musicians who work in a margin they have located between lounge jazz, psychedelia, and post-rock.

The Reveries are Eric Chenaux (guitar, harmonica, voice and mouth speaker), Ryan Driver (thumb reeds, quasi-ruler bass, voice and mouth speaker), and Doug Tielli (guitar, nose flute, bowed saw, voice and mouth speaker). The Reveries sing and play jazz standards. Some are well known ("Cry Me a River") and some are more obscure ("There's a Lull in My Life"). They have even started to compose their own. They only perform slow and languid ballads. Each member of the group usually does two or even three things at once. To keep their hands free, Chenaux's harmonica is set in a neck holder (the kind Bob Dylan uses) and Tielli's nose flute (a plastic toy instrument that changes pitch through varying the air pressure and shape of one's nasal cavity) is strapped to his face with a contraption that recalls Lector's mask in *Silence of the Lambs* (Tielli somehow manages to sing with this apparatus on). The group plays many fragile and ungainly instruments with a strange virtuosity. The bowed saw, the thumb reeds (strips of balloon rubber stretched between the thumbs and blown in a way one would a blade of grass), and the quasi-ruler bass (a strip of metal held on a table with one hand and plucked with the other, as one would pluck one's ruler while holding one end tight to one's desk) are all very hard to play stable pitches on. All three musicians have sweet, pop voices and sing consummate three-part harmonies. However, they sing with small speakers, taken from the earpieces of cellular phones, stuck inside their mouths. Every instrument has a contact microphone on it: Eric's guitar is heard coming out of the speaker in Doug's mouth; Doug's guitar or saw is heard coming out of the speaker in Ryan's mouth; everything Ryan does is heard coming out of the speaker in Eric's mouth. Because each Reverie always uses his mouth (either to sing or play an instrument), the speaker signal is filtered in a wild array of wah-wah effects caused by the changing shape of their mouth cavity.[34] The sound of their singing is further distorted by the fact that they have waterproof audio cable (attached to the speaker) hanging out of the sides of their mouths. The effect of this is that their singing is reminiscent, both in the way it sounds and looks (drool and all), of someone trying to talk when she/he has a dentist's irrigation tube hanging from her/his mouth. All of these activities are picked up by air microphones and amplified through a small home stereo.

The Reveries' music is incredibly strange/unknowably wonderful. It is dreamy and caustic at the same time. Experiencing it is like encountering delicate ultra-lounge psychedelia picked up from afar on a static-ridden short-wave radio. For all of its bizarre accoutrements, Reveries' music does not seem like theatre. The viscerality of the tasks they set themselves and their labour intensity makes it evident that they are not representing anything (as actors or Classical musicians do when they are performing their parts). Because they use all of their available energy to execute their tasks, there is none left over to strategically manipulate the audience's perception of their music through theatricality. Furthermore, the labour intensity of their activities is especially disorienting given the mellow, lymphatic slackness of the music's flow. Many listeners find humour in this music, but there are no jokes being told. As with Deleuze, for the Reveries, "art ... is never a matter of 'communication.'" They work too hard to say a thing. There is no narrative.

The experimental listener needs to come to the music and work through the aural morass of detail. This quagmire is the only locus for experimental interaction that the Reveries offer since there is very little formal variation in their music. Moreover, the entertainment values that surrounded these songs in their original milieu are dispensed with. For example, there are no dramatic contrasts to enliven their performance. Never will a fast/vigorous/exciting number follow one that is slow/reflective/heart-wrenching. One song melds into the next, separated only by minimal recovery time for the musicians and the preparing of the next set of instruments.

For all of the limits placed on the music by its eccentric apparatus, the players' traditionally nurtured musicianship is evident. They all take sensitive, distinctly personal solos on their instruments in the spirit of the jazz tradition. Yet the limits placed on the music by its apparatus enables the listener to focus on the distinctness of the playing. One is never tempted to reify this music within a jazz pantheon, to judge the musicians' places in a hierarchy of great players.

As with Chardin's still lifes, the Reveries, in building up their music, avoid priorities. Nothing has been declared unimportant. Every element is given the same degree of attention or inattention. While the near-familiarity and pop-music worldliness of the repertoire gives the Reveries' project a dreamlike coherence, these songs are not mere vehicles. Freed from the accoutrements and preconditioned codes of emotional manipulation, the specificity of each song is available to the experimental listener (if that is where her or his experiment takes her or him). There is an undefinable, strange sentimentality available with this music that cannot be held by words like happy or sad. It is the adventure of being at play with the "mystifying, in the joy of experiencing the wonderful."

Notes

1 Rudolf Komorous was born in Prague in 1931 and immigrated to Canada in 1969. In 1971, he became a professor at the University of Victoria in British Columbia, where he worked until 1989.

2 These possibilities included observing Smidra's debt to Czech surrealism; see Eric Dluhosch and Rostislav Svácha eds., *Karel Teige: L'enfant terrible of the Czech Avant-Garde* (Cambridge, MA: MIT Press, 1999); thinking about the wonderful in the context of relationships between surrealism and theories of the baroque; see Mary Ann Caws, *The Surrealist Look: An Erotics of Encounter* (Cambridge, MA: MIT Press, 1997). Also useful would be a consideration of the appropriation of the baroque in some current visual art practice and theory; see Mieke Bal, *Quoting Caravaggio: Contemporary Art, Preposterous History* (Chicago: University of Chicago Press, 1999).

3 Peter Kofron, liner notes, trans. Karolina Vocadlova, *Czech New Music of the 1960s*, perf. Agon Ensembles, F10048-2, ARTA Records [Prague] 1993, 17.

4 Peter F. Bishop, "Rudolf Komorous," *Canadian Music Centre*. 18 October 2005 <http://www.naxos.com/mainsite/default.asp?pn=composers&char=k&composerid=2579>; <www.musiccentre.ca/CMC/dac_rca/eng/k_/Komorous_Rudolf.html>.

5 Rudolf Komorous in conversation with John Abram, Victoria, BC, 1 February 2001. Recording from the private collection of John Abram.

6 There have been a few generations of Komorous students and many continue to be conspicuously active within the Canadian experimental music scene. They include, John Abram, Martin Arnold, Christopher Butterfield, Allison Cameron, Anthony Genge, Stephen Parkinson, Rodney Sharman, Linda Catlin Smith, and Owen Underhill.

7 I discovered that the use of the word "wonderful" in the term "aesthetic of the wonderful" resulted from a somewhat erroneous translation of a German program note made for an English program note shortly after Komorous arrived in Canada. The German used the word *Wunderlich* which, like *divny*, is also commonly translated as "strange." I think this was a happy accident, for the English "strange" does not project all the resonances inherent in *Wunder* and *div*. Moreover, it is worth pointing out that Komorous adopted the word "wonderful" in relation to Smidra's ideas after this translation.

8 Lorraine Daston and Katherine Park, *Wonders and the Order of Nature, 1150–1750* (New York: Zone Books, 1998), 14.

9 Daston and Park, 13.

10 Daston and Park, 16.

11 Daston and Park, 21.

12 Daston and Park, 21–23.

13 Christoph Menke, *The Sovereignty of Art: Aesthetic Negativity in Adorno and Derrida*, trans. Neil Solomon (Cambridge, MA: MIT Press, 1998), 150.

14 John Rajchman, *The Deleuze Connection* (Cambridge, MA: MIT Press, 2000), 114.

15 Rajchman, 122–23.

16 Rajchman, 135.

17 Rajchman, 139.

18 Theodor Adorno, *Aesthetic Theory*, trans. Robert Hullot Kentor (Minneapolis: University of Minnisota Press, 1997), 28.

19 "Obviously the duration to which artworks aspire is modelled on fixed inheritable possession." Adorno, 28.

20 Martin Arnold, "Olson's Fireworks Music," *Daniel Olson, Small World* (Cambridge, ON, Sackville, and Lethbridge: Cambridge Galleries, Owens Art Gallery, and Southern Alberta Art Gallery, 2000), 14.

21 Adorno, 81.

22 The word empirical refers to knowledge that is based on direct experience, observation or experiment rather than reasoning or theory.

23 Menke, 152.

24 In this context art is perceived as the wonderful was perceived in the Middle Ages. It was a wonder because the medieval person felt wonder. Today's art is art because we feel art.

25 Menke, 152.

26 Norman Bryson, *Looking at the Overlooked: Four Essays on Still Life Painting* (Cambridge, MA: Harvard University Press, 1990), 60.

27 Bryson, 61.

28 Bryson, 86.

29 Bryson, 87.

30 Bryson, 91.

31 Bryson, 90.

32 Jacques Le Goff, *The Medieval Imagination,* trans. Arthur Goldhammer (Chicago: University of Chicago Press, 1988), 33.

33 Georgina Born, "Music, Modernism and Signification," *Thinking Art,* ed. Andrew Benjamin and Peter Osborne (London: Institute of Contemporary Arts, 1991), 167.

34 To get an idea of the effect, have a friend phone you and talk to you as loudly as she or he can. While she or he speaks, put the earpiece of your phone in front of your open mouth and change the shape of its cavity. Shape the syllables "wah-wah" for example. You should be able to hear faintly your friend's voice being filtered.

16 Maîtres Chez Nous
Public Art and Linguistic Identity in Quebec

Annie Gérin

I WAS RECENTLY REMINDED OF A POSTCARD sent to a friend in France about a decade ago. The image depicted Pierryves Anger's *Le malheureux magnifique*[1] in the 1980s, in a vandalized state (fig. 1) with graffiti. I then remembered that the large-scale, white concrete sculpture of a crouching man had, throughout my memories of years lived in Montreal, been constantly modified by graffiti, a recurrent linguistic *supplement* spray-painted on its downturned forehead: *Québécois debout!*[2] The text, as a dialogue box or a thought bubble, reappeared constantly in spite of the city's efforts to keep this *malheureux* white and pristine by repainting the sculpture. Defying ideals of the artist's intellectual property rights time and again, users of the public artwork participated in meaning-making on this corner of St-Denis and Sherbrooke streets. For me, as for the recipient of the printed image sent across the ocean, the text is now inseparable from the figure. An afterimage legible to those who were exposed to the code, it determines the work's content in a way that is much more immediate than its original title, which I only learned recently.

A number of issues are raised by the appropriation of *Le malheureux magnifique* by a public who, identifying with it, claims both ownership and authorship of the sculpture when inscribing onto it a politically loaded text. This essay concentrates on one specific problem: the relationship between public art and the "linguistic question" in Quebec.[3] My inquiry stems from Roland Barthes's idea that the notion of the "author" is not necessarily the most advantageous concept for discussing significance in cultural

323

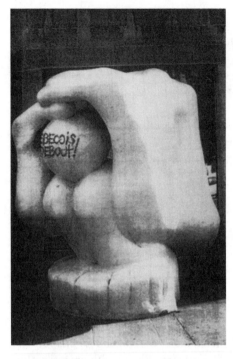

FIGURE I Pierryves Anger, *Le malheureux magnifique* with graffiti, 1980s (courtesy J.S. Revenant).

production.[4] On a more concrete level it suggests that, in the popular imagination, many works of public art such as *Le malheureux magnifique* have become monuments to a cause in particular, that of the independence of the Québécois[5] people from the Canadian federation, which is symbolized by the linguistic debate. These artworks have taken up meaning not necessarily intended by the artists, but the works are indexical, or serve as a guide, to the socio-political struggle waged in the province for over thirty years. In this context, the index, the imprint of the everyday, includes art objects in a sort of dialogue, which constantly recreates them as the political and cultural situation evolves over time.[6] While this condition might apply to all works of art, it is especially determinant with regards to public art. Because it is not cosseted by the institutional frame of the gallery, which tends to fix meaning within the narrative of a given history of art, public art simply cannot resist appropriation and regeneration.

The Gallicization of Montreal

The insertion of *Le malheureux magnifique* into its original site in 1972 corresponds to a cultural phenomenon of increased Gallicization of Montreal and other cities. This trend, which began in the 1960s, was encouraged by the institutional support of the practice of the French language in business and public affairs, as well as by the augmented material presence of Québécois culture in the public sphere.[7] Many have observed that Québécois cultural production experienced an incredible growth from that period onward. This attracted particular notice through an increased number of public art commissions, as well as the decision of many artists to carry their work processes and objects outside the gallery with the goal of reaching a broader public, such as land art, environmental sculpture, and interventions. The onset of this élan of spatial occupation by Québécois artists roughly corresponds to the Quiet Revolution, which can be laconically defined as an organized set of social, economic, and cultural reforms led by the Liberal government of Jean Lesage, elected in 1960 with the slogan *C'est le temps que ça change!*[8] Six months after the election, a variety of new institutions that favoured the Gallicization of Quebec were created, including the Quebec Arts Council and the French Language Commission. Reforms were designed to remove Quebec from the period that has become known as *la grande noirceur.*[9] Their ultimate goal was to provide Quebec with a coherent identity based on secular values. Over the decade, this identity became increasingly defined by language: "Être nous-même, c'est essentiellement de maintenir et de développer une personnalité qui dure depuis trois siècles et demi. Au cœur de cette personnalité se trouve le fait que nous parlons français. Tout le reste est accroché à cet élément essentiel, en découle ou nous y ramène infailliblement."[10]

During the Quiet Revolution, a complex social struggle was waged by the Québécois on many fronts, so that we could live, work, and represent ourselves in French. Disrupting the social and material space of the province, self-representation in the public sphere became determinant from the moment it claimed to be proof of the symbolic ownership of the province (both as culture and territory) by the francophone majority. This double emphasis on linguistic identity and territory has been pervasive since the 1960s; in political discourse, French language and the space of Quebec (the mother tongue and the motherland) tend to collapse one into the other, Quebec being "le seul endroit où il nous soit possible d'être vraiment chez nous."[11] The Quiet Revolution slogan *Maîtres chez nous!*[12] articulates this collective desire to regain control over the spatiality of *la belle province.*[13]

As the largest city in the province, Montreal rapidly became the showcase for Québécois culture.[14] Hence, when it hosted the 1967 World Fair, Quebec's cultural capital used the opportunity to create a distinct spatial identity. The Montreal Metro, inaugurated in 1966 to serve the international public of Expo 67, is an excellent illustration of this collective effort. In the city's underground network, public art established itself as an intrinsic part of the wide-ranging modernization project. Integrated to the architecture of the subway stations, it served as a platform to introduce Québécois visual arts to the world.[15] In concordance with the spatial goals set by the Quiet Revolution, a great majority of the artists who were invited to contribute artworks to the stations were Québécois; several had also been linked to the Montreal Automatiste movement in the 1940s and 1950s.[16] Under these circumstances, whether or not the themes and configurations that constituted the art displayed in the underground or the Expo 67 grounds were obviously rooted in Québécois culture (or even meant to be) seems irrelevant, since symbolic value was not only bestowed onto the artworks themselves, but also onto their producers's affiliation to a specific cultural and linguistic group. This political appropriation is where the (sometimes involuntary) nationalist involvement of the art is located.

Until that time, the predominant role of public art in Quebec had been to memorialize specific historical events or personalities.[17] During the period that concerns us, the recourse to both representational and non-representational public artworks reveals a slightly different goal. It seeks to create a specific type of presence and immediacy that would allow members of the public to recognize their contemporary selves in the space they inhabit without necessarily relying on historical representation. In other words, public art serves to claim territory for a (cultural, social, political, ideological) purpose, and it claims to anchor it by the characteristic durability of its materials. Public artworks born of the Quiet Revolution therefore produced the illusion of straightforward ownership of Québécois spatiality by the Québécois, concealing the vicariousness of public spaces as well as cultural identities.

The use of visual arts to achieve this goal of infiltrating the cultural and linguistic debate in Quebec should come as no surprise. Indeed, for Québécois sensibilities, an important aspect of mastering our space was the proliferation in the everyday of linguistic and visual signs we could relate to. These contributed to a network of interdependent strategies meant to transform our spatiality. This web, which is still being woven today, is composed of political discourse, media, popular culture, and fine arts, all referring back to *the* basic cultural-linguistic question. As art historian Johanne Lamoureux has argued, Québécois artistic production and linguistic politics are simply indissociable: "The practice of visual arts in Québec is more concerned with issues of language than with the stakes of representation.... Such a statement will be obvious to anyone familiar with the context of Québec, where linguistic difference in itself has often summarized or grounded the difference of this region."[18]

The linguistic conflict, which has persistently prevented Quebec from settling into a social and cultural status quo since 1968, is marked by the adoption of a series of laws for the protection and the propagation of the French language, such as Bill 63 (1969), Bill 22 (1974), and the notorious Bill 101 (1977), also known as La Chartre de la Langue Française, or the Sign Law. Bill 101 was designed to protect the use of the French language and therefore ensure cultural survival in Quebec by imposing French unilingual commercial display.[19] Establishing French as the common vernacular, it decisively transformed the appearance of public spaces with the expectation of creating a stable semiotic environment. In so doing, the charter materially affected the province's spatiality, literally altering the face of its cities. It also transformed social relations among the users of public spaces. On the one hand, it marginalized the public presence of communities using languages other than French. On the other, it gave voice to a segment of the population that had been previously excluded from the production of its own space. Many Québécois recognized this amendment as a major political achievement that addressed a previous injustice inherited from Quebec's colonial past.

The charter permitted the creation of a palpable francophone spatiality and contributed to the memorialization of a specific (Québécois) version of history. The possibility of affecting social space by invoking collective memory is particularly relevant in this socio-political context since one of the main concerns of the Québécois nationalist movement is to establish its own legitimacy, or the historical ownership of Quebec by the Québécois.

The Production of Memory

The monument to Félix Leclerc[20] installed in Parc Lafontaine in October 1990, two years after his death, transformed the way users of the shared green could relate to this section of the park. This larger than life naturalistic sculpture of Quebec's best-known poet straightforwardly memorializes someone who, by his prominent involvement in the linguistic debate, was already considered a symbol of Québécois culture during his life; Félix Leclerc was regarded as one of the fiercest defenders of the French language.

It seems odd that the government of Quebec did not commission a monument for Montreal. Nevertheless, responding to what he felt was a popular wish among his compatriots, Québécois artist Roger Langevin took it upon himself to conceive a public sculpture as homage to this "national" hero. Avoiding the usual political and artistic channels, Langevin sought support from the Mouvement National des Québécois et Québécoises,[21] and Québec's equivalent to credit unions, Les Caisses Populaires Desjardins, which set out to raise $150,000 in order to cast the work in bronze; 5,416 citizens of the province donated money for the erection of the monument. The names of all patrons were inscribed on a microfilm, stored safely in a case, and stashed inside the sculpture, conferring collective ownership and authorship of the work to Leclerc's public.

When Langevin offered the bronze to the city of Montreal on behalf of thousands of Québécois, the city's public art commission was placed in an extremely delicate position. It felt constrained to accept the statue and find a suitable place for it, but clearly the work did not fit the aesthetic criteria developed for the city's public art program. Moreover, it was found distasteful by a number of art specialists who made their position clear in a variety of forums. The work was critiqued on the basis that the use of one of the most conservative forms of the monument—the bronze naturalistic full-length figure—suggests unequivocally that the sculptor's preoccupations were completely unconnected with contemporary aesthetic debates. This absolute desire to signify through unambiguous forms reveals clearly the political nature of this memorializing gesture.

When the gigantic Félix was unveiled, a record five hundred people greeted the figure, singing "Mon cher Félix, c'est à ton tour de te laisser parler d'amour"[22] waving dozens of fleur de lys flags. Most artworks certainly cannot claim such a warm reception. As it turns out, the public who welcomed Félix to the park did not show up to engage with the visual arts. They came to partake in an event related to linguistic politics and the history of Québécois literary culture. They gathered to consecrate a hero.[23]

Langevin entitled the monument *Debout*[24] in reference to the poet's nationalist involvement. He described Leclerc as "notre plus grand poète, qui s'est toujours tenu debout, comme un arbre. En effet, Félix n'a-t-il pas écrit: je suis un arbre de cette terre?"[25] The title, which is meant to underscore the meaning embodied in the figure, is further echoed in the text engraved on a sequence of thirty bronze plaques displayed in a crescent configuration, at the feet of the standing figure: "Monument national des Québécois 'Nous sommes des Québécois issus de la vielle France maîtres chez nous et loin des rois après trois siècles de patience nous sommes Québécois et pour des siècles.' Félix Leclerc."[26]

In view of the absolute clarity of the subject matter and the cultural-linguistic motivation of the monument, the words seem redundant. Furthermore, when Langevin chose to iterate Leclerc's—and the Quiet Revolution's—slogan, *Maîtres chez nous*, he repeated the metaphor I outlined earlier, which allows the ownership of space and linguistic identity to stand for one another. Moreover, the legitimacy of the ownership of the land by francophone citizens, which is inferred by this metaphoric structure, claims to be rooted in an origin that can be unequivocally traced to the territory of France. The analogy that ties together political and linguistic legitimacy echoes the process of colonial exclusion from social space that once banned the Québécois from the production of our own spatiality.

Debout is indeed exclusionary on several accounts; it defines its ideal user through linguistic identity, territorial ownership, ethnic and geographical origin, and strategic use of memory. Non-francophone users of the park, those who cannot claim French ancestry and those who were not exposed to Félix Leclerc's poetry, are symbolically excluded from the transformed space. This is highly problematic since many communities share this public space.

Fortunately, not all monuments are so unsophisticated as the one produced by Roger Langevin. *Le mur archive* by artist Lisette Langevin (no relation) provides a richer example for the inscription of collective memory into public space by integrating language and visual form.[27] The work consists of brass sheets fitted into condemned doorways. The openings once led to the convent formerly occupied by the Soeurs Grises, francophone nuns who dedicated their lives to helping the poor, the sick, and orphans. The metal parchment reproduces the capricious handwriting of Louis XV who, on 3 June 1753, created the Soeurs Grises order by the authority of his signature. The text, written in old-fashioned French, contributes to a national(ist) narrative, which conveniently ignores the surrender of the colony of New France to the British Empire in 1763, just a few years after the original letter to Marguerite d'Youville was penned. Forging a myth of historical continuity for local consumption, the work refers simultaneously to New France as a period, a territory, and a cultural group, which has developed into today's Québécois population. This historical blind spot and the restructuring of history by omission are troubling, and the ensuing conception of the Quebec nation-state-space as homogeneous is quite erroneous. Inasmuch as native populations are still often ignored when the historical ethnic makeup of New France is described, the Québécois of today are time and again presented as a homogenous group, with total disregard for those whose ancestors did not emigrate from France.[28] To my mind, this type of homogenizing narrative, which necessarily invokes social exclusion, is one of the most pernicious structural flaws endemic to the process of public memorialization.

On the surface, public art, as a public form of communication, seems to convey eternal truths; yet it participates in narratives limited by circumstances, time and place. Furthermore, while public art can be appreciated in a variety of ways (aesthetic, semiotic, phenomenological, etc.), it is always also a mnemonic device implanting a material presence into the spatial reality of a community. Even if its broad role as marker of place, culture, and ideology is rarely discussed, public art contributes to establishing spatial practices. It therefore plays an important role in the creation or the legitimization of cultural codes. Its forms insert themselves into the visual vocabulary of its publics, defining or transforming how they perceive social narratives. Because of this, public artworks present their users with an opportunity to engage in a dialectical relationship between different types of authorship. These types of authorship include the artist who creates the work; different publics who author the work by including it in narratives that draw heavily on context and past experiences of art and space; and an "authoring" process that accumulates through time, and relies on the relationship between the object, the changing context of the work, and its varying users. These multiple authors, all necessary to the practice of memorialization, contribute to the potential of public art to articulate place, identity, and collective memory.

Anne Griffin has recently noted that the relationship between collective memory and political identity is particularly explicit in Quebec.[29] She also emphasizes that the concept of collective memory can never be applied straightforwardly. What, indeed, is the relationship between individual memory and social experience? How can either be understood in relation to collective memory? What is the connection between collective memory, history, and culture? Finally, by what mechanisms does collective memory influence political and cultural processes? She proposes that one of the most noticeable distinctions between the different political parties and cultural groups in Quebec is how they interpret (or ignore) the history of the New France period, the Conquest, the Revolt, and Confederation. From this, one can conclude that for all these groups, the field of historical interrogation needs to be understood as a strategic political act rather than as something recovered innocently. This suggests, for example, that when we see history as politically motivated, we can appreciate public representations, such as the monument to Leclerc, in an openly, even primarily, political way. The subject of the memorial can further be understood as a strategic historical invention rather than as a historical figure who warrants a memorial out of some kind of inescapable presence that can be traced to the facts of Quebec's history.

The concept of a Québécois collective memory, often associated with linguistic politics, serves to articulate claims and demands in the public sphere; but it concurrently functions as the base upon which paradigms are created in order to evaluate the current political or cultural situation. Griffin illustrates this point by discussing the slogan *Je me souviens*,[30] which has become ubiquitous in political discourse and the public spaces of Quebec since the 1976 victory of the Parti Québécois (the slogan has even adorned our licence plates since 1978). She argues that instead of suggesting knowledge of the past, "Je me souviens" refers to contemporary identification with a specific version of the past, which can include, to a certain degree, the incorporation into one's life of elements that happened several generations before. This condition of mnemonic promiscuity is what constitutes *Le mur archive*'s complex discourse, and what accounts for the evacuation of bits of inconvenient history (such as the English Conquest and the ethnic composition of the region) from the historical narrative it privileges.

In the national context, collective memory can therefore be understood as the capacity—and the legal right—to remember selectively, but most importantly to organize experience in a way that can repress or efface other interpretations of the past. This seems to indicate that collective forgetfulness can be as important as collective memory in this process of generating a deceptively homogenous spatiality. The aforementioned slogans *Je me souviens* and *Maîtres chez nous* therefore refer to something much larger than personal memory and individual occupation of space. They refer to a cultural and intellectual historical narrative that is very much alive today, and that still rewrites itself through repetition of historical motifs and spatial practices, which are themselves meant to define legitimate ownership of the province. In this perspective, memory and political praxis function in a dialectical relationship. This might seem peculiar since on the surface memory and praxis give the impression of belonging to disparate realms. While memory can be described as a form of inscription that concentrates the past into signs accessible in the present, praxis seeks to plant roots for future actions.

When public art serves the explicit function of memorialization, as *Debout* and *Le mur archive* do, it necessarily does so by providing a distilled and skewed version of the history it represents, a version that suits the goals of its patron, who is most often a constituted subject.[31] In this sense, memorials reflect the type of society desired by their sponsors through material contributions to collective memory and the production of historical myths. From this perspective, one can certainly intimate that the public markers of memory condition reactions to present social and political realities, and therefore shape a society's future choices. Is this not, after all, why we study history? One could hence imagine a forward-looking memory, a memory that organizes impressions from the past in relation to current and projected needs, fears, social, political, and cultural interests. Memorials such as *Le mur archive* therefore enact a progressive memory, a generative or "originary" memory. In the same way, the constant affirmation that we, the Québécois, remember (*Je me souviens*) regenerates and reconstructs the everyday. It supplements our social space through the indexical, or guided, repetition of a specific and strategic version of our history.

I previously suggested that public art, as a supplement to the city, is generative. What I meant was that public art recreates the public spaces it occupies, and it does so within the structure of iteration, of recollection; it only generates, or reproduces itself, through repetition of a narrative and/or repetitive use by its public of the skewed memory it serves up. This iterability resides in its dependence on historically antecedent visual codes or narratives. This iterability also resides in the partial, rather than total replication of these codes.[32] But there is more to this issue. In the common event when the work of art is transformed by a supplement, as *Le malheureux magnifique* is periodically, then public art acquires the authority to redirect the debate in a different direction. This is the paradoxical moment of the generative supplement, a memory later added, always conflicting with the environment it extends, since it both fixes and subverts meaning. In other words, the monument, in which a visually expressed collective memory and actual spatial practices come together, is the site of constant friction between the narrative of the nation (as a supplement to the city) and the city itself (including the people who live in it, the way they use their space, and how they might supplement this space while using it). The work transformed by a supplement concurrently maintains and exposes the illusion of a homogeneous spatiality. As I see it, this unstable situation reveals a tension: it exposes the fragility, the vulnerability of the monument-supplement to being taken over by yet another supplement.

In *The Production of Space*, Henri Lefebvre argues that monuments operate in effecting political consensus by establishing collective memory: "Monumental space offer[s] each member of a society an image of that membership, an image of his or her social visage. It thus constitute[s] a collective mirror more faithful than any personal one."[33] Lefebvre's notion of a faithful mirror is, however, open to question if the identities that partake in this memory, are (as they often are), unstable or (as they always are), political. I put forth this notion of instability in contradistinction to the usual definition of public art as a perennial marker of social identity. This idea follows on James Young's commentary that "the material of a conventional monument is usually chosen to withstand the ravages of time, the assumption being that its memory will remain as everlasting as its form."[34] The material stability of the monument is challenged by the instability of the supplement, which allows critical readings of the object outside aesthetic histories.

What is at stake here is what Lefebvre has described as the "illusion of transparency," the illusion that ideologically motivated constructions can be natural or neutral. In other words, reading public art as a supplement to space—a supplement that can also be supplemented—allows the "authoring" user to expose the narrative in which the work participates.

It also empowers the public to participate in constructing social narratives by actively contributing to their spatiality. On this topic, Lefebvre explains, "Monumental 'durability' is unable, however, to achieve a complete illusion. To put it in what pass[es] for modern terms, its credibility is never total. It replaces a brutal reality with a materially realized appearance; reality is changed into appearance. What, after all, is the durable aside from the will to endure? Monumentality imperishably bears the stamp of the will to power."[35] In the context of Quebec during the period that follows the Quiet Revolution, the "will to endure" characteristic of the monument aims to preserve francophone cultural and spatial presence in the space of the province.

The Radical Flirtatiousness of Language with Spatiality

Gilbert Boyer's 1988 project *Comme un poisson dans la ville* represents, to my mind, one of the clearest and most elegant cases of franco-spatialization in Montreal[36] (fig. 2). The title of the work adapts the French expression "like a fish in water," which can mean to be in one's element, in one's most appropriate place, or even to be the master of one's space. The work consists of a collection of a dozen white plaques fixed on exterior walls of buildings throughout the city of Montreal. Most are located on the Plateau Mt-Royal, a traditionally francophone neighbourhood. While inscriptions screwed to the walls of urban constructions usually memorialize facts and dates, these refer to a different kind of spatial practice. They refer to vanishing marks of life, of time, to the unpredictable exercise of everyday life in the spatiality of Montreal. They memorialize the banal, the ordinary. Resembling snatches of conversations or private thoughts, the open-endedness of the narratives carved on Boyer's poetic marble plaques challenge the indexical and historical function implied by the chosen material and format.

In addition, *Comme un poisson dans la ville* demands active reception from its viewers who need to walk, read, and engage with the uncanny event of memorialization. The work also reflects on the "place-specificity" of memorials.[37] Through the relationship devised by Boyer, which draws on architecture and language, the city shares an uncommon intimacy with its user, an undefined conversation, which draws attention to the space where it unfolds, and which happens to take place in the language of Molière. One plaque reads:

> *Il fallait bien un jour flou*
> *pour que je prenne le temps*
> *de regarder autour de moi.*[38]

MONTREAL S'EST INSTALLÉ ENTRE
LES 45ᵉ ET 46ᵉ DEGRÉS DE LATITUDE NORD.
SUR LE FLEUVE. AUTOUR DE LA MONTAGNE.
D'UN SOLSTICE À L'AUTRE. À CHAQUE JOUR. LE SOLEIL PASSE PAR ICI.
L'ÉTÉ. SA FIGURE CULMINE. 15 HEURES 42 DE LUMIÈRE DÉBORDANTE.
L'HIVER. IL RAMPE ET S'ÉTEINT APRÈS 8 HEURES 42 DE CLARTÉ.
ANNÉE APRÈS ANNÉE. DEPUIS SI LONGTEMPS.

FIGURE 2 Gilbert Boyer, *Comme un poisson dans la ville*, 1988 (photo courtesy of the artist).

This fragment suggests that on a misty day, in a foggy frame of mind, someone, sometime, might have taken the time to look around and appreciate his or her space in a much more layered way. This hypothetical experience is shared with the user. The intriguing idea that the world might appear in a different light if one pays closer attention can be linked to surrealist explorations of space, the experience of the city through one's senses and imagination, conjuring the strange, the wondrous, or the uncanny. This is what the work attempts to do by requiring that the viewer slow down, read, and pay attention to their environment.

The words merging with the material fibre of the city possess the capacity to recompose the street. Within these anonymous sites of everyday life, the occurrence of the inscriptions creates different kinds of (mental) spaces, which gain an intensified presence through language. As Montreal artist Alison Tett observes, "Walking and talking, urban dwellers construct other cities out of their thoughts and actions. In his public art Boyer memorializes these cities as semantic layers of place."³⁹ Within this language game, the topographic layout of the experience is not unimportant; the act of *dérive* (to "drift" aimlessly around the city in order to rediscover it), is always contained within a particular cultural geography.⁴⁰ Does this suggest that the type of referentiality Boyer draws from only fully involves those who are familiar with its language? Would the work otherwise become utterly opaque, or mute?

The importance of place-specificity for the work indicates that language is not simply an instrument of communication. As an ideological sign, language is material; it delineates a francophone symbolic sphere, concretely illustrated in Boyer's work by the petrifaction of language in a durable material.[41] For the Québécois, the ideological space delineated by language is *our* space. It signifies *Québec*, or rather what Roland Barthes might have called *Québécoisité*—a Québécois spatiality. This is because the collision of words and images in the space of one of Montreal's traditionally French-speaking neighbourhoods does not subvert, but actually reinforces the myth of the Québécois nation-state.

Boyer's work is sophisticated in the way that it invests the everyday of its users with a specific francophone sensibility, which is his own. Although the work was not meant to articulate political statements, it participates willy-nilly in a sensitive linguistic debate. This brings to mind questions which I must leave hanging. Bearing in mind that the work was conceived to be place-specific, and if language determines access to *Comme un poisson dans la ville*, what happens when users doubt the legitimacy of the myth of Quebec's ownership by the Québécois? What happens when anglophones or other groups migrate to this neighbourhood? What happens when an important section of the neighbourhood's inhabitants no longer uses the language of Molière? I would like to propose that the instability revealed by these questions is not created by the absence of meaning in the work, but rather by the radical flirtatiousness of language with spatiality—its supplement. So although this work was not intended as a political monument (but rather as a critique of this genre), the work nevertheless functions as one.

Tett understands Boyer's works within an intriguing spatial metaphor: "It is an architécriture in proposing a spatial supplement to Derrida's notion of archi-écriture, or the condition of absence that underlies writing and speech. Boyer's inscriptions *on* the city are simultaneously *about* the city. His manoeuvres between presence and absence locate the alluvial time of place."[42] This concept of "architécriture" is ultimately about the possibility of dynamic play between architectural space and linguistic meaning; yet it seems to me that it also provocatively points to Québécois logocentrism, which attempts to deny this possibility of play by attributing presence, or ownership of space, to (francophone) speech. While presence is attributed to the written text, flesh and bone users remain invisible, especially if they do not correspond to the desired public. In other words, although the work serenely stayed in place, the place-specificity of the work might have been compromised when the Plateau Mont-Royal became home to an increasingly mixed community. There might be tension between those who are invited to partake in the collective ownership of the work/space and those who actually encounter it on a daily basis. Once we acknowledge that language constitutes knowledge, underpinned by ideologies of power and disseminated through cultural fantasies, the critique of the logocentric prejudice targets specifically the separation between the text screwed to the brick wall and the everyday of users, who might no longer correspond to the intended public. As an originary supplement, language—and its lawful use in the province—also reveals the paradoxical fragility of the francophone hold over our own spatiality. Is it not appropriate, then, that the supplement of many mute public sculptures be a scribbled or sprayed-on linguistic sign? For example, in the case of the constant appropriation of the *malheureux magnifique*—shall we now call it *Québécois debout?*—the supplement proposes that users invest in places and public art in order to create for themselves narratives that do not always conform to hegemonic discourses or to the intention of the artist. This disclosure divests part of the authorship responsibility onto the user, who is not a simple viewer, not a passive consumer of images, but indeed a *user* who has been known to refuse to believe in the transparency of the monument and has often reclaimed works of art and public spaces for his or her own purposes. This is where the concept of architécriture becomes important, by refusing the distance between text and the everyday imposed by the structure of logocentricism, by fusing discourse and practice, users can transform their spaces and tailor them to their spatial needs and desires.

Notes

1 *The Magnificent Wretch* was completed in 1972. The work was first installed on Place Pasteur, off St-Denis Street, by the main campus of the Université du Québec à Montréal. It was subsequently moved in 1981 to the northwest corner of St-Denis and Sherbrooke streets. In 1991, the work was acquired by the city of Montreal and became part of its public art collection. The artist described this work as an illustration of the destiny and tragedy of the human condition.

2 "Québécois stand up (for yourselves)!" The notion of the "supplement" is drawn from Jacques Derrida's book *Of Grammatology*. The supplement is defined as a term that both adds to an already complete configuration as a surplus, and, at the same time, completes it by filling a void, or even annuls it by substituting itself for it. This non-concept attacks the traditionally dominant idea of an artwork's unity, individuality, isolation, and immutable authority. Jacques Derrida, *Of Grammatology*, trans. G.C. Spivak (Baltimore: Johns Hopkins University Press, 1976).

3 Public art is a festering ground for contradiction. According to advocates of this genre, it is a means to make a place more interesting and introduce different publics to contemporary arts. In some cases, it has also been linked to urban regeneration by raising property value. For these reasons, public artworks should never be understood straightforwardly as objects emerging from the tradition of sculpture and placed in the public

sphere. They should, on the contrary, be analyzed critically in relation to broad social discourses of a period, and their peculiar relationship to users of the space that the art modifies. The struggle to establish a critical discourse around public art has been recently examined in Suzanne Lacy, ed., *Mapping the Terrain: New Genre Public Art* (Seattle: Bay Press, 1995); W.J.T. Mitchell, ed., *Art and the Public Sphere* (Chicago: University of Chicago Press, 1990); and Rosalyn Deutsche, *Evictions: Art and Spatial Politics* (Cambridge: MIT Press, 1996).

4 In his seminal text "The Death of the Author" Roland Barthes suggests that any piece of writing is in fact a complex web of cultural meanings. Similarly, a work of art only signifies because there are strands of meaning leading to all sorts of areas of experience outside itself, as well as pictorial and linguistic references. Any work is therefore necessarily intertextual. This means that the "author function" exists as a cultural *process* and is consequently not confined to the person who signed the artwork, or to the time of its inception. Roland Barthes, *Image, Music, Text*, trans. Stephen Heath (London: Fontana, 1977), 142–48.

5 Throughout this essay, the term Québécois designates the francophone population of Quebec. The term was coined in the 1960s to distinguish culturally and politically the inhabitants of Quebec from other French Canadians.

6 The struggle for national identity and independence has evolved over time as the notion of nation itself was transformed in relation to power struggles within Quebec as well as the ideological construction of the Canadian nation. Since the 1960s, the concept of nationalism has moved from an ideal that encompassed all French Canadians to a nationalism that equates linguistic identity to the geographical borders of Quebec and demands independence from Canada.

7 It is beyond the scope of this article to discuss the series of historical events that led to the domination of the economic and cultural spaces of Quebec by an anglophone minority, within a very specific colonial structure. Suffice it to say that during the second half of the twentieth century, a shift in the population and the economy of the province contributed to the explosion of nationalism and increased francophone presence in various areas of public life. In his recent history of Montreal, Paul-André Linteau discusses this change in the balance of power, which he terms the "francization" of Montreal. Paul-André Linteau, *Histoire de Montréal depuis la Confédération* (Montreal: Boréal, 2000).

8 "It is time for a change!"

9 The "great darkness" refers to the period of Christian conservative politics under the government of Maurice Duplessis. Duplessis' administration capitalized on rural Quebec's traditional suspicions of urban life and modernization and adopted an anti-labour stance.

10 "Being ourselves essentially consists of maintaining and developing a personality which has existed for three centuries. At the heart of this personality is the fact that we speak French. Everything else is tied to this essential feature, results from it or inevitably brings us back to it." Quoted from the 1972 Parti Québécois manifesto. Conseil Exécutif du PQ, *Prochaine Étape... Quand Nous Serons Vraiment Chez Nous* (Montreal: Les Éditions du Parti Québécois, 1972), 13.

11 "The only place where we can really be at home." Conseil Exécutif du PQ, 13.

12 Masters in our home/of our space (1962).

13 Clearly, I am not concerned with space simply defined as a three-dimensional mathematical construct or a vacuum cluttered with natural and architectural objects. The concept of spatiality refers to a complex structure composed of conceived, perceived, and lived features. In other words, spatiality is produced by the assumptions a society makes about space, which determine how space is planned and constructed; spatiality is also

composed of the phenomenological response users have to it; finally, spatiality is made up of concrete and symbolic uses of the built environment, which depend on the users' worldview, as well as practical imperatives. The lived aspect of spatiality, or spatial practices, is the site of the public's interaction with public art as users instead of passive spectators. See Henri Lefebvre, *The Production of Space*, trans. Donald Nicholson-Smith (Oxford: Blackwell, 1991).

14 The need to assert linguistic identity stems from Quebec's situation as the only province in Canada with a francophone majority, which is simultaneously a minority in Canada and in North America. It is important to note that the francophone situation in Montreal is more fragile than in other parts of Quebec. While in certain regions almost 100 percent of the total population communicates in French, the Québécois represent 55 percent of the population in the metropolis. For this reason, Montreal usually sees itself as the main site and stake of the nationalist, cultural, and linguistic debates.

15 At the inception of the project, the city of Montreal viewed the Metro as a laboratory to develop Quebec culture, as well as an underground art gallery. Each station was designed in collaboration between artists and architects and displayed two types of works: memorials to the history of New France and abstract works engaging with contemporary artistic practices. Some of the artists involved included Marcelle Ferron, Jordi Bonet, Jacques de Tonnancourt, Charles Daudelin, and Pierre Granche. See Guy Desilets and André Vigneau, eds., *Répertoire des Archives Photographiques et Audiovisuelles du Fonds du Bureau de Transport Métropolitain* (Montreal: Société de Transport de la Communauté Urbaine de Montréal, 2000).

16 Inspired by the French Surrealists, this group of writers, painters, sculptors, dancers, and photographers was actively involved in Quebec politics, proposing a direct link between avant-garde artistic processes and social change. Their manifesto, *Le Refus Global* (1948), is a key document in the modern history of Quebec. The Automatist Jean-Paul Mousseau contributed to five Metro stations and served as artistic consultant for the Metro from 1971 to 1984.

17 Monuments are produced within a cultural and political structure as the material manifestations of a value system, and they participate in the construction and propagation of history. For a discussion of monuments and memorial sculpture, see Malcolm Miles, *Art, Space and the City: Public Arts and Urban Futures* (London: Routledge, 1997), 58–83.

18 Johanne Lamoureux, "French Kiss from a No Man's Land: Translating the Art of Québec." *Art Magazine* 65.6 (1991): 52. Lamoureux points out that the linguistic concerns of artists from Quebec should not be confused with the less culturally specific inquiry into language of the conceptual artists of the 1970s.

19 In 1988, the Supreme Court of Canada amended Bill 101, provoking strong reactions among the Québécois. Bill 178 (1988) required unilingual commercial display outside while permitting bilingualism inside commercial establishments. The subsequent Bill 86 (1993), allowed bilingual display outside, with clear predominance of the French language. The relationship between cultural survival and linguistic identity can only appear rational in a context where Quebec defines itself as a distinct society on the double basis of being a nation-state and a linguistic community.

20 Recognized as the father of Québécois song writing, Félix Leclerc (1914–1988) was one of the most popular Québécois poets and writers. The whole province mourned Leclerc upon his death. Several schools, libraries, streets, and parks were dedicated to his memory.

21 The MNQ is a federation of nationalist associations based in different regions of Quebec.

22 Paraphrasing Gilles Vigneault's popular nationalist "love song" *Gens du Pays* (1975).

23 While these two categories are not necessarily mutually exclusive, I choose to discuss this monument as a clear-cut example of a work that was unequivocally rejected by the artistic community but captured the affection of a population given the opportunity to celebrate its national culture and language publicly.

24 *Standing Tall.*

25 "Our greatest poet who always stood tall, like a tree. Indeed, hasn't Félix written, in one of his works: I am a tree of this land?" Roger Langevin quoted by Nathalie Petrowski, "Le Rodin de Mont-Laurier," *Le Devoir* 7 October 1989, C14.

26 "Québécois national monument: 'We are Québécois originating from old France masters of our space and far from the kings after three centuries of patience we are Québécois and will be for centuries.' Félix Leclerc."

27 *The Wall Archive* (1993) is located in the former *Soeurs Grises* convent in Old Montreal.

28 These marginalized groups are now often referred to as néo-Québécois. When one distinguishes from the Québécois on an ethnic or linguistic basis, one adopts an attitude that is also common in English Canada: attributing an ethnic identity to minorities while considering the majority, or the ruling minority, as neutral. This attitude is described in Michael Banton, *Racial and Ethnic Competition* (Cambridge: Cambridge University Press, 1983). One can also consider as an example Jacques Parizeau's infamous reference to the "ethnic vote" in order to explain the sovereigntist defeat during the 1995 referendum. This political blunder revealed whom the then-leader of the Parti Québécois considered legitimate citizens of the province. Parizeau apologized profusely for this statement and resigned shortly after.

29 Anne Griffin, "Le façonnement de la mémoire et le discours sur l'indépendence," *Les Nationalismes au Québec du XIXᵉ au XXIᵉ Siècle*, ed. Michel Sarra-Bournet (Quebec City: Les Presses de l'Université Laval, 2001), 255–75.

30 "I remember."

31 Whether a collective, a group, a community, or a nation, the constituted subject is conscious of its identity and seeks through gestures of memorialization to secure its unity and to have its identity recognized. In this case, the subject is the Québécois population.

32 For Derrida, the structure of iteration implies both similarity and difference. This means that any utterance or image can be repeated in a variety of contexts and then be used in different ways, invoking an infinity of possible meanings. Because iteration separates the motif from its original context and therefore only partially repeats it, what is left and what is recreated is never equal to itself. See Jacques Derrida, *Limited Inc*, trans. Samuel Weber and Jeffrey Mehlman (Chicago: Northwestern University Press, 1988), 82–83.

33 Lefebvre, 220.

34 James E. Young, "The Counter-Monument: Memory against Itself in Germany Today," Mitchell, 49.

35 Lefebvre, 221.

36 *Like a Fish in the City.* In 1988 and 1989, the project map was available in a number of art galleries and cafés. The plaques were, nevertheless, most often encountered by an unsuspecting public. Two plaques are now missing from the work, one destroyed, the other removed from its original site. In a conversation, Boyer told me that his objective was never to contribute to the nationalist debate, but rather to share his concern for well-spoken and well-written language. Boyer produces works in the dominant language of the region where the piece is installed. For example, the 1992 work *I Looked for Sarah Everywhere*, installed in Toronto's Sculpture Garden on King Street East, uses English text.

37 While it has often been characterized as site-specific, it might be more productive to think about this work differently. Because it is specific to spatial practices rather than

topography or architecture, one might want to describe it as place-specific, since the word "place" implies people, traditions, and spatial practices. Consequently, in the same way that removing a site-specific work from its intended environment often destroys the object, Boyer's work cannot be considered in isolation from the daily intercourse with the users of the extended space it inhabits since 1988. Because place and language in Quebec tend to collapse one into the other, the place-specificity of public artworks in Quebec often implies linguistic specificity.

38 "A hazy day was all I needed to take the time to look around me." This plaque is located on the southwest corner of St-Denis and Villeneuve Streets.

39 Alison Tett, "Gilbert Boyer's Architécriture," *Parachute* 68 (1992), 17.

40 *Dérive* was one of the principal psychogeographical tools of the Situationists International. Unlike surrealist wanderings, *dérive* was not a matter of surrendering to the dictates of an unconscious mind or irrational forces. To engage in *dérive* was to notice the way in which certain areas, streets, or buildings resonate with states of mind, inclinations, and desires, to seek out reasons for movement other than those for which an environment was designed, not only to seek the marvellous, but also to bring a critical perspective to bear on spatiality.

41 V.N. Vološinov considers words and other ideological signs to be material since they transform material objects, their physical environment and the very concrete ways users interact with them. See "The Study of Ideologies and Philosophy of Language," V.N. Vološinov, *Marxism and the Philosophy of Language* (Cambridge: Harvard University Press, 1996), 9–15. It is believed that this essay was written by Mikhail Bakhtin under the pseudonym Vološinov.

42 Tett, 19. Alison Tett draws this vocabulary from Jacques Derrida's essay "La Parole Soufflée," which can be found in translation in *Writing and Difference* (Chicago: University of Chicago Press, 1978). The concept of "archi-écriture," or "archi-writing" refers to the pure possibility of contrast, of difference, which is the primary condition for any discourse, such as architecture, the visual arts or nationalism.

IV Cultural Dissidence

Belle Sauvage
Lori Blondeau

Lori Blondeau

The images of the Indian Princess and Squaw have had a significant impact on societies' perception of Indian women and serve as inspirations for most of my work. Surprisingly, we still see popularized images of the Indian Princess being created by both native and non-native people. You can find these products being sold in Indian museums and souvenir shops across North America. These are testament to the general public's idealized perception of beautiful Native women as being exotic and hard to find—virtually non-existent. The other side of the Indian Princess is, of course, the Squaw—another of society's iconic scapegoats meant to desensitize both the general public's view of Indian women (their political, historical, and social issues, as well), and the self-perception among Native women themselves.

My work explores the influence of popular media and culture (contemporary and historical) on Aboriginal self-identity, self-image, and self-definition. I am currently exploring the impact of colonization on the traditional and contemporary roles and lifestyles of aboriginal women. I deconstruct the images of the Indian Princess and the Squaw and reconstruct an image of absurdity and insert these hybrids into the mainstream. The performance personas I have created refer to the damage of colonialism and to the ironic pleasures of displacement and resistance.

17 Black History and Culture in Canada
A Celebration of Essence or Presence

Cecil Foster

Introduction

FEBRUARY IS AN UNFORGIVING MONTH for Canadian multiculturalism—
a period when the very identity of the country and its citizenship are
openly questioned, intellectually dissected, and reassembled. This is when
the country's most vaunted boast of being a tolerant multicultural country is put to the test, challenged, and even subverted from within its own
borders.[1] The occasion is the month-long examination within Canada's
Black community, and across the country in general, of the necessity for the
continuing observation of Black History Month. Georg W.F. Hegel argues
that understanding history comes from recognizing it as an epic struggle
from the beginning of time for recognition and self-determination based on
the ability to know oneself and one's community, and the freedom to set
one's own limits and boundaries. History is memory of what, as humans
or individuals, we choose to preserve, put away, and to raise up as part of
a consciousness of who we are and what we hope to become.[2] Like a
ghost, history is a reminder of previous lives; like a spectre, it is a promise
of what we dream of becoming. Reality and existence are the awareness of
being confronted by these ghosts and spectres and the activity of freely
choosing one, the other, or none of them.

This chapter argues that the treatments and social positioning of Blacks
in modern Canada are reflective of a national consciousness. It is a hierar-

chy and a power structure that was—and still is—based on race as the main criterion for deciding belonging and entitlement within the nation-state. It shows how Canadian multiculturalism, with its norms of justice and equality, developed dialectically as a peculiar attempt to identify and maintain ethnic essences within an idealized social order. However, the search for essence was intended to discover who was good and evil, who should be included and excluded in the nation-state, and who should have power and what ranking in the society.

The dream for a lasting social order, ideologically called "a Just Society,"[3] is based on a continuation of what now obtains in the present, primarily for the continuance in national life of political and social changes that from the 1960s onwards officially positioned Canada normatively as a multicultural, multi-ethnic, and non-racist country. This chapter argues that in practice, while claiming to be founded on the recognition of ethnic groups, this order or consciousness is still based on the notion that some groups of people are better and superior to others. These elites have more rights of entitlements to the good of the nation-state and to an honoured position, so that perceptually determinations of belonging and entitlement, identity and citizenship, are race-based. In effect, in its current practice, multiculturalism still suffers from what I call a dream-deficit—the gap between the ideal and what now obtains.

Analyzing the need for, and the centrality in the Canadian imaginary of, a Black History Month provides us with an opportunity to assess and re-evaluate what it means to be a Canadian and who can claim full Canadian identity, citizenship, and belonging. It allows us to look at these issues through the lenses of an other, who is physically present among us, but who might not always feel a sense of belonging and acceptance, and who might not feel invested with the full claim to all the rights and entitlements of citizenship. This might be the case because of the social construction and placement of that other by a majority or powerful subject, even in a multicultural society whose liberal hallmark is supposedly tolerance, acceptance, and the promise of self-actualization.

Using a Hegelian dialectical analysis, the chapter contends that Blacks are not fully part of the national history, per se, in Canada, for they are not fully incorporated into the national consciousness economically, politically, or socially. This is so even though a group constructed ethnically as Black has had a presence of more than four hundred years in Canada. This is a presence that is much longer than that of many other ethnic groups that have arrived since then and have acquired official recognition as part of the Canadian mosaic. Blackness is a presence solidly on the periphery. As Charles Taylor shows in "The Politics of Recognition," tensions emanating from positioning some groups at the centre and others on the periphery are common to the kind of dialectical struggle for freedom over limits and boundaries that leads to multiculturalism as a fight for recognition.[4] Recognition amounts to being brought into consciousness and becoming fully part of the official history and of deciding who should have power and who should be ruled.

Canadian History and Cultural Imaginary

According to the ideological norms and the prevailing mythologies that explain modern Canadian identity and psychology, multicultural Canada was called into being by two founding peoples that were European and white. It is a country with a history that is primarily an epic—as suggested, for example, by the much-acclaimed CBC-TV series *Canada: A People's History*—of how Europeans dressed in liberal ideology, democratic ideals, and Judeo-Christian precepts developed and tamed a wilderness that is the northernmost tip of North America.[5]

In most versions of this narrative, there is a minor role for the Aboriginal peoples, but an almost total exclusion, and failure of recognition, of Canadians of African ancestry.[6] Lost in this idealistic reconstruction since the 1960s is any examination or analysis of the true foundations of Canada: of a country born from and shaped by the imagination of an aristocratic elite group of Europeans that showed little pretense or stomach for democracy or democratic institutions; that it was a country founded on racism and notions of ethnographic white homelands; that Canadian institutions and agencies have been shaped out of racist, functionalist norms and precepts; and that in terms of moral and ethical relations, early Canadian behaviour—in the way it treated specific groups of people—failed to meet even the accepted standards of the day that were considered to be Judeo-Christian.[7] From inception, Canadian identity and a sense of belonging were based on a dialectical struggle for inclusion between those ascribed as good and those designated as evil, between those who could become a Canadian with full benefits of belonging and those who could not.

Even when the prevailing narrative allows for discontinuities and disruptions, they are still in the form of very much what has gone before. As the myth suggests, the founding peoples by the 1960s had jettisoned most that was bad in their nation-making quest. These changes flowed from a dialectical struggle partly, among others, between English and French nationalism, and between the need for openness and growth through the adoption of a multi-ethnic immigration policy rather than sticking to a European immigration policy that resulted in stagnation, and by the demands of US capital looking to expand into Canada at a time when the traditional Canadian and British capital on which Canadian society had been built was retreating.[8] Eventually, they would create a paradisiacal country with one of the world's highest standards of living, where different ethnic groups from all parts of the world live in harmony, tolerance, and goodwill, while preserving the best of the cultures they brought to Canada. Officially, as suggested by former Prime Minister Pierre Trudeau in his pitch for an ideological change for a Just Society, while Canada may have French and English as official languages, it has no official culture. It is a country with a liberal immigration policy that looks for the "best and brightest" from around the world without regard to race, class, religion, gender, or sexuality. Once in Canada, all ethnic groups are recognized as separate cultural expressions and collectively they are all equal; individuals within those groups have equal standing before the courts, governments, and agencies through rights that are protected by a constitutionally entrenched Charter of Rights and Freedoms.[9] Canada's success is the creation of a legacy for all humanity through the establishment of what is often presented as the world's first multicultural state: one that is a working mosaic for the celebration of ethnic differences.[10] Such was the thinking behind the creation of Canada's social order, or the latest idealistic version of it.

Norms and Justice: Ideals versus Reality

In a Canada that is normatively multicultural and liberally democratic, idealistically any recognized group has a full being and identity based on prevailing modernist notions of ethnicity that appeal to a self-identified consciousness. This is not an identity or ethnicity constructed by a subject and imposed on an other. Canadian nationalism and citizenship, along with the rights and entitlements that flow from them, are not at odds with a specific ethnic consciousness, but idealistically are inclusive of all ethnicities on an equal basis. Social justice is a reflection of how, in a democracy that upholds in seeming contradiction individual and group identities, all groups can claim an equal share or entitlement to the common goods of the society and can be fully part of the Canadian consciousness. In this light, social justice would mean, among other things, that normatively individuals, regardless of their social positioning at birth or entry into the nation-state, have the right of social mobility to improve their lot and life chances according to their desires and actions. They can fully actualize themselves within the nation-state while self-identifying themselves by a specific ethnicity if they so wish. They are reconciled in a consciousness that is fully Canadian and equally fully their separate ethnic identity, a consciousness that allows them to set their own limits and boundaries and create a history struggling to extend these boundaries.

In a pragmatic sense, such is not the case for peoples constructed as part of an ethnic group called "Black" in Canada. In the first place, this construction results in the attempted homogenization of people of African ancestry into a single ethnicity with a manufactured essence—an essence that is imposed and at times accepted by those positioned as Black in Canada. Black is not based on a single ethnic consciousness. Rather it is racial, intended to decide status and positioning based on the notion of inferiority and superiority within the social order. With this construction comes a national marker, which is somatic, of inferiority and social exclusion from power and the mainstream for Blacks.

Constructed Blacks do not consent to their positioning. Individuals do not have the right to declare themselves of another ethnicity in a country where entitlement is based on ethnic ties or what Will Kymlicka calls "societal cultures" that coalesce into a national consciousness.[11] Neither are these individuals separately or collectively part of a collective consciousness struggling to remove or extend the boundaries and limits that are peculiar to their status in society. Members of this group live in a world not of their own making, but in a false consciousness that is a reaction to perceptions that other people think and have of them. Whether individually or *ethnically* imposed, limits and boundaries are not placed on Blacks as a matter of free choice, or of pretend free choices, but are prescribed by the boundaries and limits set for them by an other. Blacks must act out other people's perceptions of them in a Hegelian bondsman and slave arrangement.

This results in the kind of vertical stratification based on ethnicity and a notion of belonging that John Porter wrote about a generation ago in *The Vertical Mosaic*, and that, despite such claims as those by Jeffrey Reitz and Raymond Breton to the contrary, still holds today, particularly for Blackness in Canada.[12] A clear example of this is the experiences of Caribbean immigrants in Canada, particularly since the 1960s. Many of them arrive with big dreams for upward social mobility, but despite their high levels of education, facility with the official languages, and penchant for hard work, despite their wealth of social capital, they were quickly caught in a downward spiral, ending at the bottom of the economic pile in Canada.[13] This is a placement that has traditionally been reserved for native-born Blacks and their allies in racialized Blackness, the Aboriginal peoples. No amount of social capital can help them to escape.

Most other *ethnic* groups are in full Canadian consciousness: they contribute daily to making and preserving an inclusive Canadian history as full free agents in the Canadian epic. This is a situation where this consciousness recognizes and accepts the presence of other "histories" as part of the Canadian narrative—one that consists of many particular histories that now form a national history. They are makers of a national history and culture—part of an official national narrative—performing as the politicians, police chiefs, captains of business and industry, academics, media personalities, and the elites of the professional class that, as Engin Isin argues, are the new ruling classes of modernity.[14] This is a class from which Black Canadians and First Nations peoples are largely excluded. We shall now look at the reality of and from being constructed as Black in Canada. Does Black life come close to what is expected as the norms for Canadians fully incorporated into a national consciousness?

Black Reality in Canadian Society

Ethnicity is central to the official imaginary of what Canada was, what it is, and what it can become. Ethnicity, based on group characteristics and not race, is supposedly now central to Canadian identity and citizenship. This is an imaginary best captured in the "vision" of former Canadian Prime Minister Jean Chrétien, who in looking to the challenges of a new millennium, celebrated Canadian multiculturalism as one of its best assets and hopes for a better future. If memory and history in the Hegelian sense is what we preserve, set aside, and choose to carry forward from the past to the future, then the prime minister seems to be saying that multiculturalism ought to be venerated. In his dream, as cited by former Immigration and Citizenship minister Elinor Caplan in a press conference in November 1999, "Canada is the place to be in the twenty-first century, the place where people will want to come and stay, and learn, to pursue opportunities, to raise children, to enjoy natural beauty, to open new frontiers, to set the standard for the world of a high quality of life, a Canada that is a leader and an example to the world."[15]

A look at the conditions of those constructed as Black in Canada challenges these visions of the lived reality for Blacks in the country. Evidence of this is the economic and political position of Blacks in Canada, primarily as they themselves see their search for social justice and for entitlement to the good life. Based on economic, social, and political considerations, Blacks, as individuals and as a collective, do not enjoy the kind of social mobility that is associated with social justice, according to Canadian norms of equality and recognition, and Blacks have not yet achieved full recognition as Canadian citizens even if they may have the rights to hold a Canadian passport, to vote, or to call themselves Canadian. In the crucial area of feeling accepted and being recognized as integral to Canadian reality and as being perceived in a spirit of equality by fellow citizens as so doing—to the making of Canadian history and culture—they are still excluded. Their narrative is still not fully incorporated into the national one.

In the spring of 1999, Canada's largest and most liberal of newspapers, the *Toronto Star*, began running a series of articles that examined the achievements of a multicultural Canada in the past century and how the country was likely to fare in the new century as a liberal democracy that is multicultural.[16] A poll conducted by Goldfarb Consultants for the paper found:

- that while few Torontonians (29 percent) have personally experienced discrimination, the figures are much higher for specific ethnic and visible minority groups survey: Chinese (37 percent), Filipino (40 percent) and Hispanic communities (37 percent), and *more than double for the black community* (62 percent) [emphasis added];
- that discrimination is manifested primarily in finding work, wages and being passed over for raises or promotions. While 11 percent of Torontonians cite finding a job as their most pressing problem, the numbers are more than double for Blacks (27 percent), west Asians/Arab (24 percent) and South Asians (23 percent).[17]

Another story found that the situation was just as bleak for Blacks when it comes to enjoying the good life in Toronto. Most studies show that almost two-thirds of Canadian Blacks live in the greater Toronto area, with smaller numbers in Halifax, Montreal, Edmonton, Winnipeg, and Windsor, Ontario. How well they fared in Toronto, where some 65 percent of Canadian Blacks live, is an indication of how Blacks are treated nationally. The newspaper found that

> Blacks feel they're treated unfairly by the police, courts and the media and that other Torontonians don't understand them. Thirty-eight percent feel Toronto has become worse in the past two years and 31 percent say it will get worse in the next two. While two-thirds of Torontonians think politicians represent Toronto's diversity at least somewhat well, 38 percent of blacks think they don't represent them well at all. They also feel negative stereotyping and jobs are big problems and 28 percent feel they are not at all or only a little accepted.[18]

These findings are not the exception. In a paper prepared for Statistics Canada, economists Derek Hum and Wayne Simpson analyzed 1996 census data for wage disparities among visible minorities in Canada. "With the exception of Black men, we find no statistically significant wage disadvantages for visible minorities who are native born. It is primarily among immigrants that wage differentials for visible minority membership exists."[19] Blackness was the exception to the rule, turning all analysis of the existing world on its head when the analysis is controlled for colour.

The study highlights two other findings that speak to the lack of social justice for Blacks. First, there is no significant difference in earnings between Blacks who immigrated to Canada and those who were born in Canada, as "Blacks in general earned 19 percent less than Canadians who are not members of visible minorities."[20] Second, Black women in Canada, whether immigrant or Canadian born, earn more than Black men, more than the white Canadian female, but less than the white male. For example, in 1996 white males had an hourly wage of $17.35 and white females $13.69. This compared with an hourly wage of $15.96 for Black males and $16.70 for Black females.[21] These finding have severe implication for the Black family, indicating that their earning power is lower than that of white families, primarily because the Black female is the main breadwinner, even when she has to operate in a patriarchal society.

These trends confirmed earlier findings by Reitz and Breton.[22] Using figures from 1985 in a comparative study among immigrants in Canada, the United States, and Australia, they find that a Black male immigrant in Canada makes 26 percent less than male European immigrants. When human capital, such as levels of education, is taken into consideration, the disadvantage drops to 22 percent. In the United States, Black immigrant men receive 54 percent of wages of the top white males; in Canada they receive 70 percent.[23] Reitz and Breton make a powerful observation, however: Black immigrants to the United States start lower on the economic scale than in Canada but there is the possibility for social movement upwards.[24] This social mobility can occur within a generation, so that the children of Caribbean immigrants, for example, tend to move into a Black middle class. Native-born Blacks in the United States make 24 percent less than the benchmark white male worker, but when education is factored in, the disadvantage drops to 11 percent. This dynamic results in the children of Caribbean immigrants having to decide whether to accept social mobility and move into the wider African-American population or to forego the benefits of social mobility by remaining with their parents in Caribbean enclaves.[25] The Canadian social order does not offer Blacks this choice: their movement is downward unless they are already settled in the traditional position at the bottom of the socio-economic pile.

Is There a Need for Black History?

In light of this reality in Canada, does Black History Month have a peculiar meaning for members of the so-called Black community? Does it give them a sense of a past, present, and future in Canada as part of a Canadian dialectic and consciousness? Black History Month is, as writer André Alexis laments, an event that venerates more of what is culturally and historically non-Canadian and Black than what is Black and also Canadian.[26] So why continue this practice? The heroes celebrated, such as Malcolm X, Martin Luther King, Marcus Garvey, Sojourner Truth, and Nelson Mandela, and the remembering of historic events and achievements of Blacks that are so central to this celebration, are mainly from other countries and times. The only commonality is the colour of the skin of the celebrated and the main celebrants. For critics like Alexis, this is the most superficial argument for having such an event. For a Canadian setting, there is very little about a common nationality, shared civic duties and responsibilities, and citizenship in this celebration: there is no sense of a Canadian consciousness in this celebration.

Alexis argues that Black Canada's celebration should be about people and achievements peculiarly Canadian—the history of Blacks in the country and how as a people they are seen and perform in a Canadian space: "African Heritage ought not to become nostalgia for a place one has never been, a place always brighter, lovelier and more wonderful for being elsewhere."[27] But *pace* Alexis, the heroes and celebrants are offering a different moral consciousness of identity and belonging. They are presenting themselves as part of a Black diaspora with membership claimed through a "constructed" essentialism—the same one that is necessary in a Canada where everyone must be part of an ethnic group—that is a shared oppression based on racial categorization that is universal, and that theoretically has no respect for national borders or for most forms of constructed ethnicity. The celebration in Canada is also a form of international solidarity by those feeling oppressed because of race. Canada is a major part of the Black Diaspora, and its official recognition of *a* Black ethnicity is acknowledgement enough. This is another aspect of the Canadian historical dialectic that is not often recognized in a country that claims a historical narrative of two "founding peoples" that were English and French.

From its inception, Canada was a leading site in what has come to be called the Black Atlantic. This is the area of the globe bounded by Africa, South America, North America, and Europe. For centuries, the Black Atlantic has performed as one economic and demographic area influenced historically by African events and cultures.[28] But the observance of Black History Month also acknowledges something that is peculiar to Canada and is a hallmark of its *difference*: most of the Black heroes and acclaimed events are borrowed from abroad, and the paucity of Canadian Black heroes and historical monuments primarily undermine a long-held notion that, despite its multicultural face, Canada and Canadian identity, its cultural and historical achievements, and its notions of official memory are still presented twelve months of the year in a racialized manner that confirm norms of belonging in the national consciousness as white and European. Canada appears as barren soil still for homegrown heroes and makers of Canadian history and culture if they are essentialized as Black, and this remains the most telling reason for the continued need to celebrate a history of a struggle for inclusion while lamenting the failure to escape from an imposed essentialism.[29]

Black History Month allows those Canadians constructed as Black and those who self-identify as such to talk in their own voices about *their* history, *their* dreams, and ambitions, but also about the hurdles that are placed in the way of achieving these goals. This is a carnival-like moment when the *Black* sheep of the family, for a fleeting moment, leaves an inferior position and acts and behaves as if he or she is not only an important member of the family, but is the star of the family play. Such is the carnivalesque intoxication of hope. It is a celebration of freedom or of the quest for it.[30] It is a month-long idealistic celebration of how accepting the Canadian mainstream is—or ought to be—of a Black presence, of how the most obvious and perceptual of difference, that which is somatic by its very nature, can be integrated within the Canadian polity and consciousness.

At the same time, however, it is as much a lament of the racial discrimination that is still central to a year-long lived experienced by Canadians who are seen by fellow Canadians as different mainly because of the colour of the skin.[31] In this regard, the tolerance that is venerated by the Canadian mainstream takes on a different meaning—not of acceptance or acquiescence, but of the shortcomings and the gaps between the reality and the dream, between the lived experiences and the constructed norms, between the achieved and the promised. Sometimes, the difference is presented as cultural and geographical, so that Canadians, who emigrated from "Black" countries, such as in Africa and the Caribbean, are presented as different from other Canadians.

Black History month, therefore, is a celebration of a presence in Canada that is also an acknowledgement of exclusion.[32] This is the recognition that carnival can last for only a brief moment, before there is a return to rigidity, normalcy, and sobriety. It captures the need for an other, or a constructed stranger, to knock on the proverbial city gates—a knocking that becomes a banging in February—to demand admittance, and if that fails, to raise awareness of a continuous presence on the outside or periphery. But after one month of banging comes eleven months of silence and exclusion as the "natural" order is restored and preserved.

Within the Black community, such arguments centre around how much need there is for mentors and leaders to show the less fortunate Blacks how to succeed in Canada, as opposed to an argument that people constructed as Black need equality of opportunities to prosper rather than leaders offering them models of success. Both arguments revolve around the positioning and acceptance of Black icons—the veneration of success stories, many of them of an international flavour. Blacks in Canada need both: the mentors, but equally, the opportunities. Such is the seemingly paradoxical reasoning for celebrating Black History and what it is to be a Canadian.

Black History month challenges the official Canadian narrative by pointing to the various forms of inequality and lack of recognition by a group of people—diverse in their places of birth, languages, ancestry, regionalism, nationalism, religions, gender, and sexuality—who within a Canadian space, and to fit neatly into the prevailing ideology, societal norms, and myths, must surrender their elemental differences and be totalized and homogenized into a constructed ethnicity called Black.

Much has changed outwardly in Canada as a result of the dialectical struggle for recognition that came to a new consciousness in the 1960s, but the inner body—the structure and the functionalist position of specific groups described in Porter's *Vertical Mosaic*[33] and now reclothed by the official narrative—remains relatively unchanged. As Hegel suggests, in a lordship-bondage dialectic, there is little more than a semblance of change and duplicity of intentions.[34] By inference then, in Canada, there is less of the much-touted revolutionary change that was supposedly brought about through the adoption of official multiculturalism. For in the end, the power base—the makeup of those who officially make Canadian history and culture and enjoy full entitlement by recognition and by enjoying the good life—has hardly changed; it has merely shifted strategically to make accommodations. The elite class in Canada, even in a moment of multiculturalism, continues to exclude the two groups that have traditionally been constructed as the quintessential Canadian other—Blacks and Aboriginals.[35] The functionalism implied in Canada's idyllic quest for order and good government is still central to government and social ordering of Canada. This is not to deny that other marginalized groups such as Italians, Jews, and Ukrainians have been brought into the mainstream. However, as Charles W. Mills suggests in *The Racial Contract*, these are groups that can easily be made honorary white, shedding their former marks of racialized inferiority.[36] It is also worth noting that these accepted groups tend more likely to meet the definition of an ethnic group than the Blacks and Aboriginals, two groups without a single cultural sign, such as language, geography, religion, or lineage, to coalesce around "naturally." The latter groups are constructed racially across ethnicities, lineages, religions, and nationalities and then represented homogenously as a distinct ethnic group with a distinct culture in a multicultural Canada. This is best demonstrated in the case of African and Caribbean immigrants who themselves represent multi-ethnic groups in their different nationalities and religions but who are totalized as simply Black on arrival in Canada and are expected to automatically assume ethnic characteristics based on this construction.[37]

Therefore, there is always the need to return to Canada's primordial beginning—its ethnicity as it were—for a fuller understanding of today's race and ethnic relations and for a better understanding of the historic underpinnings of Canadian multiculturalism. On the level, then, of the very foundations of this society, Black History Month challenges the officially accepted narrative. As Homi Bhabha suggests, this demand for recognition and inclusion subverts the prevailing narrative by demanding full acceptance in the national consciousness of those traditionally excluded, so that the teaching of history in Canada would have a place for Black stories, so that Canadian history would be full of "ambivalence in the narration ... that repeats, uncounselled and unconsolable, in the midst of plenitude."[38]

In so doing, Black History Month—even though coinciding with the shortest calendar month of the year—highlights the breaks and discontinuities that are so often papered over in the construction of a singular and linear Canadian history that is by nature white and European. We should now look at the reality of living Black in Canada: the real message and story behind Black History Month.

Indeed, as Charles Taylor suggests, multiculturalism is a struggle for recognition.[39] Black History Month, therefore, is a discussion not so much about ethnicity, but of racism, in Canada. In this way, it subverts the national narrative, which talks of Canada as a heaven of pluralism, as multicultural, multi-ethnic and multiracial, with no officially recognized hierarchies within or among these many multi-identities. This discourse helps to remind us that even if Canada is indeed a paradisiacal garden, where people from all over the world can live side by side, that there is still the ageless snake in the grass in the form of racism. These ethnic groups, perhaps so that they may live in this world of make-believe harmony, still have to accept a hierarchy of claims, acceptance, and entitlement in a practical arrangement that is the social, political, and economic ordering deemed necessary for daily living. This is a hierarchy based on superiority and inferiority of these claims, acceptance, and entitlements. This is a structuralist acknowledgement *in praxis* that some groups have a more just claim to the good life in Canada, with those constructed as the Blacks historically placed at the bottom of this hierarchy and in the national imaginary considered least deserving of the good life. Black History helps Canada to recognize that on questions of belonging, citizenship, and entitlement, race, and not ethnicity, is what matters most.

Conclusion

In this chapter, I have looked at the dialectical changes that have presented us with a situation where a noticeable segment of the Canadian society feels there is a need for celebration of a particularistic history and culture that challenges and even subverts many Canadian norms and notions of identity, belonging, and well-being. There is no denying that this segment feels left out of the Canadian mainstream and that it is not part of a Canadian consciousness that professes to be based on difference, diversity, and egalitarianism. Part of the problem, I argue, is that this difference is based on the recognition and even creation of ethnicities, and that Black is not an ethnicity but a racial category, originally based on notions of superiority and inferiority as criteria for inclusion and exclusion, and later reconstituted as an ethnicity. What ways are there out of this ethical and moral problem of *appearing* to belong but not *feeling accepted* fully in a society that is still stratified along race, even if it pretends this is not the case? Part of the solution, I would argue, is equality of opportunity for everyone regardless of social standing and stratification—an equality that gives to individuals the rights to decide what of their past they want to preserve, set aside, or carry forward into the future, an equality that gives individuals, and then groups, the chance to determine who they really are, how they want to be constructed, and how they see themselves going forward from the present to the future. Equality of opportunity would at least allow Blacks to move out of a false consciousness based on a perception of feeling constrained by an other—a perception of not being free—into a different and deeper consciousness where they may feel that they are really fully accepted in the Canadian nation-state and that issues of social mobility rest entirely with the individual, and then later, the group. They would have the freedom to be the subject in a drama of life that is theirs.

Until these conditions change, Black History Month will matter.

Notes

1 Cecil Foster, *A Place Called Heaven: The Meaning of Being Black in Canada* (Toronto: Harper Collins, 1996); Neil Bissoondath, *Selling Illusion: The Cult of Multiculturalism in Canada* (Toronto: Penguin, 1994); and Will Kymlicka, *Politics in the Vernacular: Nationalism, Multiculturalism, and Citizenship* (Oxford: Oxford University Press, 2000).

2 G.W.F. Hegel, *Lectures on the Philosophy of History*, trans. J. Sibree (London: George Bell and Sons, 1878).

3 Thomas Axworthy and Pierre Elliot Trudeau, eds., *Towards a Just Society: The Trudeau Years* (Toronto: Viking, 1990), 360.

4 Charles Taylor, "The Politics of Recognition," *Multiculturalism*, ed. Amy Gutmann (Princeton, NJ: Princeton University Press, 1994), 25–40.

5 Robertson Davies, *The Merry Heart: Selections 1980–1995* (Toronto: Penguin, 1996); Margaret Atwood, *Survival: A Thematic Guide to Canadian Literature* (Toronto: Anansi,

1972); and Rick Helmes-Hayes and James Curtis, "Introduction," *The Vertical Mosaic Revisited*, ed. Rick Helmes-Hayes and James Curtis (Toronto: University of Toronto Press, 1998).

6 Robin W. Winks, *Canadian-West Indian Union: A Forty-Year Minuet* (Toronto: Oxford University Press, 1968).

7 J.S. Woodsworth, *Strangers within Our Gates; or, Coming Canadians* (Toronto: F.C. Stephenson, 1909).

8 For a fuller discussion see Joseph H. Carens, *Culture, Citizenship, and Community: A Contextual Exploration of Justice as Evenhandedness* (Oxford: Oxford University Press, 2000); Will Kymlicka, *Finding Our Way: Rethinking Ethnocultural Relations in Canada* (Toronto: Oxford University Press, 1998); Will Kymlicka, *Multicultural Citizenship: Liberal Theory of Minority Rights* (Oxford: Clarendon Press, 1995); Vic Satzewich, *Racism and Social Inequality in Canada: Concepts, Controversies and Strategies of Resistance* (Toronto: Thompson Educational, 1998); and Alan C. Cairns, *Citizen Plus: Aboriginal People and the Canadian State* (Vancouver: University of British Columbia Press, 2000).

9 Axworthy; Kymlicka, *Politics in the Vernacular*; and Carens.

10 Jon Stratton and Ien Ang, "Multicultural Imagined Communities: Cultural Difference and National Identity in the USA and Australia," *Multicultural States: Rethinking Difference and Identity*, ed. David Bennet (London: Routledge, 1998).

11 Will Kymlicka, *Finding Our Way*, 27–29.

12 John Porter, *The Vertical Mosaic: An Analysis of Social Class and Power in Canada* (Toronto: University of Toronto Press, 1985); Jeffrey G. Reitz and Raymond Breton, *The Illusion of Difference: Realities of Ethnicity in Canada and the United States* (Ottawa: C.D. Howe Institute, 1994).

13 Frances Henry, *The Caribbean Diaspora in Toronto: Learning to Live with Racism* (Toronto: University of Toronto Press, 1994); Agnes Calliste, "Canada's Immigration Policy and Domestic Blacks From the Caribbean: The Second Domestic Scheme," *The Social Basis of Law* 2nd ed., ed. Elizabeth Cormack and Stephen Brickley (Halifax: Garamond, 1991), 95–121; and Alan B. Simmons and Jean E. Turner, "Caribbean Immigration to Canada, 1967–1987," CERLAC, *York University* (Toronto) (18 February 1991), 1–32. Alan B. Simmons and Dwaine Plaza, "Breaking through the Glass Ceiling: The Pursuit of University Training among Afro-Caribbean Migrants and Their Children in Toronto," *Canadian Ethnic Studies* 30.3 (1998): 99–120.

14 Engin F. Isin, *Cities without Citizens: The Modernity of the City as Corporation* (Montreal: Black Rose, 1992).

15 Elinor Caplan, "Building Community in Multi-Ethnic Societies," address by the Honourable Elinor Caplan, minister of Citizenship and Immigration to the Metropolis Conference Plenary, Washington, DC, 10 December 1999, *Immigration and Citizenship Canada*, 2002 <http://www.cic.gc.ca/english/press/speech>.

16 Elaine Carey, "The City That Works Could Be Even Better," *Toronto Star* 1 May 1999, A1; and Ashante Infantry, "Opportunity Knocks but Not for All," *Toronto Star* 2 May 1999, A1.

17 Infantry, A1.

18 Elaine Carey, A1.

19 Derek Hum and Wayne Simpson, "Wage Opportunities for Visible Minorities in Canada," *The Income and Labour Dynamics Working Paper Series* Catalogue No. 98–17, November (1998), 14.

20 Hum and Simpson, 13.

21 Hum and Simpson, 8.

22 Reitz and Breton, 106, 107.

23 Jeffrey G. Reitz, *Warmth of the Welcome: The Social Causes of Economic Success for Immigrants in Different Nations and Cities* (Boulder, CO: Westview, 1998). 124–25.

24 Reitz, 124–26.

25 Reitz and Breton, 112.

26 Andre Alexis, "Borrowed Blackness: Canadian Blacks Are Seen as Quieter Clones of Their Bold American Counterparts," *This Magazine* 28.8 (1995): 14.

27 Alexis, 14.

28 Paul Gilroy, *The Black Atlantic: Modernity and Double Consciousness* (Cambridge, MA: Harvard University Press, 1993); John Thornton, *Africa and Africans in the Making of the Atlantic World, 1400–1680* (Cambridge: Cambridge University Press, 1995); and Paul E. Lovejoy, *Transformations in Slavery: A History of Slavery in Africa* (Cambridge: Cambridge University Press, 2000).

29 Foster, *A Place Called Heaven.*

30 George Elliott Clarke, ed., *Eyeing the North Star: Directions in African-Canadian Literature* (Toronto: McClelland and Stewart, 1997); and Rinaldo Walcott, *Black Like Who? Writing Black Canada* (Toronto: Insomniac, 1997); and Foster.

31 Neil Bissoondath, *Selling Illusion*, and Foster, *A Place Called Heaven.*

32 Satzewich, *Racism and Social Inequality in Canada.*

33 Porter, *The Vertical Mosaic.*

34 G.W.F. Hegel, *Phenomenology of Spirit*, trans. A.V. Miller (Oxford: Oxford University Press, 1977).

35 Woodsworth, *Strangers within Our Gates.*

36 Charles W. Mills, *The Racial Contract* (Ithaca: Cornell University Press, 1997).

37 See Walcott; Lawrence Hill, *Black Berry, Sweet Juice: On Being Black and White in Canada* (Toronto: Harper Flamingo Canada, 2001); Foster; and Alexis, 14.

38 Homi K. Bhabha, *Nation and Narration* (London: Routledge, 1999), 311.

39 Taylor, 25–74.

18 Decolonizing Interpretation at the Fortress of Louisbourg National Historic Site

Erna L. Macleod

Reconstructing Fortress Louisbourg

THE FORTRESS OF LOUISBOURG NATIONAL HISTORIC SITE is situated on an isolated, southeastern point of land on Cape Breton Island in Nova Scotia, Canada. The reconstruction project at Fortress Louisbourg was part of the Canadian federal government's decision to expand historic parks during the fifties and sixties. This effort was mainly directed towards developing a viable tourism industry and boosting the Canadian economy.[1] Government officials hoped that historic parks would counter alienation caused by massive urbanization and social change. They also wanted to foster feelings of unity and nationalism. Cape Breton, in particular, became the focus of government tourism efforts for a number of reasons. The island experienced a serious unemployment situation during the 1950s when its steel production and coal mining industries declined drastically. To the federal government, reconstructing Louisbourg provided a quick fix to the immediate problem of unemployment. The reconstruction also offered to establish tourism as a potential replacement for coal and steel industries.[2] From its inception, Louisbourg's reconstruction was politically motivated. Politicians had their own agendas regarding regional development, and government officials sought ways to appease dissatisfied constituents and improve their own images. They also wished to advance an acceptable political ideology. This essay examines Fortress Louisbourg's representations, illuminating the Eurocentrism embodied in the site's

361

images and narratives and exploring possibilities for more inclusive notions of history and identity.

As a national monument, Louisbourg represented the civil identity imposed on Canadians by those in power. The Interpretive Plan for the restoration project makes this objective explicit: "Louisbourg stands as a proud symbol, not only of the two great cultures whose interplay made our nation possible, but of the traditions that both have bequeathed to us. Without these disparate traditions and the dialogue stimulated by them, Canada would have few claims to nationhood."[3] Ultimately, politicians envisioned the fortress as a symbol of Canadian sovereignty, promoting patriotism by publicly representing a shared sense of history and identity to tourists and the resident population, and paying tribute to French colonists in what is now English Canada. Their vision demonstrates the limits of Canada's multiculturalism: political rhetoric and popular myth celebrate the heterogeneity of Canada's population, but cultural institutions and social practices belie claims to multicultural identity. Rhetoric such as that used in the Interpretive Plan also reveals the inability of Canada's dominant culture to confront its continuing marginalization of the other. In their attempts to defuse conflicts and differences, and promote a harmonious national culture, fortress administrators developed culturally biased representations that perpetuated exclusionary narratives characteristic of Eurocentric versions of history and identity.

Initially, the government favoured quick results rather than methodical process. In the early years, there were continuing conflicts between the historic sites and engineering services divisions of the National Parks Branch about how construction should proceed and what sort of historical image Louisbourg should represent.[4] Through ongoing negotiation, the fortress emerged as a symbol of progress, civilization, and colonial perseverance against the forces of nature: in short, the site became a celebration of colonialism.[5] Heritage consultant Ronald Way prepared a development plan for the fortress in 1961. In his report, he suggested, "The message of restored Louisbourg should be the story of the progress of Canada's two major races from armed hostility to their national partnership and unity in the Canada of today."[6] Decisions made about reconstruction and interpretation at Louisbourg thus embody the prevailing attitudes about Canadian identity that existed in the 1960s. Louisbourg's administrators presented Canada's history as a narrative of two founding cultures whose struggles in the new world eventually led to harmonious relations between French and English Canadians in present-day Canada. Fortress managers conceived of themselves as "custodians of culture" and sought to create entertaining and educational imagery that would not only attract tourists, but also enlighten citizens. Representations were designed to appeal to "popular" sentiments among like-minded people; for those with differing views, Louisbourg's images were meant to enlighten and persuade.

Louisbourg's reconstruction continued for twenty years. Today, the site consists of the reconstruction of approximately one-fifth of the original town, including military structures, warehouses, and private homes.[7] Louisbourg is a living history museum. Its focus in time is the summer of 1744, a period extolled as the pinnacle of Louisbourg's economic and imperial power. Architecture, information, and activities of costumed interpreters are organized to recreate this specific summer. Major themes include Louisbourg's military activities, administrative role in the region, economic activities, and social life. These themes are developed predominantly with costumed interpreters in buildings furnished to represent the eighteenth century. Visitors are invited to "relive a moment in time." Modern necessities like plumbing, electricity, and other services are disguised as much as possible to enhance the eighteenth-century atmosphere. Visitors park at a reception centre a short distance from the site, purchase a one-day pass to the site, and travel by bus to a drop-off destination. From here they proceed on foot to the town's main gate where they are challenged by a Compagnies Franches soldier and questioned about their purpose for visiting.

Once inside the reconstructed town, tourists can enjoy visiting the recreated homes of merchants, military officers, fishing proprietors, and civil administrators, where they can converse with employees who personify the town's inhabitants. Some dwellings have been converted into modern display areas with audiovisual media to provide background information, details, and statistics that emphasize particular themes such as military practices, community life, trade, transshipment, and commerce. There is a military bakery selling authentic "soldiers' bread," a snack shop, souvenir outlet, and several restaurants that specialize in eighteenth-century French food. Throughout the day there are cannon and musket-firing demonstrations, along with a few other rehearsed scenarios—street selling, public announcements, and drumming demonstrations to name a few. The overwhelming atmosphere at Louisbourg is that of a military fortress. The civilian aspect of life serves as a complement to the noise and pageantry of marching soldiers and exploding weapons. References to Mi'kmaq relations, slavery, and the active roles of women in society are conceptually and spatially isolated rather than integrated into the colonial narratives that dominate visitors's experiences. Despite their existence, these details seem added as an afterthought to satisfy demands for variety, clarification, or political acknowledgment. Rather than revolutionizing history, isolated references to non-dominant cultures suggest a new form of tokenism that perpetuates European patriarchal hegemony.

Multiculturalism in Eighteenth-Century Louisbourg

Although today's bus ride from the visitor reception centre to the site is an exercise in time travel, to be transported through time to eighteenth-century Louisbourg would not be a pleasant or entertaining experience. Shock, repulsion, fear, and dislocation would be much more appropriate descriptions of our reactions to the sights, sounds, and smells that would assault our senses. Our noses would be overwhelmed by the penetrating odours of human perspiration on unwashed bodies, human excrement festering in open latrines, and animal wastes wafting from streets and stable yards. Underlying these smells would be the persistent odours of drying codfish, and wood and coal smoke. More localized aromas would be tar from buildings and ships, cooking smells, and the stale breath of those standing nearest to us. The sights would be equally strange and unsettling. Faces would not be polished and "corrected" by dental practices, surgery, or modern cosmetics. Many people would exhibit birth defects, smallpox scars, and tooth decay. Hair and skin would be dirty and people would appear unkempt; many of them would be frightening to our twentieth-century sensibilities. Fashions and make-up would be grotesque and garish, and codes of etiquette would be incomprehensible, too "alien" to appeal to modern Eurocentric tastes and expectations. Eighteenth-century Louisbourg would reveal the "otherness" that the modern reconstructed fortress has been built to repress and contain.

Roaming through the streets we would encounter astonishing diversity of culture and class. Our hosts would be predominantly French, but we would notice a number of European immigrants from various countries such as Ireland, Britain, Germany, Switzerland, and Spain, along with their North American counterparts—Acadians, Québécois, and New England colonists.[8] We would recognize members of the town's elite by their elaborate fashions and pretentious etiquette, and we could distinguish these upper-class members of society from those less privileged common labourers, servants, and finally slaves who would be conspicuous by their dark complexions. It would not be unusual to meet Mi'kmaq visitors, military personnel, and members of religious orders in their distinctive clothing. We would be greeted by the unfamiliar clamour of the multitude of languages and dialects spoken by this range of people whose native tongues would include French, Basque, Mi'kmaq, Gaelic, English, German, and Spanish. If we survived the shock of our initial encounter, we would find it extremely difficult to adjust to the strange behaviours, beliefs, and values of these people from the past. Brutal physical punishment, rigid religious control, and oppressive social stratification would replace contemporary notions of institutionalization, scientific rationality, and democratic social organization. Our conceptions of government, justice, moral-ity, time, entertainment, work, and leisure would not conform to the views of this past era. For example, we do not believe that rulers govern by divine right or that criticizing monarchial authority is a blasphemous act; yet these beliefs were promoted by both the monarchy and the church in eighteenth-century French society. Similarly, we would reject a justice sys-tem that considers the accused guilty until they can prove their innocence. We would also contest social arrangements that prevent class mobility, reserving wealth and leisure for the inherited nobility and relegating the remaining population to a life of work and poverty with no hope of improving their social status. Adapting to such radical transformations would demand a long period of adjustment. If it were possible at all, it could not be accomplished within the span of several minutes or an after-noon visit.

The discrepancies between our conception of normality and the every-day experience of inhabitants of eighteenth-century Louisbourg affect the ways we perceive of and represent history. Upon close inspection, we real-ize that representations manufactured at the reconstructed fortress are largely based on twentieth-century beliefs and values. As an example, while aspects of the eighteenth-century social and religious hierarchy are represented in architecture and costumes, the oppressive nature of such rigid control recedes in the festive atmosphere of a tourism site where all "inhabitants" are approachable, accommodating, literate, and well-fed. Recreated images resemble twentieth-century norms more closely than they resemble the age they are intended to portray, and the values expressed are those considered significant by the dominant present-day powers in Canada. Once represented, these images are self-perpetuating, reinforcing existing views and silencing alternative interpretations.

Constructing National Identity

As a national historic park, Fortress Louisbourg does not simply reflect what it means to be Canadian. Instead, the fortress plays an important role in shaping the predominant views of Canadian national identity. Jeanne Cannizzo describes museums as "social artefacts" and suggests that "the cultural and ideological assumptions that have influenced their creation and their collections are a critical dimension in understanding their signifi-cance."[9] During the reconstruction of the fortress, some of those involved expressed their concerns about Louisbourg's powerful persuasiveness: "So exciting is this technique [of historic reconstruction] that one can lose sight of history itself."[10] Others suggest that museums have assumed the role once performed by monarchs and churches: "they provide the symbols through which a nation and a culture understands itself."[11]

At living history museums, particular aspects of the past are selected for interpretation and subsequently depoliticized and refashioned to present images that are marketable, non-confrontational, and appealing to a wide range of consumers.[12] In this process of depoliticization, the views of the dominant culture are often enshrined and reinforced while minority views are omitted from interpretation and, as a result, devalued or overlooked. Through selection and omission, historic parks determine what events are significant to Canadian history. Their representations perpetuate existing social hierarchies and disguise issues like oppression and cultural annihilation beneath a charming and quaint façade of colonial utopianism.[13] The appearance of depoliticization is thus more accurately described as an intensely political act of repression. Alternative interpretations of events, erased from mainstream history, continue to haunt dominant images, undermining claims of historical accuracy and completeness and complicating claims of a unified national identity. By romanticizing colonial history and cultivating nostalgia for lost community and family values, heritage sites entrench Eurocentric attitudes and resist the change necessary to alleviate the marginalization of colonized cultures.[14] In his book *Multiculturalism*, Charles Taylor argues that "the withholding of recognition can be a form of oppression."[15] He emphasizes the importance of recognition and respect for different points of view, particularly in the public sphere, stating:

> our identity is partly shaped by recognition or its absence, often by the misrecognition of others, and so a person or group of people can suffer real damage, real distortion, if the people or society around them mirror back to them a confining or demeaning or contemptible picture of themselves. Nonrecognition or misrecognition can inflict harm, can be a form of oppression, imprisoning someone in a false, distorted, and reduced mode of being.[16]

Definitions of Canadian identity are important to citizens (of the nation) because individual identities rely, in part, on public recognition of the inherent worth of one's cultural and ethnic values. Our identities are not formed in isolation; rather they are formed through continuous interaction with others in a society.[17] This process of negotiation is internalized and contributes to the formation of positive or negative individual and collective identities. Our negotiations with people and institutions also contribute to the perpetuation and transformation of social hierarchies. Institutions play active roles in the struggle between domination and oppression by selecting particular perspectives as worthy of representation and simultaneously making other views invisible or presenting them in a derogatory fashion.[18] Museums are not neutral; their interpretations function in a hegemonic way to define the boundaries of national identity.

Institutions such as Fortress Louisbourg thus enshrine and perpetuate the views of the dominant culture, but possibilities exist for more inclusive representations of history and identity.[19] If museums wish to promote more pluralistic identities, they must acknowledge the biases encapsulated in their images and strive to initiate changes in the way they represent the past. Instead of focussing on European history and the triumph of colonization, a more egalitarian interpretation of history might incorporate the accomplishments and atrocities experienced by other cultures in order to validate their roles in the development of contemporary society. Diverse representations of such non-dominant cultural groups as women, Native Canadians, and African Canadians will not eliminate the biases inherent in all forms of representation; but recognizing previously ignored cultures and ethnic groups might expand prevailing conceptions of history and identity, thus weakening discriminatory attitudes and assisting the development of a more just and tolerant society. As an agent in the formation of national identity, Fortress Louisbourg has an ethical obligation to strive to eradicate Eurocentric notions of Canadian identity to facilitate the development of a definition of Canadian-ness that is less gender-biased and more multicultural. A more pluralistic identity would include those who have been excluded and persecuted by the stereotypical images presently in place.

The Issue of Nostalgia

Fortress managers have begun incorporating references to non-dominant cultural groups within Louisbourg's historical imagery, but, as they initiate changes, managers must decide if novel ideas can match the popularity of the nostalgic images presently in place. Nostalgic commemoration of history became popular in the early twentieth century as part of anti-modernist sentiment in Western society. In Nova Scotia, this attitude coincided with government's efforts to establish a profitable tourism industry in the province.[20] Nostalgia means "homesickness," signifying a sentimental longing to return to an irrecoverable past or an imaginary state of being. Sentimental images of colonial history at museums like Fortress Louisbourg thus connote homesickness within the dominant culture for a harmonious past that never existed and a unified nation that can only be imagined. Nostalgia is growing more intense and widespread in late modern society as people search for a coping mechanism to deal with tumultuous times of change and uncertainty. Traditional values, boundaries, and hierarchies are inverted and fragmented by fast-paced technological change and increasing supremacy of the global market system.[21] Nations yield to the formation of the global village and international economy and, while many people welcome change, others face an uncertain future with apprehension. For those groups in society who profited during the modern industrial age, the longing for the safety and security of a simplified, romanticized past offers escape from the insecurity of postmodernity.[22] The prevalence of nostalgia is evident in the proliferation of living history museums like Fortress Louisbourg in the Western world in the late twentieth century. Yet, as a panacea for social ills, nostalgia can venerate the repressive elitist social structures of the past, enshrining Eurocentric history and impeding the development of original strategies to effectively confront current issues. Simply stated, nostalgia reinforces dominant values of the past and encourages resistance to change.

The spectacle of living history is both compelling and captivating, but images created in historic parks are based on twentieth-century perspectives. Historic sites are essentially recreational tourism developments; as such, they must provide entertaining and non-threatening experiences and associations for tourists. Managers often base decisions about interpretive objectives on the need to present positive images of what is conventionally popular, novel, or appealing. They often elide antagonisms between cultural groups and omit contentious issues from their representations to offer a seamless historical narrative that presents themes in their best possible light.[23] The festive atmosphere of the site tends to neutralize the horrifying realities of territorial confiscation, oppression, poverty, and patriarchy, while the repetition of signs and messages reinforces the seeming authenticity of heritage sites, obscuring the uncertain boundary between history and nostalgia. Architecture, costumes, narratives, and artifacts are arranged to create a "rhetorically meaningful memory place" that amplifies a particular point of view, suggests authenticity, and disallows conflicting interpretations.[24] By refusing to assign responsibility for past ideologies and atrocities, however, historic sites can obstruct change and sustain the existing social system. Managers may avoid representing differences because they are contentious and therefore difficult to incorporate into tourism sites seeking to attract visitors and appeal to their desires for pleasurable leisure experiences. Yet representation of difference does not necessarily conflict with tourists's expectations. Ironically, complex and sensitive depictions of historical events that celebrate cultural diversity and analyze social antagonisms may be more interesting to tourists than sanitized images of a static, homogenized past. If museums shape national identity, they should represent the cultural differences that characterize human relationships and produce ongoing hostilities. The crucial question is, can museums represent cultural difference without promoting a superficial fascination with exotic images of otherness that ultimately objectifies non-dominant cultures and perpetuates their oppression? In other words, can we craft more meaningful representations?

As contemporary architects, historians, and interpretive specialists develop increasingly vivid images of the past using modern technologies, the emphasis these sites place on perfecting the visual display for visitors threatens to eclipse the motivation to provide a balanced view of history. The need to attract visitors and provide them with pleasant experiences leads managers to downplay the conflicts that characterize the colonization of the New World. Historic sites become pure simulacra: persuasively authentic in their increasingly lifelike representation, they are often based on an idyllic, imaginary past that excludes any reference contrary to that of the dominant culture, which in this case is the European colonizers.

Native Interpretation at Fortress Louisbourg

In critiquing Fortress Louisbourg's representations, I am not suggesting that the site's historians were lax or narrow-minded in their assignment to investigate the colony's history. Reconstructing the fortress involved extensive research into many aspects of Louisbourg's history. Historians at Louisbourg devoted their efforts to providing accurate and detailed information, and it is important that the efforts of dedicated researchers are not discounted. Although much initial research focussed on French colonial history and English-French rivalry, more recently Louisbourg historians have used information found in French documents to compile several manuals outlining the roles of women, slaves, soldiers, and the Mi'kmaq at Louisbourg. Original documents are written from the French perspective, yet they provide significant insight into the various cultures that made up eighteenth-century Louisbourg society. Documenting more inclusive perspectives of history is an important element in re-evaluating the way we represent the past, but changes in academic understanding should be supplemented by more diversity in on-site interpretation. Over the years, changes in Louisbourg's focus of interpretation reflect changing values and conceptions of history, but there are questions about the ability of a colonial fortress to effectively present a decolonized, multicultural, historical narrative. Past attempts to incorporate native history, for instance, elucidate some of the potential problems.

Since the 1970s, the fortress has made several attempts to incorporate aspects of native history into the park's interpretive program. During the late 1970s and early 1980s, Mi'kmaq interpreters were hired to dress in period costume and portray native military scouts visiting Louisbourg. The program was abandoned when funding ran out but, in its aftermath, historians realized that Mi'kmaq employees had experienced incidents of racism and alienation. Historian John Johnston explains,

> the Mi'kmaq community didn't have the same perception and memory of [the program] that we had. The people who were in the program didn't feel well treated, didn't feel they were well integrated into the system, encountered some racism, they thought, in some of the reactions from staff and maybe from visitors as well. Essentially...they didn't feel that the program had been a success; they didn't have positive recollections of it. We hadn't known that at the time.... I guess that's partly management's fault here for not knowing better.[25]

In retrospect, Native-Canadian interpreters' response to the insensitivity of staff and visitors is not surprising, and managers might also be blamed for not asking these interpreters about their experiences. Yet the program was not a complete failure. Since the 1970s, fortress historians and representative members of Mi'kmaq communities in Cape Breton have formed the Unama'ki Committee and collaborated on the development of the Mi'kmaq Trail, which opened in conjunction with Louisbourg's commemorative celebrations of 1995.[26] The trail is located at the Fortress Visitor Reception Centre and consists of a short wooded walk overlooking the reconstruction. Plaques along the trail provide a brief overview of Mi'kmaq history, outlining native inhabitants' relationship with French colonists, and describing contemporary Mi'kmaq culture. The plaques are printed in Mi'kmaq as well as French and English. Since 1996, Mi'kmaq employees have been hired each summer as guides to escort visitors along the trail and provide them with additional information. The completion of the Mi'kmaq Trail is evidence of the sincere interest and co-operative effort of Louisbourg historians and the Mi'kmaq community. It provides an effective and appropriate means of communicating Mi'kmaq history to the public. The main problems with the trail are that it is isolated from the site, accessible only to the physically fit, and, as a result, visited only by a small number of tourists.

The Mi'kmaq Trail was the first of several projects undertaken by the Unama'ki Committee. Since 1995, the committee has extended its efforts to establish interpretive plaques relating to Mi'kmaq history at several other Nova Scotia parks.[27] Presently members are exploring the possibility of employing Mi'kmaq interpreters on-site at the fortress in an attempt to balance Euro-American perspectives with native history and reach a larger percentage of visitors. Such an endeavour would include sensitivity training for all interpretive staff to enhance integration of native and colonial historical representation and minimize animosity or misunderstanding between Mi'kmaq and non-native employees.[28] Johnston describes some of the intricacies involved in the presentation of Mi'kmaq history at a colonial reconstruction:

> They won't be in period costume, largely because it's difficult often for people in native dress to be accepted by visitors. Some visitors bring a lot of stereotypes and nasty remarks to them if they're dressed like that. So [costumed interpretation] might happen if we want to do a special event for an hour or so…more than likely they'll be like guides.… We may work out a base that is sort of a temporary exhibit are…but they can give tours because there are a lot of places that have connections.… We'll work out the details as we go along.[29]

In his analysis of French-Mi'kmaq relations in eighteenth-century Louisbourg, Johnston states that many Louisbourg inhabitants would have had regular ongoing interactions with the native people in surrounding areas. In particular, members of clergy, military personnel, and merchants would have maintained relationships of significant personal, political, and economic importance. He explains,

> Some of the French that were here…had very little contact.… But for some of the French…it was pretty close relationship. We know that there is some intermarriage between the French and the Mi'kmaq at some points in time. So you have actual blood relationships—people are cousins or distant relations. Some of the officers are sent off to live with the Mi'kmaq to learn the language.[30]

Stated more emphatically, French colonists at Louisbourg could never have survived in the inhospitable climate and unfamiliar surroundings of Cape Breton Island without the assistance of their Mi'kmaq allies, and the small garrison at Louisbourg relied on Mi'kmaq military support to deter English invaders.[31] Similarly, the declining Mi'kmaq population depended on French settlers to supply them with European goods and impede British settlement. In this view, French and Mi'kmaq inhabitants of Cape Breton shared a complex and intimate relationship based on mutual respect, interdependence, and tolerance of each other's differences. Seen in its complexity, the difficulty of representing this symbiotic relationship in tourist imagery becomes clearer. Johnston offers some suggestions regarding the presentation of Mi'kmaq influence in the town:

> You could spread around the indications of contact—it could be a quillwork box, furs, a hide, snowshoes—it could be a number of items. Visitors could say, "what's this?" or "what's that?" Or an interpreter could use that to say, "this reflects the connection between the two." Or you could concentrate a whole bunch of stuff in one building so that it maximizes the impact,

and let that place be where the story line is most focused. You could do a bit of both—have one major concentration and a few scattered items. Like, the De La Valliere property might be where you want to put a whole bunch of stuff because it's the one that has the closest relationship.... In the same way that the DeGannes house for a long time has been identified as the place for family life and childbirth.[32]

Despite the good intentions of those involved in research, overwhelmingly the images presented to visitors reinforce and enshrine colonial ideals. The Unama'ki Committee has initiated the process of decolonizing Louisbourg. How successful their efforts will be remains to be seen. Experimentation at the fortress illustrates that representing difference does not necessarily decolonize Eurocentric images. The best intentions can never completely decolonize representations constructed within a colonial site.

Slavery

Multiculturalism has not only affected native interpretation at the fortress. Various non-dominant cultures, including slave culture, have gained attention as part of the shift away from Eurocentrism. Cursory reports outlining the existence of slavery in Louisbourg were written twenty years ago, but, during the past few years, fortress historian Ken Donovan has researched slavery in eighteenth-century Louisbourg and published essays outlining his findings. According to Donovan's research, slaves represented a significant proportion of the town's population, with over three hundred known slaves listed among residents from 1713 to 1758. The vast majority of these people were of African origin, reflecting Louisbourg's close and nefarious relationship with the French West Indies.[33] Members of the elite, government officials, and wealthy merchants purchased slaves to display their affluent status. Most were employed in domestic service, performing duties that were essential to the functioning of the household. Considering that slaves were numerous and highly visible in Louisbourg society, there is demographic and inferential justification for a visible representation of slave culture and Black history in the reconstructed fortress. As Donovan states,

If I can find 300 [slaves], I think there are probably a lot more.... At any one time, virtually every house in the town had a slave.... And we do have evidence here of a number of baptisms and at least one wedding where black people are together as witnesses...we don't have a lot of that but we do have some.... I tend to think that there would have been a subculture. They would have known each other, but how much are they allowed to congregate? Usually, when you're a slave, your time is not your own. You're at somebody's beck and call all the time. And there's the issue of suspicion... there is always fear; you suppress people, you enslave them, but there's always fear of revolt.... So I think that [fear] limited people's freedom in getting together.... In a society in which race determined whether you were a slave or not a slave...you stand out because your skin is much darker.... The French as slave-owners...usually come across in the literature as being sympathetic slave owners. I argue that there is no evidence to support that...you have only six out of 300 slaves being freed, that tells you something.[34]

In terms of African representation, present-day interpretation virtually ignores the contribution of slave culture to Louisbourg society. Interpreters occasionally mention the existence of these inhabitants and several plaques indicate their presence in various homes, but most of the displays ignore the integral role of slavery in Louisbourg society. Donovan indicates that there are plans at Louisbourg to incorporate slavery into the interpretive focus. Fortress historians are presently consulting with members of Cape Breton's African-Canadian community to form a committee similar to the Unama'ki group that would explore possibilities for appropriate representation of Black history at Louisbourg. Donovan is optimistic about this endeavour; he comments, "it's a way of letting people have a voice," but he acknowledges that there are many pitfalls and obstacles to contend with when dealing with sensitive issues in a public, entertainment-oriented context. Research director William A. O'Shea discusses some of the issues to be confronted:

We've got to develop an approach that will give the people who will be working a level of knowledge and a level of comfort that what they are doing won't be personally debasing or embarrassing for them, that they will be able to communicate their message in a fashion where it will both mean something to them and to the people that are listening. We're going to have to talk to all of the interpreters on site so that they understand the significance of this program, and that there are to be no attempts to denigrate what is happening.[35]

Louisbourg's incorporation of Black history has many of the same problems that impede the development of First Nations history at the site. The imposing architecture is immediately conducive to thoughts of colonial history and nostalgic images of "the good old days." Such associations can only be overturned if staff members and tourists can abandon internalized racial prejudices and Eurocentric notions of history and nationhood. The challenge for museums is to overturn these largely unconscious notions of culture to expand the possibilities for identity-construction and promote heterogeneous and egalitarian communities.

Women

In comparison to other groups, women in French colonial society are quite well represented at the fortress. The numerous homes that have been reconstructed allow a broad interpretation of the diverse roles assumed by women in the town, and costumed interpreters have an opportunity to inform visitors about the varied activities performed by women in Louisbourg society. Entrepreneurial widows, in particular, exemplify the active positions many women played in social organization. The main problem with Louisbourg's interpretation of women's roles and contributions to society lies in the military emphasis of presentation. O'Shea comments, "The irony of Louisbourg is that some of our most insightful interpreters, and the majority of our interpreters are probably women. And yet... we've never really reflected the competent women who lived in Louisbourg in the eighteenth-century or talked about their role. And that's a major oversight on our part." [36]

At a glance, women's roles at the fortress appear to be limited to marriage, childbearing, and household duties. While these factors undoubtedly were central features in many women's lives, there were other women who occupied lesser-known and more socially prominent positions than such images suggest. High mortality rates, restricted opportunities for education, and unstable social and financial status often made it necessary for women to take active roles in society, acting as midwives, running businesses, securing advantageous marriages, and performing arduous labour. In addition, the difficult climate must have meant that women would have played a prominent role in securing daily needs. Although historians have written about the diversity of women's history, for the most part, women in the reconstructed fortress are presented as either upper-class ladies of leisure or servants. Stereotypical images perpetuate notions that women have always depended on men and have nothing interesting or important to contribute to history. The problem is exacerbated by the proliferation of male-oriented military images—familiar representations of colonial history—that encourage visitors to relate Louisbourg's history to their existing knowledge of the nation's past.

Finally, the numerous other non-dominant groups at Louisbourg receive virtually no recognition. There are few references to the many Irish, German, and Basque inhabitants, in spite of the fact that people from these cultures emigrated to this thriving commercial port and contributed to the composition of society. Such omissions do not only shape understandings of history; they also ignore present-day conflicts between the Canadian government and Spanish and Basque fishing ships over economic resources and territories off the Grand Banks. More inclusive representations of history at sites like Fortress Louisbourg could invite both staff and visitors to engage with current issues and consider the history of differences and contestation that engendered modern social formations and continues to shape their development.

Official Policy and Constraints at Fortress Louisbourg

Promoters of historic sites argue that museums reflect Canada's collective heritage; and yet, paradoxically, the criteria that constitute Canadian heritage are not left to the discretion of ordinary Canadians or even the local park managers. The federal Department of Heritage has sovereignty over how sites are to be selected and what they will symbolize regarding Canadian history and identity. The Department of Canadian Heritage mandate states:

> Parks Canada's purpose is to fulfill national and international responsibilities in mandated areas of heritage recognition and conservation; and to commemorate, protect, and present, both directly and indirectly, places which are significant examples of Canada's cultural and natural heritage in ways that encourage public understanding, appreciation, and enjoyment of this heritage, while ensuring long-term ecological and commemorative integrity.[37]

Official recognition of national significance is limited to sites that are formally approved by the Minister of Heritage. These sites must "provide tangible and irreplaceable links to what defines Canada as a nation and a people."[38] In addition, they must correspond with other national institutions and symbols in communicating "national significance."[39] Although the mandate states that national parks should reflect Canada's diverse cultures, geographic settings, and time periods, the document acknowledges that past commemoration activities have focussed on "marking and preserving battle and fortification sites because of their importance—real or symbolic—as landmarks in Canada's evolution."[40] Fortress Louisbourg remains a site of conflict, although the battle is now waged ideologically rather than militarily.

Louisbourg's Commemorative Integrity Statement says that "The Fortress of Louisbourg is of national significance because, between 1713 and 1768, it was a place of profound significance in the great Franco-British struggle for empire."[41] There is no mention in this document of the significance of the diverse population or the Mi'kmaq-French alliance. Yet recent efforts to expand Louisbourg's interpretive focus suggest that the Canadian government is not opposed to, and may even welcome, recognition of the contribution of other cultures to Louisbourg society. One of the most difficult issues is finding a way to combine tourism with meaningful interpretation. O'Shea comments:

One of the difficulties is not a systemic difficulty—we can do it. The difficulty will be ensuring that we do it in a way that is meaningful to both the participants and the people who are hearing it—that it's not done for shock value. It can't be a media event.... And one of the challenges that we have living in rural Canada is to understand that Canada doesn't look like us anymore. Canada looks a lot like my nephews who are Black and Chinese. And a lot of people living in rural Canada...still find that vision threatening. So we have to overcome that.... We're going to have to be gentle and persuasive in how we deal with that.[42]

O'Shea admits that Louisbourg faces numerous challenges, but he maintains that the fortress also possesses advantages that make its transition into multicultural interpretation easier than that of many other historic sites. He states,

I'm not the least bit pessimistic.... I think that presenting diversity at Louisbourg is not the challenge that perhaps other historic sites of the colonial period have.... One advantage for diversity that we have is that Louisbourg was sufficiently cosmopolitan. There was a cross-section of peoples [who are found] in twentieth-century populations.... Louisbourg has the advantage of being a closer reflection of Canada the way it is today than a lot of other historic sites. So we can move into this new era...much easier and in a more meaningful fashion than other historic sites can.[43]

In April 1999, the federal government converted the national parks system into a separate entity called the Parks Canada Agency. Formation of the agency entails a 24 percent, or $98 million, reduction in government funding for Canadian parks. Government officials claim that services will not suffer from the proposed changes.[44] Realistically, however, decreased funding can only mean increased reliance on profits, and that means that Canadian parks will find themselves increasingly dependent on corporate alliances to cover operational costs and generate revenue.

As Fortress Louisbourg faces decreasing federal government funding in the late twentieth century, the tourism industry is expanding internationally and experiencing rising profits. Faced with the need to generate revenue in order to remain operational, Louisbourg must present a marketable image of the past that will appeal to contemporary tourists from a wide range of backgrounds. The emphasis on economic factors restricts Louisbourg's potential to provide a critical look at mainstream values. Critical examination may not be popular with the public at large and the fortress might find it more profitable to capitalize on picturesque images of the colo-

nial era. As consumers of heritage history we need to critique the consequences of such complacency within our institutions.

It is important to acknowledge that we can never capture the essence of
true Canadian history because "the" historical "truth" is non-existent:
history is nothing but the record of differences between social groups.
The most we can hope to achieve is the establishment of a balanced, flexible view that demonstrates the conflicting and diverse interests, values, and
beliefs that characterize all multicultural societies—past, present, and
future. In the postmodern age, it seems that the most insightful and revolutionary forms of knowledge are constructed from fragments of history
that exemplify the complexity of human life and critique the consequences
of human actions. By including fragments and details from a variety of perspectives, we can negotiate more inclusive, self-reflexive individual and
collective identities that encourage us to engage with conflict and appreciate cultural differences as qualities to be celebrated rather than assimilated.

Decolonizing Fortress Louisbourg

A decolonized historical representation at Fortress Louisbourg would
involve de-emphasizing the military aspect of eighteenth-century life that
presently dominates interpretation of the site. To introduce more self-
reflexive, critical imagery into Louisbourg's interpretive program, managers
could develop an exhibit exploring the production and contingency of
history. The exhibit could emphasize relationships between the various
groups involved in building and rebuilding the fortress to underscore the
complexity of history and reveal the difficulty of meaningfully representing cultural differences. Accenting history's selectivity and malleability
would not only encourage innovative thinking among fortress historians
and interpreters; the exhibit could also invite audiences to be reflexive by
offering them the opportunity to act as historians. Visitors might be asked,
for example, "What would you place in an exhibit at Louisbourg? What
would you leave out? Why?" Such an exhibit could provide a creative,
persuasive, epistemologically radical, yet non-threatening resource, inviting cultural producers and audiences to consider how history is produced
in the present.

Other possibilities for a more pluralistic interpretation might include
supplementing military demonstrations with non-military activities and
dedicating modern display areas to themes such as slavery at Louisbourg
Mi'kmaq history, women's roles, the Basque community, and other non-
dominant histories. Reading material pertaining to these topics could be

provided in visitor sitting areas. Presently, fortress managers are working toward this goal: since 1995, the fortress has opened two new exhibits, one highlighting Mi'kmaq history and the other exploring the role of the Congregation of the Sisters of Notre Dame in eighteenth-century Louisbourg. As representations change, ongoing discussions with members of the respective cultural groups to negotiate historical imagery are crucial and these groups should have the ultimate voice in decision-making. This undertaking could be a learning process whereby Canadians from diverse cultural backgrounds, historians, park managers, and interpreters could determine the most effective means for promoting egalitarian, multicultural history.

Finally, the most fundamental change at the Fortress of Louisbourg would consist in changing the way we, as interpreters, talk about history. All staff should relearn the narratives of Louisbourg's development and relationships among the many cultures that intersected here. If Louisbourg is to adequately represent many different perspectives of history, epic tales about military power and mercantile progress must be replaced by a more balanced and insightful examination of the impact of colonization on oppressed cultures and the natural environment. This is a formidable task, but such a transformation could result in fundamental changes in the ways we interact with each other and the environment in the present.

Historians are making initial steps toward pluralism at Fortress Louisbourg, but it is important that efforts to expand interpretive focus do not stop at the level of historical documents and publications in scholarly journals. To enact fundamental social change, we need to reach the ordinary person, and the only effective means of achieving this end is to change the messages that are communicated by our institutions. Although we can never uncover the absolute truth about history, we can strive to create flexible, inclusive imagery that incorporates the predominant values of all members of society at this particular time and in this particular place. As yet, we have only scratched the surface of this monumental endeavour. Fortress Louisbourg's reconstruction will never be complete. Crafting meaningful representations of history is an ongoing process of selecting and combining fragments of history to reclaim historical and cultural difference and construct forms of collective memory and cultural identity that resonate with contemporary experience.

Notes

1 C.J. Taylor, *Negotiating the Past: The Making of Canada's National Historic Parks* (Montreal and Kingston: McGill-Queen's Press, 1990), xv.
2 I.C. Rand, commissioner, *Report of the Rand Commission on Coal*, Ottawa, 1960, 47.
3 "Interpretive Plan for Fortress Louisbourg," unpublished manuscript, 1970, 1.

4 Rand, 48, 49, 53.

5 Taylor, *Negotiating the Past*, 177.

6 Quoted in Taylor, *Negotiating the Past*, 180.

7 *Fortress Louisbourg National Historic Site: Commemorative Integrity Statement*. The reconstruction consists of approximately sixty-five major buildings and twenty-one associated structures.

8 A.J.B. Johnston, "The People of Eighteenth-Century Louisbourg," *Aspects of Louisbourg*, ed. Eric Krause, Carol Corbin, and William O'Shea (Sydney, NS: 1995), 152–60. According to Johnston, there is no record of a census for the year 1744; therefore, population estimates for this year are compiled from a number of documents. Existing documents indicate that Louisbourg's population would have been approximately 2,500–3,000 civilians and soldiers. Although the majority of people were from France or the French colonies, there were several hundred Basque inhabitants who emigrated to Louisbourg to fish. There were significant numbers of German and Irish inhabitants. Most German-speaking people were soldiers in the Karrer Regiment, which numbered approximately 150 men in 1744. The Compagnie Franche garrison consisted of about 560 soldiers in this year. Other minority groups included Spanish, English, Dutch, Italian, and Portuguese. There were numerous people of African origin living in the town—most were enslaved, but several lived as free citizens. Louisbourg's European population was supplemented by Native Americans. The Mi'kmaq population of Cape Breton Island was approximately 250 people in the 1740s. From 1713 to 1758 there were always significantly more men than women in Louisbourg. By the 1740s the number of women in the colony had grown, but even excluding men in the garrison from calculations, male inhabitants continued to outnumber women by three or four to one.

9 Jeanne Cannizzo, "Inside Out: Cultural Production in the Museum and the Academy," *Academic Anthropology and the Museum*, ed. Mary Bouquet (New York: Berghahn Books, 2001), 164.

10 J.D. Hebert, Chief of Historic Parks Division, Fortress Louisbourg, quoted in Taylor, *Negotiating the Past*, 178.

11 Robert Hewison, *The Heritage Industry* (London: Methuen, 1987), 84.

12 John Urry, *The Tourist Gaze* (London: Sage, 1990), 112.

13 Greg Dickenson, "Memories for Sale in Old Pasadena," *Quarterly Journal of Speech* 83.1 (1997): 5.

14 Hewison, 139.

15 Charles Taylor, *Multiculturalism*, ed. Amy Gutman (Princeton, NJ: Princeton University Press, 1994), 36.

16 Charles Taylor, *Multiculturalism*, 25.

17 Taylor, *Multiculturalism*, 32.

18 Taylor, *Multiculturalism*, 65.

19 Moira McLoughlin, *Museums and the Representation of Native Canadians* (New York: Garland, 1999). McLoughlin suggests that acknowledging the conflictual nature of human history and integrating divergent histories in museum exhibits can enhance understandings of history and expand definitions of cultural identity. Similarly, Andreas Huyssen and Marita Sturken claim that museum employees and visitors actively construct cultural memory as they produce and consume their representations. All of these writers accentuate the active processes of history-making and identity-construction. Andreas Huyssen (*Twilight Memories* [New York: Routledge, 1995]); and Marita Sturken (*Tangled Memories* [Berkeley, CA: University of California Press, 1997]).

20 Ian MacKay, "History and the Tourist Gaze: The Politics of Commemoration in Nova Scotia, 1935–1964," *Acadiensis*, 22.2 (1993): 104.

21 MacKay, 102.

22 Hewison, 45, 91, 141.

23 David Peterson, "There Is No Living History, There Are No Time Machines," *History News* 43.5 (1998): 28–30.

24 Dickenson, 2.

25 A.J.B. Johnston, interview by Erna MacLeod, 16 December 1997.

26 During our interview, historian A.J.B. Johnston stated that the Unama'ki Committee was formed in winter of 1994. Its members include Louisbourg historians William A. O'Shea, A.J.B. Johnston, and Alexander Balcom, along with Dr. Peter Christmas of the Mi'kmaq Association of Cultural Studies, and members of each Mi'kmaq band in Cape Breton.

27 A.J.B. Johnston, "Partnerships and Linkage in Native History Interpretation," unpublished manuscript, May 1993.

28 A.J.B. Johnston, interview by Erna MacLeod, 16 December 1997.

29 Johnston, interview 1997.

30 Johnston, interview 1997.

31 Harald Prins, *The Mi'kmaq: Resistance, Accommodation, and Cultural Survival* (Fort Worth, TX: Harcourt College, 1996), 151.

32 Johnston, interview 1997.

33 Kenneth Donovan, interview by Erna MacLeod, 18 December 1997.

34 Donovan, interview 1997.

35 William A. O'Shea, interview by Erna MacLeod, 25 March 1998.

36 O'Shea, interview 1998.

37 *Parks Canada Guiding Principles and Operational Policies*, Minister of Supply and Services Canada, 1994, 13.

38 *Parks Canada Guiding Principles*, 71.

39 *Parks Canada Guiding Principles*, 71.

40 *Parks Canada Guiding Principles*, 70.

41 *Fortress of Louisbourg National Historic Site: Commemorative Integrity Statement*, 3.

42 O'Shea, interview 1998.

43 O'Shea, interview 1998.

44 *Parks Canada Agency: A Discussion Paper*, Department of Canadian Heritage, June 1996, 4, 6.

19 Culture and an Aboriginal Charter of Rights

Eric Sherbert

The Kaianerekowa Great Law of Peace[1]

We must have a league of nations, so that all may live in peace and tranquillity...the chiefs must be patient, long-suffering, and courageous in the cause of right and justice....We will call it the Great Law.

We even uprooted a tall pine tree and thus made a very deep hole in the earth, at the bottom of which runs a swift current of water. Into this current we have thrown all the causes of war and strife....Under this great tree we shall rest, for its shade will be pleasant and beautiful. All the nations will look upon the law, and all will like it and desire it.[2]

An Aboriginal-Specific Charter

THE INCONGRUENCE OF CANADIAN EUROPEAN-BASED legal principles and Canadian Aboriginal culture has been the subject of much legal literature and jurisprudence. Most agree that strict application of common law to Aboriginal society is not only inappropriate in many situations, but a threat to the very existence of the culture.[3] The Supreme Court of Canada in *Guerin v. Canada*[4] firmly established the *sui generis* or unique nature of Native law issues as a fundamental principle in Aboriginal law with far-reaching effects.[5] Even human rights principles cannot be applied universally. The Canadian Charter of Rights and Freedoms[6] is built upon the notion of individual rights designed as a protective measure. Conversely, most Canadian Aboriginal cultures are based on a collective where one's rights are intrinsic to the specific responsibilities that individuals have toward their society and nature. European contact with Native cultures has tainted this collective ideal through societal influence and legislative coercion. Although not felt as intensely in modern Aboriginal society, the traditional belief in the collective ideal is still strong in the minds and hearts of Indigenous peoples. Respect for other beings, including humans

---

The views expressed in this paper are those of the author and not the Department of Justice, Canada.

381

and animals, is intrinsic to this collective ideal. This Aboriginal perception of human dignity has even fundamentally affected the Eurocentric legal paradigm. B.E. Johansen notes how the famous statesman Benjamin Franklin utilized the Iroquois Great Law of Peace as a model for his Albany Plan of 1754 and later in the Articles of Confederation, Bill of Rights, and Constitution of the United States.[7] Although elements of a native charter may be similar to existing Canadian regimes, Menno Boldt and J. Anthony Long emphasize that each society has built its model of human rights and dignity on its own conception of humankind.[8]

Many Aboriginal groups believe that any ambiguity in constitutional and charter issues can be resolved by an Aboriginal-specific charter or human rights codes based on native cultural values. This essay outlines the way Aboriginal rights open up and challenge the European cultural bias present within the Canadian legal system. Since laws are the product of cultural norms, the European nature of the Canadian legal system continues to face difficulties adapting itself to the demands of Aboriginal cultural practices. Even within a European legal system, Canada is divided between the English common law and the French Civil Code in Quebec. Common law is based upon English tradition, whereby laws are derived from custom and precedents, that is, past decisions made by judges. The French Civil Code, however, is based upon a body of systematically written statutes established by the Napoleanic Code in 1804 and other laws made by the French government. The Canadian legal system has, therefore, adapted to differences found in Quebec culture. An Aboriginal charter would simply represent another example of Canadian law adapting to yet another significant cultural group. From the point of view of both Aboriginal groups and Canadian society, an Aboriginal charter of rights would not only serve as a recognition of Aboriginal cultural identity, but would also provide a practical legal framework to assist governmental and judicial bodies on both sides confronted with the task of resolving legal issues between two different cultural groups.

Many Canadians do not understand what a charter is, and they may be surprised to learn how limited charters and human rights codes are in their effects. A charter of rights is a constitutional document that supercedes all other law and protects individuals or groups from government actions. For example, if the government were to enact a law that discriminates against a particular racial group or harms citizens in some way, a citizen or group might fight the validity of that law in court. The government enacting the law could be one of the various Canadian governments or an Aboriginal government body. The appropriate court might find that the particular law offends a charter right, rendering the law invalid. Human rights codes are usually statutes that protect individuals or groups from other individuals or groups. For example, a restaurant may exclude a particular ethnic group from its premises. In this case, the excluded individual or group could file a complaint with the provincial human rights office. The human rights authority can take legal action and force the restaurant to change its policy or face various legal penalties. Existing human rights codes do not operate on reserves. The Canadian Human Rights Act[9] exempts matters made under or pursuant to the Indian Act and provincial codes would not apply to reserves for jurisdictional reasons.

Given the fundamental need to address human rights issues in any modern society, various Aboriginal-specific human rights instruments are urgently needed to clarify Aboriginal rights collectively and individually, and to preserve human dignity in government and private activities on reserve lands. Hence, a sense of justice demands that the roots of a charter or human rights instrument for Aboriginal peoples must be firmly planted within the culture itself. Furthermore, we have acknowledged that cultural differences often exist amongst the various indigenous nations. It follows that human rights instruments developed by one Aboriginal nation could be quite different than those of another. These differences between the various First Nations merely underlines the need for not only a comprehensive external constitutional protection from intervention by the Canadian government but also an internal protection from conflicting interests within.

A History of Aboriginal Law Doctrine in Canada

The general nature of Aboriginal rights in Canada has often been explored by legal theorists, yet few have directly addressed the issue of a Canadian Aboriginal-specific human rights instrument. Aboriginal special status, land rights, traditional harvesting rights, self-determination, and self-government have been the subject of most discussions to date. Although the birth of Aboriginal rights doctrine has been placed in the early colonial times,[10] until the 1950s there was little development of Aboriginal law principles. For the most part, Canadian legal culture failed to recognize Aboriginal law as a worthwhile subject until the last forty years. As Canadians developed a desire for legal independence from the United Kingdom through the 1960s, Aboriginal peoples felt the time had come for their renewed self-determination.

The Royal Proclamation of 1763 formalized the relationship between the Indigenous nations of Canada (and the United States) and the European-based colonial governments. The proclamation gave the British Crown the role as "protector" of Aboriginal interests, especially in land, based on the role given to colonial governors in 1670 by the British Parliament. This treaty process has not ended. Many Aboriginal groups are still not signatory to any existing treaty.

Authority over Aboriginal affairs in Canada moved from the British government to the early Province of Canada in 1860. This responsibility was eventually entrenched in section 91(24) of the Constitution Act, 1867[11] which gave the Canadian government legislative powers over "Indians and Lands reserved for Indians." The first federal "Indian" legislation after confederation was the 1868 Secretary of State Act, followed by An Act for the Gradual Civilization and Enfranchisement of Indians. These statutes were consolidated in the first Indian Act[12] in 1876. This statute continued, in fact intensified, the policy of the Crown's guardianship over indigenous peoples. This previous legislation clearly indicated that the "gradual civilization and enfranchisement" or the extinction of indigenous cultures was the core of federal policy.[13] For example, the criminalization of the Sun Dance and potlatch are quintessential of Canadian Aboriginal policy. The goal of assimilation, which is the basic effect of the 1867 Constitution Act, is still intact to date.

There was little change in Canadian Indian policy until 1951, when the Indian Act was revised by John Diefenbaker's Progressive Conservative government. The prime minister's reforms included giving all Aboriginal persons the vote in federal elections,[14] appointing James Gladstone[15] as the first Aboriginal senator, and introducing the Indian Claims Commission, although the commission bill was never enacted. Most important, Diefenbaker was a strong supporter for the maintenance of special status for Indigenous peoples. This policy was later referred to in the influential Hawthorn Report[16] as "Citizens Plus," a concept that replaced the inferior status of Aboriginal persons. The term "Citizens Plus" denotes that Aboriginal persons have all the rights of Canadian citizens, plus unique Aboriginal rights based on their cultural history. Diefenbaker believed the enactment of the Canadian Bill of Rights[17] in 1960 would be a positive step for Aboriginal peoples. Unfortunately, it was the seed of great conflict between human rights legislation and Aboriginal peoples in Canada.

The Liberal Red Book policy of the late 1960s marked a complete reversal of federal support for Aboriginal special status. In 1969, Prime Minister Pierre Trudeau stated, "But aboriginal rights, this really means saying, 'We were here before you.... We want you to preserve our aboriginal rights and restore them to us.' And our answer...our answer is 'no.'"[18] These dramatic policy changes crystalized when Jean Chrétien, then minister of Indian Affairs, announced the White Paper[19] in 1969. Two key proposals in the paper were the repeal of the Indian Act and subsection

91(24) of the Constitution Act, 1867. The response by Aboriginal leaders was swift and in strong opposition to the policy. Notable briefs in response to the White Paper were the *Citizens Plus*[20] of the Alberta Chiefs (known as the Red Paper), and the *Wagbung*[21] of the Manitoba Indian Brotherhood. These papers voiced the almost unanimous position of Aboriginal peoples in Canada. Despite much criticism of the Indian Act, Aboriginal people viewed complete removal of their special status as part of a federal government agenda to avoid treaty and fiduciary commitments through assimilation of Aboriginal nations into the rest of Canadian society.[22] The White Paper was formally withdrawn in 1973.

The Liberal Red Book policy, which emphasized individual human rights, was the background for the conflict between the Canadian Bill of Rights and the Indian Act throughout the 1970s. In 1970, the Supreme Court of Canada in the *Drybones*[23] decision rendered section 95[24] of the Indian Act inoperative through the Bill of Rights. As other similar Supreme Court decisions followed,[25] by 1974, concern over the effect of the Bill of Rights superceding the Indian Act became apparent. The issue of gender discrimination in the Indian Act, here subsections 12(1)(b) and 12(1)(a)(IV), is most exemplary of the precarious position of Aboriginal societies in Canada. These sections denied Aboriginal women membership in the band if they married a "non-Indian." Ironically, Aboriginal women had to use the European-based Canadian legislation, the Bill of Rights, to protect themselves from other patriarchal legislation, the Indian Act, forced upon them by the Canadian government. Finally, after many other controversial judicial decisions and protests from many Aboriginal nations, Liberal Prime Minister Trudeau promised to change the Indian Act provisions within two years.[26] The discriminatory membership provisions were not repealed until the enactment of Bill C-31 in 1985 by the Progressive Conservative government.

The Liberal government's emphasis on individual rights culminated with the enactment of the Constitution Act, 1982.[27] Canadian Aboriginal peoples are particularly affected by four key provisions. The first three are part of the Canadian Charter of Rights and Freedoms:

> Section 15 guarantees equality, allowing temporary affirmative action programs.

> Section 25 provides that *Charter* guarantees shall not abrogate or derogate from any Aboriginal, treaty or other rights or freedoms that pertain to the Aboriginal peoples of Canada.

> Section 28 provides that notwithstanding anything in the *Charter*, the rights and freedoms referred to in it are guaranteed equally to male and female persons.

The fourth is the general constitutional guarantee:

> Section 35 (1) recognizes and affirms existing aboriginal and treaty rights.
> (2) aboriginal includes Indian, Inuit, and Metis peoples of Canada.
> (3) treaty includes land claims agreements or may be acquired so.
> (4) guaranteed equally to male and female persons.

These provisions were partially created through consultation with Canadian Aboriginal groups, including the National Indian Brotherhood (NIB), the forerunner of the Assembly of First Nations (AFN) which represents status Indians on reserves; the Native Council of Canada (NCC), which represents Metis, non-status Indians, off-reserve Indians; and the Inuit Committee on National Issues (ICNI) representing the Inuit. Many legal writers believe the inclusion of Aboriginal-specific provisions in the constitution and Native participation in their conception was a positive step for Indigenous peoples, but are cautious regarding the interpretation of the provisions.

Section 35(1) of the Constitution Act has been the most influential. This sweeping provision entrenched or "secured" any existing Aboriginal or treaty rights. Generally, this means that any custom or practice of an Aboriginal group can be continued without the agreement of the Canadian government. For example, if an Aboriginal group hunted moose in certain areas before the Europeans arrived in Canada, then that group can "legally" continue this hunting practice. Of course, there are many stipulations and limitations to this rule, which have been set out in several leading decisions of the Supreme Court of Canada.[28] The term "existing" means that any "rights" given up by Aboriginal groups before April 1982 can no longer be claimed. The full scope of section 35 and the other three sections is yet to be realized. For example, whether "existing aboriginal rights" can include the right of self-government is still a subject of much debate.

Similar to the clash with the Bill of Rights, the effect of these charter provisions on the Indian Act is even more complex and far-reaching, since they are constitutional provisions, not mere federal statutes. Federal statutes can be changed by the government at any time, while constitutional provisions require complex political consultation with all of the provinces. Few papers and jurisprudence address the interplay between these provisions or their full effect on the Indian Act and Aboriginal peoples in Canada. The balance between individual and collective rights of Aboriginal people is the key issue. Only from a historical perspective does it become clear that Canadian government has, until very recently, barely recognized Aboriginal cultural issues let alone constructed legal principles based on consultation with Aboriginal groups. These constitutional provisions have not been derived from Aboriginal cultural identity nor do they deal with the many cultural differences within Aboriginal society. An Aboriginal charter is simply the first step toward giving Aboriginal cultures the necessary protection from outside intervention while providing a framework for dealing with legal matters concerning particular Aboriginal groups and individuals. Based on our knowledge of the historical relationship between Aboriginal peoples and the federal government, we can then construct some theoretical principles for an Aboriginal charter from the law as it now exists.

The Legal Basis for an Aboriginal Charter

Any human rights regime developed by an Aboriginal group or nation would have to be based on some legal authority. The legal foundation will, of course, vary depending on the Aboriginal culture in question. However, the legal basis for the instrument will likely fall into one or more of five general categories. First, a treaty or other agreement between Canada and an Aboriginal nation may implicitly or explicitly contain such authority. This right would also be protected by section 35. Second, the authority may be a delegated federal power under section 91(24) of the Constitution Act, 1867. This channel of authority would require a bilateral agreement between the Canadian federal and Aboriginal governments. Third, having an international status could lend an Aboriginal nation the authority for a human rights document. The international arena can only be pragmatic support if the demands of Aboriginal peoples in Canada are compliant with international norms or customary international law. International covenants to which Canada is signatory would enforce such authority.

Fourth, implementation of a human rights instrument may arise from the federal government's fiduciary duty to Aboriginal peoples. This duty is unique to Aboriginal peoples of Canada and is enforceable by the Canadian courts. The fiduciary duty to Aboriginal peoples is built upon the Crown's assertion of authority over the lands, previously controlled by Indigenous nations, now called "Canada." In other words, by taking authority over the lands of Canada, the Canadian government has taken responsibility to ensure the stability of all social, political, and legal aspects of Aboriginal peoples of Canada. Further, the Canadian government must show proper conduct when negotiating with Aboriginal nations.

The fiduciary duty began historically with colonial North American treaty relationships. However, the most important authoritative source is the Supreme Court of Canada's landmark decision in *Guerin*. The Guerin case gave much-needed stability to the Aboriginal fiduciary doctrine, settling many fundamental ambiguities. Its effect on the relationship between the federal government and Aboriginal nations was unprecedented.

The Crown's fiduciary duty, like many principles in Aboriginal law, is unique in many respects in Canadian common law. Its nature and scope are based on the special relationship between the Crown and Aboriginal nations.

Fiduciary duty exists separately from other Aboriginal rights. This separation means that an Aboriginal group could base a claim on both an Aboriginal right and a fiduciary duty simultaneously. The Crown's fiduciary duty includes both federal and provincial governments; yet this duty is only a "moral" duty to Aboriginal peoples of Canada. Aboriginal peoples may therefore use the obligation of fiduciary duty to enforce the goodwill between Aboriginal people and the Canadian governments.

A fifth authoritative basis is inherent Aboriginal rights, rights that are protected by section 35 of the Constitution Act, 1982. When such a right exists, a band has unilateral power in the creation and implementation of the practice in question. By using these various doctrines established by the courts and legal literature, several viable approaches can be proffered to solve the Aboriginal human rights dilemma. All of these legal bases are processes that one might use to enact an Aboriginal charter. However, the inherent Aboriginal right doctrine is the most helpful in creating a truly "culturally based" instrument.

Human Rights Principles Inherent to Aboriginal Culture

The first legal basis for an Aboriginal charter, inherent Aboriginal rights, is the most significant source from a cultural perspective, since it is founded on traditions and practices that existed before the European invasion of Canada. Egalitarian principles are inherent to most Aboriginal cultures. Instead of the hierarchical structure found in most European-based social and political systems, key concepts in Aboriginal societies are often based on a circle. The political body of most nations is the council circle around a fire. The spiritual forces of humans and nature travel in four directions, represented in sacred circular objects like the medicine wheel and dreamcatcher. Even the core of mythical Aboriginal world, the Great Tree, rests on the circular back of the Great Turtle.

This circular paradigm in the councils represents the importance of all citizens. Some members of society do have special status. For example, elders are more experienced and their advice carries much weight. Historically, Iroquois tradition holds that clan mothers or the senior women of a family were key instructors or teachers since they "hold [own] the title [string of wampum] to chiefship."[29] However, advice and comment may be forwarded from any or all members of the nation. Final decisions are then made democratically through consensus. The chiefs merely implement the orders of the people. Within this structure lies the fundamental principles that Euro-based society would call human rights: equality, freedom of opinion and expression, and democratic rights. This inherent human rights structure could also be classified as an "inherent Aboriginal right" to develop a human rights system. If so, it would give many Aboriginal nations the unilateral power to enact a charter under the protection of section 35 of the Constitution Act, 1982.

Inherent Rights in Canadian Common Law

Inherent Aboriginal rights are unique in Canadian law. These rights exist independently and are not contingent on any treaty, executive order, or legislative enactment. The scope of possible rights is broad and can be economic, social, political, or religious. Hence, a particular right may include any facet of an Aboriginal culture, from social tradition to land title, possibly even self-government.

The affirmation of inherent Aboriginal rights by European-based governments and courts evolved slowly until the mid-1900s. Section 35 of the Constitution Act, 1982 formally entrenched any existing Aboriginal rights in Canada in the constitution; they therefore have constitutional protection. Aboriginal rights doctrine has developed more from 1982 to the present, than throughout all pre-1982 history. The Supreme Court of Canada first substantively addressed section 35 inherent rights in the *Sparrow* decision: the Musqueam Band's fishing right was inherent if it constituted "an integral part of their distinctive culture."[30] This key phrase became the basis for subsequent formalized legal doctrine and tests. These legal tests determine whether an Aboriginal practice can be protected by section 35 of the Constitution Act, 1982 as an inherent right.

An important approach to all these tests is the recognition (to some degree) of the Aboriginal perspective. This recognition is crucial since the rationale or meaning behind some customs or practices can be lost when they are formalized within the Canadian legal structure. Such is the case of human or social rights principles. These principles do exist within many, if not all, Aboriginal cultures. They are mixed throughout a cultural paradigm that differs somewhat from Canada's European-based legal system.

Human Rights Principles Inherent to Aboriginal Culture

The existence of basic human rights principles within North American indigenous cultures can be evidenced by their influence on the early governments of the United States and Canada. Aboriginal peoples' contribution toward the formulation of government based on democracy and civil rights has been a subject of controversy for many years. Some legal and political theorists believe the political system of many Aboriginal cultures was used as a model for the American government, which in turn has influenced nearly every democratic society in the world, including Canada.[31] As radical as this concept is to many conservative-minded theorists, the evidence of its validity is both demonstrable and significant.

Johansen and Wright note that the Iroquois Five Nations Confederacy or Iroquois League (now Six Nations) were studied by early political notables such as Thomas Paine and Ben Franklin. Both make references to the Great Law and the Confederacy being the models used by Franklin for his Albany Plan of 1754.[32] In the late 1700s, Ben Franklin regularly wrote about the wisdom found in Aboriginal cultures and always advocated the Iroquois Grand Council's one-house legislature.[33] He attended a speech by Canassatego, an Onondaga sachem (or chief), that extolled the strength and longevity of the Five Nations Confederacy. In that speech, Canassatego recommended that the colonists should observe "the same methods" as the Iroquois union.[34] Franklin published excerpts of the speech in 1744.[35] The *Autobiography of Benjamin Franklin*[36] makes references to the Aboriginal as "The Savages of North America," but Franklin uses the words ironically when speaking of their "kind manners" and "civility."

Thomas Paine was an influential political writer in the United States during the eighteenth century. He wrote and published works before and after the American independence from Britain in 1776. Paine's first contact with early Aboriginal peoples was on 4 February 1777 when he was sent to Pennsylvania by the Philadelphia Council of Safety to negotiate a treaty.

Samuel Edwards writes, "This was the first time that Paine had met any Indians, and he was fascinated by them. He went to great lengths to know and understand them. He became friendly with the chief of 'one of the northern tribes,' who spoke little English, and attempted to learn the language of the Iroquois.... He made progress so that...he could understand without an interpreter much that the Indians said."[37]

The critics of this "Aboriginal influence theory" often believe the early colonists based their democracy on the ancient Graeco-Roman system and other "European precedents of democracy."[38] However, Paine makes very clear his disdain and distrust of all previous government systems in one of his most famous works, *The Rights of Man*.[39] Chapter two, entitled "Of the Origin of the Present Old Governments," begins with a condemnation: "It is impossible that such governments as have hitherto existed in the world, could have commenced by any other means than a total violation of every principle sacred and moral."[40] Paine believes that only four forms of government exist: democratic, aristocratic, monarchial, and representative.[41] He notes the distinction between the ancient democracies and the present representative systems. Specifically, ancient simple democracy was "no other than a common-hall" of the ancients, where the concept of representation was "a thing unknown in the ancient democracies."[42] Accordingly, Paine believed this non-European representation system was superior and the most practical of all known government concepts. Representation is central to the Iroquois Grand Council system. Each of the Iroquois nations has a number of "seats" or representative sachems (chiefs). The sachems are chosen by the people to represent their interests, similar to the present Canadian and American government electoral seat system. The number of seats may vary amongst each nation, but this does not mean any disadvantage of power. These seats are only for the expression of different views, since any final decisions are reached by consensus.

In March of 1775, Paine became editor-in-chief of the *Pennsylvania Magazine*. Of its first issue, Edwards interestingly notes, "[Paine] wrote an editorial in which he predicted that the native Indian would be absorbed into the mainstream of American culture."[43] Hence, Paine's concern for Aboriginal culture was apparent even before his first personal experience in 1777. Franklin and Paine's keen interest in Aboriginal culture is historical fact. It is unconvincing at best to believe that they would not be aware of their political and social systems. Furthermore, Franklin and Paine both possessed exceptional knowledge of contemporary political systems and their histories, and would have appreciated the uniqueness of these representative concepts in the Iroquois political system.

Brian Slattery believes colonial countries (like Canada) should shed their "imperial constitutional models" and embrace such indigenous contributions toward a more "organic constitutional model."[44] The imperial model perpetuates a myopic legal view of Canada. Slattery's six basic canons of this model emphasize the British and French influence on Canadian culture, an influence that marginalizes or excludes all other legal and political sources. The imperial model fails to recognize the influence and legal position of Aboriginal issues Canada. This imperial approach denies, among other things, the fact of the historical occupation of Indigenous peoples and their international status, and it sees Aboriginal rights as contingent on the Crown's "good will." Slattery supports the organic model, which sees Aboriginal peoples as active participants in Canada's history. Furthermore, the model places the roots of the constitution in "Canadian soil," and not in Europe. Slattery states, "the Organic Model encourages us to broaden our conception of the sources of Canadian law and to recognize the diverse roles that Indian and Metis peoples have played in the formation of this country and its Constitution."[45] Of its six basic canons, one key is that our fundamental constitutional law need not be limited to common law sources. These approaches were taken in *Sparrow* when the Court acknowledged that Aboriginal rights are not contingent on the Royal Proclamation, but are inherent. This approach not only situates Aboriginal peoples in their proper historical place, but it acknowledges all Canadian cultural groups as a collective force that shapes the country. Regardless of how reluctantly the European-based North American cultures acknowledge the Aboriginal political history, the Aboriginal concept of representation predates contact with Europe, and already includes the very values of equality, democracy, and human rights that the European colonizers champion. The 1993 *Report of Royal Commission on Aboriginal Peoples* (RCAP)[46] states that the Iroquois Confederacy system may have dated back as far as AD 1300.[47] The birth of the Iroquois society itself could date anywhere from 500 to 4000 BC.[48] The Royal Commission on Aboriginal Peoples comments on the role of individuality in Aboriginal cultures: "In most Aboriginal societies, an individual is imbued with a strong sense of personal autonomy and an equally strong sense of responsibility to the community. Since the welfare of the community depends on ingenuity, initiative and self-reliance of its individual members, individual rights and responsibilities are viewed as serving rather than opposing collective interests."[49]

To return again to the example of Iroquois tradition, the Great Law emphasizes three key values. The first is *Gaiwoh* or "Righteousness," which represents justice practised between people and nations, as well as the desire to see justice done. The second is *Skenon* or "Health," meaning soundness of mind and body, and peace. The third is *Gashasdenshaa* or "Power," representing the authority of law and custom, as well as the power of religion or belief.[50] These concepts show an inherent practice and a desire to uphold the dignity of the individual and the society. Human dignity is not a concept unique to Europeans. These values, inherent to the Aboriginal culture, reveal the ancient Indigenous peoples' belief that all individuals (and nations) have the right to civility or human rights.

It follows that empowering these inherent social values must be part of the self-determination of Aboriginal peoples of Canada. The Royal Commission on Aboriginal Peoples states, "The right of self-determination is vested in all the Aboriginal peoples of Canada, including First Nations, Inuit, and Metis."[51] Pursuant to this goal, the fundamental values found in the Great Law should be constitutionally entrenched for those Aboriginal groups who wish to secure their traditional social rights. Such protection will guarantee no interference in key Aboriginal values by the Canadian federal or provincial governments.

These human rights and social values also satisfy the "legal" requirements set out in the various legal tests. The Aboriginal group would first identify the practices or customs they wish to protect. The fundamental nature of such values could only be of central significance or integral to the group. Further, these practices are a "defining characteristic of their culture."[52] The application of the Great Law or similar principles exists in most Aboriginal nations throughout Canada and the United States. William Fenton's prominent scholarly work *The Great Law and the Longhouse*[53] supports the existence of these practices predating European contact; his research was used as a source by the Royal Commission on Aboriginal Peoples. These key facts would be strong evidence for an inherent Aboriginal right to enact a social or human rights charter for a multitude of indigenous nations. Ironically, however, the very political systems which Aboriginal culture has helped to create has failed to ensure the rights of Aboriginal peoples to pursue their own cultural heritage.

An Aboriginal Charter Paradigm

A fundamental distinction in human rights documents is made between collective and individual rights. This distinction is important when addressing Aboriginal human rights. Section 35 of the Constitution is an example of collective rights, the rights of all Aboriginal peoples. However, section 35 is not part of the Charter. Although human rights documents most often speak of individual rights, collective rights are only occasionally provided. For example, Section 28 of the Canadian Charter, guaranteeing rights to male and female persons, is a collective right. In contrast, the African Charter on Human and Peoples' Rights[54] addresses both individual and collective rights. Interpretive or additional provisions in the existing Canadian Charter would likely remain collective in nature. Individual rights could be addressed in a general Aboriginal charter added to the existing Canadian Constitution or a local charter created by each First Nation. Another aspect of collective rights is the right of groups within Aboriginal culture, such as elders.

The paradigm used for Aboriginal charter ranges from the existing Charter model to an organically Aboriginal model. The Canadian model is based on the UN Charter. A model based more firmly in Aboriginal culture is possible. The Native Women's Association of Canada suggests a human rights code based on the Four Directions concept found in many

Aboriginal cultures. Although each Aboriginal group has its own version of this concept, the Four Directions are usually depicted as four points on a circle, like a compass. Each direction represents an aspect of the natural world, such as east, west, north, south, or earth, wind, water, and fire. These natural aspects are paired or attached to psychological, social, or spiritual human aspects.

Possible Provisions for an Aboriginal Charter

What would provisions of an Aboriginal charter look like? Many categories of rights can be protected within the Aboriginal community. Some will be unique to Aboriginal societies. These areas may include the customary or the traditional, such as right to a sentencing circle in criminal matters. Special property rights are important, since the property system of Aboriginal peoples under the Indian Act differs greatly from the non-Aboriginal context. More typical rights may include language, such as the right to government services in traditional languages.

Several general approaches may differ. For example, along with the usual negatively stated rights, positive duties can be enshrined. Such provisions are already found in other human rights documents. Section 2 of the Quebec Charter has two parts, a right of assistance and a duty to individuals:

Every human being whose life is in peril has a right to assistance.

Every person must come to the aid of anyone whose life is in danger, either personally or calling for aid, by giving him the necessary and immediate physical assistance, unless it involves danger to himself or a third person, or he has another valid reason.[55]

This pairing of rights and duties reflects the human rights code paradigm suggested by Native Women's Association of Canada above. Chapter 2 of the African Charter contains many duties of citizens. For example, Article 29 states,

The individual shall also have the duty:

1. To preserve the harmonious development of the family and to work for the cohesion and respect of the family; to respect his parents at all times, to maintain them in case of need.[56]

The rights of Elders would be of special interest to Aboriginal cultures. Article 18 of the African Charter provides rights for the elderly and disabled.[57] The African Charter also contains many provisions for the protection of African tradition and culture. These special protections would be fundamental to an Aboriginal-specific charter in Canada.

Most Aboriginal cultures are duty-based societies. Duty to the community is deeply intertwined with individual freedom. A similar balance between the community and the individual is weighed by Canadian courts everyday. Basic human rights principles can be gleaned from Aboriginal societies, but are often very group-specific, even amongst the various Aboriginal nations. The samples above are only glimpses of what an Aboriginal charter might contain.

The justice of a culturally specific charter is difficult to dismiss. The needs of each cultural group must be met because the history of their unjust exclusion from the Canadian system of justice, which calls for culture-specific recognition when addressing human rights issues. The African Charter contains very specific rights necessary for that particular social context and state history.[58] The province of Quebec, a culture similar in many respects to the rest of Canada, has slight variations in its social order that form the basis for Quebec's need of a specific charter of rights and freedoms. This difference is critical, even when English and French Canadians share similar European-based values. Aboriginal cultures in Canada have no roots in European cultures. If societies as similar as English and French Canada have specific charters, the need for an Aboriginal charter becomes clear.

The Government of Canada's "Statement of Reconciliation: Learning from the Past" gives a promise:

> In renewing our partnership, we must ensure that the mistakes which marked our past relationship are not repeated. The Government of Canada recognizes that policies that sought to assimilate Aboriginal people, women and men, were not the way to build a strong country. We must instead continue to find ways in which Aboriginal people can participate fully in the economic, political, cultural and social life of Canada in a manner which preserves and enhances the collective identities of Aboriginal communities, and allows them to evolve and flourish in the future. Working together to achieve our shared goals will benefit all Canadians, Aboriginal and non-Aboriginal alike.[59]

This statement indicates the Canadian government's hope of true independence for Aboriginal peoples of Canada. The government's promise of full participation for Aboriginal peoples must include self-government. Such independence for Aboriginal governments cannot and should not be complete without the assurance of human rights for Aboriginal individuals. Only an Aboriginal-specific charter will guarantee human rights for indigenous peoples and sustain cultural identity for indigenous peoples across Canada. Only after the call for human rights by the Aboriginal culture is heard can any claim be made for a "just society" in Canada.

Notes

1 The Great Law stems from a thousand year old Hiawatha and Deganawidah legend, spoken by the Hodenosaunee, meaning "People of the Longhouse." The people are known to the French as the Iroquois and to the English as the Five Nations Confederacy or League, which includes the Seneca, Cayuga, Onondaga, Oneida, and Mohawk. Since the Tuscarora of North Carolina joined in 1720, they are the Six Nations Confederacy. Their territorial roots span from southern Ontario, Canada, to northern New York, United States. Today, they are a strong and politically active nation.

2 E. Clark, ed., *Indian Legends of Canada* (Toronto: McClelland and Stewart, 1960), 153–54. This account of the legend was given by an Onondaga chief and fire-keeper on the Reserve of the Six Nations, Ontario, in 1888.

3 See M. Boldt and A. Long, "Tribal Philosophies and the Charter of Rights and Freedoms," *The Quest for Justice: Aboriginal Peoples and Aboriginal Rights*, ed. M. Boldt, A. Long, and L. Little Bear (Toronto: Toronto University Press, 1985).

4 *Guerin v. Canada*, [1984] 2 Canada Supreme Court Reports 335 [hereinafter *Guerin*].

5 In *Delgamuukw v. B.C.*, [1997] 3 Canada Supreme Court Reports 1010 [hereinafter *Delgamuukw*], the court allowed Aboriginal oral histories as evidence. At the very least, it was a novel and shocking allowance.

6 Part 1 of the Constitution Act, 1982, being Schedule B to the Canada Act 1982 (UK), c. 11 [hereinafter Charter].

7 B.E. Johansen, *Debating Democracy: Native American Legacy of Freedom* (Sante Fe: Clear Light, 1998) for a more comprehensive background on this point.

8 Boldt and Long, 167 n3.

9 Canadian Human Rights Act, Statutes of Canada, 1976–77, c. 33, s.67.

10 See B. Slattery, "The Hidden Constitution: Aboriginal Rights in Canada" *American Journal of Comparative Law* 32 (1984): 361.

11 Constitution Act, 1867 (UK), 30 & 31 Vict., c. 3. (formerly the British North America Act, 1867).

12 Indian Act, Revised Statutes of Canada, c. 149.

13 See for example, R.J. Surtees, *Canadian Indian Policy: A Critical Bibliography* (Bloomington: Indiana University Press, 1982), 44. References to many other similar works are noted in this excellent bibliography.

14 The right to vote was originally proposed on the condition that the tax exemption provision of the Indian Act, section 88, was repealed; however, this requirement was eventually waived.

15 Member of the Blood Indian Tribe of Alberta and president of the Indian Association of Alberta.

16 See H. Hawthorn, *A Survey of the Contemporary Indians in Canada*, Vol. 1 (Ottawa: Indian Affairs Branch, 1966), chap. 13.

17 Canadian Bill of Rights, Revised Statutes of Canada, 1970, App. III.

18 N. Cummings and H. Mickenburg, ed., *Native Rights in Canada* (Toronto: Indian-Eskimo Association, 1975).

19 The Department of Indian and Northern Development's *Statement of the Government of Canada on Indian Policy 1969* quickly became referred to as "The White Paper."

20 Indian Chiefs of Alberta, *Citizens Plus* (Edmonton: Indian Association of Alberta, 1970) became known as the "Red Paper" [hereinafter Red Paper].

21 Manitoba Indian Brotherhood, *Wahbung (Our Tomorrow)* (Winnipeg: Manitoba Indian Brotherhood, 1971).

22 D. Saunders, "The Renewal of Indian Special Status," *Equality Rights and the Canadian Charter of Rights and Freedoms,* ed. Anne F. Bayefsky and Mary Eberts (Toronto: Carswell, 1985), 529.

23 *R.v. Drybones,* [1970] Canada Supreme Court Reports 282.

24 "An Indian who (a) has intoxicants in his possession (b) is intoxicated, or (c) makes or manufactures intoxicants, off a reserve, is guilty of an offence." Indian Act, Revised Statutes of Canada, c. 1–6, s. 95.

25 For example, *A.G. Canada v. Lavell,* [1974] Canada Supreme Court Reports 1349.

26 C. Goar, "Trudeau Taken Aback in Commons as Flora Defends Indian Women," *Vancouver Sun* 8 July 1980: A7.

27 Being schedule B to the Canada Act 1982 (U.K.) m 1982, c.11.

28 These leading cases are *R. v. Sparrow,* [1990] 1 Canada Supreme Court Reports 1025 [hereinafter *Sparrow*], *R. v. Van der Peet,* [1996] 2 Canada Supreme Court Reports 507 [hereinafter *Vanderpeet*], and *Delgamuukw v. B.C.,* [1997] 3 Canada Supreme Court Reports 1010.

29 W.N. Fenton, *The Great Law and the Longhouse: A Political History of the Iroquois Confederacy* (Norman: University of Oklahoma Press, 1998), 216. Clan Mother is the modern name for the woman chief or matron. Up until the time of European influence, the families of many Aboriginal nations throughout North America were defined by matrilineage.

30 *Sparrow,* 1099.

31 Johansen; and R. Wright, *Stolen Continents: The "New World" through Indian Eyes* (Toronto: Penguin, 1993).

32 Johansen; R. Wright.

33 Johansen, 9.

34 Wright, see n. 62, 166.

35 Johansen, 8.

36 B. Franklin, *Autobiography of Benjamin Franklin* (New York: Books, n.d.), 224.

37 S. Edwards, *Rebel! A Biography of Tom Paine* (New York: Praeger, 1974), 49.

38 Johansen, 30.

39 Thomas Paine, *Collected Writings,* ed. Eric Foner (New York: Library of America, 1995).

40 Paine, 556.

41 Paine discards a republic as "not any *particular form* of government." Paine, 565.

42 Paine, 564.

43 Edwards, 25.

44 B. Slattery, "The Organic Constitution: Aboriginal Peoples and the Evolution of Canada," *Osgood Hall Law Journal* 34 (1996): 101-12.

45 Slattery, "The Organic Constitution," 112.

46 Canada, *Royal Commission on Aboriginal Peoples, For Seven Generations: An Information Legacy of the Royal Commission on Aboriginal Peoples,* (RCAP) CD ROM (Ottawa: Libraxus, 1997).

47 Canada, Royal Commission on Aboriginal Peoples, part 1, vol. 1, chap. 4.2.

48 Canada, Royal Commission on Aboriginal Peoples, part 1, vol. 1, chap. 4.2.

49 Canada, Royal Commission on Aboriginal Peoples, part 1, vol. 1, chap. 3.2.1.

50 Canada, Royal Commission on Aboriginal Peoples, part 1, vol. 1, chap. 4.2.

51 Canada, Royal Commission on Aboriginal Peoples, part 1, vol. 1, chap. 1.2.

52 *R. v. Vanderpeet,* 511.

53 Fenton, *The Great Law and the Longhouse.*

54 Africa, African Charter on Human and Peoples' Rights, 26 June 1981, OAU Doc. CAB/LEG/67/3/REV. 5, 21 I.L.M. 59 (entered into force 21 October 1986) [hereinafter African Charter].

55 Quebec Charter, Revised Statutes of Quebec c. 12 [hereinafter Quebec Charter].

56 African Charter, chap. 2.

57 African Charter, article 18.

58 See El-Obaid Ahmed El-Obaid and Kwadwo Appiagyei-Atua, "Human Rights in Africa: A New Perspective on Linking the Past to the Present" *McGill Law Journal* 41 (1996): 819–54.

59 Canada, Indian Affairs and Northern Development, "Statement of Reconciliation: Learning from the Past," *Gathering Strength: Canada's Aboriginal Action Plan* (Ottawa: Minister of Public Works and Government Services, 1997).

20 Canadian Gothic

Multiculturalism, Indigeneity, and Gender
in Prairie Cinema

Susan Lord

There she was, in the middle of nowhere with eight children to protect while her husband was away finding work. Indian men were always coming around. Imagine how scared she was! A young bride on the prairie. Indians all around in the middle of nowhere.

For years these fragments of a story, presented as truth by one who "was there," functioned to naturalize the cultural and political history of white prairie settlers' encounter with First Nations people, turning it into a tale of my sweet grandmother threatened by violence of unimaginable and inhuman proportions. Indians were just there: fully present, chthonic, wild. My grandmother had come from somewhere else, a safe place where men didn't have to go away to find work. I was told the following, just a few years ago by someone else who "was also there": "The farm was on the edge of a Reservation that had a lake. There was an arrangement: He would go to the Reservation to fish; Native men would come to the house to get produce or grain. It happened all the time. There was nothing to fear. She, in truth, was born on the prairie. He was a good friend to some of the Native men."

These two versions of the experience of prairie life[1] can be understood as representing two competing but foundational myths of nation: one sees white femininity as a fearful protector of home, and on the threshold stands the racialized other who embodies sexual violence. The other myth of nation sees multiculturalism as a successful commercial adventure—

free trade. As the following discussion will show, these tales have each their own popularized representation: the gothic and the melodrama.

How does history get into a film?[2] This question represents a wide angle on the specificities of this chapter. Through a cultural study that focusses on the dynamics of gender, multiculturalism, and indigeneity as they are represented in films made in the prairie provinces (with a focus on two films produced and directed by Film Frontiers in 1970 and on Anne Wheeler's "prairie films" of the 1980s), I hope to present something of an answer to a Canadian variation of that question: how does the history of contact get into Canadian film? By this I mean to ask about more than the depiction of Aboriginal-white encounters (as in films like *Clearcut*, *Windigo*, *Kanehsatake*, or *Blockade*);[3] rather, I am interested in the ways in which the gendered histories and discourses of cultural difference and the violence that subtends them find formal expression. That is, is there a history of form that is informed by the colonial encounter? Can this formal articulation of cultural history be productively understood as a "contact zone"?

According to Mary-Louise Pratt in her book *Imperial Eyes*, a contact zone designates the social spaces where disparate cultures meet, clash, and grapple with each other, often in highly asymmetrical relations of domination and subordination—like colonialism, slavery, or their aftermaths as they are lived out across the globe today.[4] I suggest that films that formally engage with the problematic of representing a "contact perspective"—thus, enunciating this clash and its asymmetrical power arrangements—create for the film viewer an experience closely analogous to the perspective of which Pratt writes: "the *spatial and temporal* co-presence of subjects previously separated *by geographic and historical disjunctures*, and whose trajectories now intersect.... A 'contact' perspective emphasizes how subjects are constituted in and by their relations to each other... copresence, interaction, interlocking understandings and practices, often within radically asymmetrical relations of power"[5] (emphasis mine). Certain Canadian films that employ Gothic perception or conventions can be argued to bring this history and distance into the picture of Canadian cinema. The particular distortions of time and space, self and other, and vision and blindness that produce Gothic terror will be a focus here, for they allow one to track the representation of history and land as contested territories—that is, as a space and time produced by radically asymmetrical relations of power.

I use the films of Film Frontiers and Anne Wheeler because they are exemplary in their manifestation of regional Canadian Gothic: a cultural and aesthetic response to the political and social violence of the encounter. I argue that works such as these register that past through the codes of a

Gothic aesthetic because the violence that past has produced for the present is unrepresentable in its totality, and the preconditions for its appearance are subject to the historical processes of governmentality—the discourses and institutions that constitute the citizen through the production and reception of official culture.[6] The use of the Gothic to signify the encounter has two possibilities in terms of representational politics: on the one hand, there is the enactment of a racist unconscious that ties the racialized other to fearful or mysterious forces; on the other hand, a self-reflective critique through the process of which the white/settler consciousness in its encounter with the other recognizes that its very self is constituted in great part by the projection of horror onto the other. Importantly, and as will be discussed further below, the First Nations presence is more often than not a structuring absence in the field of vision of Canadian national cinema, such that the negation or stereotyping of First Nations identity is a foundation upon which whiteness and/or Canadianness depends. Christopher Gittings discusses this as a "whiting out"[7] of the Indigenous people through the reproduction of stereotypes. Below, I add to his analysis by suggesting that this politics of representation is a reproduction of reserve systems of containment that function to remove the First Nations people from the settlers' field of vision.

The chapter is organized in a manner that allows us to trace the preconditions of the emergence of the Canadian Gothic: (1) a discussion of the history of melodrama and Gothic modes as responses to the general conditions of modernity and the modern nation; (2) the Canadian manifestation of these modes and an argument for regional variants; (3) a discussion of indigeneity in relation to the Multiculturalism Act; (4) analyses of key works of prairie cinema.

Melodrama's Other

In this section I outline the cultural and aesthetic history of the Gothic as a perversion of both the sublime and melodrama. Because the Gothic is arguably the most distinctively modern genre, a history of the Gothic can yield a history of modernity, thus helping us draw the connections between the formal and the subjective elements that correlate colonialism and gender in the visual culture of the modern, multicultural nation.

The Gothic, as I employ the concept here, is less a genre than a highly mediated mode of perception brought into being as a response to historical conditions. This approach will be outlined further below, but I follow Teresa Goddu in her critique of the psychologically centred approach to the Gothic. In her book *Gothic America: Narrative, History, and Nation,* she writes, "the Gothic disrupts the dream world of national myth with the nightmare of history."[8] Understood through this view, the Gothic perception enters a generic formulation—a melodramatic film, for example, which in its dominant formulation functions as an image of conciliation rather than critique—and disturbs its moral and aesthetic architecture. There are certainly films and novels that fully employ Gothic conventions as a genre or subgenre: horror films or possession narratives, for example. As well, there are traditions of Gothic fiction that have developed, and these traditions are read as fundamental to the cultural identity of a region (the American South) or era (nineteenth-century England) or readership (women of the emergent middle class). Gothic also functions as a subcultural style—a sign of post-punk urban youth or sado-masochistic queer culture. Even as I list these more genre-oriented formulations of the Gothic, the constant feature is illegitimacy: of taste, of gender, of region, of sexuality, of race, and so on. Hence, it is important to work the social referents in order to see what processes of social power—of governmentality—contribute to the emergence of certain formulations of disavowal and exclusion.

National cinema theory has employed the critical literature on the genre of melodrama as a means by which to discuss the repression and affect that constitute the modes of belonging and estrangement in the national imaginary.[9] The history of melodrama shows us that it too is a modern form, emerging in the eighteenth century as bourgeois entertainment; the Gothic, as a mode of perception, can be understood as infecting melodrama with the experience of the sublime, which in a colonial context plays itself out through the racialized other. Most writings on the relationship between the sublime, the Gothic, colonialism, and gender address the American literary traditions or the English domination of Ireland. Those who argue for its having been a central mode for the definition of the nation or against which the nation is defined include Louis Gross, Toni Morrison, and Teresa Goddu, mentioned above. Judith Halberstam's *Skin Shows: Gothic Horror and the Technology of Monsters* combines studies of traditional Gothic fiction and slasher films so as to analyze the mode as a space given to "the sexual outsider who is also a racial pariah, a national outcast and a class outlaw."[10] The study that I find especially informative for my attempts here is Meaghan Morris's "White Panic or, *Mad Max* and the Sublime," because she is interested in how the sublime in Australia has had practical force as a story elaborated for a "particular form of settler colonialism as it extended across the continent, Aboriginal land."[11]

Here it is important to stress that the sublime, too, is a historical experience—in both senses of having a particular condition of emergence and being that experience which comes with "falling into history."[12] In the

Enlightenment discourses provided by Immanuel Kant and Edmund Burke, the (pleasurable because painful) experience of the sublime, an experience of "man's" finitude, can be understood to be a correlate to the emergence of the infinitization of representation (conceptual, semiotic, etc.), the endlessness of industrial production (of commodity), and the views of cultural and racial radical alterity, or the views of a nothingness, an emptiness of the "new world." Kant, for instance, described the sublime as an experience of our inability to produce in the imagination (that is, by way of sensuous representation) an object adequate to the ideas of totality given by reason. In other words, the failure of the imagination to produce an image that can be used to form a concept of something, allows us to experience the sublime. Vision is thus central to sublimity: the problem of "too much to see" intensifies the inadequacy of vision—once understood as reason's most trustworthy sense—to secure a view of a knowable, material world.[13]

In modernity, the horror attributed to the feminine or to the racialized other (as instances of how in modernity nature has become an externalized, alien and alienated other) is like a hall of mirrors wherein the traditional subject finds itself in modernity to be without the characteristics that tradition had supplied: authority, originality, depth, etc. Overcoming this terror becomes less the work of the subject-qua-subject than it is the work of political technologies' modes of containment—which the subject practices in its self-governance, its governmentality. For the colonial imaginary, the projection of violence onto a presumed wilderness is then taken into the self and used as justification of acts of violence upon others.

In eighteenth- and nineteenth-century popular fiction, this "analytic of the sublime" is embodied (and Kant would say distorted) in the Gothic. The Gothic as a literary genre translates the transcendental or mastering discourse of Kant's sublime into tales of uncanny otherness that radically delimit vision. Vision in the Gothic tradition is tied to the body—to the pleasure and pain of the body's limits—and is, thus, made "impotent" from the point of view of reason. Perhaps the most well-known feature of Gothicism is the animation of the inanimate, the blurring of the knowable boundaries of life and death, human and non-human. Objects, often of the technological kind, like dolls or architectures, gain a kind of autonomy, come to life—a life that is more alive, more affective than that which the human lives. Olympia, the living doll from E.T.A. Hoffman's "The Sandman," is one of the more well-known figures of the Gothic sublime, due in part to the tale's analysis by Freud in his work on the uncanny and its later appropriation by Surrealism.[14] The other well-known tale, of course, is Horace Walpole's famous *Castle of Otranto* (1764)—the ur-text of Gothic conventions and themes of the unseen, haunting, sexual repression, and houses that are alive with violent thoughts. The tropes of living technologies, emotionalism, the undead, and so on, that comprise the Gothic perception or lens appear in popular culture from soap operas to horror.

Clearly, the psychosexual interpretation of Olympia takes us to the underside of the Enlightenment project, allowing us to see its architectures of violence beneath the *Heimlichkeit* (familiarity or homeliness) of the European family romance. Such tales have also been read as national allegories borne of modernity's revolutions: the women, masses, and technology threaten the rationalized architecture of the modern fraternal state. In the United States, however, colonial violence is explicitly written into the canon-forming texts of American literature either through the haunting that is the past of slavery or the production of literary nationalism through the deployment of indigenity. As Teresa Goddu notes, Charles Brockton Brown, in his preface to *Edgar Huntly* (1799), writes, "the field of investigation, opened to us by our own country, should differ essentially from those which exist in Europe. Puerile superstition and exploded manners; Gothic castles and chimeras might be the materials usually employed in this genre," Brown continues, but the "incidents of Indian hostility, and the perils of the western wilderness, are far more suitable" for an American Gothic.[15] Goddu goes on to argue that

> The gothicized Indian provided the nation with a distinctive literary asset as well as a politically useful cultural image. Though America did not have crumbling castles and antiquated traditions, it did have in the Indian a symbol of a ruined and conquered past.... The cultural discourse of savagism, which enabled the policies of civilization and removal, intersected with a literary discourse that took the Indian as the native material for a past specifically coded as gothic. This correlation achieved two corresponding goals: it doomed the Indian to inevitable distinction in the present and it created a unique antiquity that could be appropriated by an emerging American literature.[16]

Melodramatic versus Gothic Canada

The Gothic has an Anglo-Canadian manifestation in the "central" Canadian (Ontario, specifically) culture that is most widely known through the literature of Alice Munro, Robertson Davies (the Deptford Trilogy), and a James Reaney play about the Black Donnelly saga, *The Donnellys Must Die*. The most familiar director of Gothic Canadian cinema is David Cronenberg. There are others, however, such as the films that constitute Paul Almond's trilogy (*Isabel*, *The Act of the Heart*, and *Journey*). Almond is an Anglo-Canadian director; the trilogy is placed on the edge between protestant Anglo and Catholic Quebec cultures. Jim Leach's discussion of 1970s Anglo-Canadian cinema arguably situates films such as *Child under a Leaf* (George Bloomfield, 1974) and *Between Friends* (Don Shebib, 1973) within the Gothic: "Certainly many English Canadian films (especially) offer a vision not just of failure, but of life as a constant succession of failures, each one worse than the one before. There is often an overwhelming sense of a malevolent power against which the characters are helpless, a power which seems inevitably to create negative endings."[17] There is also, of course, the "garrison" discourse of the settler literature perpetuated by writers such as Margaret Atwood in her canonical texts *Survival* and *The Journals of Susanna Moodie*, which help to inscribe a civilization/wilderness paradigm upon the landscape of "Canadian Culture."[18]

This Ontario Gothic borrows heavily from the English traditions of sexual and familial violence that breeds a monstrosity within a private sphere generally typified as "a haven in a heartless world." While colonial history would have a bearing on the way we read one of these texts' (repressed) content, there is little evidence within the Gothic texts of Ontarian Canada of a reflection on colonialism as a foundation or precondition for the narrative of family and gender relations. What we do find is the link between technology, gender, and the violence of the family romance that informs the British tradition. A notable exception is the reflexive mix of the urban Gothic and noir conventions, used to address issues of race and racism in Clement Virgo's *Rude* (1995). In Quebec, the tradition of films featuring absent fathers makes for a specific variation on the Gothic's entanglement in melodramas of cultural marginalization and contestation. In the films of Anne Wheeler in Western Canada, the Gothic is employed in numerous films to respond to the preconditions of colonial as well as gendered violence.

The elements that distinguish the Western Canadian use of Gothic perception, seen in the films of Anne Wheeler, Norma Bailey, Mieko Ouchi, and Guy Maddin, and the writings of novelists Sinclair Ross, Sheila Watson, Margaret Laurence, and Maria Campbell, are elements that fall outside the "garrison" paradigm discussed earlier: (1) The land has history (which is often a mysterious or frightening invisible presence), and the trouble for the white settler or its surrogate is how to make a place out of the space preconditioned by national governance of land and peoples—a governance based on the racist presuppositions that Aboriginals are prehistoric and non-productive; (2) The relations between people of cultural difference are at the center of the narratives (that is, the family does not always function as allegory of the nation—or, if it does, as could be argued for Maddin's *Careful*, then it does so through highly performative and fabulist devices); (3) Related to the preceding condition, gender is often organized through extra-familiar, non-traditional or intercultural relations.

A discourse (political and cultural) of regionalism has developed since the 1960s to distinguish Western Canadian cultural articulations. The cultural statements of difference repeat very early settler descriptions, which themselves register an unmistakable connection to the Kantian sublime read through Walpole. Gerald Horne cites one such account, given by William Frances Butler in 1873:

> There is no mountain range to come up across the skyline, no river to lay its glistening folds along the middle distance, no dark forest to give shade to foreground or to bring perspective, no speck of life, no trace of man, nothing but the wilderness. Reduced thus to its own nakedness, space stands forth with almost terrible grandeur. One is suddenly brought face to face with that enigma we try to comprehend by giving to the names of endless, interminable, measureless; that dark inanity which broods upon a waste of moorland at dusk, and in which fancy sees the spectral and the shadowy.[19]

In itself there is nothing particularly regional about this discourse, except and importantly insofar as the experience of "its own nakedness" is produced through extermination of vast numbers of First Nations peoples and the subsequent containment of the survivors via the reservation system underway since the Royal Proclamation of 1763 and especially the post-Confederation treaty process, which began in 1871. The success of such policy and practice is evidenced by the complete occulting in the statements, such as those above, of the existence of Indigenous people. Here is a good example of the productivity of the process of governmentality. Regionalism appears much later (articulated by Henry Kriesel in 1968 and formulated below by Eli Mandel), in the specificities of the historical referent that made a place from space:

> the extraordinary sense of confinement by vast and seemingly unlimited space; the anxieties sharpened by this confinement; the definition of self by violation or conquest of land, a conquest which...involves much more violence than we have been yet able to admit, even in our literature; the price paid by the conqueror; the sense of being possessed by the land; the austere puritanism bred in that harsh world; and the melodramatic eruptions of passion because of such restraint; the theme of the imprisoned spirit.[20]

Here, the sublime blindness of Butler's statements are transformed by the recognition that the self is made out of the violence that cleared the land upon which that self makes its place. Not surprisingly, the inducement of selves to the new land used a language of home—melodrama.

Christopher Gittings's book *Canadian National Cinema* (2002) stakes his reading of national cinema in the melodramatic mode and analyzes a

very important historical foundation for this mode in the early representational economy of Western Canada:

> The CPR's Department of Colonization and Development encoded its mes-
> sage of white immigrant recruitment in a series of melodramas produced by
> the Edison Company to encourage American immigration to Western
> Canada. *An Unselfish Love* (1910), one of two extant melodramas from the
> CPR's Edison series of thirteen one-reel films, revolves around a male hetero-
> sexual desire for a woman that is twinned with male desire for the Canadian
> West.[21]

As both Peter Morris and Christopher Gittings uncover in the archive of
Canadian national cinema, the earliest moving images of Canada "produced in 1896 by American and European firms were 'interest' shots of
such physical features as Niagara Falls and the Rockies."[22] Such views
can be interpreted as part of the repertoire of the "safe sublime" for European and American audiences; but more importantly for the melodrama of
nation and its production of *Heimlichkeit* for potential immigrants, such
views were foundational for the development of the visual culture of
Canada as commodity. A series of the first films made in Canada and
toured in Britain, with CPR backing, presented positive immigration experiences for the white settler. As Gittings writes, "These films, which include
Harnessing the Virgin Prairie, constitute a gendered and colonizing narrative in which the territory of the Dominion of Canada is represented as a
fertile and passive terrain awaiting the cultivation or domination of the
male British settler."[23] Cinema, and the melodrama in particular, was a
foundational technology for the production of white multiculturalism. In
the rare instance when the First Nations people are depicted in these early
films, they are domesticated as part of a resource economy. In *Wonders of
Canada* (1906), for instance "through the technology of cinema, First
Nations are commodified, 'produced' for a domestic and international
market."[24]

Policies Past and Present

There is an early and important historical reality shaping the discourses of
the CPR films discussed above by Gittings and providing important regional
distinctions for (dis)appearance of First Nations people from the white
lens: the colonization and management of the land itself. The Royal Proclamation of 1763 and the post-Confederation treaty process initiated in
1871 establish two different processes of dispossession and two different
relations between colonized and colonizer. It has been argued that the

Royal Proclamation permitted the "cession or purchase" of Indian lands in Upper and Lower Canada for chiefly strategic reasons, whereas "the post-Confederation treaties were for economic development."[25] This is not to say that the British did not also have economic interests in the former territories; rather, the strategic interest was enacted "because it was important for Britain to reassert its formal adherence to the Doctrine of Discovery and to ensure that its claims to eastern North America would be respected by other European regimes."[26] The cessions and treaty processes of the western Indian nations in the post-Confederation period were entangled within a set of regional definitions of provincial authority. Regional development rather than strategic control thus drove the discourses and practices of the management of land, populations and economies. One significant technique used in this process was the "pass law."

During the period in which the early Canadian films were produced, the historical reality of the apartheid "pass law" essentially had cleared the land (now colonized by whites) from First Nations traffic. From the end of the 1885 North-West Rebellion until 1956, the majority of First Nations peoples on the prairie were not permitted to leave reservations without a "pass" provided to them by a local Indian Department official. In July 1885, Assistant Indian Commissioner Hayter Reed recommended fifteen measures for the "future management of Indians"—not just those implicated in the rebellion.[27] These were adopted by John A. Macdonald; they included hanging specific individuals, abolishing the existing tribal system, and ousting "rebel" chiefs and councillors, thus dealing with all who could be charged with crimes "in as severe a manner as the law will allow," and suspending annuity payments to rebel groups, with any further monies understood as a gift and not a right. The pass law had the effect of severely constricting the movement—and, thus, communication—of most First Nations people on the prairie. Even if the pass law was not in effect for a particular tribe, the Indian Act of 1876 had already provided the means by which to restrict movement and communication, and thus erase visibility and cultural presence, by, for instance, stating that Indians could not participate "in any show, exhibition, performance, stampede or pageant in aboriginal costume without the consent of the Superintendent General or his authorised agent."[28] The period 1876–1951, overlapping with the period of the pass law, is referred to by Gerald McMaster as "the Reservation Period," "with implications of imprisonment and the extinguishment of religious and cultural freedom."[29]

It is part of my argument that these materialities of colonial history, such as the pass law and treaty processes, are more than context and are not merely of the past: they are the latent content of the present which becomes available to representation and/or formal articulation due to particular triggers. The films of the 1970s through the 1990s on the prairies unfold this latent content in very particular ways. But why at that that time? What conditions brought this past into the visual culture of the present?

During the years between 1970 and 1990, one hundred years after the writing of the Indian Act of 1876, Canadian culture underwent a period of intense contestation in the spheres of native politics, feminist politics, and cultural politics more generally, with much public debate about artistic appropriation and systemic racism in cultural funding bodies, Japanese redress, backlash against feminism, and discourses of redemptive masculinity. Within this period, the particular struggles and strategies that constituted the politicized discourse about identity saw a full relationships: at once paralleled and overlapping, competing and in solidarity, the politics of the period produced a nuanced and complex field for the critical reception of the Canadian Multiculturalism Act, Bill C-93, passed in 1988. This reception took many forms, from direct debate and public invectives to policy analysis and scholarly publishing. Other responses, perhaps less direct but nonetheless eventful, animated the cultural sphere by highlighting issues of cultural citizenship, belonging, and exclusion that take form in racist societies. The international film and festival and symposium, In Visible Colours, that took place in Vancouver in 1989 emerged out of both the international "new cultural politics of difference" and the Canada-specific responses to racist practices in cultural institutions. Writing thru Race took place in 1994 and was met in the white press with a host of negative responses—from ridicule to charges of reverse racism to threats of defunding and disassociation.

Eva Mackey's *The House of Difference* considers the complex relationship between multiculturalist and nationalist discourses in Canadian policy and media in terms of the idealizations and ever-renewable forms of containment and control the state exercises over cultural difference and native identity:

> The New Multiculturalism Act, despite the shift to a concern with "race relations," and the transformation of dominant society, is still primarily a form of state intervention into the cultural politics of diversity. The intervention not only appropriates and institutionalises diversity for the project of nation-building in the manner of earlier multicultural policy, it now proposes that multiculturalism is a national resource in the context of global capitalism. It still limits multicultural diversity to symbolic rather than political forms, because in the political arena, members of ethnic groups are *individual* members of their groups or the larger society.... Although "multiculturalism" could be seen as vastly different from the more overtly racist and assimilationist policies of earlier governments, the institutionalisation of

difference and "tolerance" drew on previously existing patterns.... [T]he degree and form of *tolerable* differences are defined by the ever-changing needs of the project of nation-building.[30]

I quote Mackey at length because her comments succinctly reflect the analysis provided by many others. She also highlights the link between the bill and globalization (earlier she cites a 1987 policy document that clearly asserts links between "multicultural resources," free trade, and economic progress) and brings to the forefront a major point discussed by Smaro Kamboureli in her article, "The Technology of Ethnicity": Bill C-93, the Canadian Multiculturalism Act, legislates ethnicity, and as such addresses its constituents as individuals before the law. Kamboureli further notes that in the language of the act, ethnicity is mobilized as a narrative of nation: "Although a condition of difference that becomes an instrument of marginalisation in Canada, ethnicity is rendered by official multiculturalism as something residual to it.... Ethnicity loses its differential marker and becomes instead a condition of commonality: what all Canadians have in common is ethnic difference."[31] The address to everyone and to no one is common parlance in the operations of global capital. Brenda Longfellow writes about this in terms of new "international" co-productions of films such as *The Red Violin*, "Within the film itself, the proliferation of difference acts as a way of eliding any overarching parochial sense of national belonging. The enunciating location of the film is, precisely, nowhere, at least nowhere within the groundless and all enveloping textual folds of international style."[32]

A full discussion of the relationship between the global "anywhere" and the individual as "everyman" requires a different occasion. Within the terms of this article, however, it is elucidating to acknowledge this condition of liberal individualism on the free and borderless marketplace as a form of generic citizenship. The generic citizen is facilitated by cultural forms and, through the consumption of these forms, consents to techniques of power and engages in governmentality. The refusal of generic subjects and institutions in the films that emerge in the political cinemas of feminism or anti-racism or Quebec nationalism in the years between 1970 and 2000 can be read as directly engaging in a critique of governmentality and, thus, citizen production. However, as we will see in the following section, the narrative cinema of that same period engages in the problem of governmentality by disrupting the genre of melodrama (i.e., home-as-nation) with a Gothic perception of self-as-other and, thus, of home as strange, alien, and unwelcoming.

Gothic Prairie

Land as a contested territory and contact zone is a persistent trope in prairie cinema; and many of these films use the Gothic mode as a means by which to express the trouble over land and its history. Not surprisingly, the most direct and trenchant critique in filmic form of the colonial destruction of land and people was made from an explicitly Native point-of-view. *Crisis* and *Wipeout* are two films directed and produced by Film Frontiers in 1970 for the Metro Edmonton Educational Television Association. The films are interesting for their arresting politics of address and for the way in which the use of Gothic tropes dramatizes a didactic documentary on colonization and abuse of the land. These are not quintessential Canadian docu-dramas, nor is there any re-enactment footage, per se. Rather, dramatic techniques are inserted and woven through the live-action and archival footage. The films use an on-screen male subject as foil or character rather than as a historically identified real person; the music and sound effects are used to produce or convey emotional experiences (as opposed to being merely mimetic) by extending the verisimilitude of the physical or historical location through sound effects. Through such techniques, the social subjects depicted in the films and the subjects of the history narrated in voice-over are available to be on-screen surrogates for the viewer's engagement in the diegetic world of the film. The documentary tradition of an unaccented male narrator is also used in *Crisis*. The use of these generic markers initiate the viewing experience as one composed for the generic subject of white male culture. It is in the deployment of Gothic tropes that such an invitation turns into a contact zone, revealing the violence that subtends such generic citzenship.

Crisis begins with a voice-over of a Blackfoot myth about the creation of the world. This first section of the film is entitled "Land" and the image track provides beautiful long shots of plains and mountains. A dissolve then takes us to a historical genre painting of buffalo and deer. As this section of what appears to be a fairly straightforward expository documentary about a remote and mythic past comes to an end, the genre paintings of the prairie are dissolved into paintings of a buffalo hunt and the narration tells of a prophesy where the end of traditional ways was envisioned. The second section, "Imposter," opens with an image of a contemporary, young Aboriginal male—although the gender and ethnicity is somewhat and significantly ambiguous—wearing a university bomber jacket brandishing a "commerce" crest. He is looking straight ahead and standing in an undefined space. We see what he sees as our screen surrogate: a montage of archival images and shot footage depicting the destruction of the natural world and the appearance of the urban skyline. The disorienting and dislocating effect of an intensifying montage rhythm is redoubled with footage of a coyote: still, out-of-focus and very difficult to see, the texture and pacing of this shot effectively haunts the politics of the film with an image of inaccessible otherness. The film ends with a return to the image of the young man and a counter-shot of his view: a barren and stripped landscape. The Gothic tropes of a terrifyingly empty land and/or of Nature's immensity and violence and/or of the Indian as inhuman are inverted with the shift in surrogacy. Vision no longer provides a workable compass.

A similar combination of techniques is used in *Wipeout*, but here the narrator clearly speaks from a First Nations perspective, both in accent and in address. The narrator addresses the viewer as white ("when you slaughtered all the buffalo" or "you have learned little from your bloodstained history") and tropes on the white fear of Indian reprisal. The image-track opens with a shot of a man walking along a roadside toward the camera. His ethnicity is unclear. The soundtrack comprises eerie music and haunting sounds of an inhuman type; and the visual montage of animals and white hunters and walls of bones has as its counterpoint a soundtrack of gunfire and symphony. A fade to black at what we anticipate to be the end provides temporary relief from an increasingly horror-filled image/soundscape. After a ten-second pause, the screen fills with an image of a white man smiling and looking into the camera down the barrel of his rifle. The gender politics of this play on expectations works so as to situate the white male viewer (positioned as such by the address) in a position imagined for either the white woman—isolated and afraid—or the Indian subject. This feminization of the viewing position—a feature of melodramas and gothic horrors—effectively documents through a reversal the process by which the hegemonic subject displaces its fantasies of violence onto the other.

There is another equally important reading of the use of Gothic perception in these films: the expression of the land as a place haunted by a past that has no present in which to be representable. This sense of a temporal dislocation—an invisible latency—is available in other films that attempt to deal with the history of nation-building. This play on and with the imagined viewer as white and afraid and isolated, as well as the theme of the land as haunted by history, can be found throughout the films of Anne Wheeler.

As I have written elsewhere, Anne Wheeler's films from 1975 to 1986, from *Great Grandmother* to *Loyalties*, are motivated by feminism, undoubtedly of a liberal sort but informed—more than is the case for most white women working in this period—by a race politics of a particularly prairie form: Cowboys and Indians. Along with feminism, issues of colonialism (with its poverty and violence) as opposed to multiculturalism, and, thus, regionalism as opposed to nationalism, inform and motivate the stories that are told and the form in which they are presented.[33]

Wheeler's films disclose a deep commitment to their locations. That interest works either to reveal an almost structuring absence, as with *Bye Bye Blues*'s complete non-representation of First Nations, or to play upon the colonial tropes, as in *Loyalties*. As discussed above, the settler imaginary, which structures the wilderness against civilization and is evident in so much "Canadian" visual culture, is not the dominant trope in prairie visual culture. The paintings and drawings from the nineteeth and early twentieth centuries show the prairie to be peopled—or, more accurately, worked. Of course there are plenty of "wide-open spaces," but the images often contain bales of hay or tilled fields or cows.[34] In both *Bye Bye Blues* and *Loyalties*, the relationship between the symbolic value of the landscape and the point of view accorded the camera is extremely important. In both films, the white female character "arrives" from elsewhere (India in the former and England in the latter), and it is her point of view through a window that shapes our introduction to the location and its unfolding narrative. *Loyalties*' Lily Sutton arrives in Lac La Biche by air, giving us a location of unpeopled wilderness. As with films such as *Crisis* and *Wipeout*, this view is revealed to be a fantasy or projection, with the window functioning as frame and mirror. This view of landscape, formed as it is by the "dreamwork of imperialism,"[35] becomes one term in a dialectical interracial relationship between by Lily and Roseanne, the Native woman whose daughter is raped toward the end of the film by David Sutton, Lily's husband. The colonial stereotypes of Natives of/and/in nature are critiqued through a subtle series of reversals that structure the film—and include recognitions of class difference—as well as through pointed statements, such as the one made by Beatrice, Roseanne's mother. Referring to a beautiful, pristine lakeshore, Beatrice tells David that her people had lived there "until white people wanted to live here and they called us squatters." As the film's point of view moves between Lily and Roseanne, where Roseanne becomes the *primary* source of identification[36]—the "implicit feminist spectator, the film's moral and political centre"[37]—the primary location for their relationship shifts from the Sutton house to Beatrice's home on the reservation. The specificity of the relationship between land and identity is thus founded not on the transcendental sublime or pastoral imaginary but on the history of politics, power, and loss.

Containment is part of the colonial imaginary, and how Wheeler treats it, as well as the landscape upon which that imaginary projects itself, can be seen through an analysis of a key shot in her 1976 film, *Augusta*. This NFB documentary is about a Native woman who, in her eighty-eighth year, remembers "the gold rush, the cattle ranchers, Indian trails, river-steamers, stage coaches." The voice-over that opens the film belongs to the announcer for "Radio Caribou," which broadcasts messages to people in the 100 Mile House and Williams Lake area: "To Augusta Evans at Deep Creek, I'll meet you at the bus stop tomorrow morning and we can go into town and do some shopping, and that's from Edna Blankenship." As the image-track shows us Augusta preparing to leave her small house for the bus, the film's narrator, who turns out to be Edna Blankenship, a Native woman who has known Augusta for many years, tells us that Augusta lives at Deep Creek, fifteen miles north of Williams Lake, lives alone in a little cabin without electricity or running water; Augusta lost her status as a Shuswap Indian in 1903 when she married George Evans, a taxpayer.

The film carefully negotiates the ethical terrain of ethnographic filmmaking, with the image-track attentive to Augusta's physical movements and space, responding to her gestures and words by changing the shot range. And, still radical for an NFB documentary at that time, an eighty-eight-year-old Indian woman provides her own voice-over. There is one especially remarkable piece of footage: Augusta has gone to the Soda Creek Reserve for Sunday mass. We learn that she was born there and her grandfather was the chief. We are told that when she was four, she was taken to St. Joseph's Mission School, where she was forced to live for nine years without her family, culture, or language. Augusta then begins singing a bible hymn. The image-track shows an extreme long shot of largely uninhabited landscape; this view from today dissolves into an archival photograph of the mission school. With this simple technique, Wheeler twists the conventions of landscape imagery—showing an inhabited past and an empty present. This one seemingly simple convergence of two different times in the same visual space before us calls upon an ethical spectatorship perhaps more urgently than does Augusta herself: the right to amnesia is the right of the victor of history. In this simple dissolve, the landscape is remembered by the film as a space of loss.

Loyalties and *Change of Heart*, made two years earlier in 1984, are both feminist melodramas centred in the domestic sphere, and both understand that sphere to be the repository of public, political values, systems, and processes; both also employ the Gothic as a means by which to distort the home. Even while the screen time prioritizes the physical spaces of "hearth and home," those spaces are a net of signs that permit us and the female characters the ability to analyze the public sphere and its institutions. I will focus on *Loyalties* here, with reference to two other films that employ the Gothic. The early Wheeler films offer the critic a rich "Gothic" archive for an "auteurist" study: the dramatic tensions in *To Set Our House in Order*, *One's a Heifer*, *Change of Heart*, and, of course, *Loyalties*, are articulated by troping on Gothic themes of female paranoia, obscured vision, attributions of life to inanimate objects, the domestic space as terrifyingly unsafe, the undead, and, of course, the secret. As Longfellow has written about *Loyalties*,

> It appropriates melodramatic, generic conventions to feminist critique but its textual predecessors are less likely to be found among romantic melodramas than among the darker Gothic romances of *Jane Eyre* or *Rebecca*. Founded on the suspicion that the thin veneer of civility in bourgeois marriage masks a deeply malevolent brutality against women, the Gothic is preoccupied with the struggle to name the source of domestic horror. Structured by an enduring tension between the said and the unsaid, between the appearance of domestic harmony and its dark foreboding underside, the Gothic textually embodies the terror women experience as targets in a patriarchal society.[38]

While women's relationships and subjectivities form the main content of these films, the Gothic devices destabilize normative gender roles and heteronormative relations in *One's a Heifer* by presenting an encounter between a fatherless pubescent boy and an older, psychologically distressed man. The malevolence that seems to haunt the man and his house, complete with howling wind and stuffed owls and intimations of a dead woman buried somewhere on the farm, never completely vanishes, but neither does it yield anything dangerous. In fact, the boy is cared for by the old bachelor, and the momentary and fragile affection between them gives representation to a non-normative homosociality.[39] The Gothic trope is also at work in the short drama *To Set Our House in Order*, but the agent of oppression is the grandmother of our young heroine. The house is unbearably clean, lifeless, and tense with secrecy. As in the best eighteenth-century novels of the "popular sublime," the house speaks, the stairwells seem shared by ghosts, and life and death live side by side. Again, the film ends with the secret being revealed and the order of things restored; but the young girl will be forever changed by the revelation and the events leading up to it. As these two examples also show, surrogates for colonial patriarchy are not exclusively male nor are redemptive relations the sole property of women.

Wheeler's films of this period play with the Gothicism of gender and race, relaying to the viewer a history of place through the disruption of generic codes. The haunting of present by an unspeakable past can be understood as a latency of forms: a contact zone where the asymmetrical relation of domination and subordination play themselves out across the text. Reading films such as Wheeler's as texts that formally embed the history of colonial and gendered violence into an otherwise generic presentation of national/familial belonging permits images of land and identity to appear as contested territories.

At the outset of this article, I presented melodrama and the Gothic as two foundational modes of Canadian culture. They are inseparable, yet they emerge as distinct idioms in the history of modernity: one a history of visibilities, the other a history of invisibilities; one yielding tales of home and belonging and multicultural futures, the other distressing viewers with its terrors and suffering, and its horizons of racial violence. Where melodrama can be understood as productive of and for the representation of identity through the affective tension between avowal and disavowal, which yields an emotional investment in the narrative, the Gothic arises from a structuring absence that can never but disrupt the presentation of self/nation. This disaffection of the text can be understood within colonial contexts as an historical trauma, as the dream world of national myth disturbed by the nightmare of history (as Goddu paraphrases Marx), and as an invisible latency without presentability, which haunts the house of the national consciousness. Hence, the Gothic can function as a mode of perception that opens the self of nationhood to its own otherness and, thereby, to the losses upon which it is founded. While few directors of Canadian cinema take this upon themselves as a means by which to inquire into the national imaginary, the regional politics of the Prairies appears to have opened a space for such work.

Notes

1 These fragments are part of the oral history of my mother's family, as told to me by relatives.

2 This question was articulated in personal correspondence with Tom Gunning.

3 Ryszard Bugajski, *Clearcut* (Canada, 1991); Robert Morin, *Windigo* (Canada, 1994); Alanis Obomsawin, *Kanehsatake: 270 Years of Resistance* (Canada, 1993); and Nettie Wild, *Blockade* (Canada, 1993).

4 Mary Louise Pratt, *Imperial Eyes: Travel Writing and Transculturation* (New York and London: Routledge, 1992), 6–7.

5 Pratt, 7.

6 Foucault defines "governmentality" as the question of how government acts to govern the action of others, since he is said to have defined "government" as the "'conduct of conduct.'" Michel Foucault, "Governmentality" *The Foucault Effect: Studies in Governmentality*, ed. Graham Burchill, Colin Gordon, and Peter Miller (Chicago: University of Chicago Press, 1991), 2. See also Mitchell Dean, *Governmentality: Power and Rule in Modern Society* (London: Sage), 1999.

7 The phrase "whiting out" comes from Christopher Gittings, *Canadian National Cinema* (New York and London: Routledge, 2002), 198.

8 Teresa Goddu, *Gothic America: Narrative, History, and Nation* (New York: Columbia University Press, 1997), 10.

9 In Canadian cinema studies, Christopher Gittings, Brenda Longfellow, and Jean Bruce use the melodramatic lens as a means by which to critique the representation of nation in film and in film criticism. Gittings, *Canadian National Cinema*, 12–32; Brenda Longfellow, "Gender, Landscape and Colonial Allegories" *The Far Shore, Loyalties* and *Mouvements du désir*," *Gendering the Nation: Canadian Women's Cinema*, ed. Kay Armatage

et al. (Toronto: University of Toronto Press, 1999), 165–82. Other references for discussions of nation and melodrama include Julianne Burton-Carvajal, "Mexican Melodramas of Patriarchy: Specificity of a Transcultural Form," in *Framing Latin American Cinema: Contemporary Critical Perspectives*, ed. Ann Marie Stock (Minneapolis: University of Minnesota Press, 1997), 186–234; Christine Geraghty, *Women and Soap Opera* (Cambridge: Polity Press, 1991); Susan Hayward, "Framing National Cinemas," *Cinema and Nation*, ed. Mette Hjort and Scott Mackenzie (London and New York: Routledge, 2000), 88–102; Marcia Landy, *Fascism in Film: The Italian Commercial Cinema, 1930–1943* (Princeton, NJ: Princeton University Press, 1991); and Ana M. López, "Celluloid Tears: Melodrama in the 'Old' Mexican Cinema," *Iris* 13 (1991): 29–51. Feminist film theorists (particularly but not exclusively) have favoured the genre of melodrama, especially the sub-genre of "the woman's film," because the anti-realist excesses and overt ideological contradictions that strain the text are, some argue, an effect of a female point-of-view and address. More generally, the genre is gendered "feminine" due to its inversion of dominant, patriarchal forms and modes. Thomas Elsaesser, for instance, outlines a set of "feminine" terms to designate the genre against patriarchal narratives: emotionalism and internalization of violence; the social and political issues are played out in and through private contexts and family romances; the privileging of the victim's, as opposed to the victor's, point-of-view; and claustral settings and circular narratives as opposed to the domination of space (landscapes, cities, etc.) through a linear narrative structure and its attendant closure. Volumes have been written about melodrama and its sub-genres, maternal melodrama and the "woman's film." See the "debate" between Linda Williams, E. Ann Kaplan, et al. in E. Ann Kaplan, "The Case of the Missing Mother," *Heresies* 16 (1983): 81–85; and Linda Williams's "Something Else Besides a Mother," *Cinema Journal* 24.1 (Fall 1984): 2–27; *Cinema Journal* published several responses in issues 24.2, 25.1, 25.4. Also see Robert Lang, *American Film Melodrama: Griffith, Vidor, Minnelli* (Princeton: Princeton University Press, 1989); Christine Gledhill, ed., *Home Is Where the Heart Is*, Thomas Elsaesser, "Tales of Sound and Fury"; Nowell-Smith, "Minnelli and Melodrama"; Laura Mulvey, "Notes on Sirk and Melodrama"; Christine Gledhill, "The Melodramatic Field"; and Annette Kuhn, "Women's Genres: Melodrama, Soap Opera and Theory."

10 Judith Halberstam, *Skin Shows: Gothic Horror and the Technology of Monsters* (Durham: Duke University Press, 1995), 20. Other recent literature on the Gothic includes Louis Gross, *Redefining the American Gothic: From Wieland to Day of the Dead* (Ann Arbor and London: UMI Research Press, 1989); Mark Edmundson, *Nightmare on Main Street: Angels, Sadomasochism and the Culture of the Gothic* (Cambridge and London: Harvard University Press, 1997); Michelle Massé, *In the Name of Love: Women, Masochism, and the Gothic* (Ithaca: Cornell University Press, 1992); and Toni Morrison, *Playing in the Dark: Whiteness and the Literary Imagination* (Cambridge: Harvard University Press, 1992).

11 Meaghan Morris's "White Panic or, *Mad Max* and the Sublime," *Senses of Cinema* 18 (January–February 2002) <http://www.sensesofcinema.com/contents/01/18/mad_max.html>.

12 This phrase comes from my dissertation, wherein I explore the idea of the sublime experience as that which is about falling into time and about being badly timed to the chronometry of modernity. Susan Lord, "Sublime Machines: Time, Technology and the Female Body of Ocular Modernity," Diss., York University, 1999.

13 The connections between vision, technology, modern subjectivity, and the sublime require some elaboration. The terror of being overwhelmed by this fall into history is externalized in the spatial and temporal containments of the other. The other of the same—the

other that is produced by the logic of the same and thus denies a specificity to others (to other beings or to other cultural practices that are oriented toward difference) is inscribed as pathological and unproductive, as inadequate, as sterile and hollow. The positivity of adequation is constitutive of identity. The inadequacy of the non-identical is not merely trivialized (though this most certainly is the case), it is also rendered as a destablizing entity. It is not simply the case that all beings are not exchangable (capital has forced this system of exchange, which is a total system); but, in order for the adequation which is identity to be posited, it must be able to see itself thus, to recognize itself against others. (This is done in a number of ways: fetishism, in particular.) The self-identical subject must, then, recognize—re-cognize—itself in and through the gaze. The apparatus of subject formation involves a set of technicities whereby the subject sees itself as commanding its own performance. The self-directed, auto-telic individual, then, is precisely that subject whose performance is most adequate to the machine. But, as Freud attests, this adequation is unliveable. For Freud, the appearance of the uncanny (*das unheimlich*) is the ultimate scene of the inadequate. The sublime, thus, emerges as a correlative to the technological.

14 In Freud's reading of "The Sandman," the beautiful yet horrifying clockwork doll, Olympia, whose eyes were made by the optician Coppola (whose true identity is the lawyer Coppelius, the sandman, the man responsible for the death of Nathaniel's father) is only a type of, or a false, uncanny. It is clear that potential for discovering the strange (*unheimlich*) beneath the familiar (*heimlich*, home) female beauty is the reason for Nathaniel's fascination. The stillness beneath her motion, a timeless, ageless, and mechanical aspect, draws his gaze, produces his desire, and eventually brings him to a point of madness. In this gruesome scene, Olympia's co-creators (her father and Coppola) rip her apart in a battle over her origin, pull out her eyes, and fling the bloody orbs at Nathaniel. While this is certainly an instance of the uncanny, Freud reads Olympia as a front for the truly horrifying *unheimlich* of the scene of castration—a timeloop, which returns Nathaniel to the father's death. He interprets Olympia, relegated to a footnote, as "a dissociated complex of Nathaniel's which confronts him as a person." Sigmund Freud, "The 'Uncanny,'" trans. James Strachey, *Art and Literature*, Vol. 14, ed. Albert Dickson (Harmondsworth: Penguin, 1985), 335–76.

15 Goddu, 4.

16 Goddu, 55.

17 James Leach, "Second Images: Reflections on the Canadian Cinema(s) in the Seventies," *Take Two: A Tribute to Film in Canada*, ed. Seth Feldman (Toronto: Irwin, 1984), 107.

18 See Margaret Atwood, *The Journals of Susanna Moodie: Poems*, (Toronto: Oxford University Press, 1970) and *Survival: A Thematic Guide to Canadian Literature* (Toronto: Anansi, 1972).

19 Quoted in Gerald S. Horne, "Interpreting Prairie Cinema," *Prairie Forum: The Journal of Canadian Plains Research Centre* 22 (1997): 136.

20 Eli Mandel, quoted in Horne, 10.

21 Gittings, 13.

22 Gittings, 8; Morris, 12.

23 Gittings, 8.

24 Gittings, 9.

25 Juan Lindau and Curtis Cook. "One Continent, Contrasting Styles: The Canadian Experience in North American Perspective." *Aboriginal Rights and Self-Government: The Canadian and Mexican Experience in North American Perspective*, ed. Curtis Cook and Juan Lindau (Montreal and Kingston: McGill-Queen's University Press, 2000), 9.

26 Bonita Lawrence. "Rewriting Histories of the Land: Colonization and Indigenous Resistance in Eastern Canada," *Race, Space and the Law: Unmapping a White Settler Society*, ed. Sherene Razack (Toronto: Between the Lines, 2002), 37.

27 Blair Stonechild and Bill Waiser, *Loyal Until Death: Indians and the North-West Rebellion* (Calgary, Alberta: Fifth House, 1997), 215. As is well known, and well-documented in Stonechild/Waiser, the numbers of tribes and chiefs involved in the rebellion was hugely exaggerated by the state.

28 Quoted in Gerald McMaster, "Tenuous Lines of Descent: Indian Arts and Crafts of the Reservation Period," *Canadian Journal of Native Studies* 9.2 (1989): 213.

29 McMaster, 206.

30 Eva Mackey, *The House of Difference* (London: Routledge, 1999), 69–70.

31 Smaro Kamboureli, "The Technology of Ethnicity: Canadian Multiculturalism and the Language of Law," *Multicultural States: Rethinking Difference and Identity*, ed. David Bennett (New York and London: Routledge, 1989), 215.

32 Brenda Longfellow, "*The Red Violin*, Commodity Fetishism an Globalization," *Canadian Journal of Film Studies* 10 (2001): 6–20.

33 Susan Lord, "States of Emergency in the Films of Anne Wheeler," *North of Everything: English Canadian Cinema Since 1980*, ed. William Beard and Jerry White (Edmonton: University of Alberta Press, 2002), 312–26.

34 For a fascinating visual history of the prairies, see Rosemary Donegan, *Work, Weather, and the Grid: Agriculture in Saskatchewan, Exhibition Catalogue* (Regina: Dunlop Art Gallery, 1991).

35 W.J.T. Mitchell, ed., "Introduction," *Landscape and Power* (Chicago: University of Chicago Press, 1994), 10.

36 Robin Wood, "Towards a Canadian (Inter)national Cinema: Part 2: *Loyalties* and Life Classes," *CineAction!* 17 (September 1989): 23–35.

37 Brenda Longfellow, "Gender, Landscape and Colonial Allegories," 175.

38 Brenda Longfellow, "Gender, Landscape, and Colonial Allegories," 172–73.

39 For more on the non-normative relationships in Anne Wheeler and Canadian cinema in general, see Thomas Waugh, "Cinemas, Nations, Masculinities (The Martin Walsh Memorial Lecture, 1988)," *Canadian Journal of Film Studies* 8.1 (1999): 8–44.

21 Through a Canadian Lens
Discourses of Nationalism and Aboriginal Representation in Governmental Photographs

Carol Payne

> Like the state, the camera is never neutral... it arrives on the scene vested with a particular authority, authority to arrest, picture and transform daily life.... This is not the power of the camera but the power of the apparatuses of the local state which deploy it and guarantee the authority of the images it constructs to stand as evidence or register a truth.
>
> —*John Tagg*[1]

DURING ONE OF HIS TERMS AS PRIME MINISTER, Sir John A. Macdonald sat for a series of unattributed and undated portraits. Among them was a full view of the prime minister leaning on a table covered by books (fig. 1). The contrast between this image and photographic portraiture of today is striking. While we might expect a semblance of intimacy and naturalness (whether real or feigned) in our own snapshots, Macdonald's portrait seems formal and rigid. He gazes off into the distance, left hand raised in a stylized gesture familiar to orators of the time. There is a tangible sense of the first prime minister's awkwardness or even discomfort before the lens. Indeed, Macdonald probably was uncomfortable. Although photographers had been active in Canada as early as 1840, photography remained a novelty for most, and technical limitations of the time made the very business of being photographed disquieting.[2] Still, I would argue that for late-nineteenth-century viewers, this early portrait effectively imbued Macdonald with a sense of dignity appropriate to his office while presenting him as an embodiment of the dominion's very aspirations.

How does a seemingly simple image like this one confer a sense of national identity? This essay will address that question by examining,

This article has been informed by conversations about Canadian photographic representations with Jeff Thomas and Robert Evans. I also gratefully acknowledge insightful feedback from the following graduate students: Jennifer Blunt, Claudette Lauzon, Jaclyn Meloche, and Sandra Fransen.

FIGURE 1 Photographer unknown, *Sir John A. Macdonald*, c1867-1891 (courtesy of Library and Archives Canada).

through three brief case studies, how photographs commissioned by the government (and those co-opted for governmental use) have historically contributed to official constructions of Canadian identity. Throughout the country's history, still photographs have been deployed to buttress governmental authority. They helped justify Aboriginal acculturation, promote northern and western settlement, establish borders, serve military efforts, advertise Canadian industry, and provide visual endorsements for numerous other bureaucratic initiatives. In short, the Canadian government's use of photography has been varied, extensive, and influential. While a full survey is beyond the scope of this article, I will focus in each case study on one recurrent and acute example of how still photographs support national hegemony with regards to representations of First Peoples. These will be discussed in the context of the rendering of the dominant culture, as in the portrait of Macdonald. Although this essay chiefly scrutinizes the "official picture," I also acknowledge that dominant discourses are not intractable; they *can* be resisted. To present a governmentally sanctioned and, at times, suppressive view without its alternative would be tantamount to an endorsement of it. Accordingly, this article will also introduce how First Nations peoples, in particular, have resisted dominant visual models of Canadian identity in recent scholarship and art.

Until relatively recently, photographs have typically been presented as neutral and authoritative historical evidence; valued for their "transparency," they have often been invoked to "illustrate" or lend credibility to a number of historical and political positions. In contrast, this essay introduces photography as a "social practice," one which, rather than being detached from social narratives, participates in the naturalization of or resistance to discourse. Accordingly, another aim of this essay is to introduce the reader to the distinctive character of the analog photograph (the non-digital image) and of photographic meaning. Finally, in addition to exploring the specific histories narrated here, this essay offers the reader bibliographical sources for further study.[3]

Any photograph—whether a portrait of John A. Macdonald or a Polaroid snapshot of a friend—is historically inscribed; in effect, the medium is not a neutral device but encompasses the biases and concerns of the culture and times in which it was developed and viewed. The invention of analog photography, which is typically dated to about 1839 in Western Europe, reflected the cultural environment from which it emerged. Nineteenth-century European perceptions of photography still form the foundation for our thinking about the medium today. Western Europeans at that time— living in the cradle of the industrial revolution—invested tremendous authority in mechanical instruments. The camera—like the steam engine, the sewing machine, and the typewriter—was one of the most influential mechanical inventions of the time and, therefore, it crystallized both the authority of science and the cachet of the modern. To photograph a scene was to confer it with (or judge it against) the values of modern progress and power. In addition, the nineteenth century—like our own times—privileged visuality over other sensory experiences. As an implement that provided seemingly consummate visual detail, the camera responded to those biases and seemed to complement one of the key philosophical tenets of nineteenth-century Europe: positivism. With its stress on empirical observation and tangible evidence as the bases of all that was knowable, positivist philosophy, particularly in the writings of Auguste Comte from the 1820s through the 1840s, proposed that knowledge of the "actual laws of phenomena" alone could be achieved through reason and observation.[4] Photography, it seemed to many nineteenth-century viewers, was an ideal device for merging the rational and the visible. It achieved phenomenal popularity almost immediately.

At the same time, however, nineteenth-century viewers saw the photograph as a distinctive form of visual representation, a new type of realism that surpassed human optics. Not only did it provide heightened visual detail, but also—by merit of being mechanically produced—its images were typically thought to be *unmediated* by human intervention. The language used to describe photography in the nineteenth century reflects this belief in the photograph as an authoritative and neutral form of representation; it was termed variously an "exact facsimile [of nature]," the "mirror with a memory," and the "pencil of nature."[5]

Semiotics—particularly the approach developed by Charles Peirce— offers us one of the most compelling ways of accounting for photography's particular type of realism. Peirce suggests three classifications of signs: symbols (signs—such as language—developed by cultural convention with no natural relationship to their referents), icons (signs—including representational drawings—that *resemble* their referents) and, lastly, indices (signs— including footprints, shadows, and the act of pointing—that maintain a physical relationship to their referents).[6] According to this model—as interpreted by scholars of photography—a photograph is both an icon and an index.[7] The portrait of John A. Macdonald noted above, for example, is an icon in that it resembles its referent—in it we can recognize the physical appearance of the country's first prime minister; yet, for many people, this image also surpasses the mimetic by offering a seemingly direct physical connection to this historic figure, that is, an *index*. In effect, the portrait captures an historic moment when Macdonald stood in front of a camera. By looking at the photograph, we feel, in turn, transported back to that time and place, in the prime minister's presence.[8] It is for this reason that, when faced with a photograph, people often seem to forget that they are looking at a representation. This is particularly true of portraiture. Rarely, for example, would we expect someone to say, "That is how a photographer—within the limits of technology and following conventions of the time—depicted John A. Macdonald." Instead, without a second thought most of us would simply pronounce, "That *is* John A. Macdonald." The slippage in language here is telling. It reveals how pervasive the analog photograph's *indexical* character is, a character that distinguishes it from other forms of visual representation and that is at the root of photographic authority. In short, unlike a drawing or a written account, a photograph is often experienced, in the words of Roland Barthes, as a direct "emanation of its referent."[9]

Despite claims of a privileged relationship to the "real," however, photography is by no means a neutral and objective trace of the world.[10] Instead, it *mediates* the visible through subjective selection of subject matter, vantage point, and framing; alterations in depth, colour and tone; the extraction of one fraction of time from a temporal continuum; the exclusion of other sensory information and, usually, binocular vision; and recontextualization through placement, accompanying language, and reception. Moreover, it translates the effects of light on silver into the form of a two-dimensional representation employing the conventions of western Renaissance perspective.

The portrait of John A. Macdonald, for example, conveys coded meaning through props and pose. Books and other accoutrements of scholarship, which appear prominently in the image, were favoured in most nineteenth-century commercial photographers' studios; they were intended to signify the sitter's learnedness.[11] Beyond this unambiguous symbolism, the image is also encoded more subtly through technical devices. The full-length view from a low vantage point, a convention of portraiture, accentuates the subject's height, thereby conferring a sense of respect and reverence. Lighting and the prime minister's preoccupied gaze enhance those implied qualities. But the image, which was intended for public circulation, also reflects the then-emergent cult of celebrity. Middle-class audiences in the nineteenth century enthusiastically collected photographs—often in carte-de-visite or other standard formats—of performers, royalty, and, notably, politicians.[12] In the public imagination, the familiar visage of the statesman functioned as synecdoche—that is, he appeared not only as a unique individual but stood for the whole of the nation. Images like this one probably rested like faithful old friends in albums next to those of family members, fostering a sense of personal identification with and commitment to the politician and the Dominion he represented. This seemingly straightforward and utilitarian depiction is coded in a variety of ways; viewers of the time likely perceived Macdonald as a respectful, learned, and yet amiably familiar leader as well as the very embodiment of Canada.

Yet throughout most of its history, photography, as Jonathan Crary has argued, "masquerade[s] as a transparent and incorporeal intermediary between observer and world."[13] In short, photographs have been experienced as unimpeachable facts. It is precisely for this reason—because they are at once mediated or malleable carriers of meaning, and yet they almost imperceptibly disguise subjectivity as fact—that photography has become a powerful tool of persuasion, a means of encoding ideology.

Photography not only reflected the nineteenth-century predilection for mechanical innovation and Positivist philosophy but also functioned as a handmaid to contemporary Europe's most pervasive cultural program: imperialism. Under the guise of scientific discourse, photographs have been employed variously to map territories, justify invasion, promote colonial settlement, and subjugate Aboriginal peoples throughout the world.[14] As a settler colony, Canada, too, enacted colonial possession in part through photographic representations. Imperialist tendencies in Canadian photography can perhaps be seen nowhere more clearly than in the myriad images produced for the British North American and Canadian governments during the nineteenth century to facilitate northern and western expansion. In Canada, these images contributed to what Edward Said has termed an "imaginative geography"—as it applies to the construction of nationhood.[15] During the nineteenth century, photography was employed by a number of government-sponsored agencies and programs to document new territories not previously settled by non-Aboriginal peoples.[16] These included expeditions undertaken by the Royal Corps of Engineers, the Canadian Pacific Railway, and the Geological Survey of Canada.[17]

The use of photography by the Royal Corps of Engineers for the North American Boundary Commission provides an instructive example of how photography contributed to an imperialist project in nineteenth-century Canada.[18] As early as 1858, the corps began marking the British side of the forty-ninth parallel between British Columbia and the United States.[19] By 1872, following the American Civil War and after a renewed debate between the Canadian and U.S. governments, a Joint Boundary Commission was established. Work was then resumed identifying and marking the forty-ninth parallel between the Rockies and the Lake-of-the-Woods. At this point, the camera would become, as Andrew Birrell reports, "an integral part of military intelligence, research and operations."[20] Four photographers were included among the forty-four sappers on the team. Their equipment included a portable darkroom tent, two 12 x 12-inch cameras with rapid rectilinear and wide-angle lenses and two 7-1/2 x 5-inch cameras with stereographic and rapid rectilinear lenses, as well as glass plates and chemicals.[21]

Despite the arduousness of nineteenth-century field photography,[22] by the time the Royal Corps of Engineers ceased work in 1874, after just three seasons in the field, they had produced fully 250 negatives.[23] Photographic prints accompanied the commission's official report and were offered to the Colonial Office, the Foreign Office, the Canadian Department of the Interior, Governor General Lord Dufferin, and members of the expedition as souvenirs. Engravings from individual photographs were also reproduced in non-governmental publications. The images depict landscapes, corps members at work, their encampments, boundary mounds, depots, geological features, and various Aboriginal peoples encountered along the way, among other subjects. While, as Andrew Birrell suggests, the emphasis was on providing legible scientific information, a closer inspection reveals how this work buttressed the colonial project as a whole.

The Boundary Commission frequently used photography as an addendum to the act of mapping, a crucial undertaking in colonization and the construction of nationhood. Photographic images ostensibly documented the forty-ninth parallel and provided information about the surroundings and occupying peoples, information that supplemented cartographic records. Maps, of course, not only offer a symbolic rendering of space; like photographs, they also imprint geographical territory with political meaning. This is often imperceptible, partly because cartography, too, is commonly experienced as an indexical sign and a neutral science.[24] Therefore, within the context of nineteenth-century North America, maps—as used largely by European visitors and settlers—naturalized a Western European hegemony.[25] As Alan Trachtenberg has noted, a crucial component of mapping is the act of naming.[26] Naming, particularly in its ability to recast geographic locales in the linguistic shades of the colonizer, in effect performs appropriation. Photographs, in turn, perhaps because of the authority of their presumed indexical character, became integral to mapping. They buttressed the claim of ownership by, as Trachtenberg argues, attaching "a possessable image to a place name."[27] In short, mapping, naming, and photographing enact a sense of cultural and political ownership—through symbolic, linguistic, and scopic means. At the same time, they also give form to a corollary effect: erasure. For in assessing geography by European measurements, language, technology, and perspectival systems, they also negate Aboriginal culture.[28] This is compounded by the fact that for most Aboriginal peoples of the time, the very notion of possessing land not only constituted trespass but was, within their cultures, an utterly alien—even antithetical—concept.

While much of the Boundary Commission's work enacted colonial possession and Aboriginal erasure, photographic representations of First Peoples were not entirely absent from their archives. Indeed, as noted above, commission photographers also depicted members of various First Peoples living across the Prairies; but rather than asserting their presence, the images offer their subjects as the presumed European viewer's other. For example, one particularly notable and haunting image taken by a member of the Royal Corps of Engineers in 1873 depicts three unnamed Chippewas

FIGURE 2 Royal Corps of Engineers, *Untitled*, 1873 (courtesy of Library and Archives Canada).

at a grave site (fig. 2). Wrapped in blankets with their heads bowed, most viewers would assume them to be in mourning.[29] It is, however, hard not to confer the image with broader significance. It reproduces pictorially the trope of the "vanishing race"—that is to say, it functions as an emblem of Aboriginal annihilation while simultaneously implying colonial ascendency.

We might expect that First Peoples themselves would utterly shun such images, but, surprisingly, increasing numbers of Aboriginal scholars, artists, and communities are revisiting photographic representations like these, finding in them a site within which to reclaim the Native subject. One of the most engaging interventions into Euro-Canadian imaging of the First Peoples of the Prairies is found in the work of the Plains Cree artist George Littlechild.[30]

In his art practice, Littlechild explores questions of identity formation (often with direct autobiographical references) in part through the recontextualization of historic photographs. Littlechild was a member of the generation known colloquially as the "Sixties Scoop"—a group described by curator Ryan Rice as the thousands of Aboriginal children who, during the 1960s, were seized from their birth communities to be raised by non-Aboriginal foster families.[31] The artist was able to reconstruct his family tree by combing various archives and locating hundreds of photographs and textual records pertaining to his birth family. These documents were originally produced under the auspices of several anthropological, governmental, or religious organizations, who typically presented their subjects as anonymous racial types. They initially served as justifications for the very paternalistic control and acculturation that scarred Littlechild's own life; but in the artist's hands, they become emblems of a newly rediscovered heritage. In these works, Littlechild employs collage, colour, and textual amendments to reinscribe the archival material with Cree symbolism, announcing the reclamation of family history while giving form to the tensions between cultures.

Aboriginal representations continued to figure prominently in governmental photography into the twentieth century. Among the most extensive bodies of work depicting First Peoples were those produced under the auspices of the Geological Survey of Canada's Anthropology Division. Like nineteenth-century images promoting western expansion, these visual documents, too, belie an imperialist agenda.[32] The Geological Survey of Canada (GSC) was founded in 1841.[33] It was, according to Christy Vodden, crucial in stimulating the mining industry, then a pivotal part of the colonial economy.[34] Over the following decades, it would be instrumental in establishing the mineral industry, but also in mapping the country, gathering information about flora and fauna, and documenting indigenous inhabitants. In 1910, the last of these concerns was expanded upon when the survey founded an Anthropology Division.[35] The division emerged as the government's most important institution for the study of Aboriginal culture.[36]

The most influential figure associated with the GSC's Anthropology Division was C. Marius Barbeau (1883–1969). Barbeau remains well known today for his anthropological and folklore studies within both Québécois and Aboriginal cultures (including Huron and Iroquois nations as well as peoples of the Northwest coast). He joined the division in 1911 and continued to be a part of the institution until 1949. Current scholarship identifies his efforts at cataloguing and mythologizing First Peoples' culture as reflective of the "vanishing race" thesis.[37]

Like most early-twentieth-century anthropologists, Barbeau and his colleagues at the GSC's Anthropological Division adopted the camera as an invaluable tool for field research.[38] Photographic technology, at this time, had become increasingly portable and easy to use. It proved particularly helpful in both social anthropology and ethnographic research, the study of racial variations through empirical data. In this capacity, photography was often used alongside an array of other technological implements including calipers, measuring tape, audio recorders and movie cameras in order to support theories of racial difference and study the subjects' cultures. Like the camera, as already noted, these seemingly neutral tools are also culturally inscribed. As the products of the (European) interpreting culture, they naturalize Europeanness and implicitly mark their non-Western subject as other. As Elizabeth Edwards has argued, the anthropological uses of photography reflected the colonial encounter in general; they "represented technological superiority harnessed to the delineation and control of the physical world" and supported anthropology's effect of transforming "the power of knowing...into a rationalized, observed 'truth.'"[39] In nineteenth- and early-twentieth-century studies of Native North Americans, ethnographic photographs and other materials were often marshalled to support racial and evolutionary theories proposed by such then-influential figures as Henry Rowe Schoolcraft and Lewis Henry Morgan.[40] Photographs, therefore, supposedly offered verifiable proof of racial distinctions and classifications, with their inherent premise of Aboriginal inferiority and need for paternalistic care. In short, these images contributed to a justification for colonial dominance.

Among the groups Barbeau studied and photographed were the Nisga'a people in settlements along the Nass and Skeena Rivers in Northern British Columbia.[41] This group is now familiar for its recent precedent-setting land claim case against the BC government.[42] Between 1927 and 1929, Barbeau studied their social organization, arts, mythology, and history along with a Nisga'a colleague, William Beynon.[43] According to Linda Riley, Barbeau's photographs of the settlements were not chiefly concerned with visual ethnography but rather were intended as documents supporting his specific areas of research. For example, exactly one-third of the images depict totem poles, a key subject of study.[44] Others feature views of the surrounding region, housing, grave monuments, petroglyphs and other pictorial forms, social gatherings, fishery, and canning, among other sites and endeavours. However, Barbeau also made a number of portraits of the peoples of the area in both ceremonial and European dress. These portraits reflect conventions in ethnographic photography.

In 1927 and 1928, Barbeau made a series of portraits depicting the Head Chief of the Eagle clan, also known in Barbeau's records as "Old Menesk" (fig. 3). These include frontal, back, and profile views of the chief in various forms of ceremonial dress. In the example reprinted here, he wears, according to the field notes, "a button blanket cape, fringed apron with buttons and puffin beaks, a frontlet of wood with ermine trim, abalone shell inlay, sea lion whiskers and a double border of faces" in addition to carrying a rattle.[45] Nothing could mark a sharper contrast to the portrait of John A. Macdonald with which I began this essay. Although obviously staged, Macdonald's portrait nonetheless presents him as an actor, in effect performing his role of political leader and, as I suggested,

FIGURE 3 Charles Marius Barbeau, *Old Menesk*, chief of the Eagles of Gitladamks, 1927 (courtesy of Canadian Museum of Civilization, negative no. 69701).

embodiment of the Canadian dominion. The chief of the Eagle clan, on the other hand, seems inert. By posing him in a harsh frontal view against the relatively neutral backdrop of a leafy tree—a convention in ethnographic portraiture—Barbeau has removed him from the ceremonial context for which his elaborate garb was intended. The chief is denied a sense of agency. Instead, the "real" action progresses behind the lens with Old Menesk serving as little more than a prop.

Like images of western expansion, ethnographic photographs of Aboriginal peoples—such as this example—have also recently come under the scrutiny of Aboriginal scholars, artists, and communities. In 1999, for instance, Onondaga curator/photographer Jeff Thomas, a key figure in re-examining Aboriginal photographic representations in Canada, organized for the Canadian Museum of Civilization an innovative exhibition that addressed photographs made under the auspices of the GSC's Anthropology Division. The exhibition, entitled "Emergence from the Shadow: First Peoples' Photographic Perspectives," combined two ideologically and historically divergent practices: field photographs by four GSC anthropologists and photo-based work by six contemporary Aboriginal artists. Here, as in Thomas's other curatorial projects and his own photographic practice, imperialist images are not eschewed but are instead juxtaposed with those depicting a vibrant contemporary Aboriginal life. In this way Thomas engages in what Homi K. Bhabha has termed "hybridity" or "cultural translation": the space of tension between cultures.[46] For Bhabha, incidents of hybridity not only "unsettle the mimetic or narcissistic demands of colonial power but reimplicate its identifications in strategies of subversion."[47] In short, hybridity—or cultural translation—as evident in Jeff Thomas's work operates as a strategy of retranslating or reinscribing the effects of the dominant culture. By demonstrating that the dominant culture can be subverted in this way, hybridity signals the tenuousness of the colonial position and asserts the agency of the colonized. Those assertions of agency can take the form of representational intervention, as in Thomas's work, or in the case of the Nisga'a people, direct political action.

Canadian officials increasingly recognized that photography could also serve as a vehicle for public relations.[48] One of the government's most extensive uses of the promotional photograph appeared under the auspices of the National Film Board (NFB) of Canada's Still Photography Division (1941–84). In its governmentally endorsed portrait of nationhood, representations of Aboriginal peoples also played a telling role.[49]

Today, the NFB's Still Photography Division has been mainly eclipsed from public memory by the board's celebrated Motion Picture units. Nonetheless, the Still Photography Division also achieved an influential program of image production and distribution. It was founded in 1941—two years after its parent agency—under the direction of John Grierson. Like the board as a whole, the Still Photography Division was charged with the task of "interpret[ing] Canada to Canadians and to other nations." In short, its mandate called for the development of a visual rhetoric of national hegemony. In the 200,000 images and hundreds of texts it would produce, the division addressed that lofty goal by reinforcing familiar symbols of Canada—including wilderness, the North, and, by the 1960s, multiculturalism—and offering homogenized visions of the country's regions and peoples. It gave form to the "imagined community" of Canadian nationhood.[50] During the height of its activity from the 1940s to the 1960s, the Still Photography Division's distinctively jingoistic portrayal of nationhood was consumed on a regular basis by millions of Canadians and international audiences through magazines, newspapers, exhibitions, Canadian embassies, and NFB-sponsored books.

Although John Grierson's tenure at the NFB was relatively brief, his approach to documentary would continue to shape the board's cinematic and still photographic production for years. Today, of course, he is regarded as a pivotal figure in the history of non-fiction film. In 1926, Grierson coined the term "documentary."[51] While initially employed as a category of cinema, it quickly came to refer to still photographs, too. Grierson defined documentary as the "creative treatment of actuality," an acknowledgment of the disguised subjectivity of camera-made images.[52] As I have argued elsewhere, his particular approach to documentary is rooted in liberal "rational reform"—the systematic social control and planning by governments, social scientists, and industry—of the 1920s and 1930s.[53] For Grierson—and indeed, as John Tagg has demonstrated, for most documentary practice of the 1930s and after—documentary films and photographs became privileged forms in the discourse of social management.[54] Within the workings of the National Film Board of Canada, they were unabashedly at the service of governmental propaganda. As Grierson himself stated in 1942, "The materials of citizenship today are different and the perspectives wider and more difficult; but we have, as ever, the duty of exploring them and of waking the heart and will in regard to them. That duty is what documentary is about. It is, moreover, documentary's primary service to the state."[55] "Service to the state" would remain the Still Photography Division's guiding principle throughout its history. The division was staffed by a team of photographers, photo-editors, writers, librarians, and administrators. Its Ottawa office included extensive darkroom facilities and a photography library for use by government departments and the public at large.[56]

Throughout much of its history, the division's chief vehicles for disseminating its work were photo-stories: narrative layouts containing between three and nine images with accompanying captions and text. These were produced as often as weekly for national and international publications.[57] Typically, the layouts translated the linear narrative of board documentary films into pictures. Photographs were privileged over text; one visual "protagonist" emerged as a figure with whom the viewer was intended to identify, and text remained brief though glowing. Indeed, photo-stories offered an unremittingly cheerful picture of Canadian prosperity. Photo-stories were engaged, above all, with the project of constructing normative models of Canadian identity as a strategy of national unity.

The particular character of "Canadian-ness" proposed by the Still Photography Division is perhaps nowhere more evident than in photo-stories depicting children, a recurrent motif throughout its history, and particularly those featuring Aboriginal children. Children came to stand—in a variety of complex ways—for the nation itself and its citizenry. From 1955 to 1960, for example, 66 out of 250 photo-stories featured images of children.[58] They surfaced (predictably) in photo-stories addressing leisure and in others where assumptions about childhood innocence and purity were exploited, as well as children's status as embodiments of the nation's future. More surprisingly, images of children were also invoked to promote the Canadian economy in pictorials devoted to everything from agricultural production to the fur trade. They were seen most frequently—particularly in the late 1950s—in instructional settings or other institutional contexts. They were, for example, virtually ubiquitous in photo-stories on health care.

But the kids featured in photo-stories hardly seemed to act like "kids." They stoically endured medical and dental examinations, listened obediently to authority figures and looked up admiringly at all adults. Youths or children who did not fit the division's mould of happy conformity and relentless middle-class normalcy were portrayed as institutionally contained.[59] In short, children served a metonymic function in division photo-stories: they stood for an idealized model of Canadian citizenry, one that relied on a paternalistic relationship with government. In effect, these seemingly malleable kids reflected John Grierson's famous call for documentary to "mould" the materials of citizenship. In images depicting Aboriginal youth, childhood as a sign of citizenry cared for by a paternalistic government was doubly inscribed. Because Aboriginal adults were frequently described in division publications and archival records as "childlike"—an evocation of the familiar trope of Native peoples as the "childhood of mankind"[60]—Native children were presented as the neediest of the needy.

Charles Camsell Indian Hospital

For an Exclusive Clientele

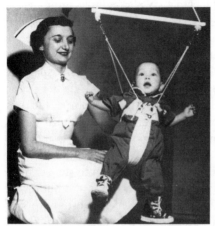

A substantial 3-storey brick building in downtown Edmonton reserves its services strictly for an exclusive clientele. The Charles Camsell Hospital was set up in 1946 with the health needs and problems of Canada's Eskimo and Indian population uppermost in mind. Today it has accommodation for over 500 and their facilities are geared to handle everyone from the newborn to the aged. Above 1-year-old Peter Tingmaniak enjoys a swing under the watchful eye of Nurse Onyshko.

Two-thirds of the hospital's patients suffer from tuberculosis as does the little girl above. In the past decade an intensive health program has succeeded in reducing the T.B. death rate from 579 to fewer than 50 per 100,000.

The hospital maintains a varied rehabilitation program which includes educational services, and handicraft training. Above, a young Indian girl who has completed her treatment is taken on a shopping tour of local department stores, her first introduction to current fashion styles.

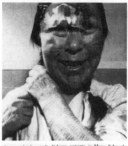

Among the hospital's Eskimo patients is Mary Edetoak from Spence Bay. She belongs to one of the few remaining groups who still use tatoo marks; the custom is losing popularity with the younger generations.

Nurse Gallagher delights 2 little Eskimo lads with a story about Eskimos. Some members of the staff are themselves of Indian or Eskimo origin.

National Film Board of Canada Photos by Gar Lunney

There's no shortage of hearty appetites in the tiny tots ward. 93 nurses tend the needs of patients together with a staff of 15 doctors and a dentist. Through a close working arrangement with the Edmonton area the hospital may call on the professional and technical skill of outsiders when necessary to supplement its own highly trained staff and modern facilities.

FIGURE 4 National Film Board of Canada, Still Photography Division, "For an Exclusive Clientele: Charles Camsell Indian Hospital." Photograph by Gar Lunney, photo-story No. 188, December 16, 1958 (courtesy NFB).

A 16 December 1958 photo-story dedicated to the Charles Camsell Indian Hospital in Edmonton exemplifies the division's treatment of Aboriginal children (fig. 4). The pictorial includes six photographs prominently featuring young Aboriginal patients seen within the institution and under the direct care of Euro-Canadian nurses.[61] Few of the children are identified by name, as if they represent interchangeable racial types rather than individual kids. Only one image takes the viewer outside the hospital. It portrays a young woman being taken on a shopping spree—apparently for a new hat—under the watch of a chaperone. Hat poised on her head, she smiles awkwardly at herself in a mirror. The emulation of Euro-Canadian middle-class status by Aboriginal peoples, as in this photograph, was another common feature in division images. She is presented as what Homi K. Bhabha terms a figure of the mimic. In addition to subject matter, the message of paternalistic Euro-Canadian authority is also buttressed by the very composition of the images themselves. As in most photo-stories, in these images the photographer adopts what we might call a "fly on the wall" view. Children and nurses seem unaware of the photographer's—and by implication, our own—presence. When they meet the gaze of the camera—as does one of the toddlers eating lunch at the lower right—their look suggests deference to authority or perhaps apprehension. As I have noted elsewhere, the all-seeing and all-powerful view became a common stylistic feature in all division photography of the time. It was, in effect, a visual equivalent of the so familiar "voice of God" narratives from documentary films produced by the board during the same years, providing a second layer of (implied) institutional guardianship.[62] Photo-stories like this one, with its representational reinforcement of institutional authority, provided a visual form for the NFB Still Photography Division's own ideological emphasis on government as paternalistic caretaker for its citizenry, its needy children—particularly Aboriginal citizen/children.

Popular culture depictions of Aboriginal peoples—such as this example from the NFB Still Photography Division, are also being reexamined by Aboriginal peoples. In an essay on popularized images of the Indian Princess typology, prominent Aboriginal scholar Gail Guthrie Valaskakis argues for the importance of engaging with and—like Jeff Thomas—reframing dominant imagery: "Like our discourse, our communities are not cemented in unity or belonging, but in the transformation and difference which is constructed in our ongoing struggle with power relations. And this dynamic process of building and re-building individual and collective identity centres in conflicting social imaginaries and their competing ideological messages."[63]

The camera has emerged as a powerful tool of official discourse in Canada. As I have suggested in the brief case studies above, photographic representations of First Peoples—whether produced under the auspices of the North American Boundary Commission, the Anthropology Division of the Geological Survey of Canada, or the National Film Board of Canada's Still Photography Division—effectively define a colonial domain and contain the official other of the nation. Drawing on the parallel assumptions of photographic authority and the logic of imperialism, these diverse historic projects marked consistent sites of Aboriginal subjugation. Yet in the face of this long institutionalized pictorial subjugation, a number of Aboriginal scholars, artists, and communities have developed effective means of resistance against them. As I have briefly noted here, by reframing dominant representations of First Peoples, such figures as George Littlechild, Jeffrey Thomas, and Gail Guthrie Valaskakis have found a way—in Bhabha's words—to "turn the gaze of the discriminated back upon the eye of power."[64]

Notes

1 John Tagg, *The Burden of Representation: Essays on Photographies and Histories* (Amherst: University of Massachusetts Press, 1988), 63–64.

2 Brian Carey, "Daguerreotypes in the National Archives of Canada," *History of Photography* 12.1 (1988): 45–60.

3 As a broad survey introducing Canadian photography, I draw extensively on the literature of Canadian photographic history, revisiting and recontextualizing others' research. I am indebted to those scholars and hope that the reader will be encouraged to read their work directly. One invaluable place where the student of Canadian photography can begin their investigation is with the 1996 special issue on Canadian photography edited by Joan Schwartz in the journal *History of Photography* 20.2 (1996).

4 Introduction to Auguste Comte, "The Nature and Importance of the Positive Philosophy," *Introduction to Positive Philosophy*, ed. Frederick Ferré (Indianapolis/Cambridge: Hackett, 1988), 2.

5 The phrase "an exact facsimile" is credited to the French Minister of the Interior and is linked to the June 1839 announcement of Daguerre's invention; the American Oliver Wendell Holmes referred to photography as a "mirror with a memory"; and "the pencil of nature" was coined by William Henry Fox Talbot, like Daguerre, an inventor of photography. See Vicki Goldberg, ed. *Photography in Print: Writing from 1816 to the Present* (Albuquerque: University of New Mexico Press, 1981), 32, 36–48, 102.

6 Charles S. Peirce, "What Is a Sign?" *The Essential Peirce*, ed. Nathan Houser and Christian Kloesel (Bloomington: Indiana University Press, 1998), 2: 4–10. Peircian semiotics, because of its inherent visual character, has been embraced by a number of recent scholars of visual culture. See, for example, Michael Leja, "Peirce, Visuality, and Art," *Representations* 72 (2000): 97–122.

7 See for example, Rosalind E. Krauss, "Notes on the Index: Part 1," *The Originality of the Avant-Garde and Other Modernist Myths* (Cambridge: MIT Press, 1985), 203.

8 The most important and moving discussion of this effect of portraiture is that proposed by Roland Barthes in his last book. Roland Barthes, *Camera Lucida: Reflections on Photography*, trans. Richard Howard (New York: Hill and Wang, 1981).

9 Barthes, *Camera Lucida*, trans. Richard Howard (New York: Hill and Wang, 1981), 80.

10 In particular, structuralist semiotics of photography reveals how photographic meaning is dependent on a nexus of cultural codes. See Roland Barthes, "The Photographic Message," *Image/Music/Text*, trans. Stephen Heath (London: Fontana, 1977), 15–31; and Victor Burgin, "Looking at Photographs," *Thinking Photography*, ed. Victor Burgin (Hampshire, UK: Macmillan, 1982), 142–53.

11 According to William C. Darrah, this austere setting of the studio was known as the "Brady" or "American" style of studio decor. William C. Darrah, *The Carte-de-Visite in Nineteenth Century Photography* (Gettysburg: W.C. Darrah, 1981), 26, 132.

12 For a detailed history of the carte-de-visite, see Elizabeth Anne McCauley, *A.A.E. Disderi and the Carte-de-Visite Portrait Photograph* (New Haven: Yale University Press, 1985).

13 Jonathan Crary, *Techniques of the Observer: On Vision and Modernity in the Nineteenth Century* (Cambridge: MIT Press, 1999), 136. For an influential discussion of this perception of photography, also see: Roland Barthes, "The Photographic Message," 15–31.

14 As James R. Ryan states succinctly in his important study of British colonial photography, "imperialism found sustenance in various photographic practices." James R. Ryan, *Picturing Empire: Photography and the Visualization of the British Empire* (Chicago: University of Chicago Press, 1997), 13.

15 Edward Said, *Orientalism* (London: Routledge, 1978).

16 A detailed historical examination of northern and western consolidation is beyond the scope of this brief study. Nonetheless, it is important to bear in mind that these programs, although various in nature, were provoked in part by a cultural climate characterized by anxieties over United States expansion and Aboriginal presence as well as various economic motivations.

17 Even before Confederation, photography was deployed for such purposes. In the late 1850s, for instance, the Assiniboine and Saskatchewan Exploratory Expedition travelled from Lake Superior to the Red River area. This excursion investigated an expanse of land that British authorities sought to acquire from the Hudson's Bay Company. See Richard J. Huyda, *Camera in the Interior: 1858, H.L. Hime, Photographer, The Assiniboine and Saskatchewan Exploring Expedition* (Toronto: Coach House Press, 1975).

18 For simplicity's sake, here I use the word "Canada" to refer to both the Dominion of Canada and the various regions constituting pre-Confederation British North America. My discussion of the Royal Corps of Engineers' use of photography draws extensively on the scholarship of Andrew Birrell. As Birrell has noted, the corps was an early advocate of photography as a scientific aid. Their first known official use of photography dates from 1851. By 1856, a photographic studio was established at their headquarters in Chatham, England, and in 1858, photography was added to the curriculum at the Royal Engineers' School. The camera was used at various times in documenting the corps' work as well as in producing portraits of ethnographic interest. Andrew J. Birrell, "The North American Boundary Commission: Three Photographic Expeditions, 1872–74," *History of Photography* 20.2 (1996): 113.

19 In the 1860s, the corps produced an extensive record of over one hundred images documenting the marking of the forty-ninth parallel between British Columbia and the United States. Birrell, "The North American Boundary Commission," 113–114; and Ralph Greenhill and Andrew Birrell, *Canadian Photography, 1839–1920* (Toronto: Coach House Press, 1979), plate 49.

20 The Canadian component of the survey was headed by Captain Donald Roderick Cameron. The scientific work on this survey—including astronomy and photography— was overseen by Captain Samuel Anderson. Birrell, "The North American Boundary Commission," 114.

21 Birrell, "The North American Boundary Commission," 114.

22 In the nineteenth century, photographing in the field was laborious. Not only did work have to be limited to the brief warm months, but contemporary photographic technology proved strikingly cumbersome. The Royal Corps of Engineers, like most photographers at this time, used the collodion wet plate process, glass-plate negatives coated with a solution of collodion (diluted gun cotton). Because plates had to be coated with the light-sensitive solution immediately before and developed soon after exposure, the photographer's entire workshop—including fragile glass plates—travelled with him over often-rough terrain. Stories of plates broken or ruined by shoddy processing are legion. For a first-hand account, see William Henry Jackson, "Time Exposure, 1940: An Excerpt," *Photography in Print: Writings from 1816 to the Present*, 168–70.

23 In fact, Andrew Birrell reports that through technological improvements and the corps' own expertise, the survey experienced few difficulties with equipment. Birrell, "The North American Boundary Commission," 119.

24 Peirce, 8.

25 José Rabasa, "Allegories of Atlas," *The Post-Colonial Studies Reader*, ed. Bill Ashcroft, Gareth Griffiths, and Helen Tiffin (London and New York: Routledge, 1995), 358–64.

26 Alan Trachtenberg, "Naming the View," *Reading American Photographs: Images as History, Mathew Brady to Walker Evans* (New York: Hill and Wang, 1989), 119–63.

27 Trachtenberg, 125.

28 For a discussion of Aboriginal erasure in another area of visual culture, see Jonathan Bordo, "Jack Pine, Wilderness Sublime—Or the Erasure of the Aboriginal Presence from the Landscape," *Journal of Canadian Studies* 27.4 (1992–93): 98–128.

29 Birrell, "The North American Boundary Commission," 119–20. Brock Silversides explains that Aboriginals' frequent lack of co-operation—as seen in Chippewas' bowed heads— was a complex and multivalent response to being photographed. He suggests that it was precipitated variously by misunderstandings about technology, fear that the photograph would strip away part of them, and the antagonism of the photographer. Brock Silversides, *The Face Pullers: Photographing Native Canadians 1871–1939* (Saskatoon: Fifth House, 1994), 6–9. Andrew Birrell also states that the figures here bow their heads "probably in reaction to the camera rather than in mourning." Birrell, "The North American Boundary Commission," 120.

30 For more scholarship offering revisionist examinations of the Aboriginal representation, see, among others, Silversides, *The Face Pullers*; Lucy R. Lippard, *Partial Recall: Photographs of Native North Americans* (New York: The New Press, 1992); and Margaret B. Blackman, "Copying People: Northwest Coast Native Response to Early Photography," *BC Studies* 52 (1981–1982), 86–112.

31 Ryan Rice, *Decolonizing the Archival Photography: George Littlechild* (Ottawa: Department of Indian and North Development, Indian Art Gallery, 1998).

32 My analysis of the GSC Anthropology Division is indebted to the work of and conversations with Jeff Thomas.

33 It was founded by the Legislature of the Province of Canada (present-day Quebec and southern Ontario).

34 Christy Vodden, *No Stone Unturned: The First 150 Years of the Geological Survey of Canada* (Ottawa: Supply and Services Canada, 1992), 1.

35 It was originally headed by Dr. Edward Sapir. As briefly noted above, anthropological images had appeared in the GSC's work before the formation of the division.

36 From 1911 until the late 1950s, it would be housed in the Victoria Memorial Museum Building (today's Canadian Museum of Nature in downtown Ottawa) and come under

the rubric of the National Museums of Canada. Its collections are the foundation of the present-day Canadian Museum of Civilization located in Hull, Quebec. Linda Riley, ed., *Marius Barbeau's Photography Collection: The Nass River*, Canadian Ethnology Service, Paper No. 109 (Ottawa: Canadian Museum of Civilization, 1988).

37 For an excellent discussion of Barbeau's relationship with avant-garde artists in Canada and his efforts to "indiginize" Euro-Canadian culture, see Sandra Jayne Dyck, "'These Things Are Our Totems': Marius Barbeau and the Indigenization of Canadian Art and Culture in the 1920s," MA thesis, Carleton University, 1995.

38 As R.G. Blackadar has shown, the survey began to employ photography in its work in the 1860s. R.G. Blackadar, *On the Frontier: Photographs by the Geological Survey of Canada* (Canada: Minister of Supply and Services Canada, 1982), 2. By the early twentieth century, field research had become the main approach to anthropological practice. Elizabeth Edwards, Introduction, *Anthropology and Photography, 1860–1920*, ed. Elizabeth Edwards (New Haven and London: Yale University Press in association with the Royal Anthropological Institute, London, 1992), 4.

39 Edwards, "Introduction," 6.

40 These two figures represented the two dominant American ethnographic theories of the late nineteenth century. Henry Rowe Schoolcraft believed that American natives had degenerated from a higher state to present primitive condition and were therefore incapable of assimilation into North American society. In contrast, Lewis Henry Morgan subscribed to a Social Darwinist theory of the stages of evolution: savagery, barbarism, civilization. He proposed that Aboriginal peoples had achieved barbarism and were capable of reaching the level of civilization, which of course was tantamount to the imitation of European culture. See Brian W. Dippie, "Representing the Other: The North American Indian," *Anthropology and Photography, 1860–1920*, ed. E. Edwards, 132.

41 For discussions of other photographers and anthropologists depicting Aboriginal peoples of the Canadian Northwest, see, among other titles, Margaret B. Blackman, *Window on the Past: The Photographic Ethnohistory of the Northern and Kaigani Haida*, Mercury Series, Paper 74 (Ottawa: National Museum of Man, 1981); and Margaret B. Blackman, "'Copying People.'"

42 For more information, see the Nisga'a Treaty Information, Forum and Voting website at <http://www.nisgaa.org/Nisgaa.htm>.

43 Riley, v.

44 Riley, v.

45 Riley, 135–36. The photograph described is numbered 69699 in the Canadian Museum of Civilization (Geological Survey of Canada) archives.

46 For a detailed discussion of Thomas's work, see Jeff Thomas and Carol Payne, "Aboriginal Interventions into the Photographic Archives: A Dialogue," *Visual Resources: An International Journal of Documentation* 18 (2002): 109–25. The term hybridity—with its reverberations of eugenics and genetic modification—has been called into question. See Jamelie Hassan, *Aldin's Gift* (North York: Art Gallery of York University, 1996), 24–28.

47 Homi K. Bhabha, "Signs Taken for Wonders," *The Location of Culture* (New York and London: Routledge, 1994), 34.

48 As Ellen Scheinberg and Melissa Rombout demonstrate, projects initiated in the 1890s by the Department of Agriculture and the Department of the Interior to promote immigration were among the earliest uses of promotional photography by the Canadian government. Ellen Scheinberg and Melissa Rombout, "Projecting Images of the Nation: The Immigration Program and Its Use of Lantern Slides," *The Archivist* 111 (1996):

13–24. The Motion Picture Bureau, which was later folded into the NFB Still Photography Division, was charged with publicizing the country by means of photographic and filmic representations.

49 See Carol Payne, *A Canadian Document: The National Film Board of Canada's Still Photography Division* (Ottawa: Canadian Museum of Contemporary Photography, 1999); Renate Wickens-Feldman, "The National Film Board of Canada's Still Photography Division: The Griersonian Legacy," *History of Photography* 20.3 (1996): 271–77; Martha Langford, "Introduction," *Contemporary Canadian Photography from the Collection of the National Film Board* (Edmonton: Hurtig Publishers, 1984), 7–16; and Melissa Rombout, "Imaginary Canada: Photography and the Construction of National Identity," *Views: The Journal of Photography in New England* 12.2 (1991): 4–9.

50 Benedict Anderson, *Imagined Communities: Reflections on the Origin and Spread of Nationalism*, rev. ed. (London: Verso, 1991).

51 The article—a review of Robert Flaherty's film *Moana*—appeared in the *New York Sun* on 8 February 1926. See Ian Aitken, *Film and Reform: John Grierson and the Documentary Film Movement* (London: Routledge, 1990), 79–80.

52 Forsyth Hardy, Introduction, *Grierson on Documentary*, ed. Forsyth Hardy (London and Boston: Faber and Faber, 1979), 11.

53 Payne, *A Canadian Document*. For a discussion of rational reform, see John M. Jordan, *Machine-Age Ideology: Social Engineering and American Liberalism, 1911–1939* (Chapel Hill and London: University of North Carolina Press, 1994), 4–6, 13, 155–84.

54 Tagg, *The Burden of Representation*.

55 John Grierson, "The Documentary Idea: 1942," *Grierson on Documentary*, 113.

56 In its first years of operation, during the Second World War, the division was largely occupied with depicting the war effort at home and serving the needs of various government agencies. Following the war, it turned fully to promoting the country's economic prosperity and fostering greater regional understanding within the nation. While the board's film production units—by the mid-1950s housed in suburban Montreal—became increasingly innovative and independent, the Still Photography Division—perhaps because of its proximity to government in Ottawa—did not deviate from its propagandistic function until the mid-1960s, when it gradually turned toward promoting the careers of individual Canadian photographers and a more subjective or "observational" mode of documentary.

57 As I have discussed elsewhere, these pictorials remained notably uniform. Carol Payne, "'How Shall We Use These Gifts?' Imaging the Land in the National Film Board of Canada's Still Photography Division," *The Virgin Beauty of Mississauga: Canadian Landscape Art and National Identity*, ed. John O'Brian and Peter White (Montreal: McGill-Queen's University Press, forthcoming 2006).

58 However, only twelve division assignment sheets or archival subject categories explicitly deal with children and their education, literacy, and health as their subject matter.

59 An example of this tendency is a 20 April 1956 photo-story about a school for the deaf. National Film Board of Canada, Still Photography Division papers, Canadian Museum of Contemporary Photography, and the Library and Archives of Canada.

60 Ryan, 153.

61 Captions, however, inform the reader that "Some members of the staff are themselves of Indian or Eskimo origin."

62 In fact, images like these relate to what Bill Nichols and Julianne Burton have termed an expository model of documentary cinema. For Nichols and Burton, expository documentary—exemplified by Grierson's own film production—directly address the viewer, are

organized around the establishment of a solution to a social ailment, and emphasize unquestioned authority. Bill Nichols, *Representing Reality: Issues and Concepts in Documentary* (Bloomington and Indianapolis: Indiana University Press, 1991), 34–38.

63 Gail Guthrie Valaskakis, "Sacajawea and Her Sisters: Images and Indians," *Indian Princesses and Cowgirls: Stereotypes from the Frontier*, ed. Marilyn Burgess and Gail Guthrie Valaskakis (Montreal: Oboro, 1992), 15–19.

64 Bhabha, *The Location of Culture*, 35.

Bibliography

Abel, Kerry. *Drum Songs: Glimpses of Dene History*. Montreal and Kingston: McGill-Queen's University Press, 1993.

Abella, Irving. "The Greatest Show Unearthed." *Globe and Mail* 15 November 2000, A15.

Acland, Charles R. "Popular Film in Canada: Revisiting the Absent Audience." *A Passion for Identity: An Introduction to Canadian Studies*. Ed. David Taras and Beverly Rasporich. Toronto: ITP Nelson, 1997. 281-96.

Adilman, Sid. "Ratings King." *Toronto Star* 16 January 1995: E7.

———. "Road Getting Smoother for Avonlea Producer." *Toronto Star* 3 January 1993.

Adorno, Theodor W. *Aesthetic Theory*. Trans. Robert Hullot-Kentor. Ed. Gretel Adorno and Rolf Tiedemann. Minneapolis: University of Minnesota Press, 1997.

Adorno, Theodor W., and Max Horkheimer. *Dialectic of the Enlightenment*. Trans. John Cumming. New York: Continuum, 1986.

Africa. African Charter on Human and Peoples' Rights, 26 June 1981, OAU Doc. CAB/LEG/67/3/Rev. 5, 21 ILM 59 (entered into force 21 October 1986).

A.G. Canada v. Lavell, [1974] Canada Supreme Court Reports 1349.

Ahmansson, Gabriella. *A Life and Its Mirrors: A Feminist Reading of L.M. Montgomery's Fiction*. Vol. 1. Stockholm: Uppsala, 1991.

Ahmed, Sarah. *The Cultural Politics of Emotion*. New York: Routledge, 2004.

Aikio, Marjut. "The Finnish Perspective: Language and Ethnicity." *Arctic Languages: An Awakening*. Ed. Dirmid R.F. Collis. Paris: UNESCO, 1990. 367–400.

Aitkin, Ian. *Film and Reform: John Grierson and the Documentary Film Movement*. London: Routledge, 1990.

Alexis, Andre. "Borrowed Blackness: Canadian Blacks Are Seen as Quieter Clones of Their Bold American Counterparts," *This Magazine* 28.8 (1995): 14. 7 July 2005 <http://proquest.umi.com/pqdweb?rqt=318&pmid=56855>.

Althusser, Louis. *Lenin and Philosophy and Other Essays*. Trans. Ben Brewster. London: New Left Books, 1971.

Amon, Trevor. "Rant Would Make Much Better Pledge." *Toronto Star* 4 May 2000, A29.

Anderson, Benedict. *Imagined Communities: Reflections on the Origin and Spread of Nationalism*. Rev. ed. London: Verso, 1991.

Angus, Ian. *A Border Within: National Identity, Cultural Plurality, and Wilderness*. Montreal: McGill-Queen's University Press, 1997.

Apostle, R., G. Barrett, A. Davis, and L. Kasdan. *Land and Sea: The Structure of Fish Processing in Nova Scotia: A Preliminary Report*. Halifax, NS: Gorsebrook Research Institute, 1985.

Appadurai, Arjun. "Disjuncture and Difference in the Global Cultural Economy." *Public Culture* 2.2 (1990): 1–23.

———. "The Production of Locality." *Counterworks: Managing the Diversity of Knowledge*. Ed. Richard Fardon. London: Routledge, 1995. 204–25.

———. "Sovereignty without Territoriality: Notes for a Postnational Geography." *The Geography of Identity*. Ed. Patricia Yaeger. Ann Arbor: University of Michigan Press, 1996. 40–58.

Aquin, Hubert. *Blackout*. Trans. Alan Brown. Toronto: Anansi, 1974. Originally published as *Trou de mémoire*. Montreal: Le Cercle du Livre de France, 1968.

Arcand, Denys, dir. *Love and Human Remains*. Atlantis Films, 1993.

Arditi, J. *A Genealogy of Manners*. Chicago: University of Chicago Press, 1998.

Arnold, Grant. "Kate Craig: Skin." *Kate Craig: Skin*. Ed. Grant Arnold. Vancouver: Vancouver Art Gallery, 1998. 1–16.

Arnold, Martin. "Olson's Fireworks Music." *Daniel Olson, Small World*. Cambridge, ON, Sackville, and Lethbridge: Cambridge Galleries, Owens Art Gallery, and Southern Alberta Art Gallery, 2000.

Atherton, Tony. "It's All in the Details, Avonlea Exec Says." *Montreal Gazette* 5 April 1999, B6.

Atwood, Margaret. *The Journals of Susanna Moodie*. Toronto: Oxford University Press, 1970.

———. *Survival: A Thematic Guide to Canadian Literature*. Toronto: Anansi, 1972.

Auslander, Philip. *Liveness: Performance in a Mediatized Culture*. New York: Routledge, 1999.

Austin, J.L. *How to Do Things with Words*. Cambridge, MA: Harvard University Press, 1962.

Axworthy, Thomas, and Pierre Elliott Trudeau, eds. *Towards a Just Society: The Trudeau Years*. Toronto: Viking, 1990.

Axworthy, Tom. "Memories Shape the Way We See Ourselves." *Toronto Star* 26 September 1997, A28.

Backhouse, Charles. *Canadian Government Motion Picture Bureau, 1917–1941.* Ottawa: Canadian Film Institute, 1974.

Badeaux, Guy, and Charles Gordon. *The Year 98 Portfolio in Canadian Caricature.* Montreal: CROC, 1998.

Badeaux, Guy, and Jay Stone. *The Year's Best Editorial Cartoons. Portfolio 15.* Toronto: Macmillan, 1999.

Badgley, Frank, prod. *Conquest of the Forest.* Canada: Canadian Government Motion Picture Bureau, 1928.

Baert, Renee. "Three Dresses, Tailored to the Times." *Material Matters: The Art and Culture of Contemporary Textiles.* Ed. Ingrid Bachmann and Ruth Scheuing. Toronto: YYZ Books, 1998. 79–82.

Bal, Mieke. *Quoting Caravaggio: Contemporary Art, Preposterous History.* Chicago: University of Chicago Press, 1999.

Balcom, Susan. "'Small-Town' Vernon in Shock over Massacre." *Vancouver Sun* 6 April 1996, A3.

Balikci, Asen. *The Netsilik Eskimos.* Garden City, NY: Natural History Press, 1970.

Bannerji, Himani. "Geography Lessons: On Being an Insider/Outsider to the Canadian Nation." *Dangerous Territories: Struggles for Difference and Equality in Education.* Ed. Leslie G. Roman and Linda Eyre. New York: Routledge, 1997. 23–41.

——. *The Dark Side of the Nation: Essays on Multiculturalism, Nationalism and Gender.* Toronto: Canadian Scholars' Press, 2000.

Banton, Michael. *Racial and Ethnic Competition.* Cambridge: Cambridge University Press, 1983.

Barber, Bruce. "Performance for Pleasure and Performance for Instruction." *Living Art Vancouver.* Ed. Alvin Balkind and R.A. Gledhill. Vancouver: Pulp Press, 1979. 78–81.

Barbour, Douglas, and Stephen Scobie. *The Maple Laugh Forever.* Edmonton: Hurtig, 1981.

Barker, Chris. *Cultural Studies: Theory and Practice.* London: Sage, 2000.

——. *Television, Globalization and Cultural Identities.* Buckingham: Open University Press, 1999.

Barthes, Roland. *Camera Lucida: Reflections on Photography.* Trans. Richard Howard. New York: Hill and Wang, 1981.

——. *Image/Music/Text.* Trans. Stephen Heath. London: Fontana, 1977.

——. *Mythologies.* London: Paladin, 1973.

Bartkowiak, Andrzej, dir. *Exit Wounds.* Warner Brothers, 2001.

Baudrillard, Jean. *The Consumer Society: Myths and Structures.* Trans. Chris Turner. London: Sage, 1998.

——. "L'esprit du terrorisme." *Le Monde.* 2 November 2001.

——. *Symbolic Exchange and Death.* Trans. Ian Hamilton Grant. London: Sage, 1993.

Beard, William. "The Canadianness of David Cronenberg." *Mosaic* 27.7 (1994): 113–33.

Bell, Lynne, and Janice Williamson. "High Tech Storyteller: A Conversation with Performance Artist Lori Blondeau." *Fuse* 24.4 (2001): 27–34.

Bell, Stewart, Lindsay Kines, Mike Bocking, and Petti Fong. "How Did Killer Get Gun Permit?: Family and Friends Ask That Question, Saying Police Already Knew Mark Chahal Had Made Threats to His Estranged Wife: Wife 'Was Too Terrified' to Press Charges." *Vancouver Sun* 8 April 1996, A1.

Berger, Thomas R. *Fragile Freedoms: Human Rights and Dissent in Canada.* Toronto and Vancouver: Clark, Irwin, 1981.

———. *Northern Frontier, Northern Homeland: The Report of the Mackenzie Valley Pipeline Inquiry,* Vol. 1. Ottawa: Minister of Supply and Services, 1977.

———. *Village Journey: The Report of the Alaska Native Review Commission.* New York: Hill and Wang, 1985.

Bergson, Henri. "Laughter." *Comedy.* Ed. W. Sypher. New York: Doubleday, 1956. 61–91.

Berlant, Lauren, and Elizabeth Freeman. "Queer Nationality." *Boundary* 2 19.1 (1992): 149–80.

Bernstein, Deborah. Personal interview. 4 October 2001.

Berry, Chris. "If China Can Say No, Can China Make Movies? Or, Do Movies Make China? Rethinking National Cinema and National Agency." *Boundary* 2 25.3 (1998): 129–50.

Berton, Pierre. *Hollywood's Canada: The Americanization of Our National Image.* Toronto: McClelland and Stewart, 1975.

———. *Why We Act Like Canadians: A Personal Exploration of Our National Character.* Toronto: McClelland and Stewart, 1982.

Bertrand, Ina. "'National Identity'/'National History'/'National Film': The Australian Experience." *Historical Journal of Film, Radio and Television* 4.2 (1984): 179–88.

"Better Than a Heritage Minute." *Ottawa Citizen* 24 October 2000, A16.

Beveridge, James, prod. *Peoples of Canada.* Canada: National Film Board of Canada, 1941.

Bewley, Marius. Introduction. *The Selected Poetry of Donne.* Ed. Marius Bewley. New York: New American Library, 1979. ix–xxxix.

Bhabha, Homi K., ed. *The Location of Culture.* New York and London: Routledge, 1994.

———. *Nation and Narration.* London: Routledge, 1990.

———. "The Third Space: Interview with Homi Bhabha." Interview with Jonathan Rutherford. *Identity: Community, Culture, Difference.* London: Lawrence and Wishart, 1990. 207–21.

Bhandar, Brenna. *A Guilty Verdict against the Odds: Privileging White Middle-Class Femininity in the Trial of Kelly Ellard for the Murder of Reena Virk.* Vancouver, BC: FREDA Centre 2000 <http://www.harbour.sfu.ca/freda/articles/bhandar.htm>.

Birket-Smith, Kaj. *The Caribou Eskimos: Material and Social Life and Their Cultural Position. Descriptive Part.* Trans. W.E. Calvert. Vol. 5. *The Report of the Fifth Thule Expedition, 1921–24.* Copenhagen: Glydenalske Boghandel, 1929.

Birney, Earle. "Can. Lit." *An Anthology of Canadian Literature in English.* Ed. Russell Brown, Donna Bennett, and Natalie Cooke. Toronto: Oxford University Press, 1990. 296.

Birrell, Andrew. *Into the Silent Land: Survey Photography in the Canadian West, 1958–1900.* Ottawa: Information Canada, 1975.

———. "The North American Boundary Commission: Three Photographic Expeditions, 1872–74." *History of Photography* 20.2 (1996): 113–21.

Bishop, Peter F. "Rudolf Komorous." *Canadian Music Centre.* 18 October 2005 < http://www.naxos.com/mainsite/default.asp?pn=composers&char=k&composerID=2579 >.

Bissoondath, Neil. *Selling Illusion: The Cult of Multiculturalism in Canada.* Toronto: Penguin, 1994.

Blackadar, R.G. *On the Frontier: Photographs by the Geological Survey of Canada.* Canada: Minister of Supply and Services Canada, 1982.

Blackman, Margaret B. "Copying People: Northwest Coast Response to Early Photography." *BC Studies* 52 (1981–82): 86–112.

———. *Window on the Past: The Photographic Ethnohistory of the Northern and Kaigani Haida.* Mercury Series. Paper 74. Ottawa: National Museum of Man, 1981.

Blackstone, Pam. "Canada Rules the Web." *Victoria Times Colonist* 1 May 2000, A9.

Blais, Marie-Claire. *A Season in the Life of Emmanuel.* Trans. Derek Coltman. 2nd ed. Toronto: McClelland and Stewart, 1992. Originally published as *Une saison dans la vie d'Emmanuel.* Paris: Éditions du Jour, 1965.

Blais, Roger, dir. *Passport to Canada.* Canada: National Film Board of Canada, 1949.

Bloomfield, George, dir. *Child Under a Leaf.* 1974.

Bocking, Mike. "Step by Gruesome Step, One Man's Killing Spree." *Vancouver Sun* 8 April 1996, B2.

Bocking, Mike, and Kim Bolan. "Killer Had Threatened Family: Nine Die in Canada's Second-Largest Mass Murder on the Eve of a Vernon Wedding, and the Murderer Commits Suicide; Killer Apologizes in Suicide Note." *Vancouver Sun* 6 April 1996, A1.

Boire, Gary. "Canadian (Tw)ink: Surviving the White-Outs." *Essays on Canadian Writing* 35 (1987): 1–16.

Boldt, Menno, A. Long, and L. Little Bear, eds. *The Quest for Justice: Aboriginal Peoples and Aboriginal Rights.* Toronto: Toronto University Press, 1985.

Bollas, Christopher. *Being a Character: Psychoanalysis and Self Experience.* New York: Hill and Wang, 1992.

———. *The Shadow of the Object: Psychoanalysis of the Unthought Known.* New York: Columbia University Press, 1987.

Bordo, Jonathan. "Jack Pine, Wilderness Sublime—Or the Erasure of the Aboriginal Presence from the Landscape." *Journal of Canadian Studies* 27.4 (1992–93): 98–128.

Born, Georgina. "Music, Modernism and Signification." *Thinking Art*. Ed. Andrew Benjamin and Peter Osborne. London: Institute of Contemporary Arts, 1991. 157–76.

Boulton, Laura, dir. *Eskimo Arts and Crafts*. Canada: National Film Board of Canada, 1943.

Bourdieu, Pierre. "The Work of Time." *The Gift: An Interdisciplinary Perspective*. Ed. Aafke Komter. Amsterdam: Amsterdam University Press, 1996. 135–47.

Brennan, Don. "Life Imitates Advertising." *Toronto Sun* 15 April 2000, N7.

Broadfoot, Dave. CBC Calgary Radio Broadcast. 24 June 2001.

Bronson, A.A. "The Humiliation of the Bureaucrat: Artist-Run Spaces as Museums by Artists." *From Sea to Shining Sea*. Toronto: Power Plant, 1987. 164–69.

Bronson, A.A., and Peggy Gale. *Performance by Artists*. Toronto: Art Metropole, 1979.

Bruzzi, Stella. "Jane Campion: Costume Drama and Reclaiming Women's Past." *Women and Film: A Sight and Sound Reader*. Ed. Pam Cook and Philip Dodd. Philadelphia: Temple University Press, 1993. 232–42.

Bryant, Adam. "Message in a Beer Bottle: Molson Cracks Open a Cool Ad for Its Canadian Brand." *Newsweek* 29 May 2000, 43.

Brydon, Diana. "Introduction: Reading Postcoloniality, Reading Canada." *Essays on Canadian Writing* 56 (1995): 1–19.

Bryson, Norman. *Looking at the Overlooked: Four Essays on Still Life Painting*. Cambridge, MA: Harvard University Press, 1990.

Bugajski, Ryszard, dir. *Clearcut*. Canada, 1991.

Bumsted, Jack. "Visions of Canada: A Brief History of Writing on the Canadian Character and the Canadian Identity." *A Passion for Identity*, 4th ed. Ed. David Taras and Beverly Rasporich. Toronto: Nelson Thomson Learning, 2001. 17–35.

Bunner, Paul. "You've Seen the Rant, Now Read the Rave: My Name Is Paul (Bunner), and I Too Am a Canadian." *Report Newsmagazine* [Alberta] 27.1 (8 May 2000), 2.

Burgess, Marilyn, and Gail Guthrie Valaskakis. *Indian Princesses and Cowgirls: Stereotypes from the Frontier*. Montreal: Oboro, 1992.

Burgin, Victor, ed. "Looking at Photographs." *Thinking Photography*. Ed. Victor Burgin. Hampshire, UK: Macmillan, 1982. 142–53.

Burton-Carvajal, Julianne. "Mexican Melodramas of Patriarchy: Specificity of a Transcultural Form." *Framing Latin American Cinema: Contemporary Critical Perspectives*. Ed. Ann Marie Stock. Minneapolis: University of Minnesota Press, 1997. 186–234.

Butler, Judith. *Bodies That Matter: On the Discursive Limits of "Sex."* New York: Routledge, 1993.

———. *Gender Trouble: Feminism and the Subversion of Identity*. New York: Routledge, 1990.

———. "Lana's 'Imitation': Melodramatic Repetition and the Gender Performative." *Genders* 9 (1990): 1–18.

———. "Performative Acts and Gender Constitution: An Essay in Phenomenology and Feminist Theory." *Writing on the Body: Female Embodiment and Feminist Theory.* Ed. Katie Conboy, Nadia Medina, and Sarah Stanbury. New York: Columbia University Press, 1997. 401-17.

———. *The Psychic Life of Power.* Stanford, CA: Stanford University Press, 1997.

Caccia, Fulvio. "L'altra riva." *Vice Versa* 16 (1986): 44-45.

Cairns, Alan C. *Citizens Plus: Aboriginal People and the Canadian State.* Vancouver: University of British Columbia Press, 2000.

"Calendar Features Women in Fishery." *Cape Breton Post* 10 June 2001, 17.

Calliste, Agnes. "Canada's Immigration Policy and Domestic Blacks from the Caribbean: The Second Domestic Scheme." *The Social Basis of Law.* 2nd ed. Ed. Elizabeth Cormack and Stephen Brickley. Halifax: Garamond, 1991. 95-121.

Cameron, Elspeth. "Heritage Minutes: Culture and Myth." *Canadian Issues* 17 (1995): 13-24.

Cameron, Heather. "Private Eyes, Public Eyes: Photography and the Surveillance Society." *Reflex Photo* 2 (2000): 9-19.

Cameron, Kirk, and Graham White. *Northern Governments in Transition: Political and Constitutional Development in the Yukon, Nunavut and the Western Northwest Territories.* Montreal: Institute for Research on Public Policy, 1995.

Campbell, Colin. "David Buchan: Lamonte Del Monte and the Fruit Cocktails." *Centerfold* 3.1 (1978): 29-32.

Campbell, Colin, dir. *Janus.* Canada: V-Tape, 1973.

———. *Modern Love.* Canada: V-Tape, 1978-80.

———. *Rendez-Vous.* Canada: V-Tape, 1997-2000.

———. *This is an Edit-This is Real.* Canada: V-Tape, 1974.

———. *True/False.* Canada: V-Tape, 1972.

———. *The Woman from Malibu.* Canada: V-Tape, 1976-77.

Canada: A People's History. Episode 1: "When the World Began…15,000 B.C. to 1800 A.D." Dir. Andrew Gregg. CBC, 2000.

Canada: A People's History. Episode 7: "Rebellion and Reform, 1815-1850." Dir. Peter Ingles. CBC, 2001.

Canada: A People's History. Episode 9: "From Sea to Sea." Dir. Jim Williamson. CBC, 2001.

Canada: A People's History. Episode 14: "The Crucible." Dir. Susan Teskey. CBC, 2001.

Canada. British North America Act, 1867.

———. Canadian Bill of Rights, Revised Statutes of Canada, 1970, App. III.

———. Canadian Charter of Rights and Freedoms, Part 1 of the Constitution Act, 1982, being Schedule B to the Canada Act, 1982 (UK), 1982, C.11.

———. Canadian Human Rights Act, Statutes of Canada, 1976-77, C.33, S.67.

———. Constitution Act, 1867 (UK), 30 & 31 Vict., C.3.

———. Constitution Act, 1982, being Schedule B to the Canada Act 1982 (UK), 1982, C.11.

———. Department of Indian and Northern Development. Statement of the Government of Canada on Indian Policy, 1969 (1969).

———. Department of Indian Affairs and Northern Development. "Statement of Reconciliation: Learning from the Past." *Gathering Strength: Canada's Aboriginal Action Plan.* Ottawa: Minister of Public Works and Government Services, 1997.

———. Indian Act, Revised Statutes of Canada, 1985, c. 1–5.

———. National Film Act. Statutes of Canada, 1939. 101–105.

———. National Film Act. Statutes of Canada, 1950. Vol. 1, 567–74.

———. Preamble. Comprehensive Land Claim Agreement Between Her Majesty in Right of Canada and the Dene...as represented by the Sahtu Tribal Council. Ottawa: Public Works and Government Services Canada, 1993.

———. Report. Royal Commission on National Development in the Arts, Letters, and Sciences. Ottawa, 1951.

———. Revised Statutes of Canada, 1985. Ottawa: Queen's Printer, 1985.

———. *Royal Commission on Aboriginal Peoples* (RCAP), Ottawa: Minister of Supply and Services Canada, 1996 in *For Seven Generations: An Information Legacy of the Royal Commission on Aboriginal Peoples*, CD ROM (Ottawa: Libraxus, 1997).

———. *Statement of the Government of Canada on Indian Policy.* Ottawa: Department of Indian Affairs and Northern Development, 1969.

"'Canadian' Beer Ad up for Award." *St. John's Telegram* 24 June 2000, 25.

Cannizzo, Jeanne. "Inside Out: Cultural Production in the Museum and the Academy." *Academic Anthropology and the Museum.* Ed. Mary Bouquet. New York: Berghahn, 2001. 162–76.

Canyon, Brice, ed. *Live at the End of the Century: Aspects of Performance Art in Vancouver.* Vancouver: Visible Art Society and Grunt Gallery, 2000.

Caplan, Elinor. "Building Community in Multi-Ethnic Societies," address by the Honourable Elinor Caplan, minister of Citizenship and Immigration, to the Metropolis Conference Plenary, Washington, DC, 10 December, 1999, *Immigration and Citizenship Canada*, 2002. <http://www.cic.gc.ca/english/press /speech>.

———. "Economic Migrants or Refugees: Trends in Global Migration Forum." Notes for an address by the Honourable Elinor Caplan, minister of Citizenship and Immigration, to the Maytree Foundation, 15 October 2005 <http:// maytree.com/pdf_ files=mrproc.pdf>.

Carens, Joseph H. *Culture, Citizenship, and Community: A Contextual Exploration of Justice as Evenhandedness.* Oxford: Oxford University Press, 2000.

Carey, Brian. "Daguerreotypes in the National Archives of Canada." *History of Photography* 12.1 (1998): 45–60.

Carey, Elaine. "The City That Works Could Be Even Better." *Toronto Star* 1 May 1999, A1.

Carleton University History Collaborative. "Press Reaction: The Reaction to Canada, A People's Reaction." *Reaction to Canada: A People's History.* 18 February 2002 <http://www.carleton.ca/historycollaborative/>.

Carter, Sarah. "First Nations Women of Prairie Canada in the Early Reserve Years, the 1870s to the 1920s: A Preliminary Inquiry." *Women of the First Nations: Power, Wisdom and Strength.* Ed. Christine Miller and Patricia Chuchryk. Winnipeg: University of Manitoba Press, 1996. 51–75.

Case, Sue-Ellen. "Toward a Butch-Femme Aesthetic." *The Gay and Lesbian Studies Reader.* Ed. Henry Abelove, Michèle Aina Barale, and David M. Halperin. New York: Routledge, 1993. 294–306.

Caws, Mary Ann. *The Surrealist Look: An Erotics of Encounter.* Cambridge, MA: MIT Press, 1997.

CBC. "Behind the Scenes—About the TV Series; Step by Step: One Story, Many Perspectives." *Canada: A People's History. Explore the Episodes.* 14 February 2002 <http://history.cbc.ca/history>.

———. "Behind the Scenes—About the TV Series; Telling the Story: Re-enacting History." *Canada: A People's History. Explore the Episodes.* 30 December 2003 <http://history.cbc.ca/history>.

———. "Canada: A People's History: Discussion Forum: Episode 14: The Crucible." 18 February 2002 <http://www.cbc.ca/mycbc/do/newsletter.cgi>.

———. "Canada: A People's History: Discussion Forums: What Did You Think of Episode One?" CBC.ca. 18 February 2002 <http://www.cbc.ca/mycbc/do/newsletter.cgi>.

———. "CBC Message Board." CBC.ca. 4 December 2000 <http://www.cbc.ca/mycbc/do/newsletter.cgi>.

———. "CBC Message Board." CBC.ca. 26 September 2001 <http://www.cbc.ca/mycbc/do/newsletter.cgi>.

———. "A Great Success Story: *Canada: A People's History/Le Canada: Une Histoire Populaire.*" CBC/Radio-Canada Annual Report 2000–2001, page 14, 14 February 2002 <http://cbc.radio-canada.ca/htmen6_2_00.htm>.

———. "A People's History of Central Canada ...Only." CBC.ca. 14 February 2002 <http://www.cbc.ca/mycbc/do/newsletter.cgi>.

———. *Let's Do It: A Vision of Canadian Broadcasting Proposed by the CBC to the Federal Task Force on Broadcasting Policy.* Ottawa: CBC, 1985.

Chanady, Amaryll. "Canadian Literature and the Postcolonial Paradigm." *Textual Studies in Canada* 5 (1994): 15–21.

Chance, Norman A. *The Iñupiat and Arctic Alaska: An Ethnography of Development.* Fort Worth: Holt, Rinehart, and Winston, 1990.

Chapman, Rosemary. *Siting the Quebec Novel: The Representation of Space in Francophone Writing in Quebec.* Oxford: Peter Lang, 2000.

Chard, Chloe. *Pleasure and Guilt on the Grand Tour: Travel Writing and Imaginative Geography 1600–1830.* Manchester: Manchester University Press, 1999.

Charland, Maurice. "Technological Nationalism." *Canadian Journal of Political and Social Theory* 10 (1986): 296–320.

Chase, Malcolm, and Christopher Shaw, ed. *The Imagined Past: History and Nostalgia.* New York: Manchester University Press, 1989.

Chouwanasai, Michael, dir. *To be or not to be. The Adventures of Iron Pussy 3.* Canada: V-Tape, 2000.

Christian, Roger, dir. *Battlefield Earth*. Warner Brothers, 2000.

Churchill, Winston S. *A History of the English-Speaking Peoples*. Vol. 2. *The New World*. New York: Dodd Mead, 1956.

Clark, Bob, dir. *Porky's*. 20th Century Fox, 1982.

Clark, E., ed. *Indian Legends of Canada*. Toronto: McClelland and Stewart, 1960.

Clarke, George Elliott, ed. *Eyeing the North Star: Directions in African-Canadian Literature*. Toronto: McClelland and Stewart, 1997.

Clarkson, Adrienne. "Installation Speech." *A Passion for Identity*, 4th ed. Ed. David Taras and Beverly Rasporich. Toronto: Nelson Thomson Learning, 2001. 11.

Clifford, James. "Museums as Contact Zones." *Routes: Travel and Translation in the Late Twentieth Century. Introduction*. Cambridge, MA: Harvard University Press, 1997. 188–219.

Clifford, James. Introduction. *Writing Culture: The Poetics and Politics of Ethnography*. Ed. James Clifford and George E. Marcus. Berkeley: University of California Press, 1986. 1–26.

Cloud, D. "Hegemony of Concordance? The Rhetoric of Tokenism in 'Oprah' Winfrey's Rags-to-Riches Biography." *Critical Studies in Mass Communication* 13 (1996): 115–37.

Coates, Kenneth S., and William Morrison. *The Forgotten North: A History of Canada's Provincial Norths*. Toronto: James Lorimer, 1992.

Cobb, Chris. "CBC's Greatest Story Ever Told." *Ottawa Citizen* 8 October 2000, A10.

Cohen, Leonard. "All There Is to Know about Adolph Eichmann." *Flowers for Hitler*. Toronto: McClelland and Stewart, 1964.

———. "The Only Tourist in Havana Turns His Thoughts Homeward." *A Passion for Identity*, 3rd ed. Ed. David Taras, Beverly Rasporich, and Eli Mandel. Toronto: Nelson Canada, 1993. 148.

———. *Stranger Music: Selected Poems and Songs*. Toronto: McClelland and Stewart, 1993.

Condit, C.W. "Hegemony in a Mass-Mediated Society: Concordance about Reproductive Technologies." *Critical Studies in Mass Communication* 11 (1994): 205–30.

Conkie, Heather. Personal interview. 9 October 2001.

Connerton, Paul. *How Societies Remember*. New York: Cambridge University Press, 1989.

Conseil Exécutif du PQ. *Prochaine Étape ... Quand Nous Serons Vraiment Chez Nous*. Montréal: Les Éditions du Parti Québécois, 1972.

Corner, John, and Sylvia Harvey, eds. *Enterprise and Heritage: Crosscurrents of National Culture*. London: Routledge, 1991.

Cottle, Simon. "'Race,' Racialization and the Media: A Review and Update of Research." *Sage Race Relations Abstracts* 17 (1992).

Crary, Jonathan. *Techniques of the Observer: On Vision and Modernity in the Nineteenth Century*. Cambridge: MIT Press, 1999.

Crawley, Mike. "Shooting Victim 'Let Down' by Vernon RCMP: Shooting Victim Isn't Looking to Blame Police, but Wants Protection for Women." *Vancouver Sun* 15 April 1996, A1.

Crawley, Radford, dir. *Iceland on the Prairies*. Canada: National Film Board of Canada, 1941.

Cronenberg, David, dir. *Crash*. Recorded Picture Co., 1996.

CRTC Public Notice 1998-44. *Canadian Television Policy Review*. CRARR Intervention, No. 13, 1998.

Cummings, N., and H. Mickenburg, eds. *Native Rights in Canada*. Toronto: Indian-Eskimo Association, 1975.

Curry, Ralph. "Robert Benchley and Stephen Leacock: An Acknowledged Literary Debt." *The American Book Collector* 7 (1957): 11–15.

Daniel, Richard. "The Spirit and Terms of Treaty Eight." *The Spirit of the Alberta Indian Treaties*. Ed. Richard Price. Edmonton: Pica Pica Press, 1987.

Darrah, William C. *The Carte-de-Visite in Nineteenth Century Photography*. Gettysburg: W.C. Darrah, 1981.

Daston, Lorraine, and Katherine Park. *Wonders and the Order of Nature, 1150–1750*. New York: Zone Books, 1998.

Davey, Frank. *Post-National Arguments: The Politics of the Anglophone-Canadian Novel since 1967*. Theory/Culture series. Toronto: University of Toronto Press, 1993.

Davidson, Arnold E. "Canadian Gothic and Anne Hébert's *Kamouraska*." *MFS: Modern Fiction Studies* 27(1981): 243–54.

Davies, Robertson. *The Merry Heart: Selections 1980–1995*. Toronto: Penguin, 1996.

Davies, Simon. "CCTV: A New Battleground for Privacy." *Surveillance, Closed Circuit Television and Social Control*. Ed. Clive Norris, Jade Moran, and Gary Armstrong. Aldershot: Ashgate, 1998. 243–54.

Davis, Arthur K. "Canadian Society and History as Hinterland versus Metropolis." *Canadian Society: Pluralism, Change, and Conflict*. Ed. Richard J. Ossenberg. Scarborough: Prentice-Hall, 1971.

Deacon, James. "The Patriot Game: I Am. A Beer Marketer." *Maclean's* 18 June 2000, 30.

Deakin, B. "Politically Correct Should Let 'Fishers' off the Hook." *Chronicle-Herald* 12 August 1997: B2.

Dean, Mitchell. *Governmentality: Power and Rule in Modern Society*. London: Sage, 1999.

Debord, Guy. *La société du spectacle*. Paris: Buchet/Chastel, 1967.

De Certeau, Michel. *The Practice of Everyday Life*. Trans. Steven F. Rendell. Berkeley: University of California Press, 1984.

De Lauretis, Teresa. *Alice Doesn't: Feminism, Semiotics, Cinema*. Bloomington: Indiana University Press, 1984.

Deleuze, Gilles. "Control and Becoming" [Interview with Antonio Negri] and "Postscript on Control Societies." *Negotiations 1972–1990*. Trans. Martin Joughin. New York: Columbia University Press, 1995. 169–82.

Delgamuukw v. B.C., [1997] 3 Canada Supreme Court Reports 1010.

Denning, Dorothy. "Activism, Hacktivism, and Cyberterrorism: The Internet as a Tool for Influencing Foreign Policy." totse.com. 2000 <http://www.totse.com/en/technology/cyberspace_the_new_frontier/cyberspc.html>.

Denniston, Stan, and Jeanne Randolph. *Reminders: Stan Denniston*. Victoria, BC: Art Gallery of Greater Victoria, 1983.

Derrida, Jacques. *Limited Inc.* Trans. Samuel Weber and Jeffrey Mehlman. Chicago: Northwestern University Press, 1988.

———. *Of Grammatology*. Trans. Gayatri Spivak. Baltimore: Johns Hopkins University Press, 1976.

———. *The Other Heading: Reflections on Today's Europe*. Trans. Pascale-Anne Brault and Michael B. Naas. Bloomington: Indiana University Press, 1992.

———. *Writing and Difference*. Trans. Alan Bass. Chicago: University of Chicago Press, 1978.

Derrida, Jacques, and Anne Dufourmantelle. *Of Hospitality*. Trans. Rachel Bowlby. Stanford: Stanford University Press, 2000.

Desbarats, Peter, and Terry Mosher, eds. *The Hecklers: A History of Canadian Political Cartooning over Two Centuries in Canada*. Toronto: McClelland and Stewart, 1979.

Désilets, Guy, and André Vigneau, eds. *Répertoire des Archives Photographiques et Audiovisuelles du Fonds du Bureau de Transport Métropolitain*. Montreal: Société de Transport de la Communauté Urbaine de Montréal, 2000.

Deutsche, Rosalyn. *Evictions: Art and Spatial Politics*. Cambridge: MIT Press, 1996.

Diamond, Elin. "Brechtian Theory/Feminist Theory: Toward a Gestic Feminist Criticism." *A Sourcebook of Feminist Theatre and Performance: On and Beyond the Stage*. Ed. Carol Martin. New York: Routledge, 1996. 120–35.

———. *Unmaking Mimesis: Essays on Feminism and Theatre*. New York: Routledge, 1997.

Dick, Ronald. "Regionalization of a Federal Cultural Institution: The Experience of the National Film Board of Canada, 1965–1979." *Flashback: People and Institutions in Canadian Film History*. Ed. Gene Walz. Montreal: Mediatexte, 1986. 107–33.

Dickenson, Greg. "Memories for Sale in Old Pasadena." *Quarterly Journal of Speech*. 83.1 (1997): 1–27.

Diekmeyer, Peter. "Should Marketers Fly the Flag?" *Montreal Gazette* 25 April 2000, D2.

Dippie, Brian W. "Representing the Other: The North American Indian." *Anthropology and Photography, 1860–1920*. Ed. Elizabeth Edwards. New Haven and London: Yale University Press in association with the Royal Anthropological Institute, 1992. 132–36.

Dirlik, Arif. *The Postcolonial Aura: Third World Criticism in the Age of Global Capitalism*. Boulder: Westview, 1997.

Dluhosch, Eric, and Rostislav Svácha, ed. *Karel Teige: L'Enfant Terrible of the Czech Avant-Garde*. Cambridge, MA: MIT Press, 1999.

Doane, Mary Ann. "Film and the Masquerade: Theorising the Female Spectator." *Screen* 23.3–4 (1982): 74–87.

———. "Masquerade Reconsidered: Some Thoughts on the Female Spectator." *Femmes Fatales: Feminism, Film Theory, Psychoanalysis*. New York: Routledge, 1991. 33–43.

Docter, Richard F. *Transvestites and Transsexuals: Toward a Theory of Cross-Gender Behavior*. New York and London: Plenum, 1988.

Dominion Institute. *Le projet memoire/The Memory Project* <www.thememory project.com>.

Donegan, Rosemary. *Work, Weather, and the Grid: Agriculture in Saskatchewan*. Exhibition Catalogue. Regina: Dunlop Art Gallery, 1991.

Donne, John. *The Selected Poetry of Donne*. Ed. Marius Bewley. New York: New American Library, 1979.

Donovan, Kenneth. Interview by Erna MacLeod. 18 December 1997.

Dorais, Louis-Jacques. "The Canadian Inuit and Their Language." *Arctic Languages: An Awakening*. Ed. Dirmid R.F. Collis. Paris: UNESCO, 1990. 185–289.

———. *From Magic Words to Word Processing. A History of the Inuit Language*. Iqaluit: Arctic College, Nunatta Campus, 1993.

———. *Inuit Uqausiqatigiit*. Iqaluit: Arctic Collage, Nunatta Campus, 1990.

Dorland, Michael. "Cultural Industries and the Canadian Experience." *Cultural Industries in Canada*. Ed. Michael Dorland. Toronto: Lorimer, 1996. 347–65.

———. *So Close to the State/s: The Emergence of Canadian Feature Film Policy*. Toronto: University of Toronto Press, 1998.

Dow, Bonnie J. *Prime-Time Feminism: Television, Media Culture, and the Women's Movement since 1970*. Philadelphia: University of Pennsylvania Press, 1996.

Downes, P.G. *Sleeping Island: The Story of One Man's Travels in the Great Barren Lands of the Canadian North*. Saskatoon: Western Producer Prairie Books, 1988.

Drain, Susan. "'Too Much Love-Making': *Anne of Green Gables* on Television." *The Lion and the Unicorn* 11.2 (1987): 63–72.

Dreisziger, N.F. "The Rise of a Bureaucracy for Multiculturalism: The Origins of the Nationalities Branch, 1939–34." *On Guard for Thee: War, Ethnicity, and the Canadian State, 1939–45*. Ed. Norman Hillmer, Bohdan Kordan, and Lubomyr Luciuk. Ottawa: Canadian Committee for the History of the Second World War, 1988. 1–29.

Druick, Zoë. "'Ambiguous Identities' and the Representation of Everyday Life: Notes Toward a New History of Production Policies at the NFB of Canada." *Canadian Issues* 20 (1998): 125–37.

Dugan, Dennis, dir. *Saving Silverman*. Columbia Tristar, 2001.

Duggan, Ginger Gregg, ed. *Fashion and Performance*. Spec. issue of *Fashion Theory* 5.3 (2001).

Duggan, Lisa. "Making It Perfectly Queer." *Socialist Review* 22 (1992): 11–31.

Durham, Jimmy. *Marginal Recession: An Installation by Edward Poitras*. Regina: Dunlop Art Gallery, 1991.

Dyck, Sandra Jane. "'These Things Are Our Totems': Marcus Barbeau and the Indigenization of Canadian Art and Culture in the 1920s." MA thesis, Carleton University, 1995.

Eagleton, Terry. *The Idea of Culture*. Oxford: Blackwell, 2000.

Edelman, Lee. "The Mirror and the Tank: 'AIDS', Subjectivity, and the Rhetoric of Activism." *Writing AIDS: Gay Literature, Language, and Analysis.* Ed. Timothy F. Murphy and Suzanne Poirier. New York: Columbia University Press, 1993. 9–38.

Edmundson, Mark. *Nightmare on Main Street: Angels, Sadomasochism and the Culture of the Gothic.* Cambridge and London: Harvard University Press, 1997.

Edwards, Elizabeth, ed. *Anthropology and Photography, 1860–1920.* New Haven and London: Yale University Press in association with the Royal Anthropological Institute, 1992.

Edwards, S. *Rebel! A Biography of Tom Paine.* New York: Praeger, 1974.

Egan, Kelly. "Things He Always Wanted to Say: 'I Am Canadian' Author Just Let It All Pour Out." *Ottawa Citizen* 19 April 2000, A3.

Ekins, Richard, and David King, eds. *Blending Genders: Social Aspects of Cross-Dressing and Sex-Changing.* London and New York: Routledge, 1996.

Elias, N. *The History of Manners.* New York: Pantheon, 1978.

———. *Power and Civility.* New York: Pantheon, 1982.

El-Obaid, Ahmed El-Obaid, and Kwadwo Appiagyei-Atua. "Human Rights in Africa: A New Perspective on Linking the Past to the Present." *McGill Law Journal* 41 (1996): 819–54.

Elsaesser, Thomas. "Tales of Sound and Fury." *Home Is Where the Heart Is.* Ed. Christine Gledhill. London: BFI, 1990. 43–69.

Emily of New Moon. Canada: CBC, 1998–2001.

Entwistle, Joanne. *The Fashioned Body: Fashion, Dress and Modern Social Theory.* Cambridge: Polity, 2000.

Ericson, Richard V., and Kevin D. Haggerty. *Policing the Risk Society.* Toronto: University of Toronto Press, 1997.

Etting, Mark. "Ambassador 'Joe.'" *Marketing* 1 May 2000, 39.

———. "The Power of Joe." *Marketing* 29 May 2000, 35.

———. "Truth about Molson." *Marketing* 10 April 2000, 47.

Evans, Gary. *In the National Interest.* Toronto: University of Toronto Press, 1989.

———. *John Grierson and the National Film Board: The Politics of Wartime Propaganda.* Toronto: University of Toronto Press, 1984.

Fanon, Frantz. "On National Culture." *The Wretched of the Earth.* Trans. Constance Farrington. New York: Grove, 1966. 167–99.

Felshin, Nina. *Empty Dress: Clothing as Surrogate in Recent Art.* New York: New York Independent Curators, 1993.

"Female Lobster Fishers in Maine." *Cape Breton Post.* 10 June 2001: 17.

Fenton, W.E. *The Great Law and the Longhouse: A Political History of the Iroquois Confederacy.* Norman: University of Oklahoma Press, 1998.

Ferguson, Marjorie, and Peter Golding, eds. *Cultural Studies in Question.* London: Sage, 1997.

Ferguson, Will. *Why I Hate Canadians.* Vancouver: Douglas and McIntyre, 1997.

Ferré, Frederick, ed. "Introduction." *Introduction to Positive Philosophy.* Auguste Comte. Indianapolis and New York: Bobbs-Merrill, 1970. 7–12.

Ferris, Lesley, ed. *Crossing the Stage: Controversies on Cross-Dressing.* London and New York: Routledge, 1993.

Fiamengo, Janice. "Belonging to the Land: Towards a Theory of the Popular Landscape in Green Gables." *Making Avonlea: L.M. Montgomery and Popular Culture.* Ed. Irene Gammel. Toronto: University of Toronto Press, 2002.

Film Frontiers. *Crisis.* Canada: Film Frontiers and Metro Edmonton Educational Television Association, 1970.

———. *Wipeout.* Canada: Film Frontiers and Metro Edmonton Educational Television Association, 1970.

Finlayson, A.C. *Fishing for Truth: A Sociological Analysis of Northern Cod Stock Assessments from 1977 to 1990.* St John's, NL: Institute of Social and Economic Research, 1994.

First Nations Circle on the Constitution: To The Source (Ottawa: Assembly of First Nations, 1992). Co-chair: Rosie Mosquito and Conrad Sioui.

Fischer, Barbara. *Pure Hell.* Toronto: Power Plant, 1990.

Fiske, John. "Popular Culture." *Critical Terms for Literary Study.* 2nd ed. Ed. Frank Lentricchia and Thomas McLaughlin. Chicago: University of Chicago Press, 1995. 321–35.

———. *Understanding Popular Culture.* Boston: Unwin, Hyman, 1989.

Flannery, John P. "Commercial Information Brokers." *Surveillance, Dataveillance, and Personal Freedoms: Use and Abuse of Information Technology.* Ed. The Staff of the Columbia Human Rights Law Review. Fair Lawn, NJ: R.E. Burdick, 1973. 215–47.

Fleras, Augie. "Walking Away from the Camera." *Ethnicity and Culture in Canada: The Research Landscape.* Ed. J.W. Berry and Jean Laponce. Toronto: University of Toronto Press, 1994. 304–84.

Fleras, Augie, and Jean Leonard Elliot. *Unequal Relations: An Introduction to Race, Ethnic and Aboriginal Dynamics in Canada.* 2nd ed. Scarborough, ON: Prentice Hall, 1996.

Fortress Louisbourg National Historic Site: Commemorative Integrity Statement. June 2001. 12 July 2005 <http://fortress.uccb.ns.ca/parks/LsbgMPE_6.htm>.

Foster, Cecil. *A Place Called Heaven: The Meaning of Being Black in Canada.* Toronto: Harper Collins, 1996.

Fothergill, Robert. "Coward, Bully, or Clown: The Dream-Life of a Younger Brother." *Canadian Film Reader.* Ed. Seth Feldman and Joyce Nelson. Toronto: Peter Martin, 1977. 234–50.

Foucault, Michel. "Governmentality." *The Foucault Effect: Studies in Governmentality.* Ed. Graham Burchill, Colin Gordon, and Peter Miller. Chicago: University of Chicago Press, 1991. 87–104.

———. *The History of Sexuality,* Vol. 1. New York: Vintage, 1980.

Francis, Daniel. *The Imaginary Indian: The Image of the Indian in Canadian Culture.* Vancouver: Arsenal Pulp Press, 1992.

———. *Imagining Ourselves: Classics of Canadian Non-Fiction.* Vancouver: Arsenal Pulp Press, 1994.

———. *National Dreams: Myth, Memory, and Canadian History.* Vancouver: Arsenal Pulp Press, 1997.

Franklin, B. *Autobiography of Benjamin Franklin.* New York: Books, n.d.

French, J.R.P., and B.H. Raven. "The Bases of Social Power." *Group Dynamics.* Ed. J.D. Cartwright and A. Zander. Evanston, IL: Row, Peterson, 1962. 607–22.

Frenkel, Vera, and Jeanne Randolph. *Vera Frenke…from the Transitbar/…du transitbar.* Toronto: Power Plant; Ottawa: National Gallery of Canada, 1994.

Freud, Sigmund. *Civilization and Its Discontents.* Trans. James Strachey. New York: Norton, 1962.

———. "Fetishism." Trans. James Strachey. *On Sexuality.* Vol. 7. Ed. Angela Richards. Harmondsworth: Penguin, 1977. 351–57.

———. "Humour." Trans. James Strachey. *Art and Literature.* Vol. 14. Ed. Albert Dickson. Harmondsworth: Penguin, 1985. 425–33.

———. "The 'Uncanny.'" Trans. James Strachey. *Art and Literature.* Vol. 14. Ed. Albert Dickson. Harmondsworth: Penguin, 1985. 339–76.

Frever, Trinna S. "How the Story Girl Lost Her Stories." Paper presented at the L.M. Montgomery and Popular Culture conference, University of Prince Edward Island, 2000.

———. "Vaguely Familiar: Cinematic Intertextuality in Kevin Sullivan's *Anne of Avonlea.*" *Canadian Children's Literature* 91/92 (1998): 36–52.

Frisch, Michael. "American History and the Structures of Collective Memory: A Modest Exercise in Empirical Iconography." *Journal of American History* 75 (1989): 1130–55.

Frye, Northrop. *The Bush Garden: Essays on the Canadian Imagination.* Toronto: Anansi, 1971.

———. "Conclusion to a *Literary History of Canada.*" *The Bush Garden: Essays on the Canadian Imagination.* Toronto: Anansi, 1971. 213–51.

———. *The Eternal Act of Creation, 1979–1990.* Ed. Robert Denham. Bloomington and Indianapolis: Indiana University Press, 1993.

———. *The Modern Century: Whidden Lectures.* Toronto: Oxford University Press, 1967.

Fuchs, Cynthia. "'Beat me outta me': Alternative Masculinities." *Boys: Masculinities in Contemporary Culture.* Ed. Paul Smith. Boulder: Westview, 1996. 171–98.

Fumoleau, René. *As Long As This Land Shall Last: A History of Treaty 8 and Treaty 11, 1870–1939.* Toronto: McClelland and Stewart [c.1975].

Garber, Marjorie. *Vested Interests: Cross-Dressing and Cultural Anxiety.* New York: Routledge, 1992.

———. *Vice Versa: Bisexuality and the Eroticism of Everyday Life.* New York: Touchstone, 1996.

Gasher, Mike. "The Audiovisual Locations Industry in Canada: Considering British Columbia as Hollywood North." *Canadian Journal of Communication* 20.2 (1995): 231–54.

Geertz, Clifford. *The Interpretation of Cultures.* New York: Basic Books, 1973.

General Idea. "Glamour." *File Megazine* 3.1 (1975): 21–22.

Genest, Michele, and Dianne Homan, eds. *Urban Coyote: A Yukon Anthology.* Whitehorse: Lost Moose, 2001.

Genosko, Gary. "The Imposition of Transparency in Canada after 9/11." Unpublished manuscript (2002). Presented in the Terror of Civilization panel of the Canadian Political Science Association Annual Meetings, Congress 2002, Toronto.

——. "The Struggle for an Affirmative Weakness." *Current Perspectives in Social Theory* 12 (1992): 179–94.

——. *Undisciplined Theory.* London: Sage, 1998.

Geraghty, Christine. *Women and Soap Opera.* Cambridge: Polity Press, 1991.

Giddens, Anthony. *The Consequences of Modernity.* Stanford: Stanford University Press, 1990.

——. "Time and Space: Time-Space, Structure, System." *The Giddens Reader.* Ed. Philip Cassell. Stanford: Stanford University Press, 1993. 176–80.

Gillespie, Beryl C. "Bearlake Indians." *Subarctic.* Ed. June Helm. *Handbook of North American Indians.* Ed. William C. Sturtevant. Washington: Smithsonian Institute, 1981. 310–13.

Gillespie, Kerry. "How That Molson Ad Hit Our Nationalist Nerve with the Rant That Rocks." *Toronto Star* 15 April 2000, A1, A30.

Gilroy, Paul. *The Black Atlantic: Modernity and Double Consciousness.* Cambridge, MA: Harvard University Press, 1993.

——. *"There Ain't No Black in the Union Jack": The Cultural Politics of Race and Nation.* Chicago: University of Chicago Press, 1987.

Gingras, Nicole. "The Movement of Things." *Kate Craig: Skin.* Ed. Grant Arnold. Vancouver: Vancouver Art Gallery, 1998. 17–29.

Girard, François, dir. *The Red Violin.* Universal Studios, 1998.

Giroux, Henry A. *The Mouse That Roared: Disney and the End of Innocence.* Lanham, MD: Bowman and Littlefield, 1999.

Gittings, Christopher. *Canadian National Cinema.* New York and London: Routledge, 2002.

——. "Imaging Canada: The Singing Mountie and Other Commodifications of Nation." *Australian-Canadian Studies* 16.2 (1998): 507–22.

——. "Re-Visioning *Emily of New Moon*: Family Melodrama for the Nation." *Canadian Children's Literature* 91/92 (1998): 22–35.

Gledhill, Christine, ed. *Home Is Where the Heart Is.* London: BFI, 1990.

——. "The Melodramatic Field: An Investigation." Gledhill, *Home,* 5–39.

Goar, C. "Trudeau Taken Aback in Commons as Flora Defends Indian Women." *Vancouver Sun* 8 July 1980, A7.

Godbout, Jacques. *Salut Galarneau!* Paris: Seuil, 1967.

Goddard, Peter. "Canadian, Eh? Then This Rant's for You, Bud." *Toronto Star* 1 April 2000, M4.

Goddu, Teresa. *Gothic America: Narrative, History, and Nation.* New York: Columbia University Press, 1997.

Goldberg, David Theo. *Racist Culture, Philosophy, and the Politics of Meaning.* Massachusetts and Oxford: Blackwell, 1993.

Goldberg, Vicki, ed. *Photography in Print: Writing from 1816 to the Present.* Albuquerque: University of New Mexico Press, 1981.

Goldie, Terry. *Fear and Temptation: The Image of the Indigene in Canadian, Australian, and New Zealand Literatures.* Kingston: McGill-Queen's University Press, 1989.

Gordon, Charles. "Let's Hear It for Canada!" *Maclean's* 1 May 2000, 62.

Goto, Hiromi. *Chorus of Mushrooms.* Edmonton: NeWest Press, 1994.

Gramsci, Antonio. *Selections from the Prison Notebooks of Antonio Gramsci.* New York: International, 1971.

Granatstein, Jack. *Who Killed Canadian History?* Toronto: HarperCollins Canada, 1998.

Green, Mary Jean. "Redefining the Maternal: Women's Relationships in the Fiction of Marie-Claire Blais." *Traditionalism, Nationalism, and Feminism: Women Writers of Quebec.* Ed. Paula Gilbert Lewis. Westport, CT: Greenwood, 1985. 125–40.

Greenberg, Clement. "Avant-Garde and Kitsch." *Partisan Review* 6.5 (1939): 34–49.

Greenblatt, Stephen. *Renaissance Self-Fashioning: From More to Shakespeare.* Chicago: University of Chicago, 1980.

Greenhill, Pauline. "Lesbian Mess(ages): Decoding Shawna Dempsey's Cake Squish at the Festival du Voyeur." *Atlantis* 23.1 (1998): 91–99.

Greenhill, Ralph, and Andrew Birrell. *Canadian Photography, 1839–1920.* Toronto: Coach House Press, 1979.

Greenlaw, Linda. *The Hungry Ocean.* New York: Hyperion, 1999.

Grenville, Bruce. Introduction. Randolph, *Psychoanalysis and Synchronized Swimming.* Ed. Bruce Grenville. Toronto: YYZ Books, 1991. 11–17.

Greyson, John, dir. *Lilies.* Triptych Media, 1996.

Grierson, John. *Grierson on Documentary.* Ed. Forsyth Hardy. London and Boston: Faber and Faber, 1979.

Griffin, Anne. "Le façonnement de la mémoire et le discours sur l'indépendence." *Les nationalismes au Québec du XIXe au XXIe siècle.* Ed. Michel Sarra-Bournet. Quebec City: Les Presses de l'Université Laval, 2001. 255–75.

Griffin, Kevin. "Violence against Women 'Isn't Cultural': Counsellors Who Deal with Domestic Violence Worry That Stereotyping Will Obscure an Issue That Affects 'All Canadians.'" *Vancouver Sun* 8 April 1996, B2.

Griffiths, Rudyard, ed. *Great Questions of Canada.* Toronto: Stoddart, 2000.

Grimm, Reinhold. "Alienation in Context: On the Theory and Practice of Brechtian Theatre." *A Bertolt Brecht Reference Companion.* Ed. Siegfried Mews. Westport, CT: Greenwood, 1997. 35–46.

Gross, Louis. *Redefining the American Gothic: From Wieland to Day of the Dead.* Ann Arbor and London: UMI Research Press, 1989.

Guattari, Félix, and Antonio Negri. *Communists Like Us: New Spaces of Liberty, New Lines of Alliance.* Trans. Michael Ryan. New York: Semiotext(e), 1990.

Guerin v. Canada, [1984] 2 Canada Supreme Court Reports 335.

Gupta, Akhil, and James Ferguson. "Culture, Power, Place: Ethnography at the End of an Era." *Culture, Power, Place: Explorations in Critical Anthropology*. Ed. Akhil Gupta and James Ferguson. Durham: Duke University Press, 1997. 1–29.

Halberstam, Judith. *Skin Shows: Gothic Horror and the Technology of Monsters*. Durham, NC: Duke University Press, 1995.

Haliburton, Thomas Chandler. *The Clockmaker: Series One, Two, and Three*. Ed. George L. Parker. Ottawa: Carleton University Press, 1995.

Hall, Lucie. Personal interview. 21 August 2001.

Hall, Stuart. Convocation Address at the University of Massachusetts at Amherst. 1989.

———. *Stuart Hall: Critical Dialogues in Cultural Studies*. Ed. David Morley and Kuan-Hsing Chen. London: Routledge, 1996.

———. "Cultural Identity and Diaspora." *Colonial Discourse and Post-Colonial Theory: A Reader*. Ed. Patrick Williams and Laura Chrisman. New York: Harvester-Wheatsheaf, 1994. 392–403.

———. "Culture, the Media, and the 'Ideological Effect.'" *Mass Communication and Society*. Ed. James Curran, Michael Gurevitch, and Janet Woollacott. London: Sage, 1979. 315–48.

———. "The Whites of Their Eyes: Racist Ideologies and the Media." *The Media Reader*. Ed. Manuel Alvarado and John O. Thompson. London: British Film Institute, 1990. 7–23.

———. "The Work of Representations." *Representation, Cultural Representation, and Signifying Practices*. Ed. Stuart Hall. London: Sage and The Open University, 1997. 15–74.

Hall, Stuart, Chas Critcher, Tony Jefferson, John Clarke, and Brian Roberts. *Policing the Crisis*. London: Macmillan, 1978.

Hamelin, Louis-Edmond. *Canadian Nordicity: It's Your North, Too*. Montreal: Harvest House, 1978.

Hamlet of Baker Lake et al. v. Minister of Indian Affairs and Northern Development et al., 107 Dominion Law Reports (3d) 513 (Fed. Ct. Trial Div.), 1980.

Hannerz, Ulf. "Cosmopolitans and Locals in World Culture." *Global Culture: Nationalism, Globalization and Modernity*. Ed. Mike Featherstone. London: Sage, 1990. 237–51.

———. *Cultural Complexity: Studies in the Social Organization of Meaning*. New York: Columbia, 1992.

Harcourt, Peter. "Imaginary Images: An Examination of Atom Egoyan's Films." *Film Quarterly* 48 (1993): 2–14.

Hardy, Forsyth, ed. Introduction. *Grierson on Documentary*. By John Grierson. London and Boston: Faber and Faber, 1979. 11–17.

Harrington, Richard. *The Face of the Arctic: A Cameraman's Story in Words and Pictures of Five Journeys into the Far North*. New York: Schuman, 1952.

———. *The Inuit Life As It Was*. Edmonton: Hurtig, 1981.

Harris, Geraldine. *Staging Femininities: Performance and Performativity*. Manchester: Manchester University Press, 1999.

Hassan, Jamelie. *Aldin's Gift*. North York: Art Gallery of York University, 1996.

Hawes, Stanley, dir. *Trans-Canada Express*. Canada: National Film Board of Canada, 1944.

Hawthorn, H. *A Survey of the Contemporary Indians in Canada*. 2 vols. Ottawa: Indian Affairs Branch, 1966.

Hawthorn, Harry B., ed. *A Survey of the Contemporary Indians of Canada: Economic, Political, Educational Needs and Policies*. 2 vols. Ottawa: Indian Affairs Branch, 1966–67.

Hayward, Susan. "Framing National Cinemas." *Cinema and Nation*. Ed. Mette Hjort and Scott Mackenzie. London and New York: Routledge, 2000. 88–102.

Hébert, Anne. *Kamouraska*. Trans. Norman Shapiro. Toronto: Stoddart, 1994. Originally published as *Kamouraska*. Paris: Seuil, 1970.

Hegel, G.W.F. *Lectures on the Philosophy of History*. Trans. J. Sibree. London: George Bell and Sons, 1878.

———. *Phenomenology of Spirit*. Trans. A.V. Miller. Oxford: Oxford University Press, 1977.

Heller, Dana. "Housebreaking History: Feminism's Troubled Romance with the Domestic Sphere." *Feminism beside Itself*. Ed. Diane Elam and Robyn Wiegman. London: Routledge, 1995. 217–33.

Helmes-Hayes, Rick, and James Curtis. "Introduction." *The Vertical Mosaic Revisited*. Ed. Rick Helmes-Hayes and James Curtis. Toronto: University of Toronto Press, 1998. 3–33.

Hennessy, Rosemary. "Queer Visibility and Commodity Culture." *Cultural Critique* 29 (1995): 31–76.

Henry, Frances. "Canada's Contribution to the 'Management' of Ethno-Cultural Diversity." *Canadian Journal of Communication* 27.2/3 (2002): 231–42.

———. *The Caribbean Diaspora in Toronto: Learning to Live with Racism*. Toronto: University of Toronto Press, 1994.

Henry, Frances, and Carol Tator. "Racist Discourse in Canada's English Print Media." Toronto: Canadian Race Relations Foundation." March 2000 <http://www.crr.ca/Load.do?section=26&subsection=38&id=322&type=2>.

Henry, Frances, Carol Tator, Winston Mattis, and Tim Rees. *The Colour of Democracy: Racism in Canadian Society*. Toronto: Harcourt Brace Canada, 1995.

Hersey, Eleanor. "'It's All Mine': The Modern Woman as Writer in Sullivan's *Anne of Green Gables* Films." *Making Avonlea: L.M. Montgomery and Popular Culture*. Ed. Irene Gammel. Toronto: University of Toronto Press, 2002.

Hewison, Robert. "Commerce and Culture." Corner and Harvey, 162–77.

———. *The Heritage Industry*. London: Methuen, 1987.

Highway, Tomson. *The Rez Sisters*. Saskatoon: Fifth House, 1988.

Higson, Andrew. "Re-Presenting the National Past: Nostalgia and Pastiche in the Heritage Film." *Fires Were Started: British Genres and Thatcherism*. Ed. Lester Friedman. Minneapolis: University of Minnesota Press, 1993. 109–29.

Hill, Lawrence. *Black Berry, Sweet Juice: On Being Black and White in Canada*. Toronto: Harper Flamingo Canada, 2001.

Hipsky, Martin A. "Anglophil(m)ia: Why Does America Watch Merchant-Ivory Movies?" *Journal of Popular Film and Television* 22.3 (1994): 98-107.

Historica Foundation. "Governance." *Histor!ca: Your Place in History.* 14 February 2002 <http://www.histori.ca>.

———. "Heritage Minutes." *Histor!ca: Your Place in History.* 14 February 2002 <http://www.histori.ca>.

———. "Historica—A Web Site Dedicated to Canadian History and Heritage." *Histor!ca: Your Place in History.* 14 February 2002 <http://www.histori .ca>.

———. "History of the Minutes." *Histor!ca: Your Place in History.* 14 February 2002 <http://www.histori.ca>.

———. "Marconi." *Histor!ca: Your Place in History.* 18 February 2002 <http:// www.histori.ca>.

———. "Search by Chronology." *Histor!ca: Your Place in History.* 14 February 2002 <http://www.histori.ca>.

———. "Search by Theme." *Histor!ca: Your Place in History.* 14 February 2002 <http://www.histori.ca>.

Hollander, Anne. *Sex and Suits.* New York: Alfred A. Knopf, 1994.

"Hollywood North Is Brimming to Become Bollywood West." (2001). *Canadian Press Newswire* 24 June 2001: 1-3. 4 October 2001 <http://www.lib.sfu.ca /cc420 1a/conv95241.conv>.

hooks, bell. "Homeplace: A Site of Resistance." *Yearning: Race, Gender, and Cultural Politics.* London: Turnaround, 1991. 41-49.

Horne, Gerald S. "Interpreting Prairie Cinema." *Prairie Forum: The Journal of Canadian Plains Research Center* 22.1 (1997): 135-51.

Hoskins, Colin, Stuart McFadyen, and Adam Finn. *Global Television and Film: An Introduction to the Economics of the Business.* Oxford: Clarendon Press, 1997.

Hougan, James. *Decadence: Radical Nostalgia, Narcissism, and Decline in the Seventies.* New York: William Morrow, 1975.

Howey, Ann F. "'She Look'd Down to Camelot': Anne and the Lady of Shalott." Paper presented at the L.M. Montgomery and Popular Culture Conference, University of Prince Edward Island, 2000.

Hum, Derek, and Wayne Simpson. *Wage Opportunities for Visible Minorities in Canada.* The Income and Labour Dynamics Working Paper Series Catalogue No. 98-17. November 1998.

Hutcheon, Linda. *As Canadian As Possible … Under the Circumstances!* Toronto: ECW, 1990.

———. *The Canadian Postmodern.* Toronto: Oxford University Press, 1988.

———. "'Circling the Downspout of Empire': Post-Colonialism and Postmodernism." *ARIEL* 20.4 (1989): 149-75.

——— ed. *Double-Talking: Essays on Verbal and Visual Ironies in Contemporary Canadian Art and Literature.* Toronto: ECW Press, 1992.

———. *The Politics of Postmodernism.* London and New York: Routledge, 1989.

———. *A Theory of Parody: The Teachings of Twentieth-Century Art Forms.* New York and London: Methuen, 1985.

Huxley, Julian. *Unesco: Its Purpose and Its Philosophy*. Washington, DC: Public Affairs Press, 1948.

Huyda, Richard J. *Camera in the Interior: 1858, H.L. Hime, Photographer, the Assiniboine and Saskatchewan Exploring Expedition*. Toronto: Coach House, 1975.

Huyssen, Andreas. *Twilight Memories*. New York: Routledge, 1995.

Indian Chiefs of Alberta. *Citizens Plus*. Edmonton: Indian Association of Alberta, 1970.

Infantry, Ashante. "Opportunity Knocks But Not for All." *Toronto Star* 2 May 1999, A1.

Innis, Harold. *The Bias of Communication*. Toronto: University of Toronto Press, 1951.

———. *The Strategy of Culture*. Toronto: University of Toronto Press, 1952.

"Interpretive Plan for Fortress Louisbourg." *Fortress Louisbourg National Historic Site: Commemorative Integrity Statement*. Manuscript, 1970.

Isin, Engin F. *Cities without Citizens: The Modernity of the City as Corporation*. Montreal: Black Rose, 1992.

Jackson, Stanley, dir. *Peoples of Canada*. Canada: National Film Board of Canada, 1941.

Jackson, William Henry. "Time Exposure, 1940: An Excerpt." *Photography in Print: Writings from 1816 to the Present*. Ed. Vicki Goldberg. Albuquerque: University of New Mexico Press, 1994. 168–70.

Jacob, Christian. *L'Empire des cartes: Approche théorique de la cartographie à travers l'histoire*. Paris: Albin Michel, 1992.

Jaimet, Kate. "'I Am'... Is Back: Molson Relaunches Ad." *Ottawa Citizen* 22 March 2000, D1.

Jameson, Frederic. "Cognitive Mapping." *Marxism and the Interpretation of Culture*. Ed. Cary Nelson and Larry Grossberg. Urbana: University of Illinois Press, 1988. 347–57.

Jameson, Fredric, and Masao Miyashi, eds. *The Cultures of Globalization*. Durham, NC: Duke University Press, 1998.

Jasmin, Claude. *Pleure pas, Germaine*. Montreal: Parti Pris, 1965; Montreal: Centre Éducatif et Culturel, 1974.

Jiminez, Marina. "Slain Teen Misfit Remembered." *Vancouver Sun* 25 November 1997, A1.

———. "Teenage Girls and Violence: The BC Reality." *Vancouver Sun* 1 December 1997, A1.

Jiwani, Yasmin. "By Omission and Commission: 'Race' and Representation in Canadian Television News." Diss., School of Communication Studies, Simon Fraser University, 1993.

———. "Erasing Race: The Story of Reena Virk." *Canadian Woman Studies* 19.3 (1999): 178–84.

———. "Mapping Violence: A Work in Progress." Report presented to the Federal Action on Family Violence Prevention Initiative in British Columbia. December 2000 <http://www.harbour.sfu.ca/freda/articles/fvpi.htm>.

———. "The Media, 'Race,' and Multiculturalism." *Proceedings of the BC Advisory Council on Multiculturalism*. Vancouver: Multiculturalism BC, 1995. 11–18 <http://www.harbour.sfu.ca/freda/articles/media.htm>.

———. "Violence against Women Is Bigger Than...Class, Racial, or Religious Affiliation." *Vancouver Sun* 13 April 1996, A25.

Johansen, B.E. *Debating Democracy: Native American Legacy of Freedom*. Sante Fe: Clear Light, 1998.

Johnson, Brian D. "The Canadian Patient." *Maclean's* 24 March 1997: 42–46.

Johnson, Cathy. Email correspondence. 16 December 2001.

Johnston, A.J.B. Interview by Erna MacLeod. 16 December 1997.

———. "Partnerships and Linkages in Native History Interpretation." Unpublished manuscript, May 1993.

———. "The People of Eighteenth-Century Louisbourg." *Aspects of Louisbourg*. Ed. Eric Krause, Carol Corbin, and William O'Shea. Sydney, NS: n.p., 1995. 152–60.

Johnston, Denis W. "Lines and Circles: The 'Rez' Plays of Thomson Highway." *Canadian Literature* 124–25 (1990): 254–64.

Jolicoeur, Nicole, and Jeanne Randolph. *La Vérité Folle*. Vancouver: Presentation House, 1989.

Jones, Amelia. *Body Art: Performing the Subject*. Minneapolis: University of Minnesota Press, 1998.

Jones, Amelia, and Andrew Stephenson. *Performing the Body/Performing the Text*. New York: Routledge, 1999.

Jordan, John M. *Machine-Age Ideology: Social Engineering and American Liberalism, 1911–1939*. Chapel Hill and London: University of North Carolina Press, 1994.

Kamboureli, Smaro. "The Technology of Ethnicity: Canadian Multiculturalism and the Language of Law." *Multicultural States: Rethinking Difference and Identity*. Ed. David Bennett. New York and London: Routledge, 1989. 208–22.

Kaplan, E. Ann. "The Case of the Missing Mother." *Heresies* 16 (1983): 81–85.

Kaprow, Allan. "The Legacy of Jackson Pollock." *Art News* 57.6 (1958): 24–26, 55–57.

Karim, Karim H. "Constructions, Deconstructions, and Reconstructions: Competing Canadian Discourses on Ethnocultural Terminology." *Canadian Journal of Communication* 18.2 (1993) <http://www.cjc-online.ca>.

———. "From Ethnic Media to Global Media: Transnational Communication Networks among Diasporic Communities." International Comparative Research Group, Strategic Research and Analysis, Canadian Heritage, Report No: WPTC-99-02, June 1998. December 2001 <http://www.transcomm.ox .ac.uk/working%20papers/karim.pdf.10>.

Kaye, Janice. "Perfectly Normal, Eh? Gender Transformation and National Identity in Canada." *Canadian Journal of Film Studies* 3.2 (1994): 63–80.

Kennedy, Janice. "Only in the Rest of Canada? Pity." *Calgary Herald* 29 April 2000, O2.

Kern, Stephen. *The Culture of Time and Space, 1880-1918*. Cambridge: Harvard University Press, 1983.

Kew, Karen, and Ed Sinclair, dir. *Chasing the Dragon*. Canada: V-Tape, 1993.

King, Thomas. "Godzilla vs. Post-Colonial." *New Contexts of Canadian Criticism*. Ed. Ajay Heble, Donna Palmateer Pennee, and J.R. (Tim) Struthers. Peterborough: Broadview, 1997. 241-48.

Kivland, Sharon, and Jeanne Randolph. *Sharon Kivland: Mes Tendresses (or, My Endearments)*. Toronto: Toronto Photographers Workshop, 1998.

Klein, Naomi. *No Logo*. New York: Picador, 1999.

Kleinhans, Chuck. "Taking Out the Trash: Camp and the Politics of Parody." *The Politics and Poetics of Camp*. Ed. Moe Meyer. New York: Routledge, 1994. 182-201.

Kofron, Peter. Liner Notes. Trans. Karolina Vocadlova. *Czech New Music of the 1960s*. Perf. Agon Ensembles. FI 0048-2. ARTA Records [Prague], 1993.

Kott, Jan. *The Theatre of Essence*. Evanston: Northwestern University Press, 1984.

Krafft-Ebing, Richard von. *Psychopathia Sexualis with Especial Reference to the Antipathic Sexual Instinct: A Medico-Forensic Study*. Trans. F.J. Rebman. New York: Physicians and Surgeons Book Company, 1934.

Krause, Michael G., and Victor Golla. "Northern Athapaskan Languages." *Subarctic*. Ed. June Helm. *Handbook of North American Indians*. Ed. William C. Sturtevant. Washington: Smithsonian Institution, 1981. 67-85.

Krauss, Rosalind. "Notes on the Index: Part 1." *The Originality of the Avant-Garde and Other Modernist Myths*. Cambridge: MIT Press, 1985.

———. "Video: The Aesthetics of Narcissism." *October* 1 (Spring 1976): 50-64.

Kroetsch, Robert. "Disunity as Unity: A Canadian Strategy." *The Lovely Treachery of Words: Essays Selected and New*. Don Mills: Oxford University Press, 1989. 21-33.

Kuhn, Annette. "Women's Genres: Melodrama, Soap Opera, and Theory." Gledhill, *Home*, 339-49.

Kunuk, Zacharias, et al., dir. *Atanarjuat: The Fast Runner*. Iglulik: Isuma Productions and the National Film Board of Canada, 2000.

Kymlicka, Will. *Finding Our Way: Rethinking Ethnocultural Relations in Canada*. Toronto: Oxford University Press, 1998.

———. *Multicultural Citizenship: Liberal Theory of Minority Rights*. Oxford: Clarendon Press, 1995.

———. "The New Debate over Minority Rights." *Canadian Political Philosophy*. Ed. Ronald Beiner and Wayne Norman. Oxford: Oxford University Press, 2001. 159-76.

———. *Politics in the Vernacular: Nationalism, Multiculturalism, and Citizenship*. Oxford: Oxford University Press, 2000.

Lacan, Jacques. "Guiding Remarks for a Congress on Feminine Sexuality." *Feminine Sexuality: Jacques Lacan and the école freudienne*. Ed. Juliet Mitchell and Jacqueline Rose. Trans. Jacqueline Rose. New York: Norton, 1982. 86-98.

Laclau, Ernesto. *Emancipation(s)*. London: Verso, 1996.

Laclau, Ernesto, and Chantal Mouffe. *Hegemony and Socialist Strategy: Towards a Radical Democratic Politics*. London: Verso, 1985.

Lacy, Suzanne, ed. *Mapping the Terrain: New Genre Public Art*. Seattle: Bay Press, 1995.

Laferrière, Dany. *How to Make Love to a Negro*. Trans. David Homel. Toronto: Coach House, 1987. Originally published as *Comment faire l'amour avec un nègre sans se fatiguer*. Montreal: VLB, 1985.

Lamoureux, Johanne. "French Kiss from a No Man's Land: Translating the Art of Québec." *Art Magazine* 65.6 (1991): 48–54.

Lamphier, Garry. "Nunavut: Canada's Final Frontier." *Edmonton Journal* 30 October 2003. Section H.

Landy, Marcia. *Fascism in Film: The Italian Commercial Cinema, 1930–1943*. Princeton, NJ: Princeton University Press, 1991.

———. *Film, Politics, and Gramsci*. Minneapolis: University of Minnesota Press, 1994.

Lang, Robert. *American Film Melodrama: Griffith, Vidor, Minnelli*. Princeton, NJ: Princeton University Press, 1989.

Langford, Martha. *Contemporary Canadian Photography from the Collection of the National Film Board*. Edmonton: Hurtig, 1984.

Lasch, Christopher. *The Culture of Narcissism*. New York: Norton, 1978.

Laucius, Joanne. "I Am Canadian…Well, I Was." *Ottawa Citizen* 20 July 2004, A1–A2.

Lawrence, Bonita. "Rewriting Histories of the Land: Colonization and Indigenous Resistance in Eastern Canada." *Race, Space, and the Law: Unmapping a White Settler Society*. Ed. Sherene Razack. Toronto: Between the Lines, 2002. 21–46.

Lawson, Alan. "Postcolonial Theory and the 'Settler' Subject." *Essays on Canadian Writing* 56 (1995): 20–36.

Leach, James. "Second Images: Reflections on the Canadian Cinema(s) in the Seventies." *Take Two: A Tribute to Film in Canada*. Ed. Seth Feldman. Toronto: Irwin, 1984. 100–110.

Leacock, Stephen. *My Discovery of the West*. Toronto: Thomas Allan, 1937.

———. "My Financial Career." *My Financial Career and Other Follies*. Ed. David Staines. Toronto: McClelland and Stewart, 1993.

———. *Sunshine Sketches of a Little Town*. London: John Lane; The Bodley Head, 1912.

Lears, T.J. Jackson. "The Concept of Cultural Hegemony: Problems and Possibilities." *American Historical Review* 90.3 (1985): 567–93.

Lee, Dennis. "Cadence, Country, Silence: Writing in Colonial Space." *Open Letter* 2.6 (1973): 34–53.

Lefebvre, Henri. *The Production of Space*. Trans. Donald Nicholson-Smith. Oxford: Blackwell, 1991.

Legate, David. *Stephen Leacock*. Toronto: Doubleday, 1970.

LeGoff, Jacques. *History and Memory*. Trans. Steven Rendall and Elizabeth Claman. New York: Columbia University Press, 1992.

———. *The Medieval Imagination*. Trans. Arthur Goldhammer. Chicago: University of Chicago Press, 1988.

Leja, Michael. "Peirce, Visuality and Art." *Representations* 72 (2000): 97–122.

Lewis, Charles. "Making Sense of Common Sense: A Framework for Tracking Hegemony." *Critical Studies in Mass Communication* 9 (1992): 277–92.

Lichtenstein, Demian, dir. *3000 Miles to Graceland*. Warner Brothers, 2001.

Lindau, Juan, and Curtis Cook. "One Continent, Contrasting Styles: The Canadian Experience in North American Perspective." *Aboriginal Rights and Self-Government: The Canadian and Mexican Experience in North American Perspective*. Ed. Curtis Cook and Juan Lindau. Montreal and Kingston: McGill-Queen's University Press, 2000.

Linteau, Paul-André. *Histoire de Montréal depuis la Conféderation*. Montréal: Boréal, 2000.

Lintvelt, Jaap, and Françoise Paré, eds. *Frontières flottantes: Lieu et espace dans les cultures Francophones du Canada/Shifting Boundaries: Place and Space in Francophone Cultures of Canada*. New York: Rodopi, 2001.

Lippard, Lucy R., ed. *Partial Recall: Photographs of Native North Americans*. New York: New Press, 1992.

Longfellow, Brenda. "Gender, Landscape and Colonial Allegories in *The Far Shore, Loyalties* and *Mouvements du désir*." *Gendering the Nation: Canadian Women's Cinema*. Ed. Kay Armatage, et al. Toronto: University of Toronto Press, 1999. 165–82.

———. "*The Red Violin*, Commodity Fetishism and Globalization." *Canadian Journal of Film Studies* 10 (2001): 6–20.

López, Ana M. "Celluloid Tears: Melodrama in the 'Old' Mexican Cinema." *Iris* 13 (1991): 29–51.

Lord, Susan. "States of Emergency in the Films of Anne Wheeler." *North of Everything: English Canadian Cinema since 1980*. Ed. William Beard and Jerry White. Edmonton: University of Alberta Press, 2002. 312–26.

———. "Sublime Machines: Time, Technology and the Female Body of Ocular Modernity." Diss., York University, 1999.

Lovejoy, Paul E. *Transformations in Slavery: A History of Slavery in Africa*. Cambridge: Cambridge University Press, 2000.

Lozano, Jorge, dir. *Samuel and Samantha*. Canada: V-Tape, 1993.

Lupack, Barbara Tepa, ed. *Nineteenth-Century Women at the Movies: Adapting Classic Women's Fiction to Film*. Bowling Green, OH: Bowling Green State University Popular Press, 1999.

Lynes, Jeanette. "Consumable Avonlea: The Commodification of the Green Gables Mythology." *Canadian Children's Literature* 91/92 (1998): 7–21.

Lyon, David. *The Electronic Eye: The Rise of Surveillance Society*. Cambridge: Polity, 1994.

Lyon, David, and Elia Zureik. "Surveillance, Privacy, and the New Technology." *Computers, Surveillance and Privacy*. Minneapolis: University of Minnesota Press, 1996. 1–18.

Lyotard, Jean-François. "On the Strength of the Weak." Trans. Roger McKeon. *Semiotext(e)* 3.2 (1978): 204–14.

———. *The Postmodern Condition: A Report on Knowledge.* Trans. Geoff Bennington and Brian Massumi. Minneapolis: University of Minnesota Press, 1984.

Macgowan, James. "My Name Is Glen and I Am an Ad Guy." *Ottawa Citizen* 19 August 2000, E2-E3.

Mackay, Ian. "History and the Tourist Gaze: The Politics of Commemoration in Nova Scotia, 1935-1964." *Acadiensis*, 22.2 (193): 102-38.

Mackey, Eva. *The House of Difference.* London: Routledge, 1999.

Magder, Ted. *Canada's Hollywood: The Canadian State and Feature Films.* Toronto: University of Toronto Press, 1993.

———. "Film and Video Production." *Cultural Industries in Canada.* Ed. Michael Dorland. Toronto: Lorimer, 1996. 145-77.

Mahtani, Minelle. "Representing Minorities: Canadian Media and Minority Identities." *Canadian Ethnic Studies* 33.3 (2001): 99-133.

Manitoba Indian Brotherhood. *Wahbung (Our Tomorrow).* Winnipeg: Manitoba Indian Brotherhood, 1971.

Mann, Michael. *The Sources of Social Power.* Cambridge: Cambridge University Press, 1986.

Mann, Steve. "Can Humans Being Clerks make Clerks be Human? Exploring the Fundamental Difference between UbiComp and WearComp." *Informationstechnik und Technische Informatik* 43.2 (2001): 97-106 <http://wearcam .org/itti/itti.htm>.

———. "Privacy Issues of Wearable Cameras Versus Surveillance Cameras." July 1995 <http://wearcam.org/netcam_privacy_issues.html>.

———. "'Reflectionism' and 'Diffusionism': New Tactics for Deconstructing the Video Surveillance Superhighway." *Leonardo* 31.2 (1998): 93-102. <http:// eyetap.org/wearcam/leonardo/my_hack_at_leonardo_html/index.htm>.

———. "Shootback Accountability Theatre." 24 December 1998 <http://wearcam .org/gat.htm>.

———. "Shooting Back." July 1995 <http://www.wearcam.org/shootingback .html>.

———. "'Smart Clothing': Wearable Multimedia Computing and 'Personal Imaging' to Restore the Technological Balance Between People and Their Environments." 7 January 1998 <http://wearcam.org/acm-mm96/index.html>.

Mann, Steve, with Hal Niedzviecki. *Cyborg: Digital Destiny and Human Possibility in the Age of the Wearable Computer.* Toronto: Doubleday, 2001.

Manuel, George, and Michael Posluns. *The Fourth World: An Indian Reality.* Don Mills: Collier Macmillan Canada, 1974.

Maracle, Lee. "The 'Post-Colonial' Imagination." *Fuse Magazine* 16.1 (1992): 12-15.

Marcel, Gabriel, *The Philosophy of Existentialism.* Trans. Marya Harari. Secaucus, NJ: Citadel Press, 1956.

Marcotte, Gilles. *Le roman à l'imparfait: La "Révolution tranquille" du roman québécois.* 2nd ed. Montreal: Éditions de l'Hexagone, 1989. Originally published as *Le roman à l'imparfait: Essais sur le roman québécois d'aujourd'hui.* Montreal: Éditions La Presse, 1976.

Mars, Tanya, and Johanna Householder, eds. *Caught in the Act: Canadian Women in Performance*. Toronto: YYZ Books, 2004.

Martin, Don. "For the Benefit of Easterners, This Is an Albertan..." *Calgary Herald* 6 May 2000, A3.

Massé, Michelle. *In the Name of Love: Women, Masochism, and the Gothic*. Ithaca: Cornell University Press, 1992.

Massey, Doreen. *Space, Place, and Gender*. Minneapolis: University of Minnesota Press, 1994.

Matthiasson, John S. *Living on the Land: Change among the Inuit of Baffin Island*. Peterborough: Broadview Press, 1992.

Mayeda, Andrew. "Brewing a Rich Heritage." *Ottawa Citizen* 23 July 2004, D1, D3.

McCauley, Elizabeth Anne. *A.A.E. Disderi and the Carte de Visite Portrait Photography*. New Haven: Yale University Press, 1991.

McDonald, Larry. "I Looked for It and There It Was—Gone: History in Postmodern Criticism." *Essays on Canadian Writing* 56 (1995): 37–50.

McGinnis, Janice Dickin. "Heritage Minutes: Myth and History." *Canadian Issues* 17 (1995): 25–36.

McGuigan, Jim. "Cultural Populism Revisited." *Cultural Studies in Question*. Ed. Marjorie Ferguson and Peter Golding. London: Sage, 1997. 138–54.

McKay, Ian. "History and the Tourist Gaze: The Politics of Commemoration in Nova Scotia, 1935–1964." *Acadiensis* 22.2 (1993): 102–38.

McKillop, A.B. "CHR Forum: Who Killed Canadian History? A View from the Trenches." *Canadian Historical Review* 80 (1999): 269–99.

McLoughlin, Moira. *Museums and the Representations of Native Canadians*. New York: Garland, 1999.

McLuhan, Marshall. *Understanding Media: The Extensions of Man*. Toronto: Signet, 1964.

McMaster, Gerald. "Tenuous Lines of Descent: Indian Arts and Crafts of the Reservation Period." *Canadian Journal of Native Studies* 9.2 (1989): 205–36.

McNaught, Kenneth. *The Pelican History of Canada*. Harmondsworth: Penguin Books, 1976.

McRoberts, Kenneth. *Misconceiving Canada: The Struggle for National Unity*. Toronto: Oxford University Press, 1997.

McSorley, Tom. "Critical Mass: Thirty Years of Telefilm Canada." *Take One* 22 (1999): 29–31.

Menke, Christoph. *The Sovereignty of Art: Aesthetic Negativity in Adorno and Derrida*. Trans. Neil Solomon. Cambridge, MA: MIT Press, 1998.

Meyer, Moe. "Introduction: Reclaiming the Discourse of Camp." *The Politics and Poetics of Camp*. Ed. Moe Meyer. New York: Routledge, 1994. 1–22.

Meyrowitz, Joshua. *No Sense of Place: The Impact of Electronic Media on Social Behaviour*. New York: Oxford University Press, 1985.

Miki, Roy. *Broken Entries: Race, Subjectivity, Writing*. Toronto: Mercury Press, 1998.

Miles, Malcolm. *Art, Space, and the City: Public Arts and Urban Futures.* London: Routledge, 1997.

Miles, Robert. *Racism.* London and New York: Routledge, 1989.

Miller, Arthur R. "Computers, Data Banks and Individual Privacy: An Overview." *Surveillance, Dataveillance, and Personal Freedoms: Use and Abuse of Information Technology.* Ed. The Staff of the Columbia Human Rights Law Review. Fair Lawn, NJ: R.E. Burdick, 1973. 11-22.

Miller, John, and Kimberly Prince. "The Imperfect Mirror: Analysis of Minority Picture and News in Six Canadian Newspapers." Toronto: School of Journalism, Ryerson Polytechnic University, 1994. 15 April 2002 <http://www.cna-acj.ca/client/cna/cna.nsf/web/DiversityAndCdnDaily>.

Mills, Charles W. *The Racial Contract.* Ithaca: Cornell University Press, 1997.

Mills, Lara. "Bud Light, Canadian Get Big Ad Push." *Marketing* 27 March 2000, 2.

Minh-ha, Trin T. "Other Than Myself/My Other Self." *Travellers' Tales: Narratives of Home and Displacement.* Ed. George Robertson, et al. London: Routledge, 1994. 9-28.

Mitchell, W.J.T., ed. *Art and the Public Sphere.* Chicago: University of Chicago Press, 1990.

Mitchell, W.J.T. "The Golden Age of Criticism: Seven Theses and a Commentary." *London Review of Books* 25 June 1987: 16-18.

———. "Introduction." *Landscape and Power.* Ed. W.J.T. Mitchell. Chicago: University of Chicago Press, 1994.

Modleski, Tania, ed. *Studies in Entertainment: Critical Approaches to Mass Culture.* Bloomington: Indiana University Press, 1986.

Molotch, Harvey, and Marilyn Lester. "News as Purposive Behaviour: On the Strategic Uses of Routine Events, Accidents, and Scandals." *American Sociological Review* 39 (1974): 101-12.

Monette, Hélène. *Unless.* Montreal: Boréal, 1995.

Monk, Philip. "Picturing the Toronto Art Community: The Queen Street Years." *C Magazine* (September–November 1998): insert, n.p.

Montgomery, L.M. *Anne of Avonlea.* Boston: L.C. Page, 1909.

———. *Anne of Green Gables.* Boston: L.C. Page, 1908.

———. *Chronicles of Avonlea.* Boston: L.C. Page, 1912.

———. *Emily of New Moon.* Toronto: McClelland and Stewart, 1923.

———. *Further Chronicles of Avonlea.* Boston: L.C. Page, 1920.

———. *The Golden Road.* Boston: L.C. Page, 1913.

———. *The Selected Journals of L.M. Montgomery,* Volume 1. Ed. Mary Rubio and Elizabeth Waterston. Toronto: Oxford University Press, 1985.

———. *The Story Girl.* Boston: L.C. Page, 1911.

Moodley, Kogila Adam. "Canadian Multiculturalism as Ideology." *Ethnic and Racial Studies* 6.3 (1983): 320-31.

Moorehead, Alan. *The Fatal Impact: An Account of the Invasion of the South Pacific, 1760-1840.* Harmondsworth: Penguin, 1968.

Moran, Albert. "Terms for a Reader: Film, Hollywood, National Cinema, Cultural Identity, and Film Policy." *Film Policy: International, National, and Regional Perspectives.* Ed. Albert Moran. London: Routledge, 1996. 1–19.

Morgan, Ceri. "There's No Place Like Home: Space, Place, and Identity in the Contemporary Francophone Novel in Quebec." Dissertation, University of Southampton, 1999.

Morgan, Joey, and Jeanne Randolph. *Joey Morgan, The Man Who Waits and Sleeps While I Dream.* Regina: Mackenzie Art Gallery, 1999.

Morice, A.G. "Hare Indians." *The Catholic Encyclopedia.* Vol. 7. Ed. Charles G. Herbermann, et al. New York: Robert Appleton, 1910.

Morin, Robert. *Windigo.* Canada, 1994.

Morley, David. *The Nationwide Audience: Structure and Decoding.* London: British Film Institute, 1980.

———. "Where the Global Meets the Local: Notes from the Sitting Room." *Screen* 32.1 (1991): 1–15.

Morris, Meaghan. "White Panic or, *Mad Max* and the Sublime." *Senses of Cinema* 18 (January–February 2002), 16 July 2002 <http://www.sensesofcinema .com/contents/01/18/mad_max.html>.

Morris, Peter. "Backwards to the Future: John Grierson's Film Policy for Canada." *People and Institutions in Canadian Film History.* Ed. Gene Walz. Montreal: Mediatext, 1986. 17–35.

———. *Embattled Shadows: A History of Canadian Cinema, 1895–1939.* Montreal: McGill-Queen's University Press, 1978.

———. "In Our Own Eyes: The Canonizing of Canadian Film." *Canadian Journal of Film Studies* 3.1 (1994): 27–44.

Morrison, Toni. *Playing in the Dark: Whiteness and the Literary Imagination.* Cambridge: Harvard University Press, 1992.

Morton, Desmond. "A Shared Past Is a Nation's Compass." *Toronto Star* 26 September 1997, A28.

Morton, Desmond, and Morton Weinfeld, ed. *Who Speaks for Canada? Words That Shape a Country.* Toronto: McClelland and Stewart, 1998.

Moss, Laura, ed. *Is Canada Postcolonial? Unsettling Canadian Literature.* Waterloo: Wilfrid Laurier University Press, 2003.

Mowat, Farley. *The Desperate People.* Boston: Little, Brown, 1959.

———. *The People of the Deer.* Boston: Little, Brown, 1952.

Mukherjee, Arun P. "Ironies of Colour in The Great White North." *Double-Talking: Essays on Verbal and Visual Ironies in Contemporary Canadian Art and Literature.* Ed. Linda Hutcheon. Toronto: ECW Press, 1992. 158–71.

———. *Postcolonialism: My Living.* Toronto: TSAR, 1998

Mulvey, Laura. "Notes on Sirk and Melodrama." Gledhill, *Home,* 75–79.

———. "Visual Pleasure and Narrative Cinema." *Visual and Other Pleasures.* Bloomington: Indiana University Press, 1989. 14–26.

Nathan, Deborah. Personal interview. 10 September 2001.

Nepveu, Pierre. *L'Écologie du réel: Mort et naissance de la littérature québécoise contemporaine.* 2nd ed. Montreal: Boréal, 1999.

New, William H. *Borderlands: How We Talk about Canada*. Vancouver: University of British Columbia Press, 1998.

New York City Surveillance Camera Project, "Overview: New York City: A Surveillance Camera Town." 13 December 1998 <http://www.mediaeater.com /cameras/overview.html>.

Newton, Esther. *Mother Camp: Female Impersonators in America*. Chicago: University of Chicago Press, 1972.

Nicol, Eric, and Dave More, eds. *The US or Us—What's the Difference, Eh?* Edmonton: Hurtig, 1986.

Nichols, Bill. "Embodied Knowledge and the Politics of Power." *CineAction* 23 (1990-91): 14-21.

———. *Representing Reality: Issues and Concepts in Documentary*. Bloomington and Indianapolis: Indiana University Press, 1991.

Nietschmann, Bernard. "Authentic, State, and Virtual Geography in Film." *Wide Angle* 15.4 (1993): 4-12.

Ninkovich, Frank A. *The Diplomacy of Ideas: US Foreign Policy and Cultural Relations, 1938-50*. Cambridge: Cambridge University Press, 1981.

Noël, Francine. *Babel, prise deux, ou Nous avons tous découvert l'Amérique*. Montreal: VLB, 1990.

Nora, Pierre. *Realms of Memory: Rethinking the French Past* Vol. 1. Trans. Arthur Goldhammer. Ed. Lawrence D. Kritzman. New York: Columbia University Press, 1996.

Norris, Clive. "The Usual Suspects." 1997 <http://merlin.legend.org.uk/~brs /archive/stories97/Suspects.html>.

Norris, Clive, and Gary Armstrong. "Introduction: Power and Vision." *Surveillance, Closed Circuit Television, and Social Control*. Ed. Clive Norris, Jade Moran, and Gary Armstrong. Aldershot: Ashgate, 1998. 3-17.

"North Star: A Proud Nation Embraces Jeff Douglas, Thanks to a Rousing Canadian Beer Ad." *People's Weekly* 24 July 2000, 126.

Northwest Territories. *Annual Report on Official Languages*. Yellowknife: Government of the Northwest Territories, Minister responsible for Official Languages, October 2004.

Northwest Territories Bureau of Statistics T-Stat (Territorial Statistics On-Line), Government of the Northwest Territories. "Population by Aboriginal Identity and Community, Northwest Territories, Census 2001." <http://www. stats.gov.nt.ca>.

Nourbese Philip, Marlene. *Frontiers: Selected Essays and Writings on Racism and Culture, 1984-1992*. Stratford: Mercury Press, 1992.

Nowell-Smith, Geoffrey. "Minnelli and Melodrama." Gledhill, *Home*, 70-75.

Nulman, Andy. "Peqs Appeal." *Montreal Gazette* 30 April 2000, C5.

Obomsawin, Alanis. *Kahnesatake: 270 Years of Resistance*. Canada, 1993.

O'Dell, Kathy. *Contract with the Skin: Masochism, Performance Art and the 1970s*. Minneapolis: University of Minnesota Press, 1998.

Offman, Craig. Interview with Jeff Douglas. *Time International* 3 July 2000, 44.

O'Shea, William A. Interview by Erna MacLeod. 25 March 1998.

Oswald, Brad. "Road Closed: Story Is Told, Kids Are Grown, So Avonlea Calls It Quits." *Winnipeg Free Press* 28 November 1995.

Oswalt, Wendell H. *Alaskan Eskimos*. Scranton, PA: Chandler, 1967.

Padolsky, Enoch. "'Olga in Wonderland': Canadian Ethnic Minority Writing and Post-Colonial Theory." *Canadian Ethnic Studies* 28.3 (1996): 16–28.

Paine, Thomas. *Collected Writings*. Ed. Eric Foner. New York: Library of America, 1995.

Palardy, Jean, dir. *Gaspe Cod Fisherman*. Canada: National Film Board of Canada, 1944.

Parker, Graham, dir. *Trans-Canada Journey*. Canada: National Film Board of Canada, 1962.

Parks Canada Agency: A Discussion Paper. Department of Canadian Heritage, June 1996.

Parks Canada Guiding Principles and Operational Policies. Minister of Supply and Services Canada, 1994.

Parpart, Lee. "Cowards, Bullies, and Cadavers: Feminist Re-Mappings of the Passive Male Body in English-Canadian and Quebecois Cinema." *Gendering the Nation: Canadian Women's Cinema*. Ed. Kay Armatage, et al. Toronto: University of Toronto Press, 1999. 253–73.

Paterson, Janet M. *Postmodernism and the Quebec Novel*. Trans. David Homel and Charles Phillips. Toronto: University of Toronto Press, 1994. Originally published as *Moments postmodernes dans le roman québécois*. Ottawa: Les Presses de l'Université d'Ottawa, 1990.

Payne, Carol. *A Canadian Document: The National Film Board of Canada's Still Photography Division*. Ottawa: Canadian Museum of Contemporary Photography, 1999.

———. "'How Shall We Use These Gifts?' Imaging the Land in the National Film Board of Canada's Still Photography Division." *The Virgin Beauty of Mississauga: Canadian Landscape Art and National Identity*. Ed. John O'Brian and Peter White. Vancouver: Arsenal Pulp Press, forthcoming 2006.

Pearlstein, Steven. "They.Are.Canadian: An American Newspaper Looks at the Peculiar Canadian Phenomenon Known as Joe's Rant." *Calgary Herald* 30 April 2000, A14.

Peirce, Charles S. "What Is a Sign?" *The Essential Peirce*. Ed. Nathan Houser and Christian Kloesel. Bloomington: Indiana University Press, 1998.

Pendakur, Manjunath. *Canadian Dreams and American Control*. Detroit: Wayne State University Press, 1990.

Pennee, Donna Palmateer. "Literary Citizenship: Culture (Un)Bounded, Culture (Re)Distributed." *Home-Work: Postcolonialism, Pedagogy, and Canadian Literature*. Ed. Cynthia Sugars. Ottawa: University of Ottawa Press, 2004.

Peter, Karl. "The Myth of Multiculturalism and Other Political Fables." *Ethnicity, Power and Politics in Canada*. Ed. Jorgen Dahlie and Tissa Fernando. Toronto: Methuen, 1981. 56–67.

Peters, John Durham. "Seeing Bifocally: Media, Place, Culture." *Culture, Power, Place: Explorations in Critical Anthropology*. Ed. Akhil Gupta and James Ferguson. Durham: Duke University Press, 1997. 15–92.

Peterson, David. "There Is No Living History, There Are No Time Machines." *History News* 43.5 (1998): 28–30.

Petrowski, Nathalie. "Le Rodin de Mont-Laurier." *Le Devoir* 7 October 1989, C14.

Pevere, Geoff, and Greig Dymond. *Mondo Canuck: A Canadian Pop Culture Odyssey.* Scarborough: Prentice Hall, 1996.

Phelan, Peggy. "Reciting the Citation of Others; or, A Second Introduction." *Acting Out: Feminist Performances.* Ed. Lynda Hart and Peggy Phelan. Ann Arbor: University of Michigan Press, 1994. 13–31.

Pirrie Adams, Kathleen. "Prior Art: Art of Record for Personal Safety." July 2001. Gallery TPW <http://www.existech.com/tpw/essay.html>.

Pollock, Griselda. "Screening the Seventies—A Brechtian Perspective." *Vision and Difference: Femininity, Feminism and Histories of Art.* New York: Routledge, 1988. 155–99.

Porter, John. *The Vertical Mosaic: An Analysis of Social Class and Power in Canada.* Toronto: University of Toronto Press, 1985.

Poster, Mark. "Databases as Discourse; or, Electronic Interpellation." *Computers, Surveillance, and Privacy.* Ed. David Lyon and Elia Zureik. Minneapolis: University of Minnesota Press, 1996. 175–92.

Potterton, Gerald, dir. *The Railrodder.* Canada: National Film Board of Canada, 1965.

"PQ Debates Horses to Healthcare." *Montreal Gazette.* 25 April 1999, A5.

Pratt, Mary Louise. *Imperial Eyes: Travel Writing and Transculturation.* London: Routledge, 1992.

Prentice, Chris. "Some Problems of Response to Empire in Settler Post-Colonial Societies." *De-Scribing Empire: Post-Colonialism and Textuality.* Ed. Chris Tiffin and Alan Lawson. London: Routledge, 1994. 45–58.

Price, Ray. *The Howling Arctic: The Remarkable People Who Made Canada Sovereign in the Farthest North.* Toronto: Peter Martin, 1970.

Price, Richard A., ed. *The Spirit of the Alberta Indian Treaties.* Edmonton: Pica Pica Press, 1987.

Prins, Harald. *The Mi'kmaq: Resistance, Accommodation, and Cultural Survival.* Fort Worth, TX: Harcourt College, 1996.

Privacy International and The Electronic Privacy Information Center <http://www.privacy.org>.

Purdy, Anthony. "Altérité, authenticité, universalité: Dany Laferrière et Régine Robin." *Dalhousie French Studies* 23 (1992): 51–59.

Quebec. Quebec Charter of Human Rights, Revised Statutes of Quebec, c. 12.

Quill, Greg. "Historical Vignettes Given a Dignified Debut." *Toronto Star* 3 May 1995, E1.

Rabasa, José. "Allegories of Atlas." *The Post-Colonial Studies Reader.* Ed. Bill Ashcroft, Gareth Griffiths, and Helen Tiffin. London and New York: Routledge, 1995. 358–64.

Rajchman, John. *The Deleuze Connection.* Cambridge, MA: MIT Press, 2000.

Rand, I.C., Commissioner. *Report of the Rand Commission on Coal.* Ottawa, 1960.

Randolph, Jeanne. *Psychoanalysis and Synchronized Swimming.* Ed. Bruce Grenville. Toronto: YYZ Books, 1991.

———. *Symbolization and Its Discontents.* Ed. Steve Reinke. Toronto: YYZ Books, 1997.

———. *Video 01, Syntax Errors: Series of Three Performed Lectures Investigating the Relationship between Authoritative Language, Presentation Technologies, and Performance Art.* Vancouver: Artspeak, 2000.

Randolph, Jeanne, and Joanne Tod. *Joanne Tod.* Victoria: Art Gallery of Greater Victoria, 1986.

Rapaport, Herman. *The Theory Mess: Deconstruction in Eclipse.* New York: Columbia University Press, 2001.

Rasporich, Beverly. "Canadian Humour in the Media: Exporting John Candy and Importing Homer Simpson." *Seeing Ourselves: Media Power and Policy in Canada.* Ed. Helen Holmes and David Taras. Toronto: Harcourt, Brace, 1996. 84–97.

Ray, Arthur J., and Donald B. Freeman, eds. *"Give Us Good Measure": An Economic Analysis of Relations between the Indians and the Hudson's Bay Company before 1763.* Toronto: University of Toronto Press, 1978.

Razack, Sherene H. *Looking White People in the Eye, Gender, Race, and Culture in Courtrooms and Classrooms.* Toronto: University of Toronto Press, 1998.

Reimer, Mavis, ed. *Such a Simple Little Tale: Critical Responses to L.M. Montgomery's* Anne of Green Gables. Metuchen, NJ, and London: Children's Literature Association and Scarecrow Press, 1992.

Reitz, Jeffrey G. *Warmth of the Welcome: The Social Causes of Economic Success for Immigrants in Different Nations and Cities.* Boulder, CO: Westview, 1998.

Reitz, Jeffrey G., and Raymond Breton. *The Illusion of Difference: Realities of Ethnicity in Canada and the United States.* Ottawa: C.D. Howe Institute, 1994.

Relph, Edward. *Place and Placelessness.* London: Pion, 1976.

Renaud, Jacques. *Broke City.* Trans. David Homel. Montreal: Guernica, 1984. Originally published as *Le Cassé.* Montreal: Parti Pris, 1964.

———. *Le cassé et autres nouvelles suivi de Le Journal du Cassé.* Collection "projection libérantes." Montreal: Parti Pris, 1981.

Rice, Ryan. *Decolonizing the Archival Photography: George Littlechild.* Ottawa: Department of Indian and North Development, Indian Art Gallery, 1998.

Rich, E.E. *Hudson's Bay Company, 1670–1870.* 3 vols. Toronto: McClelland and Stewart, 1960.

Richard, Alain-Martin. "Québec, Activism and Performance: From the Acted-Manifesto to the Manoeuvre." Alain-Martin Richard and Clive Robertson, eds. *Performance au/in Canada, 1970–1990.* Quebec: Editions Intervention; Toronto: Coach House Press, 1991. 41–47.

Richardson, Boyce. *Strangers Devour the Land.* Vancouver: Douglas and McIntyre, 1991.

Ricoeur, Paul. "Ideology and Utopia as Cultural Imagination." *Being Human in a Technological Age.* Ed. Donald M. Borchert and David Stewart. Athens, OH: Ohio University Press, 1979. 107–25.

———. *Lectures on Ideology and Utopia*. Ed. George H. Taylor. New York: Columbia University Press, 1986.

Riley, Linda, ed. *Marius Barbeau's Photographic Collection: The Nass River*. Canadian Ethnology Service, Paper No. 109. Ottawa: Canadian Museum of Civilization, 1988.

Ringley, Jennifer. "JenniCam." <http://www.jennicam.com>.

Roberts, Mike. "I Rant, therefore I Am…" *Vancouver Province* 7 May 2000, B4.

Roberts, Shari. "Western Meets Eastwood: Genre and Gender on the Road." *The Road Movie Book*. Ed. Steven Cohan and Ina Rae Hark. London: Routledge, 1997. 45–69.

Robertson, Clive. "The Complete Clichettes." *Fuse* 9.4 (1986): 9–15.

Robertson, Roland. "Glocalization: Time-Space and Homogeneity-Heterogeneity." *Global Modernities*. Ed. Mike Featherstone, Scott Lash, and Roland Robertson. London: Sage, 1995. 25–44.

Robin, Régine. "Introduction: Un Québec pluriel." *La recherche littéraire: Objets et methods*. Ed. Claude Duchet and Stéphane Vachon. Montreal: XYZ, 1993. 301–309.

"Robinson Slept Here." *Ottawa Citizen* 8 August 1997, A13.

Rombout, Luke, et al., ed. *Vancouver: Art and Artists 1931–1983*. Vancouver: Vancouver Art Gallery, 1993.

Rombout, Melissa. "Imaginary Canada: Photography and the Construction of National Identity." *Views: The Journal of Photography in New England* 12.2 (1991): 4–9.

Rosenstone, Robert A. *Visions of the Past: The Challenge of Film to Our Idea of History*. Cambridge, MA: Harvard University Press, 1995.

Roth, Moira. "Character, Costume, and Theater in Early California Performance." *Living Art Vancouver*. Ed. Alvin Balkind and R.A. Gledhill. Vancouver: Western Front, Pumps, Video Inn, 1979. 89–91.

Roy, Gabrielle. *The Tin Flute*. Trans. Alan Brown. Toronto: McClelland and Stewart, 1955. Originally published as *Bonheur d'occasion*. Montréal: Beauchemin, 1945.

Rubin, Josh. "Beer Pitcher Wows ACC: Live Performance of Canadian Rant Rocks Leaf Fans." *Toronto Star* 16 April 2000, C3.

Rubio, Mary, ed. *Harvesting Thistles: The Textual Garden of L.M. Montgomery*. Guelph, ON: Canadian Children's Press, 1994.

Rutherford, Jonathan. "The Third Space: Interview with Homi Bhabha." *Identity: Community, Culture, Difference*. London: Lawrence and Wishart, 1990. 207–21.

R. v. Drybones, [1970] Canada Supreme Court Reports 282.

R. v. Sparrow, [1990] 1 Canada Supreme Court Reports 1025.

R. v. Van der Peet, [1996] 2 Canada Supreme Court Reports 2.

Ryan, Allan J. *The Trickster Shift: Humour and Irony in Contemporary Canadian Art*. Vancouver: University of British Columbia Press, 1999.

Ryan, James R. *Picturing Empire: Photography and the Visualization of the British Empire*. Chicago: University of Chicago Press, 1997.

Sahlins, Marshall. *Stone Age Economics*. New York: Aldine, 1972.

Said, Edward. *Orientalism*. London: Routledge, 1978.

Salik, Sarah. Introduction. *The Judith Butler Reader*. By Judith Butler. Oxford: Blackwell, 2004. 1–17.

Sartre, Jean-Paul. *The Psychology of Imagination*. Trans. Bernard Frechtman. New York: Washington Square Press, 1966.

Satzewich, Vic. *Racism and Social Inequality in Canada: Concepts, Controversies and Strategies of Resistance*. Toronto: Thompson Educational, 1998.

Saunders, D. "The Renewal of Indian Special Status." Ed. Anne F. Bayefsky and Mary Eberts. *Equality Rights and the Canadian Charter of Rights and Freedoms*. Toronto: Carswell, 1985. 529–63.

Saunders, Doug. "The Myth of Hollywood North." *Report on Business* 17.10 (2001): 94–102.

Saunders, Doug, and Gayle Macdonald. "Anne's Scary Stepparents." *Globe and Mail* 16 October 1999: C1.

Sava, Sharla. "As If the Oceans Were Lemonade: The Performative Vision of Robert Filliou and the Western Front." MA thesis, University of British Columbia, 1996.

Savran, David. *Taking It Like a Man: White Masculinity, Masochism, and Contemporary American Culture*. Princeton: Princeton University Press, 1998.

Scaini, Stefan, dir. *Anne of Green Gables: The Continuing Story*. Canada: CBC, 2000.

———. *Happy Christmas, Miss King*. Canada: CBC, 1998.

Schech, Susanne, and Jane Haggis. *Culture and Development: A Critical Introduction*. Oxford and Massachusetts: Blackwell, 2000.

Scheinberg, Ellen, and Melissa Rombout. "Projecting Images of the Nations: The Immigration Program and Its Use of Lantern Slides." *Archivist* 111 (1996): 13–24.

Schimmel, Paul, ed. *Out of Actions: Between Performance and the Object, 1949–1979*. Los Angeles: Museum of Contemporary Art, 1998.

Schissel, Bernard. *Blaming Children: Youth Crime, Moral Panics and the Politics of Hate*. Halifax: Fernwood, 1997.

Schmitt, Cannon. *Alien Nation: Nineteenth-Century Gothic Fictions and English Nationality*. Philadelphia: University of Philadelphia Press, 1997.

Schneider, Rebecca. *The Explicit Body in Performance*. New York: Routledge, 1997.

Schwartz, Barry. "The Social Context of Communication: A Study in Collective Memory." *Social Forces* 61 (1982): 374–99.

Schwartz, Joan. *Canadian Photography*. Special Issue of *History of Photography* 20.2 (1996).

Schwartzwald, Robert. "Fear of Federasty: Québec's Inverted Fictions." *Comparative American Identities: Race, Sex, and Nationality in the Modern Text*. Ed. Hortense J. Spillers. London: Routledge, 1991. 175–95.

Scott, Robert. *Dominance and the Arts of Resistance: Hidden Transcripts*. New Haven, CT: Yale University Press, 1990.

Sedgwick, Eve Kosofsky. *Tendencies*. Durham: Duke University Press, 1993.

Seeing Canada. Canada: Canadian Government Motion Picture Bureau, 1919–1939.

Seymour, Michel. *Une identité civique commune.* Sherbrooke, QC: Sherbrooke GGC Éditions, 2001.

Shaheen, Jack. *The TV Arab.* Bowling Green, OH: Bowling Green State University Popular Press, 1984.

Shebib, Don, dir. *Between Friends.* National Film Board of Canada, 1973.

Shek, Ben-Zion. *French-Canadian and Québécois Novels.* Toronto: University of Toronto Press, 1991.

Shohat, Ella, and Robert Stam. *Unthinking Eurocentrism, Multiculturalism and the Media.* London and New York: Routledge, 1994.

Showalter, Elaine. *The Female Malady: Women, Madness, and English Culture 1830–1980.* 3rd ed. London: Virago, 1988.

Shurmer-Smith, Pamela. Introduction. *Doing Cultural Geography.* London: Sage, 2002. 1–7.

Silverman, Kaja. "Fragments of a Fashionable Discourse." *Studies in Entertainment: Critical Approaches to Mass Culture.* Ed. Tania Modelski. Bloomington: Indiana University Press, 1986. 139–52.

Silversides, Brock. *The Face Pullers: Photographing Native Canadians 1871–1939.* Saskatoon: Fifth House, 1994.

Simmons, Alan B., and Dwaine Plaza. "Breaking through the Glass Ceiling: The Pursuit of University Training among Afro-Caribbean Migrants and Their Children in Toronto." *Canadian Ethnic Studies* 30.3 (1998): 99–120.

Simmons, Alan B., and Jean E. Turner. "Caribbean Immigration to Canada, 1967–1987." Paper presented at the *Centre for Research on Latin American and the Caribbean Conference.* York University 18 February 1998.

Singer, Bryan, dir. *X-Men.* 20th Century Fox, 2000.

Sisler, Cathy, dir. *Mr. B.* Quebec: Groupe Intervention Vidéo, 1994.

Slattery, Brian. "The Hidden Constitution: Aboriginal Rights in Canada." *American Journal of Comparative Law* 32 (1984): 361–91.

———. "The Organic Constitution: Aboriginal Peoples and the Evolution of Canada." *Osgoode Hall Law Journal* 34 (1995): 101–12.

Slattery, Brian, and Sheila E. Stelck, eds. *Canadian Native Law Cases.* 9 vols. Saskatoon: University of Saskatchewan, Native Law Centre, 1980–1991.

Slemon, Stephen. "Unsettling the Empire: Resistance Theory for the Second World." *World Literature Written in English* 30.2 (1990): 30–41.

Slobodin, Richard. *Metis of the Mackenzie District.* Ottawa: Canadian Research Centre for Anthropology, St. Paul University, 1966.

———. "Subarctic Metis." *Subarctic.* Ed. June Helm. *Handbook of North American Indians.* Ed. William C. Sturtevant. Washington: Smithsonian Institution, 1981. 361–71.

Smart, Patricia. *Hubert Aquin, agent double: La dialectique de l'art et du pays dans Prochaine Episode et Trou de mémoire.* Montréal: Les Presses de l'Université de Montréal, 1973.

———. *Writing in the Father's House: The Emergence of the Feminine in the Quebec Literary Tradition.* Toronto: University of Toronto Press, 1991.

Originally published as *Écrire dans la maison du père: l'émergence du féminin dans la tradition littéraire du Québec* (Montréal: Éditions Québec/Amérique, 1988).

Smith, Adam. *An Inquiry into the Nature and Causes of the Wealth of Nations*. Toronto: Encyclopaedia Britannica, 1952.

Smith, A.J.M. Introduction. *The Book of Canadian Poetry: A Critical and Historical Anthology*. Chicago: University of Chicago Press, 1943. 3–31.

Smith, Dinitia. "Isn't It Romantic? Hollywood Adopts the Canon." *New York Times* 10 November 1996, sec. 4: 4.

Smulders, Marilyn. "He Is ... Truronian." *Halifax Daily News* 15 April 2000, 25.

Solomon, Alisa. "It's Never Too Late to Switch: Crossing toward Power." Ed. Lesley Ferris. *Crossing the Stage: Controversies on Cross-Dressing*. London and New York: Routledge, 1993. 144–54.

Soop, Everett. *Soop Takes a Bow*. Lethbridge: Kainai News, 1979.

Sowiak, Christine. "Contemporary Canadian Art: Locating Identity." *A Passion For Identity*, 4th ed. Ed. David Taras and Beverly Rasporich. Toronto: Nelson Thomson Learning, 2001. 251–74.

Spottiswoode, Roger, dir. *The Sixth Day*. Columbia Tristar, 2000.

Staines, David. *Stephen Leacock—My Financial Career and Other Follies*. Toronto: McClelland and Stewart, 1993.

Starowicz, Mark. "A Nation without Memory." *Globe and Mail* 6 February 1999, D1, D3.

Starowicz, Mark, dir. *The Making of Canada: A People's History*. Canada: CBC, 2001.

Statistics Canada. *Aboriginal People's Survey, 2001*. Ottawa: Statistics Canada, 2001.

Steele, Valerie. *Fetish: Fashion, Sex, and Power*. New York and Oxford: Oxford University Press, 1996.

Stefansson, Vilhjalmur. *The Friendly Arctic*. New York: Macmillan, 1921.

Steffenhagen, Janet. "Girls Killing Girls: A Sign of Angry Empty Lives." *Vancouver Sun* 25 November 1997, A1.

Stein, Jess. *The Random House Dictionary of the English Language*. New York: Random House, 1973.

Stiles, Kristine. "Uncorrupted Joy: International Art Actions." *Out of Actions: Between Performance and the Object, 1949–1979*. Ed. Paul Schimmel. Los Angeles: Museum of Contemporary Art, 1998. 227–329.

St. Laurent, Stefan/Minnie, dir. *Stand by Your Man*. Canada: V-Tape, 1998.

Stoloff, Jean-Claude. *Interpréter le narcissisme*. Paris: Dunod, 2000.

Stonechild, Blair, and Bill Waiser. *Loyal until Death: Indians and the North-West Rebellion*. Calgary: Fifth House, 1997.

Storey, Raymond. Personal interview. 30 August 2001.

Straayer, Chris. *Deviant Eyes, Deviant Bodies: Sexual Re-Orientations in Film and Video*. New York: Columbia University Press, 1996.

Stratton, Jon, and Ien Ang. "Multicultural Imagined Communities: Cultural Difference and National Identity in the USA and Australia." *Multicultural States:*

Rethinking Difference and Identity. Ed. David Bennett. London: Routledge, 1998. 135–62.

Sturken, Marita. *Tangled Memories*. Berkeley, CA: University of California Press, 1997.

Sugars, Cynthia. "Can the Canadian Speak? Lost in Postcolonial Space." *ARIEL* 32.3 (2001): 115–52.

———. "National Posts: Theorizing Canadian Postcolonialism." *International Journal of Canadian Studies* 25 (2002): 41–67.

———, ed. *Unhomely States: Theorizing English-Canadian Postcolonialism*. Peterborough: Broadview, 2004.

Sullivan, Kevin, dir. *Anne of Green Gables*. Canada: CBC, 1985.

Sullivan, Kevin, and Trudy Grant, dirs. *Road to Avonlea*. Canada–US: CBC, 1990–1996.

Surtees, R.J. *Canadian Indian Policy: A Critical Bibliography*. Bloomington: Indiana University Press, 1982.

Surveillance Camera Players. "The Surveillance Camera Players' Theatre of Cruelty." <http://www.panix.com/~notbored/artaud.html>.

———. "Time in the Shadows of Anonymity: Fighting against Surveillance Cameras, Transparency, and Global Capitalism." <http://www.notbored.org /transparent.html>.

Sutter, Stan. "Canadian Beauty, eh?" *Marketing* 8 May 2000, 42.

Swift, Jonathan. "A Modest Proposal." *The Prose Works of Jonathan Swift. Irish Tracts: 1728–1733*. Ed. Herbert Davis. Oxford: Basil Blackwell, 1964. 109–18.

Tagg, John. *The Burden of Representation: Essays on Photographies and Histories*. Amherst: University of Massachusetts Press, 1988.

Taras, David, and Beverly Rasporich, eds. *A Passion for Identity*. 4th ed. Toronto: Nelson Thomson, 2001.

Taylor, Charles. *Multiculturalism: Examining the Politics of Recognition*. Ed. Amy Gutmann. Princeton, NJ: Princeton University Press, 1994.

———. *Negotiating the Past: The Making of Canada's National Historic Parks*. Montreal and Kingston: McGill-Queen's University Press, 1990.

———. "The Politics of Recognition." *Multiculturalism*. Ed. Amy Gutmann. Princeton, NJ: Princeton University Press, 1994. 25–74.

Taylor, D.F., dir. *The Seasons of Canada*. Canada: Canadian Government Motion Picture Bureau, 1930.

Taylor, Richard. *Metaphysics*. Englewood Cliffs, NJ: Prentice-Hall, 1963.

Tennyson, Brian Douglas, ed. *Canadian-Caribbean Relations: Aspects of a Relationship*. Sydney, NS: Centre for International Studies, 1990.

Tesher, Ellie. "Moviegoers Save Their Cheering for Canada." *Toronto Star* 23 March 2000, A27.

Tester, Frank, and Peter Kulchyski. *Tammarniit (Mistakes): Inuit Relocation in the Eastern Arctic, 1939–63*. Vancouver: University of British Columbia Press, 1994.

Tett, Alison. "Gilbert Boyer's Architécriture." *Parachute* 68 (1992): 17.

Thomas, Douglas. "Criminality on the Electronic Frontier: Corporeality and the Judicial Construction of the Hacker." *Information, Communication and Society* 1.4 (1998): 382-400.

Thomas, Jeff, and Carol Payne. "Aboriginal Interventions into the Photographic Archives: A Dialogue." *Visual Resources: An International Journal of Documentation.* 18 (June 2002): 109-25.

Thomas, Lewis H. "The Constitutional Development of the North-West Territories, 1870-1888." MA thesis, University of Saskatchewan, 1941.

Thornton, John. *Africa and Africans in the Making of the Atlantic World, 1400-1680.* Cambridge: Cambridge University Press, 1995.

Tomlinson, John. *Cultural Imperialism: A Critical Introduction.* London: Pinter, 1991.

Tong, Stanley, dir. *Rumble in the Bronx.* New Line Cinema, 1995.

Toth, Derrick. "Canada Baffles Americans." *Calgary Herald* 30 March 2001, E3.

Trachtenberg, Alan. *Reading American Photographs: Images as History, Mathew Brady to Walker Evans.* New York: Hill and Wang, 1989.

Trudeau, Pierre E. *Federalism and the French Canadians.* Toronto: Macmillan, 1968.

———. "Remarks on Aboriginal and Treaty Rights." Excerpts from a speech given 8 August 1969. Peter A. Cumming and Neil H. Mickenberg, eds. *Native Rights in Canada.* Toronto: Indian-Eskimo Association of Canada in association with General Publishing, 1972. Appendix 6.

Tuer, Dot. "The CEAC Was Banned in Canada." *C Magazine* 11 (1986): 22-37.

———. "Video in Drag: Trans-Sexing the Feminine." *Parallelogramme* 12.3 (February/March 1987): 24-29.

Turner, Frederick J. *The Frontier in American History.* New York: Holt, Rinehart, and Winston, 1962.

TV Guide (Canadian Edition). "Farewells: *Road to Avonlea.*" 16-23 September 1995: 6.

TV Times. "Canadian Content." 24-30 December 1999: 6.

Tyler, Tracey. "Custody Battle over *Anne of Green Gables*: Trademark Tussle Worth Big Money." *Toronto Star* 6 March 1994. A1.

Urry, John. *The Tourist Gaze.* London: Sage, 1990.

Vail, Stephen, and Graeme Clinton. *May 2001 Nunavut Economic Outlook.* Ottawa: Conference Board of Canada, 2002.

Valaskakis, Gail Guthrie. "Sacajawea and Her Sisters: Images and Indians." *Indian Princesses and Cowgirls: Common Stereotypes of the Frontier.* Ed. Marilyn Burgess and Gail Guthrie Valaskakis. Montreal: Oboro, 1992.

Van Camp, Richard. *The Lesser Blessed.* Vancouver: Douglas and McIntyre [c. 1996].

Van Dijk, Teun A. *Elite Discourse and Racism.* Sage Series on Race and Ethnic Relations 6. Thousand Oaks, CA: Sage, 1993.

———. "Mediating Racism: The Role of the Media in the Reproduction of Racism." *Language, Power, and Ideology: Studies in Political Discourse.* Ed. Ruth Wodak. Amsterdam and Philadelphia: J. Benjamins, 1989. 199-226.

———. *Racism and the Press*. London and New York: Routledge, 1991.

Van Sant, Gus, dir. *Finding Forrester*. Columbia Tristar, 2000.

Venne, Sharon H., ed. *Indian Acts and Amendments, 1868–75: An Indexed Collection*. Saskatoon: University of Saskatchewan, Native Law Centre, 1981.

Virgo, Clement, dir. *Rude*. Conquering Lion Productions, 1995.

ViveleCanada.ca. "Why You Should Boycott Future Coors-Molson Products." *Vivele Canada: Our Country, Our Voice*. August 2004 <http://www.vivelecanada.ca>.

Vodden, Christy. *No Stone Unturned: The First 150 Years of the Geological Survey of Canada*. Ottawa: Supply and Services Canada, 1992.

Vološinov, V.N. *Marxism and the Philosophy of Language*. Cambridge: Harvard University Press, 1996.

Walcott, Rinaldo. *Black Like Who? Writing Black Canada*. Toronto: Insomniac Press, 1997.

Wallace, Joe. "A Sovereign Nation." *The Maple Laugh Forever*. Ed. Douglas Barbour and Stephen Scobie. Edmonton: Hurtig, 1981. 15.

Wallace, Mike. *Mickey-Mouse History and Other Essays on American Memory*. Philadelphia: Temple University Press, 1996.

Walsh, Kevin. *The Representation of the Past: Museums and Heritage in the Post-Modern World*. London: Routledge, 1992.

Wark, Jayne. "Kate Craig at Vancouver Art Gallery." *n.paradoxa* 2 (1988): 38–39.

Warwick, Jack. *The Long Journey: Literary Themes of French Canada*. 2nd ed. Toronto: University of Toronto Press, 1973.

Watson, Patrick. *The Canadians: Biographies of a Nation*. Toronto: McArthur, 2000.

Watson, Scott. "Hand of the Spirit." *Hand of the Spirit: Documents of the Seventies from the Morris/Trasov Archive*. Vancouver: University of British Columbia Fine Arts Gallery, 1992. 5–28.

———. "Return to Brutopia." *Return to Brutopia: Eric Metcalfe Works and Collaborations*. Vancouver: University of British Columbia Fine Arts Gallery, 1992. 7–45.

Watters, R.E. "A Special Tang: Stephen Leacock's Canadian Humour." *Canadian Literature* 5 (1960): 21–32.

Waugh, Thomas. "Cinemas, Nations, Masculinities (The Martin Walsh Memorial Lecture. 1988)." *Canadian Journal of Film Studies* 8.1 (1999): 8–44.

"We All Leave the Wharf at the Same Time." *Coastal Community News* November/December 2000.

Weber, Samuel. *The Legend of Freud*. Minneapolis: University of Minnesota Press, 1982.

Weyer, Edward. *The Eskimos: Their Environment and Folkways*. New Haven: Yale University Press, 1932.

Wheeler, Anne, dir. *Augusta*. Canada: National Film Board of Canada and Film West Associates, 1976.

———. *Bye Bye Blues*. Canada: True Blue Films, Alberta Motion Picture Development Corporation, Allarcom, Telefilm Canada, National Film Board of Canada, CFCN-TV Calgary, 1989.

———. *Change of Heart*. Canada: CBC and National Film Board of Canada, 1984.

———. *The Diviners*. Canada: Atlantis Films, Credo Group CBC, 1991.

———. *Loyalties*. Canada: Lauron International with Wheeler-Hendren Enterprises and Dumbarton Films of England, 1986.

———. *One's a Heifer*. Canada: Atlantis Films and National Film Board of Canada, 1984.

———. *To Set Our House in Order*. Canada: National Film Board of Canada and Atlantis Films, 1985.

Whittle, Stephen. "Gender Fucking or Fucking Gender?" Ed. Richard Ekins and David King. *Blending Genders: Social Aspects of Cross-Dressing and Sex-Changing*. New York and London: Routledge, 1996. 196–214.

Wickens-Feldman, Renate. "The National Film Board of Canada's Still Photography Division: The Griersonian Legacy." *History of Photography* 20.3 (1996): 271–77.

Wild, Nettie, dir. *Blockade*. Canada: Canada Wild Productions, 1993.

Williams, Colin H. "Quebec: Language and Nationhood." *Called unto Liberty! On Language and Nationalism*. Clevedon: Multilingual Matters, 1994. 187–231.

Williams, Linda. "Something Else besides a Mother." *Cinema Journal* 24.1 (1984): 2–27.

Williams, Raymond. *Keywords: A Vocabulary of Culture and Society*. Rev. ed. New York: Oxford University Press, 1983.

———. "Means of Communication as Means of Production." *Problems of Materialism and Culture*. London: Verso, 1997 [1978]. 50–63.

Wilson, Christopher P. *Jokes: Forms, Content, Use, and Function*. Toronto: Academic Press, 1979.

Winks, Robin W. *The Blacks in Canada: A History*. Montreal and Kingston: McGill-Queen's University Press, 1971.

———. *Canadian-West Indian Union: A Forty-Year Minuet*. Toronto: Oxford University Press, 1968.

Winnicott, D.W. *Playing and Reality*. Markham, ON: Penguin, 1980.

Wise, Wyndham. "Canadian Cinema from Boom to Bust: The Tax-Shelter Years." *Take One* 22 (1999): 17–24.

Wittgenstein, Ludwig. *Culture and Value*. Trans. Peter Winch. Ed. G.H. Von Wright. Chicago: University of Chicago Press, 1984.

———. *Philosophical Remarks*. Trans. R. Hargreaves and R. White. Ed. Rush Rees. Oxford: Blackwell, 1975.

Wong, Henry. "The Creative Eye: Molson Canadian." *Marketing* 8 May 2000, 32.

Wong, Paul, dir. *Miss Chinatown*. Canada: V-Tape, 1997.

Wood, Robin. "Towards a Canadian (Inter)National Cinema: Part 2: *Loyalties* and *Life Classes*." *CineAction!* 17 (1989): 23–35.

Woodsworth, J.S. *Strangers within Our Gates; or, Coming Canadians*. Toronto: F.C. Stephenson, 1909.

Wright, R. *Stolen Continents: The "New World" through Indian Eyes*. Toronto: Penguin, 1993.

Yates, Norris. *The American Humorist*. New York: Citadel Press, 1965.

Young, James E. "The Counter-Monument: Memory against Itself in Germany Today." *Landscape and Power*. Ed. W.J.T. Mitchell. Chicago: University of Chicago Press, 1994. 49–78.

Young, Robert C. *Torn Halves: Political Conflict in Literary and Cultural Theory*. Manchester: Manchester University Press, 1996.

Zelizer, Barbie. "Reading the Past against the Grain: The Shape of Memory Studies." *Critical Studies in Mass Communication* 12 (1995): 214–39.

Žižek, Slavoj. *Looking Awry: An Introduction to Jacques Lacan through Popular Culture*. Cambridge: MIT Press, 1991.

———. "Multiculturalism, Or, the Cultural Logic of Multinational Capitalism." *New Left Review* 225 (1997): 28–51.

———, ed. *Mapping Ideology*. London: Verso, 1994.

Biographical Notes

MARTIN ARNOLD is a composer and writer based in Toronto. He has studied in Canada and the Netherlands, where his teachers were Alfred Fisher, Frederic Rzewski, John Cage, Louis Andriessen, Gilius van Bergeijk, Rudolf Komorous, Douglas Collinge, and Michael Longton. He holds a doctorate from the University of Victoria. His compositions have been performed in Canada, the United States, the Netherlands, France, Germany, and Slovakia. He publishes in the areas of music and art criticism.

LORI BLONDEAU is a performance artist based in Saskatoon, Saskatchewan. She is a PhD candidate at the University of Saskatchewan, where she also teaches. In 1994 Blondeau co-founded, with Bradlee LaRocque, Tribe A Centre for Evolving Aboriginal Media, Visual and Performing Arts. Lori's performance and visual work has been exhibited nationally and internationally. Her current work consists of a series of performances based on memory, home, displacement, and decolonization.

JOANNE BRISTOL's work investigates the interplay between art, science, and history. The work in this book is part of her project, JoJo's School of Aesthetics: Services in the Arts of Projection, Attention and Photography, a series of performances involving shared activities and conversation with audiences (see www.bentaerial.net). She also teaches at the Alberta College of Art and Design.

KIRK CAMERON was born in Whitehorse, Yukon, and has studied English and history at Victoria University and Queens. He has published two books and a number of articles on northern political development, the most recent book (co-authored) being *Northern Governments in Transition*. He has worked for the governments of Yukon, British Columbia, and Canada, and is currently secretary to the Yukon Cabinet.

ALASTAIR CAMPBELL has studied history, anthropology, and semiotics in New Zealand, Canada, and Italy and has taught anthropology and sociology courses at the University of Ottawa. He has worked for the Assembly of First Nations and the governments of Canada, Yukon, Northwest Territories, and Nunavut. His work has entailed extensive analysis of Aboriginal and northern issues, and the writing of policy and informational booklets.

CAROL CORBIN is an associate professor of communication at the University College of Cape Breton, Sydney, Nova Scotia. She publishes in the areas of community, ecology, and culture, and has edited three books related to the island of Cape Breton, and a fourth on rhetoric and postmodernism with Michael Calvin McGee. She is currently working on the modernist enterprise in China from 1900 to 1949 and spent the fall of 2000 studying and teaching in Beijing.

FRANCES DORSEY is an associate professor of art at the Nova Scotia College of Art and Design in Halifax. Educated in Canada and the United States, her studio practice is based primarily in textiles and printmaking. She exhibits both nationally and internationally.

ZOE DRUICK is an assistant professor in the School of Communication, Simon Fraser University, where she teaches film and media studies. She has published in the area of Canadian film policy, with an emphasis on the history of the National Film Board of Canada. She is currently completing a book on the subject, *The Surface of Society.*

CECIL FOSTER is an author and scholar. He is an assistant professor in the Department of Sociology and Anthropology at the University of Guelph. His publications include *A Place Called Heaven, The Meaning of Being Black in Canada,* and the forthcoming books, *Where Race Does Not Matter: The New Spirit of Modernity* and *Multiculturalism: Issues of Citizenship, Culture, and Identity.*

GARY GENOSKO teaches cultural sociology at Lakehead University. His books include *Baudrillard and Signs* (1994), *McLuhan and Baudrillard* (1999), *Undisciplined Theory* (1998), and *Contest: Essays on Sports, Culture and Politics* (1999). He is editor of *The Uncollected Baudrillard* (2001), *Deleuze and Guattari: Critical Assessments,* 3 vols. (2001), and *The Guattari Reader* (1996). He is general editor of *The Semiotic Review of Books* <http://www.chass.utoronto.ca/epc/srb>.

ANNIE GÉRIN is a curator and assistant professor of art history and art theory at the Department of Visual Arts, the University of Ottawa. Educated in Canada, Russia, and the UK, her research interests encompass the areas of Soviet art and propaganda, Canadian public art, and art on the World Wide Web. She is especially concerned with art encountered by non-specialized publics, outside the gallery space.

Yasmin Jiwani is a faculty member in the Department of Communications at Concordia University. Prior to her move to Concordia, she was the executive coordinator of the BC/Yukon Feminist Research, Education, Development and Action (FREDA) Centre at Simon Fraser University.

Rachelle Viader Knowles is a visual artist working in a broad range of contemporary media, including lens, time, and text-based installation. Originally from the UK, Rachelle studied at Cardiff College of Art and the University of Wales before moving to Canada in 1994 to study at the University of Windsor. Recent solo exhibitions include: the MacKenzie Art Gallery in Regina, Chapter Gallery in Wales, Peak Gallery in Toronto, and the Art Gallery of Southwestern Manitoba. Rachelle Viader Knowles heads the intermedia area in the Visual Arts Department at the University of Regina.

Patsy Aspasia Kotsopoulos is a doctoral candidate in communications at Simon Fraser University. She is researching and writing her dissertation, "Romance and Industry on the Road to Avonlea," for which she received a SSHRC doctoral fellowship. She teaches film and interdisciplinary studies at the University of Victoria.

Joanne Lalonde is a professor of art history at UQAM and the director of the undergraduate program. She received her doctorate in semiotics from UQAM in 1999. Her research deals principally with the relationships between art and technology, media art (Canadian video), and representations of sexual and identitarian hybridization in contemporary art.

Susan Lord is an associate professor of film studies at Queen's University, where she is also cross-appointed with the Institute of Women's Studies. Her main teaching and research areas are feminist theory and film culture, and cultural studies of media and technology. She has published on gender and technology in *Public* and *CineAction*, as well as on feminist film culture in several recent anthologies, and is writing a book on multiculturalism, feminism, and the films of Anne Wheeler. She is currently co-editing a collection of essays entitled *Digital Aesthetics: Time, Technology and the Cultures of Everyday Life*, and another entitled *Killing Women: Gender, Representation, and Violence*.

Erna Macleod is a PhD student in the Department of Communication at the University of Massachusetts, Amherst. Her research interests include media criticism and identity issues, particularly those related to Canadian national identity. She is a lifelong resident of Louisbourg, Nova Scotia, and has been employed as a tour guide at the Fortress of Louisbourg National Historic Site for the past fifteen years.

Ceri Morgan received her doctorate from Southampton University in 2000. Her thesis considers representations of space, place, and identity in the contemporary francophone novel in Quebec. She is currently teaching at Keele University in the United Kingdom.

JASON MORGAN is a doctoral candidate in the Joint PhD Program in Communication at Concordia University (in conjunction with the Université de Montreal and the Université de Québec à Montréal). He has previously received a master of arts in communication studies from the University of Calgary. His current research focuses on the intersection of representations of death with the body in contemporary culture.

CAROL PAYNE is an assistant professor of art history at Carleton University's School for Studies in Art and Culture. She writes and curates exhibitions on a wide range of issues involving photographic practice and reception, including commercial images of the 1920s, Canadian governmental uses of photography, and contemporary photo-based art practice. She is currently working on a major study of the National Film Board of Canada's Still Photography Division, funded by the Social Sciences and Humanities Research Council of Canada.

SHEILA PETTY is dean of the Faculty of Fine Arts and professor of media studies at the University of Regina (Canada). She is also an adjunct scientist (New Media) at TRLabs, Regina. She has written extensively on issues of cultural representation, identity, and nation in African and African diasporic cinema, television, and new technologies. She has curated film and television series and exhibitions for galleries across Canada.

JEANNE RANDOLPH is a cultural theorist whose lectures, performances, and writings put a psychoanalytic torque on hi tech, advertising, mass media, and pop-culture phenomena. In *Psychoanalysis & Synchronized Swimming, Symbolization and Its Discontents*, and her forthcoming *Why Stoics Box*, Jeanne's collected writings embellish the value that contemporary visual arts contribute to contemporary society.

BEVERLY RASPORICH is a professor in the interdisciplinary Faculty of Communication and Culture at the University of Calgary. She teaches in the Canadian Studies program and is the author of *Dance of the Sexes: Art and Gender in the Fiction of Alice Munro*, and co-editor of *A Passion For Identity: An Introduction to Canadian Studies and Woman as Artist*. She has written numerous articles on Canadian culture on such topics as Canadian humour, Native literature, multiculturalism, and folk art. She is co-author of the thematic entry "Canadian Culture and Ethnic Diversity" in the *Encyclopedia of Canada's Peoples*. She has recently completed a compact disc on the visual arts, *Western Place/Women's Space*.

ERIC SHERBERT holds a BA and LLB from Queen's University and is currently working as legal counsel at the Department of Justice, Canada, in Toronto. He is currently completing his LLM at Queen's University with a thesis entitled "Towards an Aboriginal Charter of Rights."

GARRY SHERBERT is an associate professor in the Department of English at the University of Regina in Regina, Canada. He is the author of *Menippean Satire and the Poetics of Wit*. He is currently co-editing two volumes of *The Col-*

lected Works of Northrop Frye: Shakespeare and the Renaissance, as well as co-authoring a book entitled *In the Name of Friendship*, on Jacques Derrida and poet-philosopher Michel Deguy.

CYNTHIA SUGARS is an assistant professor in the Department of English at the University of Ottawa. She is the author of numerous articles and reviews on Canadian literature and postcolonial theory, including a forthcoming contribution to *ARIEL* entitled "Can the Canadian Speak? Lost in Postcolonial Space." She is currently editing a collection of essays entitled *Unhomely States: Theorizing English-Canadian Postcolonialism*.

JAYNE WARK is an associate professor of art history at the Nova Scotia College of Art and Design in Halifax. Her publications on contemporary visual art focus on conceptual art, video, and performance art. She is currently working on a book on feminist performance in North America.

EMILY WEST received her PhD from the Annenberg School for Communication at the University of Pennsylvania, and is currently an assistant professor in the Communication Department at the University of Massachusetts at Amherst. Her co-authored article on British nationalism as mediated by newspapers appeared in a 2004 issue of *European Journal of Communication*. In addition to her ongoing research interest in media and nationalism, she is working on major projects about two feminized and commonly denigrated forms of popular culture: greeting cards and cheerleading. Her dissertation project on expressing the self through greeting card communication was awarded a Social Sciences and Humanities Research Council of Canada Doctoral Fellowship. She teaches and writes in the areas of consumer culture, media audiences, infotainment, and freedom of expression.

Index

Cultural Studies Series

Cultural Studies is the multi- and interdisciplinary study of culture, defined anthropologically as a "way of life," performatively as symbolic practice, and ideologically as the collective product of media and cultural industries, i.e., pop culture. Although Cultural Studies is a relative newcomer to the humanities and social sciences, in less than half a century it has taken interdisciplinary scholarship to a new level of sophistication, reinvigorating the liberal arts curriculum with new theories, new topics, and new forms of intellectual partnership.

The Cultural Studies series includes topics such as construction of identities; regionalism/nationalism; cultural citizenship; migration; popular culture; consumer cultures; media and film; the body; postcolonial criticism; cultural policy; sexualities; cultural theory; youth culture; class relations; and gender.

The new Cultural Studies series from Wilfrid Laurier University Press invites submission of manuscripts concerned with critical discussions on power relations concerning gender, class, sexual preference, ethnicity, and other macro and micro sites of political struggle.

For further information, please contact the Series Editor:

Jodey Castricano
Department of Critical Studies
University of British Columbia Okanagan
3333 University Way
Kelowna BC v1v 1v7

Books in the Cultural Studies Series
Published by Wilfrid Laurier University Press

Slippery Pastimes: Reading the Popular in Canadian Culture edited by Joan Nicks and Jeannette Sloniowski
2002 / viii + 347 pp. / ISBN 0-88920-388-1

The Politics of Enchantment: Romanticism, Media and Cultural Studies by J. David Black
2002 / x + 200 pp. / ISBN 0-88920-400-4

Dancing Fear and Desire: Race, Sexuality, and Imperial Politics in Middle Eastern Dance by Stavros Stavrou Karayanni
2004 / xv + 244 pp. / ISBN 0-88920-454-3

Auto/Biography in Canada: Critical Directions edited by Julie Rak
2005 / viii + 280 pp. / ISBN 0-88920-478-0

Canadian Cultural Poesis: Essays on Canadian Culture edited by Garry Sherbert, Annie Gérin, and Sheila Petty
2006 / xvi + 530 pp. / ISBN 0-88920-486-1